Netscape Developer's Guide to JavaScript 1.2

Bill Anderson

Prentice Hall PTR
Upper Saddle River, New Jersey 07458
http://www.phptr.com

ISBN 0-13-719279-7

90000

9 780137 192793

Library of Congress Cataloging in Publication Data

Anderson, Bill.
     Netscape developer's guide to JavaScript 1.2 / Bill Anderson.
          p.   cm.
     Includes bibliographical references and index.
     ISBN 0-13-719279-7
     1. JavaScript (Computer program language) 2. NetScape. I. Title.
QA76.73.J39A53   1998
005.2′762--dc21   98-25175
                                                              CIP

Editorial/Production Supervision: *Kathleen M. Caren*
Development Editor: *Jim Markham*
Copyeditor: *Amy Constantino*
Cover Design Director: *Jerry Votta*
Cover Designer: *DesignSource*
Cover Art: *Dave Cutler*
Manufacturing Manager: *Alexis Heydt*
Marketing Manager: *Dan Rush*
Acquisitions Editor: *Greg Doench*
Editorial Assistant: *Mary Treacy*

© 1998 Prentice Hall PTR
Prentice-Hall, Inc.
A Simon & Schuster Company
Upper Saddle River, New Jersey 07458

Prentice Hall books are widely used by corporations and government agencies for training, marketing, and resale. The publisher offers discounts on this book when ordered in bulk quantities.
For more information, contact: Corporate Sales Department, Phone: 800-382-3419;
FAX: 201-236-7141; email: corpsales@prenhall.com
Or write: Corp. Sales Dept., Prentice Hall PTR, 1 Lake Street, Upper Saddle River, NJ   07458

Printed in the United States of America
10   9   8   7   6   5   4   3   2   1

ISBN 0-13-719279-7

Prentice-Hall International (UK) Limited, *London*
Prentice-Hall of Australia Pty. Limited, *Sydney*
Prentice-Hall Canada Inc., *Toronto*
Prentice-Hall Hispanoamericana, S.A., *Mexico*
Prentice-Hall of India Private Limited, *New Delhi*
Prentice-Hall of Japan, Inc., *Tokyo*
Simon & Schuster Asia Pte. Ltd., *Singapore*
Editora Prentice-Hall do Brasil, Ltda., *Rio de Janeiro*

Table of Contents

Acknowledgments

The publishing of a book is more than the solitary effort of an author typing day and night. From its conception to its final production, I owe thanks to the many people who made the journey possible. I want to thank Greg Doench, my acquisitions editor at Prentice Hall, for his support in making this book possible and for his patience in letting me pursue the latest changes in JavaScript. I owe special thanks to Jim Markham for coordinating the team that herded this book through the entire process and for his reminders that kept me focused on writing. I also want to thank Cameron Laird for his feedback in making this book technically accurate and more readable and Amy Constantino for correcting my grammatical mistakes. Kathleen M. Caren, as the Production Editor, turned this book from a manuscript into its final form.

Besides the people at Prentice Hall, I want to thank Lala Mamedov at Netscape for tracking down answers to my questions about JavaScript. There are many others involved in helping to make this book possible. The staff of SoftQuad ensured that I had the latest version of HoTMetaL Pro, which I used to develop the examples in this book. The staff of Acadia Software kept me posted with the latest versions of Acadia Infuse

ScriptBuilder (now, NetObjects ScriptBuilder). These tools saved me many hours in the writing of the examples used in this book.

There are no words that can express the thanks I owe to my wife Kay for putting up with me through the writing of this book. She created the environment that allowed me to concentrate on writing, and tolerated my impatience with any interruptions. As a road warrior, I wrote much of this book in restaurants, hotels, and even during the numerous flights. To all the staff of the restaurants and hotels, and the flight attendants of United Airlines, I owe thanks for providing me what I needed to keep writing.

Bill Anderson

About the author

Bill Anderson is an author, instructor, and consultant. As an author, he wrote *Source File Management with SCCS*, Prentice Hall, 1992, and *Building UNIX System V Software*, Prentice Hall, 1994. These books were written under the name Israel Silverberg. He was a contributing author to *Web Programming Unleashed*, Sams.net, 1996, and has written numerous courses on system administration, networking, and network management. As an instructor, Bill Anderson teaches seminars on system administration, networking, C, and C++. He is currently writing courses for Java, and JavaScript. As a consultant, he specializes in installing networks, and works with DCE/DFS.

Bill Anderson started his career in computers in 1969 as a communications computer programmer. Over the years, he worked on C, C++, and Pascal compiler, written Ethernet drivers, and worked as a Product Line Engineering Manager for a company that managed UNIX-based computers. In recent years, he was the Technical Manager for a large ISP, and implemented one of the early commercial Web sites.

Introduction

Without question, JavaScript is the most popular scripting language for extending the capabilities of HTML documents. Since its inception in Netscape Navigator 2.0, JavaScript continues to mature as a scripting language. With the release of Netscape Communicator 4.x and Netscape Server 3.x, JavaScript became a full-fledged language for developing client/server applications. The purpose of this book is to present both the client-side and the server-side dimensions of JavaScript. The combination of the two provides the basis for the development of JavaScript applications.

Who This Book Is For

This book is for anyone that writes JavaScript. It is a complete reference to the many aspects of client-side JavaScript as implemented in Netscape Communicator 4.x. However, this book also provides the information needed to develop client-side JavaScript for Netscape Navigator

2.x, Netscape Navigator 3.x, Microsoft Internet Explorer 3.x, and Microsoft Internet Explorer 4.x. This book is not a complete reference to Microsoft's version of JavaScript, which is called JScript. This is especially true for JScript in Microsoft Internet Explorer 4.0, since its implementation of DHTML differs from the approach used by Netscape.

If you are interested in writing JavaScript applications, this book includes a discussion of server-side JavaScript for the 3.x versions of Netscape Servers. If you want to learn about JavaScript Beans, this book discusses the Netscape component architecture and how to write JavaScript Bean files that comply with the JavaBean model for distributed objects.

To get the most value from this book, you need to have a background in HTML. You don't need to know Java, as the book only looks at how to incorporate Java applets into your scripts using LiveConnect. The same is true for plug-ins. If you are planning on using the LiveWire Database Service to incorporate live data into your JavaScript application, you need to know SQL.

What You'll Need

You'll need the CD-ROM that accompanies this book. You'll also need a copy of Netscape Communicator. Although you can write all of your scripts with a text editor, the CD-ROM also contains an evaluation copy of NetObjects ScriptBuilder for the Windows 95 and Windows NT platforms. It also helps to have an HTML editor, but this is not absolutely necessary.

If you want to develop server-side JavaScript scripts, you need access to Netscape's FastTrack Server 3.x, or Netscape's Enterprise Server 3.x. The Netscape servers are the only Web servers that support server-side JavaScript.

To develop JavaScript components using JavaScript Bean files, you need Netscape's Visual JavaScript and Netscape's Component Developer's Kit. The Component Developer's Kit is optional, but it provides numerous sample scripts and NetObjects JavaScript Bean Builder for the Windows 95 and Windows NT platforms.

How This Book Is Organized

This book contains three parts:

- Part 1, "Introduction to JavaScript"
- Part 2, "JavaScript Object Structure"
- Part 3, "Advanced Topics"

The following sections describe each of these parts.

Part 1: Introduction to JavaScript

The first part traces the evolution of the browser from a program used for retrieving documents, to a platform for deploying applications. The first two chapters set the stage for the material presented in this book. Chapter 1, "Evolution of the Browser," traces the change of the browser from a program that views HTML documents to being a common window environment for applications. Chapter 2, "Client/Server Methodology," reviews the characteristics of client/server software and discusses the evolution of the browser into a middleware component for distributed-object applications.

The last two chapters in this part introduce the JavaScript language. Chapter 3, "What Is JavaScript?" explains the difference between Java and JavaScript. It also discusses the methods for incorporating JavaScript into HTML documents. Chapter 4, "Fundamentals of JavaScript," describes the syntax for JavaScript data types, operators, control statements, and functions.

Part 2: JavaScript Object Structure

The second part focuses on the object structure of Netscape Navigator. Chapter 5, "JavaScript Object Model," explains a JavaScript object, describes the object hierarchy for the different versions of Netscape Navigator, and defines the syntax for the statements and operators related to objects. Chapter 6, "Built-in Objects, Methods, and Functions," describes the core objects to JavaScript that are independent of the Navigator object hierarchy.

Chapter 7, "Working with Events and Documents," presents the concept of events and the Event object, which play an important role in the user's interface to an HTML document. The chapter then discusses the document object as a reflection of the HTML document. Chapter 8, "Working with Forms," covers the Form object and its elements. Since client-side cookies and forms have a close relationship, the chapter also discusses working with cookies. Chapter 9, "Working with Windows and Frames," moves the discussion to the environment for displaying an HTML document.

Part 3: Advanced Topics

Where Parts 1 and 2 are important to anyone using JavaScript, the chapters in this part apply to those readers who which to explore the depths of JavaScript. The chapters divide into three groups: advanced client-side JavaScript, server-side JavaScript, and tools for JavaScript development.

Chapter 10, "Interfacing to Plug-ins and Java Applets," explains Live-Connect's role in interfacing JavaScript to plug-ins and Java Applets. Chapter 11, "Advanced JavaScript," concludes the discussion of client-side JavaScript with a discussion of using JavaScript with Dynamic HTML, and the Netscape Communicator security model.

Chapter 12, "Introduction to Server-Side JavaScript," introduces LiveWire and server-side JavaScript. Chapter 13, "Working with Server-Side JavaScript," explains the syntax for server-side JavaScript. Chapter 14, "LiveWire Database Service," covers the JavaScript object structure for integration with relational databases.

Chapter 15, "Building JavaScript Components," is for the advanced reader, who wants to write JavaScript components using JavaScript Bean files. Chapter 16, "JavaScript Tools" reviews the tools available to the JavaScript developer.

Conventions Used in This Book

This book uses the following conventions:

- All words that would be used in a program are shown in fixed-width Courier font.
- Brackets ([]) surround optional entries in syntax definitions.
- *Italicized* words in syntax definitions indicate that you are to substitute a variable name.

An icon set along the left side of the page highlights important points, warnings, or references to other sources of information. This book contains the following icons:

Note

 An important note that deserves special attention.

Warning

 A warning gives information about a potential problem.

Tip

 A tip discusses a shortcut or other special technique that you might want to use.

JavaScript 1.2

 This icon highlights those features that are new in JavaScript 1.2 (Netscape Communicator 4.x). If the chapter relates only to JavaScript 1.2, the icon does not appear.

Netscape Navigator

 This icon flags information that is exclusive to Netscape.

Bug

 This icon alerts you to software bugs and possible methods of avoiding them.

About the CD-ROM

The CD-ROM contains the source code for all of the listings in this book, copies of Netscape Communicator for all platforms, an evaluation copy of NetObjects ScriptBuilder for the Windows platforms, and a section for additional references. The organization of the CD-ROM is as follows:

- The examples directory contains all of the listings presented in this book. The directory contains subdirectories for each chapter. The name of the HTML files in chapter directory match the titles for the listings in the chapter.
- The tools directory contains a copy of Netscape Communicator for all platforms, and a copy of NetObjects ScriptBuilder for the Windows 95/NT platforms.

To view the contents on the CD_ROM from a Web browser, click on the index.htm file in the top-level directory. This HTML document leads you to the examples, instructions on installing the tools, and a reference page for JavaScript resources, including the Web site for this book. For details on contents of the CD-ROM in text file format, check the readme.txt file.

Part

In just a few years, the Internet evolved from a text-based environment to a new approach in developing distributed applications. The earliest browsers allowed Web pages to combine text and graphics. Then forms came along to provide a means to send information from the browser back to the Web server. The first version of JavaScript appeared in Netscape Navigator 2.0, and provided a means for doing client-side editing of forms and creating dynamic Web pages. Later, LiveWire appeared as a way to extend JavaScript to the server side. Netscape Navigator 3.0 extended the functionality of JavaScript for the browser, but LiveWire remained the same. The release of Netscape Communicator 4.0 signaled the integration of JavaScript into the distributed-object technology. Along with the

Introduction to JavaScript

release of Netscape Communicator, the 3.x version of Netscape Server incorporated LiveWire into the server and brought JavaScript to the current release. Chapters 1 and 2 set the stage for this remainder of the book, by reviewing the development of the World Wide Web and client/server technology. This part ends with an introduction to the JavaScript language in Chapters 3 and 4.

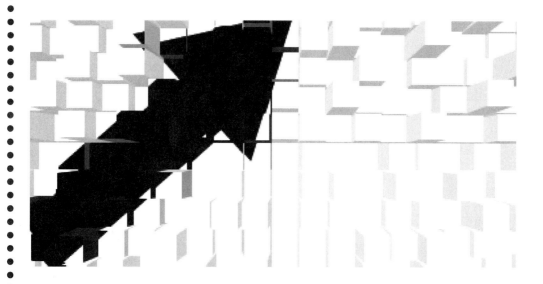

Evolution
of the Browser

Topics in This Chapter

- The Internet, HTML, and Web browsers
- The importance of interaction
- Forms and CGI

Chapter 1

The Internet, Client/Server methodology, and Object-Oriented Programming are not new technologies. Yet every day you hear announcements of new products, new innovations, and new features, which prompts the question: What is so new about these familiar technologies?

What you are seeing is a refinement and integration of technologies that have come together to create new and exciting solutions to building a distributed-network environment. Solutions that fit the needs of the industry trend for down sizing and right sizing without capsizing.

This work looks at Netscape Communicator 4.0 as a platform for building interactive, client/server applications for Internet and intranets. My objective is to present a model for building applications that are platform independent, work in a distributed network, and require a minimal investment in additional resources.

Netscape Communicator 4.0 uses JavaScript to bind together text, forms, plug-ins and Java Applets. But before discussing the practical details of JavaScript, this chapter and the next will provide a brief background and historic development of HTML, the Web browser, Java, and JavaScript.

Internet as a Flat Media

Internet, formerly called ARPAnet, was developed during the era of teletypes and ASCII terminals related to the original legacy computers. In 1969, with just three computing sites communicating at 56 Kbps, ARPAnet only provided for remote login (TELNET), file transfer, and remote printing. In 1972, e-mail joined the ranks of ARPAnet services. In terms of applications, ARPAnet continued with these basic protocols for many years with few changes.

January 1, 1983, marked the beginning of Internet as we know it when TCP/IP became the sole protocol for ARPAnet. In 1986, the Net News Transfer Protocol (NNTP) brought UseNet to ARPAnet. During this period, Internet was a very text-oriented environment with list servers, e-mail, and NetNews as the hottest means of communication. TELNET provided access to shell accounts allowing the user to experiment with the limited graphical capabilities of the host. By and large, however, this was a world of ASCII text and the only way to transfer non-ASCII files was either by ftp or by encoding them into ASCII text with uuencode.

In 1991, a team at the University of Minnesota released Gopher. Until then the only way to retrieve documents was via either ftp or archives on list servers. Gopher, with its hierarchical menu structure, made it easy to organize documents for presentation over the Internet. Gopher servers became so popular that by 1993 thousands of Gopher servers contained over a million documents. To find these documents, one used the Gopher search tool VERONICA (Very Easy Rodent Oriented Net-wide Index to Computerized Archives). Although it was text oriented, designed for dumb ASCII terminals, and was noninteractive, Gopher filled a void in the insatiable demand for information.

Development of HTML

While Gopher provided a means to link to other Gopher sites at the menu level, it could not link to other documents within a document. In 1989, Tim Berners-Lee, while consulting to CERN in Geneva, Switzerland, developed the protocols for the World Wide Web (WWW). Seeking a way to link scientific documents together, he created Hypertext Markup Language (HTML), which is a derivative of the Standard Generalized Markup

Language (SGML). The most significant enhancement was the Universal Resource Locator (URL) that allows one document to reference another within the document itself. Berners-Lee indirectly drew from the work of Ted Nelson, who in 1965 coined the word *hypertext*.

The driving force behind Berners-Lee's idea was to create a means to connect colleagues at CERN who worked on diverse and noncompatible machines. The idea was to move collaboration from the coffee room to a global information space. Scientific papers could be easily linked to other papers, eliminating the necessity for each reader to search for referenced documents. The URL is the link that binds the Web of information together.

Yet, the original HTML was text only and noninteractive. A person accessed Web pages using client-side programs such as Lynx, which runs nicely on ASCII terminals. Although Lynx itself was text oriented, the URL and the HyperText Transfer Protocol (HTTP) provided it the power to link documents across the Internet. Tim Berners-Lee designed the HTTP server to support the maximum number of clients by supporting a very simple transfer protocol. This lean and mean server required no more than 64 lines of code to implement. Under this scheme, the client side bears the burden of formatting and presentation. This approach fits well with client/server methodology, and the increasing power of workstations (including PCs) to process more complicated data.

The next key development was the Multipurpose Internet Mail Extension (MIME). MIME was developed in 1992 as a way to extend the Simple Mail Transfer Protocol (SMTP) to include attachments for non-ASCII text documents. Within a short period of time, Gopher and HTTP incorporated the MIME standard. As an extensible standard, MIME was perfect for defining the contents of a document. With MIME, the automatic execution of the proper viewing of a document was now possible. It made no difference whether it was a word processing document, a graphical image, a sound, or a movie file. The pieces of the puzzle were now in place for the development of the Web browser.

Development of the Web Browser

In 1993, the National Center for Supercomputing Applications (NCSA) released Mosaic—the first Web client (Web browser) based on a Graphical User Interface (GUI). Using the flexibility of MIME, HTML documents now included both text and graphics.

With the release of NCSA Mosaic, Internet moved into a new era. The Web now supplied documents that approached the level of printed media such as books, magazines and newspapers. Whether or not it replaces or supplements these media is an open question

With MIME's capabilities to support a variety of formats, audio and videos quickly followed text and graphics. While the recent advances in audio and videos are impressive, they still lack the richness of the actual media. These media require transmission rates that push current technology to its limits. While breaching this barrier is just a matter of time, current technology only *reflects* a vision of future possibilities. Today, we are in the infancy of a myriad of new technologies. Managing these diverse technologies has forced new approaches to browser design.

At first, browsers depended on external *helper* applications to support the protocols, other than HTTP, defined by the URL protocol definitions (called schemes) and MIME types. Since the URL schemes consist of only a few types (http, gopher, ftp, telnet, news, and mailto), browser developers quickly incorporated them into the browser. The forces behind this change were users who had less experience with computers. Experienced users found, installed, and configured the external helper applications without a problem, but for a lay Internet user, this was a daunting task.

Just as the Web browser reduced its dependency on external applications to support URL schemes, it also incorporated support for the most common MIME types for graphics such as GIF and JPEG.

Yet, the extensibility of MIME required a more flexible approach. The solution had to be transparent to the user, support the extensibility of MIME, and do this without requiring an update to the Web browser. Netscape met this challenge through the creation of plug-ins. Each plug-in responds to a particular MIME type or types. Whenever a user wants to view or hear a new MIME, they need only download the appropriate plug-in and install it. The `pluginspace` attribute of the `<EMBED>` HTML tag allows the Web page designer to define the location where the user can obtain the requested plug-in. While the process requires the user to obtain the needed plug-in, it represents a significant step forward, provided the plug-in can be downloaded and installed with minimal user intervention.

The Need for Interaction

Both Gopher and the Web started out to be information retrieval systems. Even with the MIME enhancements, they were global document distribution systems, representing a way to make information available for others to consume. In a sense, they mirrored the attributes of the media they were trying to replicate, and subsequently became another channel for distribution of information. As an information distribution channel, it fulfilled the need for immediate access to information.

Gopher clients disappeared as the browser became the window to all of the standard Internet protocols. Although Web pages continue to increase at an explosive rate, Gopher is on the decline. Gopher sparked the growth of information available on Internet, but the Web page provided the fuel to build a global on-line library. The rapid growth of the Web, lies in part with the rapid growth in the popularity of commercial Web browsers. Although the Spry Mosaic browser and Netscape Navigator browser came into being within the same period of time, Netscape now dominates the market. Microsoft's Internet Explorer was a late entry into the browser competition, and even though Internet Explorer is the number two browser, it still is in a catch-up mode. In part, Netscape achieved this dominance through innovations that took Netscape Navigator beyond the limits of document retrieval. Netscape Navigator 2.0 introduced client-side image maps, Java, and JavaScript. Netscape Navigator 3.0 introduced LiveConnect, which provided a means for Java Applets, JavaScript, and plug-ins to communicate. Netscape Communicator 4.0 introduced Dynamic HTML, Cascading Style Sheets, and major enhancements to JavaScript.

Providing information is but one dimension of the human need for gathering information. E-mail, list servers, and UseNet are successful because they provide a means for dialogue. Dialogue, whether to query a database or to get a personalized answer to a question, constitutes the fundamental difference between the potential of Internet, or intranets, and traditional media. It is in this area that Netscape made major contributions to the development of the Web.

The Impact of CGI

When first introduced, forms and the Common Gateway Interface (CGI) went hand in hand. Forms provide a standard means for the user to enter information. Single lines of text, multiple lines of text, check boxes, radio buttons, and selection lists represent the various methods for collecting information. Each of these allowed the user to enter data that provided input for diverse applications such as search criteria, e-mail messages, or database queries. The information was sent to the server, where CGI scripts handled the server-side processing of forms.

With forms, the HTML document became a collector of information. The editing and processing of this information depended on server-side CGI application programs. Perl (which originated in the UNIX community as a string processing language), shell scripts, and C were the languages of choice for development of this server-side application. In contradiction to HTTP's philosophy of keeping the server small, CGI increased the load on the server with tasks that should be accomplished on the client side such as checking the validity of form data and performing mathematical computations.

Databases store vast quantities of information, representing an additional source of data beyond that available through the standard HTML documents. Developers, who wanted to access a database via a browser, had to write the necessary server-side software to access that database. Until the release of Netscape Navigator 2.0, the HTML document could collect information from a user, but not manipulate it. Even the simplest of calculations required server-side software.

For the Web browser to emulate client-side database software, the client side had to handle the preprocessing of requests. The server side needed a more straightforward means of accessing databases, instead of each programmer having to develop their own database interface. Standard tools for database access were desperately needed. The section in this chapter on "The Impact of JavaScript," shows how the client can now perform more of the processing tasks.

Image Maps

The ability to divide a single graphical image into multiple zones (*hot spots*) that invoke defined actions, provides a means to enhance the graphical presentation of a Web page. Each hot spot has a corresponding URL. When the user clicks on the hot spot, the browser sends the coordinates to the server along with the URL of the graphic. The server then processes the coordinates according to a map data file. It then returns a *connect to URL* to the Web browser.

Like CGI, this means that the server performs tasks because of the limited capabilities of the client. This approach contains several weaknesses:

- Increases network traffic
- Increases the burden on the server
- Requires the Web page designer to create a separate file for the server

Once more, transferring this task to the client side increases performance and simplifies Web page design. This means that the HTML document needs to contain the information necessary to make the decision. Starting with Netscape Navigator 2.0, Netscape included the <MAP> tag for client-side imaging as part of its HTML extensions. The current specification for HTML 3.2 incorporates Netscape's client-side image mapping as a standard part of HTML. As more browsers shift to supporting HTML 3.2, the need for server-side image mapping will decline.

The Browser as a Common Window Environment

The browser is more than just a graphical interface for viewing Web documents. It offers a common window environment to all Internet and intranet applications. Whether it be e-mail, Netnews, the Web, or a database application, the Web browser presents the user with a single mechanism for viewing information. One of the primary features is that the user view is the same on different hardware platforms, including Microsoft Windows, Mac, or UNIX.

The single window environment possesses many advantages. It means that an application is independent of the windows environment for any particular platform. The developer is no longer concerned with a version that works for Microsoft Windows, Mac Windows, or X-Windows. The browser window hides the differences from the developer. This common window environment also reduces development time, providing one common way of creating an interactive dialogue with the user without concern for the window environment of the client machine.

The Impact of Java

In May of 1995, when Java was released to the Internet world, it was a relatively new and unknown language. Java actually existed previously under the name Oak, as a language designed for the programming of PDAs (Personal Digital Assistants), remote controllers, and other electronic devices. After failing to break into these markets, Sun decided to release Java to the Internet community in attempts to gain wider acceptance as a viable language. While new languages often take years to build a following, Java took off like a rocket. In part, Java's growth in popularity took a big leap forward when Netscape included support for Java in Navigator 2.0.

While plug-ins represented a major step forward in expanding the capability of the browser to handle new MIME types, they lacked certain features:

- Plug-ins must be installed prior to their use. This limits the dynamic content of the Web page as it forces the user to interrupt their interaction, download the plug-in, install it, and then come back to the Web page. Java Applets (small applications) are downloaded like any other object in a Web page avoiding this interruption.

- Java is not platform dependent, while plug-ins are. With the Java runtime incorporated into the browser, software developers needed to develop the application once; thereby eliminating the costs of porting the same application to multiple platforms.

- Java is not linked to MIME types, plug-ins are. Java is a powerful object-oriented programming language that supports networking. It gives software developers a simple, robust tool for developing network applications that take advantage of the browser environment.

With Java, the Web browser took a new direction. Prior to Java, talk of the Web browser providing a multiplatform GUI environment for client/server applications was a bit far fetched. Chapter 2, "Client/Server Methodology," shows why this paradigm is now possible.

Chapter 10, "Interfacing to Plug-ins and Java Applets," discusses how to interface to Java Applets, however, it is not a tutorial on Java. Chapter 10 does include a list of references on Java tutorials for those interested readers.

The Impact of JavaScript

JavaScript is not Java. Where Java is an object-oriented programming language, JavaScript is an object-based scripting language. Chapter 3, "What Is JavaScript?", discusses what this means in more detail. For the purpose of this chapter, we need only to know that Java and JavaScript are two different entities.

In the beta releases of Navigator 2.0, Netscape introduced a scripting language called LiveScript. By the time they released the final version, Netscape had changed the name to JavaScript. While this was great for marketing, it created a lot of confusion about the nature of the new scripting language.

JavaScript is an interpreted scripting language that is part of an HTML document. JavaScript provides the Web page designer with a tool that adds the following capabilities to an HTML document:

- By storing information in the *cookie* file, the Web page designer can customize the Web page for each user. Since the *cookie* file is maintained on the user's machine, the information it contains is available every time the Web page is accessed.
- Event handlers allow the Web page designer to develop HTML documents that dynamically respond to actions of the

user. They allow a Web page to respond to loading and unloading of the page; to passing over a reference, to selection of an object, and to changes in forms.

- JavaScript provides for the editing of forms, performing mathematical and string manipulations, and flow control. Prior to JavaScript, these tasks required server-side CGI scripts which increased the load on the server and network. With more work being done on the client side, the server is free to respond to more clients.

- With implementation of LiveConnect in Navigator 3.0, JavaScript provides a mechanism that allows JavaScript to communicate with Java Applets, Java Applets to communicate with other Java Applets, and JavaScript to plug-ins. With LiveConnect, the Web page designer now has the ability to take maximum advantage of the tools needed to turn Web pages into dynamic application interfaces.

- While Navigator adds JavaScript to the client side, LiveWire adds JavaScript to the server side of the client/server equation. Instead of having to learn yet more languages, the Web page developer now needs to know only one language to develop network applications. Also, LiveWire comes with SQL and ODBC libraries for accessing databases.

Although this book is about JavaScript version 1.2 as executed within Netscape Navigator, Table 1.1 shows the relationship of the different versions of JavaScript to different browser versions. Microsoft calls their version JScript. To a large extent JScript is the same as JavaScript. However, there are differences. This work attempts to note the known differences. Netscape submitted version 1.1 to the European Computer Manufacturers Association (ECMA) for approval as a language standard. As of the writing of this work, ECMA approved JavaScript 1.1 as a standard, with some changes. The standard title is ECMA-262 and their name for the language is ECMAScript.

Table 1.1 JavaScript Versions

Product	Version 1.0	Version 1.1	Version 1.2
Navigator 2.x	X		
Navigator 3.x		X	
Navigator 4.x			X
Internet Explorer 3.0	X		
Internet Explorer 4.0		X	

Summary

From the text-based orientation of HTML 1.0 with Lynx as a browser, to the multimedia, dynamic, and interactive Web browser of today is, to say the least, a radical change. What started out as a method to link documents from multiple sites, evolved step by step into a new model for client/server programming.

Through the MIME standard, Web publishing went beyond text to include graphics and then multimedia. This extensibility of MIME led to the development of plug-ins that could respond to new formats for media and documents. The Web page changed from emulating traditional media to a new form of media with new possibilities. At the same time, the drive for interaction led to the creation of forms and CGI scripts.

Even with these changes, HTML kept the Web browser oriented towards displaying Web documents. With the addition of client-side image maps, Java, and JavaScript, the Web browser entered a new world. The Web browser now takes on more of the work previously performed by the server. It also possesses the capacity to provide a new level of interactive content. The Web browser now presents a new model for client/server programming beyond the displaying of documents.

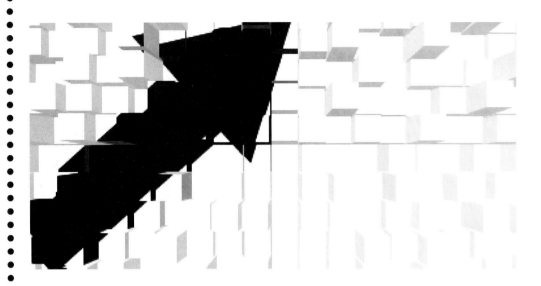

Client/Server Methodology

Topics in This Chapter

- Unlocking the client/server mystery of "What am I, a client or a server?"
- The importance of the single system image
- Netscape ONE as middleware

2

Client/server methodology began with the first computer network. Though it is not a new technology, the definition of client/server is still ambiguous. This chapter is not a comprehensive guide to the wide world of client/server programming, but it will provide the reader with a basic understanding of the terms, characteristics, and fundamental models of client/server methodology. I recommend *Essential Client/Server Survival Guide* by Robert Orfali, Dan Harkey, and Jeri Edwards for the reader who wishes a more in-depth understanding of this field. In client/server terms, Netscape Navigator falls on the client side, and the Web server on the server side. Netscape's LiveWire is a server-side product that enhances the capabilities of the Web server.

Definition of Client/Server

Client/Server; how can two words generate so much confusion? They may be just two words, but there are three pieces to this puzzle. The third piece, as shown in Figure 2.1, is *middleware* which acts to connect the client side to the server side.

Figure 2.1   *Client/server components.*

The client application makes requests to servers through the facilities provided by middleware. From this you see that the client is a consumer of services and the server is the provider for those services. In this scenario, the middleware constitutes the software that allows the client and server to communicate via a network.

Notice this model makes no assumptions about whether the client and server exist on the same machine or different machines. The client and server are simply two parts of an application separated by middleware. Thus, the question of what machine they execute on is not important. This model also does not define the client as the user interface for that is not always the case as shown in Figure 2.2.

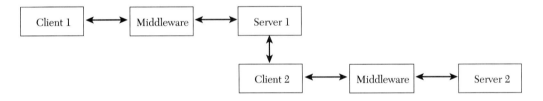

Figure 2.2   *A more complex client/server model.*

In the model shown in Figure 2.2, Client-1 makes a request to Server-1. Server-1 doesn't possess the answer, so it makes a request to Server-2 via Client-2. This model of client/server behavior appears in such applications as:

- A Web browser (client-1) sends a form for a database query to the httpd server (server-1). It starts the CGI script (client-2) to query a database server (server-2).

- A Web browser (client-1) needs to resolve the domain name part of the URL to an IP Address, so it sends a request to its domain name server (server-1). The server-1 DNS doesn't know the answer, so it queries other DNS servers (server-2) looking for the IP Address.

Although it is not delineated in Figure 2.2, the middleware involved in the first client/server relationship may be different from that involved in the second relationship. This flexible, building block approach makes the client/server paradigm a very powerful tool for building applications.

To this point, the definition of the components is rather vague. The next two sections attempt to clarify these definitions. However, before moving on, there is another set of terms that require a definition. In client/server literature, one reads about *thin clients* versus *fat servers*, or *fat clients* versus *thin servers*. To understand these terms, let's see how they apply to the relationship between a Web browser and a Web (http) server.

When HTML documents consisted of only text and graphics, the Web browser was a fat client, since it did all of the work required to display a document. On the other hand, the Web server was thin as it did no more than fetch HTML documents and graphics. With the addition of more server-side functions such as image mapping and CGI scripts, the relationship changed so that the Web browser was thin in comparison to the server. This had a dramatic affect on the Web server, since a thin server can serve more clients than a fat server. The solution was to install bigger and faster servers.

With the introduction of Java, JavaScript, and client-side image mapping, the relationship is again changing. The Web browser is getting fatter; thereby making the Web server thinner. This change allows the Web server to serve more clients, but it also means that the Web browser requires a more powerful workstation. As this discussion shows, the terms fat and thin are relative to the amount of work performed by the client versus the server.

What is not directly discussed in the client/server literature is the idea of fat versus thin middleware. The section in this chapter on "A Look at Client/Server Models" shows that there is a difference between models with fat middleware and those with thin middleware.

Client/Server Characteristics

The definition that the client consumes and the server provides says very little about the characteristics of these two components in the client/server relationship. There is no agreed upon definition for what is a client and what is a server, other than they work together over a network. Since these terms lack a common definition, this section will focus on some of the major characteristics of a client and a server. To aid in this discussion, Figure 2.3 shows a variant of the model presented in Figure 2.1 by using the four-layer TCP/IP model.

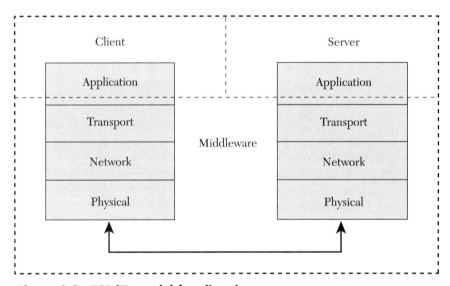

Figure 2.3   TCP/IP model for client/server components.

Figure 2.3 uses the four-layer TCP/IP model for the following reasons:

- The Web browsers and servers are Internet products that used TCP/IP for communication. Therefore, the discussion of other protocol stacks is outside the scope of this work.
- The often referred to seven-layer OSI model does not map to the TCP/IP model. The attempts to map to the two models ob-

scure the differences between the two approaches. With the TCP/IP model the application layer and physical layers are left open to varying models for these layers. This approach simplifies the discussion of how to delineate the client and server software from the middleware.

With these caveats out of the way, Figure 2.3 illustrates the following client/server characteristics:

- *Network-centric.* Whether or not it is a Local Area Network (LAN), a Wide Area Network (WAN), or on the same machine, the client and server always communicate with each other via a network defined by middleware. This characteristic excludes traditional legacy connections to a central host such as a serial RS-232 connection between a terminal and host. It includes remote terminals connected to a LAN using protocols such as SLIP (Serial Line Interface Protocol) and PPP (Point-to-Point Protocol) that extend the LAN to remote devices.
- *Shared servers.* The server application is a shared resource that responds to multiple client applications. It is the responsibility of the server application to regulate authentication and authorization to access the resources provided by the server application.
- *Client driven.* The client makes requests of the server and the server responds to those requests. Thus, the client always initiates the dialogue between the server and the client. The exception to this is IP multicasting or *server push.*
- *Location transparency.* The actual location of the server is transparent to the client. In other words, the client does not know or care whether or not the server is located on the same machine, the same LAN, or on another LAN.
- *Multiplatform.* The client and server may exist on different hardware platforms or use different operating systems
- *Scalable.* Because of the multiplatform characteristic, both client and server are scalable. The client is horizontally scalable in that the number of clients does not affect the client/server relationship. Both the client and server are vertically scalable in that either platform can be upgraded without affecting the relationship.

- *Message based.* The client and server applications communicate with each other through message-based transactions. The actual message services may come from the application itself or through the facilities of the middleware. The Remote Procedure Call (RPC) is an example of a middleware messaging mechanism.

- *Encapsulation.* As a corollary to being message based, the client and server are encapsulated in that how they perform their job is not important to the other side. Taking this one step further, different client applications may make use of the same server application.

This list does not provide a clear cut definition of what constitutes a client and server application, emphasizing the lack of a clear boundary between application and middleware. Figure 2.3 illustrates this fuzzy boundary by drawing the division between application and middleware across the application layer.

What is Middleware?

Middleware is the software that provides the foundation for the client and server applications to possess their characteristics. Middleware is all of the software that facilitates the communication between the client application and the server application. This software includes the Application Program Interfaces (APIs) used to program the client and server applications. This is a good working definition and a good starting point for seeing how it applies to the real world of software.

Once again, the discussion in this section centers on the TCP/IP protocol stack, since it relates to the focus of this book. The term *protocol stack* comes from the protocols that constitute each layer of the layered model for network communications. By assigning the protocols to each layer, the resulting diagram forms a *stack of protocols* as shown in Figure 2.4.

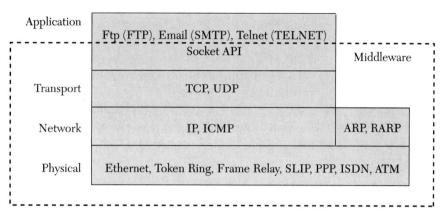

Figure 2.4 TCP/IP protocol stack.

Before proceeding with a discussion about the TCP/IP protocol stack, you need to be aware of the following limitations of the diagram in Figure 2.4:

- The diagram lists the protocols involved at each layer and not the implementation of those protocols in actual software. For the reader wishing to pursue this topic in greater detail, there are many excellent books available on TCP/IP networking.
- The purpose of the diagram is to illustrate the scope of middleware and not to discuss the details of each protocol listed.
- The application layer lists only a few of the many TCP/IP application protocols.

The middleware achieves the characteristics for client/server applications by following certain rules:

- *Encapsulation.* Each layer has a *rules for interfacing* with that layer. How it fulfills its purpose is not important to the other layers. By encapsulating each layer, the protocol and software for the layer can change as long as the interface remains constant.
- *Integrity of structure.* Each layer communicates only to the lay-

ers above and below it. Thus, layers are not skipped. Using Figure 2.3 as an illustration, the client application makes a request through the interface to the Transport Layer. This request flows through each of the layers, across the network, and back up to the application on the server side. The server answers by following the reverse path.

To illustrate how the model works, the following list takes a brief look at the function performed by each of the four layers in the TCP/IP protocol stack:

- *Application layer.* The interface between the application layer and the transport layer is the *port*. The port is not a physical port, but a software port identified by a *port number*. The port number identifies the application on the server to which the client wishes to communicate. The *services* file identifies which application relates to a particular port number. As long as both sides agree on the port numbering scheme everything is okay. On the client side, the port number is a unique number that identifies the process—for UNIX, this is the Process ID (PID). To uniquely identify each packet, the port number is combined with the IP Address to create a *socket*. The developer who writes TCP/IP applications that interface to the transport layer, uses the Sockets API or WinSock API. In addition to providing the routines necessary to interface to the transport layer, these APIs contain routines to convert the domain name to an IP Address, as the domain name is for humans and the IP Address is for machines.

- *Transport layer.* The transport layer receives a stream of data from the application layer and breaks this stream into segments. Each segment has a header that identifies the client and server port numbers. Depending on the application layer request, the transport layer uses either the Transmission Control Protocol (TCP) or the User Datagram Protocol (UDP). TCP provides a reliable, connection-oriented service to transfer the data to the destination machine. Thus, TCP is the normal protocol used to transfer files between two machines. On the other hand, UDP provides an unreliable, connectionless service for the sending of information. UDP is the protocol of choice for sending messages or other data where the overhead of a reliable, connection service is not needed. As an interesting side-light, the transport layer refers to source and destination machines and is blind to whether it acts as the client or server. Only the application layer maintains the distinction between client and server.

- *Network layer.* The Internet Protocol (IP) receives the segment from the transport layer and forms an IP Datagram by encapsulating the segment with its own header and trailer. Among other things, the header contains the source and destination IP addresses. The TCP/IP philosophy sees the network layer as the virtual network. It sees the entire Internet as one global network divided into smaller subnetworks. By comparing the IP Address to the networks subnet mask, IP knows whether or not to send the datagram to a host on the local network or forward it to a gateway, which then decides where to forward the IP Datagram on its journey to the destination host. Like UDP, IP is a connectionless, unreliable protocol. The Internet Control Message Protocol (ICMP) performs control, error reporting, and information functions for TCP/IP. The Address Resolution Protocol (ARP) and Reverse Address Resolution Protocol (RARP) are oddities in that they only relate to the transmission protocols (part of the physical layer) that use the Medium Access Control (MAC) address. They appear in the network layer because they perform the function of resolving IP addresses to MAC addresses (ARP) and the reverse (RARP).

- *Physical layer.* Within the TCP/IP model, the physical layer is seen as the physical implementation of the virtual IP network presented in the network layer. This layer encapsulates the IP datagram with the headers and trailers required by the transmission protocol supported by the network interface. Figure 2.4 lists some of the more popular transmission protocols used in building LANs and WANs. Of these, Ethernet and Token Ring use the MAC address to send packets to network interfaces in a network consisting of multiple hosts.

Once the packet arrives on the other side of the wire (or fiber), the following events take place:

- The physical layer receives the packet, strips its headers and trailers and passes it to the network layer.

- The network layer looks at the destination address in the IP Datagram and decides whether the packet belongs there or needs to be forwarded to another destination. If the packet belongs to the machine's IP Address, then it strips the headers and trailers and passes the segment to the transport layer.

- The transport layer puts the data in the segment back into a stream and signals the appropriate operating system processes that data is available on the port. While assembling the stream, TCP also performs error checking on the packet to insure that the data is correct.

- Once started, the application process reads the data from the port and performs the necessary actions.

Although this discussion gives the impression that the boundary between middleware and the client/server applications is clear, this is not always the case. For example, an ftp application uses the login portion of the telnet application to perform the authentication process with the destination host. By so doing, the login process becomes part of middleware. The fluidity of the boundary between application and middleware becomes even more apparent in Figure 2.5, which illustrates a model of the Web browser.

As shown in Figure 2.5, the HTML document acts as the client application when the boundary for middleware incorporates the Web browser. This seemingly radical view derives from changes in the HTML document. When the HTML document is a text file containing pointers to other files, the Web browser is the client application. When the HTML document contains extensions such as forms, JavaScript, Java Applets, and plug-ins that turn it into a dynamic, interactive document, the HTML document becomes a client application. This fluid boundary between client/server application and middleware ensures that any definition remains a bit hazy. On the fat versus thin scale, the Web browser model represents a thin client (the HTML document) and a thin server with fat middleware (the Web browser), which is the current trend in client/server methodology. The middleware takes on more of the burden as the client and server application become smaller.

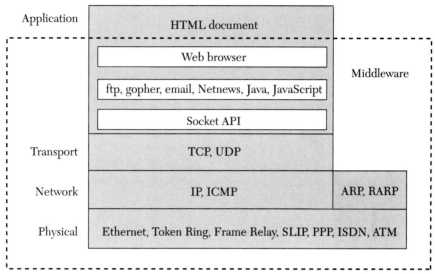

Figure 2.5   The Web broswer as middleware.

A Look at Client/Server Models

While definitions help to clarify the terminology used in client/server methodology, they don't answer the question of what are its objectives? Three phrases summarize these objectives:

- Distribute computing power.
- Make it look like a single system.
- Do it with objects.

The Orwellian image of one super computer controlling the entire world was progressive science fiction, but not science fact. The centralized computer center was a driving force into the 1970s, but this principle started to falter with the introduction of minicomputers and the idea of department-centered computing. The birth of the personal computer spawned the move to workplace- and home-based computing, and computing power became distributed into smaller and smaller units all the way down to PDAs (Personal Data Assistants).

The trouble with distributed computing is that it scatters management information and resources over an ever increasing number of isolated units. Networks were forced to expand and encompass these distributed-computing units into one distributed-computing network. LANs tied computer resources together in a building; Campus Area Networks tied LANs together in a complex of buildings; Metropolitan Area Networks tied LANs together throughout a larger geographical area (usually within distances of 75 kilometers); and Wide Area Networks tied LANs together over even a wider geographical area. LANs, CANs, MANs, and WANs are enterprise networks or intranets, with Internet being the ultimate global network that ties everything together.

Along with the building of a distributed-computing network came the objective to make it look like a single system. The *single system image* keeps the user from having to know anything about networks, since the entire network now appears as an extension to the users workstation. Achieving this is one thing when the network runs one operating system with one file system structure. It is quite another, when divergent hardware platforms with a variety of file systems are tied together.

While the first two objectives involve network design objectives, the third is a programming objective. There is no question that object-oriented programming is a favorite buzzword in software development. While it wasn't the first object-oriented programming language, C++ is the most popular, with Java quickly gaining ground. Even JavaScript is an object-based scripting language (see Chapter 3, "What Is JavaScript?," for the difference between object oriented and object based). Thus, Netscape Navigator, besides providing a common Graphical User Interface (GUI) environment, is a middleware product that manages objects on the client side. On the server side, LiveWire performs the same function.

The following descriptions of the various client/server models show that the roads to achieving these design goals follow a number of paths. Since object-oriented programming (OOP) spread very slowly, the file server, database server, and transaction server models reflect pre-OOP thinking. However, until object-oriented programs for client/server applications become common place, these models still play an important role in the development of networks.

File Servers

One of the earliest uses of a LAN was to provide a way for the users to
share access to data files, such as text, word processing, and image files,
or engineering drawings. This model provided access to the files by extending the file system of the user's operating system. For example, PC-
DOS-based networks extended the PC files system by mapping network
file systems as pseudodrives; UNIX networks extended the UNIX file
system by incorporating the network files' systems into its file system hierarchy. The file server model finds a role in networks where:

- Non-client/server applications need to share access to files.
- Work stations with small disk capacity used the resources of a
  server with a large disk capacity.
- Applications could be shared by storing them on a central server.

As hard disks became cheaper and applications larger, the last two
reasons for file servers slipped to a much lower priority. As cheap, high
capacity disks evolved, the model changed from a file server centric
model to a peer-to-peer file server model. With larger applications, the
performance degraded for downloading applications across the network,
forcing these fat applications back to the workstation. Of course these
changes brought other consequences; workstations required more computing power to support peer-to-peer networks, and moving applications
to the workstation increased the work required by system administrators
to add and maintain these applications.

The Network File System (NFS) developed by Sun Microsystems is
probably the most popular distributed file system for the UNIX platform
and for TCP/IP-based networks. As a companion package, the Network
Information System (NIS) centralizes the management of common files.
Figure 2.6 depicts the NFS model for a file server.

While NFS presents the user with a single file system view of the network, it is not without problems. In general, all file server models face
the following difficulties:

- *Portability.* Distributed file systems traditionally are operating-
  system dependent in that they reflect the operating system's
  file structure and naming conventions.
- *Scalability.* A distributed file system works best on a work

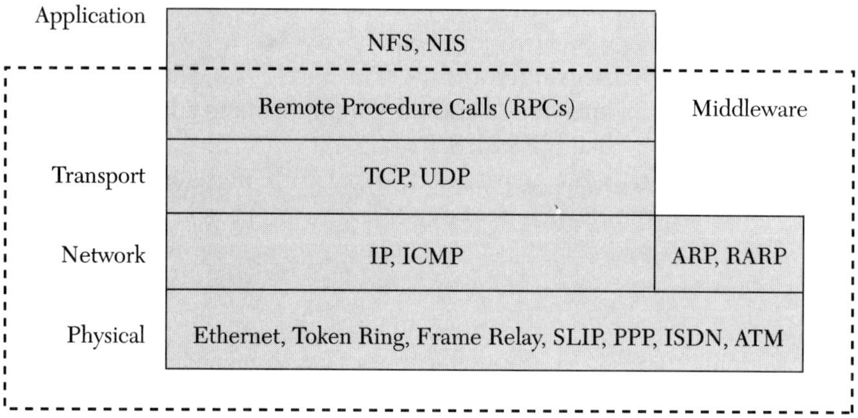

Application		NFS, NIS	
		Remote Procedure Calls (RPCs)	Middleware
Transport		TCP, UDP	
Network		IP, ICMP	ARP, RARP
Physical		Ethernet, Token Ring, Frame Relay, SLIP, PPP, ISDN, ATM	

Figure 2.6   NFS model for file server.

group centered LAN. It becomes more difficult to manage in large LANs and scales poorly to WANs.

- *Security.* Like other file server implementations, NFS is a security nightmare. Whether it is by IP Address spoofing, or breaking passwords, a security breakdown compromises the entire network file structure.

NFS and NIS together represent one of many different approaches to creating a single image for networks. Within the world of TCP/IP, the Distributed Computing Environment (DCE) from the Open Systems Foundation (OSF) is a hot alternative to NFS. The goal of DCE is to provide a heterogeneous client/server environment for the integration of multivendor servers. DCE uses an extended and secure version of RPC (DCE-RPC) to support the following main components:

- A distributed naming service based on the X.500 standard or the Domain Name System (DNS)
- A Distributed File Service (DFS)
- A security service based on Kerberos from the MIT Athena Project
- A time synchronization service

As shown in Figure 2.7, DCE is powerful when it comes to middleware. But while DCE offers many advantages in terms of a secure, multivendor client/server network, these benefits come at a price:

- *Higher administration costs.* A DCE network requires more knowledge and takes more time to administer than a system like NFS/NIS.
- *Increased network traffic.* DCE security transactions have a significant impact on network traffic.
- *Time sensitive.* Every device in the cell (DCE's administrative domain) must have the same exact time since some of the security transactions have an extremely short Time-To-Live (TTL). This short TTL creates problems when part of the cell includes low bandwidth or heavily trafficked WAN links. Also, every cell must be on the same time standard for intercell communications to function properly.
- *Requires DCE compliant applications.* The authentication and authorization features of DCE require that the applications be DCE compliant. This requirement extends to files stored under DFS. Beyond the standard applications (such as telnet, rlogin, and ftp), there are very few software packages that are DCE compliant.

This rather long section was for a purpose. It shows the evolution of the client/server models from a simple file-server model to a multivendor distributed file system.

DCE goes a step further to provide a networkwide system for authentication and authorization of all servers, workstations, applications, and users. For a DCE network, the DCE security service and name service impact on all of the subsequent client/server models.

Database Servers

While the file server model supports stand-alone applications with a shared file system, the database server model splits the database application into a client-side application and a server-side application. The world of database servers is very complex and even a short introduction to all the technologies involved is beyond the scope of this work. However, the key to understanding database client/server technology evolves

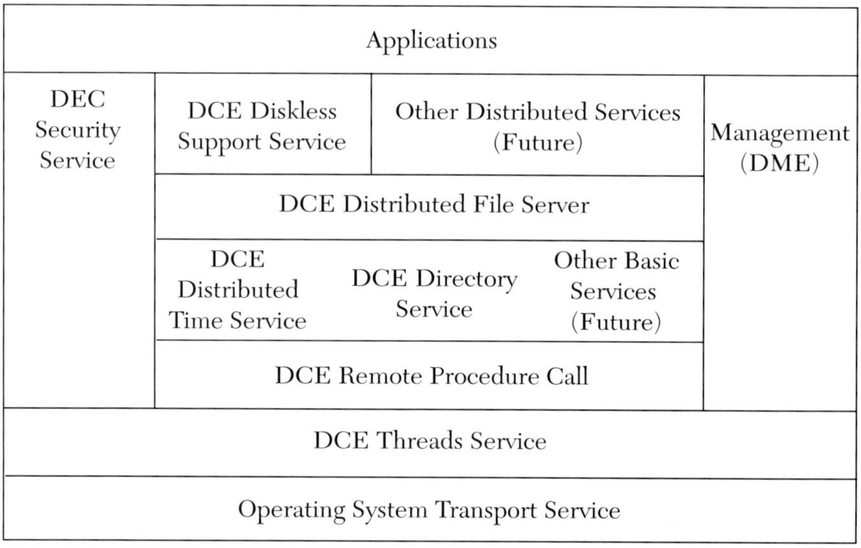

Applications			
DEC Security Service	DCE Diskless Support Service	Other Distributed Services (Future)	Management (DME)
	DCE Distributed File Server		
	DCE Distributed Time Service	DCE Directory Service	Other Basic Services (Future)
	DCE Remote Procedure Call		
DCE Threads Service			
Operating System Transport Service			

Figure 2.7   DCE protocol model.

around the Structured Query Language (SQL), which was developed by IBM in the early 1970s. SQL (pronounced as *sequel*) marks the dividing line between the client application that generates SQL queries, and the SQL server that processes the SQL queries. Figure 2.8 shows a generic model for the client side. The server side model varies depending on the database architecture.

The SQL database server model assumes a relational database on the other end. However, the SQL3 standard extends SQL to incorporate object-oriented databases. Like all areas of client/server software, new technologies continue to evolve.

The SQL Access Group (SAG) set out to define a set of standards that would provide interoperability between clients and servers from different vendors. They accomplished this goal in the following ways:

- Defining common message formats and protocols for communication between the client and the server.
- Defining a SQL Call Level Interface (CLI) that provides common definitions for SQL APIs.

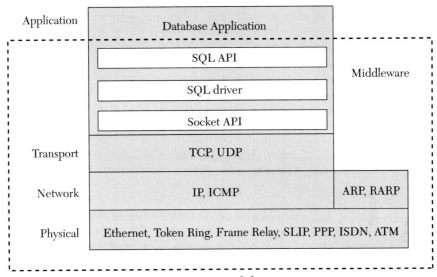

Figure 2.8   SQL database server model.

With the *Open Database Connectivity* (ODBC) Windows API standard, Microsoft extended the SAG CLI standard to include extensions for the Microsoft Windows environment plus other extensions. LiveWire provides both SQL and ODBC interfaces to databases (see "Livewire Database Service" in Chapter 14).

Transaction Servers

Transaction servers are variations of database servers, and similarly use SQL as the standard to communicate between the client and the server. The difference between the transaction server and database server is in the processing of SQL messages. A database server processes each SQL query as an independent event. On the other hand, a transaction server processes a block of SQL queries as a single event. The entire block succeeds or fails and all sides must agree on the success of an event. Thus, transaction server prevents partial updating of multiple databases that must be kept in synchronization.

The key acronym to understanding the function of transaction servers is ACID (coined in 1983 by Andreas Reuter). The acronym is defined as follows:

- *Atomicity.* Transaction servers require that all transactions succeed or fail as a unit.
- *Consistency.* The transaction must always leave the system in a stable state. If the transaction fails, then the software must return the system to the initial state.
- *Isolation.* All transactions are independent of other transactions. The software must ensure that no transaction effects another transaction.
- *Durability.* At the conclusion of a successful transaction, its affects are permanent even if the system crashes.

The applications that conform to the ACID requirements have the name *Online Transaction Processing* (OLTP). This is accomplished through Transaction Processing (TP) monitors or through stored procedures provided by the database vendor. TP monitors allow servers to control their local resources and to cooperate with other TP monitors for nonlocal resources.

Object Servers

The growth of object-oriented programming changed the very nature of client/server architecture. While OOP dates back to the early 1980s with Smalltalk and C++, its impact on client/server architecture was minimal until 1989. In that year, an international consortium of manufacturers and software houses formed the *Object Management Group* (OMG) to establish standards for distributed objects.

It is not the purpose of this work to provide a detailed discussion of OOP (Chapter 3 gives a basic introduction into the nature of objects), but it is important to understand the basic terminology and concepts of distributed objects. As this section demonstrates, OMG's work has important implications on the future direction of Netscape products.

As shown in Figure 2.9, the middleware for distributed objects consists of the following:

- *Object Request Broker (ORB).* The ORB is the mechanism that allows objects to communicate with each other. The object itself is not aware of the underlying communication process. The ORB also provides platform independence. With these characteristics, it is the foundation for building distributed object applications. OMG has defined a standard, Common Object Request Broker Architecture (CORBA), for implementing ORBs.

- *Object Services.* Object Services is a collection of services used to create (Object Factory) objects, control access to and keep track of objects, and maintain the relationship between groups of objects. These services improve the consistency of objects and the productivity of software developers.

- *Common Facilities.* End-user services (such as printing facilities, database facilities, and e-mail facilities) are grouped together as common facilities. Where every implementation of CORBA includes object services, common facilities are optional.

- *Application Objects.* These objects are specific to an application. The object classes in object services provide a base for building other application object classes.

- *Domain Interfaces.* The application domains, group applications into functional areas such as finance, healthcare, manufacturing, transportation, telecommunications, and electronic commerce. The domain interfaces are specific interfaces to the application domains.

The CORBA model works fine for stand-alone applications running on a single host. Version 2.0 of the CORBA specification provides for interoperability between ORBs through *in-line bridges* as seen in Figure 2.10. The inter-ORB bridges enables one ORB to translate the requests from another ORB.

The General Inter-ORB Protocol (GIOP) sets forth the specification for ORB interoperability. GIOP is a generic specification that maps to any connection-oriented protocol that meets its requirements. In the Internet Inter-ORB Protocol (IIOP), OMG's CORBA specification also defines a specific mapping of GIOP to TCP/IP. In addition, the CORBA specification defines an Environment Specific Inter-ORB Protocol (ES-IOP) for the Distributed Computing Environment (DCE). The DCE Common Inter-ORB Protocol (DCE-CIOP) brings distributed objects to a platform-independent network operating system.

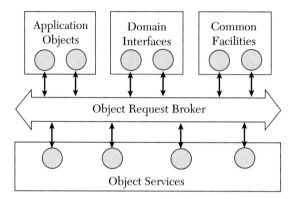

Figure 2.9 Object model.

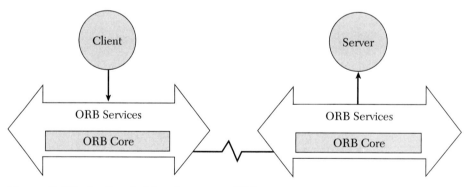

Figure 2.10 In-line bridge between ORBs.

While DCE-CIOP brings distributed objects to a specific environment, IIOP opens the door to implementing distributed objects for Internet. Using IIOP, objects can request services from one another in a multiplatform environment. Applications, such as databases, can now have object-oriented client/server relationships. It takes the Web browser beyond the limit of HTML forms. Client-side applications written in C++ or Java can communicate with server-side objects. At the same time, the browser becomes a platform-independent environment for implementing such applications.

World Wide Web Servers

In 1991, the first world Web server delivered text-only documents using Lynx as a client and a simple Web server. Its most salient features were the Uniform Resource Locator (URL) and a simple HyperText Markup Language. From this humble beginning, the World Wide Web server evolved into the information component of another Network Operating System (NOS).

Since this work focuses on the products of Netscape Communications Corporation, let's look at Netscape ONE (Open Network Environment) as an NOS. As with any modern NOS, Netscape ONE provides the following features:

- *Platform independence.* Companies no longer want to invest in a totally new infrastructure for the sake of technological advancement. Platform independence goes beyond the ability to operate on multiple hardware and software platforms. It also involves the requirement to *author once and run anywhere.* The effort required to port and customize applications to each and every platform is just too expensive.
- *Open standards.* The day of single vendor systems is gone. Applications need to work with existing applications from different vendors. This ability requires the adherence to open standards. Yet, the ongoing evolution of the network-centric model creates a fine line between the adherence to existing standards and the promotion of new standards. In the end, it becomes an issue of the promotion of open standards.
- *Scalability.* What starts out as a small intranet needs the ability to scale to a large extranet. The objective of scaling to a larger

network is to accomplish it without redesigning either the client or server applications.

- *Distributed Management.* Since the NOS views the network as the computer, distributed management is a necessity. The system administrator needs the ability to manage from any point in the network.

When the Web document was just HTML plus graphics, the Web browser presented information according to the format of the document. The Web browser looked like a client application. With the addition of plug-ins, JavaScript and Java, the nature of the Web browser changed. By adding these features, the HTML document is akin to a programming language. Thus, the Web browser becomes a part of middleware as shown in Figure 2.11.

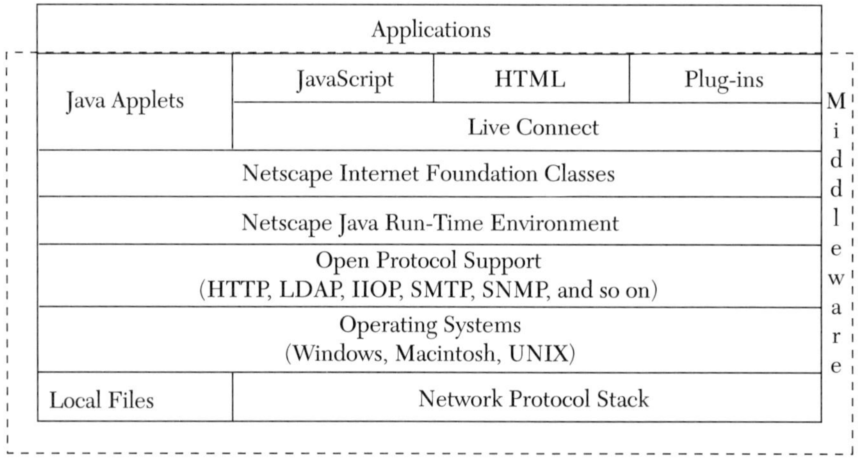

Applications			
Java Applets	JavaScript	HTML	Plug-ins
Java Applets	Live Connect		
Netscape Internet Foundation Classes			
Netscape Java Run-Time Environment			
Open Protocol Support (HTTP, LDAP, IIOP, SMTP, SNMP, and so on)			
Operating Systems (Windows, Macintosh, UNIX)			
Local Files	Network Protocol Stack		

Middleware

Figure 2.11   Browser as middleware.

As middleware, Netscape ONE becomes an application development environment. The HTML document becomes either the client or the server application program. Netscape Navigator functions as the universal desktop for client-side applications, while Netscape's LiveWire provides the development environment for server-side applications.

Netscape ONE changes the fundamental nature of client-side application development. Instead of installing the client application, the user downloads the application every time they access the Web page. This simplifies deployment of changes and the addition of new clients. The biggest change is that applications are inherently multiplatform. The end result is lower development costs for distributed applications.

As shown in Figure 2.11, the Netscape ONE development platform integrates a number of technologies. Briefly, they are as follows:

- *HTML.* This language forms the foundation for developing distributed applications. With features such as Dynamic HTML, it allows the development of sophisticated user interfaces. The administrative software for Netscape servers illustrates the power of HTML in the development of the user interface.

- *Java.* After just a few years, Java has reached a level of acceptance that other languages took many years to achieve. Initially, Java only supported self-contained *applets within the browser.* With the introduction of LiveConnect in Netscape Navigator 3.0, Java, JavaScript, and plug-ins share a common object and messaging model. This enabled a degree of interaction between each of the components. The release of Netscape Communicator 4.0 added BeanConnect and JavaBeans. BeanConnect allows separate components to communicate with each other. These components can be on the same Web page or different Web pages. JavaBeans establish an environment for BeanConnect—and Java, CORBA, plug-ins (written in C or C++), JavaScript, and even HTML can become Java-Beans. Using IIOP, client-side JavaBeans can communicate with server-side JavaBeans. The result is a distributed object oriented application.

- *JavaScript.* As a scripting language, JavaScript is a simple language when compared to C++ or Java. But it is the only HTML scripting language approved by a standards body. As such, it is a powerful tool for creating dynamic Web pages. It is also an integral component for building client/server applications.

Netscape uses the term *crossware* to define applications built around the Web server as the central application server. Through LiveWire, a developer can design application interfaces for databases stored on a wide variety of hardware platforms. By supporting CORBA and IIOP, Netscape products—both client and server—provide an application development platform for distributed objects. This unites the growth of Object Oriented Programming (OOP) and the growth of Internet technologies.

The Growth of Client/Server

Occasionally, I have read articles that declare the death of client/server methodology. Such obituaries are without a base. Client/server methodology is alive and growing, and is undergoing a metamorphosis from a desktop-centric orientation to a network-centric orientation. Even with this metamorphosis, the basic client-middleware-server model holds true.

In the desktop-centric model, the desktop workstation was the center of the user's universe. This model saw network services as ancillary to the desktop. They allowed the desktop to access printers, plotters, file servers, database servers, and other servers. The user was always aware that the network services were separate from the desktop computer.

The network-centric model changes this view. Under the network-centric model, the desktop merges into the network. It becomes another component in the distributed-computing environment. The intranet and, by extension, the extranet become a seamless single system image where the user does not see a distinction between their desktop computer resources and those of the network. In time, the lines between the desktop and Internet will cease to exist.

Summary

Network applications and client/server methodology go hand in hand. The evolution of client/server methodology points in the direction of the *single system image*. With the single system image, the line between the local host and Internet ceases to exist. Instead of Orwell's Big Brother, we have Alvin Tofler's Global Village.

The Web browser is one of the driving forces behind the growth of the Internet. It started out as a text-oriented protocol with the URL as its special feature. The incorporation of the MIME protocol into HTML opened the door to rich multimedia pages presented via the Web browser. HTML now challenges any traditional media when it comes to presenting information.

HTML forms and CGI scripts marked the beginning of integration to other services besides documents retrieved via HTTP. The introduction of plug-ins, Java, and JavaScript enhanced the capabilities of the Web browser. In the programming language arena, object-oriented programming replaced traditional methodologies for program development. However, there was no connection between client-side and server-side objects. With OMG's introduction of standards for distributed objects, distributed application development based on pure object-oriented programming became a reality. By combining the on-demand nature of HTML pages with the power of distributed objects, the Web browser offers a new mechanism for the development of distributed applications. By looking at the use of JavaScript for both the client and the server, this book will focus on the role JavaScript plays in the development of distributed applications.

What Is JavaScript?

Topics in This Chapter

- The purpose of JavaScript
- Integrating JavaScript into HTML Documents
- Security: The importance of signed scripts

3

Chapter

JavaScript first appeared in Netscape Navigator 2.0 beta as LiveScript. LiveScript was the client side scripting language for LiveWire server-side LiveScripts. Prior to the introduction of LiveScript, the editing of forms was a task performed on the server side using languages such as Perl. LiveScript offered a single language for both client and server. Moreover, it allowed the editing of forms prior to sending the data to the server.

On December 4, 1995, Netscape Communications Corp. and Sun Microsystems, Inc. announced JavaScript as an open, cross-platform object-based scripting language. The goal of the joint effort was to create an easy-to-use object-based scripting language for creating on-line applications. The vision called for JavaScript to act as the glue that linked together objects and resources of both clients and servers.

JavaScript 1.0 appeared in Netscape Navigator 2.0 and was an object-based scripting language, but it did not interact with Java applets. Netscape Navigator 3.0 moved the vision forward with the release of JavaScript 1.1 and LiveConnect. LiveConnect provided the means for JavaScript to interact with plug-ins and Java applets. Netscape

Communicator 4.0 made the leap to distributed objects with support for CORBA, IIOP and JavaScript 1.2.

With several hundred thousand Web sites using JavaScript, it is now *the* Internet scripting language for HTML documents. With the ECMA-Script standard from the European Computer Manufacturers Association (ECMA), JavaScript now has a formal industry standard specification. Although ECMAScript is a new standard, it has the potential to become the base for Internet object-based scripting languages

Java versus JavaScript

Although JavaScript resembles Java, it is not a simplified form of Java. JavaScript supports most of Java's expression syntax and flow control constructs, but does not support classes or inheritance. JavaScript is a loosely typed language that supports a small number of dynamic data types (numeric, Boolean, and string). Whereas Java supports a rich variety of data types that are static and have strong type checking.

JavaScript complements Java by allowing Web page developers to take advantage of the exposed properties of Java applets. JavaScript can get and set exposed properties, which allow it to alter the performance of both applets and plug-ins. Table 3.1 compares the features of JavaScript and Java.

Table 3.1 Comparison of Java and JavaScript

JavaScript	Java
Interpreted by the Web browser	Compiled before execution
Object-based	Object-oriented
Integrated with HTML	Applets are distinct applications
Variable types not declared	Strong typing of variables
Dynamic binding of objects references	Static binding at compile time

If JavaScript is not Java, what is it? JavaScript is a scripting language extension to HTML. By itself, HTML is a document markup language that can only statically present a document. It may contain dynamic elements such as Java applets, animated GIFs, and style sheets, but even with the addition of forms, HTML is only a collector of information. It cannot edit the forms before submitting them to the server. JavaScript adds decision-making capability to HTML and plays a distinct role in the development of client/server applications.

The power of JavaScript derives from the following characteristics:

- *JavaScript is simple*. JavaScript is a simple scripting language that allows Web developers, who are not necessarily programmers, to create dynamic Web pages. Programmers develop the more complex plug-ins and Java applets. Web page developers then use JavaScript to integrate these components into Web pages.

- *JavaScript is dynamic.* A Web page becomes dynamic when it responds to events generated by the user or other objects. Without JavaScript on the client side, the server-side program must handle all events and perform all the editing functions. JavaScript transfers these tasks back to the client side. This makes Web pages more flexible, more dynamic, and more responsive. It also reduces the load on the server, which allows the server to support more clients.

- *JavaScript is object based.* JavaScript is not an object-oriented language like C++ or Java. An object-oriented language includes classes and strong variable typing. As a scripting language, JavaScript supports *constructors* that create and initialize objects. As an object-based language, JavaScript interacts with objects that expose themselves to the scripting environment. Chapter 5, "JavaScript Object Model," discusses this in detail.

Client-Side JavaScript

Since JavaScript is an extension to an HTML document, how do you invoke JavaScript? There are four methods for invoking JavaScript:

- Within `<SCRIPT>` `</SCRIPT>` tags
- Using `javascript:` as a URL pseudoprotocol
- As HTML attribute values
- Using HTML tags to handle events

Using the <SCRIPT> Tag

It seems as if every computer programming book starts out showing how to display "Hello World." In keeping with tradition, Listing 3.1 illustrates the use of the <SCRIPT> tag.

Listing 3.1 Simple "Hello World"

```
<HTML>
<HEAD>
<TITLE>Simple &quot;Hello World&quot;</TITLE>
<SCRIPT>
document.write("Hello World")
</SCRIPT>
</HEAD>
<BODY>
   </BODY>
</HTML>
```

Figure 3.1 shows the results of the "Hello World" script. The script in Listing 3.1 placed the <SCRIPT> tag between the <HEAD></HEAD> tags. As shown in Listing 3.2, you can also place the <SCRIPT> tag between the <BODY></BODY> tags. The section below on "" discusses the guidelines for placement of JavaScript. In the "Hello World" example, the one JavaScript statement is a *method* for the *document object* (see Chapter 6 for a discussion of objects and their methods).

The LANGUAGE Attribute

Even though the script in Listing 3.1 works with both Netscape Navigator and Microsoft Internet Explorer, it assumes that the default scripting language is JavaScript. To avoid confusion, it is best to add the LAN-GUAGE attribute to the <SCRIPT> tag as shown in Listing 3.2. The valid values for JavaScript, and JScript, shows the revised script with the script between the <BODY></BODY> tags.

Listing 3.2 Better "Hello World"

```
<HTML>
<HEAD>
<TITLE>Better &quot;Hello World&quot;</TITLE>
</HEAD>
<BODY>
```

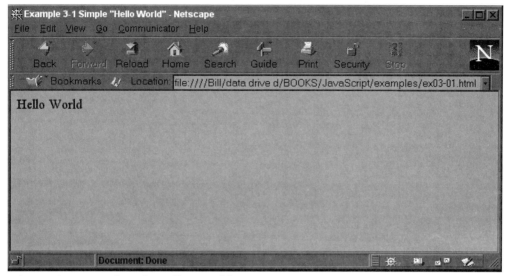

Figure 3.1   Results of "Hello World."

```
<SCRIPT LANGUAGE="JavaScript">
document.write("Hello World")
</SCRIPT>
  </BODY>
</HTML>
```

This is not the only use of the LANGUAGE attribute. With multiple versions of JavaScript in use, how can you ensure that your Web page takes advantage of the latest features, but still supports the older versions? One way is to specify the version number in the LANGUAGE attribute. The valid values are then JavaScript, JavaScript1.1, JavaScript1.2, and JScript. The JavaScript in Listing 3.3 is a simple test that illustrates the use of the version number.

Listing 3.3 Version Number Test

```
<HTML>
<HEAD>
    <TITLE>Version Number Test</TITLE>
  </HEAD>
<BODY>
<P>This tests the version number feature of the LANGUAGE
attribute</P>
```

```
<SCRIPT LANGUAGE="JavaScript">
document.write("JavaScript")
</SCRIPT>
<SCRIPT LANGUAGE="JavaScript1.1">
document.write("JavaScript 1.1")
</SCRIPT>
<SCRIPT LANGUAGE="JavaScript1.2">
document.write("JavaScript1.2")
</SCRIPT>
<SCRIPT LANGUAGE="JScript">
document.write("JScript")
</SCRIPT>
  </BODY>
</HTML>
```

Figure 3.2 shows the results of running the version test script using Netscape Communicator 4.0. Figure 3.3 shows the results of running the same test using Microsoft Internet Explorer 4.0. This is a rather primitive example of a version test script. It appears again in later chapters with additional refinements.

Table 3.2 shows how each JavaScript-enabled browser responds to the different values of the LANGUAGE attribute.

Table 3.2 JavaScript ATTRIBUTE Value Chart

LANGUAGE Value	Navigator 2.0	Navigator 3.0	Navigator 4.0	Microsoft IE 3.0	Microsoft IE 4.0
JavaScript	X	X	X	X	X
JavaScript1.1		X	X		X
JavaScript1.2			X		
JScript					X

Dealing with Non-JavaScript Browsers

Only Netscape Navigator and Microsoft Internet Explorer currently support JavaScript (the various versions of which are detailed back in Table 1.1).

If a non-JavaScript-enabled browser attempted to read an HTML document containing JavaScript code, it would generate an error message. The error message is not caused by the <SCRIPT> tag, since a browser

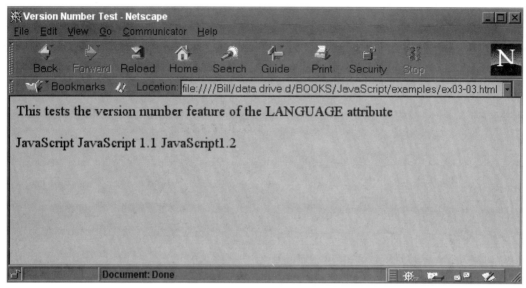

Figure 3.2   Results of version test using Netscape Communicator 4.0.

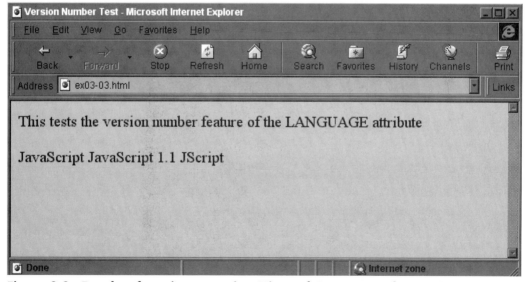

Figure 3.3   Results of version test using Microsoft Internet Explorer 4.0.

ignores any HTML tag that it doesn't support. The problem is in the JavaScript code enclosed by the `<SCRIPT>` `</SCRIPT>` tags. The trick for hiding the code is to place it within an HTML comment. This works because a non-JavaScript-enabled browser ignores the `<SCRIPT>` tags and sees the HTML comment. On the other hand, a JavaScript enabled browser sees the `<SCRIPT>` tags and ignores any HTML statements enclosed by the tags. Listing 3.4 illustrates the use of comments to hide JavaScript from browsers that do not support JavaScript.

Listing 3.4 An Improved "Hello World"

```
<HTML>
<HEAD>
<TITLE>An Improved &quot;Hello World&quot;</TITLE>
</HEAD>
<BODY>
<SCRIPT LANGUAGE="JavaScript">
<!--
document.write("Hello World")
//-->
</SCRIPT>
</BODY>
</HTML>
```

Why the "//" before the ending HTML comment? The JavaScript comment keeps the JavaScript interpreter from treating the HTML comment as JavaScript operands.

While the revised script prevents errors in non-JavaScript-enabled browsers, it fails to communicate to the user that the document uses JavaScript. Starting with JavaScript 1.1, there are the `<NOSCRIPT>` `</NOSCRIPT>` tags. Like the `<SCRIPT>` tag, non-JavaScript-enabled browsers ignore these tags. However, browsers that support JavaScript 1.1, or later, see these tags and ignore the contents. Listing 3.5 shows how to use the `<NOSCRIPT>` tag,

Listing 3.5 The Best "Hello World"

```
<HTML>
  <HEAD>
    <TITLE>The Best &quot;Hello World&quot;</TITLE>
  </HEAD>
<BODY>
<SCRIPT LANGUAGE="JavaScript1.1">
<!--
document.write("Hello World from JavaScript")
//-->
  </SCRIPT>
<NOSCRIPT>
<P>Hello World for non-JavaScript</P>
  </NOSCRIPT>
  </BODY>
</HTML>
```

This script behaves correctly in all browsers, but it has an undesirable side effect. It treats Netscape Navigator 2.0 and Microsoft Internet Explorer 3.0 as non-JavaScript browsers. However, without the version declaration, these browsers display both lines. There are no nice solutions to this dilemma short of all JavaScript users upgrading to a JavaScript 1.1 compatible browser.

The Source Attribute

Most computer languages, whether compiled or interpreted, provide a means of including source code from an external file. JavaScript accomplishes this through the SRC attribute of the <SCRIPT> tag. The format for including a JavaScript file located on the same server is shown here.

```
<HEAD>
<TITLE>Example Script</TITLE>
<SCRIPT LANGUAGE="JavaScript1.1" SRC="filename.js"
...
</SCRIPT>
</HEAD>
```

To include a file located on a different server, you need to specify the full URL as follows:

```
<HEAD>
<TITLE>Example Script</TITLE>
<SCRIPT LANGUAGE="JavaScript1.1"
        SRC="http://www.xxxx.com/filename.js"
...
</SCRIPT>
</HEAD>
```

Netscape introduced the SRC attribute in JavaScript 1.1 (Netscape Navigator 3.0). Since JScript 3.0 (Microsoft Internet Explorer 4.0) matches JavaScript 1.1, it also supports the SRC attribute. The browser only executes the JavaScript code placed between the <SCRIPT> </SCRIPT> tags when the loading of the *js* file fails. The behavior of the SRC attribute in browsers that do not support JavaScript 1.1 is inconsistent. To ensure consistent behavior, the LANGUAGE attribute value needs to include the version number. Listing 3.6 shows the HTML source and Listing 3.7 shows the *js* source of a test script that behaves correctly in all browsers.

Listing 3.6 Using the SRC attribute with "Hello World"

```
<HTML>
<HEAD>
    <TITLE>Using the SRC attribute with &quot;Hello World&quot;</TITLE>
  </HEAD>
<BODY>
<SCRIPT LANGUAGE="JavaScript1.1" SRC="ls03-07.js">
<!--
document.write("Error Reading JavaScript")
//-->
</SCRIPT>
<NOSCRIPT>
<P>Requires JavaScript 1.1 or higher.<P>
</NOSCRIPT>
  </BODY>
</HTML>
```

Listing 3.7 The JavaScript External File

```
// The JavaScript External File
document.write ("Hello World")
```

If the browser fails to load the external source file, you need to check the Web server. The server needs to map the *.js* extension to the MIME type as follows:

```
application/x-javascript          exts=js
```

When the server sends the file to the browser, the server places this MIME type in the header record of the file. Without the correct MIME type, the browser won't know what to do with the file.

There is one other restriction. The *.js* file cannot contain an SRC attribute reference because JavaScript only supports a single level for including external source files.

Even with the versions' restrictions and server requirements, the SRC attribute provides a valuable tool for Web developers. If you have a piece of JavaScript code that you want to use in other HTML documents, you can cut code from one document and paste it into another. This works until you want to make a change to the copied source code. Then you have to make the change in each HTML file to which you copied the JavaScript code. However, with external files, you make the change once and it automatically appears in the next invocation of every HTML document that references the external source file.

HTML Order of Processing

JavaScript is an extension to HTML. As such, the order of processing of an HTML document is important to the execution of JavaScripts.

Browsers process HTML files in a *top-down* fashion. Generally, the browser displays the page as it processes the HTML file. This top-down processing implies certain rules:

- *Definition precedes usage.* The browser acts on each statement as it reads the HTML document. This means that you cannot reference a variable, function, or object before the browser defines it.
- *You cannot refresh the display.* Once the browser displays a document, you cannot make any changes that forces the browser to redisplay the screen. For example, you cannot change the title of a document after the browser displays the title. However, there are two exceptions:
  - ◊ You can change the background since this does not alter the format of the HTML document itself.

◊ You can change the value displayed in a form field. However, you cannot change the layout of the form itself.

Good Web page design requires that the Web page developer understand that it is a media composed of many components. JavaScript is one of these components. The other components include HTML, Java, and plug-ins. Each has a role to play in the creation of Web-based applications.

Placement of <SCRIPT> Tags

The top-down processing of the HTML document leads to a generic model for the layout of JavaScript statements. The following JavaScript model adheres to the *definition before usage* rule by placing the variable and function definitions between the <HEAD> and </HEAD> tags. The ordering of the JavaScript statements between the <BODY> and </BODY> tags varies according to the needs of the application. However, they must follow both rules defined in the previous section.

```
<HTML>
<HEAD>
    <TITLE>JavaScript Programming Model</TITLE>
<SCRIPT LANGUAGE="JavaScript">
<!--
Declare functions and variables here
//-->
</SCRIPT>
  </HEAD>
<BODY>
<SCRIPT LANGUAGE="JavaScript">
<!--
JavaScript statements for immediate action
belong in the body of the document.
//-->
</SCRIPT>
</BODY>
</HTML>
```

Using JavaScript as a URL

In addition to the URL protocols (such as `http:`, `ftp:`, and `gopher:`), you can use the `javascript:` pseudoprotocol as a valid URL value. Listing 3.8 shows how to use `javascript:` to reload the current page. You could combine this technique with an event handler to reload a page when there is an error in loading a window, frame, or image.

Listing 3.8 Using the javascript: URL

```
<HTML>
<HEAD>
<TITLE>Using the javascript: URL</TITLE>
</HEAD>
<BODY>
<P>This reloads the page using javascript:</P>
<P><A HREF="javascript: history.go(0)">
<IMG SRC="images/reset.gif" ALT="reload page"></A></P>
</BODY>
</HTML>
```

The `javascript:` pseudoprotocol is not limited to the `history` object or the `HREF` attribute. For example, you could use it to provide the value for the `SRC` attribute of the `<IMG>` tag. The rules for `javascript:` are as follows:

- If the result of the expression following `javascript:` is undefined, a new page is not loaded.
- The browser converts any defined type to a string value (see Chapter 4, "Fundamentals of JavaScript" for an explanation of JavaScript data types).

Using JavaScript with HTML Attributes

HTML allows you to define special character entities by preceding it with an ampersand (&) and terminating it with a semicolon (;). For example, you can include a quotation mark with `&QUOT;`. JavaScript takes advantage of this HTML feature by creating a *JavaScript entity*. The JavaScript entity still requires the beginning ampersand and ending semicolon. The difference is that you need to enclose the JavaScript statement with curly braces ({}). Listing 3.9 is a short script that illustrates the use of JavaScript entities.

Listing 3.9 JavaScript as an HTML Attribute

```
<HTML>
<HEAD>
<TITLE>JavaScript as an HTML  Attribute</TITLE>
<SCRIPT LANGUAGE="JavaScript">
<!--
```

```
var barWidth=50
var barAlign="CENTER"
//-->
</SCRIPT>
</HEAD>
<BODY>
<P>This example uses variables to control the size and
 alignment of the horizontal rule.</P>
<HR WIDTH="&{barWidth};%" ALIGN="&{barAlign};">
</BODY>
</HTML>
```
Netscape

 The script in Listing 3.9 works with Netscape Navigator, version 3.0 and later, but not with Microsoft Internet Explorer. The problem is that there is no nice way to hide this code from browsers that do not support it.

This script is an example of the order in which a browser processes HTML statements. It works because the variable definitions occur before the browser processes the horizontal rule statement.

JavaScript Event Handlers

A user interacts with a Web page through URLs, forms, and events. The anchor tag controls the actions of the URLs. The form allows the user to enter data and make selections. Events provide another means of responding to user actions. Events and *event handlers* are closely tied to the object model for the browser. Since there is a close relationship between events and objects, the discussion of events appears in Chapter 7.

Signing JavaScripts

Security and flexibility are often conflicting goals. On one hand, the browser needs to protect the user's machine from unauthorized intrusion. Unauthorized intrusion includes:

- Reading or, even worse, writing files on the user's disk
- Sending mail in the user's name
- Accessing or setting restricted information such as the browser history

To solve these problems, Netscape Navigator 2.0 controlled access by seeking to prohibit unauthorized use by restricting the browser's functionality. Although these steps made the browser more secure, they also reduced the flexibility of the browser as a platform for crossware development. Netscape Navigator 3.0 used tainting as a way to restrict access to certain information to a single Web site. Netscape Navigator 4.0 replaced tainting with the signing of scripts. Signed scripts offer flexible access to restricted information, while restricting access for unsigned scripts. (Introducing the topic of signed JavaScripts this early in the book may be a bit premature. However, it is part of the discussion of the <SCRIPT> tag and it does have an impact on events and windows. So, to avoid an abundance of forward references I'm injecting it here.)

Warning

Netscape Navigator 4.0 disabled data tainting. The security model for data tainting was similar to the one used in the Perl scripting language. While it was a step forward in terms of data privacy, it lacked the robustness required for the distributed-object environment.

The security model in JavaScript 1.2 shapes the bounds of what action you can perform in JavaScript. Instead of taking away access to information, the browser gives access to signed scripts. If you don't understand everything in this section on the first pass, you can come back later and read it again.

Signed scripts have a digital signature that allows the user to confirm the validity of the certificate used to sign the script. You can sign scripts within the <SCRIPT> </SCRIPT> tags or event handlers. You cannot sign javascript: URLs or JavaScript entities. Since signing scripts requires special tools, Chapter 16, "JavaScript Tools," discusses the mechanics of signing scripts. Before signing a script, you need to ensure that the script meets the following requirements:

- The <SCRIPT> tag needs to have the ARCHIVE attribute
- An ID attribute in the <SCRIPT> tag
- A request for expanded privileges
- All scripts on the same page must be signed
- Changes to a script require re-signing the script

ARCHIVE Attribute to <SCRIPT> Tag

All signed scripts require that the <SCRIPT> tag include the ARCHIVE attribute. The value of the ARCHIVE attribute is a Java Archive (JAR) file containing the digital signature. The following snippet illustrates using the ARCHIVE attribute for a signed script specified by the SRC statement:

```
<SCRIPT LANGUAGE="JavaScript1.2" ARCHIVE="arch1.jar"
       SRC="script.js">
</SCRIPT>
```

Once you define the ARCHIVE attribute, it remains in effect until changed by another ARCHIVE attribute. When multiple JavaScript files, in-line JavaScripts, event handlers, or Java applets reference the same JAR file, you need to use the ID attribute to identify each instance.

ID Attribute to <SCRIPT> Tag

In-line scripts and event-handler scripts require the ID attribute in the <SCRIPT> tag to identify their digital signature in the JAR file. The ID attribute is a unique string that links the script to a digital signature. Here are a few rules that apply to the ID attribute:

- The ARCHIVE attribute applies only to the <SCRIPT> tag. All ID attributes following an ARCHIVE attribute refer to this JAR file, until another <SCRIPT> tag defines a different JAR file.
- Event handlers only use the ID attribute. Thus, they reference the JAR file defined by the ARCHIVE attribute in a previous <SCRIPT> tag.
- When there is more than one event handler in a single HTML tag, the entire tag has a single digital signature. Consequently, a single ID attribute covers all the event handlers.
- When the <SCRIPT> tag includes the SRC attribute, there is no ID attribute. The ID attribute only applies to in-line scripts and event handlers.

The script shown in Listing 3.10 illustrates how these rules apply. Since this script uses digital signatures, you must use the tools described in Chapter 16 to sign the script prior to loading it into Netscape Communicator 4.0.

Listing 3.10 Using the ID Attribute in a Signed JavaScript

```
<HTML>
<HEAD>
<TITLE>Using the ID Attribute in a signed JavaScript</TITLE>
<SCRIPT LANGUAGE="JavaScript1.2" ARCHIVE="arch1.jar" ID="1">
<!--
document.write("This is a signed script.")
//-->
</SCRIPT>
</HEAD>
<BODY onload="alert('alert using the first JAR')">
   onload="alert('alert using single ID attribute')" ID="2">
<SCRIPT LANGUAGE="JavaScript1.2" SRC="ls03-06a.js">
</SCRIPT>
<SCRIPT LANGUAGE="JavaScript1.2" ARCHIVE="arch2.jar" ID="1">
<!--
document.write("This is the second signed JAR file.")
//-->
</SCRIPT>
</BODY>
</HTML>
```

In Listing 3.10, the first `<SCRIPT>` tag defines the first JAR file. Since it is an in-line script, it includes the `ID` attribute. The event handlers in the `<BODY>` tag have a single `ID` attribute for both events. Since an event handler doesn't include the `ARCHIVE` attribute, the event handler depends on the previous `<SCRIPT>` to define the JAR file. The next `<SCRIPT>` tag includes a JavaScript file. Therefore, this `<SCRIPT>` doesn't need an `ID` attribute. The final `<SCRIPT>` tag establishes a new JAR file.

Requesting Expanded Privileges

The purpose of a signed script is to access Netscape's Java security classes and request expanded privileges. You need to make this request within at least one JavaScript function. This function must include the following line of code:

```
netscape.security.PrivilegeManager.enablePrivilege("target")
```

The *target* is any of those listed in Table 3.3. When the script calls this function, the browser verifies the signature before granting expanded privileges. If necessary, the browser displays a dialog box that informs the user about the author of the application, and gives the user the option to grant or deny expanded privileges. Once the browser grants expanded privileges, all functions called by the function containing the request will have expanded privileges. When the script exits the function, the expanded privileges no longer apply.

Table 3.3 lists the type of information (called *targets*) that you can access in signed scripts. Table 3.4 shows the JavaScript objects that require expanded privileges and the target needed to access these privileges. Table 3.5 provides the same information for JavaScript features. From these tables, you can see why signed scripts radically change the JavaScript security model. Many features that were not accessible in previous releases of Netscape Navigator are now accessible. Of course this security model only applies to JavaScript 1.2, which means that scripts running under different versions of JavaScript need to recognize the security models applicable to that version of JavaScript.

Table 3.3 Description of JavaScript Targets

Target	Description
UniversalBrowserRead	Permits reading of privileged data from browser.
UniversalBrowserWrite	Permits modification of privileged browser data.
UniversalFileRead	Permits a script to define a local file which the browser uploads to the server upon submission of a form.
UniversalPreferencesRead	Permits the script to use the navigator.preferences() method to read the browser preferences.
UniversalPreferencesWrite	Permits the script to use the navigator.preferences() method to set preferences.
UniversalSendMail	Permits the script to send mail in the user's name.

Table 3.4 JavaScript Objects Requiring Privileges

Object	Property	Target
`event`	setting any property	`UniversalBrowserWrite`
`DragDrop` `event`	getting the value of the data property	`UniversalBrowserRead`
`history`	getting any property	`UniversalBrowserRead`
	setting any property	`UniversalBrowserWrite`
`navigator`	getting the value of a preference	`UniversalPreferences-` `Read`
	setting the value of a preference	`UniversalPreference-` `Write`
`window`	Adding or removing: directory bar, location bar, menu bar, personal bar, scroll bar, status bar, or toolbar. Using methods: `enableExternalCapture` (when a window wants to capture events in pages loaded from different servers), `close` (unconditionally close a browser window), `moveBy` (to move a window of the screen), `moveTo` (to move a window of the screen), `open` (when using any method to make the screen smaller than 100 by 100 pixels, or larger than the screen; when creating a screen without a title bar; or, using the `alwaysRaise`, `alwaysLowered`, or `zlock` settings), `resizeTo` or `resizeBy` (when making a window less than 100 by 100 pixels). Setting the properties `innerWidth` and `inner-Height` to create a window less than 100 by 100 pixels.	`UniversalBrowserWrite`

Table 3.5 JavaScript Features Requiring Extended Privileges

Feature	Target
Setting a file for uploading on submission of a form.	`UniversalFileRead`
Submitting a form to mailto: or news: URL	`UniversalSendMail`
Using about: URL other than about:blank	`UniversalBrowserRead`

Signing of Scripts

If one script requests expanded privileges, all scripts on the HTML page or layer require a digital signature. In an HTML document containing multiple layers, unsigned scripts need to exist on a separate layer from signed scripts. You can sign JavaScript files included by the SRC attribute, in-line scripts and event handlers. If any script on the HTML page, or layer, contains a javascript: URL or a JavaScript entity, the browser treats the signed scripts as unsigned.

A change to the script's byte stream invalidates the digital signature. This protects the script from tampering. It also means that any changes to a script require a new digital signature for the script.

Warning

If you move an HTML document from one platform to another (for examples Windows to UNIX), the byte stream changes because of the differences in line termination characters. To avoid invalidating the digital signature, you need to move it as a binary file. This doesn't effect the viewing of the pages, but it does change its appearance in the new platform's text editor.

You cannot include international characters in a signed script because the process of transforming them to the local character set invalidates the digital signature. If you need to use international characters in a script, you have to use one of the following techniques:

- Escape the international characters (for example, 0x\ca)
- Put the international character string in a hidden form element and access the form element from a signed script
- Separate the signed and unsigned script into separate layers, and place the international characters in the unsigned scripts
- Remove comments that include international characters

Creating Signed Scripts

Creating a signed script is more complicated than writing and publishing the script. To create a signed script, you need to follow these three steps:

1. Include the ARCHIVE and ID attributes in the <SCRIPT> tag, and the ID attribute for event handlers.

2. Include calls to Java classes requesting expanded privileges.

3. Sign the script using the tools described in Chapter 16.

    During the development phase of a script, you can get expanded privileges without having to sign the script. By using codebase principals, Netscape Communicator allows the URL of the script to function as a principal for enabling privileges.

Warning

An unsigned script is subject to tampering. If this unsigned script contains requests for expanded privileges, using codebase principals opens the browser to potential security violations. The best practice is to sign the scripts once you complete testing.

To activate codebase principals in Netscape Communicator, you need to perform the following three steps:

1. Close all instances of Netscape Communicator.

2. Add the following line to the Netscape preferences file:

```
user_pref("signed.applets.codebase_principal_support", true);
```

3. Save the revised preferences file.

    Different platforms hide the preferences file in different places. The most likely locations are:

    - *Microsoft Windows*. \Program Files\Netscape\Users\default\prefs.js
    - *Microsoft Windows NT*. \Netscape\Uses\username\prefs.js
    - *UNIX*. ~/.netscape/preferences.js
    - *Macintosh*. System Folder:Preferences:Netscape f: (where the f is a special script character f)

Note

With codebase principals, the browser doesn't use the ARCHIVE and ID attributes. These attributes are only used on signed scripts.

When you access the script, the browser displays a dialog box similar to the one displayed for signed scripts. The difference is that the browser asks you to grant privileges to the URL without author verification. The browser also warns you that the script is not digitally signed.

Note

When you activate codebase principals and the page includes unsigned scripts, the browser treats all scripts as unsigned and uses codebase principals.

The signed script is a tight sandbox. There are several rules that apply to interfacing with information outside of the script:

- You need to use the `export` statement to provide properties, functions, and objects to other signed or unsigned scripts.
- You need to use the `import` statement in the script to accept the exported features.
- If a window with frames needs to capture events in pages loaded from other servers, you need to use the `enableExternalCapture` method in a signed script that requests `UniversalBrowserWrite` privileges. This must be done prior to using the `captureEvents` method.

Testing a signed script is also more complicated then testing an unsigned script. To check for errors, you need to open the Java Console.

Server-Side JavaScript

On the server side, LiveWire provides an alternative to CGI scripts. LiveWire simplifies software development by providing a single language environment. In addition, JavaScript interfaces with the Netscape server object model. Starting with Netscape Enterprise Server 3.0, JavaScript support is an integral part of the product. At this time, only Netscape servers support server-side JavaScripts.

Server-side JavaScripts are also part of HTML documents. This allows the intermixing of server-side executables with client-side Web pages. Chapters 12 through 14 discuss the details of how to use server-side Java-Script.

Summary

JavaScript is an HTML scripting language for both client-side and server-side application development. JavaScript is an object-based language as opposed to Java which is an object-oriented programming language. As an object-based scripting language, JavaScript dynamically interacts with objects made available to it by Java applets, C++ plug-ins, and the browser or server.

You enable JavaScript by using the `<SCRIPT> </SCRIPT>` tags, as a URL pseudoprotocol, as a value to HTML attributes, and via event handlers. Through each of these methods, JavaScript integrates with a different aspect of the HTML document.

When you write a script using JavaScript, you are immediately faced with security issues. These security issues determine how you design and write scripts. Consequently, you need to understand the security model of each browser.

Each version of JavaScript has a different security model. In JavaScript 1.0, the security model denied access to information that presented a possible security problem. The price of limiting access was a corresponding limitation to functionality. JavaScript 1.1 used the data-tainting security model. The data-tainting model allowed scripts running in different windows or frames to access information in other windows or frames as long as the servers that provided the documents shared a common domain name. JavaScript 1.2 replaced the data-tainting security model with an entirely new model based on signed scripts. Signed scripts have a digital signature that allows the user to confirm the validity of the certificate used to sign the script.

This chapter discussed how to integrate JavaScript into the HTML document. Chapter 4 focuses on the fundamentals of the JavaScript language.

Fundamentals of
JavaScript

Topics in This Chapter

- Formatting JavaScript and commenting statements
- Data types, literals, and variables
- Operators and expressions
- Writing control statements
- Using functions in JavaScript

Chapter 4

When learning a new computer language, the first thing you need to know is how to format statements and insert comments. Once you understand the syntax requirements, you need to know how JavaScript stores and manipulates data. In this respect, JavaScript follows the course of other scripting languages. Unlike a program language, JavaScript has only a few data types and they are loosely typed. In a programming language, such as Java, variables are strongly typed. When you define a variable in a programming language, you also declare its data type. On the other hand, in a scripting language, the data type is dynamically determined.

What you store in a variable determines its current data type. The data type of a variable impacts on the behavior of operators and control statements.

The next step is to discuss the operators and expressions. Operators, when formed into expressions, give you the ability to manipulate data values.

JavaScript is an object-based scripting language. As a scripting language, JavaScript has a syntax similar to many other scripting languages. JavaScript has the standard conditional and loop control statements, and as an object-based language, JavaScript also has statements to manipulate objects. Since these statements require an understanding of objects, their discussion appears in Chapter 5, "JavaScript Object Model."

In discussing the basics of JavaScript, there is a certain amount of the chicken versus the egg paradox. Thus, there are references in this chapter to objects and properties.

Formatting Statements

A *statement* is an individual unit of code that performs an action or controls the sequence of execution. This chapter discusses the following JavaScript statements:

- Setting a variable
- unary increment and decrement
- `if` statement
- `else` statement
- `switch` statement (new in JavaScript 1.2)
- `for` statement
- `while` statement
- `do ... while` statement (new in JavaScript 1.2)
- `break` statement (enhanced in JavaScript 1.2)
- `continue` statement (enhanced in JavaScript 1.2)
- `return` statement

These and the object-oriented statements covered in Chapter 5 constitute the JavaScript statements. JavaScript has three rules for writing statements:

- Use white space as a separator
- Use semicolons at the end of statements
- Use labeled statements (new in JavaScript 1.2)

White space as a Separator

In JavaScript, there is both required and optional *white space*. White space is a separator character between keywords, literals, and operators that identifies the components of a statement. The white space characters are the space, tab, and new-line characters. The JavaScript rules for white space are:

- Keywords need to be separated from the following text by a white space. The following are some examples of required white space:

```
var FirstName="John"
if (a>b)
```

- There is no white space separating the function name and the argument list. This must always be written as:

```
functionName(argument)
```

- In an argument list with multiple arguments, you need white space after each comma as the following example illustrates:

```
functionName(argument1, argument2, argument3)
```

- There is no white space after an opening parenthesis and before the closing parenthesis.
- The white space before and after operators in binary expressions is optional. The following are equivalent statements:

```
var a=b+c
var a = b + c
```

- There is no white space between a unary operator and its associated variable such as:

```
i++
```

Semicolons at the End of Statements

JavaScript requires that you separate multiple statements on the same physical line by a semicolon. For better readability, you normally start every statement on a separate physical line. When writing event handlers, you may find that including several statements on the same physical line makes the script more readable.

If you are a C programmer, you can terminate every statement with a semicolon. JavaScript ignores these extra semicolons. If you prefer not to type anything that is not necessary; leave them out.

New in JavaScript 1.2

Labeled Statements

The statement label is an identifier that precedes the statement. Only the `break` statement and `continue` statement provide a syntax for transferring control of execution to a labeled statement. The syntax for a labeled statement is as follows:

```
label :
statement
```

The syntax requires that there is a white space between the label and the colon. If you forget the white space, the JavaScript interpreter gives you an undefined label error. Since this applies only to JavaScript 1.2, you need to include the `LANGUAGE="JavaScript1.2"` attribute in the `<SCRIPT>` tag.

Warning

Since JavaScript is a scripting language, the label statement must occur before it is referenced by a `break` statement or `continue` statement.

Comments in JavaScript

JavaScript supports the following two Java style formats for comments:

- The single-line comment preceded by a double slash ("//")
- Multiple-line comments preceded by a /* and terminated by a */

The single-line comment, which Java took from C++, treats everything from the double slash to the end of the line as a comment. Thus, the following are valid examples of a single-line comment:

```
// this is a comment
if (a=b) c=1 // also a valid comment
```

The multiple-line comment, which Java took from C, can be used to bracket any comment. The following illustrates a multiple-line comment:

```
/* This is a multiple line comment.
   It can appear anywhere in a script */
```

The comment used to bracket the JavaScript statements, as shown in the previous examples, is an HTML comment. However, the last line of the comment needs the double slash to keep JavaScript from interpreting the line.

JavaScript Data Types

Unlike Java, JavaScript recognizes only a few types of values. They are as follows:

- Numeric, both real and integer, such as 4.156 and 39
- Strings, such as "Hello World"
- Logical (Boolean) values (true or false)
- Null, which is a special keyword denoting a no value

Although the number of data types is small, they are sufficient for the tasks that JavaScript performs. Notice, that there is no distinction between integer and real numbers; both data types are just numbers. Nor does JavaScript provide an explicit data type for a date. However, a built-in date object, and related methods, enable the Web page designer to manage dates.

JavaScript Literals

Literals represent the values used in JavaScript. JavaScript supports the following literals:

- Numeric literals
- Boolean literals
- String literals
- Special characters

Numeric Literals

JavaScript supports both integer and floating point literals. Each of these has a different format for representation.

The integer formats are decimal, hexadecimal or octal. A decimal integer is any sequence of digits that is not prefixed by a zero, such as 4, 89, or 157. If the integer is prefixed by a zero, it is an octal value, such as 04, 065, 0145. To express an integer in hexadecimal format, it is prefixed by 0x or 0X, such as 0xff, 0X44, or 0xAE.

A floating point literal consists of the following components:

- a decimal integer
- a decimal point (".")
- a decimal fraction
- an optional exponent.

This format allows for both fractional literals (such as 1.23, or 44.6389) or those expressed in scientific notation (3.6E-8, .4E12, or -2.7E12). Every floating point literal must have at least one digit and a decimal point or an exponent.

Boolean Literals

Boolean literals are straightforward. Their values are either true or false. You can also use yes and no to specify a Boolean literal.

String Literals

String literals can be enclosed by either single (') or double quotes ("). The beginning and ending quote mark must be the same as shown in the following examples:

```
"a double quoted literal"
'a single quoted literal'
```

Note

When writing event handlers, enclose string literals in single quotes, since HTML uses double quotes to delimit attribute values.

Special Characters

String literals may also contain special characters for formatting the string. The role these characters play in a string depends on the use of the string. For example, they do not effect the display of text in the `document.write()` method (see Chapter 7 "Working with Events and Documents"). On the other hand, \n and \r are useful in the `window.alert()` method (see Chapter 9, "Working with Windows and Frames"). Table 4.1 lists the special characters and their function.

Table 4.1 JavaScript Special Characters

Special Character	Description
\b	backspace
\f	form feed
\n	new line
\r	carriage return
\t	tab

The backslash ("\") is the escape character for JavaScript. When used at the end of a line, it acts as a line continuation character. When followed by another character, it escapes that character so that the following character loses its special function. In JavaScript, you use the backslash to escape another backslash, a single quote, or a double quote. You can also use the backslash to escape octal and hexadecimal values. The following examples show some uses of the backslash:

```
\\
\ "
\ '
\076
\x3c
```

JavaScript Variables

Variables are a fundamental part of every programming language. In a programming language, variables serve multiple purposes. Their primary function is to store information gathered in one part of the program for later use. However, variables also offer a convenient means of storing literals. Using variables to store literals makes them easier to locate and change.

The naming rules for variables require that variable names begin with a letter or underscore ("_") and that the remaining characters are either numbers (0–9), uppercase (A–Z) or lowercase letters (a–z), or the underscore. JavaScript does not allow spaces in a variable name. The following are examples of valid variable names:

```
First_Name
t99
_name
```

Reserved Words

The only other restriction on variable names is that they must not be the same as a JavaScript reserved word. Although it is not listed as a keyword, you cannot use the word *clear*, since the browser confuses this with the `clear()` method of the document object. The same applies to words such as *alert*, which the browser sees as referring to the `alert()` method. Table 4.2 lists the JavaScript reserved words.

Table 4.2 JavaScript Reserved Words

abstract	else	instanceof	super
boolean	export	int	switch
break	extends	interface	synchronized
byte	false	long	this
case	final	native	throw
catch	finally	new	throws
char	float	null	transient
class	for	package	true
const	function	private	try
continue	goto	protected	typeof
default	if	public	var
delete	implements	return	void
do	import	short	while
double	in	static	with

Netscape

Netscape has not defined the reserved word list for JavaScript 1.2. Based on the new statements in JavaScript 1.2, *export* has been added to the list of reserved words defined in JavaScript 1.1.

Some of the reserved words are for future use, so not every word in the Table 4.2 is currently used in JavaScript.

In addition to variable names, you cannot use reserved words for function names, method names, or object names.

Declaring a Variable

You declare a variable in one of two ways:

- By assigning a value to a variable name.

```
degrees = 42
```

- By using the keyword `var`.

```
var degrees = 42
```

The two methods for declaring a variable have slightly different meanings depending on the scope of the variable. JavaScript supports two scopes for variables:

- Global variables
- Local variables

Global Variables

A *global variable* is any variable declared outside of a function. For global variables, the use of the `var` keyword is optional. A good programming practice calls for the placing of all global variables at the beginning of the script. This ensures that they are defined prior to their use. Listing 4.1 is a modification of the "Hello World" script that uses global variables.

Listing 4.1 Declaration of Global Variables

```
<HTML>

  <HEAD>
    <TITLE>Global Variables</TITLE>
    <SCRIPT LANGUAGE="JavaScript">
<!--
var HelloWorld="<P>Hello World</P>"
WelWorld="<P>Welcome to JavaScript</P>"
//-->
    </SCRIPT>
  </HEAD>

  <BODY>
<SCRIPT LANGUAGE="JavaScript">
<!--
document.write(HelloWorld)
document.write(WelWorld)
//-->
</SCRIPT>
  </BODY>
</HTML>
```

There is one other way to declare a global variable. If you declare a variable in a `function` statement without using the `var` keyword, JavaScript treats it as a global variable.

Note

Declaring a variable with the `var` keyword with no assignment operator creates a variable whose value is "undefined."

Local Variables

A *local variable* is any variable defined within a `function` statement that you declare with the `var` keyword. Although it is not a recommended programming practice, you can declare a local variable with the same name as a global variable. In this case, the local variable takes precedence over the global variable, but does not alter the value of the global variable. Listing 4.2 demonstrates the scope of both local and global variables.

Listing 4.2 Declaration of Local Variables

```
<HTML>

  <HEAD>
    <TITLE>Example for Global and Local Variables</TITLE>

<SCRIPT LANGUAGE="JavaScript">
<!--
var gblvar1 = "<P>Global Variable with var</P>"
gblvar2 = "<P>Global variable without var</P>"
function lcltest() {
var lclvar1="<P>A Local Variable</P>"
var gblvar1="<P>Global variable with local declaration</P>"
gblvar2="<P>New value for Global variable</P>"
document.write(lclvar1)
document.write(gblvar1)
document.write(gblvar2)
}
//-->
</SCRIPT>
```

```
</HEAD>

<BODY>

  <P>The following displays the initial settings for two
     global variables.</P>

<SCRIPT LANGUAGE="JavaScript">
<!--
document.write(gblvar1)
document.write(gblvar2)
//-->
</SCRIPT>

  <P>The following results are from a function that
     defines a local variable, a local declaration
     of a global variable with var, and the assignment
     of a new value to a global variable.</P>

<SCRIPT LANGUAGE="JavaScript">
<!--
lcltest()
//-->
</SCRIPT>
<P> Display the settings for the two global variables.</P>
<SCRIPT LANGUAGE="JavaScript">
<!--
document.write(gblvar1)
document.write(gblvar2)
//-->
</SCRIPT>
  </BODY>
</HTML>
```

The initial global variable definitions in Listing 4.2 set the stage for demonstrating the impact of local variables on global variables. The function statement defines a new local variable (`lclvar1`), a local declaration of a global variable using the `var` keyword (`gblvar1`), and a local declaration of a global variable without the `var` keyword (`gblvar2`). With the `var` keyword, the local declaration applies only to the function and the global definition remains the same. Without the `var` keyword, the local declaration changes the value of the global variable. Although the listing declares `gblvar2` without the `var` keyword, the script produces the same output when you declare `gblvar2` with the var keyword. With either global declaration, the lack of the var keyword in a local declaration provides a means for altering the value of the global variable. Figure 4.1 shows the results of running this script.

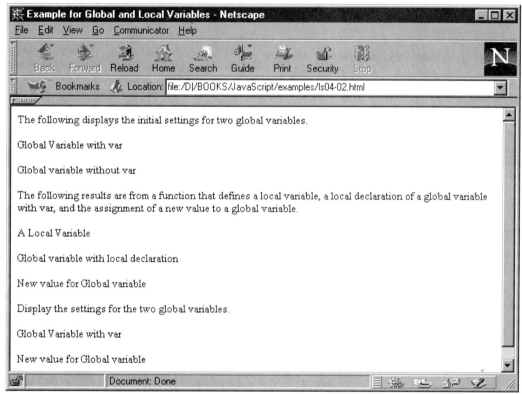

Figure 4.1   Results of running Listing 4.2.

Data Types and Variables

With JavaScript, a variable accepts all valid data. In the same script, variables can be set to different data types or even mixed data types in a single declaration. The following variable declarations are all valid:

```
temperature = 72
temperature = "The temperature is"
temperature = "The temperature is " + 72
```

In the last example, JavaScript converts the numeric literal 72 to a string. This conversion is the result of the concatenation operator. The data type of the variable is extremely important when you use operators to compare and manipulate variables.

JavaScript Expressions and Operators

When literals and variables are linked by operators, the resulting statement is an expression. The definition of an *expression* is any set of literals, variables and operators that evaluate to a single value. The resulting value is a string, number, or logical value. The assignment of a literal to a variable or the computation of several literals using mathematical operators are examples of different types of expressions. JavaScript provides a rich variety of operators that allows you to write expressions that range from the very simple to the very complex.

The JavaScript operators fall into the following categories:

- Assignment operators
- Arithmetic operators
- Bitwise operators
- Logical operators
- Comparison operators
- String operators

JavaScript includes both binary and unary operators. A binary operator has the format:

```
left-operand operator right-operand
```

The following are examples of expressions that use binary operators:

```
8 * 4
HelloWorld = "Hello World"
```

The unary operator has two formats:

```
operand operator
operator operand
```

The following are examples of expressions that use unary increment operators:

```
++x
x++
```

Assignment Operators

The assignment operator ("=") is a binary operator that assigns a value to the left operand (a variable) based on the value of the right operand. Examples of the assignment operator are as follows:

```
FirstName = "John"
x = y * 9
```

For more compact right-hand expressions, JavaScript prefixes the assignment operator with either an arithmetic or bitwise operator. Table 4.3 lists these shorthand assignment operators.

Table 4.3 JavaScript Shorthand Assignment Operators

Shorthand Operator	Meaning	Example
x += y	x = x + y	x += 7
x -= y	x = x - y	x -= 2
x *= y	x = x * y	x *= 12
x /= y	x = x / y	x /= 2
x %= y	x = x % y	x %= 8
x <<= y	x = x << y	x <<= 2
x >>= y	x = x >> y	x >>= 2
x >>>= y	x = x >>> y	x >>>= 4
x &= y	x = x & y	x &= 0xC0
x |= y	x = x | y	x |= 0x0F
x ^= y	x = x ^ y	x ^= 0XFF

Note

For those who are not familiar with C programming, be careful of the difference between and assignment operator ("=") and the comparison operator ("==").

Arithmetic Operators

The purpose of arithmetic operators is to compute a single numerical value from the numerical values of either literals or variables according to the specified arithmetic operators. JavaScript supports the standard arithmetic operators of addition ("+"), subtraction ("–"), multiplication ("*"), and division ("/"). In addition, it includes operators for modulus ("%"), increment ("++"), decrement ("– –"), and unary negation ("–").

The modulus operator ("%") is a binary operator that returns the remainder of the integral division of operand1 by operand2. For example, the result of 27 % 6 is 3.

Warning

All versions of Netscape Navigator for Windows return an incorrect value when calculating a modulus whose value is a floating-point number. For example, 27.7 % 11.3 returns 5.099999999999998, instead of 5.1. All versions of Microsoft Internet Explorer return the expected value of 5.1.

The increment and decrement unary operators respectively add or subtract one from the operand. However, the value returned depends on the operator operand order. If the operator is prefix (++x or – –x), the value returned is x+1 or x–1 accordingly. When the operator is postfix (x++ or x– –), the value returned is x before it is incremented or decremented.

The other special unary arithmetic operator is the unary negation operator. It simply reverses the sign of the value assigned to a variable. Thus, if x = –7, –x changes the value to 7.

Bitwise Operators

For those programmers who need to fiddle with bits, JavaScript provides a set of bitwise operators. For these operators, JavaScript converts the operand into a 32-bit signed integer prior to performing the operation specified by the operator. The bitwise logical operators are:

- The AND ("&") operator returns the results of the logical AND between each pair of bits. For example, 0x0f & 0x0a returns 0x0a.
- The OR ("|") operator returns the results of the logical OR between each pair of bits. For example, 0x05 | 0x0a returns 0x0f.
- The XOR ("^") operator returns the results of the logical exclusive OR of each pair of bits. For example, 0x0f & 0x0a returns 0x05.
- The NOT ("~") unary operator returns the results of a logical NOT.

JavaScript also provides a set of bitwise shift operators that shift the bits of operand1 by the amount specified in operand2. These operands are:

- The shift left ("<<") operator rotates the bits to the left by the amount specified. Excess bits shifted off to the left are discarded, while zero bits are shifted in from the right. For example, 0x0f << 2 returns 0x3c.
- The sign propagating shift right (">>") operator keeps the value of the sign while shifting bits to the right by the amount specified. Excess bits shifted to the right are discarded, while (excluding the sign bit) zero bits are shifted in from the left. For example, 10 >> 2 returns 2 and -10 >> 2 returns -2.
- The zero-fill right shift (">>>") operator does not preserve the sign bit while shifting bits to the right by the amount specified. Excess bits shifted to the right are discarded, while zero bits are shifted in from the left. For positive numbers, the results are the same as the sign propagating shift right. However, for negative numbers, the sign is lost.

Logical Operators

The logical operators require that the operands are Boolean values (true or false) and they return a logical value. In the case of logical operators, the operands are expressions that evaluate to a logical value. The logical operators are:

- Logical AND ("&&")
- Logical OR ("| |")
- Logical not ("!")

The logical *not* operator is a unary operator that reverses the Boolean value of the expression.

Note

JavaScript performs a short-circuit evaluation on logical operations such that false && expr resolves to false, and true || expr resolves to true. Under these cases, expr is not evaluated.

Comparison Operators

The comparison operators apply to numerical and string values and not to Boolean values. Both operands must be of the same data type; numbers compared to numbers, or strings compared to strings. The result of a comparison, however, is a Boolean value. The comparison operators are:

- Equal ("==")
- Not equal ("!=")
- Greater than (">")
- Greater than or equal to (">=")
- Less than ("<")
- Less than or equal to ("<=")

JavaScript also supports the conditional expression, which takes the form:

```
(condition) ? true_value : false_value
```

If the condition is true, the expression has the value of true_value. Otherwise, it has the value of false_value. Like its cousins in other C based languages, the conditional expression is a standard expression. Therefore, you can use it like any other expression. The following example illustrates the use of a conditional expression:

```
battery_status = (voltage > 1.3) ? "good" : "weak"
```

When you test for equality (== or !=), you need to know about the following:

- Changes in rules for equality operators in JavaScript 1.2
- Rules for data conversion in equality tests

Netscape

In JavaScript 1.0 and 1.1, the comparison of "undefined" with null returned true. In JavaScript 1.2, null is a separate data type, so the comparison now returns false.

Equality Operators in JavaScript 1.2

In JavaScript 1.0 and 1.1, the equality operators (== and !=) used the following rules for comparison:

- If both operands are objects, compare object references.
- If either operand is null, convert the other operand to an object and compare references.
- If one operand is a string and the other an object, convert the object to a string and compare string characters.
- If none of these rules apply, convert both operands to numbers and compare numeric identity.

While these rules make it easier to write JavaScript code, they also introduce more complexity in the language and make it more prone to errors. JavaScript 1.2 corrects these problems by changing the rules for comparison to the following:

- Operands are no longer converted from one data type to another. It is now your responsibility to ensure that the scripts are comparing like data types.
- If the operands do not have the same data type, they are not equal.

To ensure some degree of backwards compatibility, the new rules only apply when you use the LANUAGE="JavaScript1.2" attribute in the <SCRIPT> tag. This means that to use all the new features in JavaScript 1.2, you need to be careful about how the equality operator is used.

Data Conversion

With the new equality comparison rules in JavaScript 1.2, scripts must be written that qualify according to the new rules. The choice is using techniques that apply to all versions, or using techniques that depend on new built-in functions for JavaScript 1.2.

The techniques to convert data types for all versions of JavaScript are:

- To convert a numeric data type to a string data type use " " + x. For example,

```
(("" + 5) == "5"
```

- To convert a string data type to a numeric data type use x - 0. For example,

```
(("5" - 0) == 5)
```

If you want to use the built-in functions of JavaScript 1.1 and JavaScript 1.2, use the following techniques:

- To convert a numeric data type to a string data type use the function String(x). For example,

```
String(5) == "5"
```

- To convert a string data type to a numeric data type use the function Number(x). For example,

```
Number("5") == 5
```

The script in Listing 4.3 tests the conversion functions of a browser. The tests performed are:

- Test 1 depends on the browser converting the numeric data type to a string data type.
- Test 2 converts the numeric data type to a string data type.
- Test 3 depends on the browser converting the string data type to a numeric data type.
- Test 4 converts the string data type to a numeric data type.
- Test 5 converts the numeric data type using the String() function.
- Test 6 converts the string data type using the Number() function.

Listing 4.3 Data Conversion Tests

```
<HTML>
  <HEAD>
    <TITLE>Data Conversion Tests</TITLE>
  </HEAD>
  <BODY>
    <P>No LANGUAGE attribute</P>
<SCRIPT>
<!--
document.write("test1: "+(5=="5")+"<BR>")
document.write("test2: "+((""+5)=="5")+"<BR>")
document.write("test3: "+("5"==5)+"<BR>")
document.write("test4: "+(("5"-0)==5)+"<BR>")
//-->
</SCRIPT>
    <P>LANGUAGE=&quot;JavaScript&quot;</P>
<SCRIPT LANGUAGE="JavaScript">
<!--
document.write("test1: "+(5=="5")+"<BR>")
document.write("test2: "+((""+5)=="5")+"<BR>")
document.write("test3: "+("5"==5)+"<BR>")
document.write("test4: "+(("5"-0)==5)+"<BR>")
//-->
</SCRIPT>
    <P>LANGUAGE=&quot;JavaScript1.1&quot;</P>
```

```
<SCRIPT LANGUAGE="JavaScript1.1">
<!--
document.write("test1: "+(5=="5")+"<BR>")
document.write("test2: "+((""+5)=="5")+"<BR>")
document.write("test3: "+("5"==5)+"<BR>")
document.write("test4: "+(("5"-0)==5)+"<BR>")
document.write("test5: "+(String(5)=="5")+"<BR>")
document.write("test6: "+(Number("5")==5)+"<BR>")
//-->
</SCRIPT>
    <P>LANGUAGE=&quot;JavaScript1.2&quot;</P>
<SCRIPT LANGUAGE="JavaScript1.2">
<!--
document.write("test1: "+(5=="5")+"<BR>")
document.write("test2: "+((""+5)=="5")+"<BR>")
document.write("test3: "+("5"==5)+"<BR>")
document.write("test4: "+(("5"-0)==5)+"<BR>")
document.write("test5: "+(String(5)=="5")+"<BR>")
document.write("test6: "+(Number("5")==5)+"<BR>")
//-->
</SCRIPT>
  </BODY>
</HTML>
```

I ran the script shown in Listing 4.3 using Netscape Navigator 3.0 (JavaScript 1.1), Netscape Communicator 4.0 (JavaScript 1.2), Microsoft Internet Explorer 3.0 (JavaScript 1.0) and Microsoft Internet Explorer 4.0 (JavaScript 1.1). With each browser, the results were according to the version of JavaScript implemented as shown in Table 4.4. The test results confirm the data conversion rules and the techniques used to ensure the comparison of like data types.

Table 4.4 Data Conversion Test Results

	JavaScript 1.0	JavaScript 1.1	JavaScript 1.2
Test 1	true	true	false
Test 2	true	true	true
Test 3	true	true	false
Test 4	true	true	true
Test 5	Not tested	true	true
Test 6	Not tested	true	true

String Operators

The string operator ("+") concatenates two string values and returns a string that is a union of the two values. For example, the expression

```
"Java" + "Script"
```

returns

```
"JavaScript"
```

The shorthand operator (+=) concatenates the string in the left-hand operand with that in the right-hand operand and assigns the left-hand operand the new value.

Order of Precedence

In complex expressions involving more than one operator, the precedence of the operators determines the order of evaluation. By using parentheses, the programmer overrides these rules. Table 4.5 shows the order of precedence from lowest to highest.

Table 4.5 JavaScript Operator Precedence from Low to High

Description	Operators
assignment	= += -= *= /= %= <<= >>= >>>= &= ^= |=
conditional	?:
logical-or	||
logical-and	&&
bitwise-or	|
bitwise-xor	^
bitwise-and	&
equality	== !=
relational	< <= > >=
bitwise shift	<< >> >>>
addition/subtraction	+ -
multiply/divide	* / %
negation/increment	! ~ - ++ --
call, member	() []

Control Statements

For a page to be dynamic and interactive, the Web page developer needs statements that control the flow of information. Depending on computation results or input from the users, the script makes decisions that alter the path of execution. This section covers the conditional and loop statements provided in JavaScript. Chapter 5 discusses additional flow control statements that apply to objects.

Conditional Statements

In addition to the conditional expressions discussed in the previous section, JavaScript has the following conditional statements:

- `if` statement—implemented in all versions of JavaScript
- `switch` statement—new in JavaScript 1.2

The if Statement

The syntax of the `if` statement is as follows:

```
if (condition) {
    statements1 }
[else {
    statements2}]
```

The condition is any JavaScript expression that evaluates to the Boolean type of true or false. The conditional statement is a JavaScript statement (including another `if` statement) or JavaScript expression. The following is an example of a valid `if` statement:

```
if (n>3) {
    status = true
    if (j != n) j = 0 }
else j = n
```

Warning

C programmers beware that a numerical condition evaluating to nonzero is not the equivalent of a Boolean true in JavaScript. Conversely, a zero is not the same as a Boolean false. In JavaScript, the result of the condition must be a Boolean data type.

When there is only a single statement, the braces are not necessary. For example, the following is a legal `if` statement:

```
if (a=b) j=0
else j=1
```

New in JavaScript 1.2

The switch Statement

With the addition of the `switch` statement in JavaScript 1.2, the language now has the complete set of conditional statements. The `switch` statement eliminates the need to write nested `if` statements when you test a variable for multiple values. The syntax of the `switch` statement is:

```
switch (expression) {
  case label1 :
    statements;
    break;
  case label2 :
    statements;
    break;
  default :
    statements;
}
```

The `switch` statement has the following characteristics:

- The data type of the *expression* must match the data type of the *labels*.
- The statements are optional. However, you can include more than one statement in a single case.
- The semicolons are optional.
- The `break` statement causes the script to continue execution

at the next statement after the `switch` statement. It you omit the `break` statement, execution of the script continues with the next label.

- When there is no match between the *expression* and the *label*, the interpreter passes control to the default case. If there is no default case, the interpreter passes control to the next statement after the `switch` statement.

Listing 4.4 illustrates the behavior of the case statement. It requires the use of a statement that hasn't been discussed, but there was no other way to create an example that showed the `switch` statement behavior.

Listing 4.4 Example of case Statement

```
<HTML>
  <HEAD>
    <TITLE>Example of switch Statement</TITLE>
  </HEAD>
  <BODY>
<SCRIPT LANGUAGE="JavaScript1.2">
<!--
for (var i=1; i<5; i++) {
   switch (i) {
        case 2 :
            document.write("Case 2 tested.<BR>")
            break
        case 4 :
            document.write("Case 4 tested.<BR>")
            break
        default :
            document.write("Value "+i+" not a case.<BR>")
   }
}
//-->
</SCRIPT>
  </BODY>
</HTML>
```

The `switch` statement in Listing 4.4 has only two cases, while the `for` statement provides for values to `i`. The remaining values use the default case. Figure 4.2 shows the results of running this example.

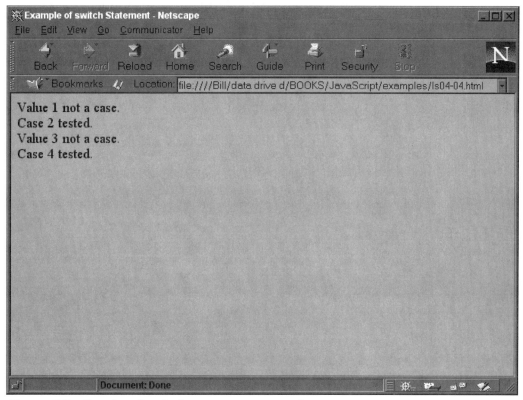

Figure 4.2   Results of switch statement example.

Loop Statements

JavaScript supports two loop structures; the `for` statement and the `while` statement. For control within the loop structure, JavaScript provides the `break` and `continue` statements.

The for Statement

The JavaScript `for` statement is the same as the one for Java and C. The `for` statement repeats a loop until the specified condition evaluates to true or the loop is exited by a `break` statement. The syntax of the `for` statement is as follows:

```
for (initial-expression; condition; increment-expression) {
   statements
}
```

The order of processing for the `for` statement is as follows:

- The browser executes the initial-expression. This expression initializes any values needed for loop control.
- The browser checks the condition. If it is True, control passes to the next step. If False, control goes to the next statement after the loop.
- The statements are then executed and, unless a break or continue statement is encountered, control goes to the next step.
- The browser executes the increment-expression which updates the variables used for loop control. The browser then returns to step 2.

Listing 4.5 illustrates one use of the `for` statement.

Listing 4.5 Example of for statement

```
<HTML>

  <HEAD>
    <TITLE>Example of for statement</TITLE>
  </HEAD>
<BODY>
<P>This example squares a series of numbers.</P>
<SCRIPT LANGUAGE="JavaScript">
<!--
for (var i=1; i<10; i++) {
   sq=i*i
   document.write("number: "+i+" square: "+sq+"<BR>")
}
//-->
</SCRIPT>
  </BODY>
</HTML>
```

Besides being an example of the `for` statement, Listing 4.5 demonstrates the use of operators and expressions. The `for` statement begins with an assignment expression that declares a variable and sets its initial value. The `for` statement's condition is a simple conditional expression that limits the number of iterations of the `for` loop. The `for` statement's increment expression is a unary arithmetic expression. The statement sq=i*i illustrates the order of precedence in resolving operators. Since multiplication has a higher precedence than assignment; JavaScript performs the multiplication before assigning it as a value to the variable. The document.write statement is an example of string concatenation where numeric data types are converted to strings.

Figure 4.3 shows the results of running the for statement example script.

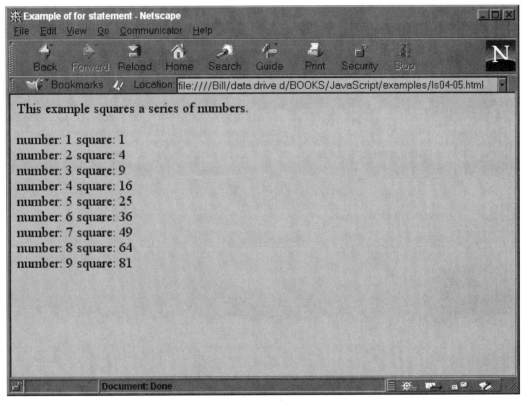

Figure 4.3   Results of for statement example.

The while Statement

The `while` statement continues to repeat the loop while the condition is true. The syntax for the `while` statement is as follows:

```
while (condition) {
    statements
}
```

The condition test occurs when the loop `while` statement is first executed and at the end of every loop. When the test returns a false, control passes to the next statement after the loop. Listing 4.6 takes the `for` statement example shown in Listing 4.5 and turns it into a `while` statement.

Listing 4.6 Example of while Statement

```
<HTML>
<HEAD>
    <TITLE>Example of while Statement</TITLE>
  </HEAD>
<BODY>
<P>This example squares a series of numbers using
   the while statement.</P>
<SCRIPT LANGUAGE="JavaScript">
<!--
var i=1
while (i<10) {
   var sq=i*i
   document.write("number: "+i+" square: "+sq+"<BR>")
   i++
}
//-->
</SCRIPT>
  </BODY>
</HTML>
```

Since the `while` statement doesn't have an argument for initializing variables, any variables used in its conditional expression need to be declared prior to the `while` statement. To avoid a perpetual loop, the `while` statement needs to include a statement that increments the value of the variable it tests. Outside of these two differences, the remainder of this example is the same as the `for` statement example.

New in JavaScript 1.2

 # The do while Statement

The addition of the do while statement in JavaScript 1.2 means that JavaScript now has all of the common loop-control statements found in other languages. The syntax for the do while statement is:

```
do {
    statements
} while (condition)
```

The do while statement is similar to the while statement with one big difference. The while statement checks the *condition* prior to executing the statements. On the other hand, the do while statement executes the statements and then checks the *condition*. The behavior of the do while statement guarantees that the interpreter executes the statements at least once. Listing 4.7 takes the example for while statement and turns it into a do while statement.

Listing 4.7 Example of the do while Statement

```
<HTML>
  <HEAD>
    <TITLE>Example of do while Statement</TITLE>
  </HEAD>
  <BODY>
    <P>This example squares a series of numbers using
       the do while statement.</P>
<SCRIPT LANGUAGE="JavaScript1.2">
<!--
var i=1
do {
    var sq=i*i
    document.write("number: "+i+" square: "+sq+"<BR>")
    i++
} while (i<10)
//-->
</SCRIPT>
  </BODY>
</HTML>
```

The script in Listing 4.7 replicates the behavior of the `while` statement. The only difference is the behavior of the two statements when the *condition* is initially false.

The break Statement

The `break` statement terminates the `for`, `while`, or `do while` loop and transfers control to the next statement following the terminated loop. Listing 4.8 illustrates how to use the `break` statement.

Listing 4.8 Example of for Statement with a break Statement

```
<HTML>
<  HEAD>
   <TITLE>Example of break statement</TITLE>
  </HEAD>
  <BODY>
    <P>This example uses the break statement to end the
       for loop statement.</P>

<SCRIPT LANGUAGE="JavaScript">
<!--
for (var i=1; i<10; i++) {
  sq=i*i
  if (sq>80) break
  document.write("number: "+i+" square: "+sq+"<BR>")
}
document.write("break at square = "+sq)
//-->
</SCRIPT>
  </BODY>
</HTML>
```

The script in Listing 4.8 illustrates the use of the `break` statement. The script tests the value of `sq` and breaks out of the loop once the value is greater than 80. The script executes correctly because the `for` statement terminated before printing the last square.

New in JavaScript 1.2

 JavaScript 1.2 revised the syntax of the `break` statement to include an optional label. The syntax for breaking out of a block of labeled statements is:

```
break label
```

This is not a `goto` statement. It is a `break` statement that transfers control to the statement following the labeled statement specified by *label*. Where the `break` statement, by itself, transfers execution out of the immediate control or `select` statement, the label option allows the `break` statement to transfer control out of multiple levels of conditional or control statements.

In Listing 4.9, the first `break` statement transfers control out of the `do while` loop. In this example, it does nothing more than a simple `break` statement. The second `break` statement transfers control out of the `for` statement from within the `do while` statement.

Figure 4.4 shows the results of running this script.

Listing 4.9 Example of break Statement with a Label

```
<HTML>
  <HEAD>
    <TITLE>Example of break Statement with a label</TITLE>
  </HEAD>
  <BODY>
    <P>Testing the break statement with labels.</P>
<SCRIPT LANGUAGE="JavaScript1.2">
<!--
bigout :
    for (var i=1; i<5; i++) {
        document.write("i = "+i)
        j=1
        littleout :
            do {
                if (i<=2) {
                    document.write(" j skipped")
                    break littleout
                }
                if (i==4) {
                    document.write(" taking the bigout.<BR>")
                    break bigout
```

```
          }
          document.write(" j = "+j++)
        } while (j<5)
      document.write("<BR>")
   }
document.write("done with the script.<BR>")
//-->
</SCRIPT>
  </BODY>
</HTML>
```

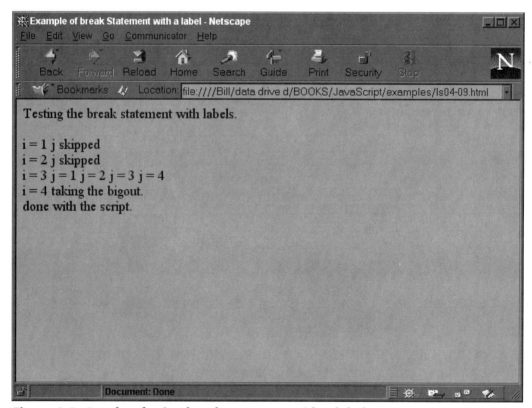

Figure 4.4   Results of using break statement with a label.

The continue Statement

Like the break statement, the continue statement terminates the current iteration of a for, while, or do while loop, it does not exit the loop. Where it picks up the next iteration depends on the type of loop:

- In a while or do while loop control passes to the condition
- In a for loop it passes to the increment-expression

Listing 4.10 illustrates how to use the continue statement within both the for statement and while statement. There is no need to include the do while statement in the script as it is just a variation of the while statement.

Listing 4.10 Example of continue Statement

```
<HTML>
  <HEAD>
    <TITLE>Example of continue statement</TITLE>
  </HEAD>
  <BODY>
    <P>The following illustrates the use of a continue
       statement in a for
       statement.</P>
<SCRIPT LANGUAGE="JavaScript">
<!--
for (var i=1; i<10; i++) {
   sq=i*i
   if (sq<25) continue
   document.write("number: "+i+" square: "+sq+"<BR>")
}
//-->
</SCRIPT>
    <P>The following illustrates the use of a continue
       statement in a while statement</P>
<SCRIPT LANGUAGE="JavaScript">
<!--
i=1
while (i<10) {
   sq=i*i++
   if (sq<25) continue
   document.write("number: "+(i-1)+" square: "+sq+"<BR>")
}
//-->
</SCRIPT>
  </BODY>
</HTML>
```

The for statement in Listing 4.10 skips printing all squares that have a value less than 25. Although the while statement performs the same task, it is a bit more complicated. To avoid a perpetual loop, the script needs to increment the value of "i" before the continue statement. Since "i" is now set for the next iteration, the document.write statement needs to subtract one.

Bug

The statement sq=i*i++ works in Netscape Communicator 4.0 and both versions of Microsoft Internet Explorer. However, Netscape Navigator 3.0 uses the incremented value of "i" when computing the square. To make this script work in all versions of JavaScript, you need to split the incrementing of "i" into a separate statement.

New in JavaScript 1.2

Like the break statement, JavaScript 1.2 added the label option to the continue statement. The label option provides a means to terminate the execution of the labeled statement and transfer control to the specified label statement. Unlike the break statement, the continue statement only applies to loop control statements. The format of the continue statement with the label option is:

continue *label*

Listing 4.11 uses the continue statement with a label to continue the while statement from within a do while statement.

Listing 4.11 Continue Statement with a Label

```
<HTML>
  <HEAD>
    <TITLE>Continue Statement with a Label</TITLE>
  </HEAD>
  <BODY>
<SCRIPT LANGUAGE="JavaScript1.2">
<!--
var i=1
bigout :
   while (i<5) {
      document.write("i = "+i)
      j=1
         do {
            if (i<=2) {
```

```
            document.write(" j skipped.<BR>")
            i++
            continue bigout
         }
         document.write(" j = "+j++)
      } while (j<5)
   document.write("<BR>")
   i++
   }
document.write("done with the script.<BR>")
//-->
</SCRIPT>
  </BODY>
</HTML>
```

The `continue` statement in Listing 4.11 transfers control to the label before the `while` statement. The result is the `while` statement is executed from the top. To keep the script from getting into a perpetual loop, the value of `i` is incremented before transferring control. When you script in Netscape Communicator 4.0, you get results shown in Figure 4.5.

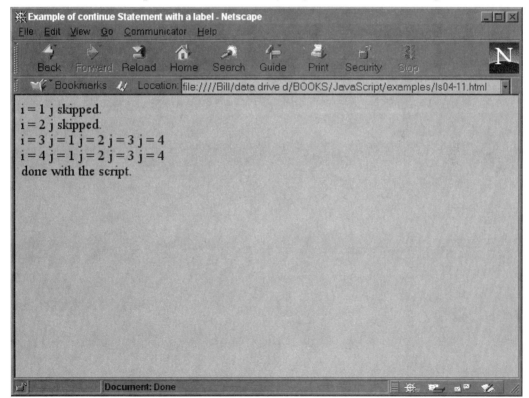

Figure 4.5   Results of running script for continue statement with label.

The function Statement

While you could write all of your code using in-line scripts and the event handlers, this is not a good programming practice. Instead, by using functions, your scripts become modular and reusable. A function is a group of JavaScript statements that perform a specified task. You can use the function by calling it from any in-line script, JavaScript entity, or event handler. The format of the function statement is as follows:

```
function FunctionName(argument list) {
    statements
}
```

Our example "Hello World" script turned into a function looks like that shown in Listing 4.12.

Listing 4.12 Hello World as a function

```
<HTML>
  <HEAD>
    <TITLE>Hello World as a function</TITLE>
<SCRIPT LANGUAGE="JavaScript">
<!--
function DisplayIt(LineToDisplay) {
  document.write(LineToDisplay+"<BR>")
}
//-->
</SCRIPT>
  </HEAD>
  <BODY>
<SCRIPT LANGUAGE="JavaScript">
<!--
DisplayIt("Hello World")
//-->
</SCRIPT>
  </BODY>
</HTML>
```

Note

Since the browser reads the statements bound by the <HEAD> ... </HEAD> tags first, it is good practice to initialize all global variables and define all functions in the HEAD of the document. This prevents errors from noninitialized variables and undefined functions.

The arguments to a function are any of the JavaScript data types or objects. The argument list to a function can contain multiple arguments by separating the arguments with commas as follows:

```
function(x, y, z) {
    ... statements
}
```

A function can include a `return` statement that returns a value to the function call. The value returned by the function can be any data type. The syntax for the `return` statement is:

```
return expression
```

Listing 4.13 changes the `for` statement script for calculating squares to make the square statement a function. Since it is unnecessary to declare a variable and then use the variable in the `document.write` statement, the script makes the function call from the `document.write` statement.

Listing 4.13 Example of return Statement

```
<HTML>
  <HEAD>
    <TITLE>Example of return statement</TITLE>
<SCRIPT LANGUAGE="JavaScript">
<!--
function square(n) {
   return n*n
}
//-->
</SCRIPT>
  </HEAD>
  <BODY>
    <P>This example squares a series of numbers.</P>
```

```
<SCRIPT LANGUAGE="JavaScript">
<!--
for (var i=1; i<10; i++) {
  document.write("number: "+i+" square: "+square(i)+"<BR>")
}
//-->
</SCRIPT>
  </BODY>
</HTML>
```

In addition to referencing arguments by the declared variable names, the array object `functionName.arguments[i]` references the function's argument array. The first argument passed to the function is referenced as follows:

```
functionName.arguments[0]
```

You can use the `functionName.arguments.length` property to get the total number of arguments passed to the function. This feature allows a variable number of arguments to be passed to the function as an argument array. Listing 4.14 shows how to write a script that uses a variable argument list.

Listing 4.14 JavaScript with Variable Number of Arguments

```
<HTML>
  <HEAD>
    <TITLE>Example of Function with a Variable Number of Arguments</TITLE>
<SCRIPT LANGUAGE="JavaScript">
<!--
var OrderedList="OL"
var UnorderedList="UL"
function displayList(ListType) {
    if (ListType==OrderedList || ListType==UnorderedList) {
        document.write("<"+ListType+">")
        for (var i=1; i<displayList.arguments.length; i++) {
            document.write("<LI>"+displayList.arguments[i])
        }
        document.write("</"+ListType+">")
        return true
    }
    else return false
}
```

```
//-->
</SCRIPT>
  </HEAD>
  <BODY>
    <P>Function call for unordered list</P>
<SCRIPT LANGUAGE="JavaScript">
<!--
if (!displayList(UnorderedList, "Bullet 1", "Bullet2")) {
   document.write("Invalid list type")
}
//-->
</SCRIPT>
  </BODY>
</HTML>
```

Listing 4.14 illustrates several important features of functions. The script shows how to use more operators in conditional tests and how to use the properties of the function object to display a variable list of arguments. It also shows how the return statement can be used to ensure that a function executed properly. Figure 4.6 shows the results of running this script.

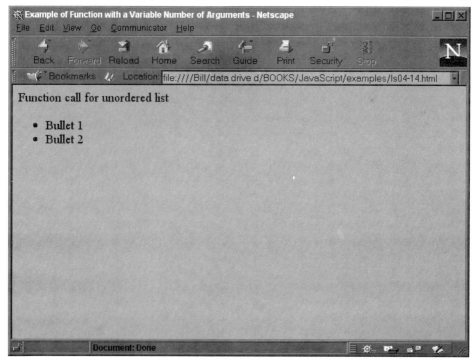

Figure 4.6 Results of script with a variable number of arguments.

Summary

In this chapter, the fundamental syntax for the JavaScript language was reviewed. You began with a look at the format for JavaScript statements including the addition of labeled statements in Netscape Communicator 4.0 (JavaScript 1.2). After a short discussion on writing comments, you moved into discussing the following areas:

- Data types and literals
- Variables
- Operators
- Conditional statements
- Loop control statements
- Functions

Chapter 5 introduces the subject of objects which form a critical part of the JavaScript language. It also includes a discussion of the remaining JavaScript statements and more object specific information about topics covered in this chapter.

Part 2

JavaScript
Object Structure

JavaScript is an object-based language that provides most of the features of an object-oriented language, such as Java and C++. As this part of the book shows, working with objects is the key to understanding JavaScript. The focus of Chapters 5 through 9 is on client-side JavaScript. The browser object hierarchy reflects the contents of an HTML document. In addition, there are objects that reflect the attributes of the browser. In total, the browser objects define the environment in which JavaScript operates. The chapters divide the browser object structure by function.

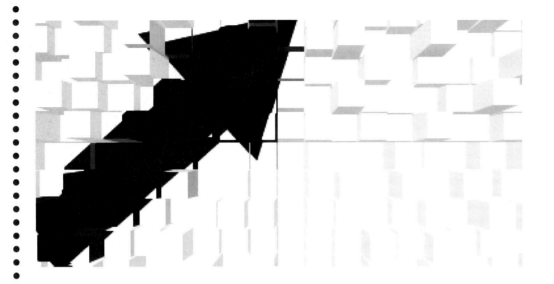

JavaScript Object Model

Topics in This Chapter

- What is the JavaScript object?
- Overview of the Navigator object model
- Referencing objects, properties, and methods
- Working with objects and custom objects
- Defining Arrays

5
Chapter

JavaScript is an object-based language, not an object-oriented programming (OOP) language. Rather than create another OOP, the designers of JavaScript sought to create a scripting language that facilitated the integration of objects created with an OOP language into HTML documents. Thus, while JavaScript lacks the encapsulation, inheritance, and abstraction features of C++ or Java, it has the means to access their external objects. While the ability to access Java applets and plug-ins is limited in Netscape Navigator 2.0, LiveConnect and the enhanced JavaScript 1.1 in Netscape Navigator 3.0, provide client-side object integration. Netscape Communicator took the next step with the implementation of CORBA (Common Object Request Broker Architecture) and IIOP (Internet Inter-ORB Protocol). With these enhancements, Netscape Communicator contains the architecture necessary for client and server objects to share information. Along with these enhancements came revised object models.

Although it lacks the Java class structure, JavaScript provides for the creation of objects that can have properties, and methods. The simplicity of JavaScript objects makes them easier to learn for those who don't have a background in object-oriented programming. The philosophy of Netscape is to divide the roles of the development staff between those who design and build components, and those who use those components to build applications.

The JavaScript Object

Trying to find a good definition of an object is the equivalent to finding a good definition of light. In both cases you know the characteristics, but lack a good definition. It is safe to say that an object is a self-contained unit of code that has the following characteristics:

- The *properties* of an object define its state.
- The *methods* of an object define its behavior. You use the methods to communicate with an object. Event handlers are a special group of methods with certain kinds of actions.
- Every object has an *identity* that makes the object unique.

Although objects created by Java or C++ have additional characteristics, these three characteristics adequately define a JavaScript object. Of these characteristics, the identity of the object is the easiest to explain as it merely says that every object has a unique name. The other two characteristics are more complicated.

Object Properties

Properties are variables or other objects. The ability of an object to include other objects creates an object hierarchy. Before making things complicated, let's start with a property that is a variable. The notational system used by JavaScript to represent an object and its properties is as follows:

```
ObjectName.PropertyName
```

When the property stores information, it has the following characteristics:

- A data type of numeric, string, logical or null.
- It is gettable, which means you can read the object.
- It is settable, which means that you can change the value of the object.

The syntax for setting a property is the same as assigning a value to a variable. The formal syntax for setting a property is as follows:

```
ObjectName assignment-operator value
```

For example, the object mydog has the properties:

```
mydog.breed="small mutt"
mydog.age=7
mydog.weight=25
```

In addition to being referenced by name, JavaScript supports two methods of array referencing; by property name, and by an index. The following examples reference a property as an array by using the property name as an index:

```
mydog["breed"]="small mutt"
mydog["age"]=7
mydog["weight"]=25
```

In Netscape Navigator 2.0, you can reference an object as an array using the following numerical index:

```
mydog[0]="small mutt"
mydog[1]=7
mydog[2]=25
```

For Netscape Navigator 3.0, Netscape Communicator 4.0, and both versions of Microsoft Internet Explorer, the rule is that if an object was created by name, you need to reference it by name. If an object was created by an index (such as arrays), you need to reference it by an index. The exception is the forms array of the document object, which you can assess by any of the three methods.

Object Methods

A function associated with an object is referred to as a *method*. Since methods are tied to a particular object, they determine the behavior of an object. The JavaScript syntax for referring to methods is as follows:

```
ObjectName.Method()
```

In Chapter 4, "Fundamentals of JavaScript," the `docu-ment.write()` method was used to write strings to the document displayed. For example, in the "Hello World" script you used:

```
document.write("Hello World")
```

As a matter of convention the names for methods are usually verbs that indicate the action taken. For `document.write`, it tells us that you are writing a string to the document.

Like functions, methods often return a value. For most methods, the value returned is a Boolean value that indicates whether or not the method succeeded. However, there are many methods that return other than Boolean values.

Navigator Object Model

From the view of JavaScript, the top of the object hierarchy is the `window` object. Some of the properties of the `window` object are themselves other objects, which in turn contain other objects. The result is a hierarchy of objects starting from the `window` object. This hierarchy of objects constitutes the Navigator Object Model. With each version of Netscape Navigator, its object model has undergone changes. The best way to understand these changes is to start with the object model for Netscape Navigator 2.0 as shown in Figure 5.1.

As Figure 5.1 shows, the `window` object is actually a property of the `navigator` object, which maintains each window as an element in a window's array. Thus, each window opened has its own object hierarchy. There are other objects in the Navigator Object Model that are arrays of objects, such as `frames`, `links`, and most of the objects under the `form` object. Each of the objects have additional properties, methods, and event handlers besides properties that are themselves objects.

The object model shown in Figure 5.1 represents the object structure. When you load an HTML document, the browser only creates those objects that are needed for that document. Thus, if the document does not contain a form, the browser does not create a `form` object. The term for this is *reflection*, since the document object hierarchy reflects the HTML document. Thus, until the browser encounters a `<FORM>` tag, there is no `form` object. If you try to reference the `form` object before the browser processes the `<FORM>` tag, you get an error message. On the other hand, you cannot change any value that alters the format of the screen after the browser displays it on the screen.

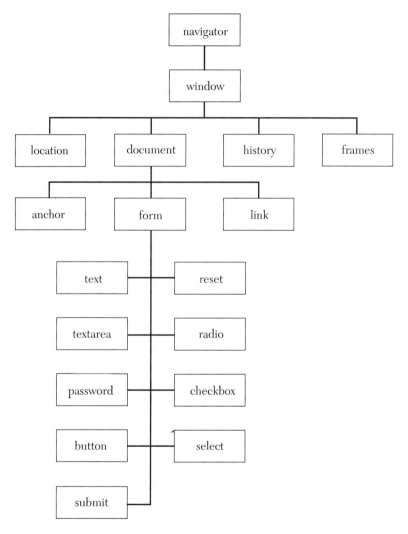

Figure 5.1   Object hierarchy for Netscape Navigator 2.0.

At a minimum, the browser creates the following objects:

- `navigator`
- `document` or `frames`
- `location`
- `history`

Netscape Navigator 3.0 didn't change the rules for referencing objects, but it did add a few new ones as shown in Figure 5.2. The new objects are `plugin`, `mimetype`, `applet`, `area`, `image`, and `fileupload`.

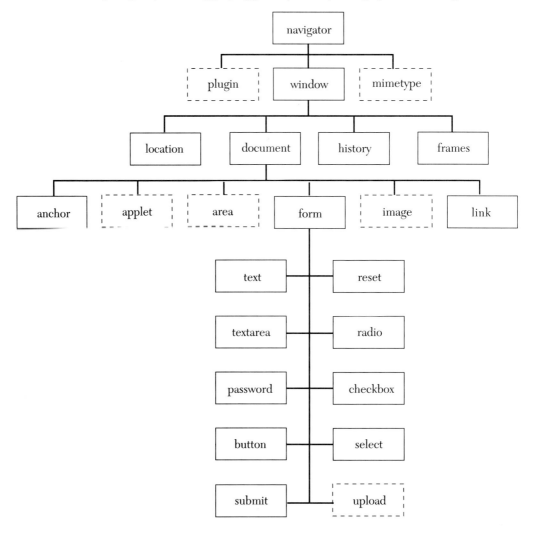

Figure 5.2 *Object hierarchy for Netscape Navigator 3.0.*

Netscape Communicator 4.0 added even more new objects (see Figure 5.3) that dramatically affected the object hierarchy and rules for processing HTML documents. The block in Figure 5.3 for toolbars actually represents six new objects; `locationbar`, `menubar`, `personal-bar`, `statusbar`, `toolbar`, and `scrollbars`. The `tags` object under the `document` object defines the styles for Cascading Style Sheets (CSS). Also under the `document` object, the `layers` object reflects the Dynamic HTML (DHTML) layers. The `layers` object has under it the full object structure for a document. With the `layers` object comes the ability to dynamically change the content of what the user sees on the screen.

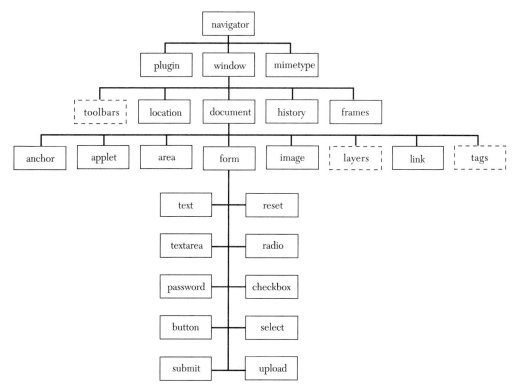

Figure 5.3   Object hierarchy for Netscape Communicator 4.0.

So where does Microsoft Internet Explorer fit into these object models? There are some minor differences in the object models of Netscape Navigator 2.0 and MSIE 3.0 , which are noted throughout this work. On the other hand, other than the object model, MSIE 4.0 has significant differences. Although its core structure is similar to that of Netscape Navigator 3.0, it has a totally different implementation for CSS and

DHTML. Once you start developing Web pages in these areas, the differences between JavaScript 1.2 and JScript become significant.

The differences start with the syntax for the `<SCRIPT>` tag and grow from there. Therefore, I am not going to attempt to discuss how to implement CSS or DHTML in JScript for Microsoft Internet Explorer 4.0.

Referencing Objects, Properties, and Methods

The naming scheme for objects reflects the hierarchical order of objects with the names separated by dots (.). In a sense, the naming convention is similar to the naming convention of the UNIX file system. Although the top of the tree is the `navigator` object, the starting point varies according to the object you are trying to reference.

The starting point for objects, properties, and methods that refer to an HTML document is the `document` object. The following are valid references relating to the current document:

```
document.write()
document.referrer.length
```

The `document.write()` reference is a reference to the `write()` method of the document property, which allows you to write data to the current document in the browser. The `document.referrer.length` reference is a reference to the `length` property of a string object that contains the URL of the document whose link invoked the loading of the current document.

When referring to a `window` property or method, you need to specify the `window` object. When you are referring to an object, property, or method in another window, you need to provide a reference starting from the `window` object. Valid window references include the following:

```
window.close()
window.innerWidth
window[1].close
```

You only need to use the `navigator` reference when you are referring to properties of the `navigator`. For example:

```
navigator.javaEnabled()
navigator.plugins[0]
```

JavaScript provides several properties that act as synonyms for referencing objects, properties and methods. These synonyms are listed in Table 5.1. When working with a single document without frames, the synonyms all refer to the same thing—the current window. These synonyms have an expanded meaning when working with frames as discussed in Chapter 9, "Working with Windows and Frames."

Table 5.1 JavaScript Properties that act as Synonyms

Property	Description	Syntax
window	Synonym for the current window or frame.	window.propertyName window.methodName()
self	Synonym for the current window or frame.	self.propertyName self.methodName()
parent	When referring to the window object, parent is a synonym for the current window. With frames, parent refers to the window containing the current frameset.	parent.propertyName parent.methodName() parent.frameName parent.frames[index]
top	Synonym for the top-most Navigator window.	top.propertyName top.methodName() top.frameName top.frames[index]

Working with Objects

Chapter 4, "Fundamentals of JavaScript," discusses operators, statements, and functions in relationship to variables and literals. Now, it is time to look at operators, statements, and methods in relationship to objects. Since much of the syntax remains the same, we only need to concern ourselves with the differences.

Operators Related to Objects

Properties, unless they are objects, behave the same as variables. Therefore, the rules for operators are the same as stated in Chapter 4.

For testing of equality (==), the browser sees variables that contain objects, arrays, or methods as having special data types. The comparison returns a Boolean value of true only when two variables contain the same object, array, or method. Two variables that contain different objects, even though they have the same properties and values, are unequal. The same applies for arrays and methods.

If you set a variable to an object property that does not exist, the variable returns an *Undefined* value. Prior to JavaScript 1.2, the following comparison returned a value of true when the property did not exist.

```
mydog.color == null
```

JavaScript 1.2 tightened the rules for comparison so that Undefined is no longer the same as null. In all versions of JavaScript, you can test whether a property or variable that refers to an object, is defined and not null by using the following code snippet:

```
if (object.property) {
      // object.property refers to a valid object
}
```

Statements Related to Objects

The manipulation of objects adds two additional statements; the for ... in statement, and the with statement. JavaScript 1.2 introduces the import and export statements for transferring objects, properties, and methods between signed and unsigned scripts. Due to the special nature of these statements, I am deferring their discussion until Chapter 11, "Advanced JavaScript," where there is a special section on signed scripts.

The for ... in Statement

The for ... in statement provides a loop mechanism for extracting the names and values of any object property currently in the browser memory. Its format is as follows:

```
for (variable in objectName) {
   statements
}
```

Listing 5.1 uses this statement to list the properties of the `window` object and its associated values.

Listing 5.1 Example of for ... in Statement

```
<HTML>
  <HEAD>
    <TITLE>Example of for ... in Statement</TITLE>
<SCRIPT LANGUAGE="JavaScript">
<!--
function listProps(obj, objName) {
   var results=""
   for (var i in obj) {
      results+=objName+"."+i+" = "+obj[i]+"<BR>"
   }
   return results
}
//-->
</SCRIPT>
  </HEAD>
  <BODY>
    <P>The properties of the window object are:</P>
<SCRIPT LANGUAGE="JavaScript">
<!--
document.write(listProps(window, "window"))
//-->
</SCRIPT>
  </BODY>
</HTML>
```

In Listing 5.1, the variable `i` is the name of the property. It then indexes the object using the property name `obj[i]`, to retrieve its value. Figure 5.4 shows the results of running this script in Netscape Communicator 4.0.

Although a primitive version, this script is a handy tool for debugging scripts. As you learn more about JavaScript, you will be able to update the script so that it is more useful.

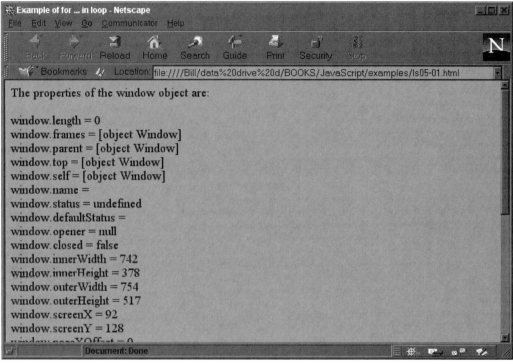

Figure 5.4 Results of running for ... in script.

Netscape

The script in Listing 5.1 works in all versions of Netscape Navigator and Microsoft Internet Explorer 4.0. It doesn't work in Microsoft Internet Explorer 3.0, since this version does not properly reflect built-in objects to the for ... in statement.

The with Statement

There are situations where the same object is referenced several times. The `with` statement establishes a default object for the bracketed set of statements. The format of the `with` statement is as follows:

```
with (objectName) {
    statements
}
```

The `objectName` is any valid object in the browser's memory. The `Math` object provides an example of how to use the `with` statement. Without the use of the `with` statement, you need to write the `math` statement as:

```
var r = 0
var x = 0
r = Math.p / (1 - Math.cos(a))
x = (2 * Math.p * Math.cos(a)) / (Math.sin(a) * Math.sin(a))
}
```

The constant repetition of the `Math` object name makes the script difficult to read. By using the `with` statement, the script becomes more readable as the following example shows:

```
var r = 0
var x = 0
with (Math) {
    r = p / (1 - cos(a))
    x = (2 * p * cos(a)) / (sin(a) * sin(a))
}
```

Functions and Methods

The methods of an object are nothing more than functions incorporated into the object. A method is the way to modify the behavior of an object without having to know anything about how the method accomplishes its task. To make object referencing transparent to the function, JavaScript has the `this` keyword. JavaScript 1.2 added the capability to nest functions providing a means to write complex methods without exposing all of the details.

The this Keyword

The this keyword refers to whatever is the current object, and is a shortcut to entering the full name of the object reference. The this keyword frequently appears with event handlers that call functions. For example, if you need to validate an account number when the account field changes, you could write the following:

```
<INPUT TYPE="text" NAME="account" VALUE=""
   onChange="chkacct(window.document.myform.account.value)">
```

With the this keyword, the code becomes:

```
<INPUT TYPE="text" NAME="account" VALUE=""
   onChange="chkacct(this.value)">
```

The this keyword applies to all object layers in the current object reference. Thus, the following are also valid uses of the this keyword:

```
this.form
this.document
```

The this keyword has a lot of uses, many of which require a knowledge of the object hierarchy to understand the shorthand object reference.

New in JavaScript 1.2

Nesting Functions

While the SRC attribute of the <SCRIPT> tag provides a means of incorporating common routines into a script, it is a legacy scripting solution and not an object-oriented solution. Netscape's Crossware development concept uses JavaBeans to tie components together to build applications. Prior to JavaScript 1.2, a method consisted of a single function. For component building, this is too restrictive. The solution is to allow nested functions, which provide for the development of complex methods. The rules for nested functions are:

- The nested function can use the arguments and variables of the outer function.
- The outer function cannot use the arguments and variables of the nested function.
- The nested function is invisible outside of the outer function.

The script in Listing 5.2 is a nested function version of the script in Listing 5.1. The listProps() function (called the outer function) contains the nested function getProps(). By using nested functions, the list-Props() function becomes a self-contained component. By using nested functions, you can write methods for objects and components for building scripts.

Listing 5.2 Example of Nested Functions

```
<HTML>
  <HEAD>
    <TITLE>Example of Nested Functions</TITLE>
<SCRIPT LANGUAGE="JavaScript1.2">
<!--
function listProps(obj, objName) {
    var results=""
    function getProps(obj, objName) {
        for (var i in obj) {
            results+=objName+"."+i+" = "+obj[i]+"<BR>"
        }
        return results
    }
    document.write(getProps(obj, objName))
}
//-->
</SCRIPT>
  </HEAD>
  <BODY>
    <P>The properties of the window object are:</P>
<SCRIPT LANGUAGE="JavaScript">
<!--
listProps(window, "window")
//-->
</SCRIPT>
  </BODY>
</HTML>
```

The Function Object

Starting with JavaScript 1.1, the function became a window object as shown in the results of running Listing 5.1. As an object, the function has properties as shown in Table 5.2. Table 5.3 shows the description for the useable properties.

Table 5.2 Properties of the Function Object

Properties	Methods	Events
arguments[ ]	none	none
arity **		
callee **		
caller **		
local variables **		
prototype *		

° *New in JavaScript 1.1;* °° *New or changed in JavaScript 1.2*

Table 5.3 Description of Properties for Function Object

Property	Description
arity **	A read-only property that returns the number of arguments expected by a function.
callee **	A read-only property that returns the current function.
caller **	A read-only property that returns the function that called the current executing function.

°° *New or changed in JavaScript 1.2*

Chapter 4 discusses two of the properties for the function object:

- functionName.arguments[index]
- functionName.arguments.length

The arguments[] property is an array of the arguments passed to a function, and arguments.length is the size of the array. On the other hand, the arity property indicates the number of arguments the function expects to receive. To use the arity property, you need the LANGUAGE="JavaScript1.2" attribute in the <SCRIPT> tag.

The value of the `caller` property points to the argument array of the outer function. When there is no outer function, the value is undefined. The `callee` property points to the current function. All local variables of a function appear as properties of the function.

Listing 5.3 Examples of Function Object Properties

```
<HTML>
  <HEAD>
    <TITLE>Example of function object properties</TITLE>
<SCRIPT LANGUAGE="JavaScript1.2">
<!--
function listProps(obj, objName) {
   var results=""
   function getProps(obj, objName) {
      for (var i in obj) {
         results+=objName+"."+i+" = "+obj[i]+"<BR>"
      }
      return results
   }
   document.write(getProps(obj, objName))
}
function testa(x, y) {
   function testb(x) {
      document.write("testb caller.x = "
                     +arguments.caller.x+"<BR>")
      document.write("testb callee.x = "
                     +arguments.callee.x+"<BR>")
      document.write("testb x = "+x+"<BR>")
   }
   testb("new-"+x)
}
//-->
</SCRIPT>
  </HEAD>
  <BODY>
    <P>Function arity for both functions:</P>
<SCRIPT LANGUAGE="JavaScript1.2">
<!--
// arity is an outside property that looks in
document.write("testa.arity = "+testa.arity+"<BR>")
document.write("testb.arity = "+testa.testb.arity+"<BR>")
```

```
//-->
</SCRIPT>
    <HR>
    <P>The caller and callee properties in testb are:</P>
<SCRIPT LANGUAGE="JavaScript">
<!--
testa("var-x", "var-y")
//-->
</SCRIPT>
    <HR>
    <P>The results of listProps for testa are:</P>
<SCRIPT LANGUAGE="JavaScript">
<!--
listProps(testa, "testa")
//-->
</SCRIPT>
  </BODY>
</HTML>
```

Listing 5.3 takes a bit of explanation. As shown in Figure 5.5, the `arguments.arity` property displays the number of arguments that each function expects. The `arguments.caller` and `arguments.callee` statements appear in the `testb` function, which is a nested function of `testa`. The `arguments.caller.x` property shows the value of x as it appears in the `testa` function. The `arguments.callee.x` property shows the value of x in the `textb` function. As the results show, there is no difference between the `callee` property and the actual value of x. The call to the `listProcs` functions show that a function is an object with properties. Those properties include the local variables of the function.

The Function Constructor

The `constructor` function provides another way to define a function. The syntax of the `constructor` function is as follows:

```
var functionName = new Function([arg1, arg2, ..., argn],
functionBody)
```

For example,

```
var square = new Function(x, "return x * x")
```

Since the function is an object that you create, it has a corresponding *constructor*. Constructors always use the new keyword followed by the

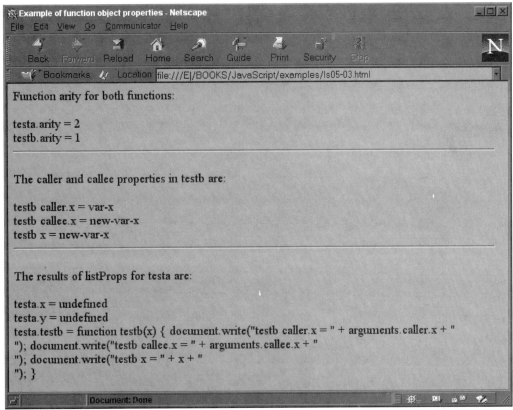

Figure 5.5 **Results of argument properties script.**

object name with the first letter capitalized. Objects that have constructors are called *Built-in objects*. The objects built into JavaScript are; `Array`, `Boolean`, `String`, `Number`, `Date`, `Function`, `Image`, `Layer`, `Math`, and `Option`. While you can use the `Function` constructor, it is not an efficient way to define a function. The reason is that the browser needs to reinterpret the constructor statement every time it encounters it. It is better to use the function statement, and let the browser apply the constructor when it loads the script.

Building Custom Objects

While JavaScript contains a large number of predefined objects, additional custom objects can be created. The custom object can a have combination of:

- Properties that hold values
- An array of values or objects
- Methods that manipulate the object
- A combination of properties, arrays, and methods

The first step is to build a simple object that has properties that contain values. From there you add arrays and methods to the custom object.

Creating a New Object

The creation of objects requires you to perform two steps:

1. Define the object type by writing a constructor function
2. Create instances of the object using the new operand

JavaScript 1.2 adds an additional method for creating objects using literal notation.

The Constructor Function

The constructor function creates an object type. The object type created by the constructor function defines the name, properties, and methods for the new object. When you define the properties of an object, you are defining its state. For example, the following constructor function defines the object type for the generic dog:

```
function dog(breed, age, weight) {
   this.breed = breed
   this.age = age
   this.weight = weight
}
```

In this example, the this keyword refers to the instance of the object being created. The name of the object type is dog and the properties are breed, age, and weight.

The new Operand

For a user-defined object type, the new operand provides a means of creating a new instance of that object type. The syntax of this operand is as follows:

```
objectName = new ObjectType(param1 [, param2,] … [, paramN])
```

Using the constructor function, the new operand defines a new instance of the object. For example:

```
mydog = new dog("small mutt", 5, 25)
```

In addition to the regular JavaScript data types (string, numeric, and Boolean), another object can be the property of an object. For example, to add a license number to the object type for a dog, the license number could refer to another object as follows:

```
function doglicense(owner, phone_number) {
    this.owner = owner
    this.phone_number = phone.number
}
```

Again, you use the new operand to create an instance of the object type for a doglicense.

```
AZ123 = new doglicense("John Smith", "999-9999")
```

You then need to modify the object type for a dog to include the new information as follows:

```
function dog(breed, age, weight, license) {
    this.breed = breed
    this.age = age
    this.weight = weight
    this.license = license
}
```

Now, you need to create an instance of the object type for a dog that includes the object instance for a particular license.

```
mydog = new dog("mixed mutt", 5, 25, AZ123)
```

To reference the owner of `mydog`, the object reference is as follows:

```
mydog.license.owner
```

New in JavaScript 1.2

Creating Object with Literal Notation

JavaScript 1.2 added another method for creating an object by using literal notation. The syntax for this method is as follows:

```
objectName = {property1:value, property2:value, ...,
propertyn:value}
```

The following statement creates `mydog` using literal notation:

```
mydog={breed:"mixed mutt", age:5, weight:25,
license:{owner:"John Smith", phone:"999-9999"}}
```

JavaScript interprets this statement only when the browser loads the HTML page. It cannot be used to dynamically define objects. However, it is a quick way to define a single instance of an object.

Adding a Property to a Custom Object

There are two ways to add a new property to a custom object: By using the `prototype` property to add a property to a previously defined object type; and by adding a new property to a single instance of an object.

The `prototype` property defines a property shared by all object instances of a particular object type. Therefore, you can use the `prototype` property to create a new property to all objects of specified object type. The format of the statement used to accomplish this is as follows:

```
objectType.prototype.propertyName = value
```

You can add a new property to a single instance of an object with the statement:

```
objectName.propertyName = value
```

Listing 5.4 contains statements for both methods of adding a property to an object. First, the script creates two instances of an object data type. Then it uses the `prototype` property to add a new property, and then, a new property is added to one object instance.

Listing 5.4 Adding New Properties to an Object

```
<HTML>
  <HEAD>
    <TITLE>Adding New Properties to an Object</TITLE>
<SCRIPT LANGUAGE="JavaScript">
<!--
function dog(breed, age) {
   this.breed=breed
   this.age=age
}
function listProps(obj, objName) {
   var results=""
   for (i in obj) {
      results+=objName+"."+i+" = "+obj[i]+"<BR>"
   }
   return results+="<HR>"
}
//-->
</SCRIPT>
  </HEAD>
  <BODY>
    <P>Define two instances of the object and display
       the properties.</P>
<SCRIPT LANGUAGE="JavaScript">
<!--
mydog=new dog("mixed mutt", 7)
document.write(listProps(mydog, "mydog"))
hisdog=new dog("spaniel", 4)
document.write(listProps(hisdog, "hisdog"))
//-->
</SCRIPT>
    <P>Use the prototype property of dog to create a
       new property.</P>
<SCRIPT LANGUAGE="JavaScript">
<!--
dog.prototype.weight=25
document.write(listProps(mydog, "mydog"))
document.write(listProps(hisdog, "hisdog"))
//-->
</SCRIPT>
    <P>Add a property to only one object.</P>
<SCRIPT LANGUAGE="JavaScript">
```

```
<!--
mydog.color="black"
document.write(listProps(mydog, "mydog"))
document.write(listProps(hisdog, "hisdog"))
//-->
</SCRIPT>
  </BODY>
</HTML>
```

JavaScript 1.1 was the first version to implement the `prototype` property. However, the script does work correctly in Microsoft Internet Explorer 3.0, which generally emulates JavaScript 1.0.

New in JavaScript 1.2

Deleting an Object's Property or Single Array Element

JavaScript 1.2 provides a means to delete a property of a custom object, or an element of an array. The syntax for the `delete` operand is as follows:

```
delete objectName.property
delete objectName[index]
```

For example, the following statement deletes the `weight` property from the `mydog` object:

```
delete mydog.weight
```

Creating Methods

If you create an object with the `new` keyword, you can add properties and methods to the object that you create. You can add them to individual objects in all releases of JavaScript or use the `prototype` property to add the new property or method to a group of objects. The `prototype` property is an advanced topic that needs separate attention (see the section "The Prototype Property" later in this chapter).

After defining a function, you can associate the function to an object using the following technique:

```
objectName.MethodName = function_name
```

The method is then referenced in the context of working with an object as follows:

```
objectName.MethodName(parameters)
```

Defining Arrays

An *array* is a collection of individual data elements whose organization appears as a single unit. The individual elements of the array have the same data type. You can address individual elements or a group of elements.

JavaScript 1.1 (Netscape Navigator 3.0) introduced the array object. JavaScript 1.2 (Netscape Communicator 4.0) enhanced the array object with more methods. JavaScript 1.0 (Netscape Navigation 2.0) lacked an array object, however, it was still possible to create an object that acted like an array.

Arrays for Netscape Navigator 2.0

While JavaScript 1.0 lacks an array data type, an equivalent function can be performed by creating an object that emulates an array. The first step is to define an array object type as follows:

```
function MakeArray(n) {
    this.length = n;
    for (var i = 1; i <= n; i++)
        this[i] = 0;
    return this
}
```

The next step is to create an instance of the `MakeArray` object type.

```
ExmpArray = new MakeArray(20)
```

Assigning values to array elements looks like assigning values to an array data type. The difference is that the array begins with one and not zero, since the zeroth property defines the length of the array.

```
exmpArray[1] = "test1"
exmpArrya[2] = "another test"
```

The Array Object

The array object has the properties and methods listed in Table 5.4. You build arrays using either the Array constructor or literal notation.

Table 5.4 Properties and Methods of the Array Object

Properties	Methods	Events
length	concat()	none
prototype	eval()	
	join()	
	reverse()	
	slice()	
	sort()	
	toString()	
	valueOf()	

The Array constructor creates an array object using one of the two following formats:

```
arrayObjectName = new Array()
arrayObjectName = new Array(arrayLength)
```

When an array is created without an `arrayLength`, the result is a zero length array. If you specify the `arrayLength`, then the browser creates an array with `arrayLength` elements. The initial values of the array elements is null. The following examples illustrate these two methods of creating an array object:

```
colorList = new Array()
colorList = new Array(3)
```

To populate the array with values, you need to assign values to the array elements:

```
colorList[0] = "red"
colorList[1] = "green"
colorList[2] = "blue"
```

The array object is not limited to its initial length. To extend an array, just add a new element such as:

```
colorList[5] = "orange"
```

For small arrays, you can set the values as part of the `Array` constructor. For example:

```
colorList = new Array("red", "green", "blue")
```

The `length` property of an array object keeps track of the size of the array. Since the array begins with an index value of zero, the last index of the array element is always one less than the length of the array.

Netscape

 Microsoft Internet Explorer 3.0 supports the `Array` constructor and the `length` property.

New in JavaScript 1.2

 JavaScript 1.2 added the literal notation as a means for creating arrays. The syntax for creating an array object using literal notation is:

```
arrayName = [element0, element1, ..., elmentn]
```

The following example uses literal notation to create the array `colorList`:

```
colorList = ["red", "green", "blue"]
```

If the `LANGUAGE` attribute in the `<SCRIPT>` tag is set to JavaScript1.2, there is a change in the behavior of the following `Array` constructor:

```
arrayName = new Array(1)
```

In previous versions of JavaScript this statement created an array of one element with a value of null. With `LANGUAGE="JavaScript 1.2"`, it creates an array such that `arrayName[0] = 1`.

Listing 5.5 modifies the script in Listing 5.2 to use an array instead of concatenating all of the results into a single variable. The use of nested functions limits this script to JavaScript 1.2.

Listing 5.5 Script to build an Array of an Object's Properties

---

```
<HTML>
  <HEAD>
    <TITLE>Build Array of Properties for an Object</TITLE>
```

```
<SCRIPT LANGUAGE="JavaScript1.2">
<!--
propsTable = new Array()
function listProps(obj, objName) {
    function getProps(obj, objName) {
        j=0
        for (var i in obj) {
            propsTable[j++]=objName+"."+i+" = "+obj[i]
        }
    }
    getProps(obj, objName)
    document.write("Total properties = "
                    +propsTable.length+"<BR>")
    for (var i=1; i<propsTable.length; i++) {
        document.write(propsTable[i]+"<BR>")
    }
}
//-->
</SCRIPT>
    </HEAD>
    <BODY>
        <P>The properties of the document object are:</P>
<SCRIPT LANGUAGE="JavaScript">
<!--
listProps(document, "document")
//-->
</SCRIPT>
    </BODY>
</HTML>
```

Listing 5.5 uses one function to build an array and then prints it in the second function. The outer function uses the `length` property of the array object to control the printing of the table. The script builds a single dimensional array as shown in Figure 5.6.

You can build a multidimensional array by making each array element an array. This is done by building one element at a time as follows:

```
var expArray = new Array(2)
expArray[0] = new Array(5)
expArray[1] = new Array[5]
```

This works fine for small arrays, but such an approach is rather tedious in large arrays. The following code snippet shows a way to build larger multidimensional arrays:

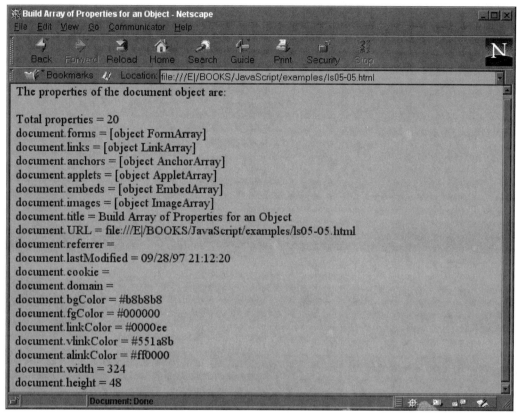

Figure 5.6   Results of building array of object properties.

```
var expArray = new Array(10)
for (var i=0, i<expArray.length, i++) {
         expArray[i] = new Array(10)
}
```

New in JavaScript 1.2

Concatenating Two Arrays

The concat() method of the array object joins two arrays to create a separate single array. The syntax of the statement to concatenate two arrays is:

arrayName3 = arrayName1.concat(*arrayName2*)

The `concat()` method does not change the two arrays. The new array is a one-level deep copy of the elements from the original array. When creating the new array, Netscape Communicator 4.0 applies the following rules:

- The object references are copied into the new array, but not the actual object. Thus, both the new array and original array point to the same object. If the referenced object changes, both arrays reflect the change.
- Strings and numbers are copied to the new array. This means that the changes to a string or number in one array are not reflected in the other.
- Any new element added to either array is not reflected in the other.

The script shown in Listing 5.6 illustrates the `concat()` method for concatenating two array objects. Figure 5.7 shows the results of running this script. The script creates two arrays and then concatenates them. Since the script displays each array, it has a `dispArray()` function that uses the array object as the only parameter.

Listing 5.6 Example for Concatenating Two Arrays

```
<HTML>
  <HEAD>
    <TITLE>Concatenate Two Arrays</TITLE>
<SCRIPT LANGUAGE="JavaScript">
<!--
function dispArray (objArray) {
   for (var i=0; i<objArray.length; i++) {
      document.write(objArray[i]+"<BR>")
   }
}
//-->
</SCRIPT>
  </HEAD>
  <BODY>
    <P>Array 1 contents:</P>
<SCRIPT LANGUAGE="JavaScript">
<!--
```

```
exArray1 = new Array("red", "green", "blue")
dispArray(exArray1)
//-->
</SCRIPT>

    <P>Array 2 contents:</P>

<SCRIPT LANGUAGE="JavaScript">
<!--
exArray2 = new Array("orange", "yellow", "purple")
dispArray(exArray1)
//-->
</SCRIPT>

    <P>Concatenated Array</P>

<SCRIPT LANGUAGE="JavaScript1.2">
<!--
exArray3 = exArray1.concat(exArray2)
dispArray(exArray3)
//-->
</SCRIPT>
  </BODY>
</HTML>
```

New in JavaScript 1.2

Extracting Part of an Array

The slice() method extracts part of an array to create a new array. The syntax for the slice() method is as follows:

```
arrayName2 = arrayName1.slice(beginSlice[, endSlice])
```

The rules for creating the elements of the new array are the same as they are for the concat() method. The rules for the arguments to the slice() method are:

- The value for both beginSlice and endSlice assume that the index for the first element in the array is zero.
- The beginSlice argument is required and is the index value for the first element that you want to extract.
- The endSlice argument is optional. If you do not specify an

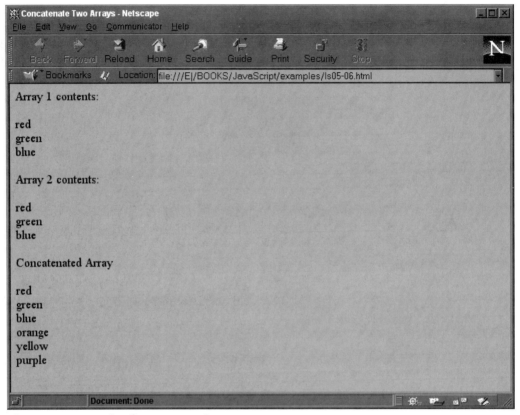

Figure 5.7 Result of concatenating two arrays.

ending index, then the method extracts all elements from be-ginSlice to the end of the array.

- A positive value for endSlice results in the method extracting all elements from beginSlice up to, but not including, the value specified in endSlice. In other words, the index value specified by endSlice is not extracted.

- A negative value for endSlice specifies an offset from the length of the array. It is the equivalent of entering the expression (arrayName.length - offset) for endSlice. A negative value does not extract the ending element.

If the rules for the slice() method seem a bit confusing, the script in Listing 5.7 provides examples for; a no endSlice argument, a positive endSlice argument, and a negative endSlice argument. For each case, the script uses the `dispArray()` function to display the extracted array. Figure 5.8 shows the results of running this script.

Listing 5.7 Example for Extracting Elements from an Array

```
<HTML>
  <HEAD>
    <TITLE>Extracting Elements from an Array</TITLE>
<SCRIPT LANGUAGE="JavaScript">
<!--
function dispArray (objArray) {
   for (var i=0; i<objArray.length; i++) {
      document.write(objArray[i]+"<BR>")
   }
}
//-->
</SCRIPT>
  </HEAD>
  <BODY>
    <P>The initial array.</P>
<SCRIPT LANGUAGE="JavaScript">
<!--
exArray1 = new Array(6)
for (var i=0; i<exArray1.length; i++) {
   exArray1[i] = "Element"+i
}
dispArray(exArray1)
//-->
</SCRIPT>
    <P>Extracting from beginSlice = 3 to the end
       of the array.</P>
<SCRIPT LANGUAGE="JavaScript1.2">
<!--
exArray2 = exArray1.slice(3)
dispArray(exArray2)
//-->
</SCRIPT>
    <P>Extracting from beginSlice = 0 to endSlice = 3.</P>
<SCRIPT LANGUAGE="JavaScript1.2">
<!--
exArray3 = exArray1.slice(0, 3)
dispArray(exArray3)
//-->
```

```
</SCRIPT>
    <P>Extracting from beginSlice = 0 to endSlice = -3</P>
<SCRIPT LANGUAGE="JavaScript">
<!--
exArray4 = exArray1.slice(0, -3)
dispArray(exArray4)
//-->
</SCRIPT>
  </BODY>
</HTML>
```

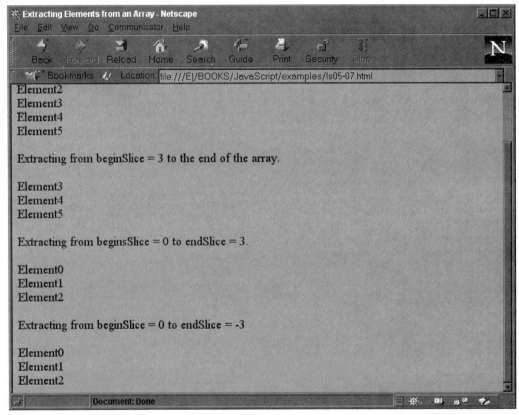

Figure 5.8   Results of extracting elements from an array.

Creating a String from Array Elements

The join() method creates a single string composed of all elements in the array. By default, the elements are separated by commas. However, you can specify another string as a separator. If the separator is not a string, the interpreter converts the argument to a string. The syntax for the `join()` method is as follows:

```
var stringVariable = arrayName.join(separator)
```

The script shown in Listing 5.8 joins the elements of an array into a string using both the default separator and ", " as a separator. By adding a space after the comma, the resulting string is easier to read. Figure 5.9 shows the results of running this script.

Netscape

Although Microsoft Internet Explorer 3.0 supports the array constructor, it does not support the `join()` method.

Listing 5.8 Joining Array Elements into a String

```
<HTML>
  <HEAD>
    <TITLE>Joining Array Elements into a String</TITLE>
<SCRIPT LANGUAGE="JavaScript">
<!--
function dispArray (objArray) {
   for (var i=0; i<objArray.length; i++) {
      document.write(objArray[i]+"<BR>")
   }
}
//-->
</SCRIPT>
  </HEAD>
  <BODY>
    <P>Array 1 contents:</P>
<SCRIPT LANGUAGE="JavaScript">
<!--
exArray1 = new Array("red", "green", "blue")
dispArray(exArray1)
//-->
</SCRIPT>
    <P>Using the default separator.</P>
<SCRIPT LANGUAGE="JavaScript1.1">
```

```
<!--
var results = exArray1.join()
document.write(results+"<BR>")
//-->
</SCRIPT>
    <P>Using &quot;, &quot; as the separator.</P>
<SCRIPT LANGUAGE="JavaScript1.1">
<!--
var results = exArray1.join(", ")
document.write(results+"<BR>")
//-->
</SCRIPT>
  </BODY>
</HTML>
```

Reversing the Order of Elements in an Array

The reverse() method of the array object inverts the order of elements in an array. This method actually changes the specified array. The syntax for the reverse() method is as follows:

```
var stringVariable = arrayName.reverse()
```

The script in Listing 5.9 creates an array and then reverses its order. The script also displays the array before and after reversing the order. The results of running this script are shown in Figure 5.10.

Netscape

Microsoft Internet Explorer 3.0 does not support the reverse() method.

Listing 5.9 Reversing the Elements in an Array

```
<HTML>
  <HEAD>
    <TITLE>Reversing the Elements in an Array</TITLE>
<SCRIPT LANGUAGE="JavaScript">
<!--
function dispArray (objArray) {
   for (var i=0; i<objArray.length; i++) {
```

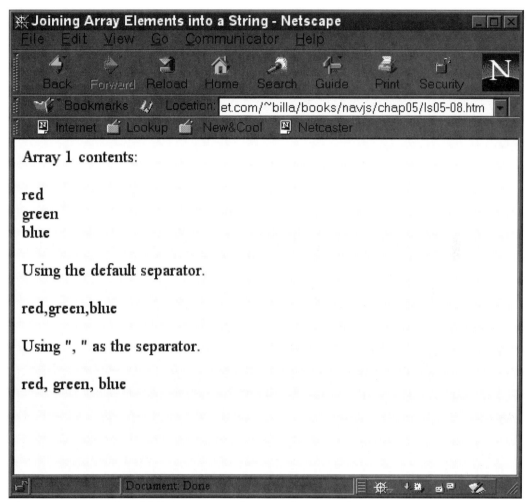

Figure 5.9   Results of joining array elements into a string.

```
        document.write(objArray[i]+"<BR>")
    }
}
//-->
</SCRIPT>
  </HEAD>
  <BODY>
    <P>Define an array with the following contents:</P>
<SCRIPT LANGUAGE="JavaScript">
<!--
```

```
exArray1 = new Array("red", "green", "blue")
dispArray(exArray1)
//-->
</SCRIPT>
     <P>Reverse the order of the array.</P>
<SCRIPT LANGUAGE="JavaScript1.1">
<!--
exArray1.reverse()
dispArray(exArray1)
//-->
</SCRIPT>
   </BODY>
</HTML>
```

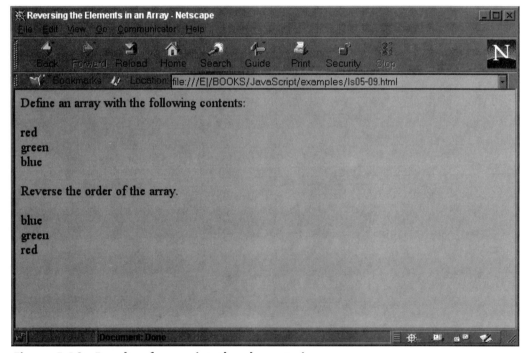

Figure 5.10   Results of reversing the elements in an array.

Sorting the Elements in an Array

By default, the sort() method orders an array into lexicographical (dictionary) order. The sort() method alters the order of the original array and returns a string in the same format as the join() method using the default separator. The sort() method also provides an optional argument that allows you to specify an alternate sorting function. The syntax for the `sort()` method is as follows:

```
var stringVariable = arrayName.sort(compareFunction)
```

Netscape

With the release of Netscape Communicator 4.0, the `sort()` method now works on all platforms. In prior releases, the `sort()` method did not function correctly on the Macintosh and UNIX platforms. In addition, the `sort()` method treats undefined elements in an array as undefined instead of null and sorts them to the high end of the array.

If you provide a *compareFunction()*, the `sort()` method orders the array elements according to the return code of the function. If element1 and element2 are the two arguments to the *compareFunction()*, then:

- If the return code of *compareFunction(element1, element2)* is less than zero, sort element2 to a lower index than element1.
- If the return code of *compareFunction(element1, element2)* is zero, leave element1 and element2 in their current order with respect to each other.
- If the return code of *compareFunction(element1, element2)* is greater than zero, sort element2 to a higher index than element1.

The script in Listing 5.10 has four examples of sorting arrays: sorting alphabetic strings; sorting numeric strings; sorting numbers; and sorting a mixture of numeric strings and numbers. The numeric sorts compare the default sort against a numeric sort that uses the compareNumbers() function.

Netscape

Microsoft Internet Explorer 3.0 does not support the sort() method.

Listing 5.10 Sorting the Elements of an Array

```
<HTML>
  <HEAD>
```

```
    <TITLE>Sorting the Elements of an Array</TITLE>
<SCRIPT LANGUAGE="JavaScript">
<!--
function compareNumbers(num1, num2) {
   return num1 - num2
}
//-->
</SCRIPT>
  </HEAD>
  <BODY>
    <P>Example of sorting a string array.</P>
<SCRIPT LANGUAGE="JavaScript">
<!--
strArray = new Array("anneal", "Annamese", "annals")
document.write("Original Array: "+strArray.join()+"<BR>")
document.write("Default Sort: "+strArray.sort()+"<BR>")
//-->
</SCRIPT>
    <P>Example of sorting a numeric string array.</P>
<SCRIPT LANGUAGE="JavaScript">
<!--
numStrArray = new Array("8", "65", "900")
document.write("Original Array: "
                +numStrArray.join()+"<BR>")
document.write("Default Sort: "+numStrArray.sort()+"<BR>")
document.write("Numeric Sort: "
                 +numStrArray.sort(compareNumbers)+"<BR>")
//-->
</SCRIPT>
    <P>Example of sorting a numeric array.</P>
<SCRIPT LANGUAGE="JavaScript">
<!--
numArray = new Array(7, 68, 895)
document.write("Original Array: "+numArray.join()+"<BR>")
document.write("Default Sort: "+numArray.sort()+"<BR>")
document.write("Numeric Sort: "
                 +numArray.sort(compareNumbers)+"<BR>")
//-->
</SCRIPT>
    <P>Example of sorting a mixed numeric string and
        numeric array.</P>
<SCRIPT LANGUAGE="JavaScript">
<!--
mixArray = numStrArray.concat(numArray)
document.write("Original Array: "+mixArray.join()+"<BR>")
```

```
document.write("Default Sort: "+mixArray.sort()+"<BR>")
document.write("Numeric Sort: "
              +mixArray.sort(compareNumbers)+"<BR>")
//-->
</SCRIPT>
  </BODY>
</HTML>
```

The script in Listing 5.10 creates three different arrays using the Array constructor. The strArray contains three words from a dictionary. The output of the sort shows that the default sort algorithm is closer to a telephone book sort than it is to a dictionary sort, because a dictionary sort ignores the case of a character. The numStrArray is an array of numbers declared as strings. The numArray is an array whose values are all numeric. The last test creates a concatenated array of numStrArray and numArray. These three tests show that a default sort converts all values to a string and then sorts them. On the other hand, the compareNumbers() function compares data as numeric values. Figure 5.11 shows the results of running this script.

The Prototype Property

JavaScript 1.1 introduced the prototype property that applies to all objects created with the new keyword, such as the following:

- The Array constructor
- The date object
- The function constructor
- The image constructor
- The select option
- The string object
- User-defined objects

When you use the prototype property to add a property or method, you modify all objects of the specified type. Prior to adding the new property or method, you need to have at least one instance of the object. Listing 5.4 shows you how to add a property to a custom object using the

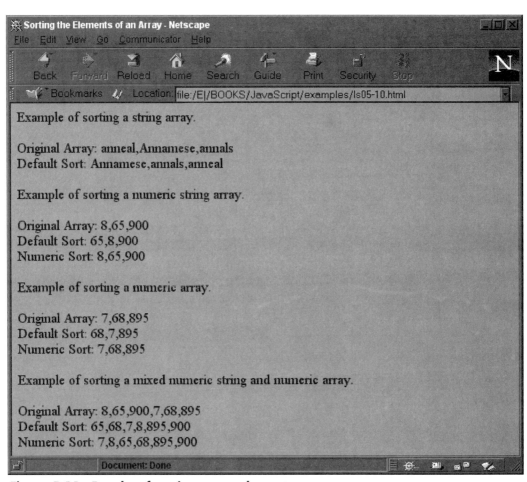

Figure 5.11 Results of sorting array elements.

`prototype` property. If you add a property or method to one of the other objects listed previously, then the `new` property or method appears in every object created with the `var` keyword.

Summary

Even though JavaScript is not an object-orient programming language, it is strongly based on objects. With JavaScript's strong object orientation, the JavaScript object and the Navigator object model form the basis for much of the material in this work. The Navigator object model is the key to understanding how to reference objects, properties and methods.

This chapter discussed the information needed to work with objects, and then to build custom objects, work with arrays, and use the prototype property to add properties and methods to objects.

This marks the end of the introduction to JavaScript. The next part puts this information to use by delving deeper into the features of the JavaScript language.

Built-in Objects, Methods, and Functions

Topics in This Chapter

- JavaScript's special object operators, built-in functions, and shared methods
- Working with strings and regular expressions
- Using the Number and Boolean objects
- Using the Date object
- More mathematics with the Math object

Chapter 6

The objects and methods described in this chapter are part of the JavaScript environment. This chapter discusses the following object and methods:

- `String`
- `Boolean`
- `Number`
- `Math`
- `Date`

In addition to these built-in objects and methods, Chapter 5, "JavaScript Object Model," previously covered the array and function objects. Chapter 7, "Working with Events and Documents," discusses the `event` object, which is new to JavaScript 1.2. Taken as a whole, these objects and their associated methods provide a powerful set of tools for building crossware applications. Before discussing these built-in objects and their associated methods, let's cover a few additional special operators, built-in functions, and shared methods that are useful in writing scripts.

Special Operators

In addition to the operators discussed in Chapter 4, "Fundamentals of JavaScript," JavaScript has four special operators:

- `delete` (new in JavaScript 1.2)
- `new`
- `typeof` (implemented in JavaScript 1.1)
- `void` (implemented in JavaScript 1.1)

Chapter 5, "JavaScript Object Model," discussed the delete and new operators. The following sections discuss the `typeof` and `void` operators.

The typeof Special Operator

The `typeof` operator returns a string that tells you the data type of the operand. The `typeof` operator identifies strings, variables, objects, functions, or expressions. The syntax for the `typeof` operand is as follows:

`typeof operand`

or,

`typeof (operand)`

The `typeof` operator returns a string containing one of the following values: string, number, boolean, object, function, or undefined. The script in Listing 6.1 checks the various data types discussed so far in this book.

Listing 6.1 Using the typeof Operand

```
<HTML>
  <HEAD>
    <TITLE>Using the typeof Operand</TITLE>
<SCRIPT LANGUAGE="JavaScript">
<!--
function dog(breed, color, age) {
   this.breed=breed
   this.color=color
   this.age=age
```

```
}
function funType(x) {
   return x * x
}
//-->
</SCRIPT>
  </HEAD>
  <BODY>
    <P>The following shows the output from different types of variables.</P>
<SCRIPT LANGUAGE="JavaScript">
<!--
var strType="A string"
var numType=3
var bolType=true
var nulType=null
var undType=
objType=new dog("mixed", "black", 7)
arrType=new Array(3)
arrType[0]="A String"
arrType[1]=5
document.write("strType = "+typeof(strType)+"<BR>")
document.write("numType = "+typeof(numType)+"<BR>")
document.write("bolType = "+typeof(bolType)+"<BR>")
document.write("nulType = "+typeof(nulType)+"<BR>")
document.write("undType = "+typeof(undType)+"<BR>")
document.write("objType = "+typeof(objType)+"<BR>")
document.write("objType.color = "+typeof(objType.color)+"<BR>")
document.write("funType = "+typeof(funType)+"<BR>")
document.write("arrType = "+typeof(arrType)+"<BR>")
document.write("arrType[0] = "+typeof(arrType[0])+"<BR>")
document.write("arrType[2] = "+typeof(arrType[2])+"<BR>")
document.write("nonType = "+typeof(nonType)+"<BR>")
//-->
</SCRIPT>
  </BODY>
</HTML>
```

Figure 6.1 shows the results of running the script in Listing 6.1 using Netscape Communicator 4.0. Microsoft Internet Explorer 4.0 produces the same results. Both Netscape Navigator 3.0 and Microsoft Internet Explorer 3.0 report an uninitialized array element as an object, while Netscape Communicator 4.0 and Microsoft Internet Explorer 4.0 report it as undefined. Notice that a variable set to null and an undefined variable are objects. This occurs because null itself is an object.

Warning

The values returned by the typeof operand contain extra spaces. Before using them in any comparison, you need to remove the spaces with a string method or a regular expression.

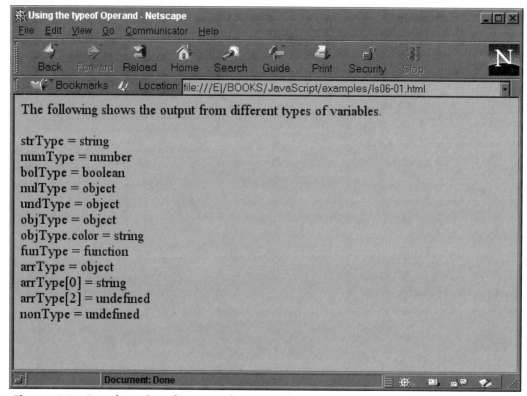

Figure 6.1 Results using the typeof operand.

The void Operator

The void operator evaluates an expression, but does not return a value. The syntax for the void operator is as follows:

```
void expression
```

or,

```
void(expression)
```

Although the parentheses are optional, it is a good programming practice to use them. Creating an entry in the Personal Toolbar in Netscape Communicator 4.0 provides an example of how to use the void operator. Besides having links to Web pages, you can add JavaScript methods to the toolbar. To add an "open new window" method to the toolbar, you need to perform the following steps:

1. In the location bar, choose Bookmarks > Edit Bookmarks.
2. From the Bookmarks window, open the Personal Toolbar Folder, and select Folder.
3. Choose File > New Bookmark.
4. In the Name field of the Bookmark Properties dialog box, enter the name that you want to appear in the tool bar, such as "Open Window."
5. In the Location(URL) field, type the command javascript:void(window.open[""]).
6. Click OK and close the Bookmarks window.

Built-in Functions

The following *built-in functions* are functions independent of any particular object.

- `parseInt()`
- `parseFloat()`
- `isNaN()`
- `Number()` (new in JavaScript 1.2)
- `String()` (new in JavaScript 1.2)
- `escape()`
- `unescape()`

The `parseInt()` and `ParseFloat()` functions operate on string variables. The `Number()` and `String()` functions operate on objects. The isNaN() function, on the other hand, checks to see if a number variable is NaN (Not a Number). The `escape()` and `unescape()` functions deal with the problem of handling special characters in HTML.

Converting String Variables to Numbers

If you need to perform a numeric comparison, use arithmetic operators, or use a `Math` method, you need to insure that the data type is numeric. For this purpose, JavaScript provides two functions: `parseInt()` and `parseFloat()`.

The `parseInt()` function converts a string containing an unsigned string integer into a number. The syntax for the function is:

```
parseInt(string[, radix])
```

The radix is the base of the string. If you do not specify the base of the string, the `parseInt()` function assumes the following:

- If the input string begins with "0x," the radix is 16 (hexadecimal).
- If the input string begins with a "0," the radix is 8 (octal).
- If the input string begins with any other number, the radix is 10 (decimal).

In processing the string, the `parseInt()` function applies these rules:

- If the first character in the string is not a valid number according to the radix, then the function returns NaN (Not a Number). NaN is not a number in any radix; rather, it is a special value. You test for NaN with the `isNaN()` function.
- When the `parseInt()` function encounters a value that is not valid according to the radix, it stops processing the string.

The script shown in Listing 6.2 demonstrates the behavior of the `parseInt()` function. The results of running this script are shown in Figure 6.2. As the results show, the `parseInt()` function acts according to the rules just stated. The only exception is Microsoft Internet Explorer 3.0. For the NaN tests, it returned 0 instead of NaN. However, this duplicates Netscape Navigator 2.0's behavior on non-UNIX platforms.

Listing 6.2 Using the parseInt() Function.

```
<HTML>
  <HEAD>
    <TITLE>Using the parseInt Function</TITLE>
  </HEAD>
  <BODY>
    <P>Although the document.write method converts the number back to a
string,
        the following examples illustrate the behavior of the parseInt func-
tion.</P>
<SCRIPT LANGUAGE="JavaScript">
<!--
document.write("<P>Without the radix argument</P>")
document.write("10 = "+parseInt("10")+"<BR>")
document.write("0x10 = "+parseInt("0x10")+"<BR>")
document.write("010 = "+parseInt("010")+"<BR>")
document.write("5 * 2 = "+parseInt("5 * 2")+"<BR>")
document.write("<P>With a radix of 10</P>")
document.write("10 = "+parseInt("10", 10)+"<BR>")
document.write("0x10 = "+parseInt("0x10", 10)+"<BR>")
document.write("010 = "+parseInt("010", 10)+"<BR>")
document.write("10A = "+parseInt("10A", 10)+"<BR>")
document.write("<P>With a radix of 16</P>")
document.write("10 = "+parseInt("10", 16)+"<BR>")
document.write("010 = "+parseInt("010", 16)+"<BR>")
document.write("A = "+parseInt("A", 16)+"<BR>")
document.write("AXX = "+parseInt("AXX", 16)+"<BR>")
document.write("<P>Examples of NaN</P>")
document.write("A5 with no radix = "+parseInt("A5")+"<BR>")
document.write("A5 with radix of 8 = "+parseInt("A5", 8)+"<BR>")
//-->
</SCRIPT>
  </BODY>
</HTML>
```

The `parseFloat()` function converts any integer, decimal, or exponent to a number. The format of the `parseFloat()` function is as follows:

```
parseFloat(string)
```

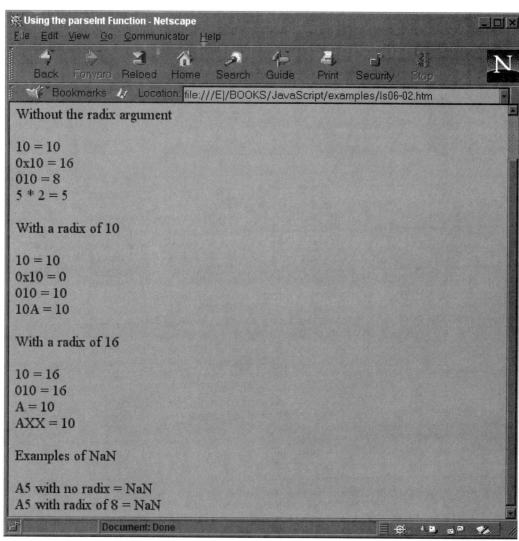

Figure 6.2   Results of using parseInt function.

The `parseFloat()` function returns a floating-point number as long as the first character it encounters is a sign (+ or –), number, or decimal point. For all other characters, the `parseFloat()` function returns NaN. If the first character is valid, `parseFloat()` continues converting the string until it reaches the end of the string or finds an invalid character.

As shown in Figure 6.3, the parseFloat() function used in Listing 6.3 behaves as expected in all browsers except Netscape Navigator 2.0, non-Unix platforms, and Microsoft Internet Explorer 3.0. On non-UNIX platforms, and Microsoft Internet Explorer 3.0, the last test returns 0 instead of NaN.

Listing 6.3 Using the parseFloat Function

```
<HTML>
  <HEAD>
    <TITLE>Using the parseFloat Function</TITLE>
  </HEAD>
  <BODY>
    <P>This test shows the behavior of the parseFloat function.</P>
<SCRIPT LANGUAGE="JavaScript">
<!--
document.write("-5 = "+parseFloat("-5")+"<BR>")
document.write("4.55 = "+parseFloat("4.55")+"<BR>")
document.write("0.035e-2 = "+parseFloat("0.035e-2")+"<BR>")
document.write("0xFF = "+parseFloat("0xFF")+"<BR>")
document.write("FF = "+parseFloat("FF")+"<BR>")
//-->
</SCRIPT>
  </BODY>
</HTML>
```

New in JavaScript 1.2

Converting Objects to Variables

The Number() and String() functions convert objects to numeric and string variables, respectively. The format of these functions is as follows:

```
Number(object)
String(object)
```

Chapter 3 shows how to use the Number() and String() functions to ensure the correct data type when comparing two values. But this is only part of the story. Table 6.1 describes how these functions behave with the various built-in objects.

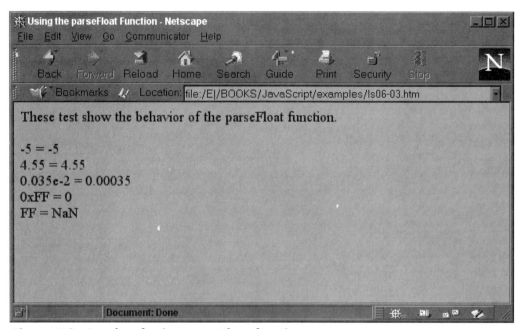

Figure 6.3   Results of using parseFloat function.

Table 6.1 Behavior of the Number() and String() Functions with Built-in Objects

Object	Number()	String()
Array	Returns the length of the array.	Returns the array in literal notation.
Boolean	Returns 0 for false and 1 for true	Returns a string with a value of false or true.
Date	Returns a value in milliseconds measured since January 1, 1970 UTC (GMT).	Returns a string such as: Thu Oct 01 09:47:53 Mountain Daylight Time 1997
Function	Returns NaN.	Returns the function in literal notation.
Number	Returns the number as a numeric data type.	Returns the number as a string data type.
String	Returns the string as a numeric data type. If the string is not a valid number, then it returns NaN.	Returns the string as a string data type.

The documentation for JavaScript 1.2 only shows how the `Number()` and `String()` functions behave with the `date` object. Through experimentation, I was able to work out the information in Table 6.1. Listing 6.4 is one of the scripts used to explore the behavior of these two functions. The results of running this script are shown in Figure 6.4.

Listing 6.4 Using the Number() and String() Functions

```
<HTML>
  <HEAD>
    <TITLE>Using String and Number Functions</TITLE>
<SCRIPT LANGUAGE="JavaScript1.2">
<!--
var strObj = new String("0.032e-2")
var errStrObj = new String("0xFF")
var numObj = new Number(12.5)
var bolObj = new Boolean(true)
var dateObj = new Date()
var strArray = new Array("12", "13", "14")
var funObj = new Function("x", "return x * x")
//-->
</SCRIPT>
  </HEAD>
  <BODY>
    <P>The following checks object conversion by String() and Number():</P>
<SCRIPT LANGUAGE="JavaScript1.2">
<!--
document.write("String to Number = "+Number(strObj)+"<BR>")
document.write("String with Error = "+Number(errStrObj)+"<BR>")
document.write("Number to String = "+String(numObj)+"<BR>")
document.write("Boolean to Number = "+Number(bolObj)+"<BR>")
document.write("Boolean to String = "+String(bolObj)+"<BR>")
document.write("Date to Number = "+Number(dateObj)+"<BR>")
document.write("Date to String = "+String(dateObj)+"<BR>")
document.write("Array to Number = "+Number(strArray)+"<BR>")
document.write("Array to String = "+String(strArray)+"<BR>")
document.write("Function to Number = "+Number(funObj)+"<BR>")
document.write("Function to Number = "+String(funObj)+"<BR>")
//-->
</SCRIPT>
  </BODY>
</HTML>
```

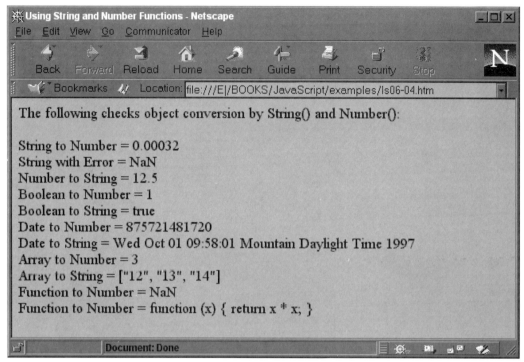

Figure 6.4 Results of using the Number() and String() functions.

Checking for NaN (Not a Number)

Since NaN is not a valid number in any radix, you need to use the `is-NaN()` function to test for a value of NaN. The syntax for this function is as follows:

```
isNaN(testValue)
```

The `isNaN()` function returns true if the *testValue* is NaN and false if it is not. The following code snippet illustrates how you might use this function:

```
var numVar = parseFloat("4.55")
if (isNaN(numVar)) {
        // statements for NaN
}
else {
        // statements for valid number
}
```

Tip

> Although JavaScript 1.0 includes the `isNaN()` function, it only works on UNIX platforms. Starting in JavaScript 1.1, the `isNaN()` function works on all platforms.

Escaping and Unescaping Strings

When browsers and servers communicate, they occasionally use nonalphanumeric characters in their messages. To insure that these characters survive the journey, they are encoded by changing the character to %xx, where xx is the hexadecimal value of the character in the ASCII ISO Latin-1 character set. For example, the space character is encoded as %20. The `escape()` function performs the task of encoding the string, and the `unescape()` function decodes it back into a regular ASCII string. These two functions have the following syntax:

```
escape("string")
unescape("string")
```

For example, the command

```
escape("#^ "}
```

produces the string

```
%23%5E%20
```

The `unescape()` function takes a string, such as a URL to a file on a hard disk, and returns it in humanly readable form. A common practice is to encode the values placed in a cookie (see Chapter 8, "Working with Forms" for more details on cookies).

Shared Methods

A *shared method* is a method that is included in several objects. The following shared methods are included in every object:

- `eval()`
- `tostring()`
- `valueOf()`

While these methods have limited use from a scripting point of view, they are very important to the function of JavaScript, which uses these methods to perform its functions.

Evaluating Strings

The `eval()` method evaluates a string and returns the results of the evaluation. In JavaScript 1.0, `eval()` is a built-in function. Starting with JavaScript 1.1, `eval()` became a method of every object. As a result, the current syntax for the `eval()` method is as follows:

```
[objName.]eval(string)
```

where the *objname* is optional.

Some of the situations where you need the eval() method are:

- When a user enters a string that includes arithmetic operators. You can't convert this string to a number, but you can use the `eval()` method to process the string and return a number. For example,

```
var numVar = eval("2 * 3")
```

- When you want a generic function to update the value of any property in a form. For example you could write a function such as the following:

```
function setValue(frmObj, newValue) {
    eval("document.forms[0]."+frmObj+".value") = newValue
}
```

The `eval()` method is not used very often. However, when you need the results of a string and not the string itself, the `eval()` method comes in handy.

The toString() Method

The `toString()` method converts the specified object to a string. Since each object has different requirements, the behavior of the `toString()` method varies according to the nature of the object. The `tostring()` method has two syntax statements:

```
objName.toString()
```

numberObjName.tostring([*radix*])

> Since the results of executing the toString() method varies with each object, the discussion of each object includes the toString() method.

The valueOf Method

The valueOf() method returns the primitive value (number, string, boolean, null, and undefined) of the object. The syntax for the valueOf() command is:

objectName.valueOf()

> The valueOf() method is rarely used in scripts. However, the browser automatically calls valueOf() to evaluate expressions. Since most objects do not have primitive data, the method provides useful information for only a few objects as shown in Table 6.2.

Table 6.2 Objects that Provide Primitive Values

Object Type	Value returned by valueOf()
Number	Returns the primitive numeric value associated with the object.
String	Returns the string associated with the object.
Boolean	Returns the primitive Boolean value associated with the object.
Date	Returns the date and time specified by the object.
Function	Returns the function reference associated with the object

The String Object

> JavaScript has both string variables and string objects. The difference between a string variable and a string object is how you define them. The two definitions are:

> • For a string variable, the syntax is:

var *stringName* = "*string*"

> • For a string object, the syntax is:

```
var stringName = new String("string")
```

If you check the two definitions with the typeof() method, the return value for a string variable is "string," and for a string object, it is "object." In practice, you don't see the difference between the two since the browser performs the necessary temporary conversions. However, a string object does have properties and methods as shown in Table 6.3. Since the browser converts string variables to string objects, why declare a string object? The answer is that if you are extensively using the properties and methods of the string object, then it is more efficient to declare the string as an object.

Table 6.3 Properties and Methods of the String Object

Properties	Methods	Events
length	anchor()	none
prototype	big()	
	blink()	
	bold()	
	charAt()	
	charCodeAt() (new in JavaScript 1.2)	
	concat() (new in JavaScript 1.2)	
	fixed()	
	fontcolor()	
	fontsize()	
	fromCharCode() (new in JavaScript 1.2)	
	indexOf()	
	italics()	
	lastIndexOf()	
	link(()	
	match() (new in JavaScript 1.2)	
	replace() (new in JavaScript 1.2)	

Table 6.3 Properties and Methods of the String Object *(Continued)*

Properties	Methods	Events
	`search()` (new in JavaScript 1.2)	
	`slice` (new in JavaScript 1.2)	
	`small()`	
	`split()` (changed in JavaScript 1.2)	
	`strike()`	
	`sub()`	
	`substr()` (new in JavaScript 1.2)	
	`substring()` (changed in JavaScript 1.2)	
	`sup()`	
	`toLowerCase()`	
	`toUpperCase()`	

There are two ways to use a string object:

- stringName.propertyName
- stringName.methodName(*parameters*)

String Object Properties

The string object has one primary property—`length`. Since it is a property, the following are all valid references:

```
strLength = stringVariable.length%
strLength = stringObject.length
strLength = "This is a string".length
```

The `prototype` property allows you to add additional properties and methods to string objects.

String Object Methods

As shown in Table 6.3, there are a large number of methods associated with the string object. The methods divide nicely into three groups:

- Wrapping a string with HTML tags
- String editing
- Regular expressions

Wrapping a String with HTML Tags

All of the methods in this category wrap the string object with HTML tags. Table 6.4 lists all of the string object methods that wrap a string with HTML tags.

Table 6.4 Methods that Add HTML Tags to a String

Method	Description
`anchor( nameAttribute)`	The `anchor()` method brackets the text with the `<A></A>` tags with the **NAME** attribute set to the value of the parameter passed to the method. For example: `document.write("Other Links".anchor("other_links"))`
`big()`	The string is wrapped with the `<BIG></BIG>` tags.
`blink()`	The string is wrapped with the `<BLINK></BLINK>` tags.
`bold()`	The string is wrapped with the `<B></B>` tags.
`fixed()`	The string is wrapped with the `<TT></TT>` tags.
`fontcolor(color)`	The string is wrapped with the `<FONT COLOR="color"></FONT>` tags. The color parameter is specified as a name from the color table in Appendix A, or in "rrggbb" format.
`fontsize(size)`	The string is wrapped with the `<FONTSIZE=size></FONTSIZE>` tags. The size can be a value from one to seven, or it can be a relative change (+ or -) to the font size specified in the `<BASEFONT>` tag.
`italics()`	The string is wrapped with the `<I></I>` tags.
`link( hrefAttribute)`	The text is wrapped with the `<A HREF=hrefAttribute></A>` tags. The argument *hrefAttribute* includes all valid URL protocols.
`small()`	The string is wrapped with the `<SMALL></SMALL>` tags.
`strike()`	The string is wrapped with the `<STRIKE></STRIKE>` tags.
`sub()`	The string is wrapped with the `<SUB></SUB>` tags.
`sup()`	The string is wrapped with the `<SUP></SUP>` tags.

The script in Listing 6.5 illustrates how to use the methods described in Table 6.4 to wrap text with HTML tags. Since there is a long list of `document.write` statements, the `with` statement sets the prefix of all the substatements to the document. Figure 6.5 shows the results of running the script.

Listing 6.5 Using the HTML Tag Methods

```
<HTML>
  <HEAD>
    <TITLE>Using the HTML Tag Methods</TITLE>
<SCRIPT LANGUAGE="JavaScript">
<!--
var strTest1=new String("This is the anchor for the link test")
//-->
</SCRIPT>
  </HEAD>
  <BODY>
<SCRIPT LANGUAGE="JavaScript">
<!--
with (document) {
   write(strTest1.anchor("test1")+"<BR>")
   write("Big text".big()+"<BR>")
   write("Blinking text".blink()+"<BR>")
   write("Bold text".bold()+"<BR>")
   write("Fixed text".fixed()+"<BR>")
   write("Colored text".fontcolor("red")+"<BR>")
   write("Bigger font text".fontsize(4)+"<BR>")
   write("Italic text".italics()+"<BR>")
   write("Linked text".link("#text1")+"<BR>")
   write("Small text".small()+"<BR>")
   write("Strikethrough text".strike()+"<BR>")
   write("This is a"+"subscript".sub()+"<BR>")
   write("This is a"+"superscript".sup()+"<BR>")
}
//-->
</SCRIPT>
  </BODY>
</HTML>
```

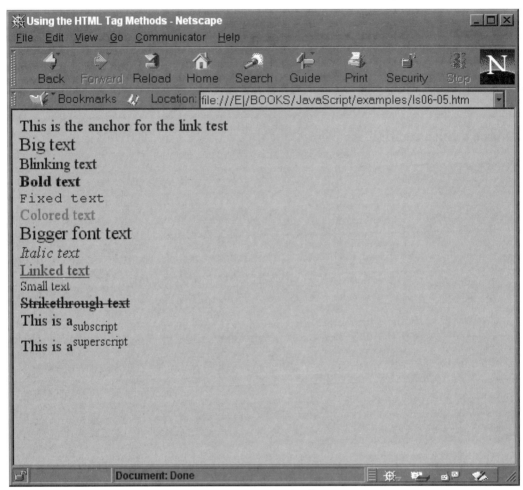

Figure 6.5   Results of using the HTML tag methods.

Converting the Case of a String

Whether you need to convert the case of a string because of server requirements or to perform a case insensitive comparison, JavaScript provides two methods for case conversion of a string. The `toLowerCase()` method converts a string to lower case, while the `toUpperCase()` method converts it to upper case. The following examples illustrate the use of these two methods:

```
newString = "Mixed Case String".toLowerCase()
newString = "Mixed Case String".toUpperCase()
```

Finding a Text within a String

The `indexOf()` method returns the position of the first character for a search string, and starts from the beginning of a string or from the optional *fromIndex*. The syntax for the `indexOf()` method is as follows:

`stringName.indexOf(searchString[, fromIndex])`

If the *searchString* is not found, the `indexOf()` method returns a -1. When the string you are searching is empty, the `indexOf()` method also returns a -1.

Instead of starting from the beginning of the string, you can search from the end of the string with the `lastIndexOf()` method. The `lastIndexOf()` method searches backwards from the end of the string, or from the optional *fromIndex*. If the `lastIndexOf()` method finds the string, it returns the index for the first character in the *search-String*. When the `lastIndexOf()` method fails to find the *searchString* in the string object, it returns a -1. The syntax for the `lastIndexOf()` method is as follows:

`stringName.lastIndexOf(searchString[, fromIndex])`

Listing 6.6 includes illustrations regarding the use of both the `indexOf()` method and the `lastIndexOf()` method. The results of running this script are shown in Figure 6.6.

Listing 6.6 Searching for Text in a String

```
<HTML>
  <HEAD>
    <TITLE></TITLE>
<SCRIPT LANGUAGE="JavaScript">
<!--
var testStr=new String("Mississippi")
//-->
</SCRIPT>
  </HEAD>
  <BODY>
    <P>Examples of the indexOf() method:</P>
<SCRIPT LANGUAGE="JavaScript">
<!--
```

```
with (document) {
    write("Search for ss in Mississippi starting at")
    write(" 0 returns: "+testStr.indexOf("ss")+"<BR>")
    write("Search for ss in Mississippi starting at")
    write(" 3 returns: "+testStr.indexOf("ss", 3)+"<BR>")
    write("Search for xx in Mississippi starting at")
    write(" 0 returns: "+testStr.indexOf("xx")+"<BR>")
    write("Search for xx in a null string starting at")
    write(" 0 returns: "+"".indexOf("xx")+"<BR>")
}
//-->
</SCRIPT>
    <P>Examples of lastIndexOf() method:</P>
<SCRIPT LANGUAGE="JavaScript">
<!--
with (document) {
    write("Search for ss in Mississippi starting at")
    write(" length-1 returns: "+testStr.lastIndexOf("ss")+"<BR>")
    write("Search for ss in Mississippi starting at")
    write(" length-7 returns: )
    write("testStr.lastIndexOf("ss", testStr.length-7)+"<BR>")
    write("Search for xx in Mississippi starting at")
    write(" length-1 returns: "+testStr.lastIndexOf("xx")+"<BR>")
    write("Search for xx in a null string starting at")
    write(" length-1 returns: "+"".lastIndexOf("xx")+"<BR>")
}
//-->
</SCRIPT>
    </BODY>
</HTML>
```

Listing 6.7 shows a revised script for listing the properties of an object. This script produces a cleaner output than the version in Listing 5.5, "Script to build anArray of an Object's Properties."

The script also illustrates the use of the methods presented in this chapter. Figure 6.7 shows a portion of the results produced by this script for the window object. It only needs to display the information in a separate window to be used as a handy debugging script (see Chapter 9, "Working with Windows and Frames").

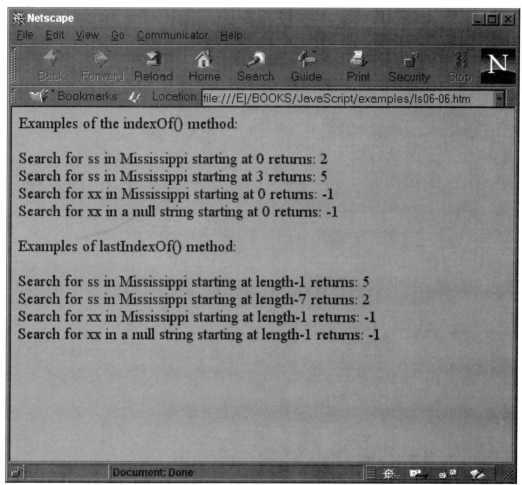

Figure 6.6   Results of searching for text in a string.

Listing 6.7 Revised List Properties of an Object

```
<HTML>
  <HEAD>
    <TITLE>Determine Data Types of Object Hierarchy</TITLE>
<SCRIPT LANGUAGE="JavaScript">
<!--
propsTable = new Array()
j=0
```

```
function getProps(obj, objName) {
   for (var i in obj) {
      propsTable[j]=new Array(3)
      propsTable[j][0]=objName+"."+i
      propsTable[j][1]=typeof(obj[i])
      if (propsTable[j][1].indexOf("str")>=0 ||
         propsTable[j][1].indexOf("num")>=0 ||
         propsTable[j][1].indexOf("boo")>=0) {
         propsTable[j][2]=obj[i].toString()
      }
      else {
         propsTable[j][2]=""
      }
      ++j
   }
}
function listProps(obj, objName) {
   getProps(obj, objName)
   document.write("Total properties = "+propsTable.length+"<BR>")
   for (var i=1; i<propsTable.length; i++) {
      document.write(propsTable[i][0]+" = ")
      document.write(propsTable[i][1])
      if (propsTable[i][1].indexOf("str")>=0 ||
         propsTable[i][1].indexOf("num")>=0 ||
         propsTable[i][1].indexOf("boo")>=0) {
      document.write(" ("+propsTable[i][2]+")")
      }
      document.write("<BR>")
   }
}
//-->
</SCRIPT>
   </HEAD>
   <BODY>
      <P>The data types of the window object are:</P>
<SCRIPT LANGUAGE="JavaScript">
<!--
listProps(window, "window")
//-->
</SCRIPT>
   </BODY>
</HTML>
```

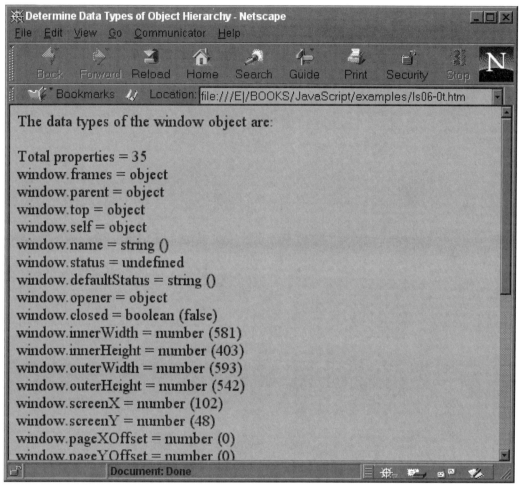

Figure 6.7   Results of listing object properties

Extracting Characters from a String

The `charAt()` method returns a single character from a string as specified by the *index*. If the *index* is outside of the bounds of the string, the `charAt()` method returns an empty string. The syntax for the `charAt()` method is as follows:

stringName.charAt(*index*)

For example,

```
charVal="test".charAt(2) // charAt() returns an "s"
```

New in JavaScript 1.2

 JavaScript 1.2 adds two more character methods to the string object. The `charCodeAt()` method returns a hexadecimal number, without the leading "0x," that indicates the ISO-Latin-1 codeset value of the character. The syntax for the `charCodeAt()` method is as follows:

```
string.charCodeAt([index])
```

The *index* is an optional argument, with a default value of 0. If the index is outside the bounds of the string, the `charCodeAt()` method returns an empty string. In the following example, the `charCodeAt()` method returns a numeric value of 66.

```
"abc".charCodeAt(1)
```

JavaScript 1.2 also includes the `fromCharCode()` as a method of the String object, although it does not extract a value from a string. The `fromCharCode()` method returns a string from the specified numbers that are ISO-Latin-1 codeset values. The syntax for the `fromCharCode()` method is as follows:

```
String.fromCharCode(num1, num2, ..., numn)
```

The following example of the `fromCharCode()` method returns the string "ABC:"

```
String.fromCharCode(65, 66, 67)
```

Extracting Part of a String

The `substring()` method extracts a contiguous set of characters from a string. The syntax of the `substring()` method is as follows:

```
stringName.substring(indexA, indexB)
```

The behavior of the `substring()` method varies according to the relationship of *indexA* to *indexB*:

- If *indexA* is less than *indexB*, `substring()` starts at *indexA* and extracts all characters up to, but not including, *indexB*.

- If *indexA* is greater than *indexB*, `substring()` starts at *indexB* and extracts all characters up to, but not including, *indexA*.
- If *indexA* equals *indexB*, the `substring()` method returns an empty string.

New in JavaScript 1.2

 If LANGUAGE= "JavaScript1.2" in the `<SCRIPT>` tag, the `substring()` method no longer swaps *indexA* and *indexB*. The new rules for the `substring()` method are:

- The `substring()` method extracts characters from *indexA* up to but not including *indexB*.
- If *indexA* is less than 0, the `substring()` method treats it as if it were 0.
- If *indexB* is greater than *stringName*.length, the `substring()` method treats it as if it were *stringName*.length.
- If *indexA* equals *indexB*, the `substring()` method returns an empty string.
- If *indexB* is omitted, the `substring()` method extracts characters from *indexA* to the end of the string.

The `slice()` method in JavaScript 1.2 behaves in a similar manner as the `substring()` method, without the implications of the LANGUAGE attribute. The syntax for the `slice()` method is as follows:

stringName.`slice(`*beginSlice*`[, `*endSlice*`])`

The behavior of `slice()` is:

- The `slice()` method extracts from *beginSlice* up to, but not including, *endSlice*.
- If *endSlice* is a negative value, the `slice()` method treats it as an offset from the end of the string.
- If *endSlice* is omitted, the `slice()` method extracts a string from *beginSlice* to the end of the string.

JavaScript 1.2 also introduces the `substr()` method. The `substr()` method extracts a string from a *start* index to the end of the string or for the number of characters specified by the *length* argument. When the *length* is 0, or negative, the `substr()` method returns an empty string. The syntax for the `substr()` method is as follows:

stringName.substr(*start*[, *length*])

The script in Listing 6.8 illustrates the use of the `substring()`, `slice()`, and `substr()` methods. The script also distinguishes between older versions of JavaScript and JavaScript 1.2. Figure 6.8 shows the results of running this script in Netscape Communicator 4.03.

Listing 6.8 Extracting a Portion of a String

```
<HTML>
  <HEAD>
    <TITLE>Extracting Portions of a String</TITLE>
<SCRIPT LANGUAGE="JavaScript">
<!--
var testStr=new String("A string test")
//-->
</SCRIPT>
  </HEAD>
  <BODY>
    <P>The substring() method with LANGUAGE=&quot;JavaScript&quot;:</P>
<SCRIPT LANGUAGE="JavaScript">
<!--
with (document) {
   write("All test use the string: "+testStr+"<BR>")
   write("substring(2, 7) returns: "+testStr.substring(2, 7)+"<BR>")
   write("substring(7, 2) returns: "+testStr.substring(7, 2)+"<BR>")
}
//-->
</SCRIPT>
    <P>The substring() method with LANGUAGE=&quot;JavaScript1.2&quot;:</P>
<SCRIPT LANGUAGE="JavaScript1.2">
<!--
with (document) {
   write("substring(2, 7) returns: "+testStr.substring(2, 7)+"<BR>")
   write("substring(7, 2) returns: "+testStr.substring(7, 2)+"<BR>")
   write("substring(2) returns: "+testStr.substring(2)+"<BR>")
   write("substring(2, -6) returns: "+testStr.substring(2, -6)+"<BR>")
}
```

```
//-->
</SCRIPT>
    <P>The slice() and substr() methods of JavaScript 1.2:</P>
<SCRIPT LANGUAGE="JavaScript1.2">
<!--
with (document) {
   write("slice(2, 7) returns: "+testStr.slice(2, 7)+"<BR>")
   write("slice(2, -5) returns: "+testStr.slice(2, -5)+"<BR>")
   write("slice(2) returns: "+testStr.slice(2)+"<BR>")
   write("substr(2, 6) returns: "+testStr.substr(2, 6)+"<BR>")
   write("substr(2) returns: "+testStr.substr(2)+"<BR>")
}
//-->
</SCRIPT>
  </BODY>
</HTML>
```

Concatenating Two Strings

In addition to the "+" operand, you can use the `concat()` method to concatenate two strings. The syntax for the `concat()` method is as follows:

string1.concat(*string2*)

Other than consistency of object methods between objects, I am not sure what is gained from using the `concat()` method over using the "+" operand.

Splitting a String into an Array

The `split()` method converts a string into an array according to the specified *separator*. The *separator* is any single character including the escaped characters shown in Table 4.1. The syntax for the `split()` method is as follows:

stringName.split([*separator*])

Although the *separator* is optional, the absence of the argument causes the `split()` method to create an array with one element containing the entire string. When `split()` parses the string, it creates an array element for each separator that it finds. The `split()` method does not

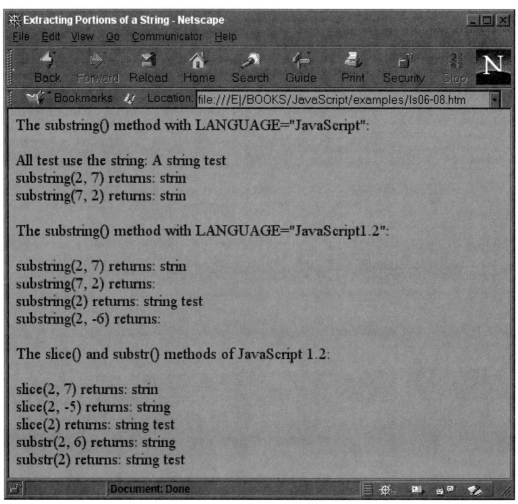

Figure 6.8   Results extracting portions of a string.

include the *separator* character in the array element. The following are some examples of the split() method:

```
strArray = someString.split(" ")   // creates an array of words
strArray = someString.split(",")   // parses a comma delimited
string
strArray = someString.split("\t")  // parses a tab delimited
string
```

New in JavaScript 1.2

 JavaScript 1.2 changed the behavior of the `split()` method and added another argument. The revised syntax for the `split()` method is:

stringName.split([*separator*][, *limit*])

The new *limit* argument defines the maximum number of splits that the split() method makes in parsing a string. The purpose of the *limit* argument is to avoid building empty entries in the array when the string ends in multiple separator characters, such as spaces when the separator is a space. This is fine, if you know the number of trailing delimiters in advance.

When LANGUAGE="JavaScript1.2" appears in the <SCRIPT> tag, the split() method does not add empty elements to the array when the separator is a space. For other separators, each occurrence of the separator generates an array element. The script in Listing 6.9 illustrates the difference between LANGUAGE="JavaScript" and LANGUAGE="JavaScript1.2" using one array with the space character as the separator and the other using the colon. Figure 6.9 shows the results of running this script.

Listing 6.9 Splitting a String into an Array

```
<HTML>
  <HEAD>
    <TITLE>Splitting a String into an Array</TITLE>
<SCRIPT LANGUAGE="JavaScript">
<!--
var spaceStr=new String("A  short test   ")
var colonStr=new String("A::short:test:::")
//-->
</SCRIPT>
  </HEAD>
  <BODY>
  <P>This example uses the split command on a string with spaces as
delimiters and aa second string with colons as delimiters. Colons are used
because document.write(array) separates the elements with commas. Since it
is hard to see spaces, the colon delimited version of the string is:</P>
  <P>A::short:test:::</P>
  <P>The results of splitting this string with LANGUAGE=&quot;Java-
Script&quot; is:</P>
```

```
<SCRIPT LANGUAGE="JavaScript">
<!--
spaceArray1=spaceStr.split(" ")
document.write("The space delimited array has "+spaceArray1.length+"
elements: ") document.write(spaceArray1+"<BR>")
colonArray1=colonStr.split(":")
document.write("The colon delimited array has "+colonArray1.length+"
elements: ") document.write(colonArray1+"<BR>")
//-->
</SCRIPT>
  <P>The results of splitting this string with
LANGUAGE=&quot;JavaScript1.2&quot;
     is:</P>
<SCRIPT LANGUAGE="JavaScript1.2">
<!--
spaceArray2=spaceStr.split(" ")
document.write("The space delimited array has "+spaceArray2.length+"
elements: ") document.write(spaceArray2+"<BR>")
colonArray2=colonStr.split(":")
document.write("The colon delimited array has "+colonArray2.length+"
elements: ") document.write(colonArray2+"<BR>")
//-->
</SCRIPT>
  </BODY>
</HTML>
```

Parsing a string using single character delimiters works for simple splitting of strings into arrays. To get around the limitation of single character parsing, JavaScript 1.2 allows a regular expression object as a separator.

New in JavaScript 1.2

Regular Expressions

Regular expressions expand the pattern matching capability of JavaScript. You are no longer limited to searching for simple strings. With regular expressions, you can create simple or complex search patterns. The regular expression feature of JavaScript contains three components:

- The regular expression pattern
- The regular expression object, which stores the pattern
- The RegExp, which relates to the actual searching for a pattern

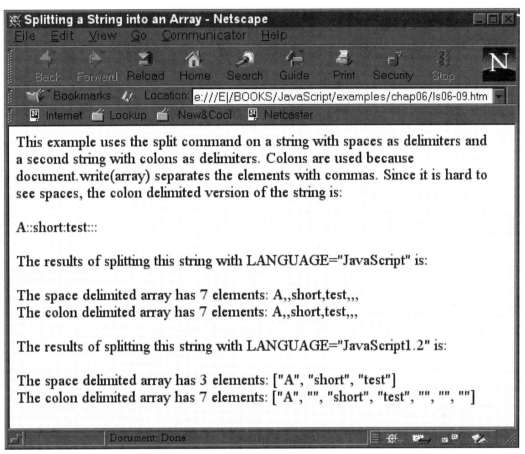

Figure 6.9   Results of splitting a string into an array.

Writing Regular Expression Patterns

The slash ("/") brackets the regular expression pattern. The pattern   /
xyz/ is a simple string pattern that matches anything containing the
string "xyz." A more complex pattern is /Chapter(\d+)\.\d*/. The
trick in writing patterns is to learn how to vocalize the pattern. You read
the last pattern as a search for a string beginning with "Chapter," followed by one or more numbers, a period, and then zero or more numbers. In addition, you want the system to remember the first set of
numbers as indicated by the parentheses.

Writing a Simple Pattern

Simple patterns are nothing more than a contiguous set of characters bounded by slashes. You use a simple pattern when you say that you are looking for anything that contains this string of characters. For example, the pattern /let/ matches character combinations that contain the characters "let" in that exact order. In the string "let the triplets wear bracelets," there are three matches for the pattern /let/, but has zero matches in the string "little Jack Horner."

Writing a Complex Pattern

Complex patterns involve searches such as: Find a match for a string that begins with "i;" has one or more of the letter "t;" and ends with the characters "le." The pattern that reflects this statement is /it*le/, which matches such words as "title" or "little." Table 6.5 lists the special characters used in regular expression patterns and gives a short example of how to use the special character. The syntax for regular expression patterns is similar to that used in Perl.

Table 6.5 Special Characters used in Regular Expression Patterns

Pattern	Definition	Example
\	If the following character has a special meaning for patterns, it means don't take the character literally.	\t says don't take the "t" as an alphabetic character, but as a tab.
	If it is a pattern match character that stands by itself, it means take this as a literal character and not a pattern matching character.	* says the following is a literal asterisk and not a pattern matching character.
^	Matches the beginning of input or a line.	/^T/ says match a line that begins with the letter "T."
$	Match the end of input or a line.	/t$/ says match a line that ends with the letter "t."
*	Match the preceding character zero or more times.	/ca*/ says match a string that has the letter "c" followed by zero or more occurrences of the letter "a."

Table 6.5 Special Characters used in Regular Expression Patterns *(Continued)*

Pattern	Definition	Example
+	Match the preceding character one or more times.	`/bo+/` says match a string that has the letter "b" followed by one or more occurrences of the letter "o."
?	Match the preceding character zero or one time.	`/a?g/` says match a string that has zero or one occurrence of the letter "a" followed by the letter "g."
.	The period (".") matches any single character except a new line.	`/.t/` says match any character followed by the letter "t."
(x)	Match x and remember the match. You can then recall the matched substring from the result array or by using the global RegExp properties of `$1` to `$9`.	`/(b.g)/` says match a string that begins with "b," followed by any character, and ends in "g." If found, remember the string.
x|y	Matches either "x" or "y."	`/big|bad/` matches a substring that contains either "big" or "bad."
{x}	Where x is a non-negative integer. Matches the previous character exactly x times.	`/e{2}/` says match a substring that contains the letter "e" exactly two times.
{x,}	Where x is a non-negative integer. Matches the previous character at least x times.	`/e{1,}/` says match a substring that contains the letter "e" at least once.
{x,y}	Where x and y are nonnegative integers. Matches the previous character at least x times but no more than y times.	`/e{1,2}/` says match a substring containing the letter "e" at least once but no more then twice.
[xyz]	The brackets define a set of characters. Matches any single character in the set of characters. You can define ranges of characters, such as `[a-z]` for all lower case characters, or `[a-zA-Z]` to define all upper and lower case characters.	`/[a-em]/` says match a single of the character set "abcdem."
[^xyz]	The `[^]` defines a negative character set. Matches any character except those listed. You can define ranges, such as `[^a-z]` that exclude all lower case characters.	`/[^a-em]/` says match any single character not including the characters "abcdem."

Table 6.5 Special Characters used in Regular Expression Patterns *(Continued)*

Pattern	Definition	Example
\b	Matches a word boundary, such as a space. The word boundary can be either the beginning or end of the word.	/\bn/ says match any word that begins with the letter "n."
\B	Matches a nonword boundary.	/[a-z]\Bn/ says match any lower case character followed by the letter "n."
\d	Matches any digit character. It is the equivalent of [0-9].	/\d{3}/ says match any three consecutive digits.
\D	Matches any nondigit character. It is the equivalent of [^0-9].	/\D/ says match any nondigit character.
\f	Matches a form-feed character.	
\n	Matches a linefeed.	
\r	Matches a carriage return.	
\s	Matches any whitespace including space, tab, form feed, linefeed, or vertical tab. It is the equivalent of [\f\n\r\t\v].	/\s[a-zA-Z]/ says match any whitespace followed by any lowercase or uppercase alphabetic character.
\S	Matches any character that is not a whitespace character. It is the equivalent of [^ \f\n\r\t\v].	/\S[a-zA-Z]/ says match any character not preceded by whitespace.
\t	Matches a tab.	
\v	Matches a vertical tab.	
\w	Matches any word character including an underscore. It is the equivalent of [A-Za-z0-9_].	/l\B\w/ says match any substring that begins with the letter "l," followed by any word character that is not on a word boundary.
\W	Matches any nonword character. It is the equivalent of [^A-Za-z0-9_].	/\W/ says match any non-word character such as a "%."
/\#/	Where # is a positive integer and is a reference to the corresponding remembered substring. If there is not a corresponding referenced substring, the \# is taken as an octal escape.	Examples of the back reference appear in the section on Using Parentheses in Regular Expression Patterns.

Table 6.5 Special Characters used in Regular Expression Patterns *(Continued)*

Pattern	Definition	Example
/x/	Where x is an octal, hexadecimal, or decimal escape value. The /x/ allows you to imbed ASCII codes into regular expression patterns.	

Using Parentheses in Regular Expression Patterns

Parentheses around any part of a substring cause JavaScript to remember that substring. Once remembered, you can recall the substring later. The following are the ways to recall a remembered substring:

- In the same pattern, you recall a remembered substring with the \# special characters. Of course, this is a back reference in the pattern, since JavaScript needs to remember the substring before recalling the substring.
- The global `RegExp` object maintains the last nine parenthesized substring matches as the properties $1 through $9. The global `RegExp` object also maintains last remembered substring as $+.
- All remembered substrings are elements of the `array` object that collects the output of the pattern match.

JavaScript numbers remembers variables according to the number of left parentheses encountered in the pattern. Thus, the first left parenthesis encountered is \1, $1, and `myArray[1]`. Although the global `RegExp` properties only track the last nine remembered substrings, the only limit to the number of remembered substrings is the amount of memory available to the browser.

Regular expression patterns form powerful tools for editing strings. For example, the following pattern edits a phone number string:

```
/\(?\d{3}\)?([-\/\.])\d{3}\1\d{4}/
```

This compact regular expression pattern assumes that a phone number takes one of the following forms:

```
(999)-999-9999 or 999-999-9999
(999)/999/9999 or 999/999/9999
(999).999.9999 or 999.999.9999
```

The following analyzes the regular expression pattern for editing phone numbers by reading the pattern:

1. The phone number may enclose the area code in parentheses. Thus, "there may be a left parenthesis" is \ (?. You need the backslash before the left parenthesis because the left parenthesis is one of the special characters. Without the backslash, JavaScript thinks this is the beginning of a remembered substring. The question mark says that there are zero or one left parenthesis.

2. "Then there is three digits for the area code" is the special characters \d{3}.

3. "Followed by an optional right parenthesis" is \ ) ?. Again, the right parenthesis requires the preceding backslash to keep JavaScript from taking the right parenthesis to mean the end of a remembered substring.

4. "Remember the next character that is a dash, slash, or period" is ([-\/ \.]). In this case, both the slash and period require the backslash to keep JavaScript from using them as special characters.

5. "Then there is three digits" is \d{3}.

6. "Then whatever character was used to separate numbers needs to appear again" is \1. The \1 recalls the remembered string.

7. "Then there is four digits" is \d{4}.

While the pattern illustrates remembered substrings, it needs some fine tuning to reflect actual valid phone numbers—one solution is to use two patterns. Handling international phone numbers is even more complex. However, for each format, you can design a pattern that edits the string.

Storing the Regular Expression Pattern

Before you can use a pattern, you need to store it in a regular expression object. There are two ways to create a regular expression object:

• Using literal notation, which has the following syntax:

```
regexp = /pattern/[i][g][gi]
```

• Using the RegExp constructor, which has the following syntax:

```
regexp = new RegExp("pattern"[, 'i'|'g'|'gi'])
```

The literal notation is more efficient, since the browser compiles the regular expression object when it loads the HTML document. You want to use the literal notation for regular expressions that remain constant. If the script constructs the regular expression pattern or the regular expression pattern comes from an outside source, you need to use the `RegExp` constructor. The resulting expression is less efficient, since the browser needs to construct the expression each time it encounters the statement. JavaScript provides a `compile()` method that allows you to optimize the efficiency of the regular expression object created by the `RegExp` constructor.

When you use the `RegExp` constructor function to create a regular expression object, you need to escape each backslash with another backslash. The extra backslash is necessary to get the desired backslash past the string processing function. For example, you need to write new `RegExp("\\w+")` instead of `/\w+/`. Also, you don't use the slash to bracket the pattern.

In addition to the regular expression pattern, you can specify one of three options:

- The "i" option sets a flag to ignore case while attempting to match a string. The default is case-sensitive matching.
- The "g" option sets a flag to find all possible matches in a string. The default is to look for the first match starting from the *lastIndex* property.
- The "gi" option sets both flags.

The result of using either the literal notation or the `RegExp` constructor is a regular expression object. Like all objects, the regular expression object has properties and methods as shown in Table 6.6.

Table 6.6 Properties and Methods of Regular Expression Object

Properties	Methods	Events
global	compile()	none
ignoreCase	exec()	
lastIndex	test()	
source		

Properties of Regular Expression Object

The *global* and *ignoreCase* properties are read-only properties that show the status of the flags. These properties are set when the browser creates the object, or when the script uses the compile() method to compile the regular expression object.

The *lastIndex* property is a read/write integer property that is the beginning index for the next match. The following rules apply to the use of the *lastIndex* property by the test() and exec() methods:

- If *lastIndex* is greater than the length of the string used in the match, the match fails, and *lastIndex* is set to zero.
- If *lastIndex* equals the length of the string and the regular expression pattern matches an empty string, it matches the input starting at *lastIndex*.
- If *lastIndex* equals the length of the string and the regular expression pattern does not match an empty string, the match fails and *lastIndex* is set to zero.
- If *lastIndex* is less than the length of the string, *lastIndex* is set to the next position in the string following the match.

The *source* property is a read-only property that contains the text of the pattern.

Methods of the Regular Expression Object

Of the three methods, this section only covers the compile() method. The section on Working with Regular Expressions discusses the exec() and test() methods.

The `compile()` method compiles a regular expression object during the execution of the script. The syntax for the `compile()` method is as follows:

```
regexp.compile("pattern"[, 'i'|'g'|'gi'])
```

The primary use of the compile() method is to compile a regular expression object created with the `RegExp` constructor function. Once you know that the regular expression pattern has a stable pattern, you need to compile the regular expression object to improve performance. If the pattern changes, you can also use the compile() method to recompile the regular expression object.

Working with Regular Expressions

After you store the pattern in the regular expression object, you can use the pattern with the methods described in Table 6.7. The special `array` object and the updates to the `RegExp` properties are special features common to a number of methods.

Table 6.7 Methods that use Regular Expressions

Method	Object	Returns	Description
exec()	regular expression	Special `Array` object Updates `RegExp` properties	Searches for a match in a specified string.
test()	regular expression	true or false	Tests for a match in a specified string.
match()	String	Special `Array` object Updates RegExp properties	Searches for a match in a specified string.
re-place()	String	Special `Array` object Updates `RegExp` properties	Searches for a match in a specified string and replaces the matched substring with a replacement substring.
search()	String	Index of match or –1 if no match	Tests for a match in a specified string.
split()	String	Array of substrings	Breaks a string into an array of substrings.

Array returned by Regular Expressions

The `exec()`, `match()`, and `replace()` methods return an array. Table 6.8 lists the properties of this array and provides a brief description of each property. The actual values returned varies according to the method and the regular expression pattern used in the match.

Table 6.8 Properties of Array returned by Regular Expressions

Property/Element	Description
input	A read-only property that contains the original string against which the method applied the regular expression.
index	A read-only property that is the zero-based index of the match in the string.
[0]	A read only element that contains the last matched characters
[1], ... [n]	If the pattern contains parenthesized matches, these elements contain the matched substrings.

Properties of the RegExp Object

The `RegExp` object is a global object with properties that the `exec()`, `match()`, and `replace()` methods set before a search for a regular string, or after they find a match. Table 6.9 provides a brief description of the `RegExp` properties. For most properties, there are two names; the longer JavaScript name, and the short Perl-like name.

Table 6.9 Properties of RegExp Object

Property	Description
input $_	A read/write property that contains the string against which the method matches the pattern.
multiline $*	A read/write Boolean property that indicates whether to search in string across multiple lines. If it is true, multiple lines are searched. If it is false, searches stop at line breaks.
lastMatch $&	A read-only property that contains the last match characters.

Table 6.9 Properties of RegExp Object *(Continued)*

Property	Description
lastParen $+	A read-only property that contains the last parenthesized match, if the match found a parenthesized substring.
leftContext $`	A read-only property that contains the string up to the most recent match.
rightContext $'	A read-only property that contains the string past the most recent match.
$1, ...$9	If there are any parenthesized substring matches, these properties contain the last nine substrings. When pattern does not contain any parenthesis, the browser interprets the $#'s literally.

The *input* property of the RegExp object is automatically set by Navigator for the following events:

- When Navigator calls an event handler for the TEXT form, Navigator sets the *input* property to the value of the contained text.
- When Navigator calls an event handler for the TEXTAREA form element, Navigator sets the *input* property to the value of the contained text and sets the *multiline* property to true.
- When Navigator calls an event handler for the SELECT form element, Navigator sets the *input* to the value of the selected text.
- When Navigator calls an event handler for the Link object, Navigator sets *input* to the value of the text between <A HREF=...> and </A>.

Warning

Except for the TEXTAREA form element, Navigator sets *multiline* to false after executing any event handler.

Searching for a Match in a String

JavaScript 1.2 has two methods for matching patterns against a string;
`regexp.exec()` and `str.match()`. The differences between the
two methods go beyond being methods of different objects. To illustrate
the differences, the discussion of `exec()` and `match()` use the same
basic script with only the method used for pattern matching changing
between the scripts.

Using exec() Method for Pattern Matching

The `exec()` method is a property of the regular expression object. The
syntax for the `exec()` method is as follows:

`regexp.exec(string)`

The `exec()` method also has a short version of the syntax:

`regexp(string)`

The script in Listing 6.10 uses one string and one pattern with regular
expression objects for; no flags, global flag, ignore case flag, and both
flags. The purpose of the script is to illustrate the behavior for matching
depending on the settings of the flags.

Listing 6.10 Using the exec() Method

```
<HTML>
  <HEAD>
    <TITLE>Using the exec() Method</TITLE>
<SCRIPT LANGUAGE="JavaScript1.2">
<!--
testStr="Checking for all Apples and Apricots."
nfre=/(\bA\w+)/
gfre=/(\bA\w+)/g
ifre=/(\bA\w+)/i
gifre=/(\bA\w+)/gi
//-->
</SCRIPT>
  </HEAD>
  <BODY>
```

```
<SCRIPT LANGUAGE="JavaScript1.2">
<!--
nTest=nfre.exec(testStr)
with (document) {
    write("The test String is: "+nTest.input+"<BR>")
    write("pattern: "+nfre.source+" produces: "+nTest)
    write(" at index: "+nTest.index+"<BR>")
    write("global flag: "+nfre.global)
    write(", ignore case flag: "+nfre.ignoreCase+"<BR>")
    write("lastParen: "+RegExp.lastParen+", $1: "+RegExp.$1+"<BR>")
    write("<HR>")
}
gTest=gfre.exec(testStr)
with (document) {
    write("The test String is: "+gTest.input+"<BR>")
    write("pattern: "+gfre.source+" produces: "+gTest)
    write(" at index: "+gTest.index+"<BR>")
    write("global flag: "+gfre.global)
    write(", ignore case flag: "+gfre.ignoreCase+"<BR>")
    write("lastParen: "+RegExp.lastParen+", $1: "+RegExp.$1+"<BR>")
    write("<HR>")
}
iTest=ifre.exec(testStr)
with (document) {
    write("The test String is: "+iTest.input+"<BR>")
    write("pattern: "+ifre.source+" produces: "+iTest)
    write(" at index: "+iTest.index+"<BR>")
    write("global flag: "+ifre.global)
    write(", ignore case flag: "+ifre.ignoreCase+"<BR>")
    write("lastParen: "+RegExp.lastParen+", $1: "+RegExp.$1+"<BR>")
    write("<HR>")
}
giTest=gifre.exec(testStr)
with (document) {
    write("The test String is: "+giTest.input+"<BR>")
    write("pattern: "+gifre.source+" produces: "+giTest)
    write(" at index: "+giTest.index+"<BR>")
    write("global flag: "+gifre.global)
    write(" ignore case flag: "+gifre.ignoreCase+"<BR>")
    write("lastParen: "+RegExp.lastParen+", $1: "+RegExp.$1+"<BR>")
}
//-->
</SCRIPT>
  </BODY>
</HTML>
```

Figure 6.10 shows the results of running Listing 6.10 using Netscape Communicator 4.03. The global flag's definition is that the method is to test the pattern against all possible occurrences in the string. Since there is only left parenthesis, there is only one remembered variable. This matches the results. The surprise is that it remembers the first occurrence and not the last. The results from running the script indicate that the exec() method stopped after finding the first match. On the other hand, the ignore case flag behaved as expected.

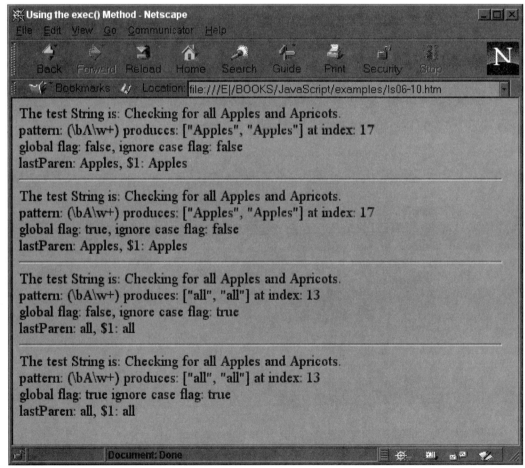

Figure 6.10   Results of using exec() method.

Using the match() Method for Pattern Matching

The match() method is a property of the String object. The syntax for the match() method is as follows:

string.match(*regexp*)

As the script in Listing 6.11 shows, the match() method has the following behavior according to the settings of the global flag and the ignore case flag:

- With neither flag set, the match() method stops after the first match and returns an array, updates the regular expression object and the global RegExp object.
- With the global flag set, the match() method returns an array of all matches and the last parenthesized substring. The *input* and *index* properties of the returned array are undefined.
- With the ignore case flag set, the match() method ignores the case when performing matches.

Listing 6.11 Using the match() Method

```
<HTML>
  <HEAD>
    <TITLE>Using the match() Method</TITLE>
<SCRIPT LANGUAGE="JavaScript1.2">
<!--
testStr="Checking for all Apples and Apricots."
nfre=/(\bA\w+)/
gfre=/(\bA\w+)/g
ifre=/(\bA\w+)/i
gifre=/(\bA\w+)/gi
//-->
</SCRIPT>
  </HEAD>
  <BODY>
<SCRIPT LANGUAGE="JavaScript1.2">
<!--
nTest=testStr.match(nfre)
with (document) {
```

```
    write("The test String is: "+nTest.input+"<BR>")
    write("pattern: "+nfre.source+" produces: "+nTest)
    write(" at index: "+nTest.index+"<BR>")
    write("global flag: "+nfre.global)
    write(", ignore case flag: "+nfre.ignoreCase+"<BR>")
    write("lastParen: "+RegExp.lastParen+", $1: "+RegExp.$1+"<BR>")
    write("<HR>")
}
gTest=testStr.match(gfre)
with (document) {
    write("The test String is: "+gTest.input+"<BR>")
    write("pattern: "+gfre.source+" produces: "+gTest)
    write(" at index: "+gTest.index+"<BR>")
    write("global flag: "+gfre.global)
    write(", ignore case flag: "+gfre.ignoreCase+"<BR>")
    write("lastParen: "+RegExp.lastParen+", $1: "+RegExp.$1+"<BR>")
    write("<HR>")
}
iTest=testStr.match(ifre)
with (document) {
    write("The test String is: "+iTest.input+"<BR>")
    write("pattern: "+ifre.source+" produces: "+iTest)
    write(" at index: "+iTest.index+"<BR>")
    write("global flag: "+ifre.global)
    write(", ignore case flag: "+ifre.ignoreCase+"<BR>")
    write("lastParen: "+RegExp.lastParen+", $1: "+RegExp.$1+"<BR>")
    write("<HR>")
}
giTest=testStr.match(gifre)
with (document) {
    write("The test String is: "+giTest.input+"<BR>")
    write("pattern: "+gifre.source+" produces: "+giTest)
    write(" at index: "+giTest.index+"<BR>")
    write("global flag: "+gifre.global)
    write(" ignore case flag: "+gifre.ignoreCase+"<BR>")
    write("lastParen: "+RegExp.lastParen+", $1: "+RegExp.$1+"<BR>")
}
//-->
</SCRIPT>
  </BODY>
</HTML>
```

As shown in Figure 6.11, the results of running the script in Listing 6.11 are exactly as expected. With the global flag set, the `match()` method found all matches of the pattern in the string. For the `match()`

method with the global flag set, the number of left parentheses in the pattern are not indicative of the number of remembered substrings.

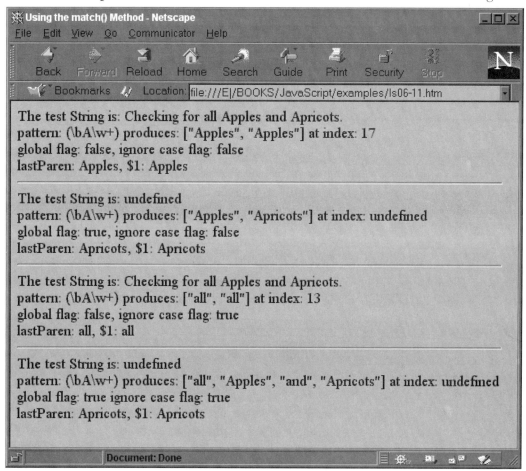

Figure 6.11   Results of using the match() method.

Testing for a Match in a String

Both the test() method of the regular expression object and the search() method of the String object test for a match between the pattern and the string. The syntax for each of these statements is as follows:

```
regexp.test(string)
string.search(regexp)
```

The test() and search() methods only return a result, they do not update either the regular expression object or the global RegExp object. Since these two methods only look for the first match, the global flag has no meaning. The difference between the two methods is:

- The test() method returns True if there was a match, and False if there was no match.
- The search() method returns the index value of the first match, or -1 if there was no match.

Note

 If you are only testing for a match, use either the test() or search() method. They are much more efficient than the exec() or match() methods.

The script in Listing 6.12 illustrates the use of both the test() method and the search() method. The results of running this script are shown in Figure 6.12.

Listing 6.12 Testing for a Match in a String

```
<HTML>
  <HEAD>
    <TITLE>Testing for a Match in a String</TITLE>
<SCRIPT LANGUAGE="JavaScript1.2">
<!--
testStr="Checking for all Apples and Apricots."
failStr="Nothing here but carrots and spinach."
nfre=/(\bA\w+)/
ifre=/(\bA\w+)/i
function listResults(inStr, pattern, caseFlag, tstRes) {
    with (document) {
        write("The test String is: "+inStr+"<BR>")
        write("pattern: "+pattern)
        write(" Ignore Case: "+caseFlag)
        write(" produces: "+tstRes+"<BR>")
        write("<HR>")
    }
}
```

```
//-->
</SCRIPT>
  </HEAD>
  <BODY>
    <P>Testing for a match in a string using the test() method.</P>
<SCRIPT LANGUAGE="JavaScript1.2">
<!--
results=nfre.test(testStr)
listResults(testStr, nfre.source, nfre.ignoreCase, results)
results=ifre.test(testStr)
listResults(testStr, ifre.source, ifre.ignoreCase, results)
results=nfre.test(failStr)
listResults(failStr, nfre.source, nfre.ignoreCase, results)
//-->
</SCRIPT>
    <P>Testing for a match in a string using the search() method.</P>
<SCRIPT LANGUAGE="JavaScript1.2">
<!--
results=testStr.search(nfre)
listResults(testStr, nfre.source, nfre.ignoreCase, results)
results=testStr.search(ifre)
listResults(testStr, ifre.source, ifre.ignoreCase, results)
results=failStr.search(nfre)
listResults(failStr, nfre.source, nfre.ignoreCase, results)
//-->
</SCRIPT>
  </BODY>
</HTML>
```

Replacing One String with Another String

The `replace()` method is a method of the `String` object, and re-places the matched substring with the new substring. The `replace()` method returns the new string. The syntax for the `replace()` method is as follows:

```
string.replace(regexp, newSubStr)
```

Listing 6.13 illustrates three techniques for replacing a substring with another substring:

- Replace a single substring after finding a match.

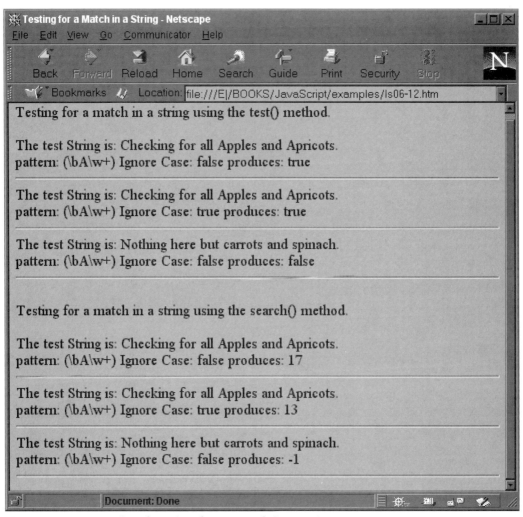

Figure 6.12   Results of testing for a match in a string.

- Replace all occurrences of one substring with another.
- Swap the order of two substrings using remembered substrings.

Figure 6.13 shows the results from running this script.

Listing 6.13 Replacing a Substring with Another String

```
<HTML>
  <HEAD>
    <TITLE>Replacing a Substring with another String</TITLE>
<SCRIPT LANGUAGE="JavaScript1.2">
<!--
testStr1="There is nothing like a holiday."
testStr2="A rose is a rose."
testStr3="John Smith"
re2=/rose/g
re3=/(\w+)\s(\w+)/
//-->
</SCRIPT>
  </HEAD>
  <BODY>
    <P>Replacing matches:</P>
<SCRIPT LANGUAGE="JavaScript1.2">
<!--
document.write("Old String: "+testStr1+"<BR>")
document.write("Replace holdiay with vacation<BR>")
testRes1=testStr1.replace(/holiday/, "vacation")
document.write("New String:: "+testRes1+"<BR>")
document.write("<HR>")
document.write("Old String: "+testStr2+"<BR>")
document.write("Replace all occurences of rose with flower<BR>")
testRes2=testStr2.replace(re2, "flower")
document.write("New String:: "+testRes2+"<BR>")
document.write("<HR>")
//-->
</SCRIPT>
    <P>Replacing remembered substrings:</P>
<SCRIPT LANGUAGE="JavaScript">
<!--
document.write("Old String: "+testStr3+"<BR>")
document.write("Swap the order.<BR>")
testRes3=testStr3.replace(re3, "$2, $1")
document.write("New String: "+testRes3+"<BR>")
//-->
</SCRIPT>
  </BODY>
</HTML>
```

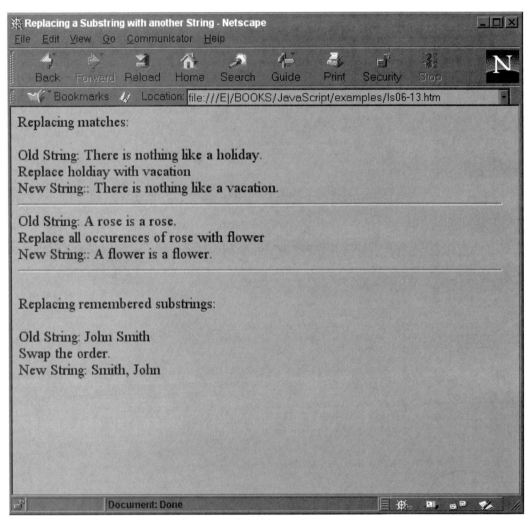

Figure 6.13   Results of replacing substrings.

Splitting a String using a Regular Expression

JavaScript 1.2 enhances the capabilities of the `split()` method to include the use of a regular expression. The syntax for the `split()` method using a regular expression is:

```
stringName.split(regexp[, limit])
```

In this case, the pattern needs to specify the match for a separator, for example:

```
/\s*;\s*/
```

The above regular expression says that there can be zero or more white space before the colon, and zero or more white space after the colon. This pattern is a generic pattern for any separator that needs to select for white space.

The Number Object

Although there is a `Number` object constructor, you never use it. Used without the new keyword, `Number()` acts as a data type conversion function that returns the numeric equivalent of its argument. The syntax for `Number()` is:

```
Number(value)
```

The `Number()` function converts decimal integers or floating-point numbers. If `Number()` cannot convert a number, it returns NaN (Not a Number). Included in the category of values the `Number()` fails to convert, are octal and hexadecimal values. `Number()` treats octal values as integers, and hexadecimal as NaN.

The Number object's properties are numeric constants as shown in Table 6.10.

Table 6.10 Properties of Number Object

Property	Description
MAX_VALUE	Defines the value of the largest number, which is approximately 1.79E+308. Any operation that exceeds this value returns POSITIVE_INIFINITY.
MIN_VALUE	Defines the value of the smallest number, which is approximately 2.22E-308. Any operation that attempts to produce a result less than this value returns NEGATIVE_INFINITY.
NaN	A special value representing a nonnumeric result.
NEGATIVE_INFINITY	A special value that acts like negative infinity.
POSITIVE_INFINITY	A special value that acts like positive infinity.

New in JavaScript 1.2

 The Number(x) function produces NaN, instead of an error, when x is a string that does not contain a well-formed numeric literal.

The Boolean Object

You use the Boolean object when you need to convert a non-Boolean value to Boolean value. You can use the Boolean object any place that JavaScript expects a primitive Boolean value. The syntax for the Boolean conversion function is:

```
booleanObjectName = new Boolean(value)
```

Boolean values that return false are 0, null, false, or an empty string. The string value of "false" actually returns true. All other values return true.

The Date Object

While JavaScript does not provide a date data type, it provides a Date object that allows the handling of date and time information. There is one caveat; all dates are dates in milliseconds from January 1, 1970 00:00:00. Due to the way it handles dates, those dates before 1970 are invalid dates.

The Date object requires that an instance of the Date object exists prior to the use of its methods. The instance can either be a new object or the property of an existing object. There are four ways to define the new instance:

```
dateObjectName = new Date()
dateObjectName = new Date("month day, year hr:min:sec")
dateObjectName = new Date(year, month, day)
dateObjectName = new Date(year, month, date, hr, min, sec)
```

When there are no arguments to the Date() function, the Date() function sets the date and time to the current date and time. If the there is no time argument, the Date() function sets the time to zero. The only property to the Date object is the prototype property. With the exception of the UTC and `parse` methods, the format for the `Date` method-od is as follows:

dateObjectName.methodName(parameters)

The exceptions are the UTC and `parse` methods, these methods have the following syntax:

```
Date.UTC(parameters)
Date.parse(parameters)
```

Extracting Information from the Date Object

Table 6.11 describes the values returned by the various methods that get information from the `Date` object. The script in Listing 6.14 writes the value returned by each of the methods in Table 6.11. Figure 6.14 shows the results of running this script.

Table 6.11 Extracting Information from the Date Object

Date Method	Returned Value
getDate()	Day of the month
getDay()	Day of the week
getHours()	Hour of the day
getMinutes()	Minutes in the hour
getMonth()	Month within the year
getSeconds()	Seconds in the minute
getTime()	Milliseconds since 1/1/1970
getTimezoneOffset()	Offset between local time and GMT in minutes
getYear()	The year in two digit format for years before 2000 and four digit format for years from 2000 and beyond.
toGMTString()	Converts the date to a GMT time zone string. The actual format of this string is platform dependent.
toLocaleString()	Converts the date to a string using local conventions. The actual format of this string is platform dependent.

Netscape

In Netscape Navigator 2.0, the `getTimezoneOffset()` method returns a negative number for offsets west of GMT. To make the value consistent with Java, Netscape Navigator 3.0 changed the value to a positive integer.

Listing 6.14 Examples of Date Methods

```
<HTML>
  <HEAD>
    <TITLE>Examples of Date Methods</TITLE>
<SCRIPT LANGUAGE="JavaScript">
<!--
testDate=new Date("November 25, 87 14:30:20")
//-->
</SCRIPT>
  </HEAD>
  <BODY>
    <P>The following examples work with the following date:</P>
<SCRIPT LANGUAGE="JavaScript">
<!--
with (document) {
   write(testDate+"<HR>")
   write("Year = "+testDate.getYear()+"<BR>")
   write("Month = "+testDate.getMonth()+"<BR>")
   write("Day = "+testDate.getDate()+"<BR>")
   write("Day Of Week = "+testDate.getDay()+"<BR>")
   write("Hour = "+testDate.getHours()+"<BR>")
   write("Minutes = "+testDate.getMinutes()+"<BR>")
   write("Seconds = "+testDate.getSeconds()+"<BR>")
   write("GMT Format = "+testDate.toGMTString()+"<BR>")
   write("Local Format = "+testDate.toLocaleString()+"<BR>")
   write("GMT Offset = "+testDate.getTimezoneOffset()+"<BR>")
   write("Milliseconds since 1/1/70 = "+testDate.getTime()+"<BR>")
}
//-->
</SCRIPT>
  </BODY>
</HTML>
```

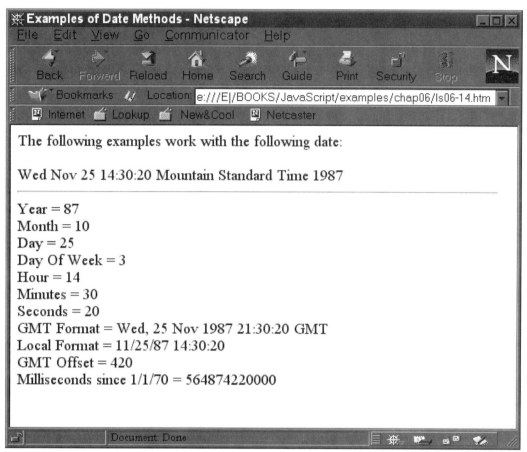

Figure 6.14   *Results of date methods examples.*

Changing the Date Object

Besides retrieving information from the Date object, the methods listed in Table 6.12 show how to change date information.

Table 6.12 Setting Information into the Date Object

Date method	Valid Values
setDate(dayValue)	1-31
setHours(hoursValue)	0-23
setMinutes(minutesValue)	0-59
setMonth(monthValue)	0-11
setSeconds(secondsValue)	0-59
setTime(timeValue)	>=0
setYear(yearValue)	>=1970

Static Date Methods

The Date object also provides two static methods for handling strings: Date.parse() and Date.UTC(). As static methods, they are not methods of an instance of the Date object. Both methods return the date converted to the number of milliseconds since January 1, 1970 00:00:00.

The Date.parse() method converts a date to milliseconds in reference to information in the *dateString*. The syntax for the Date.parse() method is:

```
Date.Parse(dateString)
```

The Date.parse() method accepts dates in a number of different formats, such as:

```
Nov 25, 1987
Wed, 25 Jan 1997 14:30:00 GMT
Wed, 25 Jan 1997 14:30:00 -0700
Wed, 25 Jan 1997 14:30:00 MST
25 Jan 97 14:30:00
01/25/97 14:30:00 MST
```

If you do not provide a *dateString*, the Date.parse() method uses the current time. The Date.parse() method provides a means for setting the date in an instance of the date object. For example,

```
aDate.setTime(Date.parse("Nov 25, 1987")
```

The `Date.UTC()` method returns the number of milliseconds since January 1, 1970 00:00:00 Universal Time Coordinate (GMT).

The syntax for `Date.UTC()` is as follows:

```
Date.UTC(year, month, day [, hrs] [, min] [, sec])
```

Listing 6.15 provides examples for both the `Date.parse()` and the `Date.UTC()` methods. This script shows that both methods produce the same result when the `Date.parse()` method specifies the time as being GMT.

Bug

The month in the `Date.UTC()` method is zero-based (January is 0). The other fields reflect the actual value, such as 2 for February.

Listing 6.15 Using the Static Date Methods

```
<HTML>
  <HEAD>
    <TITLE></TITLE>
<SCRIPT LANGUAGE="JavaScript">
<!--
testDate=new Date() // need a date object
//-->
</SCRIPT>
  </HEAD>
  <BODY>
<SCRIPT LANGUAGE="JavaScript">
<!--
testDate.setTime(Date.parse("Nov 25 96 14:30:00 GMT"))
document.write(testDate+"<BR>")
testDate.setTime(Date.UTC(96, 10, 25, 14, 30))
document.write(testDate+"<BR>")
//-->
</SCRIPT>
  </BODY>
</HTML>
```

The Math Object

The Math object provides a set of standard mathematical values and methods that augment the set of mathematical operators provided with JavaScript. As opposed to other objects, the Math object does not require an instance of the object before using them. To simplify the entering of names and to make the script more readable, the Math methods are often bounded by the with statement. The syntax for the Math object is as follows:

```
Math.propertyName
Math.methodName(parameters)
```

The Math Object Properties

The Math object provides eight properties that define various mathematical constants. Table 6.13 describes the properties and gives their values.

Table 6.13 Math Object Properties

Property	Description	Value
E	Euler's constant	2.718281828459045091
LN2	Natural logarithm of 2	0.6931471805599452862
LN10	Natural logarithm of 10	2.302585092994045901
LOG2E	Base 2 logarithm of e	1.442695040888963387
LOG10E	Base 10 logarithm of e	0.4342944819032518167
PI	Ratio of circumference to diameter	3.141592653589793116
SQRT1_2	Square root of one-half	0.7071067811865475727
SQRT2	Square root of two	1.414213562373095145

Math Object Methods

The Math object provides a number of Math methods that augment the set of mathematical operators. Table 6.14 lists the methods of the Math object and provides a short description of each method.

Table 6.14 Methods of the Math Object

Method	Description
abs(number)	This method returns the absolute value of the number.
acos(number)	The number must be a value between -1 and 1. For a valid number, acos returns arc cosine in radians. If the value of number is outside of the above range, acos() returns 0.
asin(number)	The asin() method returns the arc sine in radians. The rules for evaluation are the same as those for the acos method.
atan(number)	The atan() method returns the arc tangent in radians. The rules for evaluation are the same as those for the acos() method.
ceil(number)	This method returns the next integer greater than or equal to number.
cos(number)	The number is the angle in radians. JavaScript returns the cosine.
exp(number)	This method returns e to the power of number, where e is Euler's constant.
floor(number)	This method returns the next integer that is less than or equal to the number.
log(number)	The log method returns the natural logarithm (base e) of number, where number is any positive numeric expression or object. If the number is outside the range, the return value is always 1.797693134862316e+308.
max(number1, number2)	This method returns the greater of the two numbers.
min(number1, number2)	Conversely, this method returns the lesser of two numbers.
pow(base, exponent)	This method raises base to the power of exponent. If either the base, or the exponent is an imaginary number, JavaScript returns zero.
random()	This method is only available on UNIX platforms, where it returns a pseudorandom number between zero and one.
round(number)	JavaScript returns the value of number rounded to the nearest integer. For the purpose of rounding, any value of .5 or greater is rounded to the next highest integer.
sin(number)	This method returns the sine of the angle, where number is expressed in radians.
sqrt(number)	The sqrt() method returns the square root of any nonnegative number. If the number is out of range, JavaScript returns a zero.
tan(number)	This method returns the tangent of the angle, where number is expressed in radians.

Summary

This chapter began with the special operators, built-in functions, and shared methods that are important in working with all objects. The remainder of the chapter then focused on JavaScript's built-in objects. These objects are important as they form the basis for manipulating data in JavaScript. The objects covered in this chapter were:

- `String` object with it properties and methods.
- `Regular Expression` objects with their properties and methods.
- `Number` object and its properties.
- `Binary` object and its properties.
- `Date` object and its methods.
- `Math` object and its methods.

With the foundation in place, the next task is to understand documents and forms. An integral part of which are; events, event handlers, and the `event` object.

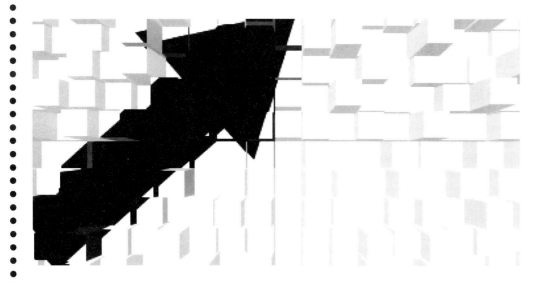

Working with Events and Documents

Topics in This Chapter

- Event models for JavaScript
- Document object
- Link and anchor objects
- Image and area objects

Chapter 7

An HTML document defines the content of a window or frame. In addition, an HTML document contains the JavaScript code that turns a static document into a dynamic interactive graphical environment. The properties of the document object reflect the HTML document, and allow you to work with the objects and properties of the document object by using JavaScript. The user interacts with the content of the HTML document through forms and events.

Events and event handlers, with the added feature of the event object (new in JavaScript 1.2), are important components of the large number of objects that compose the document object heirarchy. Since event handlers rank with properties and methods, this chapter opens with a discussion of events. From there, the topic switches to the document object. The description of forms, Java applets, and plug-ins objects is extensive enough to require separate treatment. Chapter 8, "Working With Forms," covers the forms object, while Chapter 10, "Using Plug-ins and Applets," discusses Java applets and plug-ins.

Programming Event Handlers

Events are like signals. For instance, when a friend waves to you, that is a signal, or in programming terms, an event. You respond to the event by interrupting what you are doing. A mental event handler takes control and you wave back. Computers work the same way (see Figure 7.1), an event happens, such as receiving a signal/event from the mouse interface regarding the movement of the mouse. The event takes the form of an interrupt. The operating system then has to decide—using a mouse event handler—who is going to handle the event. Since the mouse is a resource of the windows environment, the operating system transfers the event to the windows manager. The windows manager looks at the mouse event, and decides—using its own event handler—which window application needs to know about the event. The window application, such as Netscape Communicator, receives the event and passes the event to its event handler for mouse events. The mouse event handler looks at the JavaScript event handlers, such as MouseOver, and turns control over to the JavaScript statements that act as the event handler for the MouseOver event. This thumbnail sketch of events, and event handlers illustrates some important principles regarding events.

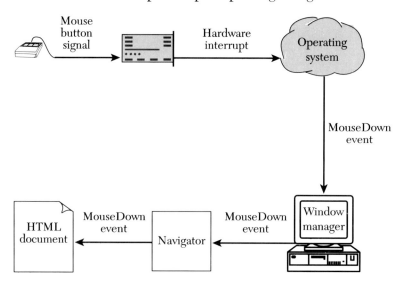

Figure 7.1   The flow of events.

- Events are signals.
- Event handlers decide how to respond to events.
- There are multiple layers of event handlers.
- One choice for the event handler, is to route the event to another event handler.

In addition to the mouse, the keyboard is another resource used by windows. Just like the mouse, the pressing of a key is an event. With reference to the user, mouse and keyboard events are *interactive* events. These events allow the document to interact with the user. There are also nonuser-oriented events called *noninteractive* events. The Load event is an example of a noninteractive event.

There is also a naming convention that needs to be understood. Mouse-Over and Load are names for events. The names onMouseOver and on-Load are the names for event handlers. Event handlers are the properties of an object that process the corresponding events for the object.

Event Handlers in JavaScript 1.0/1.1

In JavaScript 1.0, event handlers are read-only properties of their respective object. You invoke a custom action for an event by including the event handler as an HTML attribute. For example, the following HTML statement invokes a function when a field changes:

```
<INPUT TYPE="field" NAME="AGE" SIZE=3
onChange="checkAge(this)">
```

The declaration of the event handler occurs once and is part of HTML. The browser defines the event-handler property for the object just once and sets the value as read only. JavaScript 1.1 opens the door a little further by changing the event-handler property to read/write. In addition to assigning an action to an event as an HTML attribute, JavaScript 1.1 allows direct modification of the property as in this example:

```
document.forms[0].AGE.onchange=checkAge
```

With this method, the HTML statement doesn't contain the on-Change attribute. The side benefit is that you can change the value of the event handler property after the browser loads the HTML document. Besides changing the behavior of the event-handler property, JavaScript

1.1 adds new event handlers. Table 7.1 lists the event handlers available for both JavaScript 1.0 and JavaScript 1.1.

Note

 When you use an event handler as an attribute to HTML, you spell the name with *interCaps*, such as unLoad. When you refer to an event handler as the property of an object, you spell the name as all lowercase characters.

Table 7.1 JavaScript 1.0/1.1 Event Handlers

Event Handler	Syntax	Description
onabort *	imageObj.onabort onAbort="handler"	The abort event is the result of a user's action to stop the loading of an image, such as pressing the stop button, or clicking on a link in the document.
onblur **	obj.onblur onBlur="handler"	The blur event is the result of the screen focus moving from one element, window, frame, or frameset to another. The blur() method, the user clicks on another part of the screen, or the user presses the TAB key to cause a blur event. You should use the onblur event handler with care, as some actions, such as an event handler generating an alert box, may cause an infinite loop of blur events. Also, the onblur event handler in a frame overrides the onblur event handler in the <BODY> tag of a document. The onBlur attribute in a <FRAMESET> tag is not supported on Microsoft Windows platforms.
onchange **	obj.onchange onChange="handler"	The change event is the result of the screen focus moving away from a form element after the user makes a change to the form element. The blur() method, the user clicks on another part of the screen, or the user presses the TAB or ENTER key to generate a change event if the form element changed.

Table 7.1 JavaScript 1.0/1.1 Event Handlers *(Continued)*

Event Handler	Syntax	Description
onclick **	obj.onclick onClick="handler"	A click event occurs as the result of the user clicking on a related object, or the script executing the click() method. JavaScript 1.1 added the ability to cancel the click event by the event handler returning false. When a click event is canceled, the button object takes no action; radio buttons and checkboxes are not set; the submit button does not submit a form, and the reset button does not clear the form. Microsoft Windows platforms ignore the return value of false for the reset button.
onerror *	obj.onerror onError="handler"	An error event occurs when there is a JavaScript syntax error, runtime error, or an error in loading an image. Errors involving the Navigator object, or in other windows, do not generate an error event. The error event passes the error handler three arguments: a string containing the error message, a string containing the URL of the document causing the error, and the line number of the document where the error occurred. In turn, the error handler can: trace the error but return false, report the error and disable the standard error dialog by returning true, turn off error reporting by setting the error handler to null.
onfocus **	obj.onfocus onFocus="handler"	A focus event occurs when a window, frame, frameset, or form element receives focus. When you click on an object or window, or use the TAB key, the object receives focus. An event handler in the <FRAMESET> tag overrides an event handler in the <BODY> tag. If you use the alert() method in an onfocus event handler, the event handler will go into an infinite loop. On the Microsoft Windows platform, an onFocus attribute in a <FRAMESET> tag has no effect.

Table 7.1 JavaScript 1.0/1.1 Event Handlers (Continued)

Event Handler	Syntax	Description
onload **	obj.onload onLoad="handler"	A load event occurs when the browser finishes loading a window or all the frames within a <FRAMESET> tag. When working with frames, an onLoad attribute in the <BODY> tag responds to a load event before the onLoad attribute in a <FRAMESET> tag. In JavaScript 1.1, the load event occurs when the browser displays an image. This includes the display of multiple images by changing the SRC attribute or animated GIFs.
onmouseout *	obj.onmouseout onMouseOut="handler"	For client-side image maps, the mouseout event occurs when the cursor moves out of area or link inside that area. The mouseout event also occurs when the cursor leaves a link.
onmouseover **	obj.onmouseover onMouseOver="handler"	A mouseover event occurs whenever the cursor moves into an object or area from outside the object or area.
onreset *	formObj.onreset onReset="handler"	A reset event is the result of the user clicking the form's Reset button, or from the reset() method.
onselect	obj.onselect onSelect="handler"	The select event occurs whenever the user selects text within a text or textarea field.
onsubmit *	formObj.onsubmit onSubmit="handler"	The submit event occurs when the user clicks on the form's Submit button, or from the submit() method. If the event handler returns false, the browser does not submit the form.
onunload	obj.onunload onUnload="handler"	An unload event occurs as a result of any action that exits the document. The onUnload attribute in the <BODY> tag of a document receives the unload event before the onUnload attribute in the <FRAMESET> tag.

*New in JavaScript 1.1. ** Changed in JavaScript 1.1*

Table 7.2 lists the objects and their event handlers. The table splits the event handlers available in JavaScript 1.0 from those available in JavaScript 1.1. Microsoft Internet Explorer 3.0 only supports the event handlers for JavaScript 1.0. Microsoft Internet Explorer 4.0 follows the ECMAScript standard, which means that it is similar to JavaScript 1.1. However, MSIE 4.0 seems to support a variation of the event object and the additional events that appear in JavaScript 1.2. The Microsoft documentation on JScript does not mention these additional features, so I am not sure of the details.

Table 7.2 JavaScript 1.0/1.1 Objects and Their Event Handlers

Object	Event handlers for JavaScript 1.0	Event handlers for JavaScript 1.1
Window, frames, framesets	onload onunload	onblur onerror onfocus
link	onclick onmouseover	onmouseout
area *		onmouseout onmouseover
image *		onabort onerror onload
form	onsubmit	onreset
text, textarea	onblur onchange onfocus onselect	
password		onblur onfocus
button, reset, submit, radio, checkbox	onclick	onblur onfocus
select	onblur onchange onfocus	
fileUpload *		onblur onchange onfocus

* New in JavaScript 1.1.

To limit the presentation of new material, specific examples on how to use event handlers appear with their respective objects. At this point, our primary purpose is to gain an awareness of the structure of events and their relationship with event handlers.

Events in JavaScript 1.2

JavaScript 1.2 opens the event door all the way, so you now have:

- New and changed events
- More information associated with the event
- New ways of capturing and processing events

With the new event model for JavaScript 1.2, you have all the information that is passed to the browser for mouse and keyboard related events. The event model is backwards compatible. As a result, you still can write scripts using the old event models, or take advantage of the new features.

The Event Object in JavaScript 1.2

The `event` object is a global object, which contains the properties that describe an event. Table 7.3 lists the properties for the `event` object and provides a brief description of each property.

Table 7.3 Properties of the Event Object

Property	Description
target	A string containing the name of the object to which the event was originally sent.
type	A string containing the name of the event. It is the same as the name of the event handler without the prefix "on."
layerX	A number that defines, at the time of the event, the horizontal coordinate with respect to the target object's layer, or the width (in pixels) of a resized window.
layerY	A number that defines, at the time of the event, the vertical coordinate with respect to the target object's layer, or the height (in pixels) of a resized window.
width	Same as layerX, but makes more sense in regards to the resize event.
height	Same as layerY, but makes more sense in regards to the resize event.
pageX	A number that defines the horizontal coordinate relative to the target object's page.

Table 7.3 Properties of the Event Object *(Continued)*

Property	Description
pageY	A number that defines the vertical coordinate relative to the target object's page.
screenX	A number that defines the horizontal coordinate relative to the monitor screen.
screenY	A number that defines the vertical coordinate relative to the monitor screen.
which	An integer number that identifies the mouse key clicked or the ASCII value of the key pressed.
modifiers	A string specifying the modifier key associated with a mouse or key event. The modifier key values are ALT_MASK, CONTROL_MASK, SHIFT_MASK, or META_MASK.
data	An array of strings containing the URLs of the dropped objects.

The properties in the event object do not apply to every event. Table 7.4 lists the events supported in JavaScript 1.2 and the properties set by those events. It is important to note that the event sets the properties. The event handler can then access the properties of the event object.

Table 7.4 Properties of Event Object supported by Events

Event	Properties returned in Event Object
Abort	target, type
Blur	target, type
Change	target, type
Click	For a link: target, type, layerX, layerY, pageX, pageY, screenX, screenY, which, modifiers
	For a button: target, type, which, modifiers
DblClick	target, type, layerX, layerY, pageX, pageY, screenX, screenY, which, modifiers
DragDrop	target, type, data
Error	target, type (The event object is not passed to the event handler. Instead, the browser passes the arguments defined in Table 7.1.)
Focus	target, type
KeyDown	target, type, layerX, layerY, pageX, pageY, screenX, screenY, which, modifiers

---

Table 7.4 Properties of Event Object supported by Events *(Continued)*

Event	Properties returned in Event Object
KeyPress	target, type, layerX, layerY, pageX, pageY, screenX, screenY, which, modifiers
KeyUp	target, type, layerX, layerY, pageX, pageY, screenX, screenY, which, modifiers
Load	target, type
MouseDown	target, type, layerX, layerY, pageX, pageY, screenX, screenY, which, modifiers
MouseMove	target, type, layerX, layerY, pageX, pageY, screenX, screenY
MouseOut	target, type, layerX, layerY, pageX, pageY, screenX, screenY
MouseOver	target, type, layerX, layerY, pageX, pageY, screenX, screenY
MouseUp	target, type, layerX, layerY, pageX, pageY, screenX, screenY, which, modifiers
Move	target, type, screenX, screenY
Reset	target, type
Resize	target, type, width, height
Select	target, type
Submit	target, type
Unload	target, type

New and Changed Events in JavaScript 1.2

As part of the enhanced event model, JavaScript 1.2 introduces new events and changes some existing events. Some of the new events, such as mousedown and mouseup in Table 7.5, increase the granularity of events. In prior versions, the browser combines these two events into a single click event. Other new events, such as move and resize, add to the functionality of JavaScript. Some of the old events, such as click, now take advantage of the new information provided by the event object.

Table 7.6 describes the changes that JavaScript 1.2 made to the existing events.

Table 7.5 New Event Handlers in JavaScript 1.2

Event Handler	Syntax	Description
ondblclick	obj.ondblclick onDblClick= "handler"	The dblclick event occurs when a user double - clicks on a form element, link, or area. Double-clicking is a complex event because of the number of other events involved. The mousedown and mouseup combine to make a click event. After the click event follows the mousedown, mouseup, and then a double-click event.
ondragdrop	window.ondragdrop onDragDrop= "handler"	The dragdrop event occurs when a user drops an object, such as a file, onto a window. The normal response of Navigator is to load into the browser window. If the event handler returns false, Navigator cancels the drag and drop. To read the array of URLs in the event object requires a signed script.
onkeydown	obj.onkeydown onKeyDown= "handler"	The keydown event occurs when the user depresses a key. The which property of the event object contains the ASCII value of the key pressed. To get the actual value of the key, you need to use the charCodeAt() method. If the event handler returns false, Navigator blocks the keypress event. When you cancel the keypress event, Navigator does not pass the character to the text or textarea element.
onkeypress	obj.onkeypress onKeyPress= "handler"	The keypress event occurs when the user presses or holds down a key. The keypress event occurs after the keydown event. If the user holds the key down, the keypress event repeats until the user releases the key. When the event handler returns a false, Navigator cancels the individual keypress event.
onkeyup	obj.onkeyup onKeyUp="handler"	The keyup event occurs when the user releases a key.

Table 7.5 New Event Handlers in JavaScript 1.2 *(Continued)*

Event Handler	Syntax	Description
onmousedown	obj.onmousedown onMouseDown()	The mousedown event occurs when a user presses a mouse button. If the event handler returns false, Navigator cancels the default action, such as entering drag mode, entering selection mode, or arming a link. Arming a link causes the color to change to represent the new state.
onmousemove	obj.onmousemove onMouseMove= "handler"	The mousemove event occurs when the user moves the mouse. The mousemove event occurs only when an object captures events with the captureEvents() method.
onmouseup	obj.onmouseup onMouseUp= "handler"	The mouseup event occurs when the user releases a mouse button. If the event handler returns false, Navigator cancels the default action.
onmove	obj.onmove onMove="handler"	The move event occurs when a user or script moves a window or frame.
onresize	obj.onresize onResize= "handler"	The resize event occurs when a user or script resizes a window or frame.

Table 7.6 Event Handler Changes in JavaScript 1.2

Event Handler	Change
onblur	Added to the layer object.
onclick	The onclick event handler was added to the document object, which became an event handler for the window object. The big change is the additional information provided in the event object. Besides the positioning information, the event object provides information regarding which mouse button was clicked (1 for the left mouse button, 3 for the right mouse button) and any modifier keys pressed at the same time.
onload	Added to the layer object.
onmouseout	The onmouseout event handler was added to the layer object. The event handler also receives the information in the event object.
onmouseover	Added to the layer object.

Capturing and Processing Events in JavaScript 1.2

Previous versions of JavaScript provided what I call, functional events. In a functional event (such as click, mouseover, mouseout, submit) the browser took care of all the details, and you just had to create event handlers for those objects where you wanted to expand the user interface. If you didn't provide an event handler, the browser had a default action. The objects were tied to specific HTML statements, such as form elements. You could use events, with only a limited understanding of event processing. JavaScript 1.2 expands the functional events to the `layer` object, providing additional information through the `event` object, and adding new functional events such as double click. Table 7.7 lists the functional events provided in JavaScript 1.2 and their related objects.

Table 7.7 Functional Events and Their Related Objects

Event	Event Handler	Related Objects
abort	onabort	image
blur	onblur	window, frame, layer, button, checkbox, fileUpload, password, radio, reset, select, submit, text, textarea
change	onchange	fileUpload, select, text, textarea
click	onclick	document, link, button, checkbox, radio, reset, submit
dblclick	ondblclick	document, link, button
dragdrop	ondragdrop	window
error	onerror	window, frame, image
focus	onfocus	window, frame, layer, button, checkbox, fileUpload, password, radio, reset, select, submit, text, textarea
load	onload	window, frame, layer, image
mouseout	onmouseout	layer, area, image, link
mouseover	onmouseover	layer, area, image, link
move	onmove	window, frame
reset	onreset	form

Table 7.7 Functional Events and Their Related Objects *(Continued)*

Event	Event Handler	Related Objects
resize	onresize	window
select	onselect	text, textarea
submit	onsubmit	form
unload	onunload	window, frame

The order of processing for those events that impact on multiple levels (window, frame, document, layer) is from the lowest level object that references the event to the highest level object that references the event. For example, if the user clicks outside of the browser window, the order of event processing for the blur event is a form element object (such as the button object), layer object, frame object, window object.

Besides the functional event, JavaScript 1.2 provides for the processing of raw events. I use the term *raw event* to distinguish it from a functional event, which is a cooked (processed) event. The raw event is about as close as you can get to actions of the actual resource. Table 7.8 lists the raw events and their related objects.

Table 7.8 Raw Events and Their Related Objects

Event	Event handler	Related Objects
keydown	onkeydown	document, image, link, textarea
keypress	onkeypress	document, image, link, textarea
keyup	onkeyup	document, image, link, textarea
mousedown	onmousedown	document, link, button
mouseup	onmouseup	document, link, button
mousemove	onmousemove	(not an event of any object)

As Table 7.8 shows, the raw event primarily applies to objects that hold documents, with just a few exceptions. The raw events follow the same rules for order of processing, as do the functional events. The mousemove event is a special event that is part of the `captureEvents()` method.

Comments on JavaScript 1.2 Events

To this point, the discussion of events is according to the documentation available from Netscape (you can find Netscape's documentation for JavaScript at http://developer.netscape.com/one/javascript/index.html). However, writing full scripts that use the new events has generated a few interesting limitations.

The click event really only applies to the left mouse button. The default action for the mousedown event on the right mouse button (button 3) is to display the Navigator pop-up menu. If you want to kill this default action, your script needs to return false (see Listing 7.4 for an example). When you return false on a mousedown event, Navigator cancels the mouseup and click events. Therefore, there is no right mouse button click event.

Trapping a double-click event is a bit tricky, since the first click generates a click event. Listing 8.9 demonstrates the order of events when a button form element is double clicked. To see the action of a double-click event, you need to use Netscape Communicator 4.04 or above, since the double click fails to appear in earlier releases of Netscape Communicator.

For reference, my test platform was Windows 95 running Netscape Communicator 4.04. You may get different results on other platforms.

Note

The `onDblClick` event handler is not supported for the Apple Macintosh.

JavaScript 1.2 takes event management to another level. Instead of relying on the default order of processing, you can now perform traffic management for events. To make this possible, the following events are part of the window, `document`, and `layer` objects:

- `captureEvents()`
- `releaseEvents()`
- `routeEvent()`
- `handleEvent()`—not a part of the `layer` object.

Capturing Events

Advanced event management begins with capturing events before Navigator routes them to their intended targets. You can capture events at the window level (`window` object), document level (`document` object), or layer level (`layer` object) by using the `captureEvents()` method. The syntax for the `captureEvents()` method is:

```
objName.captureEvents(mask)
```

The *mask* is a property of the `Event` object. There is a mask for each of the events and is the event name in uppercase characters (such as Event.CLICK, Event.ERROR, Event.MOUSEDOWN). If you wanted to capture click events at the window level, the command is as follows:

```
window.captureEvents(Event.CLICK)
```

You can capture multiple events by using the bitwise OR operator. For example, the following statement captures the blur, focus, and click events:

```
window.captureEvents(Event.BLUR | Event.CLICK | Event.FOCUS)
```

Navigator processes any event not captured according to the default rules. For captured events, you need to write the functions that process the events.

Processing Captured Events

Once you declare that you are going to capture an event, you need to define a function to handle the event and then tell the event handler to use the new function. The code to accomplish this task looks like the following snippet:

```
function handleClick(eventObj) {
        // statements to manage the event
}
window.captureEvents(Events.CLICK)
window.onclick=handleClick
```

The last statement assigns the `handleClick()` function to the event handler. The `handleClick()` function then has the task of managing all the click events. There are three processing choices:

- The function can take action on the event.

- The function lets JavaScript route the event to other event handlers using the `routeEvent()` method.
- The function can pass the event to a specific receiver function with the `handleEvent()` method.

The tricky part is the return code of the event handler function. The function needs to return a Boolean value where:

- A value of true means continue processing the event. You only want to return true when you want Navigator to continue processing the event. If you use the `routeEvent()` or `handleEvent()` methods, you need to check the Boolean value that they return. In event processing, you need to follow the rule that the final event handler determines the fate of the event. If it cancels the event by returning false, the next level needs to cancel the event.
- A value of false means cancel further processing of the event. In other words, if the event was processed by the function or by another event handler, you want to return false.

The `routeEvent()` method says that you want JavaScript to look for other event handlers lower in the object hierarchy. If JavaScript finds an object that has an event handler, then it passes control to the next event handler in the object hierarchy. For example, if the `document` object captured the click event, then JavaScript would pass control to the document event handler. If JavaScript can't find another object event handler, it passes control to the event handler for the original target (such as a button). The syntax for the `routeEvent()` method is as follows:

```
obj.routeEvent(eventObj)
```

The following code snippet illustrates the use of the `routeEvent()` method:

```
function handleClick(ev) {
        var retval = routeEvent(ev)
        return (retval)
}
```

You can direct the event to a specific event handler, and ignore the hierarchy, by using the `handleEvent()` method. The syntax for the `handleEvent()` method is:

```
obj.handleEvent(eventObj)
```

You can pass control to the original target by using the following code snippet:

```
function handleClick(ev) {
        var retval = ev.target.handleEvent(ev)
        return (retval)
}
```

You are not limited to passing control to the target event handler. You can pass it to any event handler, including an event handler not related to the event. This allows you to simulate events or pass events from one event handler to another.

Releasing Captured Events

You can turn off event capturing with the `releaseEvents()` method. The syntax for the `releaseEvents()` method is:

```
obj.releaseEvents(mask)
```

The *mask* is the same as the mask in the `captureEvents()` method. The following examples show how to release a single event or multiple events:

```
window.releaseEvents(Event.CLICK)
window.releaseEvents(Event.BLUR | Event.CLICK | Event.FOCUS)
```

Working with Documents

The `document` object holds the properties, objects, and methods that define the presentation of the document. The `document` object reflects that part of the HTML document defined by the `<BODY></BODY>` tags. Consequently, the `document` object defines the area of the window where the user interacts with the page. The `document` object hierarchy, as shown in Figure 7.2, defines the object structure accessible to JavaScript 1.2.

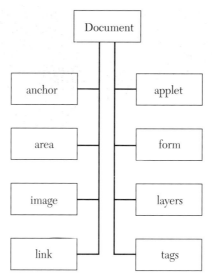

Figure 7.2 JavaScript 1.2 document object hierarchy.

In terms of the development of JavaScript, JavaScript 1.1 added the applet, area, and image objects. JavaScript 1.2 added the layers and tags objects. These additions reflect the corresponding changes in the HTML syntax for the different versions of Netscape Navigator. The tight bond between the document object and HTML also gives rise to some of the major differences between JavaScript and Microsoft's JScript. The differences become very sharp due to the wide variance in the implementation of DHTML in Netscape Communicator 4.0 and Microsoft Internet Explorer 4.0.

Table 7.9 lists the properties, methods, and event handlers associated with the document object. The <BODY> tag contains event handler attributes for onBlur, onDragDrop, onError, onFocus, onLoad, onMove, onResize, and onUnload. Although the <BODY> tag contains these attributes, they are part of the window object and not the document object.

Table 7.9 Properties, Methods, and Event Handlers of the Document Object

Properties	Methods	Event Handlers
alinkColor	captureEvents() **	onClick **
anchors[]	close()	onDblClick **
applets[] *	getSelection() **	onKeyDown **
bgColor	handleEvent() **	onKeyPress **
cookie	open()	onKeyUp **
domain *	releaseEvents() **	onMouseDown **
embeds[] *	routeEvent() **	onMouseUp **
fgColor	write()	
formName *	writeln()	
forms[]		
images[] *		
lastModified		
layers[] **		
linkColor		
links[]		
location		
plugins[]		
referrer		
title		
URL *		
vlinkColor		

*New in JavaScript 1.1, **New in JavaScript 1.2*

The remainder of this chapter discusses the components of the document object, except for:

- The form object (see Chapter 8)
- The embeds[] property, plugins[] property, and applets object (see Chapter 10)
- The layers object (see Chapter 11 for details on DHTML).

The Document Color Properties

The HTML options to the <BODY> tag define the color properties in the document object. As shown in Table 7.10, JavaScript references all of these properties, except for the background image.

Table 7.10 Document Object Color Properties

Property	Description
bgColor	Defines the background color of the document. When you change the bg-Color property, the browser immediately updates the display.
fgColor	Defines the text color of the document. After the browser completes the layout of the HTML document, the browser ignores changes to this property. Instead, the <FONT> tag or the fontcolor() method provide an alternative mechanism for changing the text color.
linkColor	Represents the color of a link defined by HREF, without prior visits.
alinkColor	Controls the color of an active link. In other words, it is the color of the link after it is selected and before the destination host replies.
vlinkColor	After the user visits a site, the browser displays this color for the link.

You can change the color properties of the document object by using either of the two following formats:

```
document.colorProperty = "#RRGGBB"
document.colorproperty = "colorName"
```

The #RRGGBB value is the hexadecimal value for the red, green, and blue components. With the hexadecimal value, #000000 is black, as it is the absence of color. On the other hand, #FFFFFF is white, as it is a complete blend of all colors. You can also use predefined colors. However, there is a considerable difference in how browsers handle color changes. Listing 7.1 is a simple script that you can use to check the behavior of different browsers.

Listing 7.1 Script for Testing Color Behavior

```
<HTML>
  <HEAD>
    <TITLE>Color Test</TITLE>
```

```
<SCRIPT LANGUAGE="JavaScript">
<!--
document.bgColor="blue"
document.vlinkColor="red"
document.linkColor="black"
document.alinkColor="yellow"
function chgColor() {
   document.bgColor="lightgreen"
   document.vlinkColor="yellow"
   document.linkColor="red"
   document.alinkColor="black"
}
//-->
</SCRIPT>
  </HEAD>
  <BODY>
    <P>This script demonstrates the effect for changing
        document colors. The colors were first defined in
        the heading using JavaScript.</P>
    <P><A HREF="http://home.netscape.com">
        home.netscape.com</A></P>
    <P><A HREF="http://www.softquad.com">
        www.softquad.com</A></P>
    <P>When you click the button, the background should
       immediately change and the links change after you
       click any link.</P>
    <FORM>
    <INPUT TYPE="BUTTON" NAME="Change" VALUE="Change"
        ONCLICK="chgColor()">
    </FORM>
  </BODY>
</HTML>
```

I ran this script on four browsers and received four different results. Netscape Communicator set the initial background colors, but then opted for the default background color as defined in the preferences. One flash of blue and then the screen changed to the value set in the preferences. When the script set the background color between the <BODY> </BODY> tags, it worked. Netscape Navigator 3.0, Microsoft Internet Explorer 3.0, and Microsoft Internet Explorer 4.0 displayed the blue background. All browsers set the link colors correctly. All browsers changed background colors when the change button was clicked. Neither version of Netscape changed the link colors, while both versions of Microsoft Internet Explorer changed them immediately. When I followed a link and then returned to the test page, all browsers resorted back to their original colors. The conclusion from this test is that changing the value of the color properties is not worth the effort.

Warning

Microsoft Internet Explorer 3.0 would not display the button when I executed the script from a local file. It worked correctly when loaded from a server.

The Document Information Properties

The properties listed in Table 7.11 are informational properties. Except for the `domain` property, these are read-only properties.

Table 7.11 Document Information Properties

Property	Description
domain	The `domain` property contains the domain name of the server from which the browser loaded the document. In JavaScript 1.1, the `domain` property was a tainted property and served an important role in the security model. Under this model, scripts could not access properties of windows loaded from different servers. For sites with multiple servers, you could modify the domain name to generalize the domain to that of the organization. Thus, you could modify the name "host.xyz.com" to just "xyz.com". With the generalized domain name, you could then read the properties in other windows that contained a document from another server within the same domain. The security model in JavaScript 1.2 no longer supports data tainting. However, JavaScript 1.2 retains the property for backwards compatibility.
lastModified	This read-only property reflects the date that the document was last modified. If the server does not provide the information, the field is set to the local time. Some servers, such as Macintosh, provide the date in an incompatible format. When this happens, the value returned does not reflect a correct date.
location	This read-only property is a synonym for the `URL` property. You should not use this property as Netscape plans on removing it in some future version of Navigator.

Table 7.11 Document Information Properties *(Continued)*

Property	Description
referrer	This read-only property contains the URL of the calling document. It contains an empty string when the user does not reach the current document by clicking on a link. The referrer property also contains an empty string when the server does not provide environment variable information.
title	A read-only property that contains the value specified by <TITLE></TITLE> tags.
URL	A read-only property that contains the URL of the file that contains the document source code. Initially, the value is the same as the location.href property.

The domain property is actually a portion of the URL property, since both contain the domain name of the server from which the browser loaded the document. Listing 7.2 is a simple script that illustrates how to use some of the document information properties.

Listing 7.2 Using Document Information Properties

```
<HTML>
  <HEAD>
    <TITLE>Using Document Information Properties</TITLE>
  </HEAD>
  <BODY>
<SCRIPT LANGUAGE="JavaScript">
<!--
document.write("Referring link was: "
              +unescape(document.referrer)+"<BR>")
document.write("Document URL is: "+unescape(document.URL))
//-->
</SCRIPT>
    <HR>
<SCRIPT LANGUAGE="JavaScript">
<!--
with (document) {
   write("<CENTER>")
   write("<P>"+document.title+"<BR>")
   write("last modified: "+document.lastModified+"</P>")
   write("</CENTER>")
}
```

```
//-->
</SCRIPT>
  </BODY>
</HTML>
```

The script in Listing 7.2 uses the unescape() function to ensure that any special characters are translated. Figure 7.3 shows the results of running this script in Netscape Communicator 4.0. In running this script using various browsers, the only one that produced different output was Microsoft Internet Explorer 3.0. For MSIE 3.0, the document.URL property was undefined and the document.referrer property returned the location of the document.

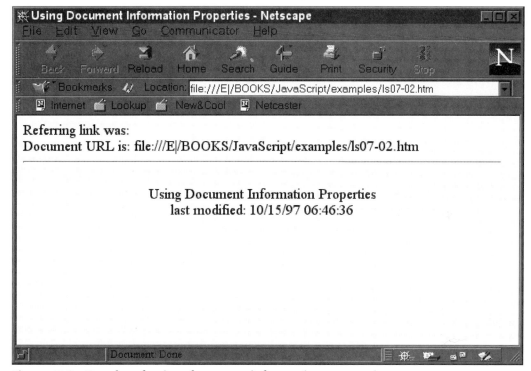

Figure 7.3   Results of using document information properties.

The cookie property contains a string value of the cookie entry from the cookies.txt file for the document. Chapter 8 describes how to use cookies since the cookie stores information collected from users.

The document Object Methods

As shown in previous examples, the document.write() method, without a window reference, writes text to the current window at the point where the statement occurs. However, when you use the docu-ment.write() method in an event handler, the browser automatical-ly opens a new document before writing the line. The opening of a new document clears the window. The document.write() uses the toString() method to convert any non-string data types to string data types. The syntax for the document.write() method is as follows:

docObj.write(*expression1*[, *expression2*, ...])

The document.writeln() method is the same as docu-ment.write(), except that it inserts a newline character at the end of the argument. The browser treats newlines as white space, except when it appears between the <PRE> </PRE> or <XMP> </XMP> tags. The format for the document.writeln() method is as follows:

docObj.writeln(*expression1*[, *expression2*, ...])

Note

> In JavaScript 1.0, the user could not print or save a Web page that included the document.write() or document.writeln() methods. JavaScript 1.1 removes this restriction.

The document.open() method opens a data stream to collect the output of the document.write() and document.writeln() methods. The syntax for the document.open() method is:

docObj.open([*mimeType*][, "replace"])

Note

> The document.open() method in JavaScript 1.0 does not clear the existing document from the window. Starting in JavaScript 1.1, the document.open(), or document.open("text/html"), method automatically clears any existing content. This change in behavior is necessary, because the document.open() method sets the default base to <BASE HREF=>. The default base allows you to use relative URLs based on the generated scripts document base.

The default MIME type is "`text/html`." However, the `docu-ment.open(mimeType)` method allows the opening of other MIME types as shown in Table 7.12. If you specify a *mimeType* other than "`text/html`," the browser assumes that you want to open the associated plug-in or viewer. You are not limited to the MIME types shown in Table 7.12. For example, the MIME type "`audio/x-liveaudio`" invokes the LiveAudio plug-in. Browsers vary on how they handle a request for a plug-in that is not installed. Either you get a file type not supported message or, as in Netscape Communicator 4.0, the browser takes you to the plug-in Web page.

Table 7.12 MIME Types for document.open() Method

MIME Type	Description
`text/html`	The document contains ASCII text with HTML formatting. This is the default MIME type.
`text/plain`	The document contains plain ASCII text with end-of-line characters that delimit line. If the document contains any HTML statements, the browser displays the tags as ASCII text.
`image/gif`	The document is a GIF image file.
`image/jpeg`	The document is a JPEG image file.
`image/x-bitmap`	The document is an XEM image file.
`plugin`	Loads the specified plug-in and uses it as the destination of all `write()` and `writeln()` methods. For example, "`application x-director`" loads the Shockwave Director plug-in from Macromedia. You need to ensure that the required plug-in is installed before opening it (see Chapter 10 for details on checking plug-in installation).

JavaScript 1.1 added the "`replace`" argument to the `docu-ment.open()` method. The "`replace`" argument reuses the history entry of the last object. If the previous history entry was a blank document or an "`about:blank`" URL, the "`replace`" argument replaces this entry with the current document. Without the "`replace`" argument, the user can press the Back button and clear the display. This argument only applies when the *mimeType* is "`text/html`."

The data stream stays open until the browser encounters a `docu-ment.close()` method. When the document is closed, the browser displays "Document: Done" in the window status bar and stops the animation of the Netscape meteor shower logo. The syntax for the document.close() method is:

docObj.close()

The document.close() method forces the browser to display contents of the data stream. It is good practice to use the document.open() and document.close() methods, as this ensures that the browser immediately displays the content written by the document.write() method.

The document.clear() method clears the content of the window. The status of the document.clear() method is somewhat questionable as the JavaScript 1.1 and JavaScript 1.2 documentation no longer reference it as a method of the document object. It is, however, part of the JavaScript 1.0 documentation and my recommendation is to treat the document.clear() method as something that exists for backwards compatibility.

New in JavaScript 1.2

 JavaScript 1.2 added the document.getSelection() method to the document object. The document.getSelection() method returns a string containing a copy of any text in the Web page that was selected by the user dragging the mouse. This method does not allow the selecting of text from any other document. The syntax for the document.getSelection() method is:

document.getSelection()

The script in Listing 7.3 brings together most of the methods for the document object including the new getSelection() method. Since the document methods are embedded in an HTML document, the document.open() method does not clear the contents of the window as shown in Figure 7.4

Listing 7.3 Using Document Object Methods

```
<HTML>
  <HEAD>
    <TITLE>Using Document Methods</TITLE>
```

```
  </HEAD>
  <BODY>
    <P>The document.write() method was used in so many
       examples that it is time to give an example of
       document.writeln().</P>
<SCRIPT LANGUAGE="JavaScript">
<!--
document.open("text/html", "replace")
with (document) {
   writeln("<P> This text is written using")
   writeln("the writeln method of the document")
   writeln("object.")
}
document.close()
//-->
</SCRIPT>
  <P>Select any text on this page and then press the
     getSelection button to see how the get selection
     method works.</P>
  <FORM>
  <INPUT TYPE="BUTTON" NAME="getSelection"
         VALUE="getSelection"
         ONCLICK="alert('you selected: \n'
                 +document.getSelection())">
  </FORM>
  </BODY>
</HTML>
```

New in JavaScript 1.2

The Document Object Event Handlers

Prior to JavaScript 1.2, the document object had no event handlers. Now, the document object plays an important role in event management since it is the intermediate object between the window object and its own objects. You register the event handlers by declaring them in the <BODY> tag. However, you also register the event handlers for the windows object in the <BODY> tag. This dual registration works because the windows object and the document object have different event handlers as shown in Tables 7.7 and 7.8.

Besides registering events via the <BODY> tag, you can manage events by using the captureEvents() method. Listing 7.4 shows a script that traps the mousedown event for a button.

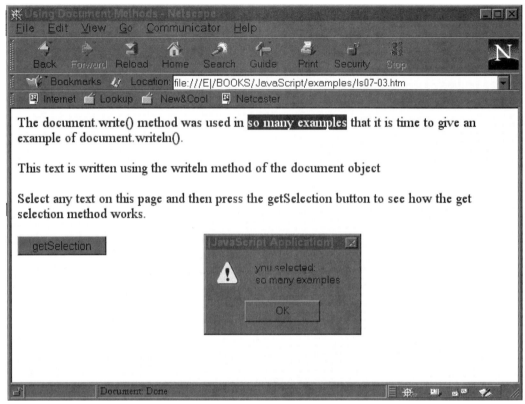

Figure 7.4   Results of using document object methods.

Listing 7.4 Using the Document Object Event Handlers

```
<HTML>
  <HEAD>
    <TITLE>Using Document Object Event Handlers</TITLE>
<SCRIPT LANGUAGE="JavaScript1.2">
<!--
function clickHdlr(ev) {
   if (ev.target.name=="dspSlct") {
      alert('you selected: \n'+document.getSelection())
      return false
   }
return true
```

```
}
document.captureEvents(Event.MOUSEDOWN)
document.onmousedown=clickHdlr
//-->
</SCRIPT>
  </HEAD>
  <BODY>
    <P>This test uses the captureEvents() method to
      trap the clicking of the mouse button. Select any
      text on this page and then press the getSelection
      button using either mouse button to show how the
      document object event handler functions.</P>
    <FORM>
    <INPUT TYPE="BUTTON" NAME="dspSlct"
        VALUE="Display Selection">
    </FORM>
  </BODY>
</HTML>
```

The script in Listing 7.4 requires a bit of explanation. The `capture-Events()` method traps the mousedown event. This is important because the default action for the mousedown event on the right mouse button is to display a Navigator window menu. Consequently, there is no mouseup event for the right mouse button. With no mouseup event, there is no right mouse button click event. When the mousedown event refers to the button, the script displays the selection without regard to which mouse button the user clicks. Once the script displays the information, it cancels the mouseup and click events by returning false. The script transfers all mouse events not related to the button back to Navigator for default processing. Since the `captureEvents()` method handles all of the events related to the display selection button, the input statement for the button has no event handler. The alert message displayed in Figure 7.4 is a result of clicking the right mouse button on the display selection button. You can experiment with this script to learn more about how Navigator processes events.

Link, Anchor, and Area Objects

The `link`, `anchor`, and `area` objects are closely related. The `link` and `anchor` objects are reflections of the `<A></A>` tags, since the `link` and `area` objects have an HREF attribute. The `document` object

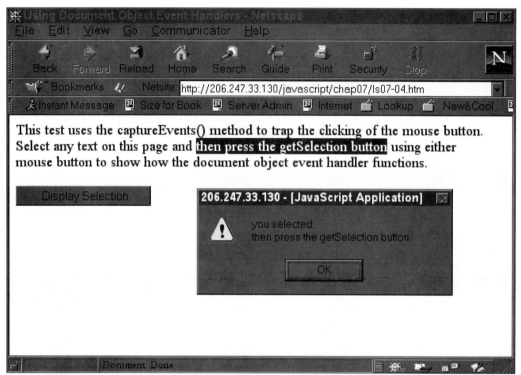

Figure 7.5 *Results of using document object event handlers.*

has two arrays that contain these objects. The `anchors[]` array property is an array of `anchor` objects. An `anchor` object has the `NAME` attribute in the `<A>` tag. The `links[]` array property is an array of `link` and `area` objects. A `link` object has the `HREF` attribute in the `<A>` tag, and an `area` object has an `HREF` attribute in the `<AREA>` tag. If the `<A>` tag contains both the `HREF` and `NAME` attributes, Navigator creates both a `link` object and an `anchor` object. The script in Listing 7.5 contains one anchor and three links. The document.write statements display the length property of the anchor and link objects.

Listing 7.5 Links versus Anchors

```
<HTML>
  <HEAD>
```

```
   <TITLE>Links versus Anchors</TITLE>
  </HEAD>
  <BODY>
   <P><A NAME="test">This</A> script illustrates the use
      of the links array and link object.</P>
   <P>
   <A HREF="http://home.netscape.com">home.netscape.com</A>
   </P>
   <P>
   <A HREF="http://www.softquad.com/">www.softquad.com</A>
   </P>
   <P><A HREF="#test">link to anchor</A></P>
   <P>The following lists the lengths of the two arrays.
   </P>
<SCRIPT LANGUAGE="JavaScript">
<!--
document.write("The link array contains "
   +document.links.length+" objects<BR>")
document.write("The anchors array contains "
   +document.anchors.length+" objects<BR>")
//-->
</SCRIPT>
  </BODY>
</HTML>
```

Figure 7.6 shows the results of running the script in Listing 7.5. The `links[]` array contains three objects that reflect the three HTML statements containing an HREF attribute. The `anchors[]` array contains just the one object reflecting the NAME attribute in the <A> tag.

The `links[]` array and `anchors[]` array are read-only arrays. The arrays are reflections of the <A> and <AREA> tags. However, the anchor() method of the `string` object also creates an anchor object entry in the `anchors[]` array. Similarly, the `link()` method of the string object creates a `link` object entry in the `links[]` array.

The Link Object

The `link` object reflects all of the hypertext links found in the document. The link is an *external object* in that there is no JavaScript constructor for building new object entries. However, you can create a new link by using the `link()` method of the `string` object. Outside of the universal methods, the `link` object has no methods of its own. It does

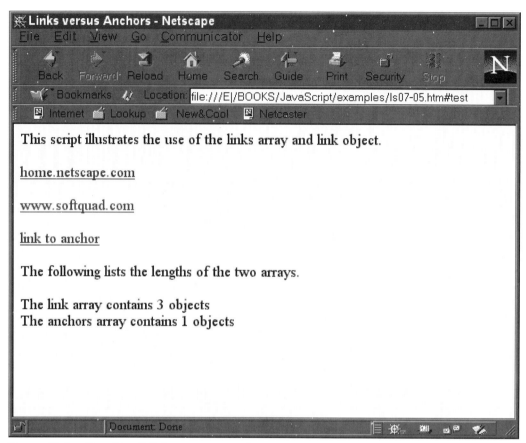

Figure 7.6 ***Results of links versus anchors.***

have the event handlers for managing mouse and keyboard events. Table 7.13 lists the properties and event handlers of the `link` object.

Table 7.13 Properties and Event Handlers of the Link Object

Properties	Methods	Event Handlers
hash	handleEvent() **	onClick
host		onDblClick **
hostname		onKeyDown **
href		onKeyPress **

Table 7.13 Properties and Event Handlers of the Link Object *(Continued)*

Properties	Methods	Event Handlers
pathname		onKeyUp **
port		onMouseDown **
protocol		onMouseOut *
search		onMouseOver
target		onMouseUp **
text **		

° *New in JavaScript 1.1,* °° *New in JavaScript 1.2*

Properties of the Link Object

Of the attributes in the HTML <A> tag, the link object deals only with the HREF and TARGET attributes, as shown in Table 7.14. The full HREF is reflected in the href property. Except for the target property, the remaining properties extract different portions of the href property.

Table 7.14 Properties of Link Object

Property	Description
hash	The hash property reflects the anchor name portion of the URL. The anchor specifies a specific location within a document. The hash property derives its name from the format of the anchor name, which begins with a hash ("#") character.
host	The host property is a string that begins after the // in the URL and ends with the character before the next /. The host property includes the host name of the server, the domain name, and the port number. In place of the host name and domain name, you may find the IP address.
hostname	The hostname property contains only the host name of the server and domain name, or IP address for the server.
href	The href property reflects the complete URL specified by the HREF attribute.
pathname	The pathname property is everything after the host property up to and including the filename.

Table 7.14 Properties of Link Object *(Continued)*

Property	Description
port	The `port` property is the port number for the server. Most URLs depend on the default port number for the server.
protocol	The `protocol` property reflects the protocol portion of the URL up to and including the colon. The protocols include `http:`, `ftp:`, `gopher:`, and `mailto:`.
search	The `search` property includes everything from the "?" to the end of the HREF attribute.
target	When the user clicks on a link, the browser normally displays the document in the current window. The `target` property reflects the TARGET attribute. The value of the `target` property is the window name in which the browser is to display the document.
text	A string that contains the text between the <A> and </A> tags.

The script in Listing 7.6 displays the properties of a `link` object. The results of running this script are shown in Figure 7.7. If you compare the results with the descriptions in Table 7.14, it will help you get a clearer understanding of the meanings of the properties.

Listing 7.6 Displaying Properties of Link Object

```
<HTML>
  <HEAD>
    <TITLE>Properties of Link Object</TITLE>
  </HEAD>
  <BODY>
    <P>The following reports the properties for
<A HREF="http://www.xyzcorp.com:81/~test/index.html#listref"
   TARGET="win2">www.xyzcorp.com</A>
     with a complete URL except for a search string.</P>
    <HR>
<SCRIPT LANGUAGE="JavaScript">
<!--
document.open()
with (document) {
   write("href: "+document.links[0].href+"<BR>")
```

```
   write("hash: "+document.links[0].hash+"<BR>")
   write("host: "+document.links[0].host+"<BR>")
   write("hostname: "+document.links[0].hostname+"<BR>")
   write("pathname: "+document.links[0].pathname+"<BR>")
   write("port: "+document.links[0].port+"<BR>")
   write("protocol: "+document.links[0].protocol+"<BR>")
   write("search: "+document.links[0].search+"<BR>")
   write("target: "+document.links[0].target+"<BR>")
}
document.close
//-->
</SCRIPT>
  </BODY>
</HTML>
```

Event Handlers for the Link Object

The link object has a number of new event handlers in JavaScript 1.2. Besides onDblClick, the link object now includes the raw event handlers for both the mouse and keyboard. Listing 7.7 is a short script that uses the onClick and onMouseOut event handlers. The standard example at this point is a script that describes how to use the onMouseOver and onMouseOut event handlers to display a message in the status bar. However, I don't like to hide the browsers use of the status bar for links.

Listing 7.7 Event Handlers and the Link Object

```
<HTML>
  <HEAD>
    <TITLE>Event Handlers and the Link Object</TITLE>
<SCRIPT LANGUAGE="JavaScript">
<!--
function dispProp(ev) {
   if (ev.which==3) {
      alert("The properties of this link are:\n"
            +"hash: "+ev.target.hash+"\n"
            +"host: "+ev.target.host+"\n"
            +"hostname: "+ev.target.hostname+"\n"
            +"href: "+ev.target.href+"\n"
```

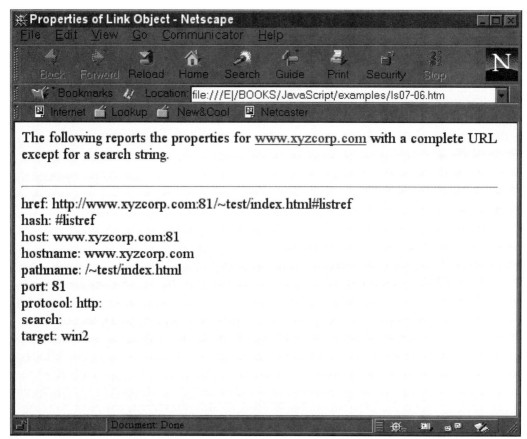

Figure 7.7   Results of displaying properties of link object.

```
                +"pathname: "+ev.target.pathname+"\n"
                +"port: "+ev.target.port+"\n"
                +"protocol: "+ev.target.protocol+"\n"
                +"search: "+ev.target.search+"\n"
                +"target: "+ev.target.target)
        return false
    }
return true
}
//-->
</SCRIPT>
  </HEAD>
  <BODY>
    <P>For the following link, the left mouse button
```

```
        produces an alert message, while the right mouse
        button displays the properties for the link object.
     </P>
     <P><A HREF=http://www.test.com:81/~test/index.htm#bookmark
        ONMOUSEDOWN="return dispProp(event)"
        ONCLICK="alert('This is a test'); return false">
        test link</A>
     </P>
   </BODY>
</HTML>
```

The script in Listing 7.7 is short, but it contains a lot of information regarding the programming of events. This example uses the event handler attributes in the <A> tag. The value for the ONCLICK attribute simply displays an alert message. It returns false to prevent the browser from taking the default action of following the link. Since the value has two statements, the statements are separated by a semicolon. The standard programming practice is to enclose the value for the attribute in double quotes and then use single quotes to quote strings within the double quotes. This practice helps prevent accidental errors in quoting strings.

The ONMOUSEDOWN attribute calls the dispProp() function to display the properties of the link object in an alert message. The function call is an argument to the return statement. By making the function call an argument, the return value of the function call passes to the browser event manager. The dispProp() function call passes the event object to the dispProp() function. The dispProp() function checks the switch property for the right mouse button. If it is the right mouse button, the function displays the properties in an alert message. The script uses the target property of the event object to address the properties of the link object. As I said, this is a short script with a lot of programming tricks. The results of clicking the right mouse are shown in Figure 7.8.

The Anchor Object

The anchors[] array of the document object is an array of anchor objects. The anchor object has no method or event handlers. However, in JavaScript 1.2, the anchor object does have properties (shown in Table 7.15). The script in Listing 7.8 displays the properties of the anchor object. Figure 7.9 shows the results of running this script in Netscape Communicator 4.0.

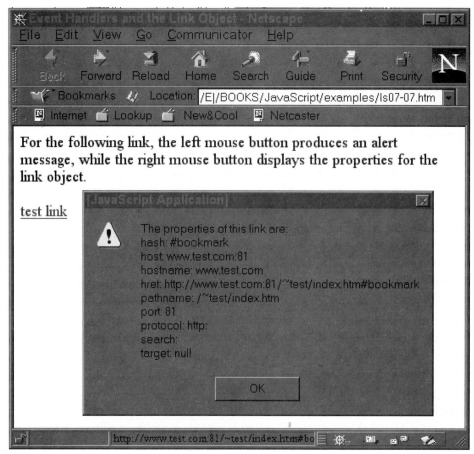

Figure 7.8 Results of event handlers and the link object.

Table 7.15 Properties of Anchor Object in JavaScript 1.2

Property	Description
name	The name of the anchor without the preceding hash ("#") character.
x	A number that specifies the horizontal position of the anchor relative to the left side of the document.
y	A number that specifies the vertical position of the anchor relative to the top of the document.

Listing 7.8 Properties of the Anchor Object

```
<HTML>
  <HEAD>
    <TITLE>Properties of the Anchor Object</TITLE>
<SCRIPT LANGUAGE="JavaScript">
<!--
function dispAnchors() {
   for (var i=0; i<document.anchors.length; i++) {
      with (document) {
         write("name: "+document.anchors[i].name)
         write(" x: "+document.anchors[i].x)
         write(" y: "+document.anchors[i].y+"<BR>")
      }
   }
}
//-->
</SCRIPT>
  </HEAD>
  <BODY>
   <H3><A NAME="Section1">Section 1</A></H3>
    <P>Some text</P>
    <H3><A NAME="Section2">Section 2</A></H3>
    <P>Some text</P>
<SCRIPT LANGUAGE="JavaScript">
<!--
dispAnchors()
//-->
</SCRIPT>
  </BODY>
</HTML>
```

In Netscape Navigator 2.0 and Netscape Navigator 3.0, the anchors[] array was an array of anchor names. However, Microsoft Internet Explorer 3.0 and Microsoft Internet Explorer 4.0 have an `array` object with just the name property. This is a situation where developing a universal script is extremely difficult.

The Area Object

The `area` object reflects only the HREF attributes of the <AREA> tag. Therefore, the `area` object has the same properties as the `link` object, although it has fewer event handlers as shown in Table 7.16.

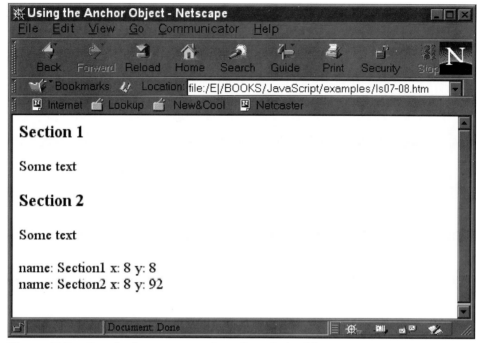

Figure 7.9 *Results from properties of anchor object.*

Table 7.16 Properties and Event Handlers of the Area Object

Properties	Methods	Event Handlers
hash		onMouseOut *
host		onMouseOver *
hostname		
href		
pathname		
port		
protocol		
search		
target		
text **		

* New in JavaScript 1.1; New in JavaScript 1.2

The area object is part of client-side image mapping. When the user clicks on the area defined by the <AREA> tag, the browser follows the associated link. Although it behaves like a link, the area object only has the two event handlers shown in Table 7.16. While there is no way to simulate the raw event handlers, you can simulate the onClick event handler by using the `javascript:` pseudoprotocol as the value to the HREF attribute. The following example shows how you might script a simulated onClick event handler:

```
HREF="javascript:clickArea('area1')"
```

Detailed examples of using the area object appear in the section on Using Client-side Image Maps. First, we need to know more about images and the image object.

Working with Images

Starting with NCSA Mosaic back in 1993, graphics have enhanced the documents that we retrieve from web servers. In spite of their importance, JavaScript 1.0 has no access to image information. The image object first appeared in JavaScript 1.1. Thus, the information provided in this section only applies to Netscape Navigator 3.0, Netscape Communicator 4.0 and Microsoft Internet Explorer 4.0.

The Image Object

The images[] array property of the document object is an array of image objects. The image object reflects most of the properties of the <IMG> tag. As shown in Table 7.17, the image object has properties and event handlers, but no methods of its own. You can reference the image object using either of the following two formats:

```
document.imageName
document.images[index]
```

Table 7.17 Properties and Event Handlers of the Image Object

Properties	Methods	Event Handlers
border	handleEvent() **	onAbort
complete		onError
height		onKeyDown **
hspace		onKeyPress **
lowsrc		onKeyUp **
name		onLoad
src		
vspace		
width		

**new in JavaScript 1.2

The image object is also a `constructor` object, which allows you to create other image objects. The syntax for the `image constructor` object is as follows:

objName = new Image(*width, height*)

Properties of the Image Object

Table 7.18 describes the properties of the `image` object. Some of the image properties are read/write and some read only. Moreover, an `image` object created by the image constructor does not have all the properties.

Table 7.18 Properties of the Image Object

Properties	Description
border	A read-only property that reflects the BORDER attribute of the <IMG> tag. The BORDER attribute specifies the width of the image border. For a constructed image object, the value of the `border` property is always zero.
complete	A read-only binary property that indicates the load status of the image. The `complete` property is false when the image is not completely loaded, and true when it is.

Table 7.18 Properties of the Image Object *(Continued)*

Properties	Description
height	A read-only property that contains the height of the image in pixels.
hspace	A read-only property that reflects the HSPACE attribute of the <IMG> tag. The HSPACE attribute specifies the space on the left and right sides of the image. For a constructed image object, the value of the hspace property is always zero.
lowsrc	A read-only property that reflects the LOWSRC attribute of the <IMG> tag. The LOWSRC attribute specifies the URL of a low-resolution image file that a browser displays while loading the image file specified in the SRC attribute. The lowsrc property is not used by a constructed image object.
name	A read only property that reflects the NAME attribute of the <IMG> tag. The NAME attribute specifies the name of the image. For a constructed image object, the value of the name property is null.
src	A read-write property that reflects the SRC attribute of the <IMG> tag. This is the URL of the image that a browser loads into the object.
vspace	A read-only property that reflects the VSPACE attribute of the <IMG> tag. The VSPACE attribute specifies the space on the top and bottom of the image. For a constructed image object, the value of the vspace property is always zero.
width	A read-only property that contains the width of the image in pixels.

The script in Listing 7.9 shows one method for using the src property to change images. This script downloads the images only when needed. The script is straightforward. However, when you write such a script, the WIDTH and HEIGHT attributes need to reflect the size of the largest image. Figure 7.10 shows how this script looks in a browser window.

Listing 7.9 Changing Images

```
<HTML>
  <HEAD>
    <TITLE>Changing Images</TITLE>
<SCRIPT LANGUAGE="JavaScript">
<!--
var imageIndex=0
var imageArray=new Array (4)
//
```

```
// The array contains the URL of the images
//
imageArray[0]="images/clipart/desstorm.jpg"
imageArray[1]="images/clipart/desert.jpg"
imageArray[2]="images/clipart/debutte.jpg"
imageArray[3]="images/clipart/dcreek.jpg"
//
// function to change src property of image object
//
function chgImage() {
   if (++imageIndex>=imageArray.length) {
      imageIndex=0
   }
   document.images[0].src=imageArray[imageIndex]
}
//-->
</SCRIPT>
  </HEAD>
  <BODY>
    <P>This script shows one way to change the src property
       of the image attribute. To change the image, just
       click on the next image button.</P>
    <CENTER>
    <P>
    <IMG SRC="images/clipart/desstorm.jpg"
         ALT="desert scenes"
         BORDER="0" WIDTH="320" HEIGHT="240">
    </P>
    <FORM>
    <P>
    <INPUT TYPE="BUTTON" NAME="nextImg" VALUE="Next Image"
         ONCLICK="chgImage()">
    </P>
    </FORM>
    </CENTER>
  </BODY>
</HTML>
```

The image constructor provides you with a mechanism for preloading images. The script in Listing 7.10 is a modified version of the script in Listing 7.9. The revised script uses the image constructor object to build an array of image objects. Again, the script sets the WIDTH and HEIGHT attributes to the size of the largest image.

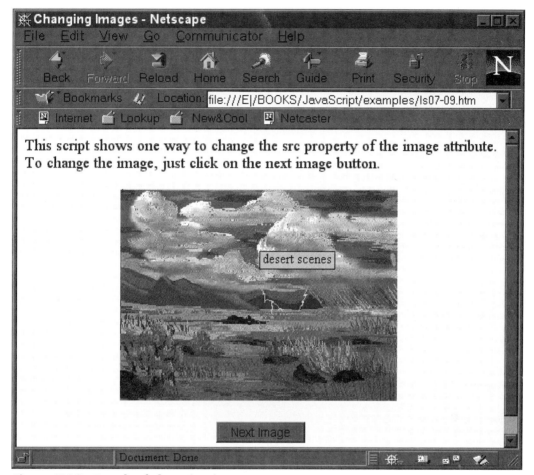

Figure 7.10   Result of changing images.

Listing 7.10 Changing Images using the Image Constructor Object

```
<HTML>
  <HEAD>
    <TITLE>
    Changing Images using the Image Constructor Object
    </TITLE>
```

```
<SCRIPT LANGUAGE="JavaScript">
<!--
var imageIndex=0
var imageArray=new Array (4)
//
// Preload the image array
//
imageArray[0]=new Image(320, 199)
imageArray[0].src="images/clipart/desstorm.jpg"
imageArray[1]=new Image(320, 240)
imageArray[1].src="images/clipart/desert.jpg"
imageArray[2]=new Image(307, 230)
imageArray[2].src="images/clipart/debutte.jpg"
imageArray[3]=new Image(320, 240)
imageArray[3].src="images/clipart/dcreek.jpg"
//
// function to change src property of image object
//
function chgImage() {
    if (++imageIndex>=imageArray.length) {
       imageIndex=0
    }
    document.images[0].src=imageArray[imageIndex].src
}
//-->
</SCRIPT>
  </HEAD>
  <BODY>
    <P>This script shows another way to change the src
       property of the image attribute. To change the
       image, just click on the next image button.</P>
    <CENTER>
    <P>
    <IMG SRC="images/clipart/desstorm.jpg"
        ALT="desert scenes"
        BORDER="0" WIDTH="320" HEIGHT="240">
    </P>
    <FORM>
    <P>
    <INPUT TYPE="BUTTON" NAME="nextImg" VALUE="Next Image"
        ONCLICK="chgImage()">
    </P>
    </FORM>
    </CENTER>
  </BODY>
</HTML>
```

Event Handlers of the Image Object

Besides the new events, one of the major features of the new event model in JavaScript 1.2 is the ability to pass the event object to the function handling the event. The script in Listing 7.11 shows how the event object provides a simple means to identify the image load error. Figure 7.11 shows the results when the browser attempts to load the image.

Listing 7.11 Handling an Error in Loading an Image

```
<HTML>
  <HEAD>
    <TITLE>Trapping an Image Load Error</TITLE>
<SCRIPT LANGUAGE="JavaScript1.2">
<!--
function imgError(ev) {
   alert("Image file "+ev.target.src+"\n"
         +"did not load.")
}
//-->
</SCRIPT>
  </HEAD>
  <BODY>
    <P>The image in this script does not exist, which
       forces the error event.</P>
    <P><IMG SRC="images/noname.jpg" ALT="no such image"
           ONERROR=" imgError(event)"></P>
  </BODY>
</HTML>
```

Warning

The onload event handler tracks both the LOWSRC and SRC attributes. Thus, the browser generates a load event for the LOWSRC attribute before it generates a load event for the SRC attribute. Moreover, the event object only tells you the image object to which the event applies. It doesn't distinguish between LOWSRC and SRC attributes. In general, events apply to objects and not to the particular properties of the object.

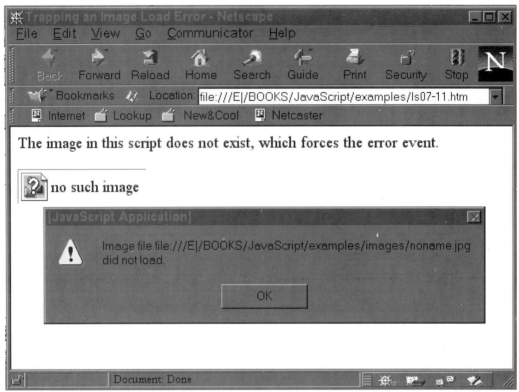

Figure 7.11   Results of handling an image load error.

Using Server-side Image Maps

Image maps provide a mechanism to divide an image into areas. By using an image map, you create a map that has multiple links within an image. Prior to JavaScript 1.1, your only choice was to use the ISMAP attribute of the <IMG> tag to generate a request to the server. The format of the server request was URL?x, y. The values *x* and *y* represent the horizontal and vertical coordinates, respectively.

The server then invokes a CGI program to process the coordinates. The CGI program, in turn, returns the designated Web page. With server-side image mapping, JavaScript has no role to play in the cycle of events.

Using Client-side Image Maps

While the server-side image maps have wide support, they do so at a price. The major problems are as follows:

- The server-side image map excludes testing of scripts on local files.

- There is an inherent delay in the server's response to user clicks. The length of the delay is often longer than the response to normal clicks.

- Server-side image maps increase the load on the server. With a heavily used server, the processing load increases, reducing the number of clients that the server can support.

Client-side image processing solves these problems at the expense of compatibility on a variety of browser platforms. Client-side image mapping first appeared in Netscape Navigator 2.0. However, JavaScript support for client-side image maps first appeared in Netscape Navigator 3.0, with the inclusion of the area object.

The script in Listing 7.12 is a long, but complete script for an image map of the United States. The HTML portion of the image map is part of SoftQuad's HoTMetaL Pro 4.0. I added the JavaScript statements that use the javascript: pseudoprotocol, and the event handlers for the mouseover and mouseout events. This works correctly with Netscape Navigator 3.0, Netscape Communicator 4.0, and Microsoft Internet Explorer 4.0. Except for the onMouseOver and onMouseOut event handlers, the script works with Microsoft Internet Explorer 3.0. Figure 7.12 shows the results of running this script.

Listing 7.12 Example of a Client-Side Image Map

```
<HTML>
  <HEAD>
    <TITLE>Example of Client-side Image Map</TITLE>
<SCRIPT LANGUAGE="JavaScript">
<!--
function clickArea(state) {
   alert("In a production script this would\n"
         +"link to a file for the state of:\n"
         +state)
}
//-->
</SCRIPT>
  </HEAD>
```

```
<BODY>
  <P>This image map is a part of the Hotmetal Pro 4.0
     package by Softquad, Inc. For this example, the
     basic map was enhanced to support JavaScript. The
     JavaScript includes use of the javascript: pseudo
     URL, the mouseover event, and the mouseout event.
  </P>
  <DIV ALIGN="CENTER">
  <IMG SRC="images/maps/unitedstates/unstsmbw.gif"
       WIDTH="200" HEIGHT="162" USEMAP="#usa2"
       ALT="Click on the map of the United States"
       BORDER="0">
  <MAP NAME="usa2">

<!-- Washington -->

  <AREA SHAPE="POLYGON"
   COORDS="20,3,20,3,43,10,41,25,19,17"
   HREF='javascript:clickArea("Washington")'
   ALT="Washington"
   ONMOUSEOVER="self.status='Washington'; return true"
   ONMOUSEOUT="self.status=''; return true">

<!-- Oregon -->

  <AREA SHAPE="POLYGON"
   COORDS="19,18,19,18,41,26,37,42,11,36"
   HREF="javascript: clickArea('Oregon')"
   ALT="Oregon"
   ONMOUSEOVER="self.status='Oregon'; return true"
   ONMOUSEOUT="self.status=''; return true">

<!--Idaho -->

  <AREA SHAPE="POLYGON"
   COORDS="43,10,43,10,46,11,53,33,58,33,58,45,38,42"
   HREF="javascript: clickArea('Idaho')" ALT="Idaho"
   ONMOUSEOVER="self.status='Idaho'; return true"
   ONMOUSEOUT="self.status=''; return true">

<!-- Montana -->

  <AREA SHAPE="POLYGON"
   COORDS="47,11,47,11,83,16,81,33,53,33"
   HREF="javascript: clickArea('Montana')" ALT="Montana"
```

```
ONMOUSEOVER="self.status='Montana'; return true"
ONMOUSEOUT="self.status=''; return true">

<!-- Wyoming -->

   <AREA SHAPE="POLYGON"
   COORDS="59,34,59,34,81,35,80,52,56,50"
   HREF="javascript: clickArea('Wyoming')" ALT="Wyoming"
   ONMOUSEOVER="self.status='Wyoming'; return true"
   ONMOUSEOUT="self.status=''; return true">

<!-- California -->

   <AREA SHAPE="POLYGON"
   COORDS="11,36,11,36,27,40,24,54,39,75,
           37,85,26,85,15,72,10,51"
   HREF="javascript: clickArea('California')"
   ALT="California"
   ONMOUSEOVER="self.status='California'; return true"
   ONMOUSEOUT="self.status=''; return true">

<!-- Nevada -->

   <AREA SHAPE="POLYGON"
   COORDS="27,40,27,40,46,44,39,74,24,54"
   HREF="javascript: clickArea('Nevada')" ALT="Nevada"
   ONMOUSEOVER="self.status='Nevada'; return true"
   ONMOUSEOUT="self.status=''; return true">

<!-- Utah -->

   <AREA SHAPE="POLYGON"
   COORDS="46,45,46,45,56,46,55,50,63,51,60,69,43,66"
   HREF="javascript: clickArea('Utah')" ALT="Utah"
   ONMOUSEOVER="self.status='Utah'; return true"
   ONMOUSEOUT="self.status=''; return true">

<!-- Arizona -->

   <AREA SHAPE="POLYGON"
   COORDS="42,67,42,67,60,70,56,96,37,88"
   HREF="javascript: clickArea('Arizona')" ALT="Arizona"
   ONMOUSEOVER="self.status='Arizona'; return true"
   ONMOUSEOUT="self.status=''; return true">
```

```
<!-- Colorado -->

    <AREA SHAPE="POLYGON"
     COORDS="63,52,63,52,87,54,86,72,61,69"
     HREF="javascript: clickArea('Colorado')"
     ALT="Colorado"
     ONMOUSEOVER="self.status='Colorado'; return true"
     ONMOUSEOUT="self.status=''; return true">

<!-- New_Mexico -->

    <AREA SHAPE="POLYGON"
     COORDS="60,70,60,70,82,73,80,94,58,95"
     HREF="javascript: clickArea('New Mexico')"
     ALT="New_Mexico"
     ONMOUSEOVER="self.status='New Mexico'; return true"
     ONMOUSEOUT="self.status=''; return true">

<!-- North_Dakota -->

    <AREA SHAPE="POLYGON"
     COORDS="83,16,83,16,104,18,106,31,82,30"
     HREF="javascript: clickArea('North Dakota')"
     ALT="North_Dakota"
     ONMOUSEOVER="self.status='North Dakota'; return true"
     ONMOUSEOUT="self.status=''; return true">

<!-- South_Dakota -->

    <AREA SHAPE="POLYGON"
     COORDS="82,31,82,31,106,32,106,47,82,44"
     HREF="javascript: clickArea('South Dakota')"
     ALT="South_Dakota"
     ONMOUSEOVER="self.status='South Dakota'; return true"
     ONMOUSEOUT="self.status=''; return true">

<!-- Nebraska -->

    <AREA SHAPE="POLYGON"
     COORDS="82,45,82,45,105,47,110,58,88,58,88,53,80,52"
     HREF="javascript: clickArea('Nebraska')"
     ALT="Nebraska"
     ONMOUSEOVER="self.status='Nebraska'; return true"
     ONMOUSEOUT="self.status=''; return true">
```

```
<!-- Kansas -->

    <AREA SHAPE="POLYGON"
    COORDS="88,59,88,59,111,59,113,73,87,72"
    HREF="javascript: clickArea('Kansas')" ALT="Kansas"
    ONMOUSEOVER="self.status='Kansas'; return true"
    ONMOUSEOUT="self.status=''; return true">

<!-- Oklahoma -->

    <AREA SHAPE="POLYGON"
    COORDS="83,73,83,73,112,73,114,87,93,84,94,75,83,74"
    HREF="javascript: clickArea('Oklahoma')"
    ALT="Oklahoma"
    ONMOUSEOVER="self.status='Oklahoma'; return true"
    ONMOUSEOUT="self.status=''; return true">

<!-- Texas -->

    <AREA SHAPE="POLYGON"
    COORDS="83,75,83,75,92,75,91,85,115,89,116,106,102,
            124,79,108,67,94,82,96"
    HREF="javascript: clickArea('Texas')" ALT="Texas"
    ONMOUSEOUT="self.status=''; return true"
    ONMOUSEOVER="self.status='Texas'; return true">

<!-- Minnesota -->

    <AREA SHAPE="POLYGON"
    COORDS="105,17,105,17,128,21,117,33,124,42,107,42"
    HREF="javascript: clickArea('Minnesota')"
    ALT="Minnesota"
    ONMOUSEOVER="self.status='Minnesota'; return true"
    ONMOUSEOUT="self.status=''; return true">

<!-- Iowa -->

    <AREA SHAPE="POLYGON"
    COORDS="107,43,107,43,124,42,128,50,124,55,109,56"
    HREF="javascript: clickArea('Iowa')" ALT="Iowa"
    ONMOUSEOUT="self.status=''; return true"
    ONMOUSEOVER="self.status='Iowa'; return true">
```

```
<!-- Missouri -->

    <AREA SHAPE="POLYGON"
     COORDS="111,57,111,57,125,57,134,74,115,75"
     HREF="javascript: clickArea('Missouri')"
     ALT="Missouri"
     ONMOUSEOVER="self.status='Missouri'; return true"
     ONMOUSEOUT="self.status=''; return true">

<!-- Arkansas -->

    <AREA SHAPE="POLYGON"
     COORDS="114,75,114,75,130,75,127,91,116,90,114,76"
     HREF="javascript: clickArea('Arkansas')"
     ALT="Arkansas"
     ONMOUSEOUT="self.status=''; return true"
     ONMOUSEOVER="self.status='Arkansas'; return true">

<!-- Louisiana -->

    <AREA SHAPE="POLYGON"
     COORDS="116,91,116,91,127,92,126,100,133,98,137,109,
             117,107"
     HREF="javascript: clickArea('Louisiana')"
     ALT="Louisiana"
     ONMOUSEOVER="self.status='Louisiana'; return true"
     ONMOUSEOUT="self.status=''; return true">

<!-- Wisconsin -->

    <AREA SHAPE="POLYGON"
     COORDS="123,27,123,27,135,32,135,46,127,46,118,33"
     HREF="javascript: clickArea('Wisconsin')"
     ALT="Wisconsin"
     ONMOUSEOUT="self.statu=''; return true"
     ONMOUSEOVER="self.status='Wisconsin'; return true">

<!-- Michigan -->

    <AREA SHAPE="POLYGON"
     COORDS="127,28,127,28,133,21,152,29,154,48,140,48,136,
     33,127,28"
     HREF="javascript: clickArea('Michigan')"
     ALT="Michigan"
     ONMOUSEOVER="self.status='Michigan'; return true"
```

```
ONMOUSEOUT="self.status=''; return true">

<!-- Illinois -->

    <AREA SHAPE="POLYGON"
     COORDS="127,47,127,47,137,47,138,67,134,72,124,57"
     HREF="javascript: clickArea('Illinois')"
     ALT="Illinois"
     ONMOUSEOUT="self.status=''; return true"
     ONMOUSEOVER="self.status='Illinois'; return true">

<!-- Indiana -->

    <AREA SHAPE="POLYGON"
     COORDS="138,49,138,49,145,49,148,61,138,67"
     HREF="javascript: clickArea('Indiana')" ALT="Indiana"
     ONMOUSEOVER="self.status='Indiana'; return true"
     ONMOUSEOUT="self.status=''; return true">

<!-- Ohio -->

    <AREA SHAPE="POLYGON"
     COORDS="146,49,146,49,160,46,161,55,157,63,148,61"
     HREF="javascript: clickArea('Ohio')" ALT="Ohio"
     ONMOUSEOUT="self.status=''; return true"
     ONMOUSEOVER="self.status='Ohio'; return true">

<!-- Kentucky -->

    <AREA SHAPE="POLYGON"
     COORDS="134,74,134,74,148,62,158,66,152,72"
     HREF="javascript: clickArea('Kentucky')"
     ALT="Kentucky"
     ONMOUSEOVER="self.status='Kentucky'; return true"
     ONMOUSEOUT="self.status=''; return true">

<!-- Tennessee -->

    <AREA SHAPE="POLYGON"
     COORDS="133,75,133,75,160,72,148,80,131,80"
     HREF="javascript: clickArea('Tennessee')"
     ALT="Tennessee"
     ONMOUSEOUT="self.status=''; return true"
     ONMOUSEOVER="self.status='Tennessee'; return true">
```

```
<!-- Mississippi -->

    <AREA SHAPE="POLYGON"
     COORDS="130,81,130,81,137,81,137,102,133,102,132,99,
            125,100"
     HREF="javascript: clickArea('Mississippi')"
     ALT="Mississippi"
     ONMOUSEOVER="self.status='Mississippi'; return true"
     ONMOUSEOUT="self.status=''; return true">

<!-- Alabama -->

    <AREA SHAPE="POLYGON"
     COORDS="137,81,137,81,147,81,151,98,142,99,142,102,
            137,102"
     HREF="javascript: clickArea('Alabama')" ALT="Alabama"
     ONMOUSEOUT="self.status=''; return true"
     ONMOUSEOVER-"self.status='Alabama'; return true">

<!-- Georgia -->

    <AREA SHAPE="POLYGON"
     COORDS="148,80,148,80,155,79,166,91,165,97,152,99"
     HREF="javascript: clickArea('Georgia')" ALT="Georgia"
     ONMOUSEOVER="self.status='Georgia'; return true"
     ONMOUSEOUT="self.status=''; return true">

<!-- Florida -->

    <AREA SHAPE="POLYGON"
     COORDS="144,99,144,99,164,98,174,112,173,122,161,110,
            155,102,143,102"
     HREF="javascript: clickArea('Florida')" ALT="Florida"
     ONMOUSEOUT="self.status=''; return true"
     ONMOUSEOVER="self.status='Florida'; return true">

<!-- South_Carolina -->

    <AREA SHAPE="POLYGON"
     COORDS="156,78,156,78,167,90,173,81,168,77"
     HREF="javascript: clickArea('South Carolina')"
     ALT="South_Carolina"
     ONMOUSEOVER="self.status='South Carolina'; return true"
     ONMOUSEOUT="self.status=''; return true">
```

```
<!-- North_Carolina -->

   <AREA SHAPE="POLYGON"
    COORDS="152,78,152,78,163,71,182,67,182,76,176,81,
           169,76"
    HREF="javascript: clickArea('North Carolina')"
    ALT="North_Carolina"
  ONMOUSEOUT="self.status=''; return true"
  ONMOUSEOVER="self.status='North Carolina'; return true">

<!-- Virginia -->

   <AREA SHAPE="POLYGON"
    COORDS="155,72,155,72,181,67,173,56"
    HREF="javascript: clickArea('Virginia')"
    ALT="Virginia"
    ONMOUSEOVER="self.status='Virginia'; return true"
    ONMOUSEOUT="self.status=''; return true">

<!-- West_Virginia -->

   <AREA SHAPE="POLYGON"
    COORDS="162,55,162,55,173,55,161,66,157,64"
    HREF="javascript: clickArea('West Virginia')"
    ALT="West_Virginia"
    ONMOUSEOUT="self.status=''; return true"
    ONMOUSEOVER="self.status='West Virginia'; return true">

<!-- Pennsylvania -->

   <AREA SHAPE="POLYGON"
    COORDS="160,45,160,45,178,42,182,50,179,53,162,55"
    HREF="javascript: clickArea('Pennsylvania')"
    ALT="Pennsylvania"
    ONMOUSEOVER="self.status='Pennsylvania'; return true"
    ONMOUSEOUT="self.status=''; return true">

<!-- Maryland -->

   <AREA SHAPE="POLYGON"
    COORDS=
    "178,52,178,52,179,54,180,58,182,61,175,60,171,55"
    HREF="javascript: clickArea('Maryland')"
    ONMOUSEOUT="self.status=''; return true"
    ONMOUSEOVER="self.status='Maryland'; return true"
```

```
      ALT="Maryland">

<!-- Delaware -->

   <AREA SHAPE="POLYGON"
    COORDS="179,54,179,54,184,58,182,60"
    HREF="javascript: clickArea('Delaware')"
    ALT="Delaware"
    ONMOUSEOVER="self.status='Delaware'; return true"
    ONMOUSEOUT="self.statu=''; return true">

<!-- New_Jersey -->

   <AREA SHAPE="POLYGON"
    COORDS=
  "179,52,179,52,181,55,185,55,185,50,184,46,180,44,182,49"
    HREF="javascript: clickArea('New Jersey')"
    ALT="New_Jersey"
    ONMOUSEOUT="self.status=''; return true"
    ONMOUSEOVER="self.status='New Jersey'; return true">

<!-- New_York -->

   <AREA SHAPE="POLYGON"
    COORDS="163,44,163,44,178,42,183,45,186,48,190,45,185,
            45,181,27,173,32"
    HREF="javascript: clickArea('New York')"
    ALT="New_York"
    ONMOUSEOUT="self.status=''; return true"
    ONMOUSEOVER="self.status='New York'; return true">

<!-- Connecticut -->

   <AREA SHAPE="POLYGON"
    COORDS="185,40,185,40,185,44,189,44,188,40"
    HREF="javascript: clickArea('Connecticut')"
    ALT="Connecticut"
    ONMOUSEOVER="self.status='Connecticut'; return true"
    ONMOUSEOUT="self.status=''; return true">

<!-- Rhode_Island -->

   <AREA SHAPE="POLYGON"
    COORDS="188,40,188,40,191,41,190,44"
    HREF="javascript: clickArea('Rhode Island')"
```

```
       ALT="Rhode_Island"
       ONMOUSEOVER="self.status='Rhode Island'; return true"
       ONMOUSEOUT="self.status=''; return true">

<!-- Massachusetts -->

    <AREA SHAPE="POLYGON"
    COORDS=
     "184,36,184,36,192,36,196,39,192,41,189,39,184,39"
    HREF="javascript: clickArea('Massachusetts')"
    ALT="Massachusetts"
    ONMOUSEOUT="self.status=''; return true"
    ONMOUSEOVER="self.status='Massachusetts'; return true">

<!-- Vermont -->

    <AREA SHAPE="POLYGON"
     COORDS="181,27,181,27,186,25,186,35,183,35"
     HREF="javascript: clickArea('Vermont')"
     ALT="Vermont"
     ONMOUSEOVER="self.status='Vermont'; return true"
     ONMOUSEOUT="self.status=''; return true">

<!-- New_Hampshire -->

    <AREA SHAPE="POLYGON"
    COORDS="186,25,186,25,187,24,193,35,186,35"
    HREF="javascript: clickArea('New Hampshire')"
    ALT="New_Hampshire"
    ONMOUSEOUT="self.status=''; return true"
    ONMOUSEOVER="self.status='New Hampshire'; return true">

<!-- Maine -->

    <AREA SHAPE="POLYGON"
     COORDS="188,24,188,24,193,33,200,24,197,12,191,12"
     HREF="javascript: clickArea('Maine')" ALT="Maine"
     ONMOUSEOVER="self.status='Maine'; return true"
     ONMOUSEOUT="self.status=''; return true">

<!-- Alaska -->

    <AREA SHAPE="POLYGON"
    COORDS="47,107,47,107,54,131,60,132,62,130,73,138,
            71,143,59,135,45,134,33,144,12,154,4,154,0,147,
```

```
          5,152,13,151,32,140,22,130,21,119,29,106"
   HREF="javascript: clickArea('Alaska')" ALT="Alaska"
   ONMOUSEOUT="self.status=''; return true"
   ONMOUSEOVER="self.status='Alaska'; return true">
  </MAP>
  </DIV>
  </BODY>
</HTML>
```

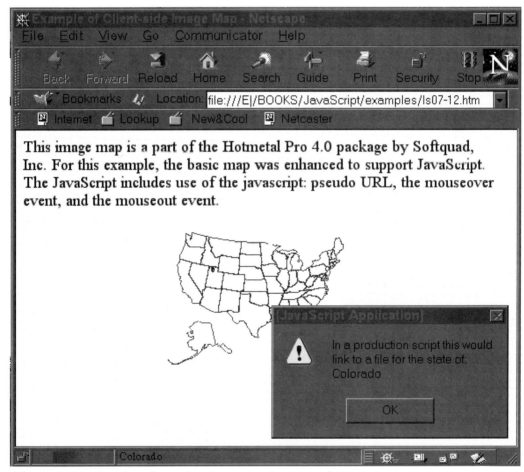

Figure 7.12 *Results of running image map example.*

Summary

The document object forms the heart of the object hierarchy, since it reflects the content of the HTML document. The document presents information, but user interaction with the document is necessary for any client/server application. This chapter started with a presentation of the idea of events. Events allow the user to dynamically interact with the document using the mouse and keyboard. Other events allow the document to respond to system events such as loading and unloading the document. Events are properties of objects just as methods are properties of objects.

From a discussion of events the chapter moved to breaking down the documentation object. The document object, itself, contains arrays of objects. The objects discussed in this chapter were the:

- Link object
- Anchor object
- Area object
- Image object

Chapter 8 "Working with Forms" tackles the forms object, since the forms object constitutes the other means for interacting with the user. The forms object allows you to gather information from the user. The applets object is a special subject that Chapter 10 "Interfacing to Plug-ins and Java Applets" covers in detail. The layer and tag objects are new to JavaScript 1.2. Since they expand our ability to dynamically present a document to a user, Chapter 11 "Advanced JavaScript" discusses these objects.

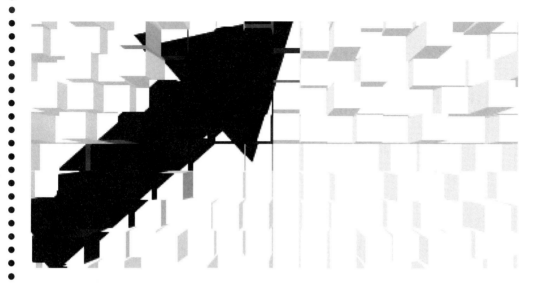

Working with Forms

Topics in This Chapter

- The Forms object
- The objects for each element of a form
- Sending data to a server
- Storing information in cookies

8

Chapter

HTML forms provide the primary means of gathering input from the user. The original purpose of forms was to send information to the server, now JavaScript extends the use of forms without depending on the server. This chapter discusses the forms object and its elements.

When the browser encounters the HTML `<FORM></FORM>` tags, it creates a `form` object and an object for each form element. Using this information, JavaScript allows you to edit the data collected from the user before submitting the form to the server. However, you don't have to submit a form to a server. You can use the data collected in forms to alter the presentation of information to the user.

You could store all the information on the server, but this requires more server capacity and reduces the responsiveness to the user. As an alternative, you can create a distributed database by using the cookie property of the document object. Netscape stores the `cookie` information in a text file. For most applications, server-side CGI scripts use the cookie information as a distributed database. Because of the close relationship to forms, this chapter includes a discussion on the use of cookies.

The Form Object

The forms[] array of the document object is an array of form objects. The browser creates a form object for each pair of <FORM></FORM> tags that it encounters in the document. Table 8.1 lists the properties, methods, and event handlers of the form object.

Table 8.1 Properties, Methods, and Event Handlers of the Forms Object

Properties	Methods	Event Handlers
action	handleEvent() **	onReset
elements[]	reset()	onSubmit
encoding	submit()	
length		
name		
method		
target		

** *New in JavaScript 1.2*

You reference the form object by using either an index to the forms[] array, or the name property of the form. The formats for these two means of referencing the form object are as follows:

```
document.forms[index]
document.formName
```

The *formName* option for addressing a form object applies only when the <FORM> tag contains the NAME attribute. The *formName* mechanism makes it easier to tie the HTML <FORM> tag to JavaScript form references. For example, the statement <FORM NAME="my-form"> creates an entry in the forms[] array. You can access the name property of this form using either of the two following references:

```
document.forms[0].name
document.myform.name
```

Properties of the Form Object

The properties of the form object reflect the attributes of the <FORM> tag and the form elements. Table 8.2 lists the properties of the form object and provides a brief description of each property.

Table 8.2 Description of the Form Object Properties

Property	Description
action	The action property is a read-write property that reflects the ACTION attribute in the <FORM> tag. The ACTION attribute specifies the destination URL for submitting the form. The URL protocols supported are http:, ftp:, and mailto:.
elements[]	An array containing any button, checkbox, fileupload, hidden, password, radio, reset, select, submit, text, and textarea objects. The elements[] array is read-only because these objects reflect the HTML form elements.
encoding	The encoding property is a read-write property that reflects the ENCTYPE attribute of the <FORM> tag. The default MIME type for the encoding property is application/x-www-form-urlencoded. If the form contains a fileupload object, the MIME type is multipart/form-data.
length	Indicates the number of form objects in the elements[] array.
name	The name property is a read-only property that reflects the NAME attribute of the <FORM> tag.
method	The method property is a read-write property that reflects the METHOD attribute of the <FORM> tag. The valid values for this property are "get" and "post."
target	The *target* property is a read-write property that reflects the *TARGET* attribute of the <FORM> tag. The *target* property specifies the window or frame to receive the form results from the server.

The form object contains both the information needed to send the information to the server and, through the objects in the elements[] array, the objects needed to collect information from the user. Figure 8.1 shows the hierarchical structure of the form object.

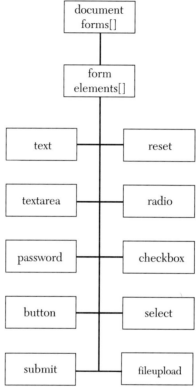

Figure 8.1
Structure of form object.

Methods of Form Object

The reset() method and submit() method simulate the behavior of a click on the Reset button or the Submit button, respectively. The syntax for these methods is as follows:

```
document.forms[index].reset()
document.formName.reset()
document.forms[index].submit()
document.formName.submit()
```

Note

> For security reasons, the `submit()` method fails if the URL proto-col in the action property is `news:`, `snews:`, or `mailto:`.

These methods allow you to use alternate graphics for these buttons. The following example shows how to provide an alternate graphic for the reset button:

```
<A HREF="javascript:document.myform.reset()">
<IMG SRC="myreset.gif"></A>
```

The `reset()` and `submit()` methods also allow you to reset or submit a form when used in conjunction with the event handlers of the `form` object (see the "Sending Data to the Server" section in this chapter). The `submit()` method also provides the means for submitting cookies to the server (see the "Working with Cookies" section of this chapter).

The `handleEvent()` method is part of the event handling system presented in Chapter 7, "Working With Events and `Handlers`." This method allows a script to directly pass an event to an event receiver (event handler). The method appears in a window or document object function that uses the `captureEvent()` method. Every form element also supports the `handleEvent()` method.

Event Handlers of Form Object

The `form` object supports only the `onReset` and `onSubmit` event handlers. A reset event occurs when the user clicks on the Reset button, or when a script calls the `reset()` method. However, the submit event only occurs when the user clicks on the Submit button. Both event handlers have two forms:

- Assign the event handler to its form object property

```
document.myForm.onreset = clearForm
document.myForm.onsubmit = checkForm
```

- Specify the event handler as an HTML attribute in the `<FORM>` tag

```
<FORM NAME="myForm" onReset="clearForm{}"
```

```
<FORM NAME="myForm" onSubmit="checkForm()"
```

If the event handler returns "false," the browser does not perform the default action. For the onSubmit event handler, the browser does not submit the form to the server when the event handler returns "false." Any other return value causes the browser to submit the form to the server. If the user disables JavaScript on their browser, the browser ignores the onSubmit attribute in the <FORM> tag and submits the form to the server. If you need to process the form prior to submitting the data to the server, you need to avoid using the submit type. Instead, you can use the standard button type as follows:

```
<INPUT TYPE="button" NAME="submitBtn" VALUE="Submit"
      onClick="checkForm">
```

Elements of the Form Object

The form object forms an outer structure for the form elements. The elements of the form object that collect information from the user are as follows:

- Checkbox
- Radio
- Select
- Text
- Textarea

Other elements allow you to control the action of the form. These elements are as follows:

- Button
- Reset
- Submit

The last group of elements provide additional functionality to the form. These elements are as follows:

- Hidden
- Password

Each element of the form is an object stored in the elements[] array of the form object. The order of the objects in the elements[] array reflects the order in which the elements appear in the form. This ordering of the elements[] array gives extra importance to using the NAME attribute in the <INPUT> tag as a means of identifying the element. The following code snippets show the difference between using the NAME attribute and referencing an object by index values:

```
document.forms[0].elements[0].value
document.custForm.custName.value
```

When you want to reference an individual element, referencing by name is easier to read. When you need to check a group of elements, you can use the index method in a loop statement. However, if you make any changes to the form, you need to check that the indexes still point to the correct element.

Common Properties, Methods, and Event Handlers

As objects, the elements of the form object share some common properties, methods, and event handlers. This section discusses those features that are common to all or, at least, most elements of the form object.

Common Properties of Form Elements

All elements possess the properties shown in Table 8.3. Except for the value property, these properties have a consistent meaning for all elements. The content of the value property varies according to the needs of the element as shown in Table 8.4.

Table 8.3 Common Properties of Form Elements

Property	Description
form	The form property is a read-only property that references the form object containing the element. The form property provides each element with a pointer to its "parent." You can use this property when your script passes the element object to a function.

Table 8.3 Common Properties of Form Elements *(Continued)*

Property	Description
name	The name property is a read-only property that reflects the NAME attribute of the HTML <INPUT> tag.
type *	The type property is a read-only property that reflects the value specified in the TYPE attribute of the HTML <INPUT> tag. The valid types are: button, checkbox, file, hidden, password, radio, reset, select, select-multiple, submit, text, and textarea.
value	The *value* property is a read-write property that initially reflects the information specified in the *VALUE* attribute of the HTML <INPUT> tag. The content of the *value* property varies according to the element.

* *New in JavaScript 1.1*

Warning

Normally, only the radio buttons have the same name so that the radio buttons form a group. However, Netscape allows you to use the same name for other elements. When this happens, the browser places the form element objects into an array, and you must then address these objects as elements of an array. The section on "Working with the fileUpload object" provides an example of the revised reference.

Table 8.4 Contents of the value Property for each Form Element

Form Element	Content of value property
button	The value property reflects the button's label that appears on the screen. If you modify the value after the page is loaded, the browser displays the new text in the button, but it does not change the size of the button to accommodate the revised value.
checkbox	The value property contains the string that the browser passes to the server when the box is checked.

Table 8.4 Contents of the value Property for each Form Element *(Continued)*

Form Element	Content of value property
FileUpload *	The value property contains a string that specifies the pathname of the file selected by the user. For the fileUpload object, the value property is read-only, except for signed scripts with the "UniversalBrowser-Write" privilege.
hidden	The value property of the hidden object is a read-write property that the browser sends to the server, but does not display on the screen.
password	The value property contains the password entered by the user.
radio	The value property contains the string that the browser passes to the server when the button is selected.
reset	The value property reflects the button's label that appears on the screen. If you modify the value after the page is loaded, the browser displays the new text in the button, but it does not change the size of the button to accommodate the revised value.
select	The select object has no value property.
submit	The value property reflects the button's label that appears on the screen. If you modify the value after the page is loaded, the browser displays the new text in the button, but it does not change the size of the button to accommodate the revised value.
text	The value property contains the text displayed in the browser window. Both the user and JavaScript can modify this property.
textarea	The value property contains the text displayed in the browser window. Both the user and JavaScript can modify this property.

° *New in JavaScript 1.1*

Common Methods of Form Elements

With the exception of the hidden object, which has no methods, the element objects of the form object share a common set of methods. As shown in Table 8.5, every element object shares the blur() and focus() methods, while only certain element objects share the click() and select() methods. These methods simulate user actions. Consequently, they trigger the corresponding event. See Chapter 7 for a description of the basic concepts of event management.

Table 8.5 Common Methods of the Form Elements

Element	blur()	click()	focus()	select()
button	X°	X	X°	
checkbox	X°	X	X°	
fileUpload *	X°		X°	X
password	X		X	X
radio	X°	X	X°	
reset	X°	X	X°	
select	X		X	
submit	X°	X	X°	
text	X		X	X
textarea	X		X	X

° *New in JavaScript 1.1*

The focus() Method

The `focus()` method sets the screen focus to the specified object and generates a focus event. The syntax for the `focus()` method is as follows:

`formObj.elementObj.focus()`

The following example sets the screen focus to a text box:

`document.forms.custForm.custName.focus()`

The blur() Method

The `blur()` method removes focus from an object and generates a blur event. The syntax of the `blur()` method is as follows:

`formObj.elementObj.blur()`

The following example removes the screen focus from a text box:

`document.forms.custForm.custName.blur()`

The click() Method

The `click()` method simulates the click of the left mouse button and generates a click event. The syntax for the `click()` method is as follows:

`formObj.elementObj.click()`

The following example submits the form by simulating a click on the Submit button:

```
document.forms.custForm.submitFrorm.click()
```

The select() Method

The `select()` method highlights the text in the specified form input element and generates a select event. The syntax for the `select()` method is as follows:

```
formObj.elementObj.select()
```

The following example selects the text in a text box:

```
document.forms.custForm.custName.select()
```

Before using the `select()` method, you need to use the `focus()` method to set the focus to the object. The reason for this requirement is that the `select()` method simulates the actions of a user. The user's action first brings focus to the object and then selects the text.

Common Event Handlers of Form Elements

As shown in Table 8.6, the common event handlers of the form elements match the methods of the form elements. The notable exception is the `password` object, which has no `onSelect` event handler even though there is a select() method. In addition, the `onChange` event handler has no corresponding method.

Table 8.6 Common Event Handlers of the Form Elements

Element	onBlur	onChange	onClick	onFocus	onSelect
button	X°		X	X°	
checkbox	X°		X	X°	
fileUpload *	X°	X °		X°	
password	X			X	
radio	X°		X	X°	
reset	X°		X	X°	

Table 8.6 Common Event Handlers of the Form Elements *(Continued)*

Element	onBlur	onChange	onClick	onFocus	onSelect
select	X	X		X	
submit	X°		X	X°	
text	X	X		X	X
textarea	X	X		X	X

° New in JavaScript 1.1

Starting with JavaScript 1.2, the browser passes the `event` object to the event handler. With the exception of the click event, the only properties of the event object available to the event handlers in Table 8.6 are the `target` property and the `type` property. The click event, on the other hand, uses all of the relevant properties of the `event` object.

The onFocus Event Handler

The focus event occurs when either the user, or `focus()` method, moves the screen focus onto a form element. You can assign an event handler to the event using either the `onfocus` property of the element object or the `onFocus` attribute of the HTML `<INPUT>` tag as shown in the following examples:

```
document.custForm.custName.onfocus = inputName
<INPUT TYPE="text" NAME="custName"
     onFocus="inputName(event)">
```

The onBlur Event Handler

The blur event occurs when either the user, or blur() method, moves the screen focus away from a form element. You can assign an event handler to the event using either the onblur property of the element object or the onBlur attribute of the HTML `<INPUT>` tag as shown in the following examples:

```
document.custForm.custName.onblur = chkName
<INPUT TYPE="text" NAME="custName" onBlur="chkName(event)">
```

You need to use the `onBlur` event handler with care. Since the blur event occurs whenever focus transfers from the element, an infinite loop can be created in onBlur event handlers that will generate an alert box. Also, you need to remember that the blur event occurs when the user temporarily transfers focus to another application.

The onClick Event Handler

The click event occurs when the user presses and releases the left mouse button. The click() method simulates the click event. You can assign an event handler to the click event using either the onclick property of the element object or the onClick attribute of the HTML <IN-PUT> tag as shown in the following examples:

```
                                   on Click
document.custForm.custSubmit.onfocus = checkForm
<INPUT TYPE="button" NAME="custName" VALUE="Submit"
        onClick="checkForm(event)">
```

The onChange Event Handler

The change event occurs when the focus moves away from a form element that the user has changed. The change of focus occurs as a result of user action or the blur() method. You can assign an event handler to the change event using either the onchange property of the element object or the onChange attribute of the HTML <INPUT> tag as shown in the following examples:

```
document.custForm.custNumber.onchange = checkNumber
<INPUT TYPE="text" NAME="custnumber"
        onChange="checkNumber(event)">
```

The difference between the change event and the blur event is that the change event only occurs when the user changes the form element. If you create event handlers for both events, you need to consider that both events occur when the text changes.

The onSelect Event Handler

The select event occurs when the user, or the select() method, highlights text in the text or textarea elements. You can assign an event handler to the select event using either the onselect property of the element object or the onSelect attribute of the HTML <INPUT> tag as shown in the following examples:

```
document.custForm.custName.onselect = saveSelect
```

```
<INPUT TYPE="text" NAME="custName"
      onSelect="saveSelect(event)">
```

Note

 The onSelect event handler is not fully implemented in the Netscape browsers, including Netscape Communicator 4.0. Netscape plans on implementing this event handler in a future release.

Working with the text Form Element

The text object reflects the text box in an HTML form. Table 8.7 lists the properties, methods, and event handlers for the text object.

Table 8.7 The Properties, Methods, and Event Handlers of the Text Object

Properties	Methods	Events
defaultValue	blur()	onBlur
form	focus()	onChange
name	handleEvent() **	onFocus
type *	select()	onSelect
value		

* *New in JavaScript 1.1; ** New in JavaScript 1.2*

The only additional property is the defaultValue property, which reflects the VALUE attribute of the HTML <INPUT> tag at the time that the browser loads the web page. Although you can modify the default-Value property, it has no effect on the appearance of the text on the screen. To change what appears on the screen, you need to use the value property.

New in JavaScript 1.2

 In addition to providing the event object to the event handlers, JavaScript 1.2 copies the text in form element to the RegExp.input property.

The script in Listing 8.1 illustrates the features of the text object. Since the script uses the event object, it will only run in Netscape Communicator 4.0.

Listing 8.1 Working with the text Form Element

```
<HTML>
  <HEAD>
    <TITLE>Working with the text Form Element</TITLE>
<SCRIPT LANGUAGE="JavaScript">
<!--
function chgFocus(formObj, msg) {
   formObj.defaultValue=formObj.value
   self.status=msg
}
function dispChange(ev) {
   alert("Old Value:\n"+ev.target.defaultValue)
}
function dispSelect() {
   alert("You selected the following text:\n"
        +document.getSelection())
}
//-->
</SCRIPT>
  </HEAD>
  <BODY ONLOAD="document.custForm.custName.focus()">
    <P>This example illustrates the various features
       of the text form element.</P>
    <FORM NAME="custForm">
    <TABLE WIDTH="100%">
      <TR>
        <TD WIDTH="97" COLSTART="1">Full Name: </TD>
        <TD WIDTH="439" COLSTART="2">

        <P><INPUT TYPE="TEXT" NAME="custName" SIZE="40"
```

```
            ONSELECT="dispSelect()"
            ONFOCUS="chgFocus(this, 'Enter your name')"
            ONBLUR="self.status=''"
            ONCHANGE="dispChange(event)"></P></TD>
</TR>
<TR>
  <TD WIDTH="97" COLSTART="1">Address 1: </TD>
  <TD WIDTH="439" COLSTART="2">

  <P><INPUT TYPE="TEXT" NAME="CustAddr1" SIZE="40"
      ONFOCUS="chgFocus(this, 'Enter your address')"
      ONBLUR="self.status=''"
      ONCHANGE="dispChange(event)"
      ONSELECT="dispSelect()"></P></TD>
</TR>
<TR>
  <TD WIDTH="97" COLSTART="1">Address 2: </TD>
  <TD WIDTH="439" COLSTART="2">

  <P><INPUT TYPE="TEXT" NAME="custAddr2" SIZE="40"
      ONSELECT="dispSelect()"
      ONFOCUS="chgFocus(this, 'Enter address line 2')"
      ONBLUR="self.status=''"
      ONCHANGE="dispChange(event)"></P></TD>
</TR>
<TR>
  <TD WIDTH="97" COLSTART="1">City: </TD>
  <TD WIDTH="439" COLSTART="2">

  <P><INPUT TYPE="TEXT" NAME="custCity" SIZE="30"
      ONCHANGE="dispChange(event)"
      ONBLUR="self.status=''"
      ONFOCUS="chgFocus(this, 'Enter your city')"
      ONSELECT="dispSelect()"></P></TD>
</TR>
<TR>
  <TD WIDTH="97" COLSTART="1">State: </TD>
  <TD WIDTH="439" COLSTART="2">

  <P><INPUT TYPE="TEXT" NAME="custState" SIZE="2"
      ONSELECT="dispSelect()"
      ONFOCUS="chgFocus(this, 'Enter your state')"
      ONBLUR="self.status=''"
      ONCHANGE="dispChange(event)"></P></TD>
</TR>
```

```
<TR>
    <TD WIDTH="97" COLSTART="1">Zip Code: </TD>
    <TD WIDTH="439" COLSTART="2">

    <P><INPUT TYPE="TEXT" NAME="custZip" SIZE="10"
        ONBLUR="self.status='';
                document.custForm.custName.focus()"
        VALUE="99999-9999" ONCHANGE="dispChange(event)"
        ONFOCUS="chgFocus(this, 'Enter your zip code')"
        ONSELECT="dispSelect()"></P></TD>
    </TR>
  </TABLE></FORM>
 </BODY>
</HTML>
```

The script in Listing 8.1 contains many features that require some explanation. The `<BODY>` statement contains an `onLoad` event handler that sets the focus of the screen to the named text element. The `onLoad` event handler works because it is not executed until the script is completely loaded. Thus, the apparent reference to an object that does not yet exist is permissible. Normally, the Tab key includes the browser location field in the list of fields through which the user cycles when pressing the Tab key. The `onBlur` event handler for the zip code element excludes the location field by setting the focus to the name field.

Every element in the form uses all of the event handlers for the text object. The `onFocus` event handler calls the `chgFocus()` function. The arguments passed to the `chgFocus()` function are the current object and a message. By using the "`this`" keyword to pass the current object, the `chgFocus()` function is compatible with all versions of JavaScript. On the other hand, the `onChange` event handler calls the `dispChange()` function with the `event` object as an argument. The `target` property of the event object provides another means of accessing the properties of the current object. When you change text in a field, the browser generates both a change event and a blur event. Figure 8.2 shows the initial screen for the script in Listing 8.1.

Bug

Netscape Communicator 4.03 on a Windows 95 platform does not generate a select event when text is highlighted.

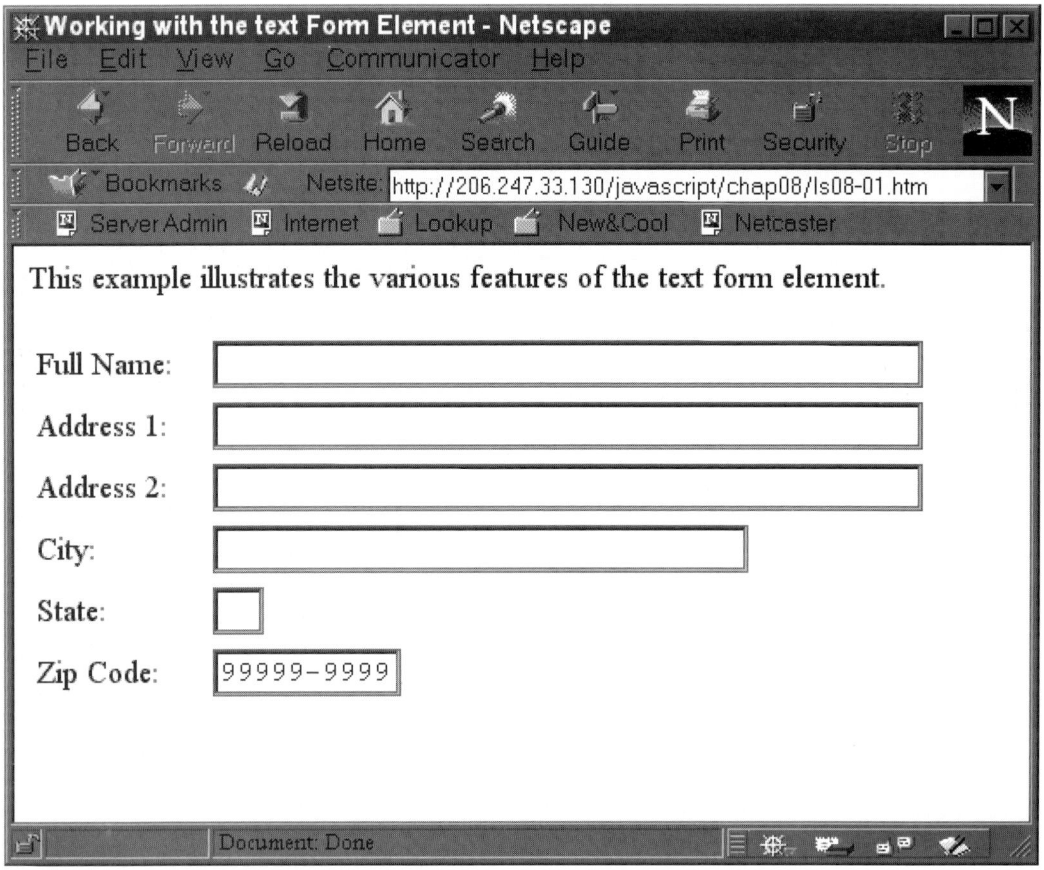

Figure 8.2 Results of working with the text form element.

Working with textarea Form Element

The textarea form element object reflects the attributes of the HTML
<TEXTAREA> </TEXTAREA> tags. Table 8.8 lists the properties, meth-
ods, and event handlers for the `textarea` object.

Table 8.8 The Properties, Methods, and Event Handlers of the Textarea Object

Properties	Methods	Events
defaultValue	blur()	onBlur
form	focus()	onChange

Table 8.8 The Properties, Methods, and Event Handlers of the Textarea Object (Continued)

Properties	Methods	Events
name	handleEvent() **	onFocus
type *	select()	onKeyDown **
value		onKeyPress **
		onKeyUp **
		onSelect

° *New in JavaScript 1.1,* °° *New in JavaScript 1.2*

The only additional property is the `defaultValue` property, which reflects text between the `<TEXTAREA>` and `</TEXTAREA>` tags at the time that the browser loads the Web page. Although you can modify the `defaultValue` property, it has no effect on the appearance of the text on the screen. To change what appears on the screen, you need to use the `value` property.

New in JavaScript 1.2

In addition to providing the `event` object to the event handlers, JavaScript 1.2 copies the text in form element to the `RegExp.input` property. Also, JavaScript 1.2 includes event handlers for `onKeyDown`, `onKeyPress`, and `onKeyUp`.

The script in Listing 8.2 illustrates the use of various elements of the `textarea` object. To maintain compatibility with different browsers, the script contains only those features implemented in JavaScript 1.0.

Listing 8.2 Working with the textarea Form Element

```
<HTML>
  <HEAD>
    <TITLE>Working with the textarea Form Element</TITLE>
<SCRIPT LANGUAGE="JavaScript">
<!--
function chgFocus(formObj, msg) {
   formObj.defaultValue=formObj.value
```

```
      self.status=msg
}
function dispChange(formObj) {
   alert("Old Value:\n"+formObj.defaultValue)
}
function dispSelect() {
   alert("You selected text.")
}
//-->
</SCRIPT>
  </HEAD>
  <BODY ONLOAD="document.custForm.custComment.focus()">
    <P>This script exercises the common event handlers of
       the textarea object.</P>
    <FORM NAME="custForm">
    <P><TEXTAREA NAME="custComment" ROWS="6" COLS="40"
       WRAP="VIRTUAL"
       ONFOCUS="chgFocus(this, 'Enter your comments.')"
       ONBLUR="self.status=''" ONCHANGE="dispChange(this)"
       ONSELECT="dispSelect()"></TEXTAREA></P>
    </FORM>
  </BODY>
</HTML>
```

The results of running this script are shown in Figure 8.3. With the exception that a change in the `dispChange()` function to use the "`this`" keyword, results in the script performing the same action as the script shown in Listing 8.1.

Netscape

The `onSelect` event handler fails to work in the Windows 95 version of all versions of Netscape. However, it does work in Microsoft Internet Explorer 4.0. In Microsoft Internet Explorer 3.0, the script hangs during the loading of the script.

Working with the Radio Button Form Element

Radio buttons enable you to provide a graphical means for users to make a single choice from multiple options. The radio object reflects the attributes of the HTML <INPUT> tag for a radio button. Table 8.9 lists the properties, methods, and event handlers of the `radio` object.

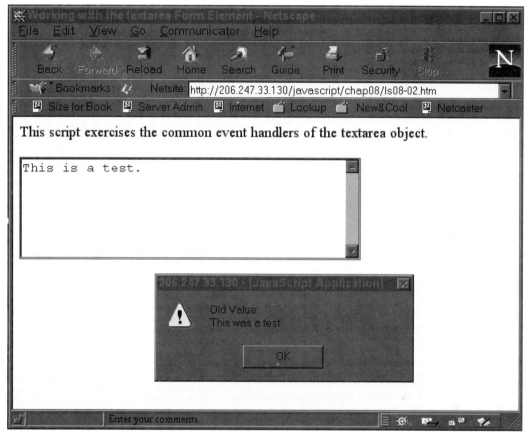

Figure 8.3   Results of working with textarea form element.

Table 8.9 Properties, Methods, and Event Handlers of the Radio Object

Properties	Methods	Events
checked	blur() *	onBlur *
defaultChecked	click()	onClick
form	focus() *	onFocus *
length	handleEvent() **	
name		
type *		
value		

*New in JavaScript 1.1; **New in JavaScript 1.2*

Radio buttons appear as a group. The NAME attribute of the HTML <INPUT> tag defines the group name of which the radio button is a member. Since the radio object reflects the attributes of a single radio button, the name property identifies the group name, and the length property of the button[] array specifies the number of radio buttons in the group. The elements[] array property of the form object arranges all radio buttons within the same group into an array, with the NAME attribute determining the first index value and the button number determining the second index as shown in the following examples:

```
document.custForm.card[0]
document.custForm["card"][0]
```

You can reference an isolated radio button using the same syntax used in referencing any element. However, common practice is to use a checkbox in this situation, rather than a radio button.

The defaultChecked property reflects the CHECKED attribute in the HTML <INPUT> tag. If you change the value of the default-Checked property, the change has no effect on the default-Checked property of other radio buttons in the group, nor does it alter the screen display of the radio button. The radio buttons on the screen reflect the checked property. The value property is the string sent to the server for a checked radio button.

The script in Listing 8.3 generates an alert message that lists the properties of the radio button when the button is clicked. Although it is listed as a property of the radio object, the length property is actually a property of the array of buttons. The dispProp() function receives a reference to the radio object itself via the "this" keyword. Since the length property is the property of the array object of which the radio object is a member, the reference to it uses the form property of the radio object. The results of running this script are shown in Figure 8.4.

Listing 8.3 Working with Radio Buttons

```
<HTML>
  <HEAD>
    <TITLE>Working with Radio Buttons</TITLE>
<SCRIPT LANGUAGE="JavaScript">
<!--
function dispProp(buttonObj) {
```

```
    var msg="Properties of "+buttonObj.value
    msg+="\n\rName: "+buttonObj.name
    msg+="\n\rNumber of buttons: "
    msg+=buttonObj.form.custCard.length
    msg+="\n\rChecked: "+buttonObj.checked
    msg+="\n\rDefault Check: "+buttonObj.defaultChecked
    alert(msg)
}
//-->
</SCRIPT>
  </HEAD>
  <BODY>
    <P>When you click on a radio button, an alert box
      appears that describes the properties of the radio
      object.</P>
    <FORM NAME="custForm">

    <P>Credit Card:
    <INPUT TYPE="RADIO" NAME="custCard" VALUE="Visa"
          CHECKED="CHECKED" ONCLICK="dispProp(this)">Visa
    <INPUT TYPE="RADIO" NAME="custCard" VALUE="Mastercard"
          ONCLICK="dispProp(this)">Mastercard
    <INPUT TYPE="RADIO" NAME="custCard" VALUE="Discovery"
          ONCLICK="dispProp(this)">Discovery</P>
    </FORM>
  </BODY>
</HTML>
```

Working with Checkboxes

Where radio buttons provide for only a single selection from a group of radio buttons, checkboxes allow the user to check zero or more boxes. Unlike the radio button, `checkbox` objects are independent elements in the `elements[]` array. Thus, a single checkbox enables you to use a graphical method for obtaining a single yes or no answer. Table 8.10 lists the properties, methods, and event handlers of the `checkbox` object.

Table 8.10 Properties, Methods, and Event Handlers of the Checkbox Object

Properties	Methods	Events
checked	blur() *	onBlur *
defaultChecked	click()	onClick

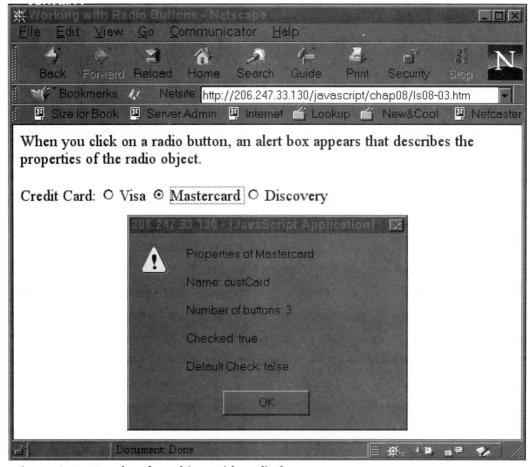

Figure 8.4 *Results of working with radio buttons.*

Table 8.10 Properties, Methods, and Event Handlers of the Checkbox Object *(Continued)*

Properties	Methods	Events
form	focus() *	onFocus *
name	handleEvent() **	
type *		
value		

* New in JavaScript 1.1; **New in JavaScript 1.2

The `checked` property is a Boolean variable that is set by: the user clicking on the checkbox; using the `click()` method; or directly setting the property. The `click()` method simulates the user clicking the left mouse button. Consequently, it toggles the value of the checked property between true and false. On the other hand, you can explicitly set the value to true or false by referencing the `checked` property itself. Although you can modify the `defaultChecked` property in a script, the new value is not reflected on the screen. The `value` property contains the string that the browser submits to the server.

The script in Listing 8.4 illustrates how to set a checkbox with the `click()` method, and how to change the value of the `checked` property. Figure 8.5 shows the results of running this script.

Listing 8.4 Working with Checkboxes

```
<HTML>
  <HEAD>
    <TITLE>Working with Checkboxes</TITLE>
  </HEAD>
  <BODY>
    <P>This example illustrates the various methods of
       changing the value of the checked property of the
       checkbox object.</P>
    <FORM NAME="testForm">
    <P><INPUT TYPE="CHECKBOX" NAME="cbox" VALUE="cbox">
            Checkbox test</P>
    <P>
     <INPUT TYPE="BUTTON" NAME="clickIt" VALUE="Click it"
            ONCLICK="document.testForm.cbox.click()">
     <INPUT TYPE="BUTTON" NAME="checkIt" VALUE="Check It"
            ONCLICK="document.testForm.cbox.checked=true">
     <INPUT TYPE="BUTTON" NAME="clearIt" VALUE="Clear It"
            ONCLICK="document.testForm.cbox.checked=false">
    </P>
    </FORM>
  </BODY>
</HTML>
```

Working with Selection Lists

The selection list gives the user a list of options from which the user chooses either a single option or multiple options depending on the type of list. The default list allows the selection of a single option like a radio button. A multiple selection list lets the user choose one or more options. The select ob-

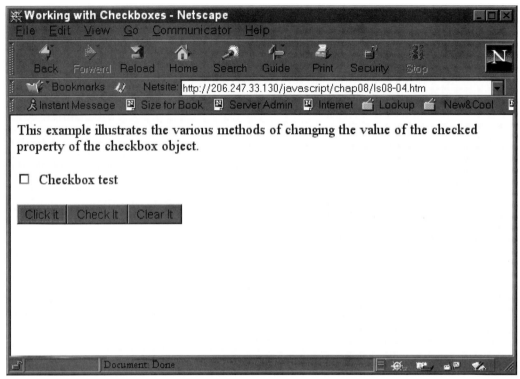

Figure 8.5   *Results of working with checkboxes.*

ject reflects the attributes of the HTML <SELECT> tag. In addition, it includes an array of option objects that reflect the attributes of the <OP-TION> tag bounded by the <SELECT> </SELECT> tags. Table 8.11 lists the properties, methods, and event handlers of the select object.

Table 8.11 Properties, Methods, and Event Handlers of the Select Object

Properties	Methods	Event Handlers
form	blur()	onBlur
length	focus()	onChange
name	handleEvent()	onFocus
options[]		
selectedIndex		
type *		

° New in JavaScript 1.1

The `type` property contains a string that indicates whether this is a single selection list (`select-one`) or multiple-selection list (`select-multiple`). The `selectedIndex` contains the index of the selected option, or the first selected option in a multiple-selection list. If no option is selected, the selectedIndex has a value of -1.

The `options[]` array property is an array of `option` objects. The `length` property contains a numeric value that defines the number of `option` objects in the `options[]` array. The `option` object reflects the attributes of the HTML `<OPTION>` tag. Table 8.12 describes the properties of the `option` object. The `option` object has no methods or event handlers.

Table 8.12 Properties of the Option Object

Property	Description
defaultSelected *	The `defaultSelected` property is a Boolean value that reflects the SELECTED attribute of the HTML `<OPTION>` tag. The `defaultSelected` property is the default selection state for an option in a selection list. The screen is not updated if you change this property. For a single-selection list, setting the `defaultSelected` property to true for an option results in the setting of the `defaultSelected` property in other option objects to false. In a multiple-selection list, you can set the `defaultSelected` property in multiple option objects.
selected	The `selected` property is a Boolean value that indicates whether the option is currently selected. Rather than modifying the `selectedIndex` property of the `select` object, you should modify the `selected` property of the `option` object. In a single-selection list this ensures that the browser clears selected properties in other option objects. For multiple-selection lists, setting the `selected` property allows you to set multiple options, where the `selectedIndex` affects only a single option.
text	The `text` property is a read-write property that initially reflects the text that appears after the HTML `<OPTION>` tag. If you change the value of the `text` property, the browser automatically updates the screen.
value	The `value` property is a read/write string that initially reflects the VALUE attribute of the HTML `<OPTION>` tag. The `value` property is sent to the server for selected options.

* *New in JavaScript 1.1*

The script in Listing 8.5 has a simple selection list that uses the on-Focus and onBlur event handlers of the select object. If you click a radio button corresponding to a selection list object, the script displays an alert message with the properties of the specified object. The results of clicking on a option object are shown in Figure 8.6.

Listing 8.5 Working with Selection Lists

```
<HTML>
  <HEAD>
    <TITLE>Working with Selection Lists</TITLE>
<SCRIPT LANGUAGE="JavaScript">
<!--
function dispSelect() {
   var msg="Properties for the select object are:"
   msg+="\n\rname: "+document.tstFrm.pSpeed.name
   msg+="\n\rtype: "+document.tstFrm.pSpeed.type
   msg+="\n\rlength: "+document.tstFrm.pSpeed.length
   msg+="\n\rselected: "
   msg+=document.tstFrm.pSpeed.selectedIndex
   alert(msg)
}
function dispOpt(idx) {
   var msg="Properties of option object "+idx+" are:"
   msg+="\n\rdefault: "
   mdg+=document.tstFrm.pSpeed.options[idx].defaultSelected
   msg+="\n\rselected: "
   msg+=document.tstFrm.pSpeed.options[idx].selected
   msg+="\n\rtext: "
   msg+=document.tstFrm.pSpeed.options[idx].text
   msg+="\n\rvalue: "
   msg+=document.tstFrm.pSpeed.options[idx].value
   alert(msg)
}
//-->
</SCRIPT>
  </HEAD>
  <BODY>
    <P>Select a speed then check the properties of the
       various objects.</P>
    <FORM NAME="tstFrm">
    <P><SELECT NAME="pSpeed" SIZE="1"
```

```
                ONFOCUS="self.status='Select CPU speed'"
                ONBLUR="self.status=''">
    <OPTION VALUE="cpu166">166 MHz</OPTION>
    <OPTION VALUE="cpu200"
                SELECTED="SELECTED">200 MHz</OPTION>
    <OPTION VALUE="cpu233">233 MHz</OPTION>
    <OPTION VALUE="cpu266">266 MHz</OPTION>
    <OPTION VALUE="cpu300">300 MHz</OPTION></SELECT></P>
  <P>Display properties for the following object:
    <BR><INPUT TYPE="RADIO" NAME="dispProp" VALUE="s"
                CHECKED="CHECKED"
                ONCLICK="dispSelect()">select
    <BR><INPUT TYPE="RADIO" NAME="dispProp" VALUE="0"
                ONCLICK="dispOpt(0)">option 0
    <BR><INPUT TYPE="RADIO" NAME="dispProp" VALUE="1"
                ONCLICK="dispOpt(1)">option 1
    <BR><INPUT TYPE="RADIO" NAME="dispProp" VALUE="2"
                ONCLICK="dispOpt(2)">option 2
    <BR><INPUT TYPE="RADIO" NAME="dispProp" VALUE="3"
                ONCLICK="dispOpt(3)">option 3
    <BR><INPUT TYPE="RADIO" NAME="dispProp" VALUE="4"
                ONCLICK="dispOpt(4)">option4</P>
   </FORM>
 </BODY>
</HTML>
```

In addition to creating option objects using HTML tags, JavaScript has an `Option constructor` object that allows you to dynamically create options. The first step is to create an object using the following syntax:

```
OptionObj = new Option(text, value, defaultSelected, selected)
```

The following example adds a new color object to a color selection list:

```
redColor = new Option("Red", "red", false, false)
```

The next task is to add the new object to the `options[]` array as follows:

```
document.myForm.colorList.option[4] = redColor
```

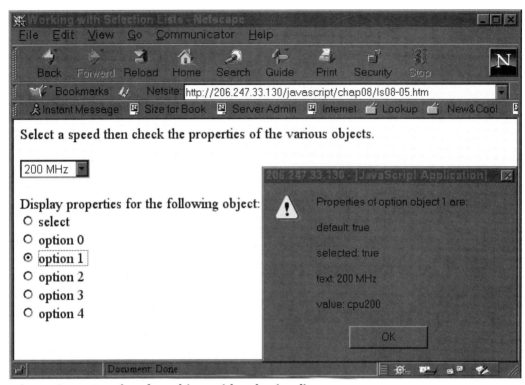

Figure 8.6 *Results of working with selection lists.*

The final step is to refresh the screen display by using the `histo-ry.go(0)` method. When the screen refreshes, variables are lost unless stored in cookies or form element values.

Besides adding `option` objects, you can delete an `option` object from the `options[]` array by setting the array element to null. To have the change reflected on the screen, you need to reload the screen with the `history.go(0)` method.

The script in Listing 8.6 adds and deletes `option` objects from a selection list of colors. The script consists of two forms. The first form contains the selection list of colors and the "Delete Selected Object" button. The second form contains the elements necessary to add an `option` object to the selection list of colors.

Listing 8.6 Adding and Deleting Option Objects

```
<HTML>
  <HEAD>
    <TITLE>Adding and Deleting Option Objects</TITLE>
<SCRIPT LANGUAGE="JavaScript">
<!--
function delColor(frmObj) {
   frmObj.clrLst.options[frmObj.clrLst.selectedIndex]=null
   history.go(0)
}
function addColor(frmObj) {
  var nClr=new Option(frmObj.clrText.value,
      frmObj.clrValue.value, frmObj.clrDefault.checked,
      frmObj.clrSelect.checked)
  clrFrm.clrLst.options[document.clrFrm.clrLst.length]=nClr
  history.go(0)
}
//-->
</SCRIPT>
  </HEAD>
  <BODY>
    <FORM NAME="clrFrm">
    <P><SELECT NAME="clrLst" SIZE="3">
      <OPTION VALUE="clr_red">red</OPTION>
      <OPTION VALUE="clr_green">green</OPTION>
      <OPTION VALUE="clr_blue">blue</OPTION>
    </SELECT></P>
    <P><INPUT TYPE="BUTTON" NAME="delButton"
            VALUE="Delete Selected Object"
            ONCLICK="delColor(this.form)"></P>
    </FORM>
    <FORM NAME="chgFrm">
    <TABLE WIDTH="80%" BORDER="0">
      <TR>
        <TD WIDTH="205" COLSTART="1">
            Color Name for List:</TD>
        <TD WIDTH="315" COLSTART="2">
        <P><INPUT TYPE="TEXT" NAME="clrText"
                SIZE="20"></P></TD>
      </TR>
      <TR>
        <TD WIDTH="205" COLSTART="1">
```

```
            Value for Submit:</TD>
      <TD WIDTH="315" COLSTART="2">
      <P><INPUT TYPE="TEXT" NAME="clrValue"
              SIZE="20"></P></TD>
    </TR>
    <TR>
      <TD WIDTH="205" COLSTART="1">Default:</TD>
      <TD WIDTH="315" COLSTART="2">
      <P><INPUT TYPE="CHECKBOX" NAME="clrDefault"></P>
      </TD>
    </TR>
    <TR>
      <TD WIDTH="205" COLSTART="1">Selected:</TD>
      <TD WIDTH="315" COLSTART="2">
      <P><INPUT TYPE="CHECKBOX" NAME="clrSelect"></P>
      </TD>
    </TR>
  </TABLE>
  <P><INPUT TYPE="BUTTON" NAME="addButton"
          VALUE="Add Color to list"
          ONCLICK="addColor(this.form)"></P>
  </FORM>
  </BODY>
</HTML>
```

As the script illustrates, the deleting of an element from an `options[]` array requires nothing more than setting the desired element to null. Although it is not really necessary, the script passes the `form` object to the `delColor()` function. The script then deletes the color identified by the `selectedIndex` property of the `select` object. Adding a color to the list is a bit more involved. The script keeps all of the elements required for the `Option` constructor object in a separate form and then passes this form to the `addColor()` function. In a zero-based array, the `length` property serves as a useful index to the next available element in the array. Both functions end with the `history.go()` method to force reloading of the script.

Navigator

The previous script works with Netscape Navigator 3.0 and Netscape Communicator 4.0. However, it fails on all versions of Microsoft Internet Explorer.

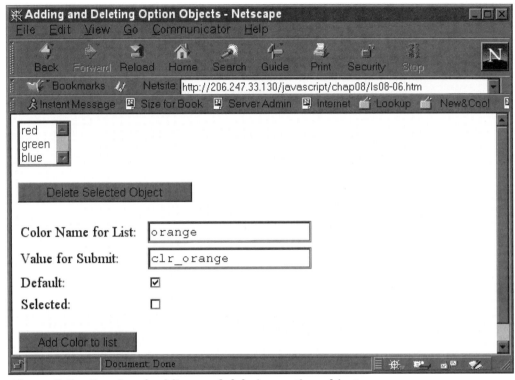

Figure 8.7 Results of adding and deleting option objects.

Working with the fileUpload Object

The fileUpload object reflects the file upload element in an HTML form, which allows a user to upload a file to the server. Table 8.13 lists the properties, methods, and event handlers of the fileUpload object.

Table 8.13 Properties, Methods, and Event Handlers of the fileUpload Object

Properties	Methods	Event Handlers
form	blur()	onBlur
name	focus()	onChange
type *	handleEvent() **	onFocus
value	select()	

* New in JavaScript 1.1; **New in JavaScript 1.2

The name property reflects the NAME attribute in the HTML <IN-PUT> tag. If the same name appears in multiple <INPUT> tags, the browser builds an array of objects with the same name. In this situation, you need to address the fileUpload objects as elements of an array as shown in the following example:

```
document.myForm.sendFile[0].value
```

The value property is a read-only property that contains the pathname of the file that the user wishes to upload to the server. In JavaScript 1.2, signed scripts with "UniversalBrowserWrite" privilege can write to the value property.

The script in Listing 8.7 demonstrates how to use the select() method to highlight text in a text input box such as the pathname for a file. The selectTest() function checks that there is a pathname before issuing the select() method. Figure 8.8 shows the initial screen for this script.

Listing 8.7 Working with the fileUpload Object

```
<HTML>
  <HEAD>
    <TITLE>Working with the fileUpload Object</TITLE>
<SCRIPT LANGUAGE="JavaScript">
<!--
function selectTest(uploadObj) {
   if (uploadObj.value!="") {
      uploadObj.select()
   }
}
//-->
</SCRIPT>
  </HEAD>
  <BODY>
    <P>For this example, you need to select a file and
       then click on the file name to give the text box
       focus. When the data entry field receives focus,
       the field is highlighted.</P>
    <FORM METHOD="POST" ENCTYPE="multipart/form-data"
         NAME="fileFrm">
    <P>Enter file name:
```

```
     <BR> <INPUT TYPE="FILE" NAME="testFile" SIZE="40"
                 MAXLENGTH="255"
                 ONFOCUS="selectTest(this)"></P>
   </FORM>
 </BODY>
</HTML>
```

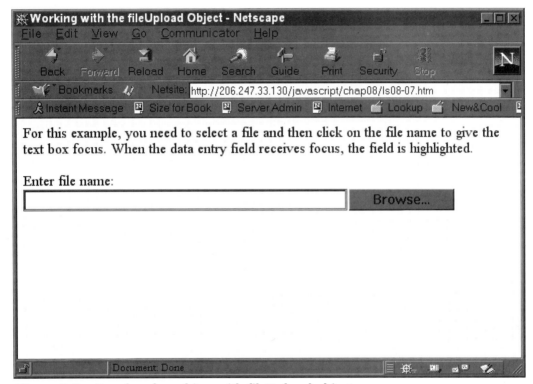

Figure 8.8   Results of working with fileUpload object.

Working with the hidden Object

The hidden object allows you to store data within a form that is not visible to the user. Table 8.14 lists the properties of the `hidden` object. The hidden object has no methods, except for the shared methods of `eval()`, `toString()` and `valueOf()` that are part of every object. Since the `hidden` object does not involve user interaction, there are no event handlers.

Table 8.14 Properties of the hidden Object

Properties	Methods	Event Handlers
form	none	none
name		
type *		
value		

° *New in JavaScript 1.1*

The `hidden` object provides a useful means of passing information to the server. The `hidden` object appears in some of the example scripts used throughout the remainder of this book.

Working with the password Object

The password field is a text field that displays asterisks when the user enters any characters. The `password` object reflects the attributes of the HTML `<INPUT>` tag for passwords. Table 8.15 lists the properties, methods, and event handlers of the `password` object.

Table 8.15 Properties, Methods, and Event Handlers of the password Object

Properties	Methods	Event Handlers
defaultValue	blur()	onBlur
form	focus()	onFocus
name	handleEvent()	
type *	select()	
value		

° *New in JavaScript 1.1*

The `defaultValue` property reflects the initial contents of the VALUE attribute of the HTML `<INPUT>` tag for passwords. Listing 8.8 is a script that illustrates the behavior of the password object. When you run this script, display the properties before entering a password. As shown in Figure 8.9, the defaultValue property does reflect the contents of the VALUE attribute. The script also uses the onFocus event handler to invoke the select() method.

Navigator

The select() method in Microsoft Internet Explorer 4.0 initially selects the contents, but then the browser immediately removes the selection highlight. Netscape Navigator 3.0 behaves in the same manner with regard to this script.

Listing 8.8 Working with the password Object

```
<HTML>
  <HEAD>
    <TITLE>Working with the password Object</TITLE>
<SCRIPT LANGUAGE="JavaScript">
<!--
function dispProp() {
  var msg="Properties of the password object are:"
  msg+="\n\rdefault: "+document.testFrm.pwdObj.defaultValue
  msg+="\n\rname: "+document.testFrm.pwdObj.name
  msg+="\n\rtype: "+document.testFrm.pwdObj.type
  msg+="\n\rvalue: "+document.testFrm.pwdObj.value
  alert(msg)
}
//-->
</SCRIPT>
  </HEAD>
  <BODY>
    <P>Enter a password and then check the properties.</P>
    <FORM NAME="testFrm">
    <P><INPUT TYPE="PASSWORD" NAME="pwdObj" SIZE="10"
            MAXLENGTH="10"
            ONFOCUS="document.testFrm.pwdObj.select()"
            VALUE="test"></P>
    <P><INPUT TYPE="BUTTON" NAME="dispBtn"
            VALUE="Display Password Properties"
            ONCLICK="dispProp()"></P>
    </FORM>
  </BODY>
</HTML>
```

Figure 8.9   Results of working with the password object.

At best, the password field provides minimal security. If you wish to use the password element, you need to consider the following security issues:

- Client-side password verification is out. All the user has to do is view the JavaScript source file to find the correct password.
- Sending the password to the server means that anyone who is capturing packets can easily discover the password. Encrypting the password with JavaScript creates a minor hurdle that merely means looking at the source file to get the encryption algorithm.
- Storing the password in a cookie file saves sending the password over the network, but still leaves it available to anyone who has access to the system or spoofs the identity of the server. Again, encrypting it in JavaScript is only a minor hurdle to someone who really wants access.

If security is important, as it should be, then use a Java applet or plug-in for collecting account names and passwords. A scripting language does not have the features necessary to support adequate authentication.

Working with Buttons

When the browser loads a Web page it creates a `button` object for each element that defines a button form element. Table 8.16 lists the properties, methods, and event handlers of the `button` object.

Table 8.16 Properties, Methods, and Event Handlers of the button Object

Properties	Methods	Event Handlers
form	blur()	onBlur
name	click()	onClick
type *	focus()	onDblClick **
value	handleEvent() **	onFocus
		onMouseDown **
		onMouseUp **

* New in JavaScript 1.1; ** New in JavaScript 1.2

The `value` property contains the text that the browser displays on the face of the button. On the Macintosh and UNIX platforms of Netscape Navigator, the `value` property is a read-only property. However, the Microsoft Windows version of Netscape Navigator allows you to modify this property. When the script is loaded, the size of the button is fixed. Thus, a new string must fit within the size of the button. If the string is too long, only a portion of the text appears in the face of the button.

There is no default action associated with a `button` object. To associate an action with a button, you need to use the `onClick`, `onDblClick`, `onMouseDown`, or `onMouseUp` event handlers. For the sake of compatibility with other browsers, you should always relate the primary action to the `onClick` event handler. The script in Listing 8.9 uses the `event` object and a textarea form element to show the events generated for a button. As shown in Figure 8.10, a single click on the "Click Me" button generates four events. Notice that the mousedown event triggers a focus event and that a mouseup event triggers a click event. In addition, the focus and blur events do not indicate the mouse button, because this property is not set for these events. You can easily modify the script to show the events for other form objects. This is a great way to learn about events, so go ahead and modify the script.

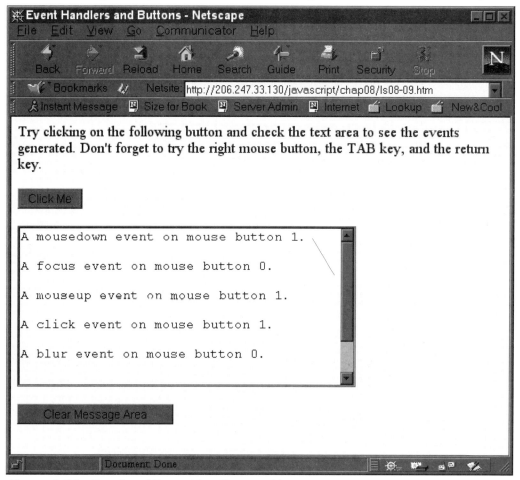

Figure 8.10   Results of Event Handlers and buttons

Navigator

This script works in both Netscape Communicator 4.0 and Microsoft Internet Explorer 4.0. However, MSIE 4.0 does not support the which property for the event object, so the mouse button appears as null.

Listing 8.9 Event Handlers and Buttons

```
<HTML>
  <HEAD>
    <TITLE>Event Handlers and Buttons</TITLE>
<SCRIPT LANGUAGE="JavaScript">
<!--
function dispMsg(ev) {
   var msg="A "+ev.type+" event"
   msg+=" on mouse button "+ev.which
   msg+=".\n\r"
   document.tstFrm.txtBox.value+=msg
}
//-->
</SCRIPT>
  </HEAD>
  <BODY>
    <P>Try clicking on the following button and check
       the text area to see the events generated. Don't
       forget to try the right mouse button, the TAB key,
       and the return key.</P>
    <FORM NAME="tstFrm">
    <P><INPUT TYPE="BUTTON" NAME="tstBtn" VALUE="Click Me"
             ONCLICK="dispMsg(event)"
             ONMOUSEDOWN="dispMsg(event)"
             ONMOUSEUP="dispMsg(event)"
             ONDBLCLICK="dispMsg(event)"
             ONFOCUS="dispMsg(event)"
             ONBLUR="dispMsg(event)"></P>
    <P><TEXTAREA NAME="txtBox" ROWS="10" COLS="40"
               WRAP="Physical"></TEXTAREA></P>
    <P><INPUT TYPE="BUTTON" NAME="clrBtn"
             VALUE="Clear Message Area"
             ONCLICK="document.tstFrm.txtBox.value=''">
             </P>
    </FORM>
  </BODY>
</HTML>
```

Sending Data to the Server

The primary purpose of forms is to collect data from the user that is then sent to the server. The previous sections in this chapter focus on the collection of data using the form object and its elements. This section concentrates on the process of sending the data to the server, which ends the client-side of the client/server equation.

On the server-side, you need to have a means for the server to receive and process the data. The Common Gateway Interface (CGI) is the bridge between the web server and the programs that process the script. The server-side programs themselves are written in a variety of languages ranging from Perl (the most common language used for CGI programs) to UNIX shell scripts. Chapters 12 through 15 of this book discuss how to use server-side JavaScript to create CGI programs. Appendix B contains references to various Web sites that explore other languages used in creating server-side CGI programs.

Validating the Form

JavaScript gives you a means of editing the form prior to sending it to the server. Client-side editing of the form reduces the load on the server and improves performance. Client-side editing does not eliminate the need for server-side editing. For browsers that do not support JavaScript, the CGI script needs to perform editing and must have access to databases that the client-side lacks (such as parts inventory for validating part numbers).

The Netscape developer's site has an excellent collection of scripts for editing forms. The collection of scripts include both US and International forms, a library of JavaScript functions, and a test script. The source code is well documented, so you can easily change it to meet your needs. The code is far too long to reproduce here, but you can find it at the following Web address:

```
http://developer.netscape.com/one/javascript/index.html
```

Although it is a bit long, the script in Listing 8.10 illustrates the editing of a basic name and address form. The script uses the onChange event handler to check for required strings after a change. The onFocus event handler calls the promptMsg() function to display a message in the status bar. The "Submit" button uses the onClick event handler to verify the form before submitting it.

Listing 8.10 An Example Form with Editing

```
<HTML>
  <HEAD>
    <TITLE>An Example Form with Editing</TITLE>
<SCRIPT LANGUAGE="JavaScript">
<!--
// The following variables ensure that string names are
// constant throughout the script
var strGivenName="Given Name (First Name)"
var strFamilyName="Family Name (Last Name)"
var strTitle="Title"
var strCompany="Company"
var strAddress="Street Address"
var strCity="City"
var strStateProvince="State or Province"
var strZip="Postal Code"
var strCountry="Country"
var strPhone="Phone Number"
var strFax="Fax Number"
var strEmail="Email address"
var strPrompt="Please enter your "
var wEmptyPrefix="The field "
var wEmptySuffix=" is required."
var errPhone="The phone number is not valid."
var errEmail="The e-mail address is not valid."
var whitespace=" \t\n\r"
// General functions
function isEmpty(str) {
   if ((str==null) || (str.length==0)) return true
return false
}
function isWhitespace(str) {
   for (var i=1; i<str.length; i++) {
      var chr=str.charAt(i)
      if (whitespace.indexOf(chr)==-1) return false
   }
   return true
}
// Functions that issue warnings
function warnEmpty(elementObj, str) {
   elementObj.focus()
   alert(wEmptyPrefix+str+wEmptySuffix)
```

```
      return false
}
function warnInvalid(elementObj, str) {
   elementObj.focus()
   elementObj.select()
   alert(str)
   return false
}
// edit functions
function isPhoneNumber(phoneStr) {
   if (parseInt(phoneStr)>0) return true
   return false
}
function isEmail(emailStr) {
   if (isWhitespace(emailStr)) return false
   // There needs to be an @ sign after the first
   // character but before the end of the string
   var idx=emailStr.indexOf("@", 1)
   if (idx==-1) return false
   // Need a period to have a domain name
   idx+=2
   if (emailStr.indexOf(".", idx)==-1)
      return false
   return true
}
// event handlers
function promptMsg(msg) {
   self.status=strPrompt+msg
}
function checkStr(theObj, fieldStr, reqField) {
   if (isEmpty(theObj.value)) {
      if (reqField==false) return true
      else return warnEmpty(theObj, fieldStr)
   }
   if (isWhitespace(theObj.value))
      return warnEmpty(theObj, fieldStr)
}
function checkPhone(theObj, fieldStr, reqField) {
   if (isEmpty(theObj.value)) {
      if (reqField == false) return true
      else return warnEmpty(theObj, fieldStr)
   }
   if (!isPhoneNumber(theObj.value))
      return warnInvalid(theObj, errPhone)
   return true
```

```
}
function checkEmail(theObj, reqField) {
   if (isEmpty(theObj.value)) {
      if (reqField==false) return true
      else return warnEmpty(theObj, fieldStr)
   }
   if (isEmail(theObj.value)) return true
   return warnInvalid(theObj, errEmail)
}
function checkForm(frmObj) {
  return(
  checkStr(frmObj.givenName, strGivenName, true) &&
  checkStr(frmObj.familyName, strFamilyName, true) &&
  checkStr(frmObj.Address, strAddress, true) &&
  checkStr(frmObj.City, strCity, true) &&
  checkStr(frmObj.stateProvince, strStateProvince, true) &&
  checkStr(frmObj.Zip, strZip, true) &&
  checkStr(frmObj.Country, strCountry, true) &&
  checkPhone(frmObj.Phone, strPhone, false) &&
  checkPhone(frmObj.Fax, strFax, false) &&
  checkEmail(frmObj.Email, false)
   )
}
//-->
</SCRIPT>
  </HEAD>
  <BODY>
    <P><I>Required fields are marked with an *.</I></P>
    <FORM NAME="userInfo">
    <TABLE BORDER="0">
      <TR>
        <TD COLSTART="1">* Given Name:</TD>
        <TD COLSTART="2">
        <P><INPUT TYPE="TEXT" NAME="givenName" SIZE="20"
            MAXLENGTH="20"
            ONFOCUS="promptMsg(strGivenName)"
            ONCHANGE="checkStr(this, strGivenName, true)">
        </P></TD>
      </TR>
      <TR>
        <TD COLSTART="1">* Family Name:</TD>
        <TD COLSTART="2">
        <P><INPUT TYPE="TEXT" NAME="familyName" SIZE="20"
            MAXLENGTH="20"
            ONCHANGE="checkStr(this, strFamilyName, true)"
```

```
        ONFOCUS="promptMsg(strFamilyName)">
  </P></TD>
</TR>
<TR>
  <TD COLSTART="1">Title:</TD>
  <TD COLSTART="2">
  <P><INPUT TYPE="TEXT" NAME="Title" SIZE="40"
      MAXLENGTH="40" ONFOCUS="promptMsg(strTitle)">
  </P></TD>
</TR>
<TR>
  <TD COLSTART="1">Company Name:</TD>
  <TD COLSTART="2">
  <P><INPUT TYPE="TEXT" NAME="Company" SIZE="40"
      MAXLENGTH="40" ONFOCUS="promptMsg(strCompany)">
  </P></TD>
</TR>
<TR>
  <TD COLSTART="1">* Street Address:</TD>
  <TD COLSTART="2">
  <P><INPUT TYPE="TEXT" NAME="Address" SIZE="40"
      MAXLENGTH="40" ONFOCUS="promptMsg(strAddress)"
      ONCHANGE="checkStr(this, strAddress, true)">
  </P></TD>
</TR>
<TR>
  <TD COLSTART="1">* City:</TD>
  <TD COLSTART="2">
  <P><INPUT TYPE="TEXT" NAME="City" SIZE="25"
      MAXLENGTH="25"
      ONCHANGE="checkStr(this, strCity, true)"
      ONFOCUS="promptMsg(strCity)">
  </P></TD>
</TR>
<TR>
  <TD COLSTART="1">* State or Province:</TD>
  <TD COLSTART="2">
  <P><INPUT TYPE="TEXT" NAME="stateProvince"
      SIZE="30" MAXLENGTH="30"
      ONFOCUS="promptMsg(strStateProvince)"
      ONCHANGE="checkStr(this, strStateProvince, true)">
  </P></TD>
</TR>
<TR>
  <TD COLSTART="1">* Postal Code:</TD>
```

```
      <TD COLSTART="2">
      <P><INPUT TYPE="TEXT" NAME="Zip" SIZE="15"
          MAXLENGTH="15"
          ONCHANGE="checkStr(this, strZip, true)"
          ONFOCUS="promptMsg(strZip)">
      </P></TD>
   </TR>
   <TR>
      <TD COLSTART="1">* Country:</TD>
      <TD COLSTART="2">
      <P><INPUT TYPE="TEXT" NAME="Country" SIZE="30"
          MAXLENGTH="30"
          ONFOCUS="promptMsg(strCountry)"
          ONCHANGE="checkStr(this, strCountry, true)">
      </P></TD>
   </TR>
   <TR>
      <TD COLSTART="1">Phone:</TD>
      <TD COLSTART="2">
      <P><INPUT TYPE="TEXT" NAME="Phone" SIZE="14"
          MAXLENGTH="14"
          ONCHANGE="checkPhone(this, strPhone, false)"
          ONFOCUS="promptMsg(strPhone)">
      </P></TD>
   </TR>
   <TR>
      <TD COLSTART="1">Fax:</TD>
      <TD COLSTART="2">
      <P><INPUT TYPE="TEXT" NAME="Fax" SIZE="14"
          MAXLENGTH="14" ONFOCUS="promptMsg(strFax)"
          ONCHANGE="checkPhone(this, strFax, false)">
      </P></TD>
   </TR>
   <TR>
      <TD COLSTART="1">E-mail:</TD>
      <TD COLSTART="2">
      <P><INPUT TYPE="TEXT" NAME="Email" SIZE="40"
          ONCHANGE="checkEmail(this, false)"
          ONFOCUS="promptMsg(strEmail)">
      </P></TD>
   </TR>
</TABLE>
<P><INPUT TYPE="BUTTON" NAME="submitBtn"
          VALUE="Submit Form"
          ONCLICK="if (checkForm(this.form)) submit()">
```

```
    <INPUT TYPE="BUTTON" NAME="resetBtn"
        VALUE="Clear Form" ONCLICK="reset()"></P>
  </FORM>
 </BODY>
</HTML>
```

The edit script in Listing 8.10 is based on the following criteria:

- It should work on all versions of Netscape Navigator. Consequently, the script uses functions (such as `isEmpty()` and `isEmail()`) to perform tasks that are simple regular expressions.

- The script addresses the international community.

- Variables store all of the string literals, which makes it easier to change a string.

- The event handlers in the script respond to both mouse and keyboard actions. Thus, the user can use the TAB key or mouse to move between fields.

Submitting a Form

The submit button is the HTML method for submitting a form to the server. When the browser loads the HTML document, it creates submit objects that reflect the submit buttons in the document. Table 8.17 lists the properties, methods, and event handlers of the `submit` object.

Table 8.17 Properties, Methods, and Event Handlers of the submit Object

Properties	Methods	Event Handlers
form	blur() *	onBlur *
name	click()	onClick
type *	focus() *	onFocus *
value	handleEvent() **	

° New in JavaScript 1.1; °°New in JavaScript 1.2

The information needed to submit the form to the server is part of the `form` object. In JavaScript 1.2, the `mailto:` and `news:` URL protocols require a signed script with the "`UniversalSendMail`" privilege.

You cannot prevent the submission of a form with the submit button's `onClick` event handler. However, the `onSubmit` event handler of the

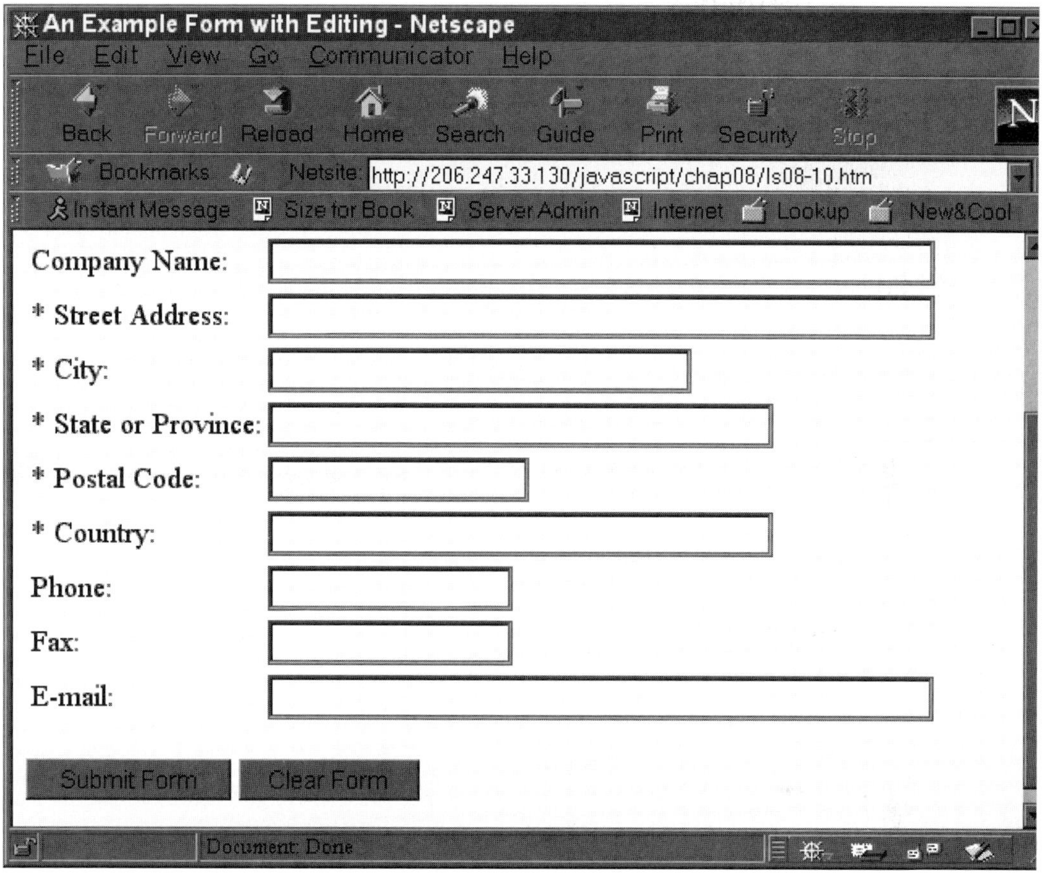

Figure 8.11   Results of example of form with editing.

form object gives you the ability to prevent the submission of a form. If the script in Listing 8.10 used the submit button and the onSubmit event handler invoked the checkForm() function, then a return value of false blocks the submission of the form. If the user disables JavaScript, the submit button causes the submission of the data to the server without any validation of the form elements. When you need to process the form with JavaScript, use the button form element as shown in Listing 8.10. With this technique, the submit() method of the form object causes the browser to submit the data.

Resetting a Form

The reset button is the HTML method for resetting a form to the defaults. When the browser loads an HTML document, it creates `reset` objects that reflect the reset buttons in the document. Table 8.18 lists the properties, methods, and event handlers of the `reset` object.

Table 8.18 Properties, Methods, and Event Handlers of the reset Object

Properties	Methods	Event Handlers
form	blur() *	onBlur *
name	click()	onClick
type *	focus() *	onFocus *
value	handleEvent() **	

* New in JavaScript 1.1; **New in JavaScript 1.2

Once the user clicks the reset button, the `onClick` event handler cannot block the resetting of the form. To query a user before resetting the form, you need to use the button object.

Working with Cookies

Cookies are elements of a distributed database that constitute an important part of client/server interaction. Another alternative is to maintain the same information in a database on the server-side in a centralized database. However, the centralized approach puts an increased load on the server in both increased server traffic and increased disk space. With a distributed database, the client stores the data. Each time the client accesses the server, it passes the data to the server, which can then modify and send back data to update the database. On the client-side, Netscape uses JavaScript to update the database and Microsoft uses Visual Basic. Figure 8.12 illustrates the maintenance of the distributed cookie database.

The server introduces a cookie to the client by including a *Set-Cookie* header as part of an HTTP response. Netscape Navigator stores the cookie in a cookie file. The location of the cookie file varies according to

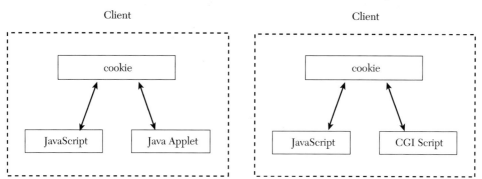

Figure 8.12   The distributed cookie database.

the platform. On the Windows and UNIX platforms, Netscape Navigator maintains the cookie file in the Navigator directory with the name `cookie.txt`. On the Macintosh platform, the MagicCookie file is in the System:Preferences:Netscape folder.

When a client contacts the server, it sends a cookie to the server by including a *Cookie* header as part of the HTTP request. The server-side decides whether to maintain the data in the cookie in its own database or rely strictly on the client to maintain the information.

For Netscape Navigator, all cookies from all servers appear in the one cookie file. The cookie file is a limited database that holds a maximum of 300 total cookies with a maximum size of 4 kilobytes per cookie. Each server or domain is limited to 20 cookies. To optimize the use of the cookie file, each cookie has an expiration date. Once this date expires, Navigator deletes the cookie from the file.

In spite of these limitations, cookies perform an important role in application development. For example, shopping applications can store information about the currently selected items for use in the current session or for future reference. Other applications can store individual preferences for loading Web pages.

Structure of a Cookie

A cookie is a series of name/value pairs that conform to the following syntax:

```
name=value[; EXPIRES=dateValue][; DOMAIN=domainName]
[; PATH=pathname][; SECURE]
```

The `name=value` pair defines the name of a cookie and its value. The semicolon, comma, and white space characters have a special meaning for the processing of cookies. To avoid any confusion, the name should only contain alphanumeric characters, the dash, the underscore, or the period. On the other hand, the value may contain any character as long as special characters are encoded with a method such as the URL %XX style of encoding. You can use the `escape()` function to encode a string and the `unescape()` function to decode the string.

The EXPIRES=dateValue pair defines the valid life time of the cookie. The format of dateValue is as follows:

```
Wdy, DD-Mon-YY HH:MM:SS GMT
```

where:

- Wdy is the day of the week (for example, Mon or Tues)
- DD is the two-digit representation of the day of the month
- Mon is a three-character abbreviation for the month
- YY is the last two digits of the year
- HH:MM:SS specifies the time in hours, minutes, and seconds, respectively

The cookie date format is similar to the date format returned by the `toGMTString()` method of the `date` object, with the exception of dashes between the day, month and year, and that the year in the cookie is only a two digit year.

Navigator automatically deletes a cookie once the expiration date passes. Without the EXPIRE=dateValue pair, the cookie expires as soon as you close Navigator.

Note

Navigator will also delete cookies before their expiration date if the number of cookies exceeds internal limits.

The `DOMAIN=domainName` pair specifies the domain attributes for a valid cookie. If the domainName is the fully qualified domain name of the server, then the cookie is sent to only that server. For more than one server, only hosts within the specified domain can set a cookie for a domain. In addition, any domain ending with com, edu, net, org, gov, mil, or int requires two periods. All other domain names require three periods. The following examples represent valid values for domainName:

```
DOMAIN=.nilenet.com
DOMAIN=.netmedia.co.il
```

The default is to use the domain name of the server which generates the cookie response. The domain name mechanism insures that servers cannot access cookies outside of their domain name.

The `PATH=pathName` pair specifies the path attributes for a valid cookie. Navigator compares the pathname component of the URL to the `pathName` attribute. Navigator uses a string pattern match so that /foo matches `/foobar` and `/foo/index.html`. A pathName attribute of `*/*` matches all paths. The default is to use the pathname of the document that created the cookie.

The `SECURE` attribute of a cookie specifies that Navigator only transmits the cookie if the communication channel to the host is secure. Currently, only HTTPS servers provide the necessary level of security through the Secure Sockets Layer (SSL). Without the SECURE attribute, Navigator will transmit cookies over any channel.

Cookie Processing

A single server response can issue multiple *Set-Cookie* headers. When Navigator saves a cookie with the same PATH and NAME attributes as an existing cookie, the new cookie replaces the existing cookie. If the PATH is the same but the cookie has a different name, Navigator adds the additional cookie. The server can delete a cookie by setting the EXPIRE attribute to a past date.

When sending cookies to the server, Navigator arranges the cookies in a specific order. All cookies with more specific pathnames are sent before cookies with less specific pathnames.

The user has the ability to set the browser preferences to query the user before accepting a cookie from the server. However, Navigator automatically sends valid cookies to the server.

Client-Side JavaScript and Cookies

The `cookie` property of the `document` object is a string that contains all valid cookies for the document. Although you can write your own functions to manage the `cookie` property, it is easier to use one of the public domain set of functions available on the Web. My preference is Bill Dortch's set of cookie functions, which are available at the following Web address:

```
http://www.hidaho.com/cookies/cookie.txt
```

You can get an example script that uses these functions at the following Web address:

```
http://www.hidaho.com/cookies/cookie.html
```

The best way to understand cookies is to experiment with creating, reading, and deleting cookies on the client-side. Since the same cookie functions apply to any application that uses cookies, the first step in creating an example is to make Bill Dortch's cookie function library a JavaScript source file as shown in Listing 8.11. The three primary functions in the library are `GetCookie()`, `SetCookie()`, and `DeleteCookie()`. This script provides extensive documentation of each function, so there is no need to add additional comments.

Listing 8.11 Bill Dortch's Library of Cookie Functions

```
//
// Cookie Functions
// -- "Night of the Living Cookie" Version (25-Jul-96)
//
// Written by:
//     Bill Dortch, hIdaho Design <bdortch@hidaho.com>
// The following functions are released to the public
// domain.
//
// This version takes a more aggressive approach to
// deleting cookies.  Previous versions set the expiration
// date to one millisecond prior to the current time;
// however, this method did not work in Netscape 2.02
// (though it does in earlier and later versions),
// resulting in "zombie" cookies that would not die.
// DeleteCookie now sets the expiration date to the
// earliest usable date (one second into 1970), and sets
// the cookie's value to null for good measure.
//
// Also, this version adds optional path and domain
```

```
//   parameters to the DeleteCookie function.  If you
//   specify a path and/or domain when creating (setting) a
//   cookie**, you must specify the same path/domain when
//   deleting it, or deletion will not occur.
//
//   The FixCookieDate function must now be called
//   explicitly to correct for the 2.x Mac date bug.  This
//   function should be called *once* after a Date object is
//   created and before it is passed (as an expiration date)
//   to SetCookie.  Because the Mac date bug affects all
//   dates, not just those passed to SetCookie, you might
//   want to make it a habit to call FixCookieDate any time
//   you create a new Date object:
//
//     var theDate = new Date();
//     FixCookieDate (theDate);
//
//   Calling FixCookieDate has no effect on platforms other
//   than the Mac, so there is no need to determine the
//   user's platform prior to calling it.
//
//   This version also incorporates several minor coding
//   improvements.
//
//   **Note that it is possible to set multiple cookies with
//   the same name but different (nested) paths.  For
//   example:
//
//     SetCookie ("color","red",null,"/outer");
//     SetCookie ("color","blue",null,"/outer/inner");
//
//   However, GetCookie cannot distinguish between these and
//   will return the first cookie that matches a given name.
//   It is therefore recommended that you *not* use the same
//   name for cookies with different paths.  (Bear in mind
//   that there is *always* a path associated with a cookie;
//   if you don't explicitly specify one, the path of the
//   setting document is used.)
//
//   Revision History:
//
//   "Toss Your Cookies" Version (22-Mar-96)
//   - Added FixCookieDate() function to correct for Mac
//     date bug
//
```

```
//   "Second Helping" Version (21-Jan-96)
//   - Added path, domain and secure parameters to SetCookie
//   - Replaced home-rolled encode/decode functions with
//     Netscape's new (then) escape and unescape functions
//
//     "Free Cookies" Version (December 95)
//
//
//   For information on the significance of cookie
//   parameters, and on cookies in general, please refer to
//   the official cookie spec, at:
//
//      http://www.netscape.com/newsref/std/cookie_spec.html
//
//***********************************************************
//
// "Internal" function to return the decoded value of a
// cookie
//
function getCookieVal (offset) {
  var endstr = document.cookie.indexOf (";", offset);
  if (endstr == -1)
    endstr = document.cookie.length;
  return
    unescape(document.cookie.substring(offset, endstr));
}
//
//   Function to correct for 2.x Mac date bug.  Call this
//   function to fix a date object prior to passing it to
//   SetCookie.
//   IMPORTANT:  This function should only be called *once*
//   for any given date object!
//
function FixCookieDate (date) {
  var base = new Date(0);
  // dawn of (Unix) time - should be 0
  var skew = base.getTime();
  if (skew > 0)  // Except on the Mac - ahead of its time
    date.setTime (date.getTime() - skew);
}
//
//   Function to return the value of the cookie specified
//     name - String object containing the cookie name.
//     returns - String object containing the cookie value,
//       or null if the cookie does not exist.
```

```
//
function GetCookie (name) {
  var arg = name + "=";
  var alen = arg.length;
  var clen = document.cookie.length;
  var i = 0;
  while (i < clen) {
    var j = i + alen;
    if (document.cookie.substring(i, j) == arg)
      return getCookieVal (j);
    i = document.cookie.indexOf(" ", i) + 1;
    if (i == 0) break;
  }
  return null;
}
//
//   Function to create or update a cookie.
//     name - String object containing the cookie name.
//     value - String object containing the cookie value.
//       May contain any valid string characters.
//     [expires] - Date object containing the expiration
//       data of the cookie.  If omitted or null, expires
//       the cookie at the end of the current session.
//     [path] - String object indicating the path for which
//       the cookie is valid. If omitted or null, uses the
//       path of the calling document.
//     [domain] - String object indicating the domain for
//       which the cookie is valid.  If omitted or null,
//       uses the domain of the calling document.
//     [secure] - Boolean (true/false) value indicating
//       whether cookie transmission requires a secure
//       channel (HTTPS).
//
//   The first two parameters are required.  The others, if
//   supplied, must be passed in the order listed above.  To
//   omit an unused optional field, use null as a place
//   holder.  For example, to call SetCookie using name,
//   value and path, you would code:
//
//   SetCookie ("myCookieName", "myCookieValue", null, "/");
//
//   Note that trailing omitted parameters do not require a
//   placeholder.
//
//   To set a secure cookie for path "/myPath", that expires
```

```
//  after the current session, you might code:
//
//  SetCookie (myCVar, cVar, null, "/myPath", null, true);
//
function SetCookie (name,value,expires,path,domain,secure)
{
  document.cookie = name + "=" + escape (value) +
  ((expires) ? "; expires=" + expires.toGMTString() : "") +
  ((path) ? "; path=" + path : "") +
  ((domain) ? "; domain=" + domain : "") +
  ((secure) ? "; secure" : "");
}


//  Function to delete a cookie. (Sets expiration date to
//  start of epoch)
//    name -   String object containing the cookie name
//    path -   String object containing the path of the
//             cookie to delete.  This MUST be the same as
//             the path used to create the cookie, or
//             null/omitted if no path was specified when
//             creating the cookie.
//    domain - String object containing the domain of the
//             cookie to delete.  This MUST be the same as
//             the domain used to create the cookie, or
//             null/omitted if no domain was specified when
//             creating the cookie.
//
function DeleteCookie (name,path,domain) {
  if (GetCookie(name)) {
    document.cookie = name + "=" +
      ((path) ? "; path=" + path : "") +
      ((domain) ? "; domain=" + domain : "") +
      "; expires=Thu, 01-Jan-70 00:00:01 GMT";
  }
}
```

The script in Listing 8.12 provides a form for each of the attributes of a cookie. You can use this form to create, modify (create with new information), read, or delete cookies. To clearly see the different actions, you should clear the form between each action.

Listing 8.12 Working with Cookies

```
<HTML>
  <HEAD>
    <TITLE>Working with Cookies</TITLE>
<SCRIPT LANGUAGE="JavaScript" SRC="ls08-11.js">
<!--
//-->
</SCRIPT>
<SCRIPT LANGUAGE="JavaScript">
<!--
// global strings
var errName="The name field is required."
var expDate=new Date()
// shared functions
function isEmpty(str) {
    return ((str==null) || (str.length==0))
}
function warnInvalid(errObj, str) {
    errObj.focus()
    errObj.select()
    alert(str)
    return false
}
// event handlers
function checkExp(frmObj) {
    if (isEmpty(frmObj.cdate.value)) {
        frmObj.cdate.value=expDate.toLocaleString()
    }
}
function cookieWrite(frmObj) {
    var tmpName=null
    var tmpValue=null
    var tmpDate=null
    var tmpPath=null
    var tmpDomain=null
    var tmpSecure=false
    if (isEmpty(frmObj.cname.value))
        return warnInvalid(frmObj.cname, errName)
    tmpName=frmObj.cname.value
    if (!isEmpty(frmObj.cvalue.value))
        tmpValue=frmObj.cvalue.value
    if (!isEmpty(frmObj.cdate.value)) {
```

```
            tmpDate=new Date(frmObj.cdate.value)
            FixCookieDate(tmpDate) //fix Mac date bug
        }
        if (!isEmpty(frmObj.cpath.value))
            tmpPath=frmObj.cpath.value
        if (!isEmpty(frmObj.cdomain.value))
            tmpPath=frmObj.cdomain.value
        tmpSecure=frmObj.csecure.checked
        SetCookie(tmpName, tmpValue, tmpDate, tmpPath,
                tmpDomain, tmpSecure)
        return true
    }
    function cookieRead(frmObj) {
        if (isEmpty(frmObj.cname.value))
            return warnInvalid(frmObj.cname, errName)
        var tmpValue=GetCookie(frmObj.cname.value)
        frmObj.cvalue.value=tmpValue
        // the getCookie function only returns the value
        // to avoid confusion, all other fields are cleared
        frmObj.cdate.value=""
        frmObj.cpath.value=""
        frmObj.cdomain.value=""
        frmObj.csecure.checked=false
        return true
    }
    function cookieDelete(frmObj) {
        if (isEmpty(frmObj.cname.value))
            return warnInvalid(frmObj.cname, errName)
        return DeleteCookie(frmObj.cname.value)
    }
    //-->
    </SCRIPT>
      </HEAD>
      <BODY>
        <P>This script allows you to write, read, and delete
          cookies.</P>
        <FORM NAME="cookieFrm">
        <TABLE>
          <TR>
            <TD>Name:</TD>
            <TD>
            <P><INPUT TYPE="TEXT" NAME="cname" SIZE="29"></P>
            </TD>
          </TR>
          <TR>
```

```
        <TD>Value:</TD>
        <TD>
        <P><INPUT TYPE="TEXT" NAME="cvalue" SIZE="30"></P>
        </TD>
      </TR>
      <TR>
        <TD>Expires:</TD>
        <TD>
        <P><INPUT TYPE="TEXT" NAME="cdate" SIZE="30"
               ONFOCUS="checkExp(this.form)"></P>
        </TD>
      </TR>
      <TR>
        <TD>Path:</TD>
        <TD>
        <P><INPUT TYPE="TEXT" NAME="cpath" SIZE="30"></P>
        </TD>
      </TR>
      <TR>
        <TD>Domain:</TD>
        <TD>
        <P><INPUT TYPE="TEXT" NAME="cdomain" SIZE="30"></P>
        </TD>
      </TR>
      <TR>
        <TD>Secure:</TD>
        <TD>
        <P><INPUT TYPE="CHECKBOX" NAME="csecure"></P></TD>
      </TR>
    </TABLE>
    <P></P>
    <P><INPUT TYPE="BUTTON" NAME="writeBtn"
               VALUE="Write Cookie"
               ONCLICK="cookieWrite(this.form)">
      <INPUT TYPE="BUTTON" NAME="readBtn"
               VALUE="Read Cookie"
               ONCLICK="cookieRead(this.form)">
      <INPUT TYPE="BUTTON" NAME="delBtn"
               VALUE="Delete Cookie"
               ONCLICK="cookieDelete(this.form)">
      <INPUT TYPE="BUTTON" NAME="clrBtn"
               VALUE="Clear the Form" ONCLICK="reset()"></P>
    </FORM>
  </BODY>
</HTML>
```

The `cookieWrite()` and `cookieDelete()` functions in Listing 8.12 format the information in the form properties for the corresponding functions in the cookie function library. The `cookieRead()` function only reads the value for the cookie name. To return all the attributes would require significant modifications to the `GetCookie()` function. Figure 8.13 shows the screen for this script.

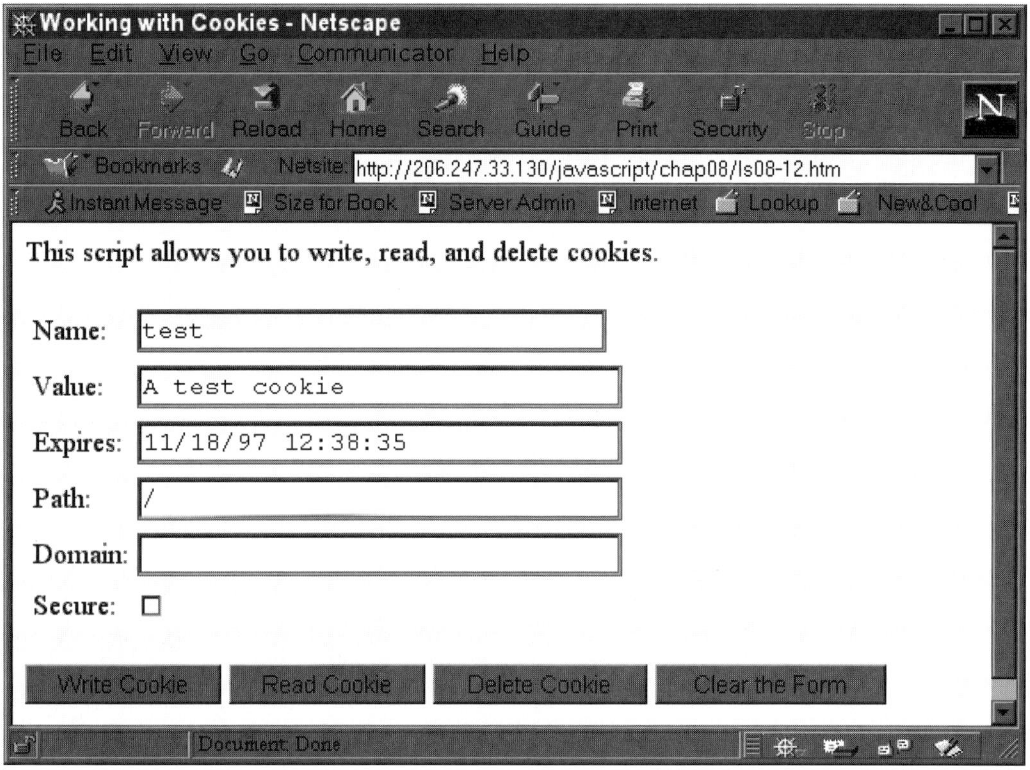

Figure 8.13   Result of working with cookies.

Guidelines for using Cookies

Cookies are a useful, but limited resource. To get the most out of cookies, you need to consider the following:

- Use as few cookies as possible. Since each cookie stores up to 4 Kilobytes of data, you should save multiple items as a single array. To store an array, you need to build the array and then convert it into a string using the `join()` method of the array object. When you retrieve a cookie, you can use the `split()` method of the string object to rebuild the array.

- Keep the expiration date reasonable. The expiration date of a cookie should reflect its useful life.
- Remember to update the expiration date when a user accesses the Web page.
- Cookies are subject to deletion by the browser. Furthermore, installation of a new version of the browser can erase the cookie file.

Summary

The HTML form provides a means for users to enter data and have it submitted to the server, or use it locally. The `form` object reflects the attributes of the HTML `<FORM>` tag. The `elements[]` array of the `form` object contains the objects for each of the elements in the form. The `submit` and `reset` objects reflect their HTML counterparts, and are the only two buttons that have a default action.

JavaScript plays a major role in extending the client-side functionality of forms. Instead of relying on the server, you can use JavaScript to edit the form prior to submission to the server. By using event handlers, the form becomes something more than a static collector of information. By using event handlers, the script responds to the actions of the user. Event handlers tie events to actions such as clicking a button object. Without events, the button object has no actions to perform.

Cookies, although totally independent of forms, provide a mechanism for storing information in a distributed database that each browser maintains. The HTML form collects information and the cookie is one alternative for storing that information. Cookies also allow server-side programs to store information related to the client on the client-side machine.

This chapter looked at a single window and its document. The next chapter explores how to manage documents in multiple windows and frames.

Working with Windows and Frames

Topics in This Chapter

- The role of the navigator object
- Retrieving the properties of the current screen
- Understanding windows and frames
- Changing the URL via the location object
- Using the history object

Chapter 9

The browser determines the environment in which HTML documents are displayed. With each new version of Netscape Navigator, new features are added enhancing your ability to control the environment through JavaScript. Chapter 3, "What Is JavaScript?," introduced the version number extension to the <SCRIPT> tag's LANGUAGE attribute as a means of distinguishing browser versions. This works with Netscape, but not for Microsoft Internet Explorer. JScript in Microsoft Internet Explorer 3.0 is JavaScript 1.0 with some features of JavaScript 1.1. Similarly, JScript in Microsoft Internet Explorer 4.0 is JavaScript 1.1 with some JavaScript 1.2 features. The navigator object provides the information needed to make these distinctions.

While the navigator object describes the browser environment, the window object defines the navigator window in which the browser displays the document. The window object specifies everything from the size of the window to the existence of scroll bars. For all practical purposes, a frame divides the window into smaller windows. Each window or frame has objects for tracking location and history.

This chapter explores the navigator environment and then the window environment. It ends with a discussion of frames and their structure.

Working with the navigator Object

Although the `navigator` object often appears as the parent of the `window` object, this abstraction is a bit misleading. It is better to view the `navigator` object as parallel to the window object, since it does not contain an array of `window` objects. You use the `navigator` object to determine the name and version number of the browser, the MIME types supported by the browser, and the installed plug-ins. Table 9.1 lists the properties and methods of the `navigator` object. The `navigator` object has no event handlers.

Table 9.1 Properties, and Methods of the navigator Object

Properties	Methods	Event Handlers
appCodeName	javaEnabled() *	none
appName	preference() **	
appVersion	taintEnabled() *	
language **		
mimeTypes[] *		
platform **		
plugins[] *		
userAgent		

° New in JavaScript 1.1; °° New in JavaScript 1.2

Properties of the navigator Object

Table 9.2 describes the properties of the `navigator` object. All of the properties of the `navigator` object are read-only properties.

Table 9.2 Description of the navigator Object Properties

Property	Description
appCodeName	A read-only string that specifies the code name of the browser.
appName	A read-only string that specifies the name of the browser.
appVersion	A read-only string that specifies the version information for the browser. For Netscape Navigator 2.0 and 3.0, the format of the string is releaseNumber (platform; country). The releaseNumber is a string that identifies the release level of the browser. The platform indicates which platform the browser is running on (for example, "Win16," or "Win95.") The country is "U" for USA, and "I" for International. For Netscape Communicator 4.0, the format of the string is releaseNumber [language] (platform; country), where language reflects the language property.
language **	A read-only string that indicates the language setting for the browser. The string is either a two character string (for example, "en") or a five character string (for example, "zh_CN").
mimeTypes[] *	A read-only array that reflects the MIME types supported by the browser (see Chapter 10, "Interfacing to Plug-ins and Java Applets" for more details).
platform **	A read-only property that reflects the machine type for which the browser was compiled. The valid platform values include Win16, Win32, Mac68k, MacPPC. Each UNIX platform also has a separate platform identifier. This platform property may differ from the actual machine type for a variety of reasons, such as emulators. For information on how SmartUpdate uses this field, see the document *Using JAR Installation Manager for SmartUpdate*. You can retrieve this document from http://developer.netscape.com/library/documentation/communicator/jarman/index.htm.
plugins[]	A read-only array of the plug-ins installed on the browser (see Chapter 10 for more details).
userAgent	A read-only string that reflects the value of the HTTP user-agent header sent to the server from the client. The server uses this information to identify the client.

* New in JavaScript 1.1; **New in JavaScript 1.2

The script in Listing 9.1 is a simple script that displays the properties of the navigator object. The script excludes the mimeTypes[] and plugins[] properties since Chapter 10 covers them in detail. Figure 9.1 shows the results of running this script in Netscape Communicator 4.04.

Navigator

 Microsoft Internet Explorer also supports the navigator object. However, it uses a different format for the appVersion property after the releaseNumber field. In addition, Microsoft Internet Explorer 4.0 supports the platform property, but not the language property.

Listing 9.1 Displaying the navigator Object Properties

```
<HTML>
  <HEAD>
  <TITLE>Displaying the navigator Object Properties</TITLE>
  </HEAD>
  <BODY>
    <P>This script displays all of the properties of the
      navigator object, except for the mimeType and plugins
      properties.</P>
<SCRIPT LANGUAGE="JavaScript">
<!--
with(document) {
   write("appCodeName: "+navigator.appCodeName+"<BR>")
   write("appName: "+navigator.appName+"<BR>")
   write("appVersion: "+navigator.appVersion+"<BR>")
   write("language: "+navigator.language+"<BR>")
   write("platform: "+navigator.platform+"<BR>")
   write("userAgent: "+navigator.userAgent+"<BR>")
}
//-->
</SCRIPT>
  </BODY>
</HTML>
```

The script in Listing 9.2 contains the getVersion() function which identifies the browser version. Since the release number is always followed by a nonnumeric character, the parseFloat() function extracts only the release number. Figure 9.2 shows the results of running

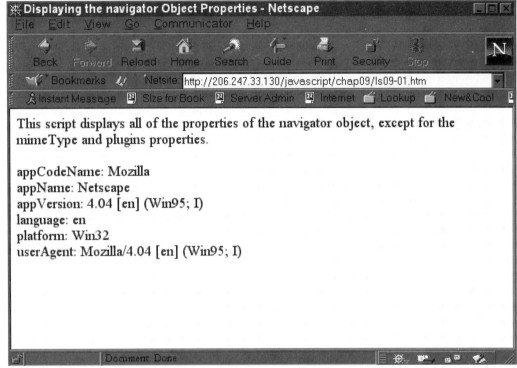

Figure 9.1 *Results of displaying the navigator object properties.*

this script in Netscape Communicator 4.04. When the script is run in Microsoft Internet Explorer 3.0, the release number is 2.0, not 3.0 as you would expect. To select only the major version number, use code similar to the following:

```
navigator.appVersion.substring(0,1)>=3
```

Listing 9.2 Identifying the Browser

```
<HTML>
  <HEAD>
    <TITLE>Identifying the Browser</TITLE>
<SCRIPT LANGUAGE="JavaScript">
<!--
var browserName=null
```

```
var browserVersion=null
function getVersion() {
   if (navigator.appName=="Netscape") browserName="NN"
   else
     if (navigator.appName=="Microsoft Internet Explorer")
       browserName="IE"
   // This field extracts only the numeric portion
   // of the release number.
   browserVersion=parseFloat(navigator.appVersion)
}
//-->
</SCRIPT>
  </HEAD>
  <BODY>
    <P>This script uses the getVersion() function to
      identify the browser version.</P>
<SCRIPT LANGUAGE="JavaScript">
<!--
getVersion()
msg="Your browser is "
if (browserName=="NN") msg+="Netscape Navigator"
if (browserName=="IE") msg+="Microsoft Internet Explorer"
msg+=" version "+browserVersion+"."
document.write(msg)
//-->
</SCRIPT>
  </BODY>
</HTML>
```

Methods of the navigator Object

For security purposes, JavaScript 1.1 added the `javaEnabled()` and `taintEnabled()` methods to the `navigator` object. The `javaEnabled()` method reflects the user preferences and is true when the user enables Java. The `taintEnabled()` method only applies to the security model for JavaScript 1.1 and returns true when the user enables data tainting through the `NS_ENABLE_TAINT` environmental variable. JavaScript 1.2 replaces the data-tainting security model with the signed-object security model, so the `taintEnabled()` always returns false.

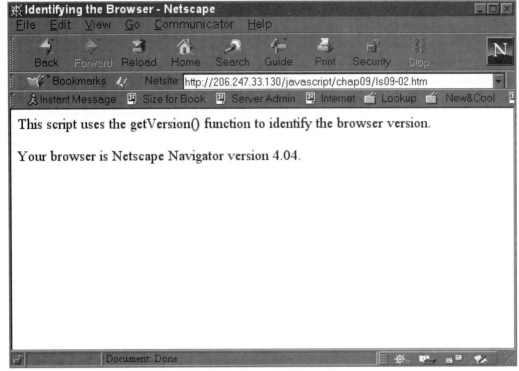

Figure 9.2   Results of Identifying the Browser.

New in JavaScript 1.2

The signed-object security model in JavaScript 1.2 extends the capability of JavaScript to reading and setting certain user preferences via the `preference()` method. The following syntax allows you to read the user preferences:

```
prefValue = navigator.preference(userPref)
```

The syntax to set a user preference is as follows:

```
PrefValue = navigator.preference(userPref, newValue)
```

Table 9.3 lists the user preferences and the values for *userPref* and *newValue* arguments to the `preference()` method. To read the preference you need a signed script with the "`UniversalPreferences-`

`Read`" privilege, and to change a preference you need a signed script with "`UniversalPreferencesWrite`."

Table 9.3 User Preference Values for preference() Method

User Preference	Preference Name (userPref)	Value (newValue)
Automatically load image	`"general.always_load_images"`	Boolean
Enable Java	`"security.enable_java"`	Boolean
Enable JavaScript	`"javascript.enabled"`	Boolean
Enable style sheets	`"browser.enable_style_sheets"`	Boolean
Enable SmartUpdate	`"autoupdate.enabled"`	Boolean
Accept all cookies	`"network.cookie.cookieBehavior"`	Numeric – 0
Accept only cookies that are returned to the originating server	`"network.cookie.cookieBehavior"`	Numeric – 1
Disable cookies	`"network.cookie.cookieBehavior"`	Numeric – 2
Warn before accepting cookie	`"network.cookie.warnAboutCookies"`	Boolean

The script in Listing 9.3 reads and modifies the user preferences defined in Table 9.3. The only new feature present in this script is the statements required for signed scripts. To test this script, you have three choices:

- Execute as a local file. The browser issues a dialogue box asking if you want to grant the requested privileges as shown in Figure 9.3.
- Execute from a server without signing the script. This option requires that you allow granting privileges based on the server by adding the following line to the Netscape preferences file:

```
user_pref("signed.applets.codebase_principal_support", true)
```

- Sign the script according to the information in Chapter 16, "JavaScript Tools."

When you run this script, review the drop-down menus on Netscape Communicator's menu bar. Notice that the options are restricted to prevent security violations.

Listing 9.3 Modifying User Preferences

```
<HTML>
  <HEAD>
    <TITLE>Modifying User Preferences</TITLE>
<SCRIPT LANGUAGE="JavaScript1.2" ARCHIVE="ls09-03.jar"
       ID="1">
<!--
function getPref() {
 netscape.security.PrivilegeManager.enablePrivilege(
   "UniversalPreferencesRead")
 document.userPref.autoLoad.checked=navigator.preference(
   "general.always_load_images")
 document.userPref.enableJava.checked=navigator.preference(
    "security.enable_java")
 document.userPref.enableJS.checked=navigator.preference(
   "javascript.enabled")
 document.userPref.enableCSS.checked=navigator.preference(
   "browser.enable_style_sheets")
 document.userPref.autoUpdate.checked=navigator.preference(
   "autoupdate.enabled")
 document.userPref.cookieBtn[navigator.preference(
   "network.cookie.cookieBehavior")].checked=true
 document.userPref.warnCookie.checked=navigator.preference(
   "network.cookie.warnAboutCookies")
}
function setPref() {
 netscape.security.PrivilegeManager.enablePrivilege(
   "UniversalPreferencesWrite")
 navigator.preference("general.always_load_images",
   document.userPref.autoLoad.checked)
 navigator.preference("security.enable_java",
   document.userPref.enableJava.checked)
 navigator.preference("javascript.enabled",
   document.userPref.enableJS.checked)
 navigator.preference("browser.enable_style_sheets",
   document.userPref.enableCSS.checked)
 navigator.preference("autoupdate.enabled",
   document.userPref.autoUpdate.checked)
 for (var i=0; i<3; i++) {
   if (document.userPref.cookieBtn[i].checked) {
   navigator.preference("network.cookie.cookieBehavior", i)
   break
```

```
    }
  }
  navigator.preference("network.cookie.warnAboutCookies",
    document.userPref.warnCookie.checked)
}
//-->
</SCRIPT>
  </HEAD>
  <BODY>
    <P>This example uses a signed script and the
      navigator.preference() method to read or update user
      preferences.</P>
    <FORM NAME="userPref">
    <TABLE>
      <TR>
        <TD WIDTH="36">
        <P><INPUT TYPE="CHECKBOX" NAME="autoLoad"></P></TD>
        <TD WIDTH="455">Automatically load images</TD>
      </TR>
      <TR>
        <TD WIDTH="36">
        <P><INPUT TYPE="CHECKBOX"
                  NAME="enableJava"></P></TD>
        <TD WIDTH="455">Enable Java</TD>
      </TR>
      <TR>
        <TD WIDTH="36">
        <P><INPUT TYPE="CHECKBOX" NAME="enableJS"></P></TD>
        <TD WIDTH="455">Enable JavaScript</TD>
      </TR>
      <TR>
        <TD WIDTH="36">
        <P><INPUT TYPE="CHECKBOX"
                  NAME="enableCSS"></P></TD>
        <TD WIDTH="455">Enable Style Sheets</TD>
      </TR>
      <TR>
        <TD WIDTH="36">
        <P><INPUT TYPE="CHECKBOX"
                  NAME="autoUpdate"></P></TD>
        <TD WIDTH="455">Enable SmartUpdate</TD>
      </TR>
      <TR>
        <TD WIDTH="36">
        <P><INPUT TYPE="RADIO" NAME="cookieBtn" VALUE="0"
```

```
                       CHECKED="CHECKED"></P></TD>
      <TD WIDTH="455">Accept all cookies</TD>
    </TR>
    <TR>
      <TD WIDTH="36">
      <P><INPUT TYPE="RADIO" NAME="cookieBtn"
                VALUE="1"></P></TD>
      <TD WIDTH="455">Accept cookies only from
           originating server</TD>
    </TR>
    <TR>
      <TD WIDTH="36">
      <P><INPUT TYPE="RADIO" NAME="cookieBtn"
           VALUE="2"></P></TD>
      <TD WIDTH="455">Disable Cookies</TD>
    </TR>
    <TR>
      <TD WIDTH="36">
      <P><INPUT TYPE="CHECKBOX"
                NAME="warnCookie"></P></TD>
      <TD WIDTH="455">Warn before accepting cookies</TD>
    </TR>
    </TABLE>
    <P><INPUT TYPE="BUTTON" NAME="readBtn"
             VALUE="Read User Preferences"
             ONCLICK="getPref()"></P>
    <P><INPUT TYPE="BUTTON" NAME="updateBtn"
             VALUE="Update User Preferences"
             ONCLICK="setPref()"></P>
    </FORM>
  </BODY>
</HTML>
```

New in JavaScript 1.2

The Windows Environment

The screen object is a built-in object that contains information about the display screen. Table 9.4 lists the properties of the screen object. All the properties of the screen object are read-only. The screen object has no methods or event handlers.

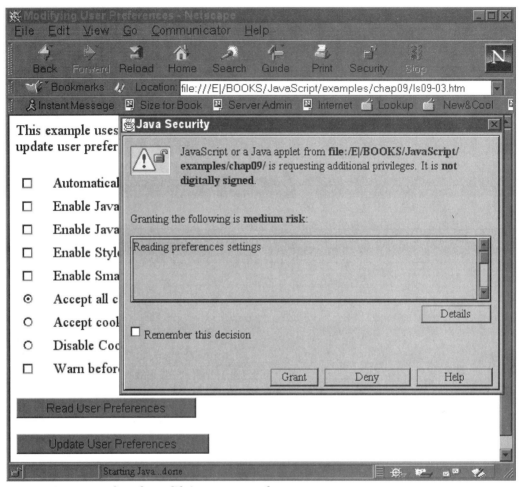

Figure 9.3   Results of modifying user preferences.

Table 9.4 Properties of the screen Object

Properties	Description
availHeight	Returns the available height, in pixels, of the display screen. The availHeight excludes any permanent or semi-permanent features such as the taskbar in Windows 95.

Table 9.4 Properties of the screen Object *(Continued)*

Properties	Description
availWidth	Returns the available width, in pixels, of the display screen. The avail-Width excludes any permanent or semi-permanent features such as the taskbar in Windows 95.
colorDepth	Returns the number of bits per pixel used in the color palette. If there is no color palette, the value is the same as the pixelDepth property.
height	Returns the height of the display screen, in pixels.
pixelDepth	Specifies the number of bits per pixel for the display screen. The pixelDepth is related to the colorDepth, since the number of bits per pixel determine the number of colors.
width	Returns the width of the display screen, in pixels.

The script in Listing 9.4 displays the properties of the current screen. Figure 9.4 shows the results of running this script in Netscape Communicator 4.04 for Windows 95. Microsoft Internet Explorer 4.0 also has a screen object, which has the same properties except for the pixelDepth property. These properties provide valuable information for the resizing of windows and for determining the number of colors the client system supports when displaying images.

Listing 9.4 Displaying the Properties of the screen Object

```
<HTML>
  <HEAD>
    <TITLE>
    Displaying the Properties of the screen Object
    </TITLE>
  </HEAD>
  <BODY>
    <P>The properties of the current screen are as follows:
    </P>
<SCRIPT LANGUAGE="JavaScript1.2">
<!--
with (document) {
   write("Screen Height: "+screen.height+"<BR>")
   write("Screen Width: "+screen.width+"<BR>")
```

```
    write("Available Height: "+screen.availHeight+"<BR>")
    write("Available Width: "+screen.availWidth+"<BR>")
    write("Color Depth: "+screen.colorDepth+"<BR>")
    write("Pixel Depth: "+screen.pixelDepth+"<BR>")
}
//-->
</SCRIPT>
  </BODY>
</HTML>
```

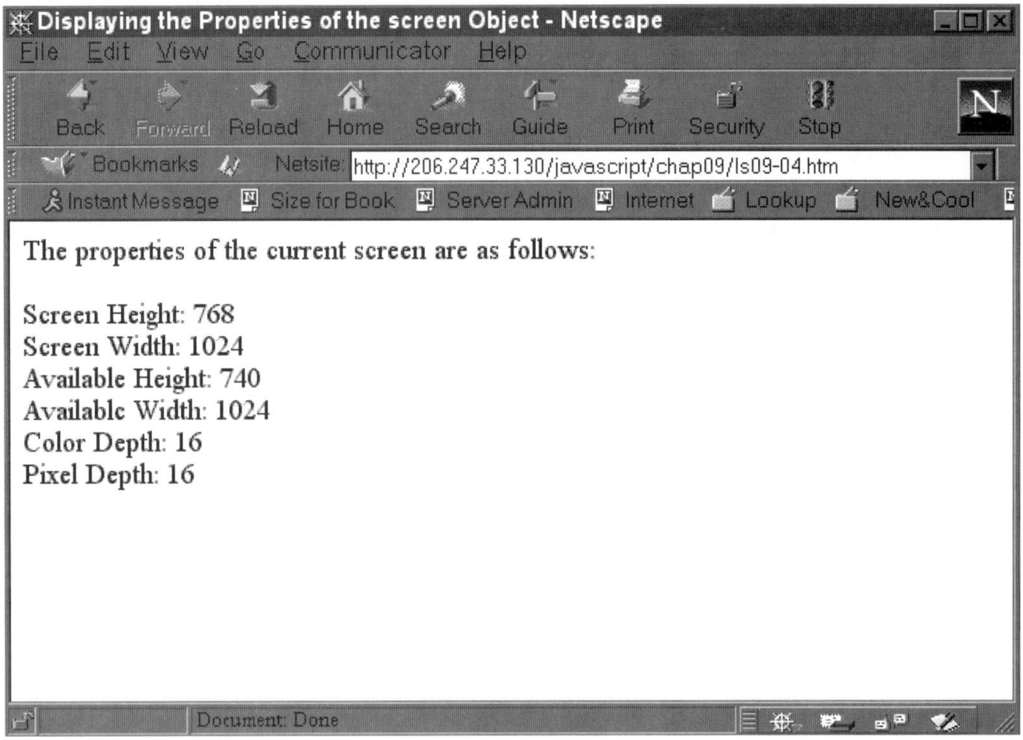

Figure 9.4   Results of Displaying Properties of the Screen Object.

Working with Windows

The document views the window as the parent object, since the document object is a property of the window object. The browser creates a window object for each <BODY> or <FRAMESET> tag that it encounters. Each <FRAME> within a <FRAMESET> also creates a window object. You can also create a new window with the window.open() method. As shown in Table 9.5, the window object contains a rich collection of properties, methods, and event handlers.

Table 9.5 Properties, Methods, and Event Handlers of the window Object

Properties	Methods	Event Handlers
closed *	alert()	onBlur *
defaultStatus	back() **	onDragDrop **
document	blur() *	onError *
frames[]	captureEvents() **	onFocus *
history *	clearInterval() **	onLoad
innerHeight **	clearTimeout()	onMove **
innerWidth **	close()	onResize **
length	confirm()	onUnload
location	disableExternalCapture() **	
locationbar **	enableExternalCapture() **	
menubar **	find() **	
name	focus() *	
opener *	forward() **	
outerHeight **	handleEvent() **	
outerWidth **	home() **	
pageXOffset **	moveBy() **	
pageYOffset **	moveTo() **	
parent	open()	
personalbar **	print() **	
scrollbars **	prompt()	
self	releaseEvents() **	
status	resizeBy() **	
statusbar **	resizeTo() **	
toolbar **	routeEvent() **	
top	scroll() *	
window	scrollBy() **	
	scrollTo() **	

Table 9.5 Properties, Methods, and Event Handlers of the window Object *(Continued)*

Properties	Methods	Event Handlers
	setInterval() **	
	setTimeout()	
	stop() **	

* New in JavaScript 1.1; ** New in JavaScript 1.2

For properties and methods, the current window is the point of reference. Consequently, you can refer to a property or method without the object reference. For the sake of readability, it is good programming practice to refer to the current window object as either window or self. The following examples are all valid references for the alert() method:

- alert()
- window.alert()
- self.alert()

Some methods, such as the open() method, are methods of more than one object. Although open(), by itself, refers to the window object, the reference to window.open() clearly separates the window method from document.open(). When working with event handlers, the object reference becomes important, as the context for an event handler is the parent of the object receiving the event. For example, the context for an event handler of a button object is the document object. In this context, the open() method, by itself, refers to document.open(). Therefore, to avoid any confusion as to the method referenced, it is better to include the object reference. When the window contains no frames, top and parent are synonyms for the current window. The section "Working with Frames" in this chapter describes the meaning of these properties in the frame environment.

The large number of properties and methods for the window object necessitates dividing them into logical groups for discussion. As the number of double asterisks in Table 9.5 indicates, many of the properties and methods are new in JavaScript 1.2.

Displaying of Status Messages

Table 9.6 lists the properties that display messages in the status bar. When you display a message in the status bar, remember that the browser also uses the status bar to display messages to the user. When you use the status bar to display a scrolling message, you prevent the user from seeing important browser messages.

Table 9.6 Properties that Display Messages in the Status Bar

Property	Description
defaultStatus	The defaultStatus message appears in the status bar when no other message appears in the status bar. When you use the defaultStatus property with the onMouseOver or onMouseOut event handlers, the event handler must return true before the message appears in the status bar.
Status	The status message is a priority or transient message that appears in the status bar. When you use the status property with an onMouseOver event handler, the event handler must return true before the message appears in the status bar.

The script in Listing 9.5 illustrates the difference between the status property and the defaultStatus property. The link uses the onMouseOver event handler to display a message in the status bar using the status property, while the onMouseOut event handler clears the message in the status property. The text boxes and their associated buttons provide the opportunity to experiment by entering different text. When you click the "Display Text in Status Bar" button, the browser displays the text in the self.status property. As soon as you move off the button, the browser clears the text from the status bar. This behavior illustrates the transient nature of the message in self.status. On the other hand, when you click the "Set Default Status Text" button, the browser displays the text you entered as default text. This text appears when there is no other message to display. Figure 9.5 shows the results of setting the defaultStatus property.

Listing 9.5 Displaying Messages in the Status Bar

```
<HTML>
  <HEAD>
    <TITLE>Displaying Messages in the Status Bar</TITLE>
  </HEAD>
  <BODY>
    <P>Move the mouse over the following link and check the
      message in the status bar:
      <A HREF=" <A HREF="http://developer.netscape.com/"
ONMOUSEOVER="self.status='Netscape Developer Site'; return true"
ONMOUSEOUT="self.status=''; return true">Netscape
        Developer Site</A>
      ONMOUSEOVER="self.status='Netscape Developer Site';
      return true"
      ONMOUSEOUT="self.status=''; return true">
      Netscape Developer Site</A></P>
    <FORM NAME="statusTest">
    <TABLE>
      <TR>
        <TD>Enter some text to display with the status
          property:</TD>
        <TD>
        <P><INPUT TYPE="TEXT" NAME="statText" SIZE="30">
        </P></TD>
      </TR>
      <TR>
        <TD></TD>
        <TD>
        <P><INPUT TYPE="BUTTON" NAME="dispStatBtn"
          VALUE="Display Text in Status Bar"
          ONCLICK="self.status=this.form.statText.value">
        </P></TD>
      </TR>
      <TR>
        <TD>Enter some text to display as the default text
          in the status bar:</TD>
        <TD>
        <P><INPUT TYPE="TEXT" NAME="defaultText" SIZE="30">
        </P></TD>
      </TR>
      <TR>
        <TD></TD>
```

Working with Windows **367**

```
       <TD>
       <P><INPUT TYPE="BUTTON" NAME="setDefaultBtn"
          VALUE="Set Default Status Text"
  ONCLICK="self.defaultStatus=this.form.defaultText.value">
       </P></TD>
     </TR>
     <TR>
       <TD></TD>
       <TD>
       <P><INPUT TYPE="BUTTON"
          NAME="clearDefaultBtn"
          VALUE="Clear Default Status Text"
          ONCLICK="self.defaultStatus=''"></P></TD>
     </TR>
   </TABLE></FORM>
 </BODY>
</HTML>
```

Using Dialog Boxes

The window object provides the three methods shown in Table 9.7 as a means of communicating with the user. You cannot change the title of the dialog box or the text that appears in the buttons. If you want more control over the content of a dialog box, you need to use the window.open() method to construct your own dialog box.

Table 9.7 Window Methods that display Dialog Boxes

Method	Description
alert()	Displays an alert dialog box with a message. You use the alert() method when you do not require the user to make a decision. The syntax for the alert() method is as follows: alert(*message*)
confirm()	Displays a confirm dialog box with a message. The confirm() method returns true if the user clicks the "OK" button and false if the user clicks the "Cancel" button. The syntax for the confirm() method is as follows: confirm(*message*)

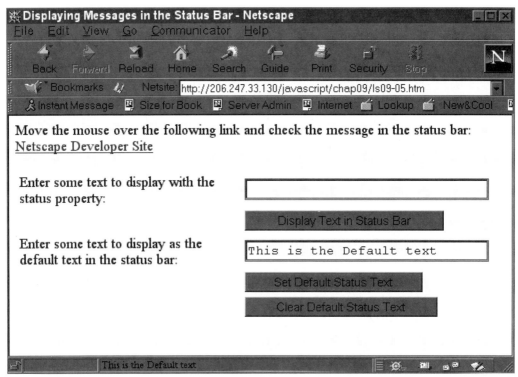

Figure 9.5 *Results of displaying messages in the status bar.*

Table 9.7 Window Methods that display Dialog Boxes *(Continued)*

Method	Description
prompt()	Displays a prompt dialog box with a message and input field. The *prompt()* method returns the text entered in the input field of the dialog box. The syntax for the *prompt()* method is as follows: prompt(message, initialValue) If you do not specify an initialValue, the dialog box displays <undefined>.

The script in Listing 9.6 illustrates different uses for dialog boxes. The script starts as a simple demonstration of different dialog boxes. However, the browser's unusual management of events results in the adding of a textarea box to track events. Clicking on the event "Check Field" button generates a change event, but does not generate a click event. If you click on any other area, you get the change event and the effect of a mousedown and mouseup events for selecting text. The script behaves the same way in Microsoft Internet Explorer 4.0, so this script needs further analysis in a later section on "Events for the window Object." Figure 9.6 shows the results of clicking on the "Check Field" button.

Listing 9.6 Using Dialog Boxes

```
<HTML>
  <HEAD>
    <TITLE>Using Dialog Boxes</TITLE>
<SCRIPT LANGUAGE="JavaScript">
<!--
var oldValue=""
function evMsg(evType, evTarget) {
   var msgStr=""
   msgStr+="A "+evType+" event"
   msgStr+=" was received for the "+evTarget
   msgStr+=" object.\n\r"
   document.testFrm.evBox.value+=msgStr
}
function clearFields(ev) {
   document.testFrm.someText.value=""
   document.testFrm.evBox.value=""
   return true
}
function saveOld(fieldObj, ev) {
   evMsg(ev.type, ev.target.type)
   oldValue=fieldObj.value
   fieldObj.focus()
   fieldObj.select()
   return true
}
function keepChange(fieldObj, ev) {
   evMsg(ev.type, ev.target.type)
   if (!confirm("Keep the change?"))
      fieldObj.value=oldValue
   return false
}
function checkField(frmObj, ev) {
   evMsg(ev.type, ev.target.type)
```

```
    if (frmObj.someText.value=="") {
       alert("The field is empty")
       frmObj.someText.focus()
       return false
    }
    alert("the field contains: "+frmObj.someText.value)
    return true
}
//-->
</SCRIPT>
  </HEAD>
  <BODY ONLOAD="clearFields(event)">
<SCRIPT LANGUAGE="JavaScript">
<!--
document.write("<P>Hello "
        +prompt("Please enter your name.", "anonymous")
        +",</P>")
//-->
</SCRIPT>
    <P>Enter some text in the following box and then click
      the &quot;Check Field&quot; button. Delete the text
      you entered and click the button again.</P>
    <FORM NAME="testFrm">
    <P>Enter text in this box: <INPUT TYPE="TEXT"
      NAME="someText" SIZE="30"
      ONCHANGE="keepChange(this, event)"
      ONFOCUS="saveOld(this, event)"></P>
    <P><INPUT TYPE="BUTTON" NAME="checkText"
       VALUE="Check Field"
       ONCLICK="checkField(this.form, event)"></P>
    <P><TEXTAREA NAME="evBox" ROWS="10" COLS="50"
       WRAP="Off"></TEXTAREA></P>
    </FORM>
  </BODY>
</HTML>
```

Opening and Closing Windows

When you open a new window from JavaScript, you have the ability to define the document loaded into the window, the name of the window, and the characteristics of the window. The syntax for the open() method of the window object is as follows:

winVar = winObj.open(*URL, windowName, features*)

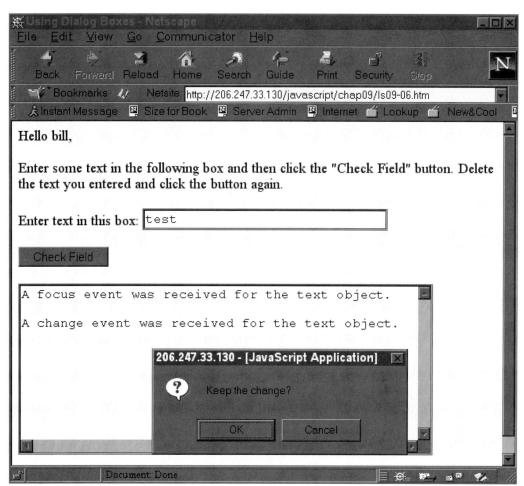

Figure 9.6   Results of using dialog boxes.

The *winVar* variable holds the new window object, or null, if the open() method fails. You use *winVar* to reference a window object. The *windowName* parameter only applies to referencing a window via the TARGET attribute in a <FORM> or <A> tag. The *winObj* reference is the name of an existing window: self, window, top, parent, or the name of a window object. The *winObj* reference determines the parent window for the new window.

The *URL* defines the document that the browser is to load into the new window. If the URL is an empty string, then the window has no document. However, there are no event handlers until a window contains a document. You can also use the empty URL to create an object reference to an existing window, which then allows you to access the properties of the window.

The *features* parameter is a comma-separated string that defines the characteristics of the new window. Table 9.8 lists the features, their data type, default value, and a brief description for the open() method.

Table 9.8 Features of the open() Method

Feature	Data Type	Default	Description
alwaysLowered **	Binary	no	If yes, the window always appears below all other windows, even when the window is active. This feature requires a signed script.
alwaysRaised **	Binary	no	If yes, the window always appears above all other windows, even when the window is not active. This feature requires a signed script.
dependent **	Binary	no	If no, the window is not a child of the current window. A dependent window automatically closes when the parent window closes, and does not appear in the task bar on the Windows platform.
directories	Binary	yes	If yes, the new window includes the director bar, also called the personal toolbar.
height	Numeric		For JavaScript 1.0 and 1.1; specifies the height of the viewing area of the window in pixels. JavaScript 1.2 uses the innerHeight feature in place of the height feature. The feature continues to exist for backward compatibility.
hotkeys **	Boolean	yes	If no, most hotkeys in the new window that have menu bars, are disabled. The security and exit hotkey remain enabled.
innerHeight **	Numeric		Specifies the height of the window's viewing area in pixels. A value of less than 100 pixels requires a signed script.
innerWidth **	Numeric		Specifies the width of the window's viewing area in pixels. A value of less than 100 pixels requires a signed script.
location	Boolean	yes	If yes, the window includes the location, or URL bar.

Table 9.8 Features of the open() Method *(Continued)*

Feature	Data Type	Default	Description
menubar	Boolean	yes	If yes, the window includes the menu bar.
outerHeight **	Numeric		Specifies the height of the entire window and takes precedence over the innerHeight, if both are set. A value of less than 100 pixels requires a signed script.
outerWidth **	Numeric		Specifies the width of the entire window and takes precedence over the innerWidth, if both are set. A value of less than 100 pixels requires a signed script.
resizable	Boolean	yes	If yes, allows a user to resize the window.
screenX **	Numeric		Specifies the distance, in pixels, from the left edge of the screen to the left edge of the window. A value that forces the window to go off-screen requires a signed script.
screenY **	Numeric		Specifies the distance, in pixels, from the top of the screen to the top edge of the window. A value that forces the window to go off-screen requires a signed script.
scrollbars	Boolean	yes	If yes, the browser creates horizontal and vertical scroll bars when the text exceeds the dimensions of the viewing area.
status	Boolean	yes	If yes, the window includes a status bar.
titlebar **	Boolean	yes	If yes, the window includes a title bar. Changing the value requires a signed script.
toolbar	Boolean	yes	If yes, the window includes a tool bar.
Width	Numeric		For JavaScript 1.0 and 1.1, specifies the width of the viewing area of the window in pixels. JavaScript 1.2 uses the innerWidth feature in place of the width feature. The feature continues to exist for backward compatibility.
z-lock **	Boolean	no	If yes, the new window does not rise above other windows when activated. This feature requires a signed script.

***New in JavaScript 1.2*

The *features* string has the following requirements:

- The binary values are yes (1) and no (0). Not specifying a value is the same as yes. Thus, the following are equivalent phrases:
  ```
  toolbar
  toolbar=yes
  toolbar=1
  ```
- It is a quoted string with no embedded spaces. For example,

```
"directories=yes,location=yes,menubar=yes"
```

- If *windowName* does not specify an existing window and you do not provide the *features* parameter, the features follow the defaults shown in Table 9.8.
- If *windowName* does not specify an existing window and you do set at least one Boolean feature in the *features* parameter, all the remaining Boolean features are set to no except for title-bar and hotkeys parameters, which remain yes.

The behavior of `alwaysLowered`, `alwaysRaised`, and `z-lock` depends on the platform as follows:

- For Windows, `alwaysLowered` and `z-lock` are always below all windows open in all applications.
- For Macintosh, `alwaysLowered` and `z-lock` are below all browser windows, but not necessarily below all applications.
- The `alwaysRaised` feature behaves in a similar manner.

Before presenting example scripts showing how to use the `open()` method for the `window` object, we need to discuss the `close()` method, the `opener` property, and the `closed` property. The syntax for the `close()` method is as follows:

```
winObj.close()
```

The behavior of the `close()` method varies with each version of the browser as follows:

- In Netscape Navigator 2.0, `close()` method closes any window.
- In Netscape Navigator 3.0, the `close()` method closes only those windows opened by the `open()` method.
- In Netscape Communicator 4.0, the `close()` method in a signed script can unconditionally close any window. The `close()` method in an unsigned script can only close win-

dows opened by the open() method.

- In Netscape Navigator 3.0 and Netscape Communicator 4.0, any attempt to close a window not opened by the open() method generates a user confirmation dialog box. This is a security measure to prevent "mail bombs" that contain a self.close().

If you set the dependent feature equal to yes, the open() method forms a parent/child relationship with the new window. Of course, the child window can open another window, and Netscape Communicator allows a maximum of 100 open windows, which is more than sufficient. With dependent windows, the closing of a parent window closes all children.

On the other hand, if the dependent feature is equal to no, then closing the parent does not close the child, and the parent window object remains. This occurs because the opener property contains an object reference to the window from which it is opened. This is where the closed property comes to play, since it indicates whether the window object represents an open or a closed window. If the parent window is closed, then the child window needs to set the opener property to null to release the parent window object to the browser's garbage collection mechanism. The following snippet shows how you might accomplish this:

```
if (window.opener.closed) window.opener=null
```

You could also use the opener property to reference any property in the parent window, for example:

```
window.opener.document.bgcolor="white"
```

Table 9.9 Window Properties related to Opening and Closing Windows

Property	Description
closed	A Boolean read-only property that returns true when the window is closed.
name	A read/write property that identifies the name of the window for reference by the TARGET attribute in the <FORM> or <A> tags. The name is limited to alphanumeric characters and the underscore (_). It is not the name used in a *winObj* reference.
opener	A read/write property that specifies the *window* object that opened the window. The property is undefined for a window opened by the browser. To release a parent *window* object after the parent is closed, you can set the opener property to null.

Although you cannot use the `name` property to reference a `window` object, you can use it to establish a reference to the `window` object as shown in the following example:

```
WinObj = window.open("", "winName")
```

The script in Listing 9.7 allows you to experiment with setting different parameters for opening a new window. Each window that it opens uses the same document, so you can open multiple windows. The script also contains buttons to close the window, check the status of the closed property in the parent window, close the parent window, and release the parent `window` object.

Listing 9.7 Opening and Closing Windows

```
<HTML>
  <HEAD>
    <TITLE>Opening and Closing Windows</TITLE>
<SCRIPT LANGUAGE="JavaScript">
<!--
var parentName="undefined"
var win_obj=new Array()
var winNameErr="Please enter a name for the window."
var errNum="Not an interger."
var intPat=/^\d+$/
function warnError (fieldObj, errMsg) {
   alert(errMsg)
   fieldObj.focus()
   fieldObj.select()
   return false
}
function isEmpty(str) {
   return(str==null || str=="")
}
function isInteger(str) {
   return intPat.test(str)
}
function needComma(str) {
   if (str!="") return ","
   return ""
}
function openWin(frmObj) {
```

```
if (isEmpty(frmObj.winName.value))
    return warnError(frmObj.winName, winNameErr)
if (!frmObj.winFeatures.checked) {
    win_obj[win_obj.length]=window.open("ls09-07.htm",
        frmObj.winName.value)
    return true
}
var featureStr=""
if (frmObj.winDependent.checked)
    featureStr+="dependent=yes"
if (frmObj.winDirectories.checked)
    featureStr+=needComma(featureStr)+"directories=yes"
if (frmObj.winHotkeys.checked)
    featureStr+=needComma(featureStr)+"hotkeys=yes"
if (frmObj.winLocation.checked)
    featureStr+=needComma(featureStr)+"location=yes"
if (frmObj.winMenubar.checked)
    featureStr+=needComma(featureStr)+"menubar=yes"
if (frmObj.winResizable.checked)
    featureStr+=needComma(featureStr)+"resizable=yes"
if (frmObj.winScrollbars.checked)
    featureStr+=needComma(featureStr)+"scrollbars=yes"
if (frmObj.winStatus.checked)
    featureStr+=needComma(featureStr)+"status=yes"
if (frmObj.winToolbar.checked)
    featureStr+=needComma(featureStr)+"toolbar=yes"
if (!isEmpty(frmObj.winInnerHeight.value)) {
    if (isInteger(frmObj.winInnerHeight.value)) {
        featureStr+=needComma(featureStr)+"innerHeight="
        featureStr+=frmObj.winInnerHeight.value
    }
    else return warnError(frmObj.winInnerHeight, errNum)
}
if (!isEmpty(frmObj.winInnerWidth.value)) {
    if (isInteger(frmObj.winInnerWidth.value)) {
        featureStr+=needComma(featureStr)+"innerWidth="
        featureStr+=frmObj.winInnerWidth.value
    }
    else return warnError(frmObj.winInnerWidth, errNum)
}
if (!isEmpty(frmObj.winOuterHeight.value)) {
    if (isInteger(frmObj.winOuterHeight.value)) {
        featureStr+=needComma(featureStr)+"outerHeight="
        featureStr+=frmObj.winOuterHeight.value
    }
```

```
        else return warnError(frmObj.winOuterHeight, errNum)
    }
    if (!isEmpty(frmObj.winOuterWidth.value)) {
        if (isInteger(frmObj.winOuterWidth.value)) {
            featureStr+=needComma(featureStr)+"outerWidth="
            featureStr+=frmObj.winOuterWidth.value
        }
        else return warnError(frmObj.winOuterWidth, errNum)
    }
    if (!isEmpty(frmObj.winScreenX.value)) {
        if (isInteger(frmObj.winScreenX.value)) {
            featureStr+=needComma(featureStr)+"screenX="
            featureStr+=frmObj.winScreenX.value
        }
        else return warnError(frmObj.winScreenX, errNum)
    }
    if (!isEmpty(frmObj.winScreenY.value)) {
        if (isInteger(frmObj.winScreenY.value)) {
            featureStr+=needComma(featureStr)+"screenY="
            featureStr+=frmObj.winScreenY.value
        }
        else return warnError(frmObj.winScreenY, errNum)
    }
    win_obj[win_obj.length]=window.open("ls09-07.htm",
      frmObj.winName.value, featureStr)
    return true
}
function checkParent() {
    if (window.opener==null) {
        alert("There is no parent window.")
        return false
    }
    if (window.opener.closed)
        alert("Window "+window.opener.name+" closed.")
    else alert("Window "+window.opener.name+" open.")
    return true
}
function relParent() {
    if (window.opener==null) return false
    if (window.opener.closed) window.opener=null
    return true
}
//-->
</SCRIPT>
  </HEAD>
```

```
  <BODY ONLOAD="document.winTest.winName.focus()">
<SCRIPT LANGUAGE="JavaScript">
<!--
if (self.opener) parentName=self.opener.name
document.write("The parent window name is: "
              +parentName+"<BR>")
while (self.name==null || self.name=="") {
   self.name=prompt("Please enter a name for this window",
      "")
}
document.write("The current window name is: "+self.name)
//-->
</SCRIPT>
    <P>Select the features you want for a new window:</P>
    <FORM NAME="winTest">
    <TABLE WIDTH="100%" BORDER="1">
      <TR>
        <TD WIDTH="25%">Name:</TD>
        <TD COLSPAN="3" WIDTH="25%">
        <P><INPUT TYPE="TEXT" NAME="winName" SIZE="20"
                VALUE=""></P></TD>
      </TR>
      <TR>
        <TD WIDTH="25%">Set features:</TD>
        <TD COLSPAN="3" WIDTH="25%">
        <P><INPUT TYPE="CHECKBOX" NAME="winFeatures"
                CHECKED="CHECKED"></P></TD>
      </TR>
      <TR>
        <TD WIDTH="25%">dependent:</TD>
        <TD WIDTH="25%">
        <P><INPUT TYPE="CHECKBOX" NAME="winDependent"
                VALUE="yes"></P></TD>
        <TD WIDTH="25%">outerWidth:</TD>
        <TD WIDTH="162">
         <P><INPUT TYPE="TEXT" NAME="winOuterWidth"
                SIZE="4" MAXLENGTH="4"></P></TD>
      </TR>
      <TR>
        <TD WIDTH="25%">directories:</TD>
        <TD WIDTH="25%">
        <P><INPUT TYPE="CHECKBOX" NAME="winDirectories"
                CHECKED="CHECKED" VALUE="yes"></P></TD>
        <TD WIDTH="25%">resizable:</TD>
        <TD WIDTH="162">
```

```
    <P><INPUT TYPE="CHECKBOX" NAME="winResizable"
            CHECKED="CHECKED" VALUE="yes"></P></TD>
</TR>
<TR>
  <TD WIDTH="25%">hotkeys:</TD>
  <TD WIDTH="25%">
  <P><INPUT TYPE="CHECKBOX" NAME="winHotkeys"
            VALUE="yes" CHECKED="CHECKED"></P></TD>
  <TD WIDTH="25%">screenX:</TD>
  <TD WIDTH="162">
  <P><INPUT TYPE="TEXT" NAME="winScreenX" SIZE="4"
            MAXLENGTH="4"></P></TD>
</TR>
<TR>
  <TD WIDTH="25%">innerHeight:</TD>
  <TD WIDTH="25%">
  <P><INPUT TYPE="TEXT" NAME="winInnerHeight"
            SIZE="4" MAXLENGTH="4"></P></TD>
  <TD WIDTH="25%">screenY:</TD>
  <TD WIDTH="162">
  <P><INPUT TYPE="TEXT" NAME="winScreenY" SIZE="4"
            MAXLENGTH="4"></P></TD>
</TR>
<TR>
  <TD WIDTH="25%">innerWidth:</TD>
  <TD WIDTH="25%">
  <P><INPUT TYPE="TEXT" NAME="winInnerWidth" SIZE="4"
            MAXLENGTH="4"></P></TD>
  <TD WIDTH="25%">scrollbars:</TD>
  <TD WIDTH="162">
  <P><INPUT TYPE="CHECKBOX" NAME="winScrollbars"
            VALUE="yes" CHECKED="CHECKED"></P></TD>
</TR>
<TR>
  <TD WIDTH="25%">location:</TD>
  <TD WIDTH="25%">
  <P><INPUT TYPE="CHECKBOX" NAME="winLocation"
            VALUE="yes" CHECKED="CHECKED"></P></TD>
  <TD WIDTH="25%">status:</TD>
  <TD WIDTH="162">
  <P><INPUT TYPE="CHECKBOX" NAME="winStatus"
            VALUE="yes" CHECKED="CHECKED"></P></TD>
</TR>
<TR>
  <TD WIDTH="25%">menubar:</TD>
```

```
      <TD WIDTH="25%">
      <P><INPUT TYPE="CHECKBOX" NAME="winMenubar"
                VALUE="yes" CHECKED="CHECKED"></P></TD>
      <TD WIDTH="25%">toolbar:</TD>
      <TD WIDTH="162">
      <P><INPUT TYPE="CHECKBOX" NAME="winToolbar"
                VALUE="yes" CHECKED="CHECKED"></P></TD>
    </TR>
    <TR>
      <TD WIDTH="25%">outerHeight:</TD>
      <TD WIDTH="25%">
      <P><INPUT TYPE="TEXT" NAME="winOuterHeight"
                SIZE="4" MAXLENGTH="4"></P></TD>
      <TD WIDTH="25%"></TD>
      <TD WIDTH="162"> </TD>
    </TR>
    <TR>
      <TD WIDTH="25%" COLSPAN="2">
      <P><INPUT TYPE="BUTTON" NAME="openBtn"
                VALUE="Open New Window"
                ONCLICK="openWin(this.form)"></P></TD>
      <TD WIDTH="25%" COLSPAN="2">
      <P><INPUT TYPE="BUTTON" NAME="winCloseBtn"
                VALUE="Close Current Window"
                ONCLICK="window.close()"></P></TD>
    </TR>
    <TR>
      <TD WIDTH="25%" COLSPAN="2">
      <P><INPUT TYPE="BUTTON" NAME="closeParentBtn"
                VALUE="Close Parent Window"
  ONCLICK="if (window.opener!=null) window.opener.close()">
        </P></TD>
      <TD WIDTH="25%" COLSPAN="2">
      <P><INPUT TYPE="BUTTON" NAME="checkParentBtn"
                VALUE="Check Parent Window"
                ONCLICK="checkParent()"></P></TD>
    </TR>
    <TR>
      <TD WIDTH="25%" COLSPAN="2">
      <P><INPUT TYPE="BUTTON" NAME="relParentBtn"
                VALUE="Release Parent Window"
                ONCLICK="relParent()"></P></TD>
      <TD WIDTH="25%" COLSPAN="2"></TD>
    </TR>
  </TABLE></FORM>
  </BODY>
</HTML>
```

Although the script in Listing 9.7 is a bit long, it includes all the properties that do not require a signed script. If you want to experiment with these properties, you can create a signed script by adding a request for the "`UniversalBrowserWrite`" privilege. The script stores the window objects in an array, which allows you to open multiple windows. If the "Set Features" checkbox is unchecked, the script creates a window based on the default properties. When you initially load the script, you are prompted for the window name if the window has no name. Figure 9.7 shows the initial window.

Note

Since the script uses references that are new in JavaScript 1.2, it only runs on Netscape Communicator 4.0. Microsoft Internet Explorer does not support the JavaScript 1.2 features. MSIE 4.0 does have additional features not supported in JavaScript 1.1, such as `fullscreen`, `channelmode`, `top` (same as `screenY`), and left (same as `screenX`).

The script in Listing 9.8 is a revised version of the script in Listing 6.7. The script is a JavaScript source file that has a single accessible function—`listProps()`. The `listProps()` function prompts the user for an object name and then displays the properties of the object in a separate window. The new window is dependent of the parent window, so that closing the parent window automatically closes the window containing the list of properties.

Netscape

The JavaScript source file in Listing 9.8 only works with Netscape Communicator 4.0. Microsoft Internet Explore 4.0 does not support nested functions or the `dependent` feature of the `window.open()` method.

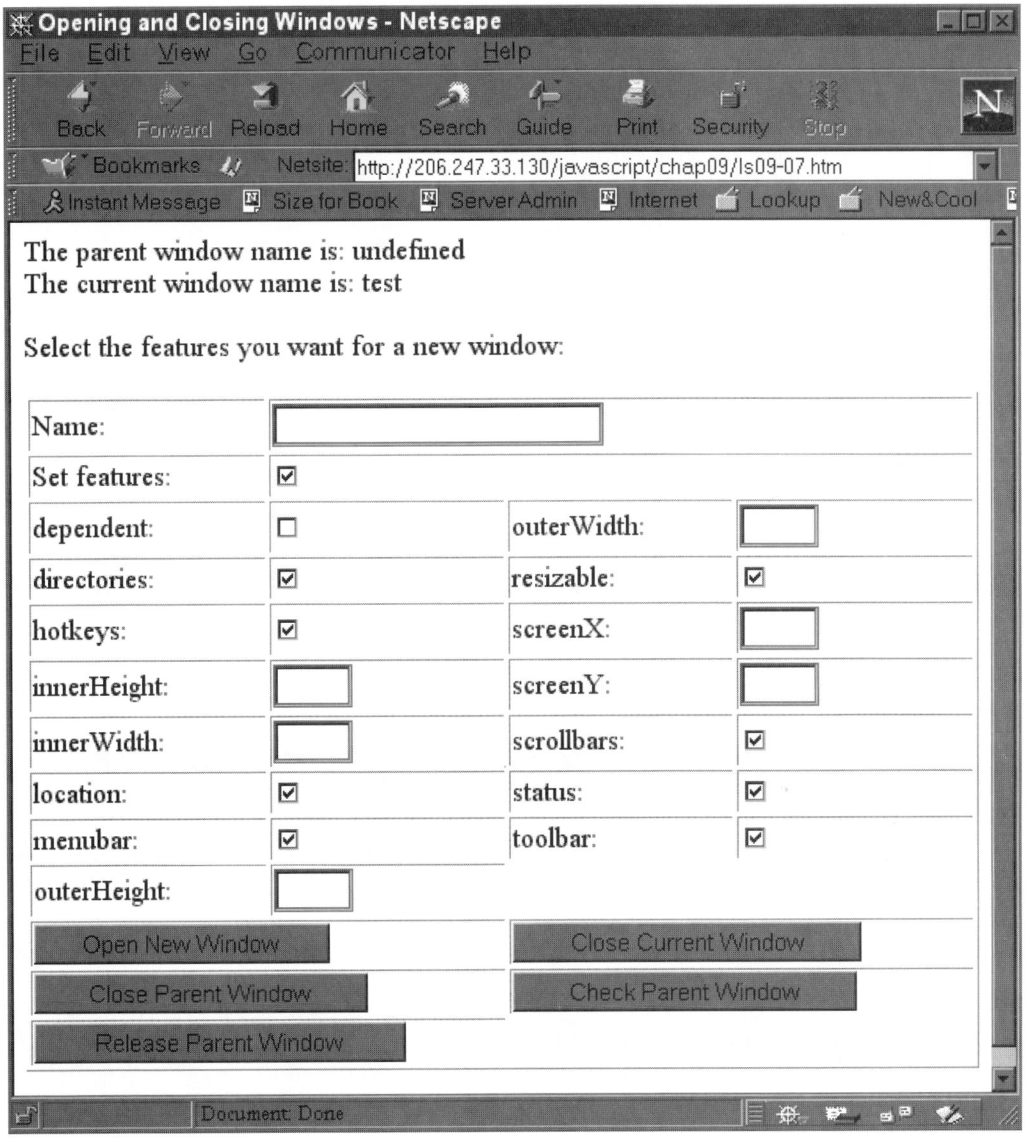

Figure 9.7 Results of opening and closing windows.

Listing 9.8 Display Properties of an Object

```
//
// This source file lists the properties of any object.
// The document only needs to call listProps() without
// any arguments.
//
function listProps() {
      var objName=""
      var propsTable = new Array()
      var j=0
      function getObjName() {
         while ( objName=="" ) {
            objName=prompt("Enter the name of the object:", "")
         }
         return objName
      }
      function getProps(obj, objName) {
         for (var i in obj) {
            propsTable[j]=new Array(3)
            propsTable[j][0]=objName+"."+i
            propsTable[j][1]=typeof(obj[i])
            if (propsTable[j][1].indexOf("str")>=0 ||
                propsTable[j][1].indexOf("num")>=0 ||
                propsTable[j][1].indexOf("boo")>=0) {
               propsTable[j][2]=obj[i].toString()
            }
            else {
               propsTable[j][2]=""
            }
            ++j
         }
         return true
      }
      getObjName()
      if ( objName==null ) return false
   getProps(eval(objName), objName)
   debugWin=window.open("", "debugWin",
         "dependent=yes,scrollbars=yes")
   debugWin.document.open()
   debugWin.document.write("Total properties = "
         +propsTable.length+"<BR>")
   for (var i=1; i<propsTable.length; i++) {
```

```
        debugWin.document.write(propsTable[i][0]+" = ")
        debugWin.document.write(propsTable[i][1])
        if (propsTable[i][1].indexOf("str")>=0 ||
            propsTable[i][1].indexOf("num")>=0 ||
            propsTable[i][1].indexOf("boo")>=0) {
          debugWin.document.write(" ("+propsTable[i][2]+")")
        }
        debugWin.document.write("<BR>")
    }
    debugWin.document.close
    return true
}
```

The script in Listing 9.9 includes the JavaScript source in Listing 9.8. The script invokes the `listProps()` function with the `onClick` event handler of the "List Properties of an Object" button. Figure 9.8 shows the results of running the script in Listing 9.9. Figure 9.9 shows the results of listing the `document` object for this script.

Listing 9.9 Object Properties Test

```
<HTML>
  <HEAD>
    <TITLE>Object Property Test</TITLE>
<SCRIPT LANGUAGE="JavaScript1.2" SRC="ls09-08.js">
<!--
alert("JavaScript source file not found")
//-->
</SCRIPT>
  </HEAD>
  <BODY>
    <P>This document shows how to invoke the listProps()
      function, which is part of a JavaScript source file.
      To invoke the script, press the button below and see
      what happens.</P>
    <FORM>
    <P><INPUT TYPE="BUTTON" NAME="debugBtn"
            VALUE="List Properties of an Object"
            ONCLICK="listProps()"></P>
    </FORM>
  </BODY>
</HTML>
```

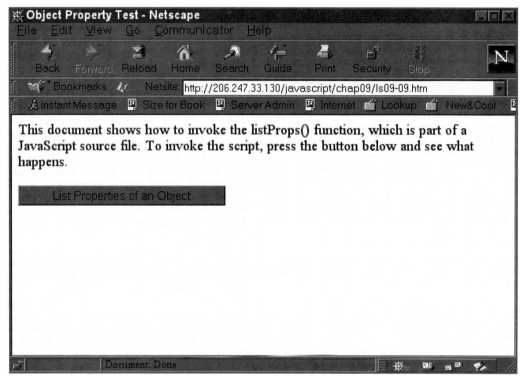

Figure 9.8   Results of object propertytest.

New in JavaScript 1.2

Modifying the Properties of a Window

The properties of the `window` object listed in Table 9.10 are new in JavaScript 1.2. Since these properties effect an existing window, you need to use them in a signed script with the "`UniveralBrowserWrite`" privilege. However, you can change the dimensions of the screen as long as the result is not less than 100 x 100 pixels.

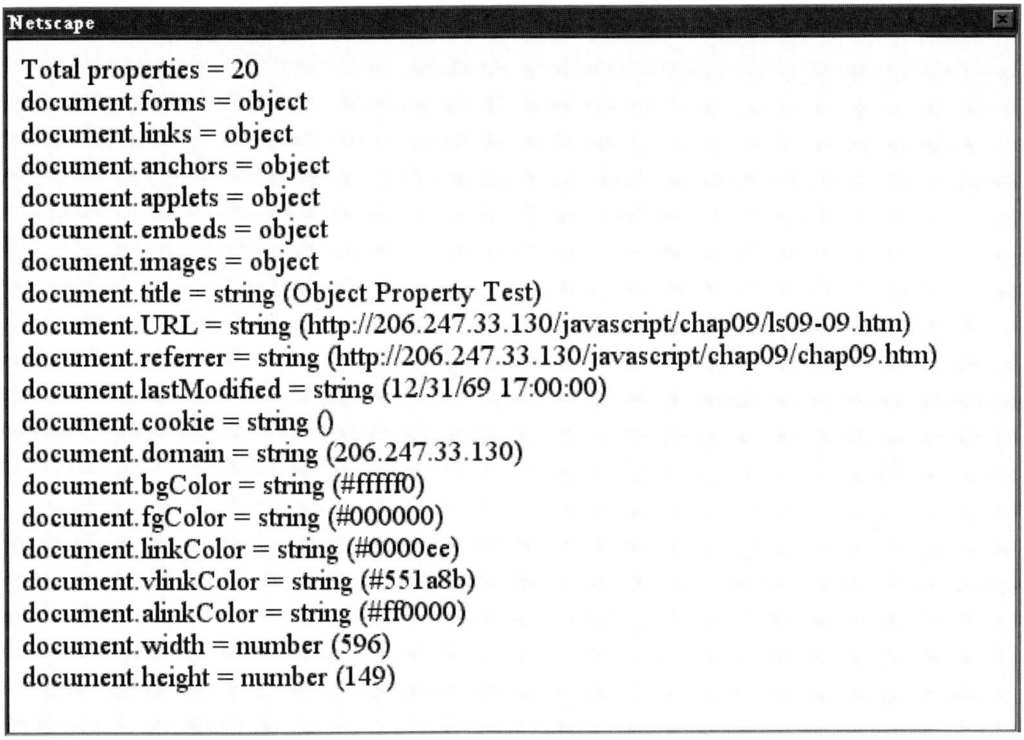

```
Netscape                                                              ☒
Total properties = 20
document.forms = object
document.links = object
document.anchors = object
document.applets = object
document.embeds = object
document.images = object
document.title = string (Object Property Test)
document.URL = string (http://206.247.33.130/javascript/chap09/ls09-09.htm)
document.referrer = string (http://206.247.33.130/javascript/chap09/chap09.htm)
document.lastModified = string (12/31/69 17:00:00)
document.cookie = string ()
document.domain = string (206.247.33.130)
document.bgColor = string (#ffffff0)
document.fgColor = string (#000000)
document.linkColor = string (#0000ee)
document.vlinkColor = string (#551a8b)
document.alinkColor = string (#ff0000)
document.width = number (596)
document.height = number (149)
```

Figure 9.9   Results of object properties display.

Table 9.10 Window Object Properties that modify the Window

Property	Description
innerHeight	Specifies the height, in pixels, of the window's viewing area. To set a height of less than 100 pixels requires a signed script with the "UniversalBrowser-Write" privilege.
innerWidth	Specifies the width, in pixels, of the window's viewing area. To set a width of less than 100 pixels requires a signed script with the "UniversalBrowser-Write" privilege.
locationbar	The visible property is the only property of the locationbar property and, if false, the location bar is hidden. For example, self.locationbar = false.

Table 9.10 Window Object Properties that modify the Window *(Continued)*

Property	Description
menubar	The visible property is the only property of the menubar property and, if false, the menu bar is hidden. For example, self.menubar = false. Setting the visible property requires a signed script with "UniversalBrowser-Write" privilege.
outerHeight	Specifies the height, in pixels, of the window's outside boundary. To set a height of less than 100 pixels requires a signed script with the "Universal-BrowserWrite" privilege.
outerWidth	Specifies the width, in pixels, of the window's outside boundary. To set a width of less than 100 pixels requires a signed script with the "UniversalBrowser-Write" privilege.
personalbar	The visible property is the only property of the personalbar property and, if false, the personal bar is hidden. For example, self.personalbar = false. Setting the visible property requires a signed script with "Universal-BrowserWrite" privilege.
scrollbars	The visible property is the only property of the scrollbars property and, if false, the scroll bars are hidden. For example, self.scrollbars = false. Setting the visible property requires a signed script with "Universal-BrowserWrite" privilege.
statusbar	The visible property is the only property of the statusbar property and, if false, the status bar is hidden. For example, self.statusbar = false. Setting the visible property requires a signed script with "Universal-BrowserWrite" privilege.
toolbar	The visible property is the only property of the toolbar property and, if false, the tool bar is hidden. For example, self.toolbar = false. Setting the visible property requires a signed script with "UniversalBrowser-Write" privilege.

The script in Listing 9.10 is another signed script and has the same conditions for execution as the script in Listing 9.3. The script allows you to modify the properties of a test window. Other than the requirement for signing, the script does not introduce any new techniques. Figure 9.10 shows the results of creating a window with the properties shown in the form.

Netscape

 The properties in Table 9.10 are not supported by Microsoft Internet Explorer 4.0.

Listing 9.10 Modifying the Properties of a Test Window

```
<HTML>
  <HEAD>
    <TITLE>
    Modifying the Properties of a Test Window
    </TITLE>
<SCRIPT LANGUAGE="JavaScript1.2">
<!--
var errNum="Not an interger."
var intPat=/^\d+$/
USB="UniversalBrowserWrite"
function warnError (fieldObj, errMsg) {
   alert(errMsg)
   fieldObj.focus()
   fieldObj.select()
   return false
}
function isEmpty(str) {
   return(str==null || str=="")
}
function isInteger(str) {
   return intPat.test(str)
}
function openTestWin() {
   twin=window.open("", "testWin")
   twin.document.open()
   twin.document.write("This is the test window.")
   twin.document.close()
   return true
}
function closeTestWin() {
   if (!twin.closed) twin.close()
}
function setInner(frmObj) {
   netscape.security.PrivilegeManager.enablePrivilege(USB)
```

```
     if (!isEmpty(frmObj.winInnerHeight.value)) {
        if (isInteger(frmObj.winInnerHeight.value)) {
         twin.innerHeight=Number(frmObj.winInnerHeight.value)
        }
        else return warnError(frmObj.winInnerHeight, errNum)
     }
      if (!isEmpty(frmObj.winInnerWidth.value)) {
        if (isInteger(frmObj.winInnerWidth.value)) {
           twin.innerWidth=Number(frmObj.winInnerWidth.value)
        }
        else return warnError(frmObj.winInnerWidth, errNum)
     }
     return true
}
function setOuter(frmObj) {
   netscape.security.PrivilegeManager.enablePrivilege(USB)
   if (!isEmpty(frmObj.winOuterHeight.value)) {
      if (isInteger(frmObj.winOuterHeight.value)) {
       twin.outerHeight=Number(frmObj.winOuterHeight.value)
      }
      else return warnError(frmObj.winOuterHeight, errNum)
   }
   if (!isEmpty(frmObj.winOuterWidth.value)) {
      if (isInteger(frmObj.winOuterWidth.value)) {
         twin.outerWidth=Number(frmObj.winOuterWidth.value)
      }
      else return warnError(frmObj.winOuterWidth, errNum)
   }
   return true
}
function setInterface(frmObj) {
   netscape.security.PrivilegeManager.enablePrivilege(USB)
   twin.locationbar.visible=frmObj.winLocationbar.checked
   twin.menubar.visible=frmObj.winMenubar.checked
   twin.personalbar.visible=frmObj.winPersonalbar.checked
   twin.scrollbars.visible=frmObj.winScrollbars.checked
   twin.statusbar.visible=frmObj.winStatusbar.checked
   twin.toolbar.visible=frmObj.winToolbar.checked
   return true
}
//-->
</SCRIPT>
  </HEAD>
  <BODY ONLOAD="openTestWin()" ONUNLOAD="closeTestWin()">
    <P>When you set the following properties, you are
```

```
  modifying the properties of the current screen.</P>
<FORM NAME="testFrm">
<TABLE WIDTH="100%" BORDER="2">
  <TR>
    <TD COLSPAN="2" WIDTH="30%">
    <P>innerHeight: <INPUT TYPE="TEXT"
      NAME="winInnerHeight" SIZE="4" MAXLENGTH="4">
    </P></TD>
    <TD WIDTH="30%">
    <P>innerWidth: <INPUT TYPE="TEXT"
      NAME="winInnerWidth" SIZE="4" MAXLENGTH="4">
    </P></TD>
    <TD>
    <P><INPUT TYPE="BUTTON" NAME="innerBtn"
             VALUE="Set Inner Dimensions"
             ONCLICK="setInner(this.form)"></P></TD>
  </TR>
  <TR>
    <TD COLSPAN="2" WIDTH="30%">
    <P>outerHeight: <INPUT TYPE="TEXT"
      NAME="winOuterHeight" SIZE="4" MAXLENGTH="4">
    </P></TD>
    <TD WIDTH="30%">
    <P>outerWidth: <INPUT TYPE="TEXT"
      NAME="winOuterWidth" SIZE="4" MAXLENGTH="4">
    </P></TD>
    <TD>
    <P><INPUT TYPE="BUTTON" NAME="outerBtn"
             VALUE="Set Outer Dimensions"
             ONCLICK="setOuter(this.form)"></P></TD>
  </TR>
  <TR>
    <TD COLSPAN="2" WIDTH="30%">
    <P>locationbar: <INPUT TYPE="CHECKBOX"
      NAME="winLocationbar" CHECKED="CHECKED">
    </P></TD>
    <TD WIDTH="30%">
    <P>menubar: <INPUT TYPE="CHECKBOX"
      NAME="winMenubar" CHECKED="CHECKED"></P></TD>
    <TD ROWSPAN="3">
    <P><INPUT TYPE="BUTTON" NAME="userBtn"
             VALUE="Set User Interface"
             ONCLICK="setInterface(this.form)">
    </P></TD>
  </TR>
```

```
<TR>
  <TD COLSPAN="2" WIDTH="30%">
  <P>personalbar: <INPUT TYPE="CHECKBOX"
    NAME="winPersonalbar" CHECKED="CHECKED">
  </P></TD>
  <TD WIDTH="30%">
  <P>scrollbars: <INPUT TYPE="CHECKBOX"
    NAME="winScrollbars" CHECKED="CHECKED"></P></TD>
  </TR>
  <TR>
  <TD COLSPAN="2" WIDTH="30%">
  <P>statusbar: <INPUT TYPE="CHECKBOX"
    NAME="winStatusbar" CHECKED="CHECKED"></P></TD>
  <TD WIDTH="30%">
  <P>toolbar: <INPUT TYPE="CHECKBOX"
    NAME="winToolbar" CHECKED="CHECKED"></P></TD>
  </TR>
  </TABLE></FORM>
</BODY>
</HTML>
```

New in JavaScript 1.2

Moving and Resizing Windows

JavaScript 1.2 provides the methods shown in Table 9.11 for moving and resizing windows. If the resulting window goes beyond the screen, you need to sign the script.

Table 9.11 Methods of Window Object for resizing and moving a Window

Method	Description
moveBy(horizontal, vertical)	Moves the window by the number of pixels specified by the *horizontal* and *vertical* arguments. A negative argument moves the window to the left or up, respectively. Moving part or the entire window off the screen requires a signed script with the "UniversalBrowserWrite" privilege.

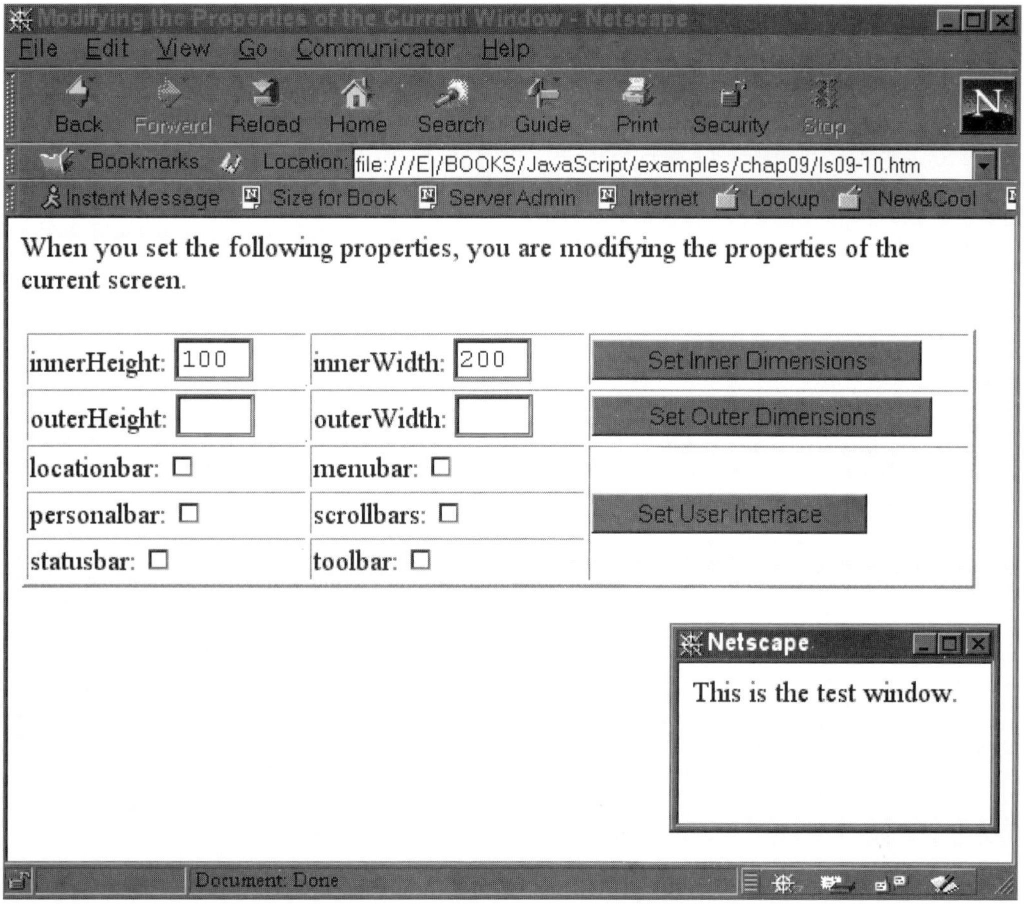

When you set the following properties, you are modifying the properties of the current screen.

innerHeight: `100`	innerWidth: `200`	Set Inner Dimensions
outerHeight:	outerWidth:	Set Outer Dimensions
locationbar: ☐	menubar: ☐	
personalbar: ☐	scrollbars: ☐	Set User Interface
statusbar: ☐	toolbar: ☐	

This is the test window.

Figure 9.10   Results of modifying the properties of a test window.

Table 9.11 Methods of Window Object for resizing and moving a Window (Continued)

`moveTo(horizontal, vertical)`	Moves the top-left corner of the window to the position, in pixels, specified by the *horizontal* and *vertical* arguments. Moving part or the entire window off the screen requires a signed script with the "`UniversalBrowserWrite`" privilege.

Table 9.11 Methods of Window Object for resizing and moving a Window *(Continued)*

`resizeBy(horizontal, vertical)`	Resizes the window by moving the bottom-right corner the number of pixels specified in the *horizontal* and *vertical* arguments. A negative argument decreases the size of the window. If any or all of the resized window exceeds the boundaries of the screen or the window size is less than 100 x 100 pixels, the script requires "`UniveralBrowserWrite`" privileges.
`resizeTo(horizontal, vertical)`	Resizes the window to the number of pixels specified by the horizontal and vertical arguments. The top-left corner of the window remains anchored when the browser resizes the window. If any or all of the resized window exceeds the boundaries of the screen or the window size is less than 100 x 100 pixels, the script requires "`UniveralBrowserWrite`" privileges.

The script in Listing 9.11 allows you to move and resize a test window (see Figure 9.11 as well). The script also shows one of the problems with a dependent window. If you make the dependent window hide under the primary window, you need to move the primary window to get to it. To solve this problem, you need to set the `alwaysRaised` feature in a signed script.

Navigator

The methods referenced in Table 9.11 are not supported by Microsoft Internet Explorer 4.0.

Listing 9.11 Moving and Resizing Windows

```
<HTML>
  <HEAD>
    <TITLE>Moving and Resizing Windows</TITLE>
<SCRIPT LANGUAGE="JavaScript1.2">
<!--
var featureStr="dependent=yes,resizable=yes"
featureStr+=",screenX=50,screenY=50"
var errNum="Not a valid interger."
var errX="Missing the horizontal position."
```

```
var erry="Missing the vertical position."
var intPat=/^\d+$/
var intSignedPat=/^[+-]*\d+$/
function warnError (fieldObj, errMsg) {
   alert(errMsg)
   fieldObj.focus()
   fieldObj.select()
   return false
}
function isEmpty(str) {
   return(str==null || str=="")
}
function isInteger(str) {
   return intPat.test(str)
}
function isSignedInteger(str) {
   return intSignedPat.test(str)
}
function openTestWin() {
   twin=window.open("", "testWin", featureStr)
   twin.document.open()
   twin.document.write("This is the test window.")
   twin.document.close()
   return true
}
function checkBy(fieldX, fieldY) {
   if (isEmpty(fieldX.value))
      return warnError(fieldX, errX)
   if (!isSignedInteger(fieldX.value))
      return warnError(fieldX, errNum)
   if (isEmpty(fieldY.value))
      return warnError(fieldY, errY)
   if (!isSignedInteger(fieldY.value))
      return warnError(fieldY, errNum)
   return true
}
function checkTo(fieldX, fieldY) {
   if (isEmpty(fieldX.value))
      return warnError(fieldX, errX)
   if (!isInteger(fieldX.value))
      return warnError(fieldX, errNum)
   if (isEmpty(fieldY.value))
      return warnError(fieldY, errY)
   if (!isInteger(fieldY.value))
      return warnError(fieldY, errNum)
```

```
      return true
}
function doMoveBy(frmObj) {
    if (checkBy(frmObj.winX, frmObj.winY)) {
       twin.moveBy(frmObj.winX.value, frmObj.winY.value)
       return true
    }
    return false
}
function doMoveTo(frmObj) {
    if (checkTo(frmObj.winX, frmObj.winY)) {
       twin.moveTo(frmObj.winX.value, frmObj.winY.value)
       return true
    }
    return false
}
function doResizeBy(frmObj) {
    if (checkBy(frmObj.winX, frmObj.winY)) {
       twin.resizeBy(frmObj.winX.value, frmObj.winY.value)
       return true
    }
    return false
}
function doResizeTo(frmObj) {
    if (checkTo(frmObj.winX, frmObj.winY)) {
       twin.resizeTo(frmObj.winX.value, frmObj.winY.value)
       return true
    }
    return false
}
//-->
</SCRIPT>
  </HEAD>
  <BODY ONLOAD="openTestWin()">
    <P>You can move and resize a test window by using the
       form below.</P>
    <FORM NAME="testForm">
    <TABLE WIDTH="100%">
      <TR>
        <TD>
        <P>horizontal: <INPUT TYPE="TEXT" NAME="winX"
           SIZE="4" MAXLENGTH="4"></P></TD>
        <TD>
        <P>vertical: <INPUT TYPE="TEXT" NAME="winY"
           SIZE="4" MAXLENGTH="4"></P></TD>
```

```
      </TR>
      <TR>
        <TD></TD>
        <TD></TD>
      </TR>
      <TR>
        <TD>
        <P><INPUT TYPE="BUTTON" NAME="winMoveByBtn"
                  VALUE="Move By"
                  ONCLICK="doMoveBy(this.form)"></P></TD>
        <TD>
        <P><INPUT TYPE="BUTTON" NAME="winResizeBy"
                  VALUE="Resize By"
                  ONCLICK="doResizeBy(this.form)"></P></TD>
      </TR>
      <TR>
        <TD>
        <P><INPUT TYPE="BUTTON" NAME="winMoveToBtn"
                  VALUE="Move To"
                  ONCLICK="doMoveTo(this.form)"></P></TD>
        <TD>
        <P><INPUT TYPE="BUTTON" NAME="winResizeToBtn"
                  VALUE="Resize To"
                  ONCLICK="doResizeTo(this.form)"></P></TD>
      </TR>
    </TABLE></FORM>
  </BODY>
</HTML>
```

The `checkBy()` and `checkTo()` functions in Listing 9.11 check the values for both moving and resizing. Two functions are used because the `checkBy()` function has signed integers, while the `checkTo()` function does not. Since there is a features string in the `window.open` statement for the test window, the script needs to declare that the window is resizable.

New in JavaScript 1.2

Scrolling Documents

JavaScript 1.1 implemented the `scroll()` method. As shown in Table 9.12, JavaScript 1.2 replaces the `scroll()` method with the `scroll-To()` method. However, the `scroll()` method continues to exist for backward compatibility.

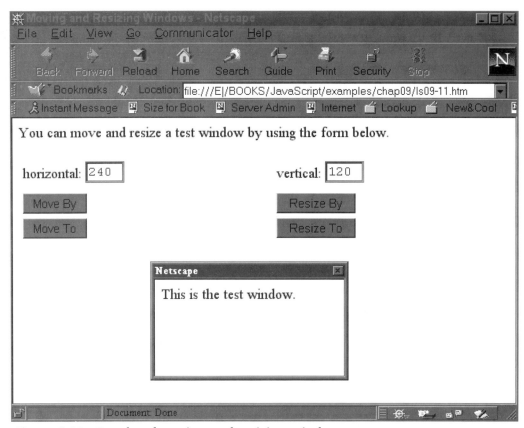

Figure 9.11 Results of moving and resizing windows.

Table 9.12 Window Methods for scrolling Documents

Method	Description
scroll(horizontal, vertical)	Using the upper-left corner of the display area as a reference, the scroll() method moves the document to a specific position. JavaScript 1.2 replaces the scroll() method with the scrollTo() method.
scrollBy(horizontal, vertical)	Scrolls the document by the values, in pixels, specified by the *horizontal* and *vertical* arguments. This method requires that scrollbars.visible is true.

Table 9.12 Window Methods for scrolling Documents *(Continued)*

ScrollTo(horizontal, vertical)	Scrolls the document to the position specified, in pixels, by the horizontal and vertical arguments. The horizontal and vertical coordinates become the coordinates for the upper-left corner of the viewing area. This method requires that scrollbars.visible is true.

To aid in the positioning of text in the view area of the window, Java-Script 1.2 provides the properties listed in Table 9.13. The pageXOff-set and pageYOffset properties indicate the current position in the document relative to the top-left corner of the content area.

Table 9.13 Window Properties for scrolling Documents

Property	Description
pageXOffset	Specifies the current horizontal position of a page as it relates to the upper-left corner of the content area in the screen. The property is useful in testing the value of the *horizontal* argument of the scrollBy() method.
pageYOffset	Specifies the current vertical position of a page as it relates to the upper left corner of the content area of the screen. The property is useful in testing the value of the vertical argument of the scrollBy() method.

Navigator

The methods in Table 9.12 and properties in Table 9.13 are not supported by Microsoft Internet Explorer 4.0.

New in JavaScript 1.2

Window Methods of the Toolbar

JavaScript 1.2 adds methods to the window object that represent the functions provided on the toolbar. Table 9.14 lists these methods along with a brief description of each.

Table 9.14 Methods related to the Toolbar

Method	Description
back()	Undoes the last step anywhere in the top-level window, whether it occurs in the same frame or any other frame within the frame tree. The back() method of the window object differs from the back() method of the history object, as the back() method of the history object only undoes the last step in the current frame. It is equivalent to pressing the back button on the toolbar.
find()	Finds the specified string in the contents of the specified window. The syntax of the find() method is as follows: find(*string, casesensitive, backward*) The *string* argument specifies the test string to find in the document. The *casesensitive* argument is a Boolean value, where true indicates a case-sensitive search. The *backward* argument is a Boolean value, where true specifies a backward search through the document. The find() method returns true if the search finds the *string*. If you do not specify a string, the method displays a find dialogue box, which allows the user to enter a string.
forward()	Moves forward to the next URL in the current history. It is equivalent to pressing the forward button on the toolbar.
home()	Points the browser to the URL in user preferences as the user's home page. It is equivalent to pressing the home button on the toolbar.
print()	Prints the contents of the current window or frame and is equivalent to pressing the print button on the toolbar.
stop()	Stops the current download and is equivalent to pressing the stop button on the toolbar.

These methods allow you to create a custom toolbar for a page. For such a page, you really need frames so that one frame emulates the content area of the standard browser window.

Navigator

Microsoft Internet Explorer 4.0 does not support the methods referenced in Table 9.14.

Setting Timers

The `setTimeout()` method evaluates an expression or calls a function once after the specified period of milliseconds. It does not stop the execution of the script during the timeout period. Instead, the script schedules the event and then continues execution. The `setTimeout()` method was actually implemented in JavaScript 1.0. However, it was limited to evaluating an expression as shown in the following syntax:

```
timerID = setTimeout(expression, msec)
```

JavaScript 1.2 extends the `setTimeout()` method to include a function call as shown in the following syntax:

```
timerID = setTimeout(function, msec[, arg1, ..., argn])
```

The clearTimeout() method cancels the timeout set with the `set-Timeout()` method. The syntax for the `clearTimeout()` method is as follows:

```
clearTimeout(timerID)
```

JavaScript 1.2 introduced the `setInterval()` method. Where the `setTimeout()` method executes just once, the `setInterval()` method evaluates an expression or calls a function every time a specified number of milliseconds passes. The `setInterval()` method has the same syntax as the `setTimeout()` method. The two formats are as follows:

```
timerID = setInterval(expression, msec)
timerID = setInterval(function, msec[, arg1, ..., argn])
```

The `clearInterval()` method cancels the timeout set with the `setInterval()` method. The syntax for the `clearInterval()` method is as follows:

```
clearInterval(timerID)
```

The script in Listing 9.12 illustrates the use of both the `setTimeout()` method and the `setInterval()` method. The first `<SCRIPT> </SCRIPT>` tags define the functions needed to display the local date and time every second using the `setTimeout()` method.

Since the setTimeout() method executes only once, the disp-Time() function needs to set the event on each invocation. The next set of <SCRIPT></SCRIPT> tags uses the LANGUAGE attribute to limit the script to JavaScript 1.2. It includes a new definition of the functions that use the setInterval() method. Besides illustrating both the setTimeout() method and the setInterval() method, the script also shows how to implement the same functions for different versions of JavaScript. Figure 9.12 shows the results of running this script.

Listing 9.12 Displaying the Local Date and Time

```
<HTML>
  <HEAD>
    <TITLE>Displaying the Local Date and Time</TITLE>
<SCRIPT LANGUAGE="JavaScript">
<!--
var timerID=null
var timerOn=false
function dispTime() {
   var cDate=new Date()
   document.clock.clockDisplay.value=cDate.toLocaleString()
   timerID=setTimeout("dispTime()", 1000)
   timerOn=true
}
function stopClock() {
   if (timerOn) clearTimeout(timerID)
   document.clock.clockDisplay.value=""
   timerOn=false
}
function startClock() {
   stopClock()
   dispTime()
}
//-->
</SCRIPT>
<SCRIPT LANGUAGE="JavaScript1.2">
<!--
function dispTime() {
   var cDate=new Date()
   document.clock.clockDisplay.value=cDate.toLocaleString()
}
function stopClock() {
```

```
   if (timerOn) clearInterval(timerID)
   document.clock.clockDisplay.value=""
   timerOn=false
}
function startClock() {
   stopClock()
   timerID=setInterval("dispTime()", 1000)
   timerOn=true
}
//-->
</SCRIPT>
  </HEAD>
  <BODY>
    <FORM NAME="clock">
    <TABLE WIDTH="60%">
      <TR>
        <TD COLSPAN="2">
        <P><INPUT TYPE="TEXT" NAME="clockDisplay"
               SIZE="30"></P></TD>
      </TR>
      <TR>
        <TD>
        <P><INPUT TYPE="BUTTON" NAME="startClockBtn"
               VALUE="Start Clock"
               ONCLICK="startClock()"></P></TD>
        <TD>
        <P><INPUT TYPE="BUTTON" NAME="stopClockBtn"
               VALUE="Stop Clock"
               ONCLICK="stopClock()"></P></TD>
      </TR>
    </TABLE></FORM>
  </BODY>
</HTML>
```

Events for the Window Object

As shown in Table 9.15, the window object supports a number of event handlers. The window object represents the top of the event handler tree. Thus, the event handler for the window object receives the event before lower level objects such as frames, documents, form elements, or layers.

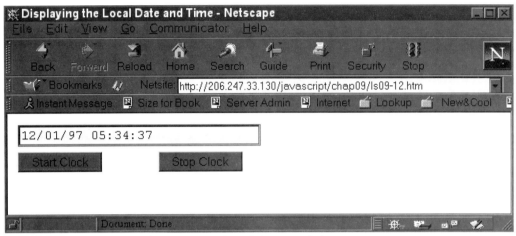

Figure 9.12 Results of displaying local date and time.

Table 9.15 Event Handlers for the window Object

Event Handler	Description
onBlur *	The blur event for a window occurs when the window loses focus or from the window.blur() method. You can include the onBlur attribute in the <BODY> tag or the <FRAMESET> tag. However, the Windows platform does not support the onBlur attribute in the <FRAMESET> tag in Netscape Navigator 3.0.
onDragDrop **	The DragDrop event occurs when the user drags and drops a file or shortcut into the browser window using the native system's drag-and-drop mechanism. The normal behavior for the browser is to attempt to load the item into the browser window. The data property of the event object contains an array of the URLs dropped onto the browser window. To read the data property, you need a signed script with the "UniversalBrowserRead" privilege.
onError *	The error event occurs when there is a JavaScript syntax or runtime error. A browser error, such as attempting to link to an invalid URL, does not generate an error event.
onFocus *	The focus event for a window occurs from the window.focus() method or when a user clicks the mouse on an object or uses the TAB key on the keyboard. You can include the onFocus attribute in the <BODY> tag or the <FRAMESET> tag. However, the Windows platform does not support the onFocus attribute in the <FRAMESET> tag in Netscape Navigator 3.0.

Table 9.15 Event Handlers for the window Object *(Continued)*

Event Handler	Description
onLoad	The load event occurs when the browser finishes loading a window or all the frames within a <FRAMESET> tag.
onMove **	The move event occurs when the user or the script moves a window or frame.
onResize **	The resize event occurs when the user or the script resizes a window or frame. The event occurs after the browser finishes adjusting the HTML layout within the new window's inner dimensions.
onUnload	The unload event occurs when the user exits a document.

* *New in JavaScript 1.1;* ** *New in JavaScript 1.2*

Unless the script manages the events, the browser makes the decisions regarding the passing of events to event handlers. When an event handler returns true, the browser performs the default actions associated with the event. If the event handler returns false, the browser terminates further processing of the event. Since events are interrupts to the flow of processing, an event can interrupt the processing of other events. The script in Listing 9.13 illustrates the behavior of events. Using the script in Listing 9.13 as a starting point, the script has every event handler for the window (minus, the onError event handler), document, text, and button objects. Every event is recorded in the textarea box. To clear the textarea box, you need to press the reload button on the toolbar. The results are shown in Figure 9.13.

Listing 9.13 Events for a Window with a Single Document

```
<HTML>
  <HEAD>
  <TITLE>Events for a Window with a Single Document</TITLE>
<SCRIPT LANGUAGE="JavaScript">
<!--
var oldValue=""
function evMsg(evType, evTarget) {
   var msgStr=""
   msgStr+="A "+evType+" event"
```

```
      msgStr+=" was received for the "+evTarget
      msgStr+=" object.\n\r"
      document.testFrm.evBox.value+=msgStr
}
function logWin(ev) {
   evMsg(ev.type, "window")
   return true
}
function logDoc(ev) {
   evMsg(ev.type, "document")
   return true
}
function logForm(ev) {
   evMsg(ev.type, ev.target.type)
   return true
}
function clearFields(ev) {
   document.testFrm.someText.value=""
   document.testFrm.evBox.value=""
   return true
}
function saveOld(fieldObj, ev) {
   evMsg(ev.type, ev.target.type)
   oldValue=fieldObj.value
   fieldObj.focus()
   fieldObj.select()
   return true
}
function keepChange(fieldObj, ev) {
   evMsg(ev.type, ev.target.type)
   if (!confirm("Keep the change?")) {
      fieldObj.value=oldValue
      return false
   }
   return true
}
function checkField(frmObj, ev) {
   evMsg(ev.type, ev.target.type)
   if (frmObj.someText.value=="") {
      alert("The field is empty")
      frmObj.someText.focus()
      return false
   }
   return true
}
```

```
//-->
</SCRIPT>
  </HEAD>
  <BODY ONUNLOAD="clearFields(event)"
        ONBLUR="return logWin(event)"
        ONFOCUS="return logWin(event)"
        ONLOAD="return logWin(event)"
        ONDRAGDROP="return logWin(event)"
        ONMOVE="return logWin(event)"
        ONRESIZE="return logWin(event)"
        ONCLICK="return logDoc(event)"
        ONDBLCLICK="return logDoc(event)"
        ONKEYDOWN="return logDoc(event)"
        ONKEYPRESS="return logDoc(event)"
        ONKEYUP="return logDoc(event)"
        ONMOUSEDOWN="return logDoc(event)"
        ONMOUSEUP="return logDoc(event)">
    <P>Enter some text in the following box and then click
      the &quot;Check Field&quot; button. Delete the text
      you entered and click the button again.</P>
    <FORM NAME="testFrm">
    <P>Enter text in this box: <INPUT TYPE="TEXT"
        NAME="someText" SIZE="30"
        ONCHANGE=" return keepChange(this, event)"
        ONFOCUS="return saveOld(this, event)"
        ONBLUR="return logForm(event)"
        ONSELECT="return logForm(event)"></P>
    <P><INPUT TYPE="BUTTON" NAME="checkText"
        VALUE="Check Field"
        ONCLICK="return checkField(this.form, event)"
        ONBLUR="return logForm(event)"
        ONDBLCLICK="return logForm(event)"
        ONFOCUS="return logForm(event)"
        ONMOUSEDOWN="return logForm(event)"
        ONMOUSEUP="return logForm(event)"></P>
    <P><TEXTAREA NAME="evBox" ROWS="15" COLS="60"
        WRAP="Off"></TEXTAREA></P>
    </FORM>
  </BODY>
</HTML>
```

The script in Listing 9.6 seems to ignore a click on the "Check Field" button after making any changes in the text box. From a functional view, one may separate the change event as being totally independent of the click event. However, this is not the case. The mousedown event on the button removes focus from the text box. After the focus moves away from the text box, the browser generates a change event. The `onChange` event handler catches this event and generates a dialog box to confirm the change. Alas, the dialog box removes focus from the button and transfers it to the dialog box. Once you respond to the dialog box, focus goes back to the button. By now the mouseup event for the button, which would have generated a click event, gets lost in the shuffle of the mouse actions relating to the dialog box.

To get a clear picture of what happens, consider the mouse action (or, keyboard action) as a raw event. The raw mousedown event on the button generates several cooked events. The first cooked event is a blur event from the original object. The browser sees the blur event, looks at the text field, generates a change event (another cooked event), releases the blur event, and finally generates a focus event for the button. All these events are the result of one raw event. Of course, the event cycle becomes much more complicated with the generation of the dialog box. The dialog box is a separate window, which removes focus from the button and from the window. The dialog box is a bit selfish in that it blocks all events to the original window until you respond to it. After it goes away, focus returns to the window and then to the button. The mouseup event waits for the change event to complete, but the dialog box blocks the mouseup event and it gets lost.

The moral of this story is beware of what you do in event handlers, especially when working with cooked events. Just as over-cooked foods destroy part of the original raw food, so do over-cooked events destroy some raw events.

Navigator

The script in Listing 9.13 only works with Netscape Communicator 4.0. The event object for Microsoft Internet Explorer 4.0 does not support the `target` property. Instead of the `target` property, MSIE 4.0 has the `srcElement` property. Of the properties in the event object, MSIE 4.0 only supports the `type`, `screenX`, and `screenY` properties.

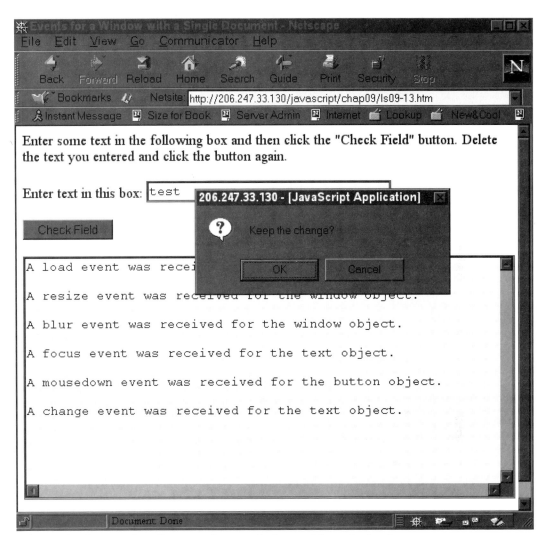

Figure 9.13   Results of events for a window with a single document.

Using the onError Event Handler

The error event triggers the onError event handler. As mentioned in Table 9.15, the error event covers only JavaScript syntax errors and run-time errors. Browser errors, such as an invalid link, are not among the errors reported by the error event. However, a bad URL in an `<IMG>` tag or a corrupted image file are included in the reported errors.

You can take the following actions in the `onError` event handler:

- Suppress all errors with the following JavaScript code:

```
window.onerror=null
```

- Handle image errors, but suppress JavaScript errors with the above entry plus the following:

```
<IMG NAME="imgName" SRC="imageSource" onError="errorFunc()"
```

- Trace all errors and allow the standard JavaScript error dialog by providing an event handler function that returns false (this is opposite of other event handlers that return true to allow default error handling).
- Report the errors and disable the standard JavaScript error dialog by providing an event handler function that returns true.

The browser passes the onError event handler three arguments:

- Message text
- URL of the document
- Line number on which the error occurred

The following snippet places the arguments in an array for later processing:

```
msgArray=new Array()
urlArray=new Array()
lnoArray=new Array()
function errorHandler(msg, url, lno) {
   msgArray[msgArray.length]=msg
   urlArray[urlArray.length]=url
   lnoArray[lnoArray.length]=lno
}
```

New in JavaScript 1.2

Managing Events

JavaScript 1.2 opens the door to event management so that you have more control over the handling of events. Chapter 7 introduced the subject of advanced event management and now it is time to tie the pieces together to form a total picture. Table 9.16 lists the `window` object methods used in advanced event management.

Table 9.16 Window Object Methods for Managing Events

Method	Description
`captureEvents (eventType)`	Capture all events of the specified types (see the "Capture Events" section in Chapter 7).
`disableExternal Capture()`	Disables external event capturing set by the `enableExternalCapture()` method.
`enableExternal Capture()`	Enables a window with frames to capture events in documents loaded from different locations. This method requires a signed script. You need to request "`UniversalBrowserWrite`" privilege before the `captureEvents()` method.
`handleEvent(event)`	Allows you to bypass the event handling hierarchy and pass the event to an event receiver. An event receiver is an event handler for a specific event. For example, if you wanted to pass a click event to the `onClick` event handler for a checkbox, you would write something like: `document.myform.acheckbox.handleEvent(event)`
`releaseEvents (eventType)`	Releases the specified event types for default processing.
`routeEvent(event)`	Passes the event along the normal event hierarchy.

The script in Listing 9.14 uses the script in Listing 9.13 as a base. Except for the `onLoad` and `onUnload` attributes in the `<BODY>` tag, the only event receivers are in the text object and the button object. For the `window` and document object, the click, mouseup, and mousedown events are captured. The window object event handler uses the `routeEvent()` method to direct the event along the normal event hierarchy. The document object event handler uses the `handleEvent()` method to directly assign the event to a particular object. In this script, the event goes to the targeted object. However, you can direct the event to any object that has an event receiver to handle the event.

Listing 9.14 Advanced Event Management

```
<HTML>
  <HEAD>
    <TITLE>Advanced Event Management</TITLE>
<SCRIPT LANGUAGE="JavaScript">
<!--
// The evMsg function displays a message in the
// textarea box.
function evMsg(evType, evTarget) {
   var msgStr=""
   msgStr+="A "+evType+" event"
   msgStr+=" was received for the "+evTarget
   msgStr+=" object.\n"
   document.testFrm.evBox.value+=msgStr
}
// The following functions handle the routing of
// events.
function winHandler(ev) {
   evMsg(ev.type, "window")
   routeEvent(ev)
   return true
}
function docHandler(ev) {
   evMsg(ev.type, "document")
   ev.target.handleEvent(ev)
   return true
}
function setWinCapture(evType) {
   var evStr="Event."+evType.toUpperCase()
   if (setWinCapture.arguments.length>1) {
     for (var i=1; i<setWinCapture.arguments.length; i++) {
        evStr+=" | Event."
        evStr+=setWinCapture.arguments[i].toUpperCase()
     }
   }
   window.captureEvents(eval(evStr))
   return true
}
function relWinCapture(evType) {
   var evStr="Event."+evType.toUpperCase()
   if (relWinCapture.arguments.length>1) {
     for (var i=1; i<relWinCapture.arguments.length; i++) {
```

```
         evStr+=" | Event."
         evStr+=relWinCapture.arguments[i].toUpperCase()
      }
   }
   window.releaseEvents(eval(evStr))
   return true
}
function setDocCapture(evType) {
   var evStr="Event."+evType.toUpperCase()
   if (setDocCapture.arguments.length>1) {
      for (var i=1; i<setDocCapture.arguments.length; i++) {
         evStr+=" | Event."
         evStr+=setDocCapture.arguments[i].toUpperCase()
      }
   }
   document.captureEvents(eval(evStr))
   return true
}
function relDocCapture(evType) {
   var evStr="Event."+evType.toUpperCase()
   if (relDocCapture.arguments.length>1) {
      for (var i=1; i<relDocCapture.arguments.length; i++) {
         evStr+=" | Event."
         evStr+=relDocCapture.arguments[i].toUpperCase()
      }
   }
   document.releaseEvents(eval(evStr))
   return true
}
// assign the event handler functions
window.onclick=winHandler
window.onmousedown=winHandler
window.onmouseup=winHandler
document.onclick=docHandler
document.onmousedown=docHandler
document.onmouseup=docHandler
// The following functions handle the receiving
// of events. Consequently, they are called receivers
var oldValue=""
function logEv(ev) {
   evMsg(ev.type, ev.target.type)
   return true
}
function startDoc(ev) {
   document.testFrm.someText.value=""
```

```
      document.testFrm.evBox.value=""
      evMsg(ev.type, ev.target.type)
      setWinCapture("click", "mousedown", "mouseup")
      setDocCapture("click", "mousedown", "mouseup")
      return true
}
function exitDoc(ev) {
      evMsg(ev.type, ev.target.type)
      relWinCapture("click", "mousedown", "mouseup")
      relDocCapture("click", "mousedown", "mouseup")
      return true
}
function saveOld(fieldObj, ev) {
      evMsg(ev.type, ev.target.type)
      oldValue=fieldObj.value
      fieldObj.focus()
      fieldObj.select()
      return true
}
function keepChange(fieldObj, ev) {
      evMsg(ev.type, ev.target.type)
      if (!confirm("Keep the change?")) {
         fieldObj.value=oldValue
         rcturn false
      }
      return true
}
function checkField(frmObj, ev) {
      evMsg(ev.type, ev.target.type)
      if (frmObj.someText.value=="") {
         alert("The field is empty")
         frmObj.someText.focus()
         return false
      }
      return true
}
//-->
</SCRIPT>
  </HEAD>
  <BODY ONLOAD="return startDoc(event)"
        ONUNLOAD="return exitDoc(event)">
    <P>Enter some text in the following box and then click
      the &quot;Check Field&quot; button. Delete the text
      you entered and click the button again.</P>
    <FORM NAME="testFrm">
```

```
    <P>Enter text in this box:
       <INPUT TYPE="TEXT" NAME="someText" SIZE="30"
              ONCHANGE=" return keepChange(this, event)"
              ONFOCUS="return saveOld(this, event)"
              ONBLUR="return logEv(event)"
              ONSELECT="return logEv(event)"></P>
    <P><INPUT TYPE="BUTTON" NAME="checkText"
              VALUE="Check Field"
              ONCLICK="return checkField(this.form, event)"
              ONBLUR="return logEv(event)"
              ONDBLCLICK="return logEv(event)"
              ONFOCUS="return logEv(event)"
              ONMOUSEDOWN="return logEv(event)"
              ONMOUSEUP="return logEv(event)"></P>
    <P><TEXTAREA NAME="evBox" ROWS="10" COLS="56" WRAP="Off">
       </TEXTAREA></P>
    </FORM>
  </BODY>
</HTML>
```

As shown in Figure 9.14, the script in Listing 9.14 produces the same results as the script in Listing 9.13. The essential difference is that it shows that the browser never transfers the mouseup event to the script. Since the mousedown event generates the change, blur, and focus events, the normal event hierarchy handles these cooked events. When you click on the button a second time, you will see the expected series of events.

Working with Frames

Frames are a way of dividing a window into distinct sections, where each section has its own URL. To divide a window into frames, the document loaded into the top-level window has a `<FRAMESET>` tag instead of a `<BODY>` tag. Within the `<FRAMESET>` `</FRAMESET>` tags, the `<FRAME>` tags define the document loaded into the frame and the frame's characteristics.

The window object reflects the attributes of the `<FRAMESET>` tag. For each `<FRAME>` in the `<FRAMESET>`, the browser creates a `frame` object in the `frames[]` array. The `frame` object is really a window object that has all the properties and methods of the top-level window object with the following caveats:

- For the top-level window, which contains the `<FRAMESET>`,

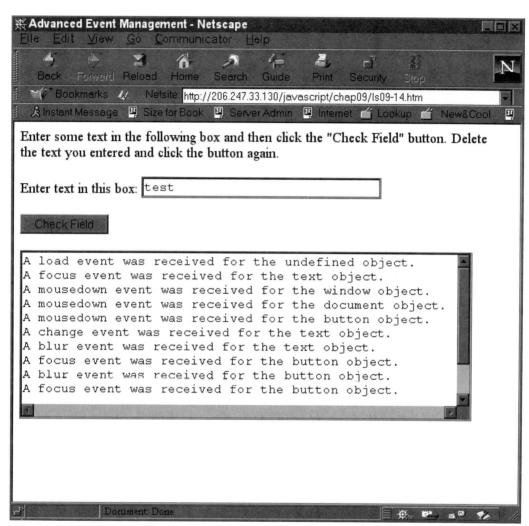

Figure 9.14 Results of advanced event management.

the parent and top properties are references to the top-level window itself.

- For the document in a frame, the top property refers to the top-level window, and the parent property refers to the parent window of the frame. This becomes more apparent if a frame contains a <FRAMESET>.

- For a top-level window, the `defaultStatus` and `status` properties set the text that appears in the browser status bar. For a frame, the `defaultStatus` and `status` properties only set the status bar text when the cursor is over the frame.
- The `close()` method of the `window` object serves no function in a frame.
- To create window event handlers for the blur and focus events, you need to use the `window.onblur` and `window.onfocus` properties, respectively.
- The SRC and NAME attributes of the `<FRAME>` tag allow you to reference a sibling frame of the parent with the following syntax:

```
parent.frameName
```

The following syntax statements show the two methods for referencing frames:

```
winObj.frames["frameName"]
winObj.frames[index]
```

The `length` property of the `window` object indicates the number of window objects in the `frames[]` array. You can use the `parent.length` property as a means of detecting if a document is loaded into a frame. The `length` property is greater than zero only when the document is a `<FRAMESET>`.

Figure 9.15 shows the relationships of the `parent` and `top` properties of various frames. It helps to remember that the `<FRAMESET>` is nothing more than a specialized document whose task is to divide the window into frames. Furthermore, the `<FRAMESET>` is not limited to the top-level window. The SRC attribute of a `<FRAME>` tag can load another `<FRAMESET>` document.

The following scripts implement the diagram shown in Figure 9.15. The script in Listing 9.15 is the top-level frameset and defines the top-level `window` object. This frameset divides the window into two frames. The browser loads the document in Listing 9.16 into the first frame. The second frame contains the document described in Listing 9.17. Since the `window.name` property is undefined for the top-level window, the script sets the `name` property equal to "topWin."

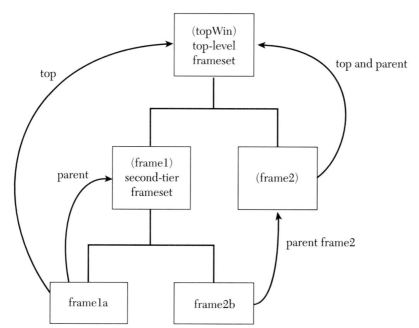

Figure 9.15 Diagram of frameset relationships.

Listing 9.15 Top-Level Frameset

```
<HTML>
  <HEAD>
    <TITLE>Top-Level Frameset</TITLE>
<SCRIPT LANGUAGE="JavaScript">
<!--
window.name="topWin"
//-->
</SCRIPT>
  </HEAD>
  <FRAMESET ROWS="50%,50%" NAME="topFrame">
    <FRAME SRC="ls09-16.htm" NAME="frame1"
           MARGINWIDTH="3" MARGINHEIGHT="3"
           SCROLLING="NO" NORESIZE="NORESIZE">
    <FRAME SRC="ls09-17.htm" NAME="frame2b"
           MARGINWIDTH="3" MARGINHEIGHT="3"
           SCROLLING="NO" NORESIZE="NORESIZE">
```

```
<NOFRAMES>
  <BODY>
  <P>This test requires frames.</P>
  </BODY>
</NOFRAMES>
</FRAMESET>
</HTML>
```

The source file for the first frame is another `<FRAMESET>` document that splits the frame into two columns, with each containing a `<FRAME>` tag. The script described in Listing 9.17 is loaded into both frames.

Listing 9.16 Second-Tier Frameset

```
<HTML>
  <HEAD>
    <TITLE>Second-Tier Frameset</TITLE>
  </HEAD>
    <FRAMESET COLS="50%,50%">
      <FRAME SRC="ls09-17.htm" NAME="frame1a"
             MARGINWIDTH="3" MARGINHEIGHT="3"
             SCROLLING="NO" NORESIZE="NORESIZE">
      <FRAME SRC="ls09-17.htm" NAME="frame1b"
             MARGINWIDTH="3" MARGINHEIGHT="3"
             SCROLLING="NO" NORESIZE="NORESIZE">
    </FRAMESET>
</HTML>
```

The script in Listing 9.17 simply displays the `window.name`, `self.name`, `top.name`, and `parent.name` properties. As shown in Figure 9.16, the `window.name` and `self.name` properties always refer to the current window object. The `top.name` property always refers to the top-level window. The `parent.propety`, however, varies according to the location of the frame in the frame hierarchy. The results match those shown in Figure 9.15.

Listing 9.17 Frame Relationships

```
<HTML>
  <HEAD>
    <TITLE>Frame Relationships</TITLE>
```

```
  </HEAD>
  <BODY>
    <P>The relationships of this frame are:</P>
<SCRIPT LANGUAGE="JavaScript">
<!--
with (document) {
   open()
   write("window: "+window.name+"<BR>")
   write("self: "+self.name+"<BR>")
   write("top: "+top.name+"<BR>")
   write("parent: "+parent.name+"<BR>")
   close()
}
//-->
</SCRIPT>
  </BODY>
</HTML>
```

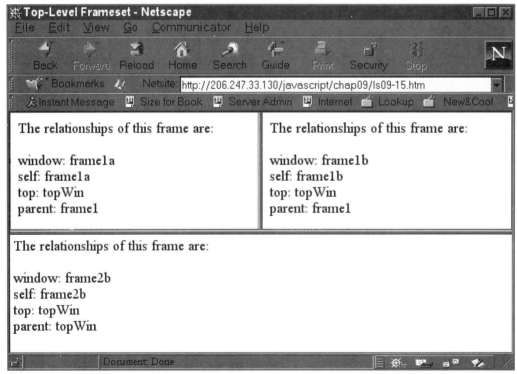

Figure 9.16 Results of frame relationships.

Working with the location Object

The `location` object reflects the URL of the web page currently loaded into the window. Table 9.17 lists the properties and methods of the `location` object.

Table 9.17 Properties and Methods of the location Object

Properties	Methods	Event Handlers
hash	reload() *	None
host	replace() *	
hostname		
href		
pathname		
port		
protocol		
search		

°New in JavaScript 1.1

The properties of the `location` object correspond to the structure of a URL. Table 9.18 lists the properties of the `location` object along with a brief description. Figure 9.17 provides a diagram that relates the definitions to an actual URL.

Table 9.18 Description of the Properties of the location Object

Property	Description
hash	Represents the anchor name portion of the URL. The `hash` property only applies to the HTTP URL and includes the hash (#) mark. Although it is safer to set the entire URL via the `href` property, you can set only the hash property. By setting the `hash` property, you can navigate to the anchor without reloading the document. For example, you could have one frame as an index to a document in the second frame. The script in the index frame could then set the `hash` property in the document frame.

Table 9.18 Description of the Properties of the location Object *(Continued)*

Property	Description
host	Represents the server name, domain name, and port number portion of the URL. Although the hostname property is a read-write property, you should always use the href property to define a new URL.
hostname	Represents the server name and domain name portion of the URL. The host property is a substring of the hostname property. You can set the host property; however, it is better to set the entire URL using the href property.
href	Represents the entire URL for the document. The other location object properties are substrings of the href property. You should always use the href property to change the URL, since it correctly sets the other properties in the location object. Using the window.location reference to set a URL is equivalent to window.location.href.
pathname	Represents the file pathname of the URL and begins with a slash (/) character.
port	Represents the port number through which the server application communicates to the clients. The port number is necessary only when communicating to a server through a port number that is not the default port number for the protocol.
protocol	Represents the protocol portion of the URL including the trailing colon (:).
search	Represents the query portion of the string, beginning with a question mark (?). The format of the string is as follows: ?var1=xxx&var2=yyy

The protocol property determines the protocol used to communicate with a server. Table 9.19 lists the common URLs used in Web pages.

Table 9.19 Common URL Protocols

Protocol	Description	Example
file:/	Reference to local file. The additional slash is required.	file:///E|/JavaScript/ls09-15.htm
ftp:	File Transfer Protocol	ftp://ftp.xxx.com/public/zzz.zip
gopher:	Menu oriented text retrieval.	gopher://sv1.xxx.com

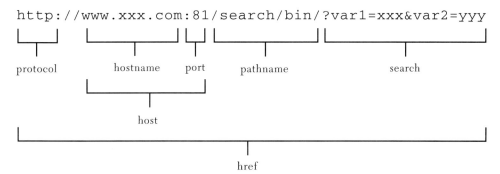

Figure 9.17   Diagram of the properties of the location object.

Table 9.19 Common URL Protocols *(Continued)*

Protocol	Description	Example
http:	World Wide Web protocol.	http://home.netscape.com
javascript:	JavaScript code. The void() method results in the browser not loading a new page.	Javacript:void(0)
mailto:	Send e-mail message.	mailto:billa@nilenet.com
news:	Usenet	news://news.xx.com/ comp.lang.javascript
telnet:	TELNET protocol	telnet://sv1.xxx.com

Navigator

 Microsoft Internet Explorer 3.0 does not support the `mailto:` protocol.

The script in Listing 9.18 opens a test window and then displays the properties of the location object in the text boxes of the primary window. As written, the script is limited to URLs within the same domain. For the script to work with all URLs, you need to add a request for "Universal-BrowserRead" privilege, and sign the script. Figure 9.18 shows the results of listing a URL from the test window. Except for the hash and `search` properties, the results illustrate the breakdown of the `href` object into separate components.

Listing 9.18 Viewing the Properties of the Location Object

```
<HTML>
  <HEAD>
    <TITLE>
    Viewing the Properties of the location Object
    </TITLE>
<SCRIPT LANGUAGE="JavaScript">
<!--
function checkLoc(frmObj) {
   frmObj.checkHref.value=testWin.location.href
   frmObj.checkProtocol.value=testWin.location.protocol
   frmObj.checkHostname.value=testWin.location.hostname
   frmObj.checkHost.value=testWin.location.host
   frmObj.checkPort.value=testWin.location.port
   frmObj.checkPathname.value=testWin.location.pathname
   frmObj.checkHash.value=testWin.location.hash
   frmObj.checkSearch.value=testWin.location.search
}
//-->
</SCRIPT>
  </HEAD>
  <BODY ONLOAD="testWin=window.open('', 'testWin')">
    <P>This screen shows you the properties of the
     location object for the URL entered in the second
     screen. After entering a URL in the second window,
      press the &quot;Check It&quot; button.</P>
    <FORM>
    <P><INPUT TYPE="BUTTON" NAME="checkBtn"
            VALUE="Check It"
            ONCLICK="checkLoc(this.form)"></P>
    <P>href: <INPUT TYPE="TEXT"
                  NAME="checkHref" SIZE="50"></P>
    <P>protocol: <INPUT TYPE="TEXT"
                      NAME="checkProtocol" SIZE="20"></P>
    <P>hostname: <INPUT TYPE="TEXT"
                      NAME="checkHostname" SIZE="40"></P>
    <P>host: <INPUT TYPE="TEXT"
                  NAME="checkHost" SIZE="40"></P>
    <P>port: <INPUT TYPE="TEXT"
```

```
                        NAME="checkPort" SIZE="4"></P>
    <P>pathname: <INPUT TYPE="TEXT"
                        NAME="checkPathname" SIZE="40"></P>
    <P>hash: <INPUT TYPE="TEXT"
                        NAME="checkHash" SIZE="20"></P>
    <P>search: <INPUT TYPE="TEXT"
                        NAME="checkSearch" SIZE="40"></P>
      </FORM>
    </BODY>
</HTML>
```

Reloading a Document

The reload() method emulates the behavior of the reload button in the toolbar. The syntax for the reload() method is as follows:

```
reload(forceGet)
```

The *forceGet* argument is a Boolean value. If *forceGet* is false, the reload() method follows the policies set in the user preferences for reloading the document. By default, the reload() method retrieves the document from the cache unless the user specifies to check it every time. In that case, the reload() method performs a conditional HTTP GET using the "If-modified-since" HTTP header.

If *forceGet* is true, the browser performs an unconditional HTTP GET from the server. You should not use this option unless there is an error in the loading of a document or an image.

Replacing a URL in the History

The replace() method loads the specified URL over the current history entry. The syntax for the replace() method is as follows:

```
replace(URL)
```

The specified *URL* is the URL that becomes the current history entry. By using the replace() method, the user cannot use the back button to go back to the page that contains the replace() method. For Netscape Navigator 2.0, you can emulate the behavior of the replace() method with the following snippet:

```
if (location.replace == null) location.replace = location.assign
```

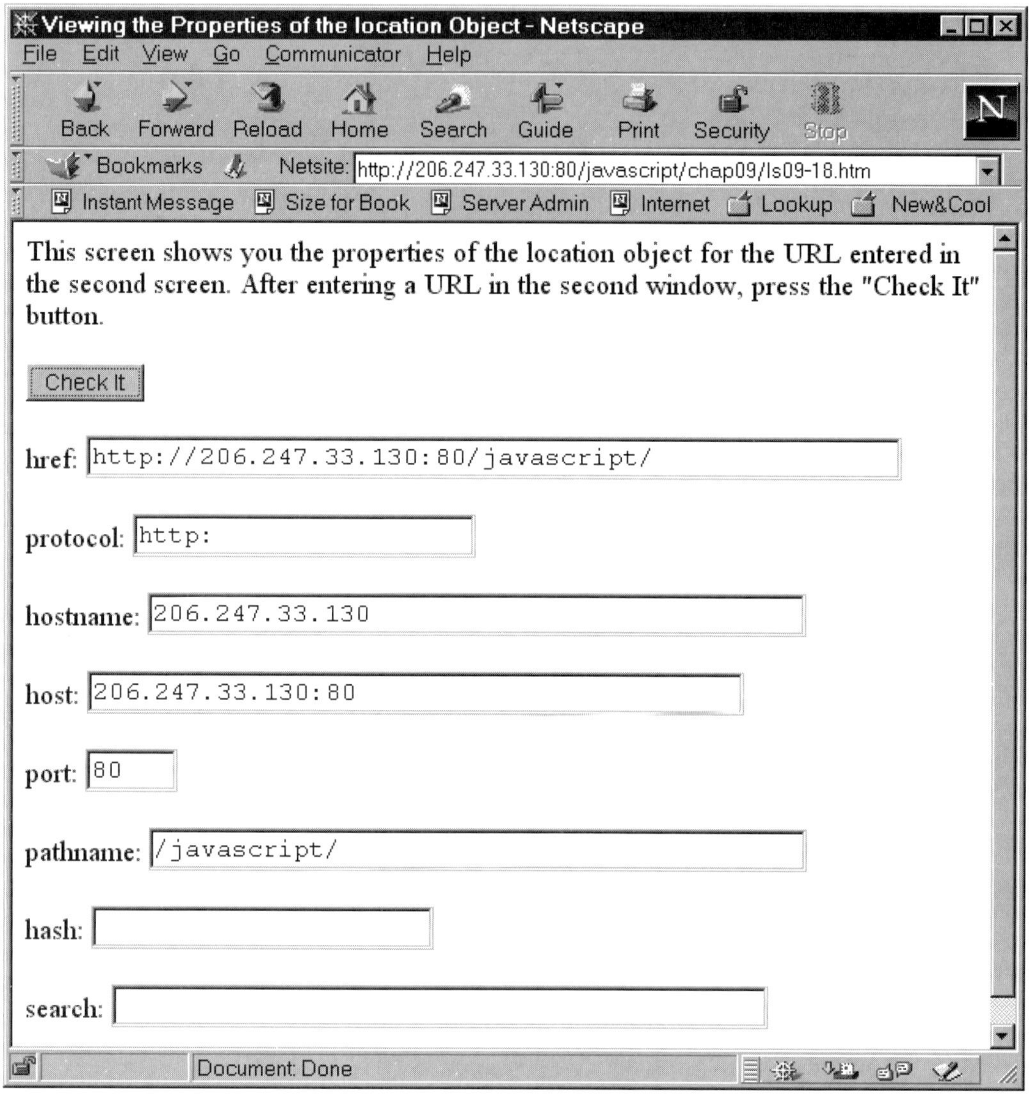

Figure 9.18 Results of viewing the properties of the location object.

Working with the history Object

The `history` object maintains the history of pages visited in this session for the current window. Table 9.20 lists the properties and methods of the `history` object. The `history` object has no event handlers.

Table 9.20 Properties and Methods of the history Object

Property	Method	Event Handler
current *	back()	None
length	forward()	
next *	go()	
previous *		

* *New in JavaScript 1.2*

The `history` object is actually an array of all locations visited by the browser during the current session. The first URL visited is `history[0]`. As the user visits other sites, those sites are added to the array. The only exception to this rule is a document that uses the `location.method()` to replace the current URL in the history array with another URL.

Table 9.21 describes the properties of the `history` object. In JavaScript 1.2, you need a signed script with the "UniversalBrowserRead" privilege to access any of these properties.

Table 9.21 Description of Properties for history Object

Property	Description
current *	A read-only string that contains the complete URL of the current history entry.
length	A read-only number that specifies the number of elements in the `history[]` array.
next *	A read-only string that contains the complete URL of the next history entry.
previous *	A read-only string that contains the complete URL of the previous history entry.

* *New in JavaScript 1.1*

The security requirements protect the user from scripts gaining access to their history list. However, you can use the methods described in Table 9.22 to navigate the current history.

Table 9.22 Descriptions of the Methods of the history Object

Method	Description
back()	Takes the browser back to the previous history entry.
forward()	Takes the browser forward to the next history entry.
go(delta)	Navigates the browser according to the specified parameter.
go(location)	The delta parameter is a signed integer that moves the browser forward or back the specified number of entries in the history table. The back() method is equivalent to history.go(-1). The forward() method is equivalent to history.go(1). The location.reload() method is equivalent to history.go(0). The location parameter is a string that causes the browser go to the nearest history entry that contains location as a substring. The match is case sensitive. The go() method creates a new history entry. To avoid creating a new history entry, you need to use the location.replace() method.

The methods of the history object navigate the browser forward or back in the history of the current window or frame. In contrast, the window.back() method and the window.forward() method navigate according to the history of the top-level window. For example, the history.back() method in a frame takes the browser back to the last history entry for the frame. On the other hand, the window.back() method takes the browser back to the last history entry even though it is in a different frame. You need to remember that each window object, whether it is in the top-level window, a frame, or a window opened by the window.open() method, maintains its own history object.

The next three scripts illustrate the difference between the history that the top-level window object maintains and the history that a frame window object maintains. For this test to work, you must establish a current history for the top-level window before invoking the script in Listing 9.19. This script divides the window into two frames and loads the next two scripts into each frame.

Listing 9.19 Navigating with Window and History Methods

```
<HTML>
  <HEAD>
  <TITLE>Navigating with window and history Methods</TITLE>
  </HEAD>
  <FRAMESET ROWS="*,60">
  <FRAME SRC="ls09-20.htm" NAME="docFrame" SCROLLING="YES"
        NORESIZE="NORESIZE">
  <FRAME SRC="ls09-21.htm" NAME="controlFrame"
        MARGINWIDTH="3" MARGINHEIGHT="3" SCROLLING="NO"
        NORESIZE="NORESIZE">
  <NOFRAMES><BODY>
    <P>This example requires the use of frames.</P>
  </BODY></NOFRAMES></FRAMESET>
</HTML>
```

The upper frame displays the document shown in Listing 9.20. When you press the "Start Test" button, the script replaces the index.htm that is on the CD-ROM. You need to navigate down to another test in this window.

Listing 9.20 Start Test

```
<HTML>
  <HEAD>
    <TITLE>Start Test</TITLE>
  </HEAD>
  <BODY>
    <P>This test starts by replacing this page with the
      index.html page for the listings in this book. By
      replacing the page, the index.html page becomes
      the first page in the frame history. Press the
      &quot;Start Test&quot; button to begin the test.</P>
    <FORM>
    <P><INPUT TYPE="BUTTON" NAME="startBtn"
        VALUE="Start Test"
        ONCLICK="window.location.replace('../index.htm')">
    </P>
    </FORM>
  </BODY>
</HTML>
```

The lower frame contains the document shown in Listing 9.21. Once you reach a lower-level window, you can test the difference between the two histories by using the navigation buttons in the lower frame.

Listing 9.21 Control Panel

```
<HTML>
  <HEAD>
    <TITLE>Control Panel</TITLE>
  </HEAD>
  <BODY>
    <FORM>
    <TABLE WIDTH="100%">
      <TR>
        <TD>
        <P><INPUT TYPE="BUTTON" NAME="winBackBtn"
                  VALUE="Window Back"
                  ONCLICK="top.back()"></P></TD>
        <TD>
        <P><INPUT TYPE="BUTTON" NAME="winForwardBtn"
                  VALUE="Window Forward"
                  ONCLICK="top.forward()"></P></TD>
        <TD WIDTH="10%"></TD>
        <TD>
        <P><INPUT TYPE="BUTTON" NAME="historyBackBtn"
                  VALUE="History Back"
                  ONCLICK="parent.docFrame.history.back()">
        </P></TD>
        <TD>
        <P><INPUT TYPE="BUTTON" NAME="historyForwardBtn"
                VALUE="History Forward"
                ONCLICK="parent.docFrame.history.forward()">
        </P></TD>
      </TR>
    </TABLE></FORM>
  </BODY>
</HTML>
```

Figure 9.19 shows the initial screen for this test. This script works best if you use the CD-ROM or load the contents of the CD-ROM onto a server.

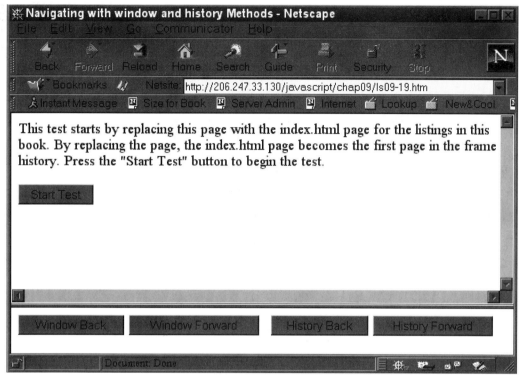

Figure 9.19 *Results of navigating with window and history methods.*

Summary

The top of the object hierarchy has three important objects: the navigator object, the screen object, and the window object. The navigator object defines the browser environment. The screen object defines the entire display screen. The top-level screen object defines the browser window. Taken together, these three objects define the total environment in which the document exists. JavaScripts access to the navigator and screen objects provides you with the ability to make decisions about how to display the document within these environments. While you cannot make adjustments to the navigator and screen environment, you can make changes to the window environment through the properties and methods of the `screen` object.

The `window.open()` method gives you the ability to open customized windows. JavaScript 1.2 expands the number of properties and methods to give you tremendous latitude in the design of windows. For example, you can create your own dialog boxes by designing always-raised windows that are dependent on the parent window.

In addition to creating additional windows, you can divide a window into frames by using the `<FRAMESET> </FRAMESET>` tags in place of the `<BODY> </BODY>` tags. Within the `<FRAMESET>` tags, you define frames with the `<FRAME>` tag, which defines the document loaded into the frame. The frame object in the `frames[]` array is really a window object that has the same properties and methods as the top-level window object, with just a few differences.

Once the browser loads a document into a window, the browser enables event management for the window. There are two kinds of events: raw events (such as mousedown) and functional events (such as blur). As the examples in this chapter illustrate, the mousedown event triggers the blur event. The blur event then triggers the change event. The browser's default routing mechanism routes the events to the appropriate receiver (event handler). By using the `captureEvents()` method, you can manage the event hierarchy for events. You have the option of routing events with the `routeEvent()` method or transferring events to a particular receiver with the `handleEvent()` method. Before embarking on writing exotic event management code, you need to take the time to experiment with events and understand how the browser processes them.

This chapter concludes with a discussion of the `location` and `history` objects. Both of these objects play an important role in the user's navigation from document to document. Without signed scripts, you are limited to window and history methods for moving between documents. With signed scripts, you have more control over the navigation process.

It took five chapters to work through the Netscape object model, but this chapter finally reaches the apex of the object hierarchy. The next two chapters fill in the missing holes by looking at LiveConnect (integrating plug-ins and applets with JavaScript) and Dynamic HTML.

Part

3

Advanced Topics

The chapters in this section explore the advanced aspects of JavaScript. Chapters 10 and 11 conclude the discussion of client-side JavaScript with discussions of LiveConnect, layers, and the JavaScript security model. Chapters 12 through 14 discuss LiveWire, which is the name for server-side JavaScript. Chapter 15 moves to a discussion of JavaScript components and JavaScript Beans. Chapter 16 reviews the tools available for JavaScript development.

Interfacing to Plug-ins and Java Applets

Topics in This Chapter

- JavaScript interface with Java Applets
- JavaScript interface with Plug-ins
- Interfacing with LiveAudio
- Interfacing with LiveVideo

Chapter 10

Netscape's LiveConnect technology adds a new dimension to plug-ins and Java Applets. HTML provides a means for including plug-ins and applets and setting the initial parameters. This approach is the same as executing a program. What is lacking is a dynamic relationship between the HTML document and the applet or plug-in. As shown in Figure 10.1, LiveConnect provides the interface mechanism to allow JavaScript, JavaApplets, and plug-ins to communicate with each other.

Of the three interfaces illustrated in Figure 10.1, this chapter discusses the JavaScript interfaces to Java Applets and plug-ins. The interface between a Java Applet and a plug-in is beyond the scope of this work. This chapter concludes with a discussion of LiveAudio and LiveVideo. These products, which are a part of Netscape Navigator 3.0 and Netscape Communicator 4.0, are LiveConnect enabled.

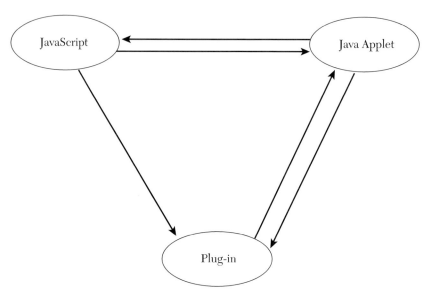

Figure 10.1   Model of LiveConnect Interfaces.

Working with Java Applets

The Java language is an object-oriented, device-independent, programming language developed by Sun Microsystems. Java's philosophy of "program once, run anywhere" has taken the world by storm. This book is not about the Java language. For those readers interested in learning about Java, there are a number of introductory books available. One excellent book is *Core Java: Volume 1—Fundamentals* by Cay S. Horstmann and Gary Cornell (Prentice Hall, 1997). You can get the Java SDK (Software Development Kit) from the Sun web site at http://java.sun.com.

This book concentrates on the interface between JavaScript and Java, which takes the following forms:

- The `<PARAM>` tag with the `<APPLET> </APPLET>` tags
- By setting the public parameters of the Java applet
- Using Java code to access JavaScript methods and properties

The user preferences have a direct bearing on the use of LiveConnect. The use of Java applets requires that Java is enabled. The communication between JavaScript and Java requires that JavaScript is enabled. If the user disables JavaScript, you are left with the `<NOSCRIPT>` `</NOSCRIPT>` tags as a means of communicating any message to the user regarding the need for JavaScript. If JavaScript is enabled, you can check the return value of the `navigator.javaEnabled()` method to verify that Java is enabled.

The applets Object

For each `<APPLET>` tag, the browser creates an `applet` object in the `document.applets[]` array. If the `<APPLET>` tag contains the NAME attribute, you can reference the applet by its name. Consequently, the valid methods for referencing applets are as follows:

```
document.AppletName
document.applets[index]
document.applets["AppletName"]
```

The `length` property of the `document.applets[]` array tells you the number of Java applets in the document. The public properties of the Java applet are properties of the applet object. Similarly, the public methods of the Java applet are methods of the applet object. It is through the public properties and methods that Java opens the door for JavaScript to interact with a Java applet.

Using the <PARAM> Tag

If you think of the Java applet as an application program, then it only makes sense that you can pass the applet parameters. To set the parameter, HTML provides the `<PARAM>` tag, which has the NAME and VALUE attributes. To receive the parameter, the Java applet uses the `getParameter()` method.

Listing 10.1 shows the code for a Java applet that uses the `<PARAM>` tag to display a string. The purpose of this applet is to illustrate the use of the `getParameter()` method and not to show off the capabilities of Java.

Listing 10.1 Code for DisplayMsg Java Applet

```
import java.applet.*;
import java.awt.*;

public class DisplayMsg extends Applet {
    public void paint(Graphics g) {
        String msgStr = getParameter("msg");
        g.drawString(msgStr, 25, 50);
    }
}
```

Listing 10.2 illustrates the implementation of the Java applet in an HTML document. The <PARAM> tag defines the message that the applet displays.

Listing 10.2 Using Applet Parameters

```
<HTML>
  <HEAD>
    <TITLE>Using Applet Parameters</TITLE>
  </HEAD>
  <BODY>
    <P>This document displays the text set as an applet
       parameter.</P>
    <APPLET CODE="DisplayMsg.class"
            ID="DisplayMsg"
            ALT="display a message" NAME="DisplayMsg"
            WIDTH="200" HEIGHT="100">
    <PARAM NAME="msg" VALUE="Hello World"></APPLET>
  </BODY>
</HTML>
```

Since the Java applet retrieves the parameter through the `getParameter()` method, the parameter is not a public parameter and does not appear as a property of the applet. This method of interfacing to a Java applet only sets the initial parameters for the applet as shown in Figure 10.2. For dynamic interaction with a Java applet, you need to use the features of LiveConnect.

Note:

If you are using a Java applet written by someone else, you need to read the documentation for that applet to know how to interface with the applet.

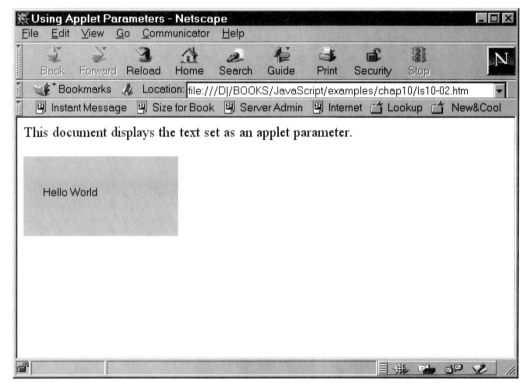

Figure 10.2   Results of using applet parameters.

Interfacing with a Java Applet's Public Properties and Methods

Where the <PARAM> tag provides a static, non-JavaScript method of passing parameters to a Java applet, LiveConnect opens the door to dynamic interaction with the applet with the aid of JavaScript. JavaScript has access to all public variables, properties and methods of Java applets.

As shown in the section on *"Understanding Netscape Packages,"* Java-Script's access to Java extends to its ancestor classes and packages.

The code for the Java applet shown in Listing 10.3 illustrates a Java public method. The applet displays a default string when it is started. The public `setString()` method dynamically changes the string displayed by the applet. Since it is a public method, `setString()` is a property of the applet object.

Listing 10.3 Java Applet with a Public Method

```
import java.applet.*;
import java.awt.*;

public class DisplayStr extends Applet {
   String dispStr;
   public void init() {
      dispStr =  new String("Default String");
   }
   public void paint(Graphics g) {
      g.drawString(dispStr, 25, 50);
   }
   public void setString(String newStr) {
      dispStr = newStr;
      repaint();
   }
}
```

The HTML document in Listing 10.4 incorporates the Java applet shown in Listing 10.3 and uses JavaScript to access the public `set-String()` method. When you click on the "Display String" button, the script invokes the `setString()` method to change the displayed string to that entered in the text box.

Listing 10.4 JavaScript Interface to Java

```
<HTML>
  <HEAD>
    <TITLE>JavaScript Interface to Java</TITLE>
  </HEAD>
```

```
<BODY>
   <P>This example illustrates how JavaScript can use a
     Java method to control an applet.</P>
   <APPLET CODE="DisplayStr.class"
          ID="DisplayStr" ALT="Display a String"
          NAME="strD" WIDTH="200" HEIGHT="100">
   </APPLET>
   <P>Enter a string in the following box and then press
     the &quot;Display String&quot; button.</P>
   <FORM NAME="test">
   <P ALIGN="RIGHT"><INPUT TYPE="TEXT" NAME="str"></P>
   <P><INPUT TYPE="BUTTON" NAME="dispButton"
            VALUE="Display String"
ONCLICK="document.strD.setString(document.test.str.value)">
   </P>
   </FORM>
   </BODY>
</HTML>
```

Both the code for the Java applet and the JavaScript are simple, but they show the principle that drives the interface between JavaScript and Java. Figure 10.3 shows the results of running the HTML document shown in Listing 10.4. Although Java provides for public variables, the public method is the most common method for interfacing with Java. The Java public method provides a way to dynamically interface with the Java applet. It is the Java applet's responsibility to convert the JavaScript data types to Java data types. Thus, the person who develops Web pages only needs to know what the Java applet expects from a JavaScript perspective.

Understanding Netscape Packages

Java allows the grouping of classes into a collection called *packages*. Packages provide a means to organize classes and separate libraries. Starting with Netscape Navigator 3.0, Netscape incorporated Netscape packages into its products. The java_30 file includes the following packages:

- *netscape* packages to facilitate JavaScript and Java communication
- *java* and *sun* packages to enhance the security of LiveConnect

The java and sun packages replace packages in Sun's Java Development ment Kit (JDK). These packages exist only to provide enhanced security

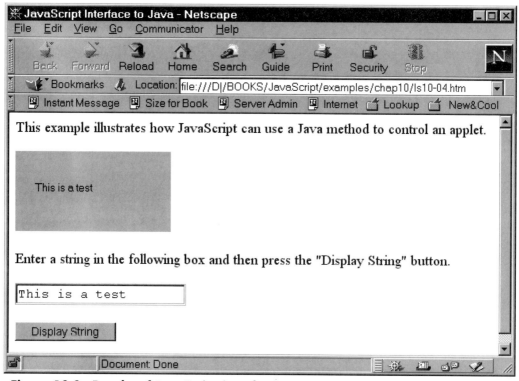

Figure 10.3   Results of JavaScript interface to Java.

and may be discontinued in the future. The packages specific to Netscape are as follows:

- *netscape.applet* replaces the Sun JDK package *sun.applet*.
- *netscape.net* replaces the Sun JDK package *sun.net*.
- *netscape.javascript* implements the JSObject class to allow Java applets to access JavaScript methods and properties. It also implements JSException to handle JavaScript errors.
- *netscape.plugin* implements the Plugin class to enable JavaScript and Java plug-in communications.

To use these packages for Netscape Navigator 3.0, you need to modify the CLASSPATH environment variable to specify the path for the java_30 file. For the Windows environment, the CLASSPATH could be as follows:

```
.;C:\JDK\java\lib\classes.zip;C:\Program
Files\Netscape\Navigator\Program\Classes\java_301
```

The name of the file changes according to the release of Netscape Navigator. Instead of a single package file, Netscape Communicator provides a number of JAR (Java ARchive) files that implement Navigator classes for Java. A JAR file consists of a compressed set of Java class files, JavaScript scripts, Communicator plug-ins, or any other kind of document or application. The JAR format allows you to digitally sign any member of a JAR file. JDK 1.1 introduced JAR files as a means of packaging elements to build components. Since this time the discussion of components involves the Visual JavaScript tool, this topic is covered in Chapter 16, "JavaScript Tools."

Warning

The Java applets used in this book were compiled using JDK 1.1.5. While JDK 1.1.5 is the most current release of Java as of this writing, Netscape Communicator is edging towards full compliance with JDK 1.1.4. To add to the confusion, Microsoft's foundation classes are not fully compliant with Sun's standard foundation classes. Just as JavaScript is evolving into a mature object-oriented scripting language, Java continues to evolve as an object-oriented programming language. When reading any reference documentation about the interface between JavaScript and Java, you need to be aware of the impact of the change from the package file to the JAR file. From the perspective of LiveConnect, this marks the difference between Netscape Navigator 3.0 and Netscape Communicator 4.0, as LiveConnect was not a feature of Netscape Navigator 2.0.

As mentioned previously, the public Java method is the mechanism used to facilitate the JavaScript interface to Java. Besides any custom methods declared in a Java applet, every applet has a set of common methods. The script in Listing 10.5 is the script in Listing 10.2, with the addition of a button to display the properties of the applet. Figure 10.4 shows the initial screen for this document. When you click the "Display

Properties of Applet Object" button, the script displays the window shown in Figure 10.5.

Listing 10.5 Common Public Methods of Java Applets

```
<HTML>
  <HEAD>
    <TITLE>Common Public Methods of Java Applets</TITLE>
<SCRIPT LANGUAGE="JavaScript1.2">
<!--
function listProps(objName) {
      var propsTable = new Array()
      var j=0
      function getProps(obj, objName) {
          for (var i in obj) {
              propsTable[j]=new Array(3)
              propsTable[j][0]=objName+"."+i
              propsTable[j][1]=typeof(obj[i])
              if (propsTable[j][1].indexOf("str")>=0 ||
                  propsTable[j][1].indexOf("num")>=0 ||
                  propsTable[j][1].indexOf("boo")>=0) {
                  propsTable[j][2]=obj[i].toString()
              }
              else {
                  propsTable[j][2]=""
              }
              ++j
          }
          return true
      }
  getProps(eval(objName), objName)
  debugWin=window.open("", "debugWin",
          "dependent=yes,scrollbars=yes")
  debugWin.document.open()
  debugWin.document.write("Total properties = "
          +propsTable.length+"<BR>")
  for (var i=1; i<propsTable.length; i++) {
     debugWin.document.write(propsTable[i][0]+" = ")
     debugWin.document.write(propsTable[i][1])
     if (propsTable[i][1].indexOf("str")>=0 ||
         propsTable[i][1].indexOf("num")>=0 ||
         propsTable[i][1].indexOf("boo")>=0) {
         debugWin.document.write(" ("+propsTable[i][2]+")")
```

```
      }
      debugWin.document.write("<BR>")
   }
   debugWin.document.close
   return true
}
//-->
</SCRIPT>
  </HEAD>
  <BODY>
    <P>The following Java applet displays the text
      specified in the parameter:</P>
    <APPLET CODE="DisplayMsg.class"
            ID="DisplayMsg" ALT="display a message"
            NAME="DisplayMsg" WIDTH="200" HEIGHT="100">
      <PARAM NAME="msg" VALUE="Hello World">
    </APPLET>
    <FORM>
    <P><INPUT TYPE="BUTTON" NAME="dispObj"
            VALUE="Display Properties of Applet Object"
            ONCLICK="listProps('document.applets[0]')">
    </P>
    </FORM>
  </BODY>
</HTML>
```

The screen in Figure 10.5 indicates that there are 137 common public methods that are part of this Java applet. Most of the methods require additional Java code to take advantage of the method. However, the methods that control the life cycle of an applet play an important role for all Java applets. The Java runtime automatically calls these methods as needed; therefore, you do not need to call them from JavaScript. Table 10.1 presents these methods to show how the Java runtime interacts with a Java applet.

Table 10.1 Java Methods that control the Life Cycle of an Applet

Method	Description
init()	The browser calls the init() method when Java first launches the applet. The applet uses this method to perform all initialization functions.

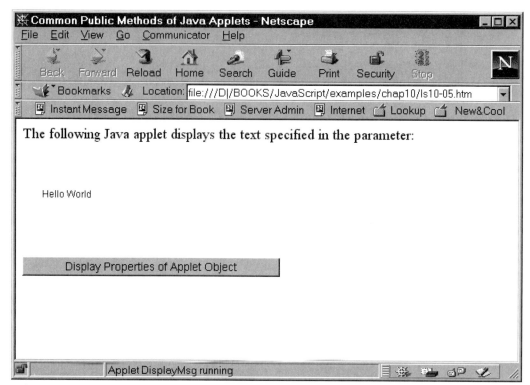

Figure 10.4   The initial window for Display Applet properties.

Table 10.1 Java Methods that control the Life Cycle of an Applet *(Continued)*

Method	Description
start()	After Java calls the init() method, Java automatically calls the start() method. When the user leaves the page and then returns to it, Java automatically calls the start() method.
stop()	Java automatically calls this method when the user leaves the page containing the applet. You should not call this method directly.
destroy()	Java calls this method when the user closes the browser. Java automatically calls the stop() method before calling the destroy() method.

```
Netscape                                                                    ×
Total properties = 137
document.applets[0] paint = function
document.applets[0].destroy = function
document.applets[0].stop = function
document.applets[0].start = function
document.applets[0].init = function
document.applets[0].play = function
document.applets[0].getParameterInfo = function
document.applets[0].getLocale = function
document.applets[0].getAppletInfo = function
document.applets[0].getAudioClip = function
document.applets[0].getImage = function
document.applets[0].showStatus = function
document.applets[0].resize = function
document.applets[0].getAppletContext = function
document.applets[0].getParameter = function
document.applets[0].getCodeBase = function
document.applets[0].getDocumentBase = function
document.applets[0].isActive = function
document.applets[0].setStub = function
document.applets[0].addNotify = function
```

Figure 10.5   Results of Display Applet properties.

The Java Console

The Java Console is a special Netscape Navigator window that displays Java messages. Although the Java Console is primarily a debugging tool for Java, it is also a useful tool for JavaScript programmers. You can use the Java Console as follows:

- Check the status of applets on a page
- Use Java methods to write to the console

Navigator

Microsoft Internet Explorer does not support the Java Console.

To start the Java Console in Netscape Communicator, you need to click "Communicator" on the menu bar, and then click "Java Console." For Netscape Navigator 3.0, you need to click "Options" on the menu bar, and then click "Java Console." To find out the options available to you, type a "?" ("h" in Netscape Navigator 3.0). Figure 10.6 shows the options available to the user of the Java Console. For a JavaScript programmer, the useful options are as follows:

- Clear console window
- Dump applet context state to console
- Print current memory use to console

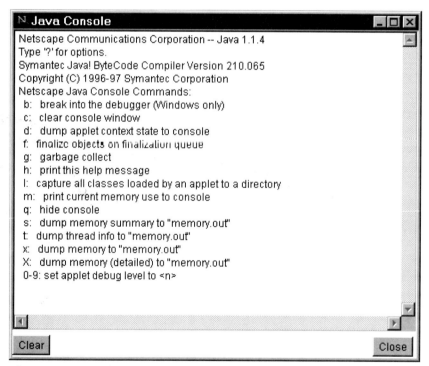

Figure 10.6 Help display for Java console.

Using the script in Listing 10.4 as an example, Figure 10.7 shows the applet context and memory usage for the DisplayStr applet.

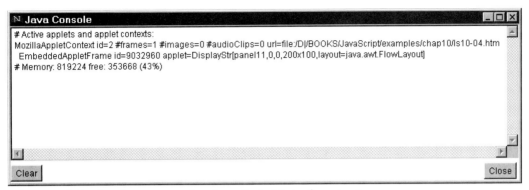

Figure 10.7 Applet context for JavaScript interface to Java.

The JavaScript `Packages` object reflects the Java packages and classes. Thus, the `Packages` object gives you a means of accessing the classes for the Java, Sun, and Netscape packages. The syntax for referencing a method for a class is as follows:

```
[Packages.]packageName.className.methodName
```

The name Packages is optional for Java, Sun, and Netscape packages. To simplify references to packages, JavaScript provides the following aliases:

- `java` is an alias for `Packages.java`
- `sun` is an alias for `Packages.sun`
- `netscape` is an alias for `Packages.netscape`

For example, you can refer to the `println()` method using either of the following two references:

```
Packages.java.lang.System.err.println(text)
Java.lang.System.err.println(text)
```

The `println()` method prints the string specified by *text* to the Java Console. As seen by the class name, this method uses part of Java's error handling. As the script in Listing 10.6 shows, you can use the `println()` method from JavaScript to write text to the Java Console.

Listing 10.6 Writing to the Java Console

```
<HTML>
  <HEAD>
    <TITLE>Writing to the Java Console</TITLE>
<SCRIPT LANGUAGE="JavaScript">
<!--
function dispText(frmObj) {
   var System=java.lang.System
   System.err.println(frmObj.str.value)
}
//-->
</SCRIPT>
  </HEAD>
  <BODY>
    <P>For this example, you need to open the Java Console,
       enter some text in the following text box, and then
       click the display button.</P>
    <FORM NAME="test">
    <P><INPUT TYPE="TEXT" NAME="str" SIZE="40"></P>
    <P><INPUT TYPE="BUTTON" NAME="dispBtn"
              VALUE="Display Text in Java Console"
              ONCLICK="dispText(this.form)"></P>
    </FORM>
  </BODY>
</HTML>
```

Figure 10.8 shows the browser window for the script in Listing 10.6. When you click on the "Display Text in Java Console" button, the script uses the `println()` method to print the string to the Java Console, as shown in Figure 10.9. Thus, the Java Console becomes an alternate screen for displaying JavaScript errors and debugging information.

Java access to JavaScript

Conversely, Java can access JavaScript objects, properties, and methods. The `netscape.javascript.JSObject` class controls the Java-to-JavaScript interface. The class contains the methods described in Table 10.2. These methods provide Java access to JavaScript features (such as window control and browser information) to which Java is not exposed.

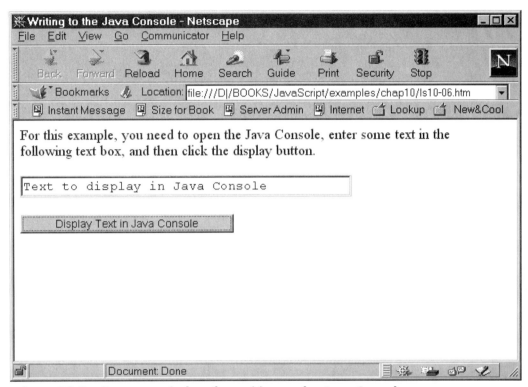

Figure 10.8   Browser window for writing to the Java Console.

Table 10.2 Methods of JSObject Class

Method	Description
call()	Calls a JavaScript method.
eval()	Evaluates a JavaScript expression.
getMember()	Retrieves the named member of a JavaScript object.
getSlot()	Retrieves an indexed member of a JavaScript object.
setMember()	Sets a named member of a JavaScript object.
setSlot()	Sets an indexed member of a JavaScript object.
toString()	Converts a JSObject to a string.
removeMember()	Removes a named member of a JavaScript Object.
getWindow()	A static method that gets a JSObject for the window containing the applet.

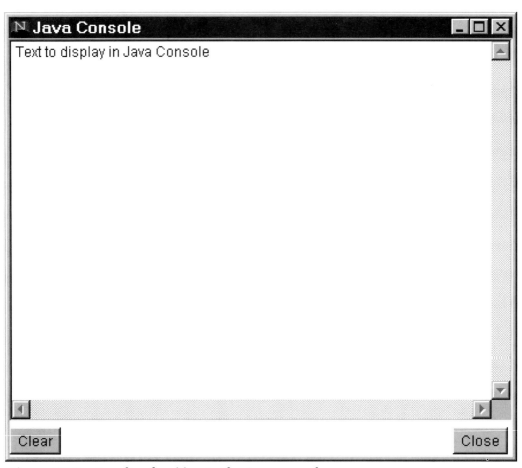

Figure 10.9 Results of writing to the Java console.

To use these methods, the author of the Java applet needs to import the Netscape javascript package with the following line:

```
import netscape.javascript.*
```

The author of the HTML page permits a Java applet to access Java-Script by specifying the MAYSCRIPT attribute in the <APPLET> tag. The MAYSCRIPT attribute prevents an applet from accessing JavaScript without the permission of the Web page's author. The MAYSCRIPT tag is not needed for JavaScript to access Java.

The Java-to-JavaScript interface involves understanding Java beyond the scope of this book. For readers who wish to explore this topic in more detail, reference the JavaScript Reference manual and the JavaScript Guide. You can obtain this documentation in Adobe Acrobat's PDF format, or zipped HTML format, from the following URL:

```
http://developer.netscape.com/library/documentation/index.html
```

Working with Plug-ins

If you strip away all of the extensions, HTML is simply a text-oriented language for displaying documents. To incorporate other media types into an HTML document, you need a formatting syntax for HTML and a means of identifying the media type. The <IMG> and <EMBED> tags are the HTML format statements for alternate media types. The Multi-purpose Internet Mail Extensions (MIME) standard establishes a mechanism for identifying the type of data in a file. Table 10.3 lists some of the most common MIME types. For a complete list of MIME types, check the latest MIME standard from IETF (Internet Engineering Task Force). As of this writing, the latest RFCs for the MIME type standard are RFC 2045, RFC 2046, RFC 2047, RFC 2048, and RFC 2049.

Table 10.3 Some Common MIME Types

Mime Type	Description	File Extensions
application/acad	AutoCAD Drawing Files	dwg. DWG
application/excel	Microsoft Excel	xl
application/msword	Microsoft Word	word, w6w, doc
application/pdf	Adobe Acrobat PDF	pdf
application/postscript	PostScript	ai, PS, ps, eps
application/rtf	Rich Text Format	rtf
application/x-director	Macromedia Director	dir, dcr, dxr
application/x-mif	FrameMaker MIF Format	mif
application/x-gzip	GNU Zip	gz, gzip

Table 10.3 Some Common MIME Types *(Continued)*

Mime Type	Description	File Extensions
application/x-latex	LaTeX source	latex
application/x-tex	TeX source	tex
application/zip	ZIP archive	zip
audio/basic	Basic audio (usually μ-law)	au, snd
audio/x-aiff	AIFF audio	aif, aiff, aifc
audio/x-pn-realaudio	RealAudio	ra, ram
audio/x-wav	Windows WAVE audio	wav
image/gif	GIF image	gif
image/jpeg	JPEG image	jpg, JPG, JPE, jpe, JPEG, jpeg
image/tiff	TIFF image	tiff, tif
image/x-xbitmap	X Bitmap	xbm
image/x-xpixmap	X Pixmap	xpm
text/html	HTML	html, htm
text/plain	Plain text	txt, g, h, C, cc, hh, m, f90
video/mpeg	MPEG video	mpeg, mpg, MPC, MPE, mpe, MPEG
video/quicktime	QuickTime Video	qt, mov
video/msvideo	Microsoft Windows Video	avi
x-world/x-vrml	VRML Worlds	wrl

The SRC attribute of the <IMG> and <EMBED> tags defines the name of the file. When the browser downloads this file, the server places the MIME type in the header message. The browser then decides whether to process a file according to the following choices:

- Internal routine
- Plug-in
- Helper application

There are two aspects to the use of plug-ins. On one side, the browser tracks installed plug-ins via the `Plugin` objects in the `plugins[]` array, and the relationship between MIME types and plug-ins via the `Mime-Type` objects in the `mimeTypes[]` array. On the other side, the Embed objects in the `embeds[]` array tracks the `<EMBED>` tags in the HTML document.

The Plugin Object

A *plug-in* is a software module that extends the browser's capability to handle additional MIME types. Users install plug-ins to upgrade Navigator without having to modify or upgrade the browser itself. Since the plug-in is a separately installed component, there is no connection between plug-ins a user installs and the HTML document. JavaScript 1.1 introduces the `plugins[]` array to expose the installed plug-ins to JavaScript as a means for the HTML document to determine the availability of plug-ins needed to present the document. Table 10.4 lists the properties and methods of the `plugins[]` array.

Table 10.4 Properties and Methods of the plugins[] Array

Properties	Methods	Event Handlers
length	refresh()	None

The `plugins[]` array is an array of Plugin objects. Like all arrays, it includes a `length` property that indicates the number of objects in the array. In addition, the `plugins[]` array includes the `refresh()` method, which makes newly installed plug-ins available to the browser. The `refresh()` method takes either of the following formats:

```
navigator.plugins.refresh(true)
navigator.plugins.refresh(false)
```

With the true option, the `refresh()` method refreshes the `plugins[]` array to include any newly installed plug-ins and reloads all documents that contain an `<EMBED>` tag. The false option to the `refresh()` method refreshes the `plugins[]` array, but does not reload the documents. Unless the plug-ins are LiveConnect aware, you need to reload a document to use the new plug-in. Without the `refresh()`

method, the user must close and reopen the browser to make the plug-in available.

A `Plugin` object is an element in the `plugins[]` array and reflects an installed plug-in. Table 10.5 describes the properties of the `Plugin` object. All properties of the `Plugin` object are read-only.

Table 10.5 Properties of the Plugin Object

Property	Description
name	A string that specifies the plug-in's name as supplied by the plug-in.
description	A description of the plug-in.
filename	The pathname for the plug-in. The pathname varies from platform to platform and is also dependent on the install path selected by the user.
length	Number of elements in the plug-in's array of `MimeType` objects.

A plug-in can support multiple MIME types. To accommodate multiple MIME types, the Plugin object contains an array of `MimeType` objects. The `length` property of the Plugin object specifies the number of MIME types supported by the plug-in. You can address the `Plugin` object using either an index to the `plugins[]` array or the name of the plug-in as shown in the following examples:

```
navigator.plugins[0]
navigator.plugins["LiveAudio"]
```

To reference a `MimeType` object in a `Plugin` object, you can use either the index value of the object or the MIME type as shown in the following examples:

```
navigator.plugins[0][0]
navigator.plugins["LiveAudio"]["audio/wav"]
```

The script in Listing 10.7 prints a list of the plug-ins installed on the machine. For each plug-in, the script lists the properties of the `Plugin` object. Figure 10.10 shows the result of running this script.

Listing 10.7 Working with the Plugin Object

```
<HTML>
  <HEAD>
    <TITLE>Working with the Plugin Object</TITLE>
  </HEAD>
  <BODY>
    <P>The script in this example lists the installed
      plugins.</P>
<SCRIPT LANGUAGE="JavaScript1.1">
<!--
for (var i=0; i<navigator.plugins.length; i++) {
   with (document) {
      writeln("<HR>")
      writeln("Name: "+navigator.plugins[i].name+"<BR>")
      writeln("Filename: "+navigator.plugins[i].filename
              +"<BR>")
      writeln("Description: "
              +navigator.plugins[i].description+"<BR>")
      writeln("# of MIME Types: "
              +navigator.plugins[i].length+"<BR>")
   }
}
//-->
</SCRIPT>
  </BODY>
</HTML>
```

The MimeType Object

Beginning with JavaScript 1.1, the mimeTypes[] array contains a Mi-meType object for every MIME type supported by the browser. Table 10.6 describes the properties of the MimeType object. The mime-Types[] array and MimeType objects are read-only.

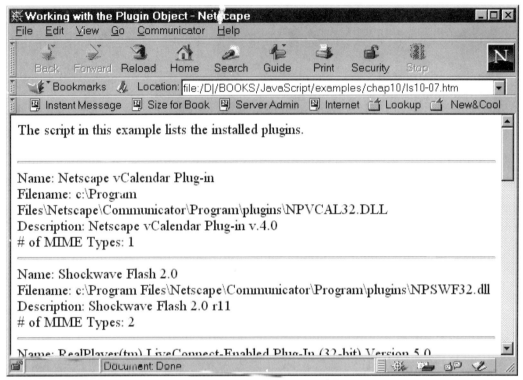

Figure 10.10 Results of working with the Plugin object.

Table 10.6 Properties of the MimeType object

Property	Description
description	A string that describes the MIME Type
enabledPlugin	Contains the Plugin object enabled to support the MIME type. If there is no Plugin object configured for the MIME type, the value is null. Although more than one plug-in may support the same MIME type, there is only one enabled plug-in.
suffixes	A comma separated string of file extensions for the MIME type.
type	A string that defines the unique name of the MIME type.

If there is a `MimeType` object, but the `enabledPlugin` property is null, then the `MimeType` object indicates that the MIME type is supported internally or via helper applications. As shown in the following examples, you can reference a `MimeType` object using either an index to the array or the MIME type name.

```
navigator.mimeTypes[0]
navigator.mimeTypes["audio/wav"]
```

The script in Listing 10.8 prints a list of the MIME types supported by the browser. Figure 10.11 shows the results of running this script. The `for` statement limits the script to only the first five MIME types. For some reason, Netscape Communicator for Windows NT crashed when attempting to list the entire array.

Listing 10.8 Working with the MimeType Object

```
<HTML>
  <HEAD>
    <TITLE>Working with the MimeType Object</TITLE>
  </HEAD>
  <BODY>
    <P>This browser supports the following MIME types:</P>
<SCRIPT LANGUAGE="JavaScript">
<!--
for (i=0; i < 5; i++) {
   document.writeln("<HR>")
   document.writeln("type: "+navigator.mimeTypes[i].type
                 +"<BR>")
   document.writeln("description: "
                 +navigator.mimeTypes[i].description
                 +"<BR>")
   document.writeln("suffixes: "
                  +navigator.mimeTypes[i].suffixes
                  +"<BR>")
   document.writeln("plug-in enabled: ")
   if (navigator.mimeTypes[i].enabledPlugin==null) {
      document.writeln("None<BR>")
   } else {
      document.writeln(
         navigator.mimeTypes[i].enabledPlugin.name)
      document.writeln("<BR>")
```

```
    }
}
//-->
</SCRIPT>
  </BODY>
</HTML>
```

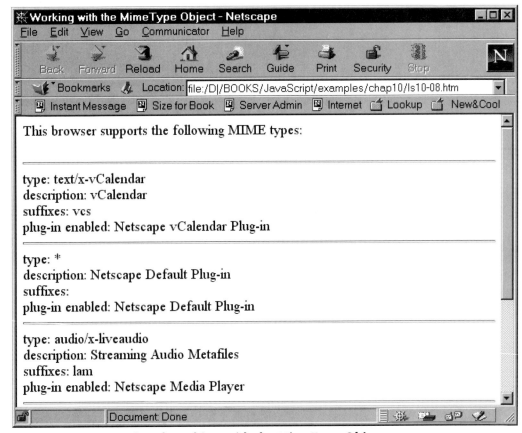

Figure 10.11 **Results of working with the MimeType Object.**

The Embed Object

The embeds[] array is a read-only array of the document object that reflects the files embedded in the document by the <EMBED> tag. The elements of the embeds[] array are Embed objects that reflect the audio, video, or other files embedded in the document. Embed objects that are LiveConnect aware may have properties and methods. The `length` property of the embeds [ ] array indicates the number of embedded objects in the document. As shown in the following examples, you can reference an Embed object in the embeds [ ] array using either an index or the value specified by the NAME attribute in the <EMBED> tag.

```
document.embeds[0]
document.embeds["embed1"]
```

LiveConnect Aware Plug-ins

A plug-in that uses the Java class `netscape.plugin`.Plugin is Live-Connect aware. This class allows access to its static variables and methods in the same way that you access a Java applet's variables and methods. The LiveAudio and LiveVideo plug-ins are examples of Live-Connect aware plug-ins.

Interfacing to LiveAudio

The LiveAudio plug-in plays audio files that use the audio/basic, audio/midi, audio/x-aiff, and audio/x-wav MIME types. LiveAudio allows you to create an audio console with the views described in Table 10.7. The `HEIGHT` and `WIDTH` attributes of the <EMBED> tag determine the elements displayed by the browser.

Table 10.7 LiveAudio Console Alternatives

View	Description
Console	Consists of play, pause, stop, and volume control lever.
Small Console	Similar to the console view, but with smaller buttons. In addition, this view automatically starts playing the sound file.
Play Button	A button to start playing the specified sound file.
Pause Button	A button that pauses the playing of the specified sound file without unloading it.
Stop Button	A button that stops playing the specified sound and unloads it.
Volume Lever	A lever that adjusts the volume level of the sound.

The LiveAudio plug-in provides a comprehensive set of attributes that are part of the `<EMBED>` tag. You can find the specifications for these attributes, along with the documentation for the LiveAudio plug-in, at the following URL:

```
http://search.netscape.com/comprod/products/navigator/
version_3.0/multimedia/audio/how.html
```

Additional documentation on the LiveAudio plug-in can be found by performing a search of Netscape documentation. This book limits this discussion to the JavaScript interface to LiveAudio through the use of LiveConnect. Table 10.8 lists the methods of the LiveAudio plug-in exposed to JavaScript.

Table 10.8 LiveAudio Methods

Method	Description
`play(loop, 'URL of sound')`	Causes the sound to play. The value of *loop* is true, false, or an integer indicating the number of loops.
`stop()`	Stops playing of the sound file.
`pause()`	Pauses playing of the sound file without unloading the file.
`start_time(seconds)`	Designates the number of *seconds* into the sound file to begin playing.
`end_time(seconds)`	Designates the number of *seconds* into the sound file where playing is to end.
`setvol(percent)`	Sets the volume to the specified percentage.
`fade_to(to_percent)`	Fades the volume level to the designated percentage.
`fade_from_to(from_percent, to_percent)`	Fades the volume level from *from_percent* to *to_percent*.
`start_at_beginning()`	Overrides the value set by `start_time()`.
`stop_at_end()`	Overrides the value set by `end_time()`.
`IsReady()`	Returns true if the plug-in is ready to play the sound.
`IsPlaying()`	Returns true if the sound is currently playing.
`IsPaused()`	Returns true if the sound is currently paused.
`GetVolume()`	Returns the current volume as a percentage.

The methods in Table 10.8 are part of the `Embed` object associated with the LiveAudio `<EMBED>` tags. Thus, you can reference using the `embeds[]` array as follows:

```
document.embeds[index].method()
```

If the `<EMBED>` tag includes the `NAME` attribute, you can reference it by name as follows:

```
document.embedName.method()
```

Note:

When you use the `NAME` attribute in the `<EMBED>` tag for LiveAudio, you must include the `MASTERSOUND` attribute for the sound to play. The requirement for the `MASTERSOUND` attribute applies even when there are no other LiveAudio `<EMBED>` tags with the same name.

The HTML document in Listing 10.9 illustrates how to use JavaScript to interface to the LiveAudio plug-in. Although the script uses buttons to control the sound, it could easily be adapted to an image with an image map for the controls.

Listing 10.9 Using the LiveAudio Plug-in

```
<HTML>
  <HEAD>
    <TITLE>Using the LiveAudio Plug-in</TITLE>
<SCRIPT LANGUAGE="JavaScript">
<!--
function playSound() {
   document.testSnd.play(true)
}
function pauseSound() {
   document.testSnd.pause()
}
function stopSound() {
   document.testSnd.stop()
}
```

```
function volUp() {
   var currentVol=document.testSnd.GetVolume()
   var newVol=currentVol+5
   if (newVol>100) newVol=100
   document.testSnd.setvol(newVol)
}
function volDown() {
   var currentVol=document.testSnd.GetVolume()
   var newVol=currentVol-5
   if (newVol<0) newVol=0
   document.testSnd.setvol(newVol)
}
function dispStatus() {
   var msg="The current status is:\n"
   msg+="Sound file ready: "
   msg+=document.testSnd.IsReady()+"\n"
   msg+="Sound playing: "
   msg+=document.testSnd.IsPlaying()+"\n"
   msg+="Sound paused: "
   msg+=document.testSnd.IsPaused()+"\n"
   msg+="Volume percentage: "
   msg+=document.testSnd.GetVolume()
   alert(msg)
}
//-->
</SCRIPT>
  </HEAD>
  <BODY>
    <P>When you press the play button, the browser will
       load and continuously play a sound file. You can then
       use the other controls to experiment with the
       LiveAudio plug-in.</P>
    <EMBED HIDDEN="TRUE" MASTERSOUND="MASTERSOUND"
    NAME="testSnd" AUTOSTART="FALSE"
    SRC="../sounds/classical.wav">
    <FORM>
    <P><INPUT TYPE="BUTTON" NAME="playBtn" VALUE="Play"
           ONCLICK="playSound()">
       <INPUT TYPE="BUTTON" NAME="pauseBtn" VALUE="Pause"
           ONCLICK="pauseSound()">
       <INPUT TYPE="BUTTON" NAME="stopBtn" VALUE="Stop"
           ONCLICK="stopSound()">
       <INPUT TYPE="BUTTON" NAME="volUpBtn"
           VALUE="Increase Volume"
           ONCLICK="volUp()">
```

```
        <INPUT TYPE="BUTTON" NAME="volDwnBtn"
               VALUE="Lower Volume"
               ONCLICK="volDown()">
        <INPUT TYPE="BUTTON" NAME="statusBtn"
               VALUE="Display Status" ONCLICK="dispStatus()">
    </P>
    </FORM>
    <P>The classical.wav sound file came from the royalty
       free music collection at
       <A HREF="http://www.partnersinrhyme.com/">
       http://www.partnersinrhyme.com/</A></P>
  </BODY>
</HTML>
```

The <EMBED> tag defines a hidden sound file with the AUTOSTART attribute set to false. With this definition, the sound file loads, but does not play until the "Play" button is pressed. Except for the "Display Status" button, the buttons simulate the behavior of the LiveAudio console. Figure 10.12 shows the Web page for this document. If your initial sound level is not an integer value, increase and decrease the sound results in increments that are not exactly five percent.

Interfacing to LiveVideo

The LiveVideo plug-in plays AVI video files with a MIME type of video/ msvideo. The LiveVideo plug-in currently only works on the Windows 95 and Windows NT platforms. The following URL provides documentation on the HTML syntax for the <EMBED> tag:

```
http://home.netscape.com/comprod/products/navigator/
version_3.0/multimedia/video/how.html
```

The LiveVideo plug-in has the controls built into the plug-in so that clicking on the video with the left mouse button starts and stops the video. If you click on the video with the right mouse button, the LiveVideo plug-in displays a pop-up menu with the full set of options. In addition, you can add external control through the methods exposed to JavaScript as listed in Table 10.9.

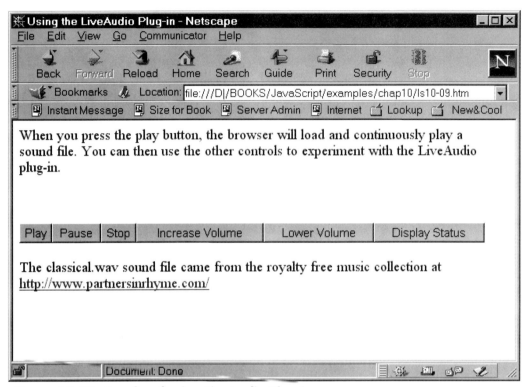

Figure 10.12   Results of using LiveAudio Plug-in.

Table 10.9 LiveVideo Methods

Methods	Description
play()	Starts playing the video at the current location in the source file.
stop()	Stops the currently playing video.
rewind()	Rewinds the currently loaded video.
seek(frame-number)	Sets the current frame to that specified by *frame-number*.

You can see a demonstration of the LiveVideo plug-in at the following URL:

```
http://home.netscape.com/comprod/products/navigator/
version_3.0/multimedia/video/index.html
```

Summary

Java applets and plug-ins provide two ways to extend the capabilities of the browser: the Java applet uses the browser window as a platform independent display for small applications; and, the plug-in extends the capabilities of the browser to support other media types as specified by the MIME type. While the Java applet is dynamically loaded as part of the HTML document, the plug-in requires prior installation before it can be used.

Through Netscape packages, Netscape's LiveConnect allows the Web page developer to interact with Java applets and plug-ins. JavaScript can access the public properties and methods of both Java applets and plug-ins. In addition, Java applets can access the JavaScript object hierarchy.

The Web page developer does not need to know how Java applets or plug-ins perform their functions. All the Web page developer needs is documentation regarding the publicly available properties and methods. This approach fits with Netscape's concept of a reusable component architecture that separates the duties of Web page developers from the programming tasks required to write Java applets and plug-ins.

The next Chapter concludes the discussion of the client-side features of JavaScript with discussion of Dynamic HTML, Cascading Style Sheets, and more on Java Security. After this, the attention of the book addresses the use of JavaScript on the server-side.

Advanced JavaScript

Topics in This Chapter

- Enhancing the appearance of a Web page with style sheets
- Expanding the behavior of a Web page with positioned content
- The security model in Netscape Communicator 4.0

Chapter 11

Cascading style sheets, positioned content, and downloadable fonts are the three components of Dynamic HTML (DHTML). When combined with JavaScript, these new features provide the tools that extend control over the layout and appearance of your Web pages. Style sheets control the stylistic attributes of the typographical elements on a Web page. Content positioning controls the positioning of content and its behavior when the user loads the Web page. The ability to download fonts ensures that the user's machine has the correct fonts available for displaying the Web page.

The use of JavaScript in managing style sheets and positioned content represents only part of the DHTML picture. Since there is no JavaScript involved with downloadable fonts, the subject is not covered in this chapter. To learn about the HTML portion of DHTML, you should read Netscape's "Introducing Dynamic HTML" document, which is available at the following URL:

```
http://developer.netscape.com/one/dynhtml/index.html
```

While DHTML is a hot topic, the security model is a topic that every advanced JavaScript user needs to understand. The security model for

Netscape Communicator 4.0 is a balancing act. On one hand, the user needs to protect the integrity of their machine. Conversely, the application developer needs to use the browser as a platform for cross-platform applications. The security model attempts to meet the needs of both parties.

This chapter focuses on Netscape's approach to DHTML and security as implemented in JavaScript for Netscape Communicator 4.0. The changes to Microsoft's JScript for Microsoft Internet Explorer 4.0 are significantly different from JavaScript 1.2. Consequently, compatibility notes will not be included in this chapter.

Cascading Style Sheets

Without style sheets, it was difficult to control the typographical presentation of the Web page. Although you could specify headings, you had little control over their placement and the fonts used. Fonts were a problem for all text, as you were limited to the fonts available on the user's machine.

The development of cascading style sheets provides the ability to control the stylistic aspects of your Web page, such as text color, margins, element alignment, font styles, font sizes, and font weights. Netscape Communicator supports two types of style sheets:

- Cascading Style Sheet (CSS) syntax
- JavaScript style sheets using the World Wide Web Consortium's Document Object Model (DOM)

When you write a style sheet you declare it as either "text/css" or "text/javascript." Style sheets written in CSS syntax comply with the World Wide Web Consortium standard for CSS1. Since CSS style sheets are defined in HTML, they are not covered in this book. This section covers JavaScript style sheets and the Document Object Model (DOM).

The Document Object Model (DOM)

The Document Object Model is a subset of the document object properties that specifically relate to style sheets, rather than a new model that attempts to replace the JavaScript Object Hierarchy. The DOM for style sheets adds three new objects to the `document` object as follows:

- `tags`
- `classes`
- `ids`

All three objects reflect the statements between the `<STYLE> </STYLE>` tags. The `tags` object reflects styles that apply to particular HTML tags. The `classes` property defines a generic style, while the `ids` property defines exceptions to the `classes` property. The following sections explore these properties in more detail.

The *<STYLE> Tag*

The `<STYLE> </STYLE>` tags define a style sheet. The `tags`, `classes`, and `ids` objects reflect the statements specified within the `<STYLE> </STYLE>` tags. The `<STYLE>` tag needs to appear between the `<HEAD> </HEAD>` tags. The `TYPE` attribute is the only attribute of the `<STYLE>` tag and it defines whether the style sheet uses CSS or JavaScript syntax. The following snippet defines a style sheet using CSS:

```
<STYLE TYPE="text/css">
<!—
  P (font-size:18pt; color:red;)
-->
</STYLE>
```

When the style sheet `TYPE="text/css"` uses CSS syntax, the CSS syntax requires that you bracket the CSS statements with comments to keep browsers that do not understand style sheets from processing the statements. In contrast, you do not bracket the JavaScript statements as the following snippet of JavaScript syntax illustrates:

```
<STYLE TYPE="text/javascript">
  document.tags.P.fontSize = "18pt"
  document.tags.P.color = "red"
</STYLE>
```

Since the `tags` property always applies to the current document object, you can omit specifying the `document` object and simply write, for example, `tags.P.fontSize`. You can shorten the expression even further by using the `with` statement as shown in the following snippet:

```
<STYLE TYPE="text/javascript">
  with (tags.P) {
    fontSize = "18pt"
    color = "red"
  }
</STYLE>
```

As the CSS and JavaScript snippets show, the only difference between the two methods is the syntax for coding the styles. As with other HTML statements, the CSS statements are reflected in the JavaScript object model. The real core of style sheets lies within the statements between the `<STYLE> </STYLE>` tags.

The tags Property

The `tags` property has the following syntax:

`tags.HTMLtag.styleProperty`

The *HTMLtag* object specifies the HTML tag to which the *styleProperty* applies. The *HTMLtag* value is the name of the HTML tag without the surrounding `<>`. The *HTMLtag* object divides the HTML tags into the following levels:

- The body object applies to the entire document. For example, `tags.body.fontSize` sets font size for the entire document.
- Block-level elements, such as H1 and P, apply a style to a block of text. For example, `tags.P.fontSize` sets the font size for paragraphs.
- Inline-level elements, such as EM and B, apply to a text string within a block-level element. For example, `tags.EM.fontSize` sets the font size for emphasized text.

The breaking of HTML tags into levels creates a hierarchy in terms of applying a specific style. The block-level objects override any styles defined by the body object. The text-level objects override any styles defined in the block-level objects or the body object. However, not every style is inherited from a higher level element. Inheritance is one of the attributes of a particular style.

The *styleProperty* parameter defines the typographical style. The typographical styles fall into the following categories:

- Font properties
- Text properties
- Block-level formatting properties
- Color and background properties
- Classification properties

The Font Properties

The font properties define the font size, font family, font style, and font weight for any element. Table 11.1 describes the font properties and Table 11.2 defines the characteristics for these font properties.

Table 11.1 Description of Font Properties

Property	Description
fontSize	Defines the size of the font for the specified element.
fontFamily	Defines the font family to use. A font family consists of a set of fonts with different styles and weights that share a common font design, such as Times and Ariel.
fontStyle	Determines whether the font has a normal or italic style.
fontWeight	Defines the darkness of a font.

Table 11.2 Characteristics of Font Properties

Property	Default Value	Applies To	Inherited	Percentage Values
fontSize	medium	all elements	yes	relative to parent font size
fontFamily	defined by user preferences	all elements	yes	not applicable
fontStyle	normal	all elements	yes	not applicable
fontWeight	normal	all elements	yes	not applicable

The font properties provide complete control over the typographical appearance of a Web page. If there is one danger to such control, it is the tendency to define too many different fonts on a single page. Good typographical design uses the minimum number of fonts to carry the intended message. Too many fonts or conflicting font families distract the reader from the content that you are attempting to communicate.

The fontSize Property

The fontSize property defines the length (width in typography terminology) of a font. The values for the fontSize property allow you to specify the length of a font in the following terms:

- Absolute size
- Relative size
- Length
- Percentage of parent

The values for absolute size are as follows:

- xx-small
- x-small
- small
- medium
- large
- x-large
- xx-large

The values for relative size are as follows:

- smaller
- larger

When you define a font in terms of length, you specify the size in relationship to a specific unit, such as 18pt. Table 11.3 describes the different units of measure used for specifying the value for the fontSize property.

Table 11.3 Units for specifying the Length of a Font

Unit	Description
pt	A point is an absolute unit, where there are approximately 72 points to an inch. The point is the smallest typographical unit.
pc	A pica is an absolute unit, where there are approximately 6 picas per inch. The tricky part is that font families have different typeface efficiencies. For example, a 10pt Helvetica font has an average of 2.68 characters per pica. Whereas, a 10pt Times Roman font has an average of 2.81 characters per pica.
px	A pixel is an absolute unit. However, the number of pixels per inch is a function of the rendering device. For example, 10 pixels on a 640x480 pixels per inch screen are going to appear much larger than 10 pixels on a 1024x768 screen.

Table 11.3 Units for specifying the Length of a Font *(Continued)*

Unit	Description
in	The inch is an absolute unit.
mm	The millimeter is an absolute unit.
cm	The centimeter is an absolute unit.
em	A relative unit of measure that refers to the width of the capital letter "M."
ex	A relative unit that refers to half the height of the letter "x."

There are different ways to specify the font size, for example:

```
tags.P.fontSize = "x-large"
tags.P.fontSize = "smaller"
tags.P.fontSize = "16pt"
tags.P.fontSize = "120%"
```

Note:

 When a child inherits the font size from its parent, the browser converts relative values to points. For example, if the body object defines the font size as "large," then a paragraph inherits the point size and not the relative size.

The fontFamily Property

In typographical terms, the `fontFamily` property refers to a typeface family. The various weights and styles of a particular typeface (such as Helvetica) constitute a typeface family. When you specify a value for the `fontFamily` property, you have the following choices:

- Gamble that the font exists on the user's machine
- Download a font definition file
- Use a generic font family

The generic font family gives you a way to specify a category for a typeface family without knowing the exact typeface family. Which typeface family the browser uses for a generic font family depends on the typeface families (fonts) available on the user's machine. The generic font families are as follows:

- `serif`
- `sans-serif`
- `cursive`
- `monospace`
- `fantasy`

Although the generic family insures that the value for the fontFamily is valid, you have no control over the exact typeface family used by the user's browser. Another option is to specify a list of typeface families. The browser first tries to use a typeface family from the list before it uses the typeface family defined in the user preferences. The following example shows how to specify a list for the fontFamily property:

```
tags.P.fontFamily = "Garamond, Times, serif"
```

By ending a list with a generic family, you prevent the browser from defaulting to the user's preferences. This approach is faster than downloading fonts and marginally better than exclusively using generic families.

The fontStyle Property

Style sheets only support two values for the `fontStyle` property:

- `normal`
- `italic`

The fontWeight Property

You can specify the weight of a character in relative or absolute terms. The values for the relative weights of a character are as follows:

- `normal`
- `bold`
- `bolder`
- `lighter`

You can specify even finer degrees of weight with numerical values that range from 100 to 900. The lightest weight is represented by a value of 100 and the heaviest by 900.

Example of Font Properties

The HTML document shown in Listing 11.1 illustrates the use of various font properties. Besides showing how to set font properties, the document illustrates the inheritance of properties. The value for `tags.H2.fontSize` is not 120% of `tags.H1.fontSize`; rather, it is 120% of `tags.body.fontSize`. Similarly, the <B> tag inherits the properties of the body object, except for the `tags.B.fontWeight`. Figure 11.1 shows the results of loading the document.

Listing 11.1 Using Font Parameters

```
<HTML>
  <HEAD>
    <TITLE>Using Font Parameters</TITLE>
<STYLE TYPE="text/javascript">
  tags.body.fontFamily = "serif"
  tags.body.fontSize = "11pt"
  tags.H1.fontFamily = "sans-serif"
  tags.H1.fontSize = "18pt"
  tags.H1.fontWeight = "bold"
  tags.H2.fontFamily = "sans-serif"
  tags.H2.fontSize = "120%"
  tags.H2.fontStyle = "italic"
  tags.B.fontWeight = "bold"
</STYLE>
  </HEAD>
  <BODY>
    <H1>Main Heading</H1>
    <P>The main heading displays according to a style
      sheet. So do the <B>bold</B> characters.</P>
    <H2>A Second Level Heading</H2>
    <P>All of the paragraphs are styled according to the
      default properties set by the body object.</P>
  </BODY>
</HTML>
```

The Text Properties

The text properties alter how the browser displays a font. Table 11.4 describes the text properties and indicates the valid values for each property. Table 11.5 lists the characteristics of the text properties.

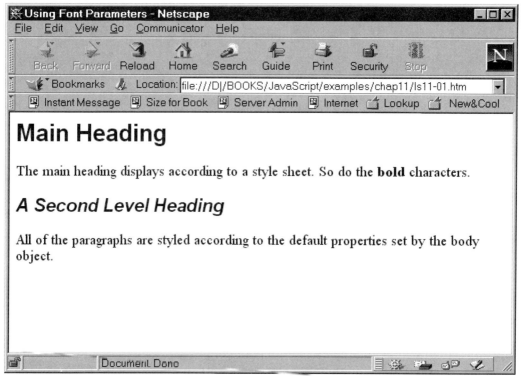

Figure 11.1   Results of using Font Properties.

Table 11.4 Description of Text Properties

Property	Description	Values
lineHeight	Sets the distance between the baselines of two adjacent lines. This property applies only to block-level elements.	The possible values are a number, a length, a percentage, or normal.
textDecoration	Defines the decorations that are added to the text of an element. If the element has no text, such as <IMG>, the property is ignored.	none, underline, line-through, blink
textTransform	Defines the text case.	none, capitalize, uppercase, lowercase
textAlign	Describes the alignment of the text within an element.	left, right, center, justify
textIndent	Defines the indentation for the first line of text in an element.	length, percentage

Table 11.5 Characteristics of the Text Properties

Property	Default Value	Applies To	Inherited	Percentage Values
lineHeight	normal	block-level elements	yes	refers to the font size
textDecoration	none	all elements	no	not applicable
textTransform	none	all elements	yes	not applicable
textAlign	left	block-level elements	yes	not applicable
textIndent	0	block-level elements	yes	refers to parent element's width

Except for the lineHeight and textIndent properties, the text properties require no additional explanation.

The lineHeight Property

The lineHeight property defines the spacing between lines by setting the space between the baselines of adjacent lines. The baseline is an imaginary line below the bottom of the characters that have no descenders. A descender is the portion of some characters that go below the line, such as the letter "g." You can adjust the line spacing by specifying a value according to Table 11.6.

Table 11.6 Values for lineHeight Property

Value	Description
number	When you specify a number without a unit, the browser multiples the font size by the *number* to create the lineHeight. For a *number*, the child inherits the *number* itself, and the resultant value.
percentage	This is a percentage of the font size. For a *percentage*, a child inherits the resultant value.
length	The height is expressed in the units of measurements defined in Table 11.3.

Following are examples of how to set the lineHeight property:

```
tags.P.lineHeight = "1.2" // the same as 120%
```

```
tags.P.lineHeight = "120%"
tags.P.lineHeight = "0.4in"
```

The textIndent Property

The `textIndent` property indents the first line of a block-level element. You can create hanging paragraphs by setting the `textIndent` to a negative value. You specify the indentation by setting `textIndent` to either a number or percentage. When you specify a number, you need to append it with a unit of measurement from Table 11.3. If you specify a percentage, it is a percentage of the parent element's width. Examples of how to set the `textIndent` property are as follows:

```
tags.P.textIndent = "0.5in"
tags.P.textIndent = "5%"
```

Note:

 An HTML <BR> tag does not force the next line to be indented.

Example of Text Properties

The HTML document in Listing 11.2 illustrates the use of the text properties. The `textIndent` is five percent of the width of the line. The `lineHeight` is set to one and a half times the length of the font. The best way to learn the behavior of various text properties is to experiment with different values. Figure 11.2 shows the results of loading this document.

Listing 11.2 Using Text Properties

```
<HTML>
  <HEAD>
    <TITLE>Using Text Properties</TITLE>
<STYLE TYPE="text/javascript">
   tags.H1.textTransform = "uppercase"
   tags.H2.textDecoration = "underline"
   tags.P.textIndent = "5%"
   tags.P.textAlign = "justify"
```

```
    tags.P.lineHeight = "1.5"
</STYLE>
  </HEAD>
  <BODY>
    <H1>An Uppercase Heading</H1>
    <P>This is a sample paragraph. The paragraph
      illustrates the text properties set in the style
      sheet. These tags apply to block-level elements such
      as the paragraph.</P>
    <H2>An Underlined Heading</H2>
    <P>The last paragraph did not contain line breaks. This
      paragraph contains a break to illustrate what happens
      with breaks.<BR>This line should not be indented.</P>
  </BODY>
</HTML>
```

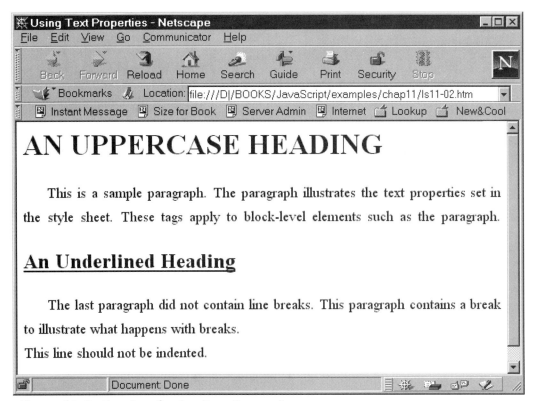

Figure 11.2   Results of using Text Properties.

The Block-Level Properties

The block-level properties treat the block-level element as if it where surrounded by a box. Table 11.7 describes the block level properties and lists the valid values for each property. You define the *length* values according to the units of measurement given in Table 11.3. Table 11.8 lists the characteristics of the block-level properties.

Table 11.7 Description of Block-Level Properties

Property/Method	Description	Values

`marginLeft`
`marginRight`
`marginTop`
`marginBottom`
`margins()`
	The margins set the minimal distance between the borders of the virtual box between two block-level elements. For the `margins()` method, the order of elements is top, right, bottom, and then left.	*length*, *percentage*, auto

`paddingTop`
`paddingRight`
`paddingBottom`
`paddingLeft`
`paddings()`
	The paddings set the distance between the border of an element and its content. For the `paddings()` method, the order of elements is top, right, bottom, and then left.	*length*, *percentage*

`borderTopWidth`
`borderBottom-`
`Width`
`borderLeftWidth`
`borderRightWidth`
`borderWidths()`
	The border width properties set the width of the border. For the `borderWidths()` method, the order of elements is top, right, bottom, left.	length

`borderStyle`	Sets the style of the border around a block-level element.	none, solid, double, inset, outset, grove, ridge
`borderColor`	Sets the color of the border. The *colorvalue* is either a color name or the hexadecimal RGB value. For a list of color names and their RGB values, see Appendix A.	colorvalue
`width`	Sets the width of the elements content. If you define both the margins and width property, the margins take precedence over the width.	*length*, *percentage*, auto

Table 11.7 Description of Block-Level Properties *(Continued)*

Property/Method	Description	Values
align	Defines the alignment of the element with regards to its parent. The `align` property allows other elements to wrap around it. If you use the `align` property, do not set margins, as the two are incompatible.	`left, right, none`
clear	Defines the sides where floating elements are not excepted.	none, left, right, both

Table 11.8 Characteristics of Block-Level Properties

Property/Method	Default Value	Applies To	Inherited	Percentage Values
marginLeft marginRight marginTop marginBottom margins()	0	block-level elements	no	Refers to parent element's width.
paddingTop paddingRight paddingBottom paddingLeft paddings()	0	block-level elements	no	Refers to parent element's width.
borderTopWidth borderBottom- Width borderLeftWidth borderRight- Width borderWidths()	none	block-level elements	no	not applicable
borderStyle	none	block-level elements	no	not applicable
borderColor	none	block-level elements	no	not applicable

Table 11.8 Characteristics of Block-Level Properties *(Continued)*

Property/Method	Default Value	Applies To	Inherited	Percentage Values
width	auto	block-level and re-placed elements	no	Refers to parent element's width.
align	none	block-level elements	no	not applicable
clear	none	block-level elements	no	not applicable

For margins, paddings, and border widths, JavaScript provides a method for setting all of the properties in one statement. For all three properties, the order is top, right, bottom, and then left. The HTML document in Listing 11.3 illustrates the use of these methods. It also shows the use of borders for paragraphs. Figure 11.3 shows the results of loading this script into Netscape Communicator.

Listing 11.3 Using the Block-Level Properties

```
<HTML>
  <HEAD>
    <TITLE>Using the Block-Level Properties</TITLE>
<STYLE TYPE="text/javascript">
   tags.P.margins("20pt", "10pt", "20pt", "10pt")
   tags.P.paddings("10pt", "10pt", "10pt", "10pt")
   tags.P.borderWidths("4pt", "2pt", "4pt", "2pt")
   tags.P.borderStyle = "ridge"
   tags.P.borderColor = "blue"
</STYLE>
  </HEAD>
  <BODY>
    <H1>Example for Paragraphs</H1>
    <P>The paragraphs should have margins, paddings, and
      blue borders. The top and bottom borders are wider
      than the side borders.</P>
  </BODY>
</HTML>
```

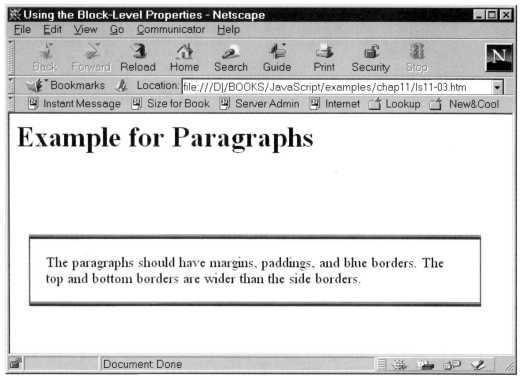

Figure 11.3   Results of using the Block-Level Properties.

Color and Background Properties

The color and background properties allow you to define the colors and background for the document as a whole or for block-level elements. Table 11.9 provides a description of the color and background properties, while Table 11.10 describes the characteristics of these properties.

Table 11.9 Description of Color and Background Properties

Property	Description	Values
color	Defines the color of the foreground element.	colorname, hexvalue
backgroundImage	Defines the background image for an element. When you use a relative URL, the browser interprets the relative location from the style sheet and not the document.	URL
backgroundColor	Defines the background color for an element.	colorname, hexvalue

Table 11.10 Characteristics of Color and Background Properties

Property	Default Value	Applies To	Inherited	Percentage Values
color	black	all elements	yes	not applicable
background-Image	empty	all elements	no	not applicable
background-Color	empty	all elements	no	not applicable

Besides using the name of a color, you can set the RGB value using the following methods:

- Hexadecimal value
- Decimal value for each color in the range of 1 to 255
- Percentage of each color

For example, you can define the color blue in the following ways:

```
tags.body.backgroundColor = "blue"
tags.body.backgroundColor = "#0000FF"
tags.body.backgroundColor = "0, 0, 255"
tags.body.backgroundColor = "0%, 0%, 100%"
```

The HTML document in Listing 11.4 sets the background for the document and creates a separate background for the <BLOCKQUOTE> tag. It also changes the color for the <H1> tag. Figure 11.4 shows the results of loading this document into Netscape Communicator.

Listing 11.4 Using the Color and Background Properties

```
<HTML>
  <HEAD>
   <TITLE>Using the Color and Background Properties</TITLE>
<STYLE TYPE="text/javascript">
   tags.body.backgroundColor = "white"
   tags.H1.color = "blue"
   tags.BLOCKQUOTE.backgroundColor = "lightblue"
   tags.BLOCKQUOTE.borderWidths("2pt", "2pt", "2pt", "2pt")
   tags.BLOCKQUOTE.paddings("10pt", "10pt", "10pt", "10pt")
   tags.BLOCKQUOTE.borderSytle = "groove"
   tags.BLOCKQUOTE.borderColor = "blue"
 </STYLE>
  </HEAD>
  <BODY>
    <H1 ALIGN="CENTER">Example for Colors</H1>
    <P>The following quote should appear within a bordered
      box and have a light blue background.</P>
    <CENTER>
      <BLOCKQUOTE>When all else fails, read the
      instructions.</BLOCKQUOTE>
    </CENTER>
  </BODY>
</HTML>
```

The Classification Properties

The classification category indirectly controls the visual parameters. As shown in Table 11.11, the properties alter the behavior of HTML tags. Table 11.12 lists the characteristic for the classification properties.

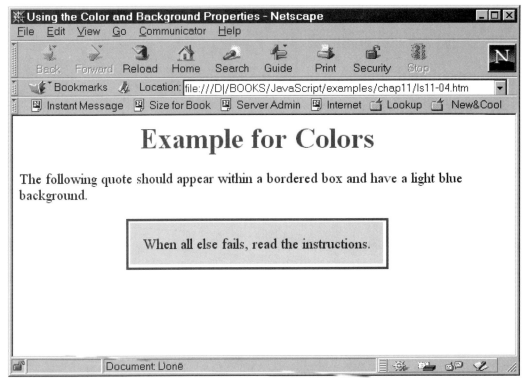

Figure 11.4   Results of using the Color and Background Properties.

Table 11.11 Description of the Classification Properties

Property	Description	Values
display	Overrides the HTML specification for an element, by allowing you to define an element as follows:	
	• none—The element is not available.	none
	• block—The element is treated as a block level item.	block
	• inlin—The element is an inline item, such as <B>.	inline
	• list-item—The element is treated as a list item, such as <LI>.	list-item

Table 11.11 Description of the Classification Properties *(Continued)*

Property	Description	Values
listStyleType	Defines the formatting for list-item elements. You can define the property for any element, such as body, but it only applies to those elements defined as list-item.	disc circle square decimal lower-roman upper-roman lower-alpha upper-alpha none
whiteSpace	Sets the rules for handling white space. The choices are as follows: • normal—White space is collapsed. • pre—Behaves like the <PRE> HTML tag.	normal pre

Table 11.12 Characteristics of the Classification Properties

Property	Default Value	Applies To	Inherited	Percentage Values
display	according to HTML	all elements	no	not applicable
listStyle-Type	disc	all elements with the property value of list-item.	yes	not applicable
whiteSpace	according to HTML	block-level elements	yes	not applicable

Warning

The inline value for the display property does not alter the behavior of HTML block-level elements.

The HTML document in Listing 11.5 uses a style sheet to place a border around the <UL> tag and to change the bullet for the list to a square. When you define alternate styles for a <LI> element, you need to separate the styles that apply to an unordered list from those that apply to an ordered list. Figure 11.5 shows the results of loading this document into Netscape Communicator.

Listing 11.5 Using the Classification Properties

```
<HTML>
  <HEAD>
    <TITLE>Using the Classification Properties</TITLE>
<STYLE TYPE="text/javascript">
  tags.UL.display = "block"
  tags.UL.paddings("10pt", "10pt", "10pt", "10pt")
  tags.UL.borderWidths("2pt", "2pt", "2pt", "2pt")
  tags.UL.borderSytle = "inset"
  tags.UL.borderColor = "blue"
  tags.UL.backgroundColor = "lightblue"
  tags.LI.listStyleType = "square"
</STYLE>
  </HEAD>
  <BODY>
    <P>The example illustrates the following properties:</P>
    <UL>
      <LI>Defining UL as a block element</LI>
      <LI>Setting borders for the list items</LI>
      <LI>Setting the border style</LI>
      <LI>Defining the bullet style for the list</LI>
    </UL>
  </BODY>
</HTML>
```

The classes Property

The `tags` property creates a style that applies to every occurrence of the specified tag. However, there are cases where you want to apply different styles to the same tag. You can accomplish this by creating *classes*. The creation of a class requires two operations:

- Define the class in the style sheet
- Declare the class to use in the tag with the HTML CLASS attribute

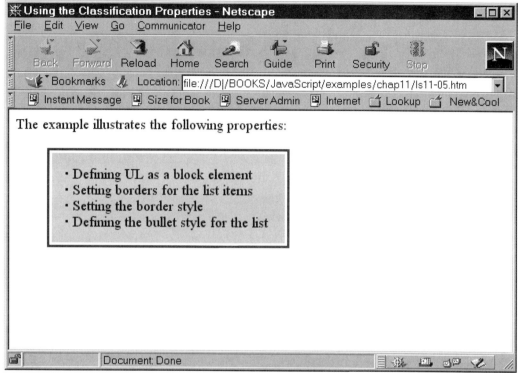

Figure 11.5   Results of using the Classification Properties.

The syntax for defining a class using JavaScript syntax in a style sheet is as follows:

```
classes.className.HTMLtag.styleProperty
```

When you use the JavaScript syntax for style sheets, the *className* cannot include any JavaScript operators, such as -, +, °, %, and /. To insure that your *className* is valid, use only alphanumeric characters and the underscore (_). When defining the *HTMLtag*, you can use the keyword all to apply to all elements.

To use a class name, you add the CLASS attribute to an HTML tag as shown in the following example:

```
<H1 CLASS="className">
```

You can define only one CLASS attribute in an HTML tag. The browser ignores any additional CLASS attributes within a single HTML tag.

The style sheet used in Listing 11.6 defines two classes for formatting paragraphs. Figure 11.6 shows the results of applying each class to a different paragraph.

Listing 11.6 Using the classes Property

```
<HTML>
  <HEAD>
    <TITLE>Using the classes Property</TITLE>
<STYLE TYPE="text/javascript">
   classes.test1.P.fontFamily = "serif"
   classes.test1.P.fontSize = "large"
   classes.test1.P.textAlign = "justify"
   classes.test2.P.fontFamily = "sans-serif"
   classes.test2.P.fontSize = "x-large"
   classes.test2.P.textAligh = "justify"
</STYLE>
  </HEAD>
  <BODY>
    <P CLASS="test1">This is an example of using the test1
      class. The text is serif, large font size, and
      justified.</P>
    <P CLASS="test2">This paragraph uses the test2 class.
      The text is sans-serif, extra large, and justified.
    </P>
  </BODY>
</HTML>
```

The ids Property

By using the ids property, you can define an individual style sheet. The individual style sheet provides a means of altering properties defined in a class style sheet. Since the individual style sheet makes changes to a class style sheet you need to do the following:

- Define the class style sheet
- Define the individual style sheet
- Use the CLASS and ID attributes in the HTML tag

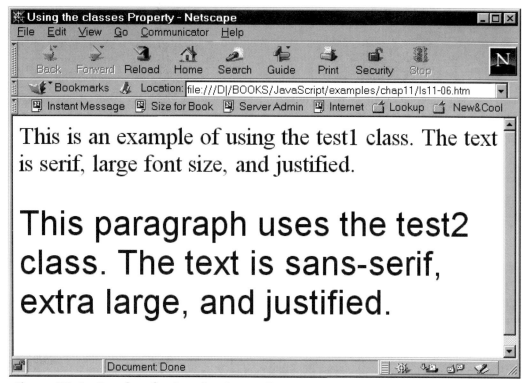

Figure 11.6 *Results of using the classes Property.*

The syntax for defining a individual style sheet using Java syntax is as follows:

```
ids.IDname.HTMLtag.styleProperty
```

The rules for defining an *IDname* are the same as those for a *class-Name*. The rules for the *HTMLtag* are also the same as for the classes property.

The following example shows how to implement the individual style sheet in an HTML tag:

```
<H1 CLASS="className" ID="IDname">
```

By combining an individual style sheet with a class style sheet, the HTML document in Listing 11.7 changes the font size of the second paragraph, as shown in Figure 11.7. The individual style sheet provides a way to control positioning between layers.

Listing 11.7 Using the ids Property

```
<HTML>
  <HEAD>
    <TITLE>Using the ids Property</TITLE>
<STYLE TYPE="text/javascript">
  classes.test1.P.fontFamily = "serif"
  classes.test1.P.fontSize = "large"
  classes.test1.P.textAlign = "justify"
  ids.test2.fontSize = "medium"
</STYLE>
  </HEAD>
  <BODY>
    <P CLASS="test1">This paragraph uses the test1 class
      style sheet without an indivdual style sheet.</P>
    <P CLASS="test1" ID="test2">This paragraph uses the
      test1 class style sheet with the test2 individual
      style sheet.</P>
  </BODY>
</HTML>
```

Limiting the Context of a Style

Although the ids property provides a way to create exceptions to a style sheet, you must enter the ID attribute for each exception. Use the `contextual()` method for creating context sensitive styles. For example, if you want italicized text to display in red when it appears in block quotes, you could define this context as follows:

```
contextual(tags.BLOCKQUOTE, tags.I).color = "red"
```

In a two-level unordered list, you can have different colors for each level of list item with the following context statements:

```
contextual(tags.UL, tags.LI).color = "red"
contextual(tags.Ul, tags.UL, tags.LI).color = "blue"
```

You can use contextual selection criteria to apply to the tags, classes, or ids properties in any combination. The following example illustrates the combining of different properties to obtain the desired result:

```
classes.myclass.all.color = "blue"
contextual(tags.DIV, classes.myclass.P).fontStyle = "italic"
```

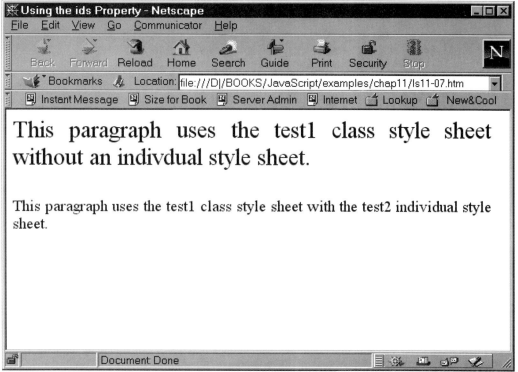

Figure 11.7   Results of using the ids Property.

Now, all paragraphs with a <DIV> tag that use myclass will appear in italics. You could think of the contextual() method as nested if statements. In terms of a condition, the above contextual() method reads that if the <DIV> tag and the <P> tag use myclass, then the font style is italic.

The <LINK> Tag

External style sheets offer a means for creating a template that can be used with any HTML document. By using the <LINK> tag, you can incorporate a style sheet template into all the documents for a Web site to give a consistent look.

The syntax for defining an external style sheet is the same as for defining a style sheet within a document, except that you do not need the opening and closing <STYLE> </STYLE> tags. By convention, the filename extension for cascading style sheets is ".css". The following is an example of an external style sheet:

```
/* An external style sheet using JavaScipt Syntax */
classes.test1.P.fontFamily = "serif"
classes.test1.P.fontSize = "large"
classes.test1.P.textAlign = "justify"
ids.test2.fontSize = "medium"
```

To use the external style sheet in a document, use the <LINK> tag as shown in the following example:

```
<LINK REL=STYLESHEET TYPE="text/javascript"
 HREF="http://www.xyz.com/styles/mainstlye.htm">
```

Like the <STYLE> tag, you must place the <LINK> tag between the <HEAD> </HEAD> tags.

Specifying Styles using HTML Attributes

The classes and ids properties require the use of the CLASS and ID HTML attributes to activate the class style sheet and individual style sheet. By the same token, you can define a style for an HTML tag, with the STYLE attribute. The following example uses JavaScript syntax to define a style for a single paragraph:

```
<P STYLE="fontSize='12pt'; color='blue';
textAlign='jsutified'">
```

Since each property represents a JavaScript statement, you need to separate them with semicolons. The rules of inheritance apply to the STYLE attribute just as they apply to the tags property.

The <SPAN> Tag

The inline <SPAN> </SPAN> tags allow you to define a style for a text string. The <SPAN> tag allows you to define a style or a class as shown in the following examples:

```
<P>The word is <SPAN style="color='blue'">blue</SPAN>.</P>
<P><SPAN class="initcap">t</SPAN>he letter is special.</P>
```

In the first example, the `<SPAN>` tag sets a style for a text string. In the second example, the `<SPAN>` tag applies a class style sheet to the first letter of a paragraph.

Positioning Content

With standard HTML, you have little control over how the browser positions content. Furthermore, once the browser displays the page, you have no means of dynamically altering the displayed content. DHTML breaks these barriers by providing dynamic control over the appearance of Web pages. By combining positioned content with JavaScript, you can:

- Move layers
- Hide layers
- Expand and contract layers
- Change the order of overlap
- Change the characteristics of a layer
- Change the content of a layer
- Dynamically create new layers

The subject of positioned content is much broader than the scope of this book. Consequently, this section focuses on JavaScript and the JavaScript object model. To get a complete view on how to design Web pages with positioned content, refer to the following URL:

```
http://developer.netscape.com/one/dynhtml/index.html
```

Creating Positioned Content

Netscape Communicator provides three alternatives for creating positioned content:

- Style sheets
- The `<LAYER>` and `<ILAYER>` tags
- The `Layer` object constructor

The term "positioned content" fails to adequately describe the visual nature that it creates. However, the term "layers" is more descriptive of the visual impact on Web pages. The underlying structure of the Web page is still the HTML document. On top of that document, you can add layers that are transparent or opaque. The layer itself, is a document, which may have additional layers. When defining a layer, you specify the parameters of that layer. Table 11.13 lists the parameters available for defining a style sheet and includes both HTML syntax for the <LAYER> tag (identified as tag) and the CSS syntax (identified as CSS). If there is a JavaScript style sheet syntax for defining layers, I have not found a reference to it.

Table 11.13 Parameters for defining a Layer

Parameter	Description	Values
position (CSS)	The position parameter applies only to layers created with style sheets. The absolute value equates to creating a layer with the <LAYER> tag, while the relative value equates to the <ILAYER> tag. For example, `position:absolute`	absolute relative

ID (tag)	The ID parameter applies to only the <LAYER> and <ILAYER> tags and provides a name to identify the layer. When you define a layer using style sheets, the name of the layer is part of the syntax. To avoid any conflicts with JavaScript, the name should consist of only alphanumeric characters and the underscore. For example,
	`<LAYER ID=topLayer>`
	`#toplayer (position:absolute);`
		name

LEFT (tag) left (CSS)	Specifies the horizontal position of the top-left corner of a layer with respect to the containing layer or, for top-level layers, the document. When using style sheets, you need to add the unit of measurement for pixels.	pixels

Table 11.13 Parameters for defining a Layer *(Continued)*

Parameter	Description	Values

TOP (tag)
top (CSS)
	Specifies the vertical position of the top-left corner of a layer with respect to the containing layer or, for top-level layers, the document. When using style sheets, you need to add the unit of measurement for pixels. For example,
	`<LAYER TOP=200 LEFT=70>`
	`#toplayer (position:absolute; top:200px; left:70px;)`
		pixels

PAGEX (tag)	Specifies the horizontal position of the top-left corner of a layer with respect to the enclosing document, rather than the enclosing layer. This parameter is not available to style sheets.	pixels
PAGEY (tag)	Specifies the vertical position of the top-left corner of a layer with respect to the enclosing document, rather than the enclosing layer. This parameter is not available to style sheets. For example, `<LAYER PAGEX=100 PAGEY=100>`	pixels

SRC (tag)
include-source (CSS)
	Specifies the URL of an external HTML document to display in the layer. For example,
	`<LAYER SRC="../includes/special.htm">`
	`include-source:url("../includes/spe-cial.htm");`
		URL

WIDTH (tag)
width (CSS)
	Defines the width of the layer at which the content wraps. If the layer contains an image that extends beyond the width, the width expands accordingly. When you specify the width as a *percentage*, it is a percentage of the enclosing layer. For example,
	`<LAYER WIDTH=200>`
	`width:80%; /* CSS */`
		pixels
		percentage

Table 11.13 Parameters for defining a Layer *(Continued)*

Parameter	Description	Values

HEIGHT (tag)
height (CSS)
	Determines the initial height of the clipping region of the layer. If the content does not fit within the specified height, then the height expands to fit the content. The primary purpose of the HEIGHT parameter is to act as a reference height for child layers. By default, the height is the minimum required to display the contents of the layer. When you specify the height as a *percentage*, it is a percentage of the enclosing layer. For example,
	`<LAYER HEIGHT=200>`
	`height:80%;  /* CSS */`
		pixels
		percentage

CLIP (tag)
clip (CSS)
	Defines the clipping rectangle for a layer. The left and right values are specified as pixels from the left edge. The top and bottom values are specified as pixels from the top edge. The format is as follows:
	`CLIP="left,top,right,bottom"`
	`CLIP="10,40,20,100"`
	Or,
	`clip:rect(left,top,right,bottom);`
	`clip:rect(10,40,20,100); /* CSS */`
		pixels

Z-INDEX (tag)
z-index (CSS)
	Defines the stack order for the layers. Layers with higher numbers are stacked above those with lower numbers. A child layer is always above the parent layer, so the Z-ORDER only applies to siblings. For example
	`<LAYER Z-INDEX=4>`
	`z-index:4;  /* CSS */`
		integer

ABOVE (tag)	The new layer is created immediately above the specified layer. This option is not available to style sheets. For example, `<LAYER ABOVE=layer1>`	layerName
BELOW (tag)	The new layer is created immediately below the specified layer. This option is not available to style sheets. For example, `<LAYER BELOW=layer1>`	layerName

Table 11.13 Parameters for defining a Layer *(Continued)*

Parameter	Description	Values

VISIBILITY (tag)
visibility (CSS)
	Determines whether the layer is visible or hidden. If set to inherit, the value is inherited from the parent. For a top-level layer, the parent is the document and the document is always visible. For example,
	`<LAYER VISIBILITY=HIDE>`
	`visibility:hide;  /* CSS */`
		show
		hide
		inherit

BGCOLOR (tag)
background-color (CSS)
	Sets the background color for the layer. By default, the layer is transparent, which means that the lower layers show through the transparent area of the layer's text and other content. You can specify the background color either by name or hexadecimal value (see Appendix A). For example,
	`<LAYER BGCOLOR="WHEAT">`
	`bgcolor:F5DEB3;  /* CSS */`
		colorName
		hexValue

BACKGROUND (tag)
background-image (CSS)
	Defines the titled image to draw across the background of a layer. For example,
	`<LAYER BACKGROUND="../images/marble.gif">`
	`background-image:url("../images/mar-`
	`ble.gif");`
		URL

Note:

> Although the NAME attribute is still supported for the <LAYER> and <ILAYER> tags, you should use the ID attribute to define the name of the layer.

Without the ability to create layers, the largest piece of content is the block-level element. With layers, you create a frame in which to place content. The properties described in Table 11.13 show how to build the special frame, which is called a layer. The next task is to get a better understanding of the features of layers.

Absolute versus Relative Positioning

An absolute layer is considered out-of-line because it can be placed anywhere within the document view and does not take up space in the document flow. You can specify the position of the layer by setting the LEFT and TOP parameters. You declare an absolute layer by using the <LAYER> </LAYER> tags, or, with style sheets, by setting the position property equal to "absolute."

In contrast, a relative layer is called an inflow layer, and appears wherever it falls within a document. A relative layer is inflow because it occupies space in the document flow. It is inline, because it shares line space with other HTML elements. For the relative layer, the left and top parameters set the offset of the layer's top-left corner from the current position in the document. You declare a relative layer by using the <ILAYER> </ILAYER> tags, or, with style sheets, by setting the position property to "relative."

If you find the difference between absolute and relative layers a bit obscure, you are not alone. The topic of positioning requires more explanation for it is the key to understanding positioned content.

Specifying the Position of a Layer

For absolute layers, the origin is the top-left corner of the document or containing layer. For relative layers, the origin is the natural position of the layer within the flow of the document. Thus, the difference is the starting point for positioning the layer.

The HTML document in Listing 11.8 contains both absolute and relative positioning of layers. The best way to understand the results is to compare the document to the results shown in Figure 11.8. The absolute layer appears below the relative layer even though it is written first in the document. Also, the absolute layer is not part of the document flow since the paragraph before the relative layer appears at the top of the screen. The relative layer is preceded and followed by a paragraph. The position of the relative layer is in relation to its location in the document, and it does alter the flow of the document.

Listing 11.8 Example of Absolute versus Relative Positioning

```
<HTML>
  <HEAD>
    <TITLE>
    Example of Absolute versus Relative Positioning
    </TITLE>
  </HEAD>
  <BODY>
    <LAYER LEFT="50" TOP="200" WIDTH="400"
          HEIGHT="200" BGCOLOR="wheat">
    <P>First Layer with absolute position</P>
      <LAYER BGCOLOR="teal" LEFT="20" TOP="50" WIDTH="200"
          HEIGHT="100">
      <P>This is an embedded absolute layer within the
        first layer.</P>
      </LAYER>
    </LAYER>
    <P>Paragraph above a relative layer.</P>
    <P><ILAYER BGCOLOR="lightblue" LEFT="10"
              WIDTH="200" HEIGHT="50">
      This is a relative layer that is positioned to the
      left.</ILAYER></P>
    <P>Paragraph after a relative layer.</P>
  </BODY>
</HTML>
```

The Layer Object

JavaScript represents each layer as a `layer` object within the `layers[]` array of the `document` object. Table 11.14 lists the properties, methods, and event handlers for the `layer` object.

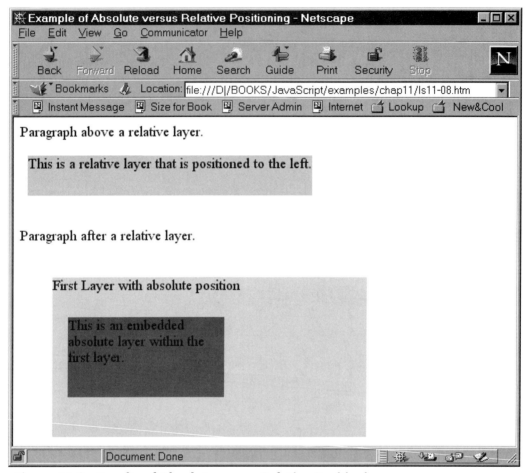

Figure 11.8 Results of Absolute versus Relative Positioning.

Table 11.14 Properties, Methods and Event Handlers of the Layer Object

Properties	Methods	Event Handlers
document	moveBy()	onMouseOver
name	moveTo()	onMouseOut
left	moveToAbsolute()	onLoad
top	resizeBy()	onFocus

Table 11.14 Properties, Methods and Event Handlers of the Layer Object *(Continued)*

Properties	Methods	Event Handlers
pageX	resizeTo()	onBlur
pageY	moveAbove()	
zIndex	moveBelow()	
visibility	load()	
clip.top		
clip.left		
clip.right		
clip.bottom		
clip.width		
clip.height		
background		
bgColor		
siblingAbove		
siblingBelow		
above		
below		
parentLayer		
src		

You can reference the properties, methods, and event handlers of the `layer` object using any of the following formats:

```
document.layerName.property
document.layers["layerName"].property
document.layer[index].property
```

The order of the `layer` objects in the `layers[]` array is according to the z-order (stacking order). The layer with the lowest z-order value has an index value of zero. The *index* value is not the same as the z-order value, since multiple layers may have the same z-order value. As with all arrays, the `lengths` property of the `layers[]` array tells you the number of objects in the array.

The document object in the `layer` object is a regular document object with all of the properties, methods, and event handlers of the window document object. Thus, to reference a layer in the layer `document` object, you would use a reference similar to the following:

`document.layerName1.document.layerName2.property`

Properties of the Layer Object

The properties of the `layer` object reflect the attributes set in the `<LAYER>` or `<ILAYER>` tags. For style sheets, the properties of the layer object reflect the properties of the style sheet. Table 11.15 provides a description of the properties of the `layer` object and indicates whether they can be modified with JavaScript.

Table 11.15 Properties of the Layer Object

Property	Modifiable	Description
document	no	Each layer has a `document` object that reflects the content of the layer. You can use the methods of the `document` object only to change the content of the layer.
name	no	Reflects the ID attribute of the `<LAYER>` or `<ILAYER>` tags. For style sheets, it reflects the name of the style sheet.
left	yes	Reflects the LEFT attribute of the `<LAYER>` or `<ILAYER>` tags. For style sheets, it reflects `left` property. When setting this property, you can specify an integer value in either pixels or a percentage.
top	yes	Reflects the TOP attribute of the `<LAYER>` or `<ILAYER>` tags. For style sheets, it reflects the `top` property. When setting this property, you can specify an integer value in either pixels or a percentage.
pageX	yes	Reflects the PAGEX attribute of the `<LAYER>` or `<ILAYER>` tags. When setting this property, you need to specify number of pixels.
pageY	yes	Reflects the PAGEY attribute of the `<LAYER>` or `<ILAYER>` tags. When setting this property, you need to specify number of pixels.
zIndex	yes	Reflects the Z-INDEX attribute of the `<LAYER>` or `<ILAYER>` tags. For style sheets, it reflects the z-index property. When setting this property, the legal values are 0 or a positive integer.

Table 11.15 Properties of the Layer Object *(Continued)*

Property	Modifiable	Description
visibility	yes	Reflects the VISIBILITY attribute of the <LAYER> or <ILAYER> tags. For style sheets, it reflects the visibility property. The valid values for this property are "show," "hide," or "inherit."
clip.top	yes	All the clip properties reflect the CLIP attribute or property. The values for clip.top, clip.left, clip.right, and clip.bottom are in the layer's coordinate system as described in Table 11.13. The valid values are 0 or a positive integer.
clip.left	yes	See clip.top.
clip.right	yes	See clip.top.
clip.bottom	yes	See clip.top.
clip.width	yes	The width is computed by subtracting clip.left from clip.right. If you specify a new width as some integer value w, clip.right is set as follows: clip.right = clip.left + w
clip.height	yes	The height is computed by subtracting clip.top from clip.bottom. If you specify a new height as some integer h, clip.bottom is set as follows: clip.bottom = clip.top + h
background	yes	Reflects the BACKGROUND attribute of the <LAYER> or <ILAYER> tags. For style sheets, it reflects the background-image property. The value is null if the layer has no background image.
bgColor	yes	Reflects the BGCOLOR attribute of the <LAYER> or <ILAYER> tags. For style sheets, it reflects the background-color property. When setting the property, the valid values are a color name (see Appendix A) or a hexadecimal value. For a transparent layer the value is null.
sibling-Above	no	Specifies the sibling layer object above the layer in the stack order. The property is null when there is no sibling layer above this layer.
sibling-Below	no	Specifies the sibling layer object below the layer in the stack order. The property is null when there is no sibling layer below this layer.

Table 11.15 Properties of the Layer Object *(Continued)*

Property	Modifiable	Description
above	no	Specifies the `layer` object above the layer in the stack order. The `layer` object need not be a sibling and is the `window` object for the topmost layer.
below	no	Specifies the `layer` object below the layer in the stack order. The `layer` object need not be a sibling and is null for bottommost layer.
parentLayer	no	Specifies the `layer` object of the enclosing layer, or the window object if the `layer` is not nested in another layer.
src	yes	A URL that reflects the SRC attribute of the `<LAYER>` or `<ILAYER>` tags. For style sheets, it reflects the `include-source` property.

Except for the `visibility`, `background`, and `bgColor` properties, there is a matching method that modifies the `layer` object properties. When the object has a method that modifies a property, always use the method, since it contains editing routines and takes care of all housekeeping details.

The *Fancy Flowers Farm Example* in Netscape's *Dynamic HTML for Netscape Communicator* provides a good example of how to use the `visibility` property to display a selected layer. To see the example, go to the following URL and then scroll down to Chapter 10 in the index frame:

```
http://developer.netscape.com/library/documentation/
communicator/dynhtml/index.htm
```

Methods of the Layer Object

Table 11.16 describes the methods of the `layer` object.

Table 11.16 Methods of the Layer Object

Method	Description
moveBy(dx, dy)	Move the layer from its current position by *dx* pixels to the left and *dy* pixels down.

Table 11.16 Methods of the Layer Object *(Continued)*

Method	Description
moveTo(x, y)	Equivalent to setting both the left and top properties of the layer object. For absolute layers the position is relative to the containing layer or document. For relative layers, it is relative to the natural position of the layer in the contents in the containing layer or document. Both *x* and *y* are in pixels.
moveToAbsolute(x, y)	Equivalent to setting both the pageX and pageY properties. This method moves the layer to the specified position within the page. Both *x* and *y* are in pixels.
resizeBy(dwidth, dheight)	Resizes the layer according to the number of pixels specified by *dwidth* and *dheight*. It is the equivalent of adding *dwidth* and *dheight* to the clip.width and clip.height properties, respectively. The values for *dwidth* and *dheight* may be positive or negative integers. The method does not relayout the contents of the layer. If the new boundaries of the layer are less than the current boundaries, the content may be clipped.
resizeTo(x, y)	Equivalent of setting both the clip.width and clip.height properties. The method does not relayout the contents of the layer. If the new boundaries of the layer are less than the current boundaries, the content may be clipped.
moveAbove(layer)	Stacks the current layer above the specified layer object.
moveBelow()	Stacks the current layer below the specified layer object.
load(sourceString, width)	Loads the file specified by sourceString into the current layer and sets the width for wrapping the HTML content to the value specified by width. The sourceString must be a valid URL.

When working with layers, you commonly use methods in conjunction with the handling of events. Consequently, examples for using methods appear with the discussion of other topics.

Event Management for Layers

Since a layer object contains a document object, it has the same event handling capabilities as the top-level window. This includes the ability to capture and route events. Table 11.17 describes how the browser invokes the event handlers for layer objects.

Table 11.17 Description of Events for the Layer Object

Event Handler	Description
onMouseOver	Invoked when the cursor passes into a layer.
onMouseOut	Invoked when the cursor moves from the area of a layer.
onLoad	Invoked when the document that contains the layer is displayed. It makes no difference whether the layer is hidden or visible.
onFocus	Invoked when the layer gets keyboard focus.
OnBlur	Invoked when the layer loses keyboard focus.

In a situation where there are overlapping layers, the top-most layer receives the event, even if it is a transparent layer. Hidden layers, however, do not receive events.

The *Changing Wrapping Width Example* (Chapter 14 of Netscape's *Dynamic HTML in Netscape Communicator*) is an excellent example of how to manage captured events. The URL for the document is as follows:

```
http://developer.netscape.com/library/documentation/
communicator/dynhtml/index.htm
```

JavaScript and Layers

When writing JavaScript code for layers, the following JavaScript features play an important role:

- JavaScript statements within a layer
- Changing the content of the layer
- Inline JavaScript

When you include JavaScript within blocks of positioned content, the scope of the JavaScript is the block. This limited scope is especially important to the coding of event handlers. The following snippet illustrates the use of localized JavaScript:

```
<LAYER ID=layer1
    onMouseOver="changeImg('testBtnOvr.gif')"
    onMouseOut="changeImg('testBtn.gif')>
  <IMG NAME="tstBtn" SRC="testBtn.gif"
```

```
          WIDTH="100%" HEIGHT="100%">
      <SCRIPT LANGUAGE="JavaScript">
        function changeImg(newBtn) {
           src=newBtn
        }
      </SCRIPT>
</LAYER>
```

As with any document, you can use the `document.write()` and `document.writeln()` methods to define the initial content of the document. With a layer, you are using the layer's document methods, since the `layer` object contains a `document` object. With an HTML document, you cannot change the content displayed on the screen. However, when you write to a layer document after the browser loads the document, the browser erases the original content and replaces it with the new content. The HTML document shown in Listing 11.9 illustrates both ways of writing to a layer. Figure 11.9 shows the initial screen after loading the document into Netscape Communicator.

Listing 11.9 Writing to a Layer

```
<HTML>
  <HEAD>
    <TITLE>Writing to a Layer</TITLE>
<SCRIPT LANGUAGE="JavaScript">
<!--
function chgLayer() {
   var newHeader="<H1>New Content</H1>"
   var newContent="<P>The new content for the layer.</P>"
   document.testLayer.document.writeln(newHeader)
   document.testLayer.document.writeln(newContent)
   document.testLayer.document.close()
}
//-->
</SCRIPT>
  </HEAD>
  <BODY>
    <FORM NAME="testFrm">
    <P><INPUT TYPE="BUTTON" NAME="chgBtn"
             VALUE="Change Content"
             ONCLICK="chgLayer(); return false;">
```

```
    </P>
    </FORM>
    <LAYER ID="testLayer" BGCOLOR="wheat" LEFT="20"
        TOP="100" WIDTH="400">
    <H1>Original Content</H1>
<SCRIPT LANGUAGE="JavaScript">
    document.write("The original content for the layer.")
</SCRIPT>
    </LAYER>
  </BODY>
</HTML>
```

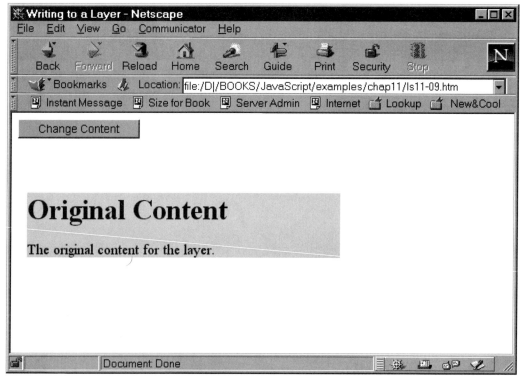

Figure 11.9 *Resulting of writing to a Layer.*

When setting the LEFT and TOP attributes of the <LAYER> tag, you can use inline JavaScript to position a layer. The HTML document in Listing 11.10 uses inline JavaScript to position the second layer with respect to the first layer. Figure 11.10 shows the output.

Listing 11.10 Using Inline JavaScript

```
<HTML>
  <HEAD>
    <TITLE>Using Inline JavaScript</TITLE>
  </HEAD>
  <BODY>
    <LAYER ID="scene1" LEFT="20" TOP="20">
      <IMG SRC="../images/clipart/desert.jpg"
           ALT="desert scene" WIDTH="320" HEIGHT="240">
      <P>A Desert Scene</P>
    </LAYER>
    <LAYER ID="scene2"
           LEFT="&{window.document.scene1.left + 200};"
           TOP="&{document.scene1.top
                + document.scene1.document.height  - 160};">
      <IMG SRC="../images/clipart/desstorm.jpg"
           ALT="desert storm" WIDTH="320" HEIGHT="199">
      <P>A Desert Storm</P>
    </LAYER>
  </BODY>
</HTML>
```

Inline JavaScript requires a special syntax as shown in Listing 11.10. The syntax for an inline JavaScript statement is as follows:

```
&{JavaScript statement};
```

The inline JavaScript statement can then reference the `position` properties of another layer as a point of reference. For absolute layers, this technique helps position each layer relative to another layer.

Warning

 The syntax described in the version of Netscape's *Dynamic HTML for Netscape Communicator* is incorrect. You do not precede the statement with '&{"&"};', as shown in the Netscape document.

Dynamically Creating Layers

In addition to creating layers via DHTML and CSS, you can dynamically create a new absolute layer using the `Layer` object constructor. The syntax for the `Layer` object constructor is as follows:

```
newLayerObject = new Layer(width[, parentLayer])
```

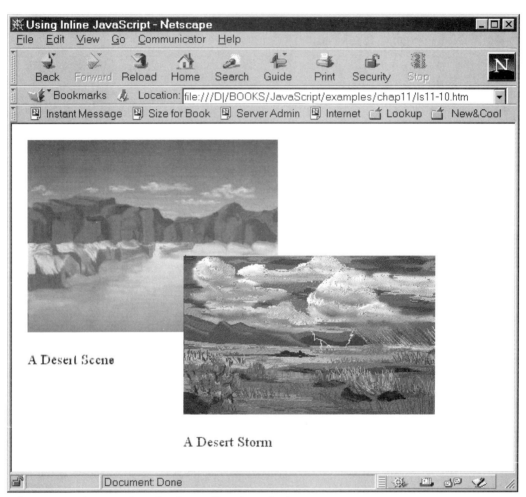

Figure 11.10 *Results of using Inline JavaScript.*

When you create a new layer using the `Layer` object constructor, it has no content. You can add the content by using either of the following methods:

- Use the `load()` method to load an HTML document into the layer
- Use the `document.write()` and `document.writeln()` methods to dynamically create the content

In addition, you can use the properties and methods of the `layer` object to further define the properties and position of the newly created layer. The default is to place the new layer at coordinates 0,0, and set the visibility to hide. The HTML document shown in Listing 11.11 illustrates how to dynamically create a new layer.

Listing 11.11 Creating a Layer using JavaScript

```
<HTML>
  <HEAD>
    <TITLE>Creating a Layer using JavaScript</TITLE>
<SCRIPT LANGUAGE="JavaScript">
<!--
function createLayer() {
   var msg="<H1>New Layer</H1>"
   tstLayer=new Layer(400)
   tstLayer.bgColor = "wheat"
   tstLayer.pageX=50
   tstLayer.pageY=100
   tstLayer.document.open()
   tstLayer.document.writeln(msg)
   tstLayer.document.close()
   tstLayer.visibility="show"
}
//-->
</SCRIPT>
  </HEAD>
  <BODY>
    <FORM NAME="testFrm">
    <P><INPUT TYPE="BUTTON" NAME="createBtn"
             VALUE="Create a New Layer"
             ONCLICK="createLayer(); return false;"></P>
    </FORM>
  </BODY>
</HTML>
```

As shown in Listing 11.11, there are several things you need to consider when creating a new layer. When creating a top-level layer, you do not need to specify the parent object. The reference to the properties of the new layer begins with the object name of the new layer. To avoid having the user see the changes that you are making to the new layer, place the statement to show the layer at the end of the function. There is one other caveat. You cannot dynamically create a new layer until the Web page is loaded. This means that the function to generate new layers is an event handler. Figure 11.11 shows the results of clicking on the "Create a New Layer" button, which uses the onClick event handler.

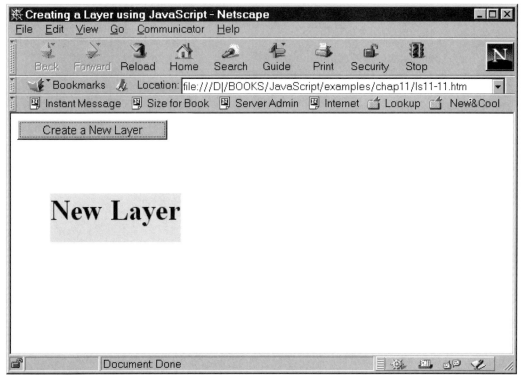

Figure 11.11   Results of creating a Layer using JavaScript.

Animating Content

By using the setInterval() function, setTimeOut() function, and event handlers, you can simulate animation with JavaScript. The following are two methods for creating the illusion of animation:

- Incrementally move the position of a layer by using the setInterval() or setTimeOut() functions. (For example, moving it from being off the viewing area to being within the viewing area of the screen.) You can also change a hidden layer to a visible area and then move the layer to a new position.
- Change the source for an image. In combination with the mouse-Over, mouseOut, and mouseDown events, you can create the il-

lusion of clicking a button. You can even add a click sound file to the mouseDown event. You can also use the focus and blur events to control the highlighting of the area that has keyboard focus.

The HTML document in Listing 11.12 illustrates the process of sliding an image from the edge to the center of the screen. Try resizing the screen and see what happens.

Listing 11.12 Animating Content with JavaScript

```
<HTML>
  <HEAD>
    <TITLE>Animating Content with JavaScript</TITLE>
<SCRIPT LANGUAGE="JavaScript">
<!--
var cntrX=0
var cntrY=0
var sTopX=0
var sTopY=0
var cTopY=0
var slideRate=5
function cntrTop() {
   sTopX=cntrX-Math.round(document.scene.clip.width / 2)
   sTopY=cntrY-Math.round(document.scene.clip.height / 2)
   document.scene.moveTo(sTopX, 0)
   document.scene.visibility="show"
}
function runAnim() {
   if (cTopY < sTopY) {
      cTopY+=5
      document.scene.moveTo(sTopX, cTopY)
      slideIt=setTimeout("runAnim()", slideRate)
   }
}
function initVar() {
   cntrX=Math.round(window.innerWidth / 2)
   cntrY=Math.round(window.innerHeight / 2)
   cTopY=0
   cntrTop()
   slideIt=setTimeout("runAnim()", slideRate)
}
function resetVar() {
```

```
    clearTimeout(slideIt)
    document.scene.visibility="hide"
    initVar()
}
window.onresize=resetVar
//-->
</SCRIPT>
  </HEAD>
  <BODY ONLOAD="initVar()">
    <LAYER ID="scene" VISIBILITY="HIDE">
      <IMG SRC="../images/clipart/desert.jpg"
           ALT="desert image" WIDTH="320" HEIGHT="240">
    </LAYER>
  </BODY>
</HTML>
```

As soon as the browser loads the document shown in Listing 11.12, the initVar() function calculates the center of the viewing area of the browser window. The cntrTop() function then calculates the positions for working with the top-left corner of the layer, since this is the corner referenced by the moveTo() method. Once the layer is correctly positioned, the visibility is set to "show." Then the setTimeout() method invokes the runAnim() function to move the layer to the center of the screen. If you resize the screen, the onresize event handler calls the resetVar() function to reinitialize the sliding of the image. When the image has completed its movement, it is centered in the viewing area as shown in Figure 11.12.

The Security Model for Netscape Communicator 4.0

JavaScript security consists of two policies:

- The *same origin* policy, which first appears in Netscape Navigator 2.0. It is the default policy.
- The *signed script policy*, which is new in Netscape Communicator 4.0. The signed script policy's *object signing* model is a JavaScript security model.

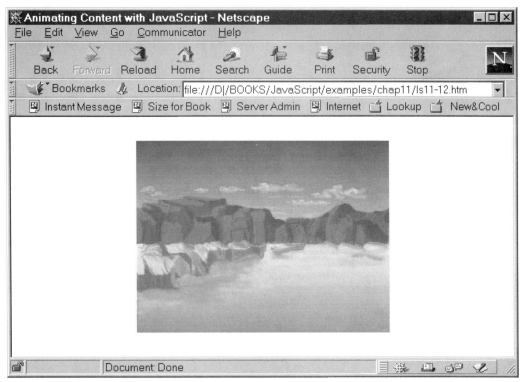

Figure 11.12   Results of Animating Content with JavaScript.

The Same Origin Policy

The same origin policy holds that documents loaded from different origins cannot get or set certain properties in the original document. To be from the same origin, Netscape Communicator requires that the protocol and host—which includes the port number—portions of the URL be identical. For example, the following URLs are not the same:

```
http://www.xyz.com/dir/index.html
http://xyz.com/dir/index.html (domain is different)
http://www.xyz.com:81/dir/index.html (port is different)
ftp://www.xyz.com/dir/index.html (protocol is different)
```

By setting the `document.domain` property to a suffix of the current domain, the browser uses the shorter domain name for subsequent same origin checks. For example, if a script from www.xyz.com includes the statement:

```
document.domain = "xyz.com"
```

then subsequent documents from www2.xyz.com or xyz.com fulfill the requirements of the same origin policy. The suffix must specify at least two levels of the domain name (three for domain names that end with the country code). Thus, com and co.uk are not valid suffixes.

Table 11.18 lists the properties and methods subject to the same origin check. The `toString()` method appears in the table, because it provides access to the properties that are subject to the same origin policy.

Table 11.18 Properties and methods subject to Origin Check

Object	Properties	Methods
button	name value	toString()
checkbox	checked defaultChecked name value	toString()
document	cookie domain forms lastModified links referrer title URL	
fileUpload	name	
form	action name	
hidden	name value	toString()
history	current next previous	toString()
image	name lowsrc src	

Table 11.18 Properties and methods subject to Origin Check *(Continued)*

Object	Properties	Methods
layer	src	
link	All properties	toString()
location	All properties	toString()
option	defaultSelected selected text	
password	All properties	toString()
plugin	length	
radio	checked defaultChecked name value	toString()
reset	name	toString()
select	name selectedIndex	toString()
submit	name value	toString()
text	defaultValue name value	toString()
textarea	defaultValue name value	toString()
window	defaultStatus find name status	

To improve security, Netscape Communicator has a stricter same origin policy than Netscape Navigator 3.0. The differences are as follows:

- In Netscape Navigator 3.0, named forms were not subject to an origin check even though the forms[] array was. In Netscape Communicator, both the named forms and forms[] array are subject to the same origin check.

- In Netscape Navigator 3.0, the protocol of the URL for the SRC attribute in the `<SCRIPT>` tag could be different than the protocol for the document containing the tag. In Netscape Communicator, if you load a document with a protocol other than `file:`, the SRC attribute of a `<SCRIPT>` tag cannot use the file: protocol.

For layers, JavaScript checks the origins of the layers before any interaction with the parent document. If an `<APPLET>` tag contains the MAYSCRIPT attribute, the applet is subject to same origin checks when the applet calls JavaScript.

The Signed Script Policy

Chapter 3, "What Is JavaScript?," introduced the JavaScript security model and signed script. Subsequent chapters presented the signing requirements for restricted objects and their properties. Now, it is time for a look at the principles behind the JavaScript security model for Netscape Communicator 4.0. There are five areas of concern as follows:

- Signed objects
- Secure servers
- Codebase principals
- Scripts signed by different principals
- Impact of windows and layers

Signed Objects and the JavaScript Security Model

The Java security model for signed objects is the foundation of the JavaScript security model. JavaScript with the `<SCRIPT>` tags, event handlers, JavaScript entities, and JavaScript source files are all candidates for signing. Through the Java SecurityManager class, a signed script allows access to restricted information beyond the "sandbox." Java uses the term "sandbox" to define the limits within which Java code operates.

In the Java security model, a *principal* defines who is allowed access, and a *target* specifies objects that require extended *privileges*. A principal must prove their identity before Java will grant access to a specific target. The proof of identity is the digital signature implemented as a *certificate*. A trusted third party maintains the certificate information for the principal.

A particular principal, which includes both individuals and companies, owns a digital signature. Although a single principal signs the scripts in most Web pages, the security model allows for a single HTML document to contain scripts signed by multiple principals. The Java ARchive (JAR) file holds the digital signatures. For inline scripts, event handlers, and JavaScript entities, the Page Signer stores only the signature and an identifier for the script in the JAR file. For a JavaScript source file, the Page Signer places the entire source file in the JAR file.

A signed scripts says who signed it and provides the certificate as proof of authorship. With this information, the user makes the final decision whether to grant the privileges requested by the script. A good programming practice requires that a signed script provide for a graceful way to handle a denial by the user.

Secure Servers and Unsigned Scripts

The secure server offers an alternative to using the Page Signer tool to sign scripts. By default, Netscape Communicator treats all pages received from a Secure Sockets Layer (SSL) server as signed pages. For dynamically generated pages, an SSL server offers the only solution for access to extended privileges.

Codebase Principals

JavaScript also supports Java's codebase principals. A *codebase principal* derives its privileges from the origin of the script, rather than from a digital signature. Because they offer a weaker form of security, Netscape Communicator disables codebase principals. However, Netscape Communicator uses codebase principals as the mechanism for enforcing the same origin security policy.

For the record, both signed and unsigned scripts use codebase principals. The crucial difference centers on the proof of identity. A signed script gets its proof of identity from the certificate's digital signature. Signed scripts prove the identity of the author of the script. If the user enables codebase principals (see Chapter 3 for instructions on how to modify the preferences file), Netscape Communicator presents a dialog box similar to that of the signed script when the script requests extended privileges. With codebase principals, the proof of identity is the URL of the server, without proof of the author.

Scripts Signed by Different Principals

Although JavaScript uses the Java model for signed scripts, JavaScript presents unique problems which are not an issue with Java. Java protects classes and uses the public/private/protected mechanism to protect the methods of those classes. For example, you cannot extend any Java class or method marked as *final*.

In contrast, JavaScript lacks the concept of public and private methods. Furthermore, as a scripting language, JavaScript allows runtime changes by adding properties to objects, replacing existing properties, and replacing existing methods. The changes to a document may come from within the document, or from a document in another frame, window, or layer.

To ensure security, signed scripts in JavaScript assume that privileges apply to the common principals when there are multiple scripts on a page. Following are a few examples:

- If one script was signed by two principals (X and Y) and a second script signed only by X, then JavaScript acts as if both scripts were only signed by X.
- Using the same rule, when there is a signed script and an unsigned script, JavaScript treats both as unsigned. The latter case is true, because both scripts use codebase principals.

Impact of Windows and Layers

Netscape Communicator 4.0 considers windows and layers as containers for documents. When there are multiple containers in a Web page, Netscape Communicator applies cross-container checks to most properties. First, Netscape Communicator resolves the principals for each container in the Web page. After resolving the principals in a container, the browser can compare principals between containers. All comparisons start with the outermost document, which is reflected in the top-most window. The outermost document opens other windows and layers. From this model of behavior, the container-check encounters the following possibilities:

- When the containers are signed by the same principal, the inner container can reference the outer container.
- When the inner layer is unsigned and the outer layer signed, the inner layer cannot access most properties in the outer container.

However, the outer container can access the inner container.
- Certificates themselves have a hierarchical structure. When scripts are signed by different principals that are part of the same super-set, then access is permitted.

The following properties are exempted from the cross-container check:
- `closed`
- `height`
- `outerHeight`
- `outerWidth`
- `pageXoffset`
- `pageYoffset`
- `screenX`
- `screenY`
- `secure`
- `width`

To avoid any potential access errors with an unsigned layer with a signed container, you need to take the following steps:
- Set the `parentLayer` property to null to prevent unauthorized access to the parent layer.
- Use the `initStandardObjects()` method to create a copy of the standard window objects (such as string, date, and array) within the layer's scope.

Summary

Netscape Communicator 4.0 added DHTML to the HTML document. DHTML extends the capabilities for creating dynamic content through Cascading Style Sheets and positioned content. You create style sheets using either the CSS or JavaScript syntax. This chapter presented the JavaScript syntax for writing style sheets. While style sheets add a new level of typographical capabilities to a Web page, positioned content adds the ability to create layers. This chapter concentrated on the `<LINK>` and `<ILINK>` tags as a means of creating positioned content. However, you can create positioned content with the CSS syntax.

Netscape Communicator also changed the JavaScript security model for the browser to use the Java security model for signed objects. The new JavaScript security model has two policies: the same origin policy and the signed script policy. The same origin policy was used by prior versions of Netscape Navigator. The signed script policy extends the access to restricted information through assigning privileges to principals. The certificate provides the digital signature that identifies the author of the signed script. Both signed and unsigned scripts use codebase principals as the mechanism for managing security. The problem of ensuring a secure environment in a page that contains multiple windows or layers, was solved when Netscape Communicator added rules for checking the privileges between containers.

This chapter concludes the client-side discussion of JavaScript. Next the server-side JavaScript will be discussed.

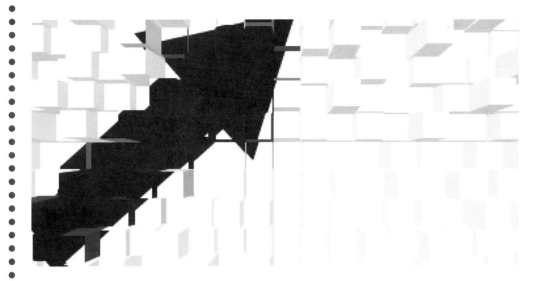

Introduction to
Server-Side JavaScript

Topics in This Chapter

- Client/server JavaScript architecture
- Implementing JavaScript on a Netscape server
- The development cycle for JavaScript applications

Chapter

12

LiveWire is the Netscape component that implements server-side Java-Script. The original LiveWire and LiveWire Pro products were based on JavaScript 1.0 and sold separately from server software. LiveWire Pro differs from LiveWire in the following ways:

- LiveWire Pro includes support for SQL relational databases from Informix, Oracle, Sybase, and Microsoft
- LiveWire Pro includes Crystal Software's Crystal Reports Professional

Netscape first bundled LiveWire with the FastTrack Server 3.01, and LiveWire Pro with the Enterprise Server 3.0. At the same time Netscape updated LiveWire to support JavaScript 1.2.

This chapter opens with a discussion of how server-side JavaScript fits into the structure of the JavaScript language. We will then learn how to configure the server to support server-side JavaScript. The chapter ends with a discussion of the development cycle for client/server JavaScript applications.

JavaScript Architecture

A large majority of Web pages use only the client-side of JavaScript. Interaction with the server is limited to document retrieval, or interfacing to Common Gate Interface (CGI) programs on the server-side. For client/server applications built on a Netscape server, LiveWire offers JavaScript as an alternative for building the server-side of an application. LiveWire has several advantages over CGI programs:

- LiveWire is tightly integrated with HTML
- The developer needs to learn one language—JavaScript
- Platform independent byte code for files that contain server-side JavaScript

The JavaScript language has three components: client-side, core, and server-side. Figure 12.1 illustrates the relationship of these three components.

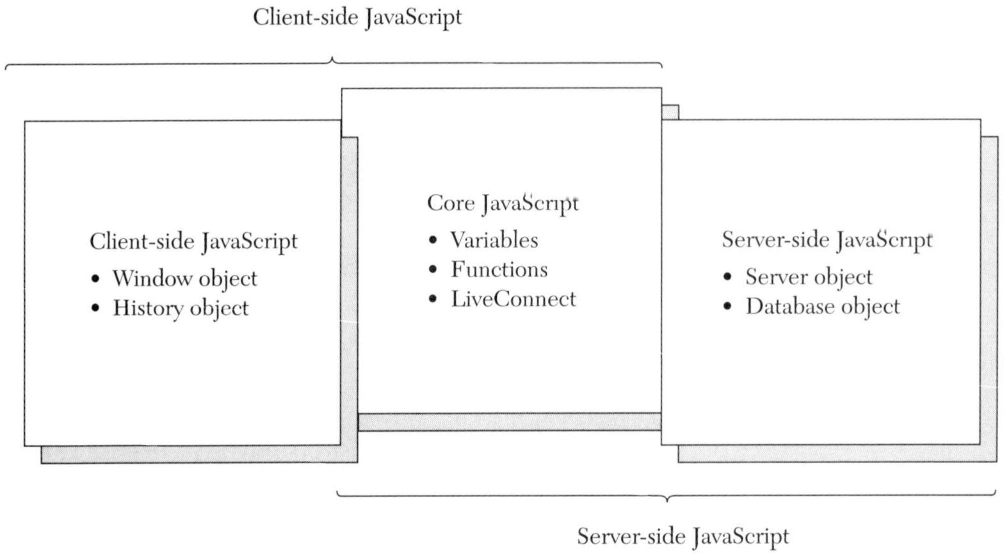

Figure 12.1   Components of JavaScript language.

Client-side JavaScript incorporates the core language and the extensions necessary to run JavaScript in a browser. The browser interprets client-side JavaScript at runtime. *Server-side JavaScript* includes the core language and the extensions needed to run JavaScript on a server. To meet the performance requirements of a server, server-side Java-

Script is compiled into byte-code web files before deployment. A *Java-Script application* uses both client-side and server-side JavaScript.

JavaScript Application Architecture

Like client-side JavaScript, server-side JavaScript uses embedded HTML tags. The server-side statements allow you to perform the following tasks:

- Connect to relational databases
- Share information between users of an application
- Access the file system on the server
- Communicate with other applications through LiveConnect and Java

The LiveWire Database Service connects a JavaScript application to a relational database. Such an application has three tiers as shown in Figure 12.2.

A typical scenario for the three tiers is as follows:

- The browser (tier 1) requests a Web page from the Netscape server (tier 2). The Web page contains a form for a database query, which includes client-side JavaScript routines for editing the form. The user completes the form and sends it back to the Netscape server. From the view of the browser, tier 2 is the server-side. The browser has no knowledge of how the tier 2 server handles the returned data.

- The Netscape server receives the form data. Since the application is a database query, the Netscape server has to query a relational database (tier 3). From the view of the Netscape server, now acting as a client, the database server represents the server-side. Like the browser, the Netscape server has no knowledge of how the database server processes the request.

- The database server sends the requested data back to the Netscape server. The Netscape server, using JavaScript, formulates an HTML document and sends it back to the browser.

- The browser displays the results of the query.

Although the tiers are not delineated, the client/server diagram shown in Figure 12.2 represents a three-tier client/server model. Another ex-

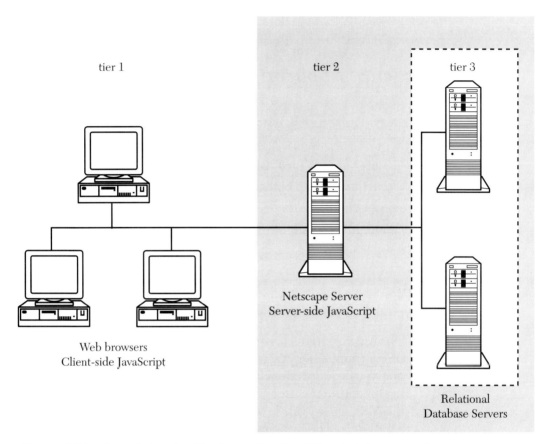

Figure 12.2 *JavaScript Application using LiveWire database service.*

ample of the three-tier model is when the server-side JavaScript uses LiveConnect to communicate with a second application.

Server-Side JavaScript Architecture

The Netscape FastTrack server and the Netscape Enterprise server are Web servers. Server-side JavaScript is an extension to the server features. Figure 12.3 is a conceptual diagram of the server-side JavaScript architecture. As such, the diagram illustrates the connection between the Netscape Web server and JavaScript applications.

As shown in Figure 12-3, the JavaScript runtime has three major components as follows:

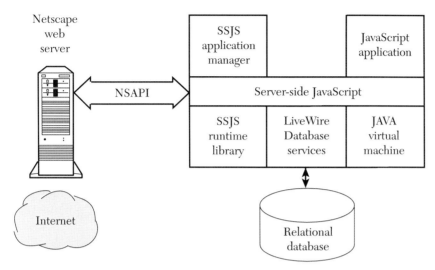

Figure 12.3 Server-side JavaScript architecture.

- The *JavaScript runtime library* provides the routines for basic JavaScript functionality.
- The *LiveWire Database Service* provides the classes and objects necessary to interface to external relational databases.
- The *Java Virtual Machine* is used by JavaScript applications. LiveConnect provides the interface to Java applets.

JavaScript applications include HTML documents and JavaScript source files that contain both client-side and server-side JavaScript. In the HTML document, the <SCRIPT> tag defines client-side JavaScript, and the <SERVER> tag delimits server-side JavaScript. JavaScript source files contain either client-side or server-side JavaScript, but not both. The separation of source files is necessary, since the source file does not contain the <SCRIPT> or <SERVER> tags.

The JavaScript compiler compiles HTML documents containing JavaScript source files—which contain server-side JavaScript—into a single JavaScript executable file for the application. The executable file uses bytecodes that are platform-independent. The extension for the compiled file is .web. The JavaScript Application Manager installs the executable files on the Netscape server.

When a browser requests a page from a server-side JavaScript application, the runtime engine locates the representation of the file in the application's *web* file. The runtime engine then runs the server code and creates an HTML document to send to the browser. The HTML document, itself, may contain client-side JavaScript statements. The server executes all server-side JavaScript.

Server Configuration

Before developing and running JavaScript applications on a Netscape server, you need to enable the JavaScript runtime engine. You must also consider the security of the server, its access to Java applets, and the path for the JavaScript compiler.

Enabling JavaScript

To enable server-side JavaScript, perform the following steps from the Server Manager:

1. Select the server for which you wish to enable JavaScript.
2. Click the "Programs" button.
3. Select "Server-Side JavaScript." (see Figure 12.4).
4. Click the "Yes" button for the question "Activate Server-Side JavaScript application environment?"
5. Click the "Yes" button for the question "Require administration server password for Server-Side JavaScript?"
6. Click "OK."
7. In the next screen, click the "Save and Apply" button to apply the changes.

Server-Side Security

Because the Application Manager controls JavaScript applications, you need to protect it from unauthorized access. By clicking the "Yes" button, you establish the requirement to enter the administration server password to access the Application Manager. If you selected "No," then anyone can add, remove, modify, start, and stop applications.

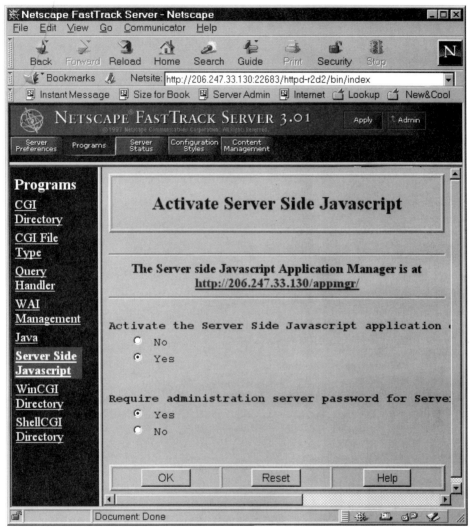

Figure 12.4   Enabling server-side JavaScript.

Without question, if the server is outside of the firewall, you must password protect the server. This server is known as the *deployment server*. In larger sites, you may not want the developers to have access to the password of the deployment server. In this circumstance, the *development server* should reside within the bounds of the firewall. For security reasons, this server should also be protected with a password used by the developers. Once the JavaScript application is ready for deployment, the site administrator can deploy the application to the deployment server.

Remote administration presents an additional problem. Unless the server uses the Secure Sockets Layer (SSL), the account name and password for the Server Manager are passed over the network as clear text. This could allow an intruder to gain access to the server by monitoring the packets on the network. Consequently, you need SSL for complete server security for a server that resides outside of the firewall.

Preparing the Server for LiveConnect

Netscape servers include Java classes that can be used with JavaScript. By default, the CLASSPATH for these Java classes is set to $NSHOME/js/samples directory, where $NSHOME is the install directory for the server. On Windows NT, the default path is c:\Netscape\Suite-Spot\js\samples. Although you can define a CLASSPATH environmental variable to point to a different directory for Java classes, the best solution is to modify the obj.conf file in the config directory for the server.

To use server-side Java you must first enable it. The procedure for enabling server-side Java is the same as for server-side JavaScript (see Figure 12.5), except that you click on "Java" instead of "Server-Side JavaScript." Once you enable Java, you can modify the obj.conf file to incorporate your new path. For the path to take effect, shutdown and restart your server.

Note

The CLASSPATH environmental variable includes other directories that contain Java classes besides those for use with JavaScript.

Preparing the Server for the JavaScript Compiler

The installation of a Netscape server does not change the system's PATH environmental variable to include the directory that contains the JavaScript application compiler. To avoid using the complete pathname of the compiler, you need to modify the PATH environmental variable. Table 12.1 lists the location of the JavaScript application compiler for the

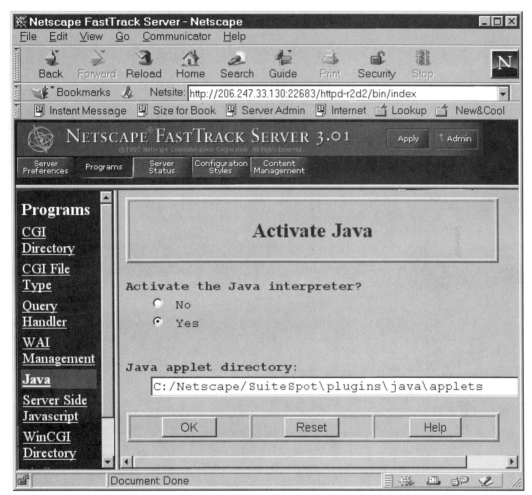

Figure 12.5 Enabling Server-side Java.

Enterprise server and FastTrack server on both the UNIX and Windows NT platforms. If you have any questions on how to set the PATH environmental variable, check with your system administrator.

Table 12.1 Location of JavaScript Application Compiler

Server	UNIX *	Windows NT **
Enterprise 3.x	$NSHOME/bin/https	%NSHOME%\bin\https
FastTrack 3.x	$NSHOME/bin/httpd	%NSHOME%\bin\httpd
	* $NSHOME is the install directory for the server.	** %NSHOME% is the install directory for the server.

Application Development Cycle

The development of a JavaScript application involves a different development cycle than client-side only JavaScript. Assuming that there is a development server and a deployment server, the steps involved in the development of a JavaScript application are as follows:

1. Create the source files.
2. Compile the JavaScript application using the JavaScript Application Compiler.
3. Publish the web files on the development server.
4. Install the application using the Application Manager.
5. Test and debug the application.
6. Publish and install the application on the deployment server.

Creating Source Files for JavaScript Applications

The web file for a JavaScript application contains the following types of files:

- HTML files, with the extension .htm or .html, containing standard HTML and JavaScript statements. The HTML file may contain both client-side and server-side JavaScript.
- JavaScript source files, with the extension .js, containing either client-side or server-side JavaScript. A single source file cannot contain both client-side and server-side JavaScript.

You can create these files with a text editor or a JavaScript tool, such as NetObject's ScriptBuilder or HoTMetaL Pro. Other HTML editors may also include the ability to create server-side JavaScript. If your HTML editor supports JavaScript, check to see if it supports the `<SERVER>` tag in addition to the `<SCRIPT>` tag.

Compiling a JavaScript Application

After developing an application, you need to compile the HTML files and JavaScript source files that contain server-side JavaScript into a `.web` file. The web file is a platform-independent bytecode file which you install using the Application Manager. The syntax for the JavaScript Application Compiler is as follows:

```
jsac [-h] [-c] [-v] [-d]
     [-l characterSet]
     [-o outfile.web]
     [-i inputFile]
     [-p pathName]
     [-f includeFile]
     [-r errorFile]
     [-a 1.2]
     script1.html [... scriptn.html]
     [jsSource1.js ... jsSourcen.js]
```

For clarity, the syntax for `jsac` splits the options onto different lines. However when you enter the compile command, all the options occur on the same line. Table 12.2 lists the options for the JavaScript Application Compiler.

Table 12.2 Options to JavaScript Application Compiler

Option	Description
-h	Display the syntax for the JavaScript Application Compiler. The -h option excludes all other options.
-c	Check syntax only. If you specify the -c option, you do not need to specify the -o option.
-v	Display additional information (verbose) about the compilation of the application.
-d	Display contents of generated JavaScript.

Table 12.2 Options to JavaScript Application Compiler *(Continued)*

Option	Description
-l	Specifies the character set (such as iso-8859-1, x-sjis, euc-kr) to use when compiling an application.
-o	Specifies the name of the bytecode output file. The format of the output file name is `outfile.web`. If you do not specify this option, the compiler does not create an output file.
-i	Allows you to specify an input file using the absolute pathname instead of a relative pathname. You can specify only one *inputFile* using this option. When you need to specify multiple input files using the absolute pathname, use the –f option.
-p	Specifies the pathname to use as the root for all relative pathnames. This option must proceed any option that uses relative pathnames.
-f	Specifies a file that contains a list of the input files. The list of input files are white-space delimited. Filenames containing a space must be enclosed in double quotes. The –f option provides a means of circumventing input line length restrictions.
-r	Redirects the error output to the specified filename.
-a 1.2	Specifies that the compiler should use JavaScript 1.2 rules for comparison operators (see Chapter 4, "Fundamentals of JavaScript").

For all platforms, you can use either the dash (-) or forward slash (/) to specify options, as shown in the following examples.

```
jsac -h
jsac /h
```

The use of the forward slash for options creates a problem for UNIX absolute pathnames that begin with slash. To specify a UNIX absolute pathname for an input file, you must use the -i option.

A typical command line for the JavaScript Application Compiler looks like the following:

```
jsac -v -o myapp.web main.html hello.html support.js
```

As an alternative, you can specify the input files using the -f option as follows:

```
jsac -v -f filelist.txt -o myapp.web
```

The `filelist.txt` file would then contain the following lines:

```
main.html
hello.html
support.js
```

Using the Application Manager

You can use the Application Manager to perform the following tasks:

- Install a new JavaScript application
- Modify the attributes of an installed application
- Start, stop, and restart an installed application
- Run and debug an installed application
- Remove an installed application

The Application Manager, itself, is a JavaScript application that you invoke by entering the following URL in Netscape Navigator:

```
http://server.domain/appmgr
```

Figure 12.6 shows the initial window for the Application Manager. The left frame shows a list of installed applications and the action buttons. The right frame displays the following information:

- Application name
- Pathname for the application
- Default and initial Web pages for the application
- Maximum number of database connections allowed
- External libraries
- Method used to maintain the client object
- Status of the application

Installing an Application

After you compile and publish your application, use the Application Manager to install it on the Web server by clicking the "Add Application" button. The browser then displays the form shown in Figure 12.7. Table 12.3 describes the requirements for the input fields for the application installation form.

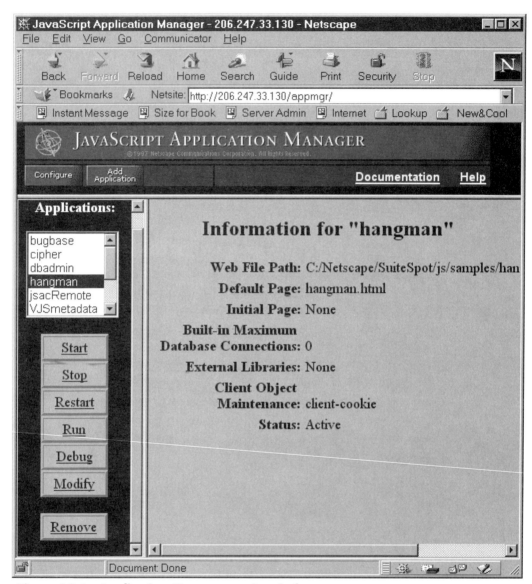

Figure 12.6 Application Manager main window.

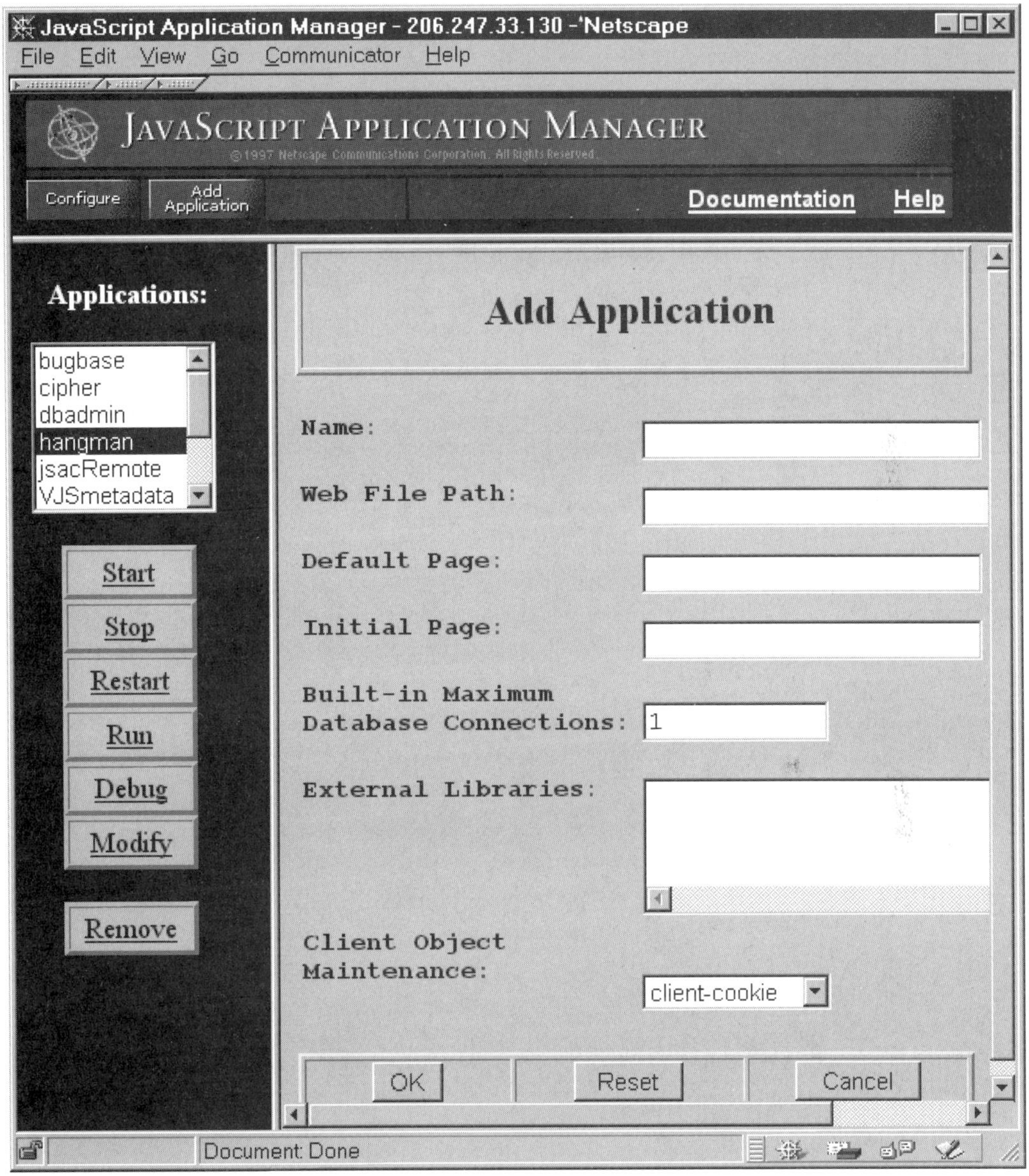

Figure 12.7 Form for installing an application.

Table 12.3 Description of Installation Form Fields

Field	Description
Name	The name of the application for use in the application URL. For example, the URL for "myApp" would be `http://server.domain/myapp`. The name needs to be a unique application name and not conflict with any other URLs on the server.
Web File Path	The full pathname to the application's web file on the server.
Default Page	The default page the server is to run when the user does not specify a particular page.
Initial Page	An optional page that the JavaScript runtime engine executes when you start the application from the Application Manager. Use this page to initialize values, create locks, and establish database connections. This page cannot contain references to the `request` or `client` objects.
Built-in Maximum Database Connections	An optional field that specifies the default value for the maximum number of database connections that the application can have open at one time. You can override this setting in the JavaScript code with the `database.connect()` method.
External Libraries	A comma or semicolon separated list of external libraries used by the application. See Chapter 13, "Working with Server-Side JavaScript," for more details on external libraries.
Client Object Maintenance	Specifies the technique used to save the properties of the `client` object. The valid choices are `client cookie`, `client URL`, `server IP`, `server cookie`, or `server URL`. See Chapter 13 for more details on the `client` object.

After completing the form, click the "OK" button and the Application Manager will install the new application. Once installed, you do not need to reinstall the application when installing new versions of the application.

Modifying an Application

The Application Manager allows you to change all of the installation fields except the application name. To modify an application, select the application name in the selection list and then click the "Modify" button. If you modify the fields of a stopped application, the Application Manager automatically starts the application. If you modify the fields of an active application, the Application Manager stops and restarts the application.

To change the name of an application, you need to remove the application and reinstall it. When you change an application's name, you also change the URL for accessing the application.

Removing an Application

You can remove an application from the server by selecting the application's name and clicking the "Remove" button. Removing an application only removes it from the list of applications that the server can run. It does not remove the files from the server.

Starting, Stopping and Restarting an Application

After installation, you must start the application before running it. When you start an application the status changes from stopped to active. If you have access privileges to the Application Manager, you can also start an application with the following URL:

```
http://server.domain/appmgr/control.html?name=appName&cmd=start
```

You can stop an application by clicking the "Stop" button. This changes the status of the application from active to stopped. Users cannot access a stopped application. You must stop an application if you want to remove the web file. If you have access privileges to the Application Manager, you can also stop an application with the following URL:

```
http://server.domain/appmgr/control.html?name=appName&cmd=stop
```

When you rebuild an active application, you must restart the application by clicking the "Restart" button. Essentially, restarting an application is the same as reinstalling it. If you have access privileges to the Application Manager, you can also restart an application with the following URL:

```
http://server.domain/appmgr/control.html?name=appName&cmd=restart
```

Running an Application

Once you have compiled, installed, and started an application, you can run the application by either of the following methods:

- Click the "Run" button in the Application Manager, and the Application Manager will open a new browser window and display the application's Web page.

- Type the URL in the Location bar of any browser to load the application.

Debugging an Application

The Application Manager provides a debugging tool that traces the execution of an application's server-side. When you trace the execution of an application from the Application Manager, the Application Manager opens the application in a new window with two frames as shown in Figure 12.8. This example traces the execution of the "World" application, which is one of the sample applications provided with the server.

The left-hand frame of the window shown in Figure 12.8 displays the results of the trace. The right-hand frame displays the application. As the client interacts with the server, the trace routine displays the actions of the server. The trace utility displays the following debugging information:

- Values of object properties and arguments of the debug() functions called by the application
- Before and after properties of the request and client objects
- Property values of the project and server objects
- New values that the application assigns to properties
- Indication of when the runtime engine sends content to the client

If you have Application Manager privileges, you can achieve the same trace results by using the following URL:

```
http://server.domain/appmgr/debug.html?name=appName
```

For example, to trace the hangman application provided with the Netscape servers, you need to enter the following URL:

```
http://www.xyz.com/appmgr/debug.html?name=hangman
```

If you want the trace utility to display the trace results in a separate window, use the following URL:

```
http://server.domain/appmgr/trace.htrml?name=appName
```

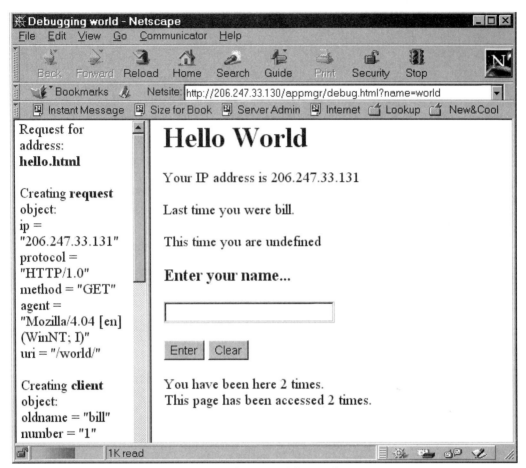

Figure 12.8   Results of debugging the "World" application.

Once you start the debugging operation, the start and stop functions are not functional. If you try to stop or start an application and you receive the message "Trace is active," perform the following steps:

1. Close any windows running the debugger.
2. Close any windows running the application.
3. In the Application Manager, select the application and click the "Run" button.

Upon completion of these steps, you can start or stop an application.

Configuring the Application Manager

You can configure the Application Manager's default settings by clicking on the "Configure" button on the top button bar for the Application Manager window. Figure 12.9 shows the lower portion of the configuration form.

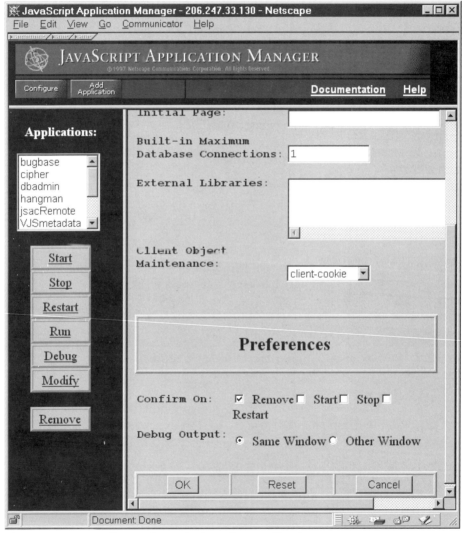

Figure 12.9   Configuration window for Application Manager.

Default values can be set for the following:

- Web file path
- Default page
- Initial page
- Built-in maximum database connections
- External libraries
- Client object maintenance

In addition, you can set the following preferences:

- Confirmation on the remove, start, stop, and restart buttons for an application
- Sending debug output to the same window or a different window

Summary

Server-side JavaScript is the flip side of client-side JavaScript. When combined the two sides form a JavaScript application. As a language, JavaScript consists of core components, plus extensions for client-side JavaScript and server-side JavaScript.

Server-side JavaScript is similar to a CGI program. The biggest difference is the tight integration between HTML and server-side JavaScript. With server-side JavaScript, you can perform the following tasks:

- Connect to relational databases
- Share information between users of an application
- Access the file system on the server
- Communicate with other applications through LiveConnect and Java

Before using server-side JavaScript, you need to configure the Netscape server to enable server-side JavaScript. If using server-side Java applets, you must also enable the Java runtime environment and establish the CLASSPATH environmental variable.

The development cycle of a JavaScript application is different from only using client-side JavaScript. After writing the source files, you need to compile the HTML files that contain server-side JavaScript and the server-side JavaScript source files into a single web file. Once the web file is compiled, you can publish the JavaScript application. Before using the application, you need to install it by using the Application Manager. Besides installing applications, the Application Manager allows you to start, stop, restart, remove, and debug applications.

This chapter established the environment for the development of server-side JavaScript. The next chapter takes a closer look at server-side JavaScript as a language.

Working with
Server-Side JavaScript

Topics in This Chapter

- Process for writing server-side JavaScript
- Understanding the Session Management Service
- Review built-in functions for server-side JavaScript
- Special server-side JavaScript utilities
- Impact of Java and CORBA on server-side JavaScript

Chapter

13

Server-side JavaScript combines JavaScript core functions with server-side extensions to support the requirements of server-side programming. JavaScript applications start with client-side HTML documents. These documents include server-side code which the server acts upon before passing the document to the client. Where only Netscape servers support server-side JavaScript, client-side browsers can be any browser that supports the generated HTML document. Thus, if the generated document is pure HTML 3.2, then any browser that supports HTML 3.2 can act as a client. Conversely, if the document includes client-side JavaScript that is unique to JavaScript 1.2, then the browser must support JavaScript 1.2.

The process of writing JavaScript applications that integrate client-side and server-side JavaScript into a single document, differs from writing HTML documents containing only client-side JavaScript. Server-side JavaScript contains client-side built-in functions, and additional built-in functions for server-side processing. The heart of server-side JavaScript lies in the objects and properties of the Session Management Service, since these objects and properties add the dimension for client/

server interaction. Server-side JavaScript also comes with utilities for handling mail and working with files. The Common Object Request Broker Architecture (CORBA) and Java reach their full potential when Java applets interact on both sides of the client/server application.

Writing Server-Side JavaScript

The development process for writing a JavaScript application, differs from that of just retrieving and displaying documents. The process starts with the design of a JavaScript application. It is then necessary to consider the runtime order of processing, how to incorporate server-side JavaScript into HTML documents, and some important differences between client-side and server-side JavaScript.

Designing JavaScript Applications

After defining the overall requirements of an application, you must decide which tasks are client-side and which tasks are server-side. The decision is not always clear-cut, since either the client or the server can perform many of the same tasks. As a general guideline, the client should perform as many tasks as possible, so that the server is free to support the maximum number of clients. Using this general guideline, the tasks could be divided along the lines shown in Table 13.1.

Table 13.1 Guidelines for Separating Client-Side and Server-Side Tasks

Client-Side Tasks	Server-Side Tasks
• Validate user input to forms.	• Maintain information for multiple accesses by the same client.
• Prompt users for errors or additional information.	• Maintain information for shared clients or applications.
• Perform calculations for data retrieved from the server.	• Access relational databases or files on the server.
• Format content of the Web page.	• Call external libraries on the server.
• Perform other tasks that do not require server support.	• Dynamically customize Java applets.

In addition to the general guideline, you need to consider the following:

- The server-side Session Management Service allows you to preserve information over time
- Servers can maintain information across multiple clients or multiple applications
- Servers provide access to databases and files
- Client-side objects only exist during the session

Runtime Processing of Applications

In working with client/server applications, you need to consider the sequence of events during the actual running of an application. The flow-chart shown in Figure 13.1 describes the order of processing for JavaScript applications.

The web file contains only those HTML documents and JavaScript source files that use server-side JavaScript. Before sending an HTML document in the web file to the server, the server's runtime engine needs to retrieve the document from the web file, process all server-side JavaScript, and generate an HTML document. All other HTML documents, JavaScript source files, images, and Java applets follow the same retrieval process as does any file managed by the server. Thus, a JavaScript application consists of both regular HTML documents and generated HTML documents.

Embedding Server-Side JavaScript in an HTML Document

There are two methods for embedding server-side JavaScript into an HTML document:

- The `<SERVER> </SERVER>` tags act like the `<SCRIPT> </SCRIPT>` tags. However, the `<SERVER>` tag has no attributes. Instead of using the `SRC` attribute to include JavaScript source files, you specify all JavaScript source files on the command line for the JavaScript Application Compiler. You also cannot include any HTML tags or the `<SCRIPT> </SCRIPT>` tags between the server tags. Since the browser never sees the `<SERVER>` tag, you do not need to comment the JavaScript

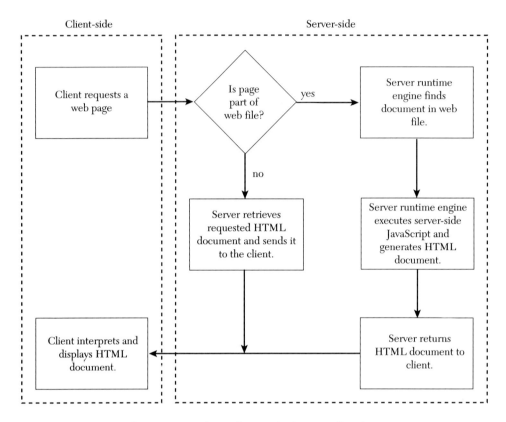

Figure 13.1   Runtime processing of JavaScript applications.

statements to protect them from non-JavaScript enabled browsers.

- Use backquotes (`) to enclose server-side JavaScript expressions as substitutes for HTML attribute names or attribute values. When you backquote a JavaScript expression that is a substitute for an attribute value, the JavaScript runtime engine automatically adds quotation marks around the entire value. Within a backquoted expression, the runtime engine treats all double quoted text as literals.

The JavaScript statements that appear within the <SERVER> </SERVER> tags often do not alter the HTML document sent to the client (for example, an HTML document that sends a mail message). However, you can use the write statement to alter the HTML document as shown in the following example:

```
<SERVER>
   var testStr="test"
   write("<P>This is a dynamically generated string</P>")
   write "<P>This is a " + testStr + " string.</P>")
</SERVER>
```

When you use backquotes as an attribute value, remember that the JavaScript runtime engine automatically supplies the necessary quotation marks. The following line from the hangman application—included as a sample application with the server—illustrates the use of backquotes:

```
<IMG SRC=`"images/hang"+client.num_misses+".gif"`>
```

If the value of client.num_misses equals 1, then the string sent to the client is as follows:

```
<IMG SRC="images/hang1.gif">
```

Note

 You cannot specify a server-side JavaScript statement as an event handler.

Overview of Server-Side JavaScript

The original LiveWire and LiveWire Pro products implement server-side JavaScript version 1.0. The changes in JavaScript 1.1 apply only to the client-side. With the release of the Netscape FastTrack Server 3.01 and the Netscape Enterprise Server 3.0, LiveWire became a bundled part of the servers, and the server-side JavaScript moved to version 1.2. Since LiveWire no longer exists as a separate product, I am not including a discussion of the difference between server-side JavaScript 1.0 and server-side JavaScript 1.2. Instead, the discussion focuses strictly on the current implementation of LiveWire.

For the core components of JavaScript, client-side JavaScript behaves in much the same manner as server-side JavaScript. However, there are differences in the handling of comparison operators and prototypes.

As mentioned in Chapter 4, "Fundamentals of JavaScript," JavaScript 1.1 provides for automatic conversion of operands for comparison operators. However, JavaScript 1.2 does not provide for automatic conversion of operators. On the client-side, this difference is relevant only when the `LANGUAGE` attribute of the `<SCRIPT>` tag is set to JavaScript1.2. Since the `<SERVER>` tag has no attributes, use JavaScript 1.1 rules for conversion of operands as the default behavior. If you want to enforce the JavaScript 1.2 rules of comparison operators, you need to include the `-a 1.2` option on the command line for the JavaScript Application Compiler (`jsac`).

Chapter 5, "JavaScript Object Model," describes how to use the `prototype` property to add to an object and all of its instances. Server-side JavaScript also supports the prototype property as follows:

- You can use the `prototype` property to add new properties to the `Blob`, `Connection`, `Cursor`, `DbPool`, `File`, `Lock`, `Resultset`, `SendMail`, and `Stproc` objects. In addition, you can use the prototype property of the `DbBuiltin` object to add properties to the database object provided by the JavaScript runtime engine.

- The `prototype` property is not available for the `client`, `project`, `request`, and `server` objects.

- You can use the `prototype` property for any object that you define.

Since all server-side JavaScript applications run in the same environment, a property added to server-side objects by the prototype property is available to all applications running on the server. This feature enables you to add new functionality to all JavaScript applications on a server. However, if you use the prototype property to add a property to an object that you define in an application, the new property is available only in that application.

Core Built-in Functions

The core JavaScript language provides the common built-in functions described in Table 13.2. Chapter 6, "Built-in Objects, Methods, and Functions," discusses these functions in detail.

Table 13.2 List of Core Built-in Functions

Function	Description
escape()	Returns the hexadecimal of an argument in the ISO Latin-1 character set.
unescape()	Returns the ASCII string of an escape string.
isNAN()	Evaluates the argument to determine if it is Not a Number.
parseFloat()	Evaluates the string argument and returns a floating point number.
parseInt()	Evaluates the string argument and returns an integer.

Core Objects and Properties

Table 13.3 lists the core objects available to both client-side JavaScript and server-side JavaScript. The properties and methods of these objects are also core components.

Table 13.3 List of Core Objects

Object	Description
Array	Defines an array of elements (see Chapter 5).
Boolean	Represents a Boolean value (see Chapter 6).
Date	Represents a date (see Chapter 6).
Function	Specifies a JavaScript string to be compiled as a function (see Chapter 5).
Math	Provides math constants and functions (see Chapter 6).
MimeType	Reflects the MIME types supported by the client (see Chapter 10, "Interfacing to Plug-ins and JavaApplets").
Number	Represents numeric values (see Chapter 6).
Object	Constructor for building objects (see Chapter 5).
Packages	The Java packages required to interface to JavaScript (see Chapter 10).
String	Represents a string value (see Chapter 6).

Session Management Service

JavaScript processes are asynchronous in that many users can access the same application at any given point in time. The JavaScript runtime engine handles requests from multiple users as they arrive, and processes them in the order received. This means an application needs to support the interleaving of multiple users. To make the process more difficult, the Hypertext Transfer Protocol (HTTP), which is the message protocol for transferring information between the client and the server, is a *stateless* protocol. As a stateless protocol, HTTP does not preserve information between requests. Therefore, any information needed to process a request needs to be sent with the request. In traditional client/server programming, the author of the program has the responsibility to sort out these issues. However, in a JavaScript application, the Session Management Service of the JavaScript runtime engine handles these details so that the application developer can concentrate on the requirements of the application.

The Session Management Service provides the objects needed to share data among multiple client requests to an application, among multiple users of a single application, or among multiple applications on the same server. The JavaScript runtime engine makes this possible by automatically maintaining the `client`, `server`, `project`, and `request` objects.

When a Netscape server receives a client request for an application page, it first performs an authorization check. If the client request fails the server authorization check, the process ends and the JavaScript runtime engine takes no further steps. If the authorization check succeeds, the JavaScript runtime engine takes the following steps:

1. The JavaScript runtime engine initializes the built-in properties of the `request` object, such as the requester's IP address and any form elements associated with the request. In addition, the JavaScript runtime engine initializes any other properties specified by the URL of the request. If the `client` object already exists, the JavaScript runtime engine retrieves the object according to the specified client-maintenance technique. If there is not a `client` object, the JavaScript runtime engine constructs a new object with no properties. The actual order for constructing these objects varies, so your application should not depend on a specific order of construction.

2. The JavaScript runtime engine finds the requested source page and begins the construction of the HTML document for the client. As it creates the

page, the JavaScript runtime engine stores the page in a memory buffer until it is time to send the contents of the buffer to the client.

3. The JavaScript runtime engine continues building a page until one of the following conditions occur:

    - The buffer reaches the limit of 64KB. At this point, the runtime engine performs steps 4 and 5 and then returns to step 3 to continue processing the page.

    - When the runtime engine encounters a `flush()` function, it performs steps 4 and 5 and then returns to step 3 to continue processing the page.

    - When the runtime engine encounters a `redirect()` function, it skips to step 4 and does not process any of the remaining statements in the source file. The runtime engine immediately loads the new page and discards any previous content.

    - When it reaches the end of the page, the runtime engine continues with step 4.

4. The JavaScript runtime engine saves the `client` object's properties before it sends the first part of an HTML page to the client. Even though the runtime may return to step 3, it only performs this step once. Thus, any properties of the client object that you want to preserve must be set prior to reaching the 64KB limit by executing either a `flush()` function or a `redirect()` function. Any properties set after this point affect the remainder of the session, but are discarded at the end of the session.

5. The server sends the page in the memory buffer to the client.

6. The JavaScript runtime engine destroys the `request` object constructed for this client request. It destroys the JavaScript `client` object. It does not destroy the `server` or the `project` object.

The flow of a single request forms the basis for understanding the Session Management Service objects. The discussion of these objects builds on the handling of one request to form a picture of the management of a client/server session.

The request Object

The JavaScript runtime engine automatically creates a `request` object each time a client makes a request of the server. The runtime engine destroys the `request` object upon completion of the request. Table 13.4 lists the properties of the request object along with a description of the property. All of the properties of the request object are read-only. The request object has two methods: the `httpHeader()` method and the `getPostData()` method. The section "Working with the Request and Response Headers," in this chapter, discusses the use of these methods. Like all server-side objects, the `request` object has no event handlers.

Table 13.4 Properties of the request Object

Property	Description
agent	Provides name and version information about the client browser. This information is the same as the `userAgent` property of the `navigator` object (see Chapter 9, "Working with Windows and Frames").
auth_type	Netscape servers support the *basic* authorization type. This property corresponds to the CGI `AUTH_TYPE` environmental variable.
auth_user	If HTTP access authorization is activated for the URL of the page, this property contains the name of the local HTTP user of the Web browser. This property corresponds to the CGI `REMOTE_USER` environmental variable.
imageX	Provides the horizontal position of the mouse pointer over an image map. The client sends this information to the server when the `<IMG>` tag includes the `ISMAP` attribute, which indicates that this is a server-side image map.
imageY	Provides the vertical position of the mouse pointer over an image map. The client sends this information to the server when the `<IMG>` tag includes the ISMAP attribute, which indicates that this is a server-side image map.
inputName	Creates a property for each name in an HTML form. The value of the property is equal to the value property of the form element.
ip	Provides the IP address of the client.
method	Provides the HTTP method associated with the request. The value of the method property is the same as the value of the method property for the form object. You use the property to determine the proper response to a request. This property corresponds to the CGI `REQUEST_METHOD` environmental variable.
protocol	Provides information regarding the HTTP protocol level supported by the client browser. The current version of the HTTP protocol is "HTTP/1.0." Since there is only one correct value, you use this property to check the validity of the protocol. This property corresponds to the CGI `SERVER_PROTOCOL` environmental variable.
query	Reflects the search portion of the URL, which is the string after the "?." This property corresponds to the CGI `QUERY_STRING` environmental variable.
uri	A portion of the URL that excludes the protocol, host name, and port number.

By setting the search portion of the URL, you can pass custom information to the server. The syntax for encoding additional information into the URL is as follows:

```
<A HREF="URL?propertyName1=value1&propertyName2=value2 ...">
```

Of course if the string contains any nonalphanumeric characters, you need to escape the string before sending it to the server. This technique provides an interesting method to pass information from one request to another, since it can be used with any HREF attribute.

Note:

The initial page—the page that initializes any properties and makes the database connection—cannot contain any reference to the request object. When this page is run, the runtime engine has not created the `request` object. However, the default page can contain the `request` object.

The HTML document in Listing 13.1 illustrates how to incorporate server-side JavaScript into an HTML document. If you view the source for the document from the browser, you will see no server-side JavaScript statements. Figure 13.2 shows the results of loading this document.

Comment on CD for Chapter 13

The examples for Chapter 13, "Working with Server-Side JavaScript," are organized differently than the examples for previous chapters. All of the examples are compiled into a single web file called `ls13.web`. The index to the examples (`chap13.htm`) does not contain any server-side JavaScript statements. Consequently, `chap13.htm` is not compiled into the web file. To simplify the compilation, all of the compiled files are maintained in `chap13.txt`. The web file is compiled with the following command line:

```
jsac -v -f chap13.txt -o ls13.web
```

The application is installed with the name `chapter13` and the default page is set to `chap13.htm`. Although all of the HTML documents for the chapter are included in the directory, you do not need them in an actual production environment. By not including the files on the deployment server, you avoid the possibility of anyone viewing the source files that include server-side JavaScript.

Listing 13.1 Using the request Object

```
<HTML>
  <HEAD>
    <TITLE>Using the request Object</TITLE>
  </HEAD>
  <BODY>
    <H1 ALIGN="CENTER">Welcome</H1>
    <P>This example displays the following selected
      properties of the request object:<BR>
      Your IP address is
    <SERVER>write(request.ip)</SERVER><BR>
      Your browser is
    <SERVER>write(request.agent)</SERVER><BR>
      Your protocol is
    <SERVER>write(request.protocol)</SERVER><BR>
      The uri property value is
    <SERVER>write(request.uri)</SERVER></P>
  </BODY>
</HTML>
```

The client Object

The client object provides the means to maintain client information over multiple requests to an application. By constructing a client object for each client/application pair, the JavaScript runtime engine can support multiple clients accessing the same application.

The JavaScript runtime engine constructs and destroys a client object for each client request. While processing a request, the runtime engine saves the names and values of the client object's properties. By so doing, the runtime engine can reconstruct the client object upon subsequent requests from the same client to the same application. This process of reconstruction of the client object allows information to persist across an entire session.

Figure 13.2 Results of using the request Object.

The JavaScript runtime engine only saves the `client` object when it has properties to save. There are no predefined properties for the `client` object. When a client first connects to an application, any properties for the `client` object must be created. The method used by the runtime engine to preserve properties across requests, requires that the properties contain string values. This means that you cannot assign an object to a property, since there is no mechanism for converting an object into a string. To improve performance, you need to assign a client property to a variable, work with the variable, and then set the `client` object property to the new value.

While the `client` object has no properties it does have methods. These methods play an important role in working with `client` objects.

Methods of the client Object

Table 13.5 describes the methods of the client object. The impact of these methods depends on the mechanism used to save the client object.

Table 13.5 Methods of the client Object

Method	Description
destroy()	This method destroys the client object and its properties. If you do not explicitly issue the destroy() method, the JavaScript runtime engine automatically destroys the client object when its lifetime expires. The default lifetime is 10 minutes. While the destroy() method removes the client object on the server, it does not destroy client objects stored in URLs and client-side cookies. Following is an example of the destroy() method: `<SERVER>client.destroy()</SERVER>`
expiration(seconds)	This method sets the expiration time for a client object in seconds. You must use the expiration() method in every page that you want an expiration period other than the default. Following is an example of the expiration() method that sets the expiration of a client object to one hour: `<SERVER>client.expiration(3600)</SERVER>`

Saving the Client Object

You have a number of options for saving the client object between client requests. The technique used to maintain the client object is set at the time you install the application with the Application Manager. However, the client object maintenance method also affects how you develop your applications. Consequently, you need to ensure that you develop and install an application with the same method.

You can save the client object on either the client or the server. The client-side methods are client cookie and client URL encoding. The server-side methods are server cookie, server URL encoding, and server IP address. Each technique has its advantages and disadvantages. You need to choose the technique whose advantages outweigh the disadvantages for your application requirements.

Using the Client Cookie

Saving a property and its value in a client cookie is a popular method of preserving information between requests. When a client makes a request to the server, the client sends the information in the client cookies related to the requested application, as part of the HTTP header. The JavaScript runtime engine on the server sets the properties of the `client` object according to the name/value pairs that it receives from the client. Conversely, the server sends a cookie to the client the first time it sends the contents of the buffer to the client. This means that you need to perform all cookie maintenance before the runtime engine sends the first buffer to the client. Figure 13.3 illustrate the client cookie technique.

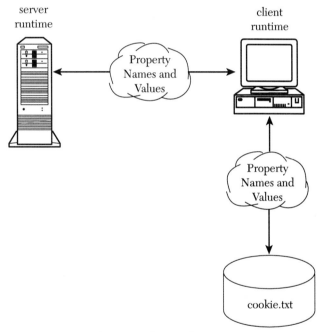

Figure 13.3   Client cookie technique.

To avoid any conflicts with other application cookies, the runtime engine automatically prefixes every property name with `NETSCAPE_LIVEWIRE`. For example, the `client.custID` property has a cookie name of `NETSCAPE_LIVEWIRE.custID`. If the value contains any special characters, the runtime engine automatically escapes the value before sending it to the client.

Chapter 8, "Working with Forms," discusses the limits for client cookies and the client-side techniques for working with cookies. Of key importance is that each name/value pair constitutes a single cookie, and each application is limited to 20 cookies. The client cookie technique requires that the client browser support the Netscape cookie protocol. This presents a problem for users of Microsoft Internet Explorer, since Microsoft's implementation of cookies does not comply with the Netscape cookie protocol. This is especially true if you attempt to use client-side JavaScript to maintain cookies.

By default, the expiration time for cookies is ten minutes. If you want to change the expiration time for a cookie, you need to use the `expiration()` method. While the `destroy()` method removes the server-side client object and its properties, it does not remove the cookie from the client-side cookie file. To remove a cookie from the client cookie file, you need to set the expiration time to zero. Of course, this needs to occur before sending the first buffer and before destroying the `client` object.

You are not limited to waiting for the JavaScript runtime engine to set a cookie on the client. The following function sets a client cookie and it does so even for other `client` object maintenance methods:

```
function setCookic(name, value, expires, path, domain, secure) {
        document.cookie =
                name + "="
                + escape(value)
                + ((expires) ? "; expires=" +
expires.toGMTString() : "")
                + ((path) ? "; path=" + path : "")
                + ((domain) ? "; domain=" domain : "")
                + ((secure) ? "; secure" : "")
}
```

This function works because it is part of the client-side JavaScript. As such, it does not involve the server in the maintenance of the cookie.

Using Client URL Encoding

With the client URL encoding scheme, the JavaScript runtime engine appends the client cookie to URLs in the generated HTML document. Thus, all links in the document carry the properties of the `client` object. Figure 13.4 shows a conceptual drawing of the client URL encoding scheme.

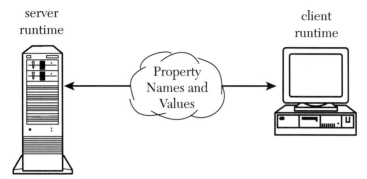

Figure 13.4   Client URL Encoding.

The single advantage of the client URL encoding scheme is that it does not depend on the browser using the Netscape cookie protocol. However, it does possess the following disadvantages:

- The maximum size of the URL string is 4KB. Any data that goes beyond the 4KB limit is truncated.
- Every URL on the generated Web page carries the client object properties. If the size of the properties is very large, the client URL encoding scheme has a significant impact on the amount of network traffic.
- The properties persist only as long as the session is active. Once the user goes to another application, the information is lost.

Since the JavaScript runtime engine stores the client object as part of the URL, the client URL encoding technique lacks an expiration time. Also, URLs that follow the destroy() method are not encoded, since the client object no longer exists.

Common Features of Server-Side Methods

The server-side methods for saving the client object share the following features:

- The JavaScript runtime engine stores the client object in the server memory
- A client index points to the data structure for a particular client
- The client object and its properties are not saved on the server disk

- Other than memory restrictions, there is no limit to the amount of information stored
- There is minimal impact on the amount of network traffic

The only difference between these server-side methods is how they store the client index for accessing the data structure.

Using the Server Cookie

For the server cookie method, the JavaScript runtime engine uses the Netscape cookie protocol to store the index on the client's disk. Since the server cookie method only stores the index, it needs only a single cookie. Figure 13.5 illustrates the workings of the server cookie method for saving the index into the data structure.

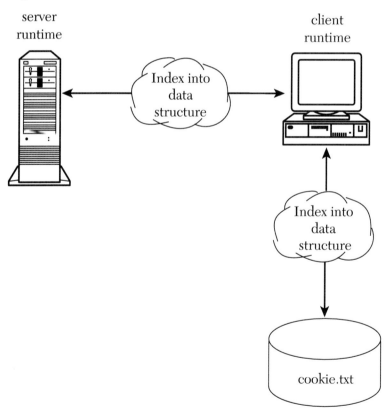

Figure 13.5   Server Cookie Method.

Since only the index is stored on the client's disk, you can make changes to the `client` object anywhere within the Web page. The properties and values of the `client` object are saved into the server's data structure as the final step in processing the Web page.

By default, the JavaScript runtime engine sets the expiration of the server data structure to ten minutes and does not set an expiration of the cookie sent to the client. You can use the `expiration()` method to change the expiration time. The `expiration()` method sets the expiration time for both the data structure and the client cookie.

Since the `destroy()` method removes the `client` object and its properties, the properties are not saved in the data structure. If the `destroy()` method occurs after the first buffer is sent to the client, the index points to an empty data structure.

Using Server URL Encoding

Server URL encoding is the same as client URL encoding, with the exception that the JavaScript runtime engine only appends the index to every URL in the generated HTML document. Figure 13.6 illustrates the server URL encoding scheme for saving the index into the data structure.

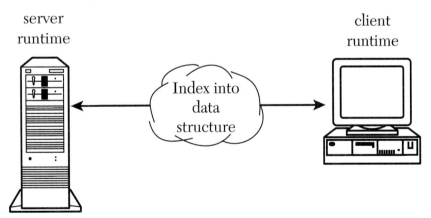

Figure 13.6   Server URL Encoding.

If you have a URL whose link is outside of the application, you may not want the client index appended to the URL. To keep the JavaScript runtime engine from appending the client index to a URL, you need to use backquotes to generate the URL as shown in the following example:

```
<A HREF=`"mailto:info@xyz.com"`>
```

With server URL encoding, you lose the client index when you submit a form using the GET method. The client index is lost because the form data replaces everything after the "?" in the URL.

Using the Server IP Address Method

The server IP address method uses an index composed of the server's IP address and the client's IP address. Since IP addresses are used, the server IP address method does not send any information to the client as shown in Figure 13.7.

server
runtime

client
runtime

Figure 13.7 Server IP Address Method.

The server IP address method is fast and has no impact on network traffic. However, the server IP address method depends on the client having a unique and fixed IP address. Thus, this method does not work under the following conditions:

- The client leases an IP address using the Dynamic Host Configuration Protocol (DHCP)
- A terminal server assigns the client an IP address from a pool of addresses
- The client sits behind a proxy server, which provides a single IP address for all users

The project Object

The project object provides a mechanism for sharing data between multiple clients who are accessing the same application. The JavaScript runtime engine constructs a new project object when the application is started via the Application Manager, and destroys the project object when the application is stopped. Each client accessing an application shares the same project object.

If you happen to have multiple Netscape servers using different port numbers on the same machine, then a project object is created for each server. For example, if you have a server running on port 80 and another running on port 142, the JavaScript runtime engine creates two separate project objects.

Like the client object, the project object has no predefined properties. Although you can create a new property at any time, you normally create properties for the project object in the initial page. The initial page is the HTML document run when the Application Manager starts an application. If you store a reference to an object created during the processing of a client request, the JavaScript runtime engine does not destroy the object upon completion of the request.

The JavaScript runtime engine does not automatically save the project object to disk when the Application Manager stops an application. If you store any data in the project object, you need to write the data to a database or file on the server.

The project object has two methods as shown in Table 13.6.

Table 13.6 Methods of the project Object

Method	Description
lock()	Obtains the lock for the project object. If another client request has the project object, the method waits until it can get the lock. Although locks are voluntary, they are necessary to avoid client requests updating the project object simultaneously.
unlock()	Releases the lock. The unlock() method returns false when there is an internal JavaScript error or you attempt to unlock a lock that you do not own.

A typical example of these methods is updating a customer ID key as shown in the following snippet:

```
project.lock()
```

```
project.lastID = 1 + parseInt(project.lastID, 10)
client.custID = project.lastID
project.unlock()
```

Tip

Since the `lock()` method suspends other lock requests, you should keep the code between the `lock()` and `unlock()` statements to a minimum.

The server Object

The `server` object stores information that is common to all applications. The JavaScript runtime engine creates the `server` object when the server starts, and destroys the `server` object when the server is stopped. If there are multiple servers running on a machine, the runtime engine creates a separate instance of the `server` object for each server process.

The `server` object has the read-only properties described in Table 13.7 In addition to the predefined properties, you can create custom properties.

Table 13.7 Properties of the server Object

Property	Description
host	Specifies the server name, subdomain, and domain name of the server.
hostname	Specifies the full host name of the server, which is the host property plus the port number of the server. When the port number is 80, the default port for a Web server, the host, and hostname properties are the same.
port	Specifies the port number used by the server.
protocol	Specifies the communication protocol used by the server. The protocol property indicates the protocol portion of a URL including the first colon. For a Web server, the protocol is "http:".
jsVersion	Specifies the version of the JavaScript runtime engine and the platform.

If you store a reference to an object created during the processing of a client request, the JavaScript runtime engine does not destroy the object upon completion of the request. However, when the server stops, the runtime engine destroys all properties of the `server` object. If you want to preserve any information stored in the `server` object, you need to store the data in a database or file on the server.

The `server` object has the methods described in Table 13.8.

Table 13.8 Methods of the server Object

Method	Description
`lock()`	Obtains the lock for the `server` object. If another client request has the server object, the method waits until it can get the lock. Although locks are voluntary, they are necessary to avoid client requests updating the server object simultaneously.
`unlock()`	Releases the lock. The *unlock()* method returns false when there is an internal JavaScript error or you attempt to unlock a lock that you do not own.

The HTML document shown in Listing 13.2 uses server-side JavaScript to display the properties of the `server` object. Figure 13.8 shows the results of loading this document.

Listing 13.2 Example of using server Object

```
<HTML>
  <HEAD>
    <TITLE>Using the server Object</TITLE>
  </HEAD>
  <BODY>
    <H1 ALIGN="CENTER">Properties of the Server Object</H1>
    <P>The server object has the following predefined
      properties:</P>
    <P>server.host =
      <SERVER>write(server.host)</SERVER><BR>
      server.hostname =
      <SERVER>write(server.hostname)</SERVER><BR>
      server.port =
      <SERVER>write(server.port)</SERVER><BR>
      server.protocol =
      <SERVER>write(server.protocol)</SERVER><BR>
      server.jsVersion =
      <SERVER>write(server.jsVersion)</SERVER></P>
  </BODY>
</HTML>
```

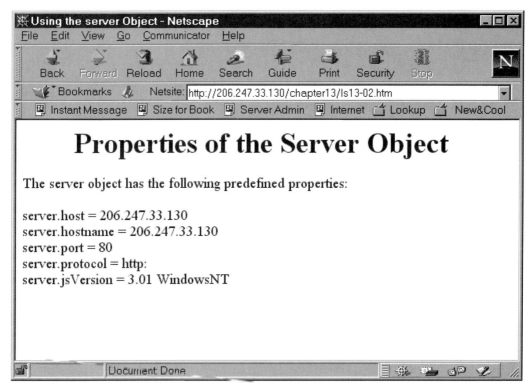

Figure 13.8 Results of using the server Object.

The Lock Object

Starting with version 3.x, Netscape servers operate in a multithreaded environment, allowing processes to handle multiple requests at the same time. If multiple threads attempt to access the same object, the result of the changes is undetermined. To prevent this behavior, you must establish control over the *critical section* of code that accesses shared objects. The `project` and `server` objects provide the `lock()` method to establish control over a critical section. In addition to these objects, you can create other objects that are shared by the application or between applications. You can create instances of the `Lock` object to control access to multiple objects, and to provide access control to the properties of shared objects. You can also create multiple instances of the `Lock` object for different objects or properties of an object.

Although it is not required, you should create all instances of the Lock object in the initial Web page. The initial Web page is only run once when the application is started, ensuring that only a single instance of a lock is created. Creating an instance of a Lock object in another HTML document, allows that multiple clients might attempt to create instances of the same Lock object at the same time. In this situation, you may end up with multiple instances of the Lock object for the same object, which defeats the whole purpose of creating locks.

When you create an instance of the Lock object, the new lock object has the methods described in Table 13.9.

Table 13.9 Methods of the Lock Object

Method	Description
`lock([timeout])`	Obtains the lock. The default is to wait indefinitely for the lock. You can specify a *timeout* period in seconds, where the value 0 causes an indefinite wait.
`isValid()`	Verifies that the new `lock` object was properly constructed.
`unlock()`	Releases the lock.

To construct a lock for a customer order and save the new object in the `project` object, use the following code:

```
project.ordersLock = new Lock()
// Check the validity of the new lock
if (! project.ordersLock.isValid) {
   // unable to create lock - redirect to error page
   redirect("sysfailure.htm")
}
```

Although rare, the failure to create a valid lock indicates that the JavaScript runtime engine ran out of resources while constructing the object. To prevent the creation of multiple instances of a new lock record, place the code to create a new `lock` object in the initial Web page. You need to save the lock in the `project` object, since all client requests to an application share the project object.

The difference between the `lock()` method of a `lock` object constructed with the `Lock` object constructor and the `lock()` method of the `project` and `server` objects is the addition of the *timeout* option. The following snippet demonstrates the use of the *timeout* option:

```
// Beginning of a critical section
if (project.ordersLock.lock(10)) {
   // work with the data and then store it
   var x = project.orders.count
   x += 1
   project.orders.count = x
   // end of critical section
   project.ordersLock.unlock()
}
// lock not available
else
   redirect("comebacklater.html")
```

This snippet uses a custom `lock` object for managing the `project.orders.count` property. You could create additional locks for such properties as the customer ID. Although the JavaScript runtime engine does not enforce the use of locks, you should develop the habit of using the lock() and unlock() methods when modifying any shared data.

Built-in Functions

In addition to the core built-in functions, server-side JavaScript provides additional built-in (also referred to as global) functions. Table 13.10 lists the built-in functions for server-side JavaScript and provides a brief description of each function. Subsequent sections break the table into functions related according to function and provide a more detailed discussion of each function.

Table 13.10 Built-in Functions for Server-Side JavaScript

Function	Description
addClient(*URL*)	Adds the properties of the client object to a dynamically generated HTML or the URL of the redirect() function.
addResponseHeader(*field, value*)	Places additional information in the header sent to the client.

Table 13.10 Built-in Functions for Server-Side JavaScript *(Continued)*

Function	Description
blob(*path*)	Assigns BLOb data to a column in a cursor (see Chapter 14, "Live wire Database Service," for details).
callC(*JSFunction, arg1, ..., argN*)	Calls an external function and returns a value from the function.
debug(*expression*)	Displays a JavaScript expression in the trace utility.
deleteResponseHeader(*field*)	Removes information from the header sent to the client.
flush()	Sends data from the memory buffer to the client.
getOptionValue(*name, index*)	Returns the text of a selected OPTION in the SELECT form element.
getOptionValueCount(*name*)	Returns the number of options selected by the user in a SELECT form element.
redirect(*URL*)	Redirects the client to the specified URL.
registerCFunction(*JSFunction, libraryPath, external-Function*)	Registers an external function for use with a JavaScript application.
ssjs_generateClientID()	Returns a string that you can use to identify a client object.
ssjs_getCGIVariable(*variableName*)	Returns the value of the specified environmental variable set in the server process.
ssjs_getClientID()	Returns the index for the client object used by the server maintenance methods.
write(expression)	Generates HTML based on an expression and sends it to the client.

Working with Generated HTML

The `write()` function is the workhorse of server-side JavaScript. The `write(`*expression*`)` function analyzes the expression and writes the output to the memory buffer. From the view of the client, the document is a normal HTML document. In terms of syntax for the expression, the server-side `write()` function is similar to the client-side `document.write()` method. Following is an example of the `write()` function:

```
write("<P>Your IP address is "+request.ip+".</P>")
```

For the IP address 192.168.30.10, the generated HTML, which is all that the browser receives, is as follows:

```
<P>Your IP address is 192.168.30.10.</P>
```

As the JavaScript runtime engine processes the document, it places the HTML document in a memory buffer. The runtime engine automatically sends the buffer to the client after each 64KB of input. With the `flush()` function, you control when to send the contents of the memory buffer to the client. You may want to flush the memory buffer in the following circumstances:

- Prior to a database request, so that the user sees something happening
- After so many rows of data from a database retrieval, so that the browser continuously displays some action

The following snippet shows how to use the `flush()` function prior to a database query and then after processing each row from the query.

```
flush()
conn.beginTransaction()
cursor = conn.cursor("SELECT * FROM CUSTOMER", true)
while (cursor.next()) {
   // code to process the row
   flush()
}
conn.commitTransqction()
cursor.close()
```

Note

> If you use the client cookie method for maintaining the `client` object, you need to complete all `client` object changes before issuing the `flush()` function. With the client cookie method, the first header contains the cookie information.

The `redirect(URL)` function, provides a means of redirecting the flow to another HTML document. When the JavaScript runtime engine encounters a `redirect()` function, it immediately discards the current document and loads the new HTML document. The following example redirects the browser to another URL when there is a system failure in creating a lock:

```
if (! project.ordersLock.isValid) {
   // unable to create lock – redirect to error page
   redirect("sysfailure.htm")
```

If you need to preserve the `client` object, you can use the `addClient()` function to add the `client` object information to the redirected URL.

While developing a JavaScript application, you occasionally encounter problems. While the trace utility of the Application Manager provides the basic information, the `debug()` function allows you to write additional information to the trace output. The syntax for the `debug()` function is as follows:

```
debug(expression)
```

The *expression* has the same syntax as the expression for the `write()` function. The following example displays the value of the last customer ID in the trace output:

```
debug("The last customer ID is "+project.lastCustID)
```

When the Application Manager encounters a `debug()` function, it prints "Debug message:" and then the output of the `debug()` function.

Working with Forms

The primary purpose of a form is to collect input from the user and send it to the server. When a user submits a form, it is sent to the URL specified in the ACTION attribute of the <FORM> tag. The METHOD attribute of the <FORM> tag specifies either GET or POST. The GET method uses URL encoding to pass the form data to the server. The POST method passes the information as a continuous stream to standard input. The GET method assigns the data to the QUERY_STRING environmental variable, which has size limits depending on the operating system. The POST method does not assign the data to an environmental variable, and therefore, does not possess restrictions as to the amount of data passed to the server. With both methods, the JavaScript runtime engine assigns the name/value pairs as properties of the request object. With JavaScript applications, POST is the preferred method of passing form data to the server, as shown in the following example:

```
<FORM METHOD="POST" ACTION="procForm.html">
```

With one exception, the form elements are string values, which you access as request.*elementName*. The one exception is the SELECT form element with the MULTIPLE attribute. The getOptionValue() function allows you to retrieve each selected value. The syntax for the getOptionValue() function is as follows:

```
getOptionValue(name, index)
```

The *name* parameter is the same as the NAME attribute of the <SELECT> tag. The *index* is the zero-based index to the array of selected options. To find the number of options selected, use the getOptionValueCount() function, whose syntax is as follows:

```
getOptionValueCount(name)
```

The *name* parameter is the value of the NAME attribute of the <SELECT> tag. The following snippet illustrates how to use the getOptionValue() and getOptionValueCount() functions:

```
<SERVER>
var i = 0
var numOpt = getOptionValueCount("opSysUsed")
while (i < numOpt) {
   var optVal = getOptionValue("opSysUsed", i)
   write(optVal+"<BR>")
   i++
}
</SERVER>
```

Warning

 Server-side JavaScript applications do not automatically support the file upload form element. You need to manually handle the file as shown in the section on "Working with the Response Header."

Working with CGI Variables

Although Netscape servers do not set up a separate environment for all of the CGI variables, the `ssjs_getCGIVariable()` function gives you access to the CGI environmental variables. Table 13.11 lists the CGI variables that you can access via the `ssjs_getCGIVariable()` function. Table 13.4 lists the CGI variables reflected in the `request` object.

Table 13.11 CGI Variables accessible by ssjs_getCGIVariable()

CGI Variable	Description
AUTH_TYPE	The authorization type, when any type of authorization protects the request. Netscape servers support the "basic" authorization type.
HTTPS	If security is active on the server, the value is "ON;" otherwise, it is "OFF."
HTTPS_KEYSIZE	Specifies the number of bits in the session key used for encryption.
HTTPS_SECRETKEYSIZE	Specifies the number of bits used to generate the server's private key.
PATH_INFO	Specifies the path information sent by the browser.
PATH_TRANSLATED	Specifies the full system path for the pathname specified in PATH_INFO.
QUERY_STRING	Specifies the string following the "?" in the URL.
REMOTE_ADDR	Specifies the IP address of the host that submitted the request.
REMOTE_HOST	Specifies the domain name of the host that submitted the request. This variable requires that DNS is operating on the server.
REMOTE_USER	When authorization is in effect for the requested document, this variable contains the name by which the user obtained authorization.
REQUEST_METHOD	Reflects the METHOD attribute of the <FORM> tag.
SCRIPT_NAME	Specifies the name of the HTML document accessed for server-side JavaScript.

Table 13.11 CGI Variables accessible by ssjs_getCGIVariable() *(Continued)*

CGI Variable	Description
SERVER_NAME	Specifies the domain name or IP address of the server.
SERVER_PORT	Specifies the port through which the request accessed the server.
SERVER_PROTOCOL	Specifies the HTTP protocol supported by the server.
SERVER_URL	Specifies the URL the client used to access the server.

The syntax for the ssjs_getCGIVariable() function is as follows:

```
CGIValue = ssjs_getCGIVariable(varName)
```

The following example retrieves the value for the REMOTE_HOST variable:

```
RemHost = ssjs_getCGIVariable("REMOTE_HOST")
```

If you supply an argument that is not listed in Table 13.11, the JavaScript runtime engine looks for a variable by the specified name in the systems environment. If the runtime engine finds the variable, it returns its value, otherwise, it returns null. The following example retrieves the value for the CLASSPATH environmental variable:

```
classpath = ssjs_getCGIVariable("CLASSPATH")
```

Note

Server-side   JavaScript   does   not   support   the GATEWAY_INTERFACE   and   SERVER_SOFTWARE   CGI variables.

Working with the client Object

If you use client or server URL encoding to preserve the client object, the JavaScript runtime engine does not automatically encode the URLs in the redirect() function or dynamically generated URLs. You need to encode these URLs with the addClient() function.

The following example encodes the client objected in a redirected URL:

```
redirect(addClient("neworder.html"))
```

The following example preserves the `client` object for a dynamically generated URL:

```
<A HREF=`addClient("page"+project.pageno+".html")`>
```

If you have an application that needs to store information related to a specific client/application pair in the `server` or `project` objects, you need to use either the `ssjs_generateClientID()` function or the `ssjs_getClientID()` function. The function that you use depends on the `client` object maintenance method for the application.

If your application uses a client-side method for preserving the `client` object, you need to generate a unique key for the client/application pair with the `ssjs_generateClientID()` function. Each time you call the `ssjs_generateClientID()` function, the JavaScript runtime engine generates a unique key. Thus, once you create a key for a client/application pair, you need to preserve the key between requests. If you store the key in the `client` object, you need to be careful that an intruder cannot get access to the key and use the key to access sensitive information.

For applications that use server-side methods for preserving the `client` object, you need to use the `ssjs_getClientID()` function to retrieve the key automatically generated by the JavaScript runtime engine. You do not need to worry about saving the key, since the key is the only value saved in the server-side methods.

Working with the Request and Response Headers

The JavaScript runtime engine normally performs all tasks related to the request and response headers, however, the following situations require manual intervention in the processing of headers:

- The request header contains a content type other than blank or `application/x-www-form-urlencoded`
- The request is for a file upload

- The content type of the response header is something other than `text/html`

A detailed discussion of the HTTP header formats is beyond the scope of this book. You can find detailed information regarding the HTTP header formats at the following URL:

```
http://www.w3.org/Protocols/
```

Working with the Request Header

You can access the client request header record with the `request.httpHeader()` method. The `httpHeader()` method returns an object whose properties correspond to the name/value pairs in the header. The following snippet illustrates how to list the information in the client request header:

```
<SERVER>
var headerObj = request.httpHeader()
var i
for (i in headerObj) {
    write(i+": "+headerObj[i]+"<BR>")
}
```

Table 13.12 lists the CGI variables that you can obtain from the client request header. This is not a complete list of the properties present in the client request header.

Table 13.12 CGI Variables in the Client Request Header

CGI Variable	Property	Description
CONTENT_LENGTH	content-length	Contains the number of bytes being sent by the client.
CONTENT_TYPE	content-type	Contains the type of data being sent by the client.
HTTP_ACCEPT	accept	Lists the type of data the client can accept. This property occurs when the POST method is used for a form.

Table 13.12 CGI Variables in the Client Request Header *(Continued)*

CGI Variable	Property	Description
`HTTP_USER_AGENT`	`user-agent`	Identifies the browser being used by the client. This value is also reflected as the `request.agent` property.
`HTTP_IF_MODIFIED_SINCE`	`if-modified-since`	A date, in GMT format, that specifies a response is to be sent if it is newer than this date.

When uploading a file to the server from the client using the file form element, the `content-type` property is `multipart/form-data` and the method is `POST`. Since the JavaScript runtime engine does not process this content type, you need to write the code to handle a file upload. In this case, the file comes as an attachment to the header record. To read the attachment, you need to use the `request.getPostData()` method. The syntax for the `getPostData()` method is as follows:

```
postData = request.getPostData(length)
```

If the *length* is set to 0, the JavaScript runtime engine returns the entire contents of the attached data. You can also retrieve smaller chunks of data by setting the *length* to the size of chunk that you wish to retrieve. The following snippet illustrates how you would retrieve 100 byte chunks of data.

```
<SERVER>
var headerObj = request.httpHeader()
var datalength = parseInt(headerObj.content-length, 10)
var i = 0
while (i < datalength) {
   postData = request.getPostData(100)
   // process the data
   i += 100
}
```

Working with the Response Header

The `addResponseHeader()` and `deleteResponseHeader()` functions allow you to modify the header record sent to the client. The content-type is one field that you may change. The JavaScript runtime engine automatically returns a header with the content type set to `text/html`. If you need to change the content-type to a custom type, you must delete the old type from the header and add a new one as shown in the following example:

```
<SERVER>
deleteResponseHeader("content-type")
addResponseHeader("content-type", "mycustom-format")
</SERVER>
```

Note

All modifications to the header must occur before the JavaScript runtime engine first sends the contents of the memory buffer to the client.

Working with External Libraries

External libraries are functions written in languages such as C, C++, or Pascal. From a JavaScript perspective, these functions are called *external functions* or *native functions*. Libraries of external functions, called *external libraries*, are Dynamic Link Libraries (DLL) on Windows operating systems and shared objects on UNIX operating systems.

Although the recommended approach is to use the capabilities of Live-Connect, you may want to use native functions in the following cases:

- You already have complex native functions that you wish to use
- The application requires computation-intensive functions, which perform better in native functions than in JavaScript
- The application requires a task that you cannot perform in JavaScript

To use external libraries, you need to perform the following steps:

1. Write and compile the native functions in a form compatible with JavaScript.

2. Use the Application Manager to identify the external libraries for an application.

3. Restart the server to load the external libraries for your application. The functions are now available to all applications on your server.

4. In the application, use `registerCFunction()` to identify the function, and `callC()` to call the function.

5. Recompile and restart your application for the changes to take affect.

Writing Native Functions

Although you may write the native function in any language, JavaScript uses C calling conventions. The function must include the `jsaccall.h` header file in the `js/samples/jsaccall` directory. The directory also contains a sample function called `jsaccall.c`. For JavaScript to call the function, it must be exported and must conform to the following type definition:

```
typedef void (*LivewireUserCFunction)
   (int argc, struct LivewireCCallData argv[],
    struct LivewireCCallData* result, pblock* pb,
    Session* sn, Request* rq);
```

Registering Native Functions

Before you can use a native function in an application, you need to register it with `registerCFunction()`. The syntax for this function is as follows:

```
registerCFunction(JSName, libraryPath, CfunctionName)
```

The *JSName* is the name by which the `callC()` function refers to the native function. The *libraryPath* is the full pathname to the library. The pathname must be exactly as you entered it in the Application Manager. The *CfunctionName* is the name of the function as defined in the external library. The following snippet is an example of how to register a native function:

```
<SERVER>
```

```
var isRegisterd = registerCFunction("myFunc",
   "c:\\mydir\\mylib.dll", "mylib_myFunc()")
if (isRegistered == false) {
   write("Failure to register a function")
}
</SERVER>
```

Note

 Since the backslash ("\") is a special character in JavaScript, you need to use either the forward slash ("/") or a double blackslash ("\\") to separate directory names and the file name for the Windows operating systems.

Since you only need to register the function once before using it, the initial page is the recommended place for registering native functions. Once you register a function, you can use it any number of times.

Using Native Functions

Once you have registered a function, use the `callC()` function to call the native function by its JavaScript name. The syntax for the `callC()` function is as follows:

```
callC(JSname, arg1[, ..., argN])
```

All the arguments are converted to strings before calling the function. Thus, you can pass JavaScript string values, Boolean values, numbers, or null. Although you can pass an object, the string conversion makes the object rather useless.

Server-Side Utilities

Server-side JavaScript includes additional functionality for sending email messages and accessing the server file system. These utilities round out the basic functionality of server-side JavaScript.

The File System Service

The `File` object provides applications with the ability to read and write files from the server's file system. This allows you to save uploaded files, attach files to email messages, and save data that needs to persist even when the server goes down.

Warning

The ability to read and write files on the server opens the door to security violations. It is the developer's responsibility to insure that their applications do not allow intruders to read or write sensitive system files. To make it more difficult for intruders to access applications, you should never use filenames that match the names of properties of the `client` or `request` object.

To use the file service, you need to start by creating an instance of the `File` object for the file that you want to open. The syntax for creating a `File` object with the `File` object constructor is as follows:

```
fileObjectName = new File("pathname")
```

The *fileObjectName* is the name by which you refer to the file. The *pathname* is the absolute pathname to the file. The format of the *pathname* is the format used by the server's file system, and not in URL format. Do not use a relative pathname, as you have no control over the current working directory. You can display the pathname of a file by using the `write()` function and passing it the *fileObjectName*, as shown in the following example:

```
<SERVER>
fileObj = new File("d:\Netscape\pub\test\myfile.txt")
write(fileObj)
</SERVER>
```

The only property to the `File` object is the `prototype` property. You can use the prototype property to add a property to all instances of the `File` object. When you add a property to the `File` object, the new property becomes available to all instances of the `File` object on the server, and not just the instances of the `File` object for the application.

Table 13.13 summarizes the methods of the File object. The following sections provide additional details on each of these methods.

Table 13.13 Methods of the File Object

Method	Description
byteToString(*number*)	Converts a *number* that represents a byte into a string.
clearError()	Clears the current file error status.
close()	Closes an open file on the server.
eof()	Determines whether the position pointer is beyond the end of the file.
error()	Returns the current error status.
exists()	Tests whether the file already exists.
flush()	Flushes the file buffer to a file.
getlength()	Returns the length of the file.
getPosition()	Returns the current pointer position in the file.
open("*mode*")	Opens a file on the server.
read(*count*)	Reads the number of characters specified by the *count* argument.
readByte()	Reads the next byte from the file and returns it as a number.
readln()	Reads the current line from the server and returns it as a string.
setPosition(*position*, *reference*)	Sets the position in an open file according to the *position* and *reference* arguments.
stringToByte(*string*)	Converts the first character of a string and returns a number that represents a byte.
write(*string*)	Writes the specified string to an open file on the server.
writeByte(*count*)	Writes the number of bytes specified by *count* to a file on the server.
writeln(string)	Writes the string plus a ("\n") on UNIX platforms or ("\r\n") on Windows platforms.

Opening and Closing Files

You need to use the `open()` method to open a file on the server before you can read from the file or write to the file. The syntax for the `open()` method is as follows:

```
result = fileObjectName.open("mode")
```

Table 13.14 lists the options for the *mode* argument. By default, the `open()` method opens the file as a text file. On the Windows platforms, you can open a file as a binary file by appending "b" to the *mode*. The *result* returned by the `open()` method depends on the *mode*.

Table 13.14 Options for the Mode Argument

Mode	Description
`r[b]`	Opens a file for reading. If the file exists, the `open()` method returns true; otherwise, it returns false.
`w[b]`	Opens a file for writing. If the file exists, the `open()` method overwrites the file; otherwise it creates a new file. This mode always returns true.
`a[b]`	Opens a file for appending data to the end of the file. If the file does not exist, the `open()` method creates the file. This mode always returns true.
`r+[b]`	Opens a file for reading and writing. If the file exists, the open() method returns true; otherwise, it returns false. Both reading and writing start at the beginning of the file. When writing, the existing data is overwritten.
`w+[b]`	Opens a file for reading and writing. If the file exists, it is overwritten; otherwise, the open() method creates the file. This mode always returns true.
`a+[b]`	Opens a file for reading and writing. If the file does not exist, the open() method creates a file. Reading and writing start at the end of the file. This mode always returns true.

Once you are finished working with a file, you need to close the file with the `close()` method. The syntax for the `close()` method is as follows:

```
result = fileObjectName.close()
```

If the file is not open, the `close()` method returns false; otherwise, it returns true.

When a file is shared in an application or between applications, you need to lock the file before using it. The best method is to create a `lock` object for each shared file using the `Lock()` constructor in initial Web page. The following example creates a lock file for an application log file:

```
<SERVER>
project.appLogLock = new Lock()
if (! project.appLogLock.isValid) {
   redirect("sysfailure.htm")
}
</SERVER>
```

Any application that uses the log file needs to lock the file before performing any operations on the file. The following snippet illustrates how you might accomplish this task:

```
<SERVER>
logFile = new File("/var/adm/logs/applog.txt")
if (project.appLogLock.lock()) {
   logFile.open("a")
   // code for writing log entry
   logFile.close()
   project.appLogLock.unlock()
}
</SERVER>
```

Positioning within a File

The `File` object maintains a pointer that indicates the current position in the file. The initial position in a file depends on the mode in which you opened the file. You use the `setPosition()` method to reposition the pointer in a file. The syntax for the `setPosition()` is as follows:

```
result = setPosition(position, reference)
```

The *position* specifies the character offset from the indicated *reference*. You can use either a positive or negative value for the *position* value. If positioning relative to the beginning of the file, the value must be positive. If positioning relative to the end of the file, you can position beyond the end of the file. Table 13.15 lists the optional values for the *reference* argument. If successful, the `setPosition()` method returns true; otherwise, it returns false.

Table 13.15 Options for the reference Argument of the setPosition() Method

Option	Description
0	Relative to the beginning of the file.
1	Relative to the current position.
2	Relative to the end of the file.
Other value or unspecified	Relative to the beginning of the file.

The `getPosition()` method returns the current position in the file. The syntax for the `getPosition()` method is as follows:

```
position = fileObjectName.getPosition()
```

When there is an error, the `getPosition()` method returns a –1; otherwise, it returns the current position in the file. The position is zero-based. Consequently, the position of the beginning of the file is 0.

The `eof()` method tests whether the position of the pointer is beyond the end of the file. The syntax for the `eof()` method is as follows:

```
result = fileObjectName.eof()
```

The `eof()` method returns true if the pointer position is beyond the end of the file; otherwise, it returns falls. When reading a file, the reading of the last data in the file places the pointer beyond the end of the file. You can also use the `setPosition()` method to place the pointer beyond the end of the file as shown in the following example:

```
myFile.setPosition(1, 2)
```

Reading from a file

The File service provides three methods for reading files: `read()`, `readByte()`, and `readln()`. The `read()` method gets the specified number of characters from a text file and returns them as a string. The syntax for the `read()` method is as follows:

```
charString = fileObjectName.read(count)
```

The value of the *count* argument is any positive integer. If you attempt to read more characters than remain in the file, the `read()` method returns a string up to the end of the file. The `read()` method automatically moves the pointer the number of characters specified by the *count* argument. The following example illustrates the use of the `read()` method:

```
<SERVER>
var charStr = ""
txtFile = new File("d:\pub\junk.txt")
if (txtFile.open("r")) {
    while (! txtFile.eof) {
        charStr = read(100)
        // code to process the string
    }
    txtFile.close()
}
</SERVER>
```

The `readln()` method reads the current line of characters from a text file, starting from the current position of the pointer. The syntax of the `readln()` method is as follows:

charString = *fileObjectName*.readln()

The `readln()` method retrieves data from the file until in finds a "\n" character, or reaches the end of the file. On the Windows platform, the `readln()` method drops the "\r" that precedes the "\n." The "\n" is not passed to the returned string. The `readln()` method automatically positions the pointer to the next line in the text file.

You use the `readByte()` method to read a binary file. The syntax for the `readByte()` method is as follows:

byteValue = *fileObjectName*.readByte()

The `readByte()` method reads the next byte from a file and returns a numeric value of the byte. The `readByte()` method updates the pointer by one position. If you attempt to read beyond the end of the file, the `readByte()` method returns a –1.

Writing to a File

The `File` object has methods for writing a file that parallels those for reading a file. The `write()` method sends the specified string to the file buffer. The syntax for the `write()` method is as follows:

```
result = fileObjectName.write(string)
```

If the write is successful, the `write()` method returns true; otherwise, it returns false. You use the `write()` method to write data to a text file. The following snippet uses the `write()` method to copy a text file:

```
<SERVER>
var data = ""
srcFile = new File("c:\pub\test\file1.txt")
if (srcFile.open("r")) {
    trgtFile = new File("c:\pub\test\file2.txt")
    trgtFile.open("w")
    while (!srcFile.eof()) {
        data = srcFile.read(1)
        trgFile.write(data)
    }
    srcFile.close()
    trgtFile.flush()
    trgtFile.close()
}
</SERVER>
```

The `writeln()` method writes a string to a text file. It automatically appends the string with a "\n" on UNIX platforms, and a "\r\n" on Windows platforms. The syntax for the `writeln()` method is as follows:

```
result = fileObjectName.writeln(string)
```

If the write operation is successful, the `writeln()` method returns true; otherwise, it returns false. When reading and writing to files, the `readln()` method pairs with the `writeln()` method.

You use the `writeByte()` method to write data to a binary. The `writeByte()` method takes a number representing a byte and writes it to a binary file. The syntax for the `writeByte()` method is as follows:

```
result = fileObjectName.writeByte(number)
```

The `writeByte()` method returns true for a successful operation; otherwise, it returns false. To copy a binary file, use the `readByte()` method and the `writeByte()` method.

When you use any write method of the `File` object, the data is sent to an internal buffer. The `flush()` method writes the buffer to a physical file. The syntax for the `flush()` method is as follows:

```
result = fileObjectName.flush()
```

The flush() method returns true if the process is successful; otherwise, it returns false.

Warning:

Do not confuse the flush() function with the flush() method of the File object. The flush() function sends the data in the memory buffer to the client, while the flush() method sends the data to a physical file on the server.

Converting Data

The byteToString() and stringToByte() methods convert data between ASCII and binary formats. The byteToString() method converts a byte value, represented by a number, to a character. The format of the byteToString() method is as follows:

```
character = File.byteToString(number)
```

The byteToString() method is a static method. Therefore, you always write it as File.byteToString(*number*) and not as a method of the File object that you created. If the argument is not a number, the method returns an empty string.

The stringToByte() method takes the first character of the string argument and converts it to a number. The syntax for the stringToByte() method is as follows:

```
number = File.stringToByte(string)
```

The stringToByte() method is a static method. Therefore, you always write it as File.stringToByte(*string*) and not as a method of the File object that you created. If the conversion fails, the method returns a 0.

Getting Information about a File

The File object has methods that provide information about files and errors. The `error()` method returns an integer that indicates the error status. The syntax for the `error()` method is as follows:

```
errorCode = fileObjectName.error()
```

An *errorCode* of 0 indicates that there is no error. An *errorCode* of –1 indicates that the file is not open. Any other value for *errorCode* is operating system dependent.

The `clearError()` method clears both the file error status and the end of file status. The syntax for the `clearError()` method is as follows:

```
fileObjectName.clearError()
```

The following example illustrates the use of the `error()` and `clearError()` methods:

```
<SERVER>
var inFile = new File("c:\pub\test\infile.txt")
inFile.open("r")
if (inFile.error() == 0) {
   // code to process the file
}
else {
   // code for error handling
}
inFile.clearError()
</SERVER>
```

The `exists()` method returns true if a file exists; otherwise, it returns false. The syntax for the `exists()` method is as follows:

```
result = fileObjectName.exists()
```

The `getLength()` method returns the number of bytes in a binary or text file, or –1, if it fails. The syntax for the `getLength()` method is as follows:

```
length = fileObjectName.getLength()
```

The following example combines several methods to copy a file:

```
<SERVER>
var data = ""
var inFile = new File("d:\pub\test\infile.txt")
if (inFile.exists()) {
    if (inFile.open("r")) {
        var outFile = new File("d:\pub\test\outfile.txt")
        outFile.open("a")
        for (var x = 0; x < inFile.getLenght(); x++) {
            inFile.setPosition(x)
            data = inFile.read(1)
            outFile.write(data)
        }
        inFile.close()
        outFile.flush()
        outFile.close()
    }
}
</SERVER>
```

Example for Saving an Uploaded File

The set of HTML documents in this section completes the discussion of uploading a file from the client to the server. The process starts with the document shown in Listing 13.3. As shown in Figure 13.9, the document is limited to strictly uploading a file. The METHOD attribute must be "POST" and the ENCTYPE must be "multipart/form-data" for a file upload form.

Listing 13.3 Form for uploading a File

```
<HTML>
  <HEAD>
    <TITLE>Form for uploading a File</TITLE>
  </HEAD>
  <BODY>
    <H1 ALIGN="CENTER">File Upload Form</H1>
    <P>Enter the name of the file to upload in the dialog
      box below and then press submit.</P>
    <FORM ACTION="http://www.xyz.com/chapter13/ls13-04.htm"
        METHOD="POST" ENCTYPE="multipart/form-data"
```

```
              NAME="tstForm">
  <P><INPUT TYPE="FILE" NAME="tstFile" SIZE="40"
            MAXLENGTH="256"></P>
  <P><INPUT TYPE="BUTTON" NAME="subBtn"
            VALUE="Upload File" ONCLICK="submit()"></P>
  </FORM>
  </BODY>
</HTML>
```

Figure 13.9   Results of loading Form for uploading a File.

Although there is not much to the HTML document for uploading a file, the HTML document for the server-side processing of the file is more complicated. The HTML document in Listing 13.4 contains the server-side JavaScript necessary to process the uploaded file.

Listing 13.4 File Upload Script

```
<HTML>
  <HEAD>
    <TITLE>File Upload Script</TITLE>
  </HEAD>
  <BODY>
    <H1 ALIGN="CENTER">Results of File Upload</H1>
    <P>Following is the information from the header
       record:</P>
    <P>
<SERVER>
var header=request.httpHeader()
var i
for (i in header) {
   write(i+": "+header[i]+"<BR>")
}
var contentType=header["content-type"]
var j=contentType.lastIndexOf("boundary=")+9
var boundaryStr=contentType.slice(j)
</SERVER></P>
    <P>Information about the file upload follows:</P>
    <P>
<SERVER>
flush()
var contentLength=parseInt(header["content-length"], 10)
var tstStr=""
var i=0
function getData(srchChar) {
   var tmpData=""
   var nextChar=""
   while (i < contentLength) {
      nextChar=request.getPostData(1)
      tmpData+=nextChar
      i++
      if (nextChar==srchChar) break
   }
   return tmpData
}
// find the first -
getData("-")
// get past the initial boundary string
getData("\n")
```

```
// get next block of POST data
tstStr=getData("\n")
// get Content-disposition
var j=tstStr.indexOf(":")
var k=tstStr.indexOf(";")
var contentDisp=tstStr.substring(j+2, k)
// get the name of the form file
j=tstStr.indexOf("=", k)
k=tstStr.indexOf(";", j)
formName=tstStr.substring(j+2, k-1)
// get the name of the source file
j=tstStr.indexOf("=", k)
k=tstStr.lastIndexOf("\"")
upPath=tstStr.substring(j+2, k)
// get filename from pathname
userAgent=header["user-agent"]
if (userAgent.indexOf("Win") > 0) {
    j=upPath.lastIndexOf("\\")
}
else {
    j=upPath.lastIndexOf("/")
}
var upFile=upPath.substring(j+1)
var outPath="C:\\Temp\\"+upFile
// get next block of POST data
tstStr=getData("\n")
// extract the content-type
var j=tstStr.indexOf(":")
var contentType=tstStr.substring(j+2, tstStr.length-2)
// The input is now positioned to extract the data
// First write the information found to this point
write("Content Disposition = "+contentDisp+"<BR>")
write("Form Name = "+formName+"<BR>")
write("Content Type = "+contentType+"<BR>")
write("Source Path = "+upPath+"<BR>")
write("Output Path = "+outPath+"<BR>")
flush()
// Open the output file and process data
var outFile=new File(outPath)
if (outFile.exists()) {
    write("File already exists - overwriting file<BR>")
}
// The data terminates with the boundary string
// plus two dashes and the extra CRLFs
var dataLength=contentLength-boundaryStr.length-8
```

```
// get rid of extra CRLF
request.getPostData(2)
i+=2
// treat everything as a binary file
outFile.open("wb")
while (i < dataLength) {
   tmpData=request.getPostData(1)
   outFile.write(tmpData)
   i++
}
outFile.flush()
outFile.close()
</SERVER></P>
   <P>File save successful.</P>
  </BODY>
</HTML>
```

As shown in Figure 13.10, the HTML document in Listing 13.4 writes a lot of information to the screen that is not necessary in a production script. However, this output helps to explain the server-side JavaScript code. Since the JavaScript runtime engine does not process this content type, the script needs to read the request header record to obtain the content type, boundary string, and user agent.

The main part of the script involves reading the request body using the `request.getPostData()` method. The request body uses the same format as a MIME attachment. Consequently, it is wrapped with the boundary string. The initial boundary string begins with a dash ("-") and ends with a carriage return/linefeed (CRLF), so the script finds the first dash and then skips to the ending linefeed ("\n"). The next block of data that ends with a CRLF contains the content disposition, form name, and source file name fields. The only field that really matters is the source file name field, as the script needs to extract the file name from the path name. The script uses the user agent field to account for the differences in the formatting of pathnames between different platforms.

The next block of data that ends with a CRLF defines the content type of the actual file. Although you could devise a script that handles different content types, this script treats all files as binary files. Before the beginning of the actual data, there is another CRLF that you need to skip over. The end of the data is the content length minus the border length, which has two extra trailing dashes, minus a CRLF before the boundary string and two CRLFs after the boundary string. The script writes the output one byte at a time, until it reaches the end of the data. The script takes the easy way out, and simply overwrites a file that already exists on the server. You could modify the script to create a unique file name.

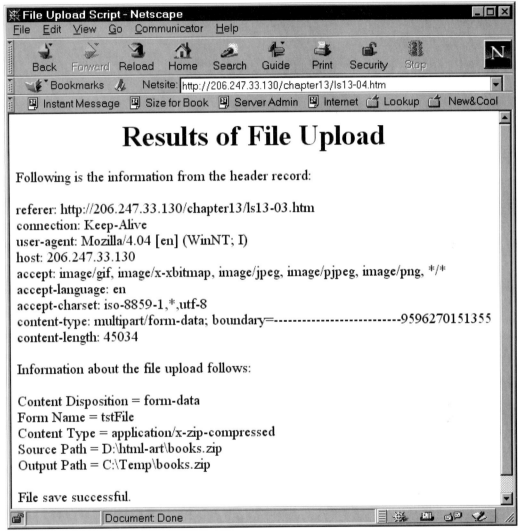

Figure 13.10   Results of File Upload Script.

The Mail Service

The mail service allows you to send mail messages from the server. The mail service uses the SendMail Java class, and it supports both text messages and messages with attachments. To send a message, you need to create a mail object using the `SendMail()` constructor. The syntax for the `SendMail()` constructor is as follows:

```
sendMailObject = new SendMail()
```

The `SendMail` object has the properties described in Table 13.16.

Table 13.16 Properties of the SendMail Object

Property	Description
Bcc	A comma delimited list of recipients who are to receive a blind carbon copy of the message.
Body	Contains the text of the message.
Cc	A coma delimited list of recipients who are to receive a carbon copy of the message.
Errorsto	Contains the address to send error messages regarding the message. The default is the sender's address.
From	Specifies the mail address of the person sending the message
Organiza-tion	Contains the name of the organization.
prototype	Allows you to add new properties to all instances of the SendMail class.
Replyto	The address to which replies are to be sent. The default is the sender's address.
Smtpserver	The domain name of the mail (SMTP) server. The default is the value set in the Administration server.
Subject	Contains the subject of the message.
To	A comma delimited list of the primary recipients of the message.

Table 13.17 lists the methods of the `SendMail` object.

Table 13.17 Methods of the SendMail Object

Method	Description
errorCode()	Returns an integer error code that indicates the results of sending a message.
error-Message()	Returns the error as a message string.
send()	Sends the message and returns true if the send is successful; otherwise, it returns false.

Table 13.18 lists the error codes and their associated messages. The errorCode() method returns an error code, while the errorMessage() method returns the associated message.

Table 13.18 Error Codes and Messages for the SendMail Object

Error code	Associated Message
0	Successful send.
1	SMTP server not specified.
2	Specified mail server is down or does not exist.
3	At least one receiver's address must be specified to send the message.
4	Sender's address must be specified to send the message.
5	Mail connect problem; data not sent.

Although the SendMail Java class allows you to write a complete server-side mail application, including attachments, the development of such an application is a daunting task. In regards to the attachments, the files need to exist on the server. This means you have to download the file to the server from the client's machine, and then attach the file to a message. It is far easier for the user to send attachments from the client-side mail program. If you are interested in pursuing the subject of MIME attachments to email messages, you need to read RFCs 2045, 2046, 2047, 2048, 2049, and 2112. You can obtain these RFCs from the following Web address:

```
http://www.internic.net/
```

A more typical use of the SendMail class is to send the results of a form as an email message. The next four listings illustrate how you might accomplish this task. Listing 13.5 shows a simple form that allows a user to request information. Figure 13.11 shows a completed form ready for transmittal. Although this form has only a few elements, you could expand it to include any number of items. The amount of data sent is not important, since the form uses the POST method. In addition to the form elements completed by the user, this form requires the following HIDDEN elements:

- The recipient of the form is set in the HIDDEN element with the NAME="recipient" attribute. This becomes the To property of the mail message.
- The Subject property is set from the data defined by the HIDDEN element with the NAME="subject" attribute.
- To provide a custom response page, the HIDDEN element with the NAME="thankURL" attribute provides a URL for a thank you message.

Listing 13.5 Information Request Form

```
<HTML>
  <HEAD>
    <TITLE>Information Request Form</TITLE>
  </HEAD>
  <BODY>
    <H1 ALIGN="CENTER">Information Request</H1>
    <FORM ACTION="http://www.xyz.com/chapter13/ls13-06.htm"
        METHOD="POST">
    <H4>Please complete the following form:</H4>
    <PRE>
      <I>Your First Name    </I>
      <INPUT NAME="firstName" SIZE="25" MAXLENGTH="50">
      <I>Your Last Name     </I>
      <INPUT NAME="lastName" SIZE="25" MAXLENGTH="50">
      <I>Position           </I>
      <INPUT NAME="Position" SIZE="25" MAXLENGTH="50">
      <I>Company            </I>
      <INPUT NAME="Company" SIZE="25" MAXLENGTH="50">
      <I>Location           </I>
```

```
        <INPUT NAME="Location" SIZE="25" MAXLENGTH="50">
        <I>EMail              </I>
        <INPUT NAME="Email" SIZE="25" MAXLENGTH="50">
     </PRE>
     <P>
        <INPUT TYPE="HIDDEN" NAME="recipient"
               VALUE="billa@nilenet.com">
        <INPUT TYPE="HIDDEN" NAME="thankURL"
            VALUE="http://www.xyz.com/chapter13/ls13-07.htm">
        <INPUT TYPE="HIDDEN" NAME="subject"
               VALUE="Information Request">
     </P>
     <INPUT TYPE="SUBMIT" VALUE="Send Survey">
     <INPUT TYPE="RESET" VALUE="Clear Values">
     </FORM>
   </BODY>
</HTML>
```

The script in Listing 13.6 is the script that actually formats the email message. Since the JavaScript runtime engine automatically handles the content type of the form, the runtime engine stores the input variables in the `request` object. The script handles any form, as it filters out the predefined properties of the `request` object, and only processes the input from the form. The script displays no information to the user. Rather, the script redirects the client to the thank you page or the error page. There is one subtle point in this script. The `Body` property cannot end with a CRLF. If the `Body` property ends with a CRLF, the `send()` method fails to include it in the body of the message.

Listing 13.6 Mail Form Script

```
<HTML>
  <HEAD>
    <TITLE>Mail Form Script</TITLE>
  </HEAD>
  <BODY>
<SERVER>
var mailObj=new SendMail()
mailObj.From="billa@nilenet.com"
mailObj.Smtpserver="nilenet.com"
mailObj.Body="----\r\n"
```

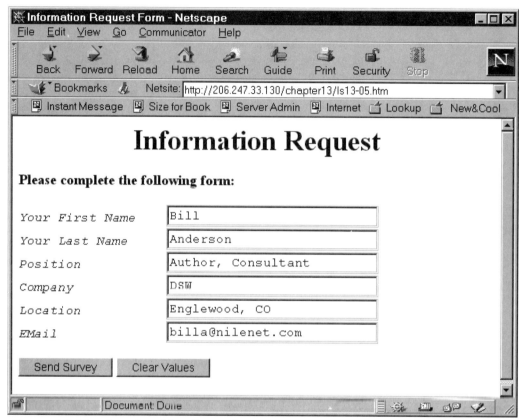

Figure 13.11   *Results of loading Information Request Form.*

```
var i=0
for (i in request) {
   switch (i) {
      case "agent":
      case "ip":
      case "method":
      case "protocol":
      case "thankURL":
      case "uri":
         break
      case "recipient":
         mailObj.To=request[i]
         break
      case "subject":
```

```
            mailObj.Subject=request[i]
            break
       default:
          mailObj.Body+=i+": "
          mailObj.Body+=request[i]+"\r\n"
    }
}
mailObj.Body+="----"
if (!mailObj.send()) {
   client.errorMsg=mailObj.errorMessage()
   redirect(addClient(
     "http://www.xyz.com/chapter13/ls13-08.htm"))
}
redirect(request["thankURL"])
</SERVER>
  </BODY>
</HTML>
```

If the send() method succeeds, the redirect() function sends the browser to the URL specified in the request.["thankURL"] property, which comes from the client input. Listing 13.7 is a simple thank you message. If you want the message to include information from the original form, you need to add the information to the client object in the mail processing script and then modify the redirect() function to include the addClient() function. Figure 13.12 shows the result of redirecting the client browser to the thank you message. Figure 13.13 shows the mail message generated by the script in Listing 13.6.

Listing 13.7 Thank You Message

```
<HTML>
  <HEAD>
    <TITLE>Thank You Message</TITLE>
  </HEAD>
  <BODY>
    <H1 ALIGN="CENTER">Thank You</H1>
    <P>Thank you for requesting information about our
      company.</P>
  </BODY>
</HTML>
```

If the send() method fails, the script in Listing 13.6 creates a client object property containing the error message. The script then uses the addClient() function to add the client properties to the error message

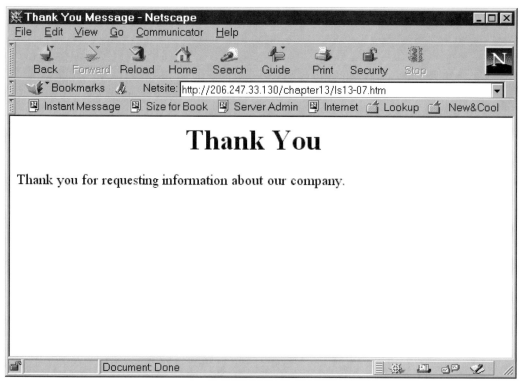

Figure 13.12   *Results of Thank You Message.*

URL. The HTML document shown in Listing 13.8 redirects the client to the error message page, which includes the text of the error message.

Listing 13.8 SendMail Error Message

```
<HTML>
  <HEAD>
    <TITLE>SendMail Error Message</TITLE>
  </HEAD>
  <BODY>
    <H1 ALIGN="CENTER">Warning</H1>
    <P>The mail message failed for the following reason:
    </P>
    <P>
    <SERVER>write(client.errorMsg)</SERVER></P>
  </BODY>
</HTML>
```

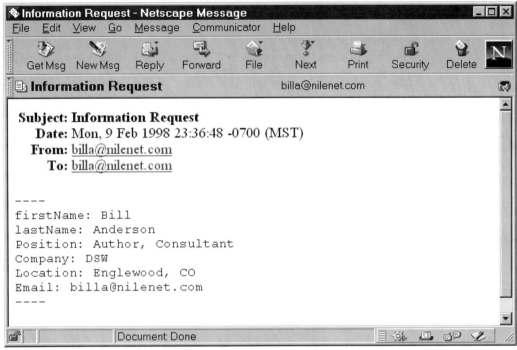

Figure 13.13   Results of Sending Message.

Working with Java and CORBA

LiveConnect allows you to communicate with Java applets. To communicate with programs written in other languages, you have the following alternatives:

- Wrap the code in Java and use LiveConnect
- Wrap the code as a CORBA-compliant distributed object and use LiveConnect in concert with an object request broker
- Use the external library facility of server-side JavaScript

Since this book is not about programming in other languages, this section only discusses the interface between Java and JavaScript. The URLs for more information on this topic are the same as those given in Chapter 10.

The Server-Side JavaScript Interface to Java

For all available Java classes in the CLASSPATH, you can access the static public properties or methods of the class. If you create an instance of the Java class, such as the Lock, File, and SendMail classes, you can access the public properties and methods of the instance that you create. With client-side JavaScript, you are able to access Java applets in any window, frame, or layer. However, in server-side JavaScript you can only access the Java classes defined for an application, or classes stored as a property of the server object. Therefore, you cannot access the properties or methods of a Web Application Interface (WAI) plug-in, NSAPI extension, or a Java Applet defined in an HTML <APPLET> tag.

You can access the packages in serv3_0.zip, which are included with the Netscape servers. This file allows you to access the following Java packages:

- The netscape.javascript package implements the JSObject and JSException classes that allow Java code to access JavaScript methods and properties and to handle JavaScript errors.
- The netscape.server package implements some of the server-side Java classes. The only class you can use with JavaScript is the netscape.server.serverenv class.
- The netscape.net package replaces the Sun JDK package sun.net.
- The sun and java packages replace the packages in the Sun JDK classes.zip.

To reference the constructor, static methods, and static properties of a Java class, you need to use corresponding syntax as follows:

```
new Packages.javaClassName(arguments)
Packages.javaClassName.staticMethod(arguments)
Packages.javaClassName.staticProperty
```

The Packages prefix is optional when you access netscape, sun, or java packages.

The Server-Side Java Interface to Java

When you call a Java method from server-side JavaScript, you can pass a JavaScript object to the Java class. Java can then interact with the properties and methods of the JavaScript object. This is the only way for Java classes to interact with JavaScript objects. The requirement to pass the JavaScript object to the Java class differs from client-side JavaScript, which allows the Java applet to access a JavaScript object in the JavaScript hierarchy. The reason for the difference is that server-side JavaScript lacks an explicit JavaScript hierarchy.

For a Java class to access the properties and methods of a JavaScript object, the Java class needs to import the `JSObject` and `JSException` classes. With the exception of the `GetWindow()` method of the `JSObject` class, the `JSObject` and `JSException` classes work the same on server-side JavaScript and client-side JavaScript.

Working with CORBA

Chapter 2, "Client/Server Methodology," describes the principles of the Common Object Request Broker Architecture (CORBA). Netscape implements an Object Request Broker (ORB) through its Internet Service Broker (ISB) for Java. The ISB for Java uses the Internet Inter-ORB Protocol (IIOP) to communicate with itself and other object request brokers.

Through ISB for Java, JavaScript can access CORBA-compliant distributed objects deployed in an IIOP-capable ORB. To access a distributed object, you need a Java stub that exists within the `CLASSPATH`. Through the facilities of Java and LiveConnect, you can expose JavaScript objects to CORBA-compliant distributed objects.

While the development of distributed objects is beyond the scope of this book, the diagram in Figure 13.14 helps illustrate how a JavaScript application interfaces to CORBA. The JavaScript application interfaces to Java stubs using LiveConnect. In turn, the Java stubs interface to ISB for Java. Through the facilities of IIOP, the Java stubs interact with CORBA-compliant distributed objects.

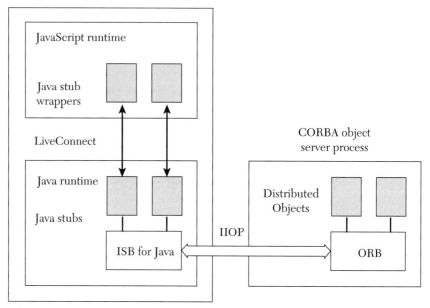

Figure 13.14   JavaScript application as a CORBA client.

Summary

Since server-side and client-side JavaScript share core components, server-side and client-side JavaScript are extensions to the core components. This chapter covered all of the server-side extensions not related to interfacing with a relational database.

Server-side JavaScript breaks down into three components:

- The JavaScripts objects incorporated in the Session Management Service
- The built-in functions
- The File Service and Mail Service utilities

The Session Management Service holds the key to understanding the flow of processes for server-side JavaScript. The Session Management Service includes the following objects:

- The `request` object, which contains information related to a single client request
- The `client` object, which maintains information across multiple requests from a client
- The `project` object, which allows sharing of information between clients
- The `server` object, which allows sharing of information between applications

With just a few differences, LiveConnect allows server-side JavaScript to interact with Java in much the same manner as client-side JavaScript. The major difference is that server-side JavaScript only interacts with public properties and methods of an instance of a Java class. In addition, Java can only communicate with JavaScript after JavaScript first calls a method of the Java class and passes a JavaScript object as an argument to the method.

The next chapter closes the discussion of server-side JavaScript, by addressing its interface with relational databases. From the view of server-side JavaScript, the LiveWare Database Service is just another service available to JavaScript application developers.

LiveWire Database Service

Topics in This Chapter

- Configuring your database for Netscape servers
- Establishing a database connection
- Retrieving and storing information
- Conversion of data types
- Handling database errors

14
Chapter

Netscape 3.x servers include the LiveWire Database Service which allows you to develop JavaScript applications that connect to Open Database Connectivity (ODBC) compliant database servers. Servers supported by ODBC compliant databases include Microsoft SQL, Informix, Oracle, Sybase, and DB2.

Since it is a separate product, you first need to install and configure the database server before developing JavaScript applications that interact with the database server. Before working with a database, you need to establish a connection between your application and the database server. Once you establish the connection to the database, the Structured Query Language (SQL) is used to retrieve and store database information. You will also need to convert JavaScript data types to SQL data types and visa versa. This chapter covers all of these topics and ends with a discussion of error handling for the LiveWire Database Service.

This chapter is not a tutorial on SQL or database administration. SQL is a subject unto itself, and database administration varies with each vendor's database. This chapter is a reference for those who know SQL and want to develop JavaScript applications that interact with an ODBC compliant database.

Database Configuration

The LiveWire Database Service is an integral part of Netscape 3.x servers. For specific information about the database servers supported and any restrictions, check the release notes for your Netscape server. You can find the release notes for both the Netscape FastTrack server and the Netscape Enterprise server at the following URL:

```
http://home.netscape.com/eng/server/webserver/3.0/
```

From this URL, choose the Netscape server product that you are using and the hardware platform. From the next Web page, follow the links for LiveWire database service.

Note

Starting with the Netscape 3.x servers, the libraries required to connect to a database are no longer part of the Netscape server product distribution. To obtain these libraries, check the Netscape server release notes for the required driver and then obtain the driver from the database vendor.

Once you have installed and configured your database server, you can test the connectivity to the server with the dbadmin application provided with your Netscape server. For this chapter, I used Microsoft SQL Server 6.5 running on a Windows NT 4.0 server. To access the dbadmin application, use the following URL:

```
http://server.domain/dbadmin
```

The dbadmin application requires that you have server-side Java-Script application administration privileges. After entering the server administrator's account name and password, the dbadmin application displays the screen shown in Figure 14.1.

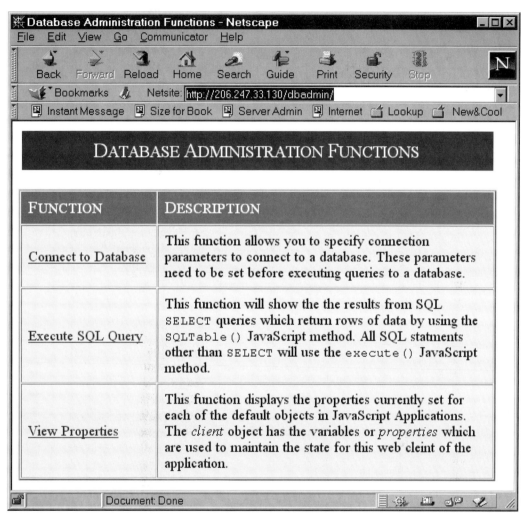

Figure 14.1   Initial window for the dbadmin Application.

From the initial window, select the "Connect to Database" link. The "Connect to Database" screen is a generic screen for connecting to the database server as a database administrator. The values you enter for each field depend on the database server that you are using. For the Microsoft SQL Server, use the ODBC option for type of database server. As an initial check for connectivity, I connected to the "LocalServer" Data Source Name as a database administrator. Figure 14.2 shows a partial view of the "Connect to Database" window.

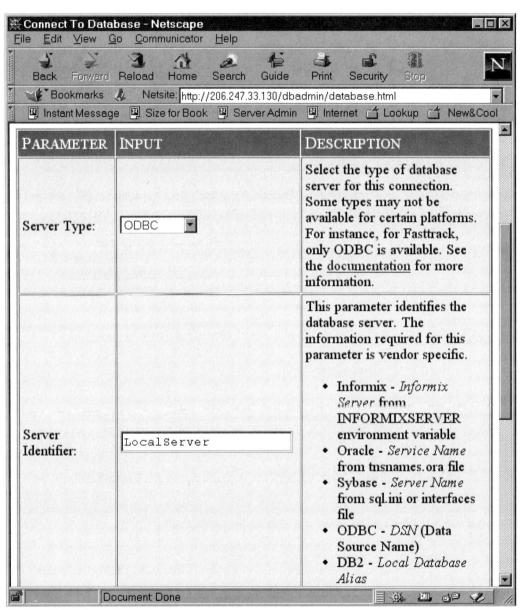

PARAMETER	INPUT	DESCRIPTION
Server Type:	ODBC ▼	Select the type of database server for this connection. Some types may not be available for certain platforms. For instance, for Fasttrack, only ODBC is available. See the <u>documentation</u> for more information.
Server Identifier:	LocalServer	This parameter identifies the database server. The information required for this parameter is vendor specific. • Informix - *Informix Server* from **INFORMIXSERVER** environment variable • Oracle - *Service Name* from tnsnames.ora file • Sybase - *Server Name* from sql.ini or interfaces file • ODBC - *DSN* (Data Source Name) • DB2 - *Local Database Alias*

Figure 14.2   The dbadmin "Connect to Database" window.

If the connection is successful, the dbadmin application displays the "Execute Query" Web page shown in Figure 14.3. Should the connection fail, the dbadmin application displays the "Database Connection

Error" Web page shown in Figure 14.4. The error codes depend on which SQL server you are using. Refer to the documentation for your SQL server to determine the reason for the error. Once you achieve a successful connection, the initial configuration phase is finished.

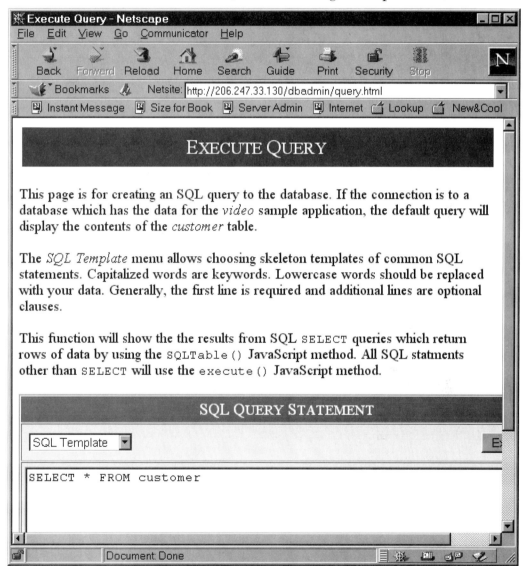

Figure 14.3   The dbadmin "Execute Query" window.

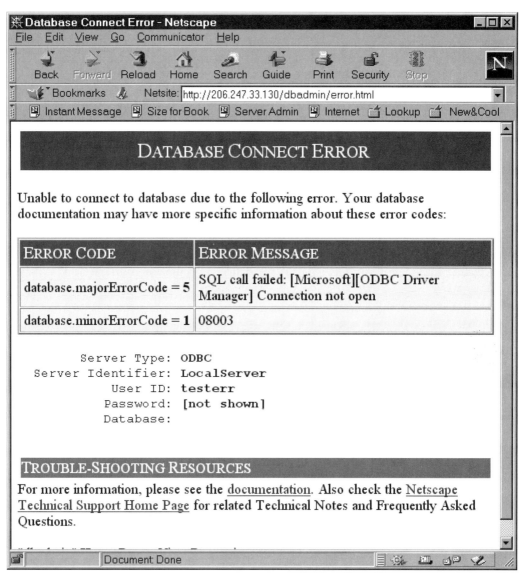

Figure 14.4 The dbadmin "Database Connection Error" window.

With the dbadmin application, you can create and populate a database from your Web browser. However, it is easier to use the graphical tools designed for this purpose to initially create, populate, and test your database. Once your database is working, you are ready to use the dbadmin tool to test the connection to the database, and to test whether you can query and update the database.

Netscape servers come with videoapp and oldvideo applications. These applications provide sample databases that can be used as models for building your own JavaScript applications. To install the videoapp and oldvideo applications, read Chapter 13 of *Writing Server-Side Java-Script Applications*. This document is available in PDF format from the following URL:

```
http://developer.netscape.com/library/documentation/index.html
```

Connecting to a Database

The LiveWire Database Service provides the following ways to establish a connection to a database:

- Establish a connection using the DbPool and Connection objects
- Establish a connection using the connect() method of the database object

The DbPool and Connection objects give you more flexibility in designing database applications. The DbPool object establishes a pool of database connections. The connection() method of the DbPool object makes the connections to a database, and creates the Connection objects. These objects separate the activities of establishing and managing connections from the activities of accessing a database through a connection. This separation allows you to create multiple connections from multiple accounts to the databases accessible to a specific user. You can also create multiple pools to manage connections for different databases and different users.

When using the connect() method of the database object, multiple connections to a single database can be established. When LiveWire was a separate product, the Netscape servers were single threaded and allowed only a single connection to a database. Since the Netscape 3.x servers are multithreaded, the new DbPool object provides the capability to create multiple connections to multiple databases and different users. The database object has been retained for backward compatibility, and was enhanced to support multiple connections. Thus, current database objects represent a pool of connections to a single database.

The DbPool and Connect objects split the properties of the database object. The DbPool object manages the connection to a database, while the Connect object manages the interaction to a database.

Although the DbPool and Connect objects offer greater flexibility with multiple connections, you must have a database driver that supports multiple threads. If the database driver only supports single threads, then only one connection can be open at any one time, even when there is a pool of connections. For single-threaded drivers, the connect() method of the database object is simpler to manage, since in a single-threaded environment you need to consider the following:

- Database interactions need to be short so that other clients can access the database. Therefore, you need to release connections and close open cursors and stored procedures to prevent undue waits.

- Use only explicit transaction control.

- An open connection that is waiting for user input imposes delays for other users wanting to establish a connection.

- A user is less likely to complete, in a timely manner, a cursor or transaction that spans multiple pages.

Although these design considerations are critical in a single-threaded environment, you should also follow them in a multithreaded environment. In a multithreaded environment, each open connection does consume its share of system resources.

The DbPool Object

The DbPool object reflects a pool of connections to a particular database configuration. Use the DbPool() constructor to create an instance of the DbPool object. The syntax for the DbPool() constructor has several formats as follows:

```
newDbPoolObj = new DbPool()
newDbPoolObj = new DbPool(dbtype, serverName, userName,
password, databaseName)
```

```
newDbPoolObj = new DbPool(dbtype, serverName, userName,
password, databaseName, maxConnections)
newDbPoolObj = new DbPool(dbtype, serverName, userName,
password, databaseName, maxConnections, commitFlag)
```

The first version of the DbPool() constructor creates an instance of the DbPool object. This version also creates and caches one connection. The second version of the DbPool() constructor creates an instance of the DbPool object and then calls the connect() method to establish a database connection. The third and fourth versions of the DbPool() constructor creates an instance of the DbPool object and then calls the connect() method to establish a database connection. In addition, the JavaScript runtime engine attempts to create the number of requested connections. If the runtime engines fails to create all of the requested connections, the DbPool() constructor returns an error. In all versions, except the fourth version of the DbPool() constructor, pending transactions are rolled back. The action of the fourth version depends on the value of the *commitFlag*. Table 14.1 describes the parameters of the DbPool() constructor.

Table 14.1 Parameters of the DbPool() Constructor

Parameter	Description
dbtype	Set to one of the following values: ORACLE, SYBASE, INFORMIX, DB2, or ODBC.
serverName	Specifies the name of the server to which you connect. Typically, you define the server name at the time the database server is installed. The name varies according to the database server.
	For Oracle, it is the service name as specified in the tsnames.ora file. When the Oracle server is on the same machine, this is an empty string.
	For Informix, it is the server name. On Windows NT, you set the server name with the setnet32 utility; on UNIX, it is in the sqlhosts file.
	For Sybase, it is the server name set by the sqledit utility on Windows NT, and the sybinit utility on UNIX.
	For DB2, it is the local database alias.
	For ODBC, it is the Data Source Name (DSN).

Table 14.1 Parameters of the DbPool() Constructor *(Continued)*

Parameter	Description
userName	Specifies the name of the user to connect to the database. Depending on the database server, it is either the login name, or the user name defined as part of database administration.
password	Specifies the user's password. If there is no password, you need to specify an empty string.
databaseName	Specifies the database name to which you want to connect for a given *server-Name*. For Oracle, DB2, and ODBC, the *databaseName* is always an empty string.
max-Connections	Specifies the number of connections that are part of the pool. The JavaScript runtime engine attempts to create the number of connections specified. The default value is 1. For single-threaded databases, the value is 1.
commitFlag	A Boolean value that indicates whether to commit a pending transaction when the connection is released or the object finalized. If the parameter is false, the pending transaction is rolled back. If true, the transaction is committed. The default for the *DbPool* object is false. If you specify the commitFlag, you must also set the maxConnections property.

Following are examples of the different versions of the DbPool() constructor.

```
pool = new DbPool()
pool = new DbPool("ORACLE", "myserver", "testAcct", "pwd1")
progject.pool = new DbPool("ORACLE", "myserver", "testAcct",
"pwd1", 5)
server.pool = new DbPool("ODBC", "LocalServer", "testAcct",
"pwd1", 5, true)
```

The lifetime of the *newDbPoolObj* object varies according to which object you assign the object that you create with the DbPool() constructor. The choices are as follows:

- The project.newDbPoolObj remains until the application terminates, the property is assigned another value, or the property is set to null
- The server.newDbPoolObj remains until the server is shut down, the property is assigned another value, or the property is set to null

- A newDbPoolObj, by itself, is a property of the request object and remains only as long as the request is active, the property is assigned another value, or the property is set to null

It is your responsibility to close any open cursors and stored procedures, and then release the connection. If you release a connection before closing any open cursors and stored procedures, the JavaScript runtime engine waits until they are closed before releasing the connection.

The property of the DbPool object is the prototype property, which allows you to add a new property to the DbPool object. The new property appears in all instances of the DbPool object, including instances in other applications.

The DbPool object has the methods described in Table 14.2.

Table 14.2 Methods of the DbPool Object

Method	Description
connect()	Connects the pool to a particular configuration of database and user.
connected()	Tests whether the connections in a database pool are connected to a database.
connection()	Retrieves an available connection from the pool.
disconnect()	Disconnects all connections in the pool from the database.
majorErrorCode()	Returns the major error code received from the database server or ODBC. For more information regarding this method see the "Handling Database Errors" section in this chapter.
majorErrorMess()	Returns the major error message received from the database server or ODBC. For a database server, the message typically corresponds to the server's SQLCODE. For more information regarding this method see the "Handling Database Errors" section in this chapter.
minorErrorCode()	Returns a secondary error code from the database vendor's library. For more information regarding this method see the "Handling Database Errors" section in this chapter.
minorErrorMess()	Returns a secondary error message from the database vendor's library. For more information regarding this method see the "Handling Database Errors" section in this chapter.
storedProcArgs()	Creates a prototype for DB2, ODBC, or Sybase stored procedures.

The following sections discuss each of the methods shown in Table 14.2. The `database` object uses these same methods, and the `Connection` object uses some of these methods. Therefore, the discussion references these objects when they behave differently than the DbPool method.

The connect() Method

Use the `connect()` method when the `DbPool()` constructor is used without any parameters, or you wish to reconnect the pool to a different database or user. You can use any of the following formats for the connect() method:

```
result = poolObj.connect(dbtype, serverName, userName, password,
databaseName)
result = poolObj.connect(dbtype, serverName, userName, password,
databaseName, maxConnections)
result = poolObj.connect(dbtype, serverName, userName, password,
databaseName, maxConnections, commitFlag)
```

The parameters for the `connect()` method are the same as those for `DbPool()` constructor (see Table 14.1 for a detailed description of each parameter). The `DbPool()` constructor automatically calls the `connect()` method when you specify the parameters for the `DbPool()` constructor.

If the `connect()` method makes the connections, it returns 0. If the `connect()` method returns any other value, you need to use `majorErrorCode()` or `majorErrorMess()` methods to determine the cause of the error.

When you call the `connect()` method, the `connect()` method first releases any open connections. To avoid the loss of any pending transaction, you need to close all transactions.

The connection() method

The `connection()` method retrieves an available connection from the available pool created by the `DbPool()` constructor. The syntax for the `connection()` method is as follows:

```
connObj = connection([name[, timeout]])
```

The connection() method returns a Connect object. The optional *name* parameter is used for debugging. The *timeout* parameter specifies the number of seconds to wait for a connection before returning. The default is to wait indefinitely. If you specify the *timeout* parameter, you also need the *name* parameter.

The connected() Method

The connected() method checks whether its associated object is connected to the database. The syntax for the connected() method is as follows:

```
result = poolObj.connected()
```

The connected() method returns true if the pool is connected to a database; otherwise, it returns false. If the connected() method returns false for a Connection object, then you cannot use any other method of the Connection object. In this case, you need to reconnect to the database using the DbPool object, which generates a new Connection object. If the connected() method returns false for a database object, you need to reconnect before using any methods of the database object.

Following is an example of how to use the connected() method of the Connection object:

```
if (!dbConn1.connected()) {
    dbPool.connect("INFORMIX", "svr01", "SYSTEM", "pwd1",
"testdb", 4)
    dbConn1 = dbPool.connection()
}
```

The disconnect() Method

For connections created with either the DbPool object or the database object, the disconnect() method disconnects all connections in the pool from the database. The syntax for the disconnect() method takes the following forms:

```
result = poolObj.disconnect()
result = database.disconnect()
```

The `disconnect()` method returns 0, if the disconnect succeeds. Otherwise, the `disconnect()` method returns an error message passed by the database. If the return code is nonzero, use the `majorErrorCode()` method or the `majorErrorMess()` method to determine the cause of the failure.

Prior to calling the `disconnect()` method, you need to release all connections in the database pool. If you do not release all connections, the `disconnect()` method waits until all connections are released. Following is an example of how to use the `disconnect()` method:

```
if (database.connected()) {
   database.disconnect
}
```

The storedProcArgs() Method

The `storedProcArgs()` method applies only to Sybase stored procedures, which are processed by DB2, ODBC, and Sybase databases. The purpose of the `storedProcArgs()` method is to declare the name of the procedure and whether each argument is input ("IN"), output ("OUTPUT"), or both input and output ("INOUT"). The syntax for the `storedProcArgs()` method is as follows:

```
objName.storedProcArgs(procName, type1[, ..., typeN])
```

Since the `storedProcArgs()` method is a method of both the `Db-Pool` and `database` objects, the *objName* is the name of the referenced object. The values for the *type* parameter are "IN", "OUT", or "INOUT". The `storedProcArgs()` method has no return value. LiveWire allows you to declare an INOUT Sybase stored procedure as either INOUT or OUT. If you define an INOUT Sybase stored procedure as OUT in the `storedProcsArgs()` method, LiveWire implicitly passes a null parameter for that argument. The `storedProcArgs()` method works in conjunction with the `storedProc()` method of the `Connection` and `database` objects. For information about writing stored procedures, see the "Working with Stored Procedures" section of this chapter. Following is an example of the `storedProcArgs()` method:

```
database.storedProcArgs("demoproc", "IN", "INOUT")
stprocObj=database.storedProc("demoproc", 6, 100)
answer=stprocObj.outParameters(0)
```

The Connection Object

When you execute the `connection()` method of a `DbPool` object, the `connection()` method creates an instance of the `Connection` object. The only property of the `Connection` object is the `proto-type` property, which allows you to create a new property for all instances of the `Connection` object. The `Connection` object provides the methods that interact with a database as described in Table 14.3. The methods of the `Connection` object are also methods of the `data-base` object. A few methods are also methods of the `DbPool` object. To avoid redundant explanations, Table 14.3 provides references to the original description of the method.

Table 14.3 Methods of the Connection Object

Method	Description
`beginTransaction()`	Initiates a new SQL transaction.
`commit-Transaction()`	Commits the current transaction.
`connected()`	Tests the existence of a database connection. For information on this method see "The Connected() Method" section in this chapter and the associated discussion.
`cursor()`	Creates a Cursor object for the specified SQL SELECT statement.
`execute()`	For SQL statements that are not queries, this method performs the specified SQL statement.
`majorErrorCode()`	Returns the major error code received from the database server or ODBC. For more information regarding this method see the "Handling Database Errors" section in this chapter.
`majorErrorMess()`	Returns the major error message received from the database server or ODBC. For a database server, the message typically corresponds to the server's SQLCODE. For more information regarding this method see the "Handling Database Errors" section in this chapter.
`minorErrorCode()`	Returns a secondary error code from the database vendor's library. For more information regarding this method see the "Handling Database Errors" section in this chapter.
`minorErrorMess()`	Returns a secondary error message from the database vendor's library. For more information regarding this method see the "Handling Database Errors" section in this chapter.

Table 14.3 Methods of the Connection Object *(Continued)*

Method	Description
rollback- Transaction()	Rolls back the current transaction.
SQLTable()	Creates the HTML statements needed to display the results of a SQL query.
storedProc()	Creates a stored procedure object and executes the stored procedure.

The beginTransaction() Method

Once you have a database connection, you need to start the process of interacting with the database. The first step in the process is to mark the beginning of the *current transaction* with the beginTransaction() method. The syntax for the beginTransaction() method is as follows:

```
result = objName.beginTransaction()
```

The beginTransaction() method returns 0 if the command succeeds. Otherwise, the beginTransaction() method returns an error message passed by the database. If the return code is nonzero, use the majorErrorCode() method or the majorErrorMess() method to determine the cause of the failure.

For the database object, the scope of the transaction is limited to the current request. If the application exits the page before executing the commitTransaction() method or the rollbackTransaction() method, the JavaScript runtime engine commits or rolls back a transaction according to the setting of the *commitFlag* of the database.connect() method.

For the Connection object, the scope of the transaction is limited to the lifetime of the object. If the connection is released or the pool of connections is closed before executing the commitTransaction() method or the rollbackTransaction() method, the JavaScript runtime engine will commit or roll back a transaction according to the setting of the *commitFlag* of the DbPool() constructor or the connect() method of the Connection object.

Note

> The LiveWire Database Service does not support nested transactions. Before starting a new transaction, you must commit or roll back the current transaction. If you attempt to initiate a new transaction before completing the current transaction, the `beginTransaction()` method will return an error.

The cursor() Method

The `cursor()` method issues a SQL SELECT query and returns the results in a `Cursor` object. The syntax of the `cursor()` method is as follows:

```
cursorObj = connObj.cursor(sqlStatement [, updateable])
```

The `cursor()` method always creates an instance of the `Cursor` object with the name defined by *cursorObj*. However, the `Cursor` object contains the rows returned by the SQL query. Thus, a SQL query that finds no matches in the database results in a `Cursor` object with no rows.

The `cursor()` method is either a method of the `Connection` object or the `database` object as specified by *connObj*. The *sqlStatement* is any valid SQL SELECT string. The optional *updateable* parameter is a Boolean value that defines whether the SQL SELECT statement is to return an updateable answer. The default value is false. For information on how to construct an updateable query, refer to your database vendor's documentation.

The `cursor()` method only stores the returned rows in the `Cursor` object. You then must decide how you want to modify, update, or display the returned rows. The following snippet illustrates the use of the `cursor()` method:

```
database.beginTransaction()
custInfo = database.cursor(
    "select * from customer where customerID = "
    + request.customerID)
```

The execute() Method

The `execute()` method allows you to execute any Data Definition Language (DDL) or Data Manipulation Language (DML) SQL statement supported by the database server. The syntax for the `execute()` method is as follows:

```
result = connObj.execute(sqlStatement)
```

The `execute()` method returns 0 if the command succeeds. Otherwise, the `execute()` method returns an error message passed by the database. If the return code is nonzero, use the `majorErrorCode()` method or the `majorErrorMess()` method to determine the cause of the failure.

Every database supports a core of DDL and DML statements. The database vendor's documentation defines the DDL and DML statements supported by their database product. The syntax of the *sqlSatement* must conform to the syntax specified by the vendor. You cannot use the `execute()` method to call functions that are not DDL or DML SQL statements.

Although the `execute()` method can be used to perform data modification statements (such as, INSERT, UPDATE, and DELETE), this practice increases your dependence on the features of a particular database. To insure database independence, you should always use the `Cursor` object to modify data.

The `execute()` statement is an exception to the rule that every transaction needs to begin with the `beginTransaction()` method. If there is no current transaction, the `execute()` method automatically commits the single transaction.

The SQLTable() Method

The `SQLTable()` method builds an HTML table to display the results of a SQL SELECT statement. Like the server-side JavaScript `write()` function, the `SQLTable()` method writes the output directly to the memory buffer for the client. The syntax for the SQLTable() method is as follows:

```
connObj.SQLTable(sqlStatement)
```

The `SQLTable()` method is either a method of the `Connection` object or the database object as specified by *connObj*. The *sqlStatement* is any valid SQL SELECT string.

Although the `SQLTable()` method provides an easy way to retrieve and display data, the `SQLTable()` method does not create a Cursor object. Therefore, you cannot modify, navigate, or control the format of the output. Following is an example of the `SQLTable()` method.

```
database.beginTransaction()
database.SQLTable(
   "select * from customer where customerID = "
   + request.customerID)
```

Note

The `SQLTable()` method does not display Binary Large Objects (BLOb) stored in a database. To work with a BLOb, you need to use the `cursor()` method.

The storedProc() Method

The `storedProc()` method creates an instance of the `Stproc` object and runs the stored procedure. The syntax for the `storedProc()` method is as follows:

```
stprocObj = connObj.storedProc(procName[, inArg1, ..., inArgN])
```

The `storedProc()` method creates an instance of the `Stproc` object with the name specified by *stprocObj*. The `storedProc()` method is either a method of the `Connection` object or the `database` object as specified by *connObj*. The parameters *inArg1* through *inArgN* are the input parameters to the stored procedure.

The scope of a `Stproc` object is limited to a single request. Thus, all methods for an instance of the `Stproc` object need to be executed on the same page as the `storedProc()` method. For information on writing stored procedures, see the "Working with Stored Procedures" section of this chapter.

The stored procedure may contain default values for some of the parameters. When you use the `storedProc()` method, you need to explicitly declare a default value by entering "/Default/" in place of a parameter. Following is an example of the storedProc() method:

```
stObj = connObj.storedProc("newcust", "/Default/")
```

The commitTransaction() Method

The commitTransaction() method commits all transactions since the beginTransaction() method. The syntax of the commit-Transaction() method is as follows:

```
result = connObj.commitTransaction()
```

The commitTransaction() method returns 0 if the command succeeds. Otherwise, the commitTransaction() method returns an error message passed by the database. If the return code is nonzero, use the majorErrorCode() method or the majorErrorMess() method to determine the cause of the failure. The commitTransaction() method is either a method of the Connection object or the database object as specified by *connObj*.

For the database object, the scope of the commitTransaction() method is the current HTML document. If the application exits the HTML document before executing the commitTransaction() method or the rollbackTransaction() method, the JavaScript runtime engine either commits or rolls back the transaction according to the setting of the *commitFlag* for the connection.

For the Connect object, the scope of the commitTransaction() method is limited to the lifetime of the object. If you release the connection or close the pool of connections before executing the commitTransaction() or the rollbackTransaction() method, the JavaScript runtime engine either commits or rolls back the transaction according to the setting of the *commitFlag* for the connection.

If there is no preceding beginTransaction() method, The JavaScript runtime engine ignores the commitTransaction() method or the rollbackTransaction() method.

The rollbackTransaction() Method

The `rollbackTransaction()` method undoes all transactions since the `beginTransaction()` method. The syntax of the `rollbackTransaction()` method is as follows:

```
result = connObj.rollbackTransaction()
```

The `rollbackTransaction()` method returns 0 if the command succeeds. Otherwise, the `rollbackTransaction()` method returns an error message passed by the database. If the return code is non-zero, use the `majorErrorCode()` method or the `majorErrorMess()` method to determine the cause of the failure. The `rollbackTransaction()` method is either a method of the `Connection` object or the `database` object as specified by *connObj*.

For the database object, the scope of the `rollbackTransaction()` method is the current HTML document. If the application exits the HTML document before executing the `commitTransaction()` method or the `rollbackTransaction()` method, the JavaScript runtime engine either commits or rolls back the transaction according to the setting of the *commitFlag* for the connection.

For the `Connect` object, the scope of the `rollbackTransaction()` method is limited to the lifetime of the object. If you release the connection or close the pool of connections before executing the `commitTransaction()` or the `rollbackTransaction()` method, the JavaScript runtime engine either commits or rolls back the transaction according to the setting of the *commitFlag* for the connection.

If there is no preceding `beginTransaction()` method, The JavaScript runtime engine ignores the `commitTransaction()` method or the `rollbackTransaction()` method.

The release() Method

The `release()` method returns the connection back to the connection pool. The syntax for the `release()` method is as follows:

```
result = connObj.release()
```

The `release()` method returns 0 if the command succeeds. Otherwise, the `release()` method returns an error message passed by the database. If the return code is nonzero, use the `majorErrorCode()` method or the `majorErrorMess()` method to determine the cause of the failure. The `release()` method is a method of an instance of the `Connection` object as specified by *connObj*.

Before executing the `release()` method, you need to close all open instances of the `Cursor` object. If there are open instances of the `Cursor` object, the JavaScript runtime engine does not release the connection to the pool until they are closed.

If you do not execute the `release()` method, the connection remains open until the JavaScript runtime engine destroys the `Connection` object. The lifetime of a `Connection` object depends on which object it is a property of. If the `Connection` object is a property of the `server` object, the JavaScript runtime engine does not destroy the `Connection` object until the server is shutdown. If the `Connection` object is a property of the `project` object, the JavaScript runtime engine does not destroy the `Connection` object until the application is stopped. If the `Connection` object is a property of the `request` object, the JavaScript runtime engine destroys the `Connection` object when it completes processing the current HTML document.

You must call the `release()` method for all open connections before you call the `disconnect()` method of the `DbPool` object. If there are active connections, the JavaScript runtime engine waits until they are released before it disconnects all of the connections.

The database Object

The JavaScript runtime engine automatically creates a database object. You initiate use of the object by calling the database.connect() method. For the database object, the scope of a connection is a single HTML document. Since the JavaScript runtime engine closes the connection at the end of the HTML document, you need to close all instances of the Cursor, Stproc, and Resultset objects before the end of the HTML document. To prevent multiple clients from trying to manipulate the status of a connection at the same time, you should connect to the database in the initial Web page.

The sole property of the database object is the prototype property. If you create a new property using the prototype property, the new property is part of all instances of the database object.

Table 14.4 lists the methods of the database object and provides a brief description of each method. All of the methods of the database object are described in the sections in this chapter on the `DbPool` object and the `Connection` object. Table 14.4 references where in this chapter to find the full description of the `database` object's methods.

Table 14.4 Methods of the database Object

Method	Description
beginTransaction()	Initiates a new SQL transaction. For information on this method, see "The beginTransaction() Method" section and the associated discussion.
commit-Transaction()	Commits the current transaction. For information on this method, see "The commitTransaction() Method" section and the associated discussion.
connect()	Connects the pool to a particular configuration of database and user. For information on this method see "The connectTransaction() Method" section and the associated discussion.
connected()	Tests the existence of a database connection. For information on this method see "The connected() Method" section and the associated discussion.
cursor()	Creates a Cursor object for the specified SQL SELECT statement. For information on this method, see "The cursor() Method" section and the associated discussion.
disconnect()	Disconnects all connections in the pool from the database. For information on this method see "The disconnect() Method" section and the associated discussion.
execute()	For SQL statements that are not queries, this method performs the specified SQL statement. For information on this method, see "The execute() Method" section and the associated discussion.
majorErrorCode()	Returns the major error code received from the database server or ODBC. For more information regarding this method see the "Handling Database Errors" section in this chapter.
majorErrorMess()	Returns the major error message received from the database server or ODBC. For a database server, the message typically corresponds to the server's SQLCODE. For more information regarding this method see the "Handling Database Errors" section in this chapter.

Table 14.4 Methods of the database Object (Continued)

Method	Description
minorErrorCode()	Returns a secondary error code from the database vendor's library. For more information regarding this method see the "Handling Database Errors" section in this chapter.
minorErrorMess()	Returns a secondary error message from the database vendor's library. For more information regarding this method see the "Handling Database Errors" section in this chapter.
rollback-Transaction()	Rolls back the current transaction. For information on this method, see "The rollbackTransaction() Method" section and the associated discussion.
SQLTable()	Creates the HTML statements needed to display the results of a SQL query. For information on this method, see Table 14.3 and the associated discussion.
storedProc()	Creates a stored procedure object and executes the stored procedure. For information on this method, see Table 14.3 and the associated discussion.
storedProcArgs()	Creates a prototype for DB2, ODBC, or Sybase stored procedures. For information on this method see Table 14.2 and the associated discussion.

Working with a Database

The cursor() method of the Connection or database objects creates an instance of the Cursor object. If the cursor has a column that contains an image, the Cursor object creates an instance of the blob object for each image. This section looks at the Cursor and blob objects.

The Cursor Object

A database query returns a virtual table called a *cursor*. The pointer into the virtual table is the *current row*. Most of the methods of the Cursor object work with the current row. You can add, change, and delete rows in the virtual table. The `Cursor` object is a repository for data. To display the data, you need to create your own HTML code.

When the `cursor()` method creates the `Cursor` object, the pointer for the current row is positioned before the first row. To advance the pointer, use the `next()` method of the `Cursor` object. When the `next()` method reaches the end of the table, it returns false. Thus, the `next()` method immediately returns false when the SQL SELECT operation fails to find any matching data.

After you are finished working with the cursor, use the `close()` method to close the cursor and release the memory used by the cursor. When the JavaScript runtime engine attempts to destroy a `DbPool` or `database` object, the runtime engine closes all open `Cursor` objects. Table 14.5 lists the properties of the `Cursor` object.

Table 14.5 Properties of the Cursor Object

Property	Description
`cursorColumn`	An array of objects corresponding to the columns in a cursor. Each field in the SQL SELECT statement is a column in a cursor and appears in the order presented in the SELECT statement.
`prototype`	Allows you to create new properties of the `Cursor` object. The new property appears in all instances of the `Cursor` object.

Table 14.6 lists the methods of the `Cursor` object and provides a brief description of each method.

Table 14.6 Methods of the Cursor Object

Method	Description
`close()`	Closes an instance of the `Cursor` object and frees allocated memory.
`columnName(number)`	Returns the name of the column specified by *number*.
`columns()`	Returns the number of columns in the cursor.
`deleteRow(table)`	Deletes a row in the specified *table*.
`insertRow(table)`	Inserts a row in the specified *table*.
`next()`	Moves the current row to the next row in the cursor.
`updateRow(table)`	Updates the row in the specified table.

The next() Method

The next() method moves the pointer for the current row to the next row in the cursor. The syntax for the next() method is as follows:

```
result = cursorObj.next()
```

If the next row places the pointer for the current row beyond the last row in the table, the next() method returns false; otherwise, it returns true. The initial pointer for the current row is just before the first row in the cursor. Thus, to access the first row, you need to use the next() method. If the cursor is empty, the next() method immediately returns false.

The following example shows how to create an HTML table for displaying the rows in a cursor:

```
// Create an HTML table
<TABLE BORDER>
<TR>
<TH>Customer ID</TH>
<TD>Order number</TD>
<TD>Order Date</TD>
</TR>
<SERVER>
custOrder=database.cursor(
    "SELECT custID, ordNbr, ordDate FROM custOrders")
// Display each order for a customer
while (custOrder.next()) {
</SERVER>
// Display the cursor row in an HTML table
    <TR>
    <TH><SERVER>write(custOrder.custID)</SERVER></TH>
    <TD><SERVER>write(custOrder.ordNbr)</SERVER></TD>
    <TD><SERVER>write(custOrder.ordDate)</SERVER></TD>
    </TR>
<SERVER>
}
</SERVER>
</TABLE>
```

The columns() Method

The `columns()` method returns the number of named and unnamed columns in the cursor. The syntax for the `columns()` method is as follows:

```
numberColumns = cursorObj.columns()
```

If you use a wildcard in the SQL SELECT statement, you do not know the number of columns returned. The following example shows how to use the `columns()` method to determined the number of columns in a cursor.

```
custSet=database.cursor("SELECT * FROM customer")
nbrCols=custSet.columns()
```

The columnName() Method

The `columnName()` method returns the name of the specified column number in the cursor. The syntax for the `columnName()` method is as follows:

```
columnName = cursorObj.columnName(columnNumber)
```

The *columnNumber* is a zero-based index to the columns in the cursor. When you specify specific names in the SQL SELECT statement, the JavaScript runtime engine creates properties of the `Cursor` object for each of the names. Thus, the following SQL SELECT statement has named columns:

```
cust=connObj.cursor("SELECT custID custName FROM customer")
```

However, if you use wildcards in the SQL SELECT statement, you do not know in advance the names of the columns in the cursor or their order. The following SQL SELECT statement is an example of this case:

```
cust=connObj.cursor("SELECT * FROM customer")
```

The `columnName()` method gives you a means of determining the names of the returned columns, as shown in the following example:

```
write(connObj.columnName(0))
```

There are two cases when columns have no names:

- The result sets for Informix and DB2 stored procedures have no column names (for more information on result sets, see the section on "Working with Stored Procedures" in this chapter).
- Computed values in the SQL SELECT statement (such as "MAX(salary)") have no names.

When a column in the cursor has no name, you must refer to it by a zero-based column number. The following example illustrates the case of a computed value that has no name:

```
empSalary=database.cursor(
   "SELECT name, MAX(salary) FROM employee")
if (empSalary.next()) {
   write(empSalary[1])
}
```

The deleteRow() Method

The `deleteRow()` method uses an updateable cursor to delete the current row from a database table. The syntax for the `deleteRow()` method is as follows:

```
result = cursorObj.deleteRow(table)
```

If the delete is successful, the `deleteRow()` method returns 0; otherwise, it returns a nonzero status code. To determine the cause of the error, use the `majorErrorCode()` or `majorErrorMess()` methods. For more information, see the section "Handling Database Errors" in this chapter.

The following example shows how to remove a customer record from a database:

```
database.beginTransaction()
custRec=database.cursor("SELECT * from customer where
   customerID = "+request.custID, true)
if (custRec.next()) {
   retCode=custRec.deleteRow("customer")
   custRec.close()
   if (retCode==0) {
      database.commitTransaction()
```

```
    }
    else {
        database.rollbackTransaction()
    }
}
else {
    custRec.close()
    database.rollbackTransaction()
}
```

The insertRow() Method

The `insertRow()` method uses an updateable cursor to insert the current row into a database table. The syntax for the `insertRow()` method is as follows:

```
result = cursorObj.insertRow(table)
```

If the insert is successful, the `insertRow()` method returns 0; otherwise, it returns a nonzero status code. To determine the cause of the error, use the `majorErrorCode()` or `majorErrorMess()` methods. For more information, see the section "Handling Database Errors" in this chapter.

The location of the row in the database table, after an insert, depends on the database vendor. If you need to use the row after inserting it in the database table, close the current cursor and open a new cursor.

You have several ways to set the values for a new row as follows:

- Explicitly assign values to each column in the cursor.
- Navigate to a row with the `next()` method and then assign values to the columns that you wish to change. The remaining columns retain their original values.
- Without navigating to another row with the `next()` method, assign values to only some of the columns. In this case, the remaining columns are null.

The following example shows how to insert a customer record into a database by using a default customer for the initial values:

```
database.beginTransaction()
custRec=database.cursor("SELECT * from customer where
```

```
   customerID = default", true)
if (custRec.next()) {
   custRec.custID=request.custID
   custRec.custName=request.custName
   custRec.custPhone=requeset.custPhone
   retCode=custRec.insertRow("customer")
   custRec.close()
   if (retCode==0) {
      database.commitTransaction()
   }
   else {
      // send some error message
      database.rollbackTransaction()
   }
}
else {
   custRec.close()
   database.rollbackTransaction()
}
```

The updateRow() Method

The updateRow() method uses an updateable cursor to update the records for the current row in a database table. The syntax for the up-dateRow() method is as follows:

result = *cursorObj*.updateRow(*table*)

If the update is successful, the updateRow() method returns 0; oth-erwise, it returns a nonzero status code. To determine the cause of the error, use the majorErrorCode() or majorErrorMess() meth-ods. For more information, see the section "Handling Database Errors" in this chapter.

The update() method allows you to modify some columns in the cursor. The unmodified columns retain their current value.

The following example shows how to update a customer record in a database:

```
database.beginTransaction()
custRec=database.cursor("SELECT * from customer where
   customerID = "+request.custID, true)
if (custRec.next()) {
```

```
    custRec.custName=request.custName
    custRec.custPhone=request.custPhone
    retCode=custRec.updateRow("customer")
    custRec.close()
    if (retCode==0) {
        database.commitTransaction()
    }
    else {
        database.rollbackTransaction()
    }
}
else {
    custRec.close()
    database.rollbackTransaction()
}
```

The close() Method

The `close()` method closes the cursor, or result set, and releases the memory used by the cursor. The syntax for the `close()` method is as follows:

```
result = cursorObj.close()
```

If the close is successful, the `close()` method returns 0; otherwise, it returns a nonzero status code. To determine the cause of the error, use the `majorErrorCode()` or `majorErrorMess()` methods. For more information, see the section "Handling Database Errors" in this chapter.

You should always close open cursors when you are finished working with the cursor. If you do not close the cursor, the JavaScript runtime engine automatically closes the cursor when it attempts to delete the `Cursor` object.

The blob Object

The JavaScript runtime engine creates a `blob` object for a `Cursor` object property that holds Binary Large Objects (BLObs). Table 14.7 lists the methods of the `blob` object.

Table 14.7 Methods of the blob Object

Method	Description
blob- Image()	Displays BLOb data stored in a cursor column.
blobLing()	Displays a link that references BLOb data stored in a cursor column.

The blobImage() Method

The blobImage() method creates an HTML <IMG> tag for a graphic image in GIF, JPEG, or any other MIME image format. The syntax for the blobImage() method is as follow:

```
CursorObj.colName.blobImage(format, altText, align,
widthPixels, heightPixels, borderPixels, ismap)
```

Table 14.8 describes the parameters for the blobImage() method.

Table 14.8 Parameters of the blobImage() Method

Parameter	Description
format	Specifies the image format as GIF, JPEG, or any other MIME image format. However, both the server and the browser must support the image type.
altText	An optional value for the ALT attribute of the <IMG> tag.
align	An optional value for the ALIGN attribute of the <IMG> tag.
widthPixels	An optional value for the WIDTH attribute of the <IMG> tag.
heightPixels	An optional value for the HEIGHT attribute of the <IMG> tag.
borderPixels	An optional value for the BORDER attribute of the <IMG> tag.
ismap	An optional Boolean value. If the value is true, the <IMG> tag includes the IS-MAP attribute; otherwise, it does not.

The blobImage() method retrieves the BLOb image from the database and stores it as a temporary file with the file extension set to the value of the *format* parameter. The SRC attribute of the generated <IMG> tag points to the temporary file. Once the server sends the generated Web page to the client, the JavaScript runtime engine deletes the temporary file.

While building the HTML document, JavaScript maintains the BLOb image in memory. Thus, a large number of requests for image data may exceed the available dynamic memory on the server.

The following example illustrates the use of the `blobImage()` method:

```
database.beginTransaction()
empRec=database.cursor("SELECT * from employee where
    empID = "+request.empID, true)
if (empRec.next()) {
    write("<H4>"+empRec.empName+"</H4>")
    empRec.empPic.blobImage("GIF", "Photo", "LEFT",
        200, 400, 10, false)
}
empRec.close()
database.rollbackTransaction()
```

The blobLink() Method

The `blobLink()` method generates an HTML tag containing a link to the BLOb data. The syntax for the `blobLink()` method is as follow:

```
cursorObj.colName.blobLink(mimeType, linkText")
```

The *mimeType* parameter is a valid MIME type for binary data that is supported by the server. The *linkText* parameter is any valid JavaScript expression.

The `blobLink()` method retrieves the BLOb data from the cursor column and stores the data in a temporary file. The `blobLink()` method generates a hypertext link to the temporary file.

While building the HTML document, JavaScript maintains the BLOb data in memory. Thus, a large number of requests for image data may exceed the available dynamic memory on the server.

Instead of displaying the employee photo, the following example creates a link to the photo:

```
empRec=database.cursor("SELECT * from employee where
    empID = "+request.empID, true)
if (empRec.next()) {
```

```
    write("<P>Select the following link for photo.</P>")
    empRec.empPic.blobLink("image/gif", "Employee photo")
}
empRec.close()
```

The `blobLink()` method generates the following link text in the generated HTML output:

```
<A HREF="LIVEWIRE_TEMP1">Employee photo</A>
```

The blob() Function

The built-in `blob()` function assigns BLOb data to a cursor column. The syntax for the `blob()` function is as follows:

```
blob(path)
```

The *path* parameter is the path to the binary data that you want to store in a cursor column. You use the `blob()` function with an update-able cursor, as shown in the following example:

```
database.beginTransaction
empRec=database.cursor("SELECT * from employee where
    empID = "+request.empID, true)
if (empRec.next()) {
    empRec.empPic=blob("d:\\employee\\photos\\emp22.gif")
    retCode=empRec.updateRow("employee")
    empRec.close()
    if (retCode==0) {
        database.commitTransaction()
    }
    else {
        database.rollbackTransaction()
    }
}
else {
    empRec.close()
    database.rollbackTransaction()
}
```

Note

With DB2, BLObs are limited to 32K.

Working with Stored Procedures

Stored procedures and result sets are features of the database. The rules for writing stored procedures and results vary with each database vendor. For information on writing stored procedures and result sets, refer to the documentation provided by your database vendor. This section concentrates on how you retrieve and run stored procedures and result sets using server-side JavaScript.

Tip

Since JavaScript only retrieves and runs stored procedures and result sets, you need to write and test them with the tools provided by the database vendor. This approach will save you a lot of debugging time when it comes to using stored procedures and result sets in your JavaScript application.

The Stproc Object

The `storedProc()` method of the `database` or `Connection` object creates an instance of the `Stproc` object. When you are finished using a stored procedure, you need to close the stored procedure with the `close()` method. If you attempt to release a connection before closing a stored procedure, the JavaScript runtime engine waits until the stored procedure is closed before releasing the connection.

When the JavaScript runtime engine needs to destroy the `Stproc` object, the runtime engine automatically closes all stored procedures before destroying the `Stproc` object. The forced closing of stored procedures by the JavaScript runtime engine can cause unpredictable results.

The `prototype` property is the only property of the `Stproc` object. If you create a new property using the prototype property, the new property becomes available to all instances of the `Stproc` object.

Table 14.9 lists the methods of the `Stproc` object.

Table 14.9 Methods of the Stproc Object

Method	Description
`close()`	Closes a stored procedure.
`out-ParamCount()`	Returns the number of output parameters that the stored procedure returns.
`out-Parameters()`	Returns the value of the specified output parameter.
`resultSet()`	Creates a new `Resultset` object.
`returnValue()`	Returns the return value of the stored procedure.

The outParamCount() Method

The `outParamCount()` method returns the number of output parameters for the stored procedure. The syntax for the `outParamCount()` method is as follows:

paramCount = *stprocObj*.`outParamCount()`

To ensure that the stored procedure has output parameters, you should always execute the `outParamCount()` method before using the `outParameters()` method. However, Informix stored procedures do not have output parameters. Consequently, the `outParamCount()` method always returns zero for Informix databases.

The outParameters() Method

The `outParameters()` method returns the value of an output parameter of a stored procedure. The syntax of the `outParameters()` method is as follows:

paramValue = *stprocObj*.`outParameters(`*index*`)`

The returned value from a stored procedure has string, number, double, or object data types. For information on conversion of data types see the section on "Converting Data Types" in this chapter. If the stored procedure has result sets, you need to execute the `resultSet()` method before retrieving output parameters with the `outParameters()` method. Once you execute the `outParameters()` method, the result set data is no longer available.

Warning

Since Informix stored procedures do not have output parameters, do not use the `outParameters()` method for Informix stored procedures.

The resultSet() Method

The `resultSet()` method creates an instance of the `Resultset` object for a result set. The syntax for the `resultSet()` method is as follows:

rsObj = *stprocObj*.resultSet()

When the `storedProc()` method runs a stored procedure, the stored procedure may create result sets. For each result set that a stored procedure creates, you need to execute the `resultSet()` method. There is no method that tells you how many result sets a stored procedure creates. You will find this information by analyzing the stored procedure itself.

The returnValue() Method

If the stored procedure provides a return value, the `returnValue()` method returns the returned value of the stored procedure. The syntax for the `returnValue()` method is as follows:

retValue = *stprocObj*.returnValue()

The results of running the `returnValue()` method depends on the database as the following indicates:

- For Sybase, the `returnValue()` method always returns the returned value of the stored procedure.
- For Oracle, the `returnValue()` method returns null when the stored procedure has no return value. If the stored procedure has a return value, the `returnValue()` method returns the returned value of the stored procedure.
- For Informix, DB2, and ODBS, the `returnValue()` method always returns null.

Before calling the `returnValue()` method, you need to retrieve all result sets with the `resultSet()` method. Once you execute the `returnValue()` method, you cannot retrieve result sets.

The close() Method

The `close()` method closes the stored procedure and releases any memory allocated to the stored procedure. The syntax for the `close()` method is as follows:

```
result = stprocObj.close()
```

If the close is successful, the `close()` method returns 0; otherwise, it returns a non-zero status code. To determine the cause of the error, use the `majorErrorCode()` or `majorErrorMess()` methods. For more information, see the section "Handling Database Errors" in this chapter.

You should always close an open stored procedure when you are finished working with it. If you do not close the stored procedure, the JavaScript runtime engine automatically closes the stored procedure when it attempts to delete the corresponding `Cursor` object.

The Resultset Object

The `resultSet()` method creates an instance of the `Resultset` object. The number of result sets created by running a stored procedure depends on the database as the following indicates:

- For DB2, ODBC, Oracle, and Sybase stored procedures, the stored procedure creates a result set for each SELECT statement executed by the stored procedure.

- Informix stored procedures always create a single result set.

A result set is a read-only version of a cursor. Since a result set is similar to a cursor, there is a property for each column in the SELECT statement. However, the naming of columns for a result set depends on the database as follows:

- For Oracle, ODBC, and Sybase stored procedures, you can reference the columns by name.
- For Informix and DB2 stored procedures, you need to reference the column by an index.

Any interactions with the database can invalidate a result set. In particular, you need to avoid the following:

- The `commitTransaction()` and `rollbackTransaction()` methods terminate access to the current result sets and preclude retrieval of other result sets.
- The `returnValue()` and `outParameters()` methods of the `Stproc` object terminate access to the current result sets and preclude retrieval of other result sets.
- The `cursor()` and `SQLTable()` methods of the `database` and `Connection` objects terminate access to the current result sets.

You always need to close a result set when you are finished working with it. If you release a connection before closing a result set, the JavaScript runtime engine keeps the connection open until all result sets are closed. The JavaScript runtime engine automatically closes all result sets when it destroys the `database` and `DbPool` objects.

The `prototype` property is the only property of the `Resultset` object. If you create a new property using the prototype property, the new property becomes available to all instances of the `Resultset` object.

Table 14.10 lists the methods of the `Resultset` Object. Except as noted, the behavior of the methods of the result set are the same as for a cursor.

Table 14.10 Methods of the Resultset Object

Method	Description
close()	Closes the result set and releases the memory allocated to the result set.
columnName()	Returns the name of the specified column. For Informix, this method always returns the value "Expression."
columns()	Returns the number of columns in the result set.
next()	Moves the pointer for the current row to the next row in the result set.

Converting Data Types

Databases support a richer variety of data types than does JavaScript. The JavaScript runtime engine automatically performs the conversion between the data types for a relational database and the JavaScript data types. Conversely, when you update a cursor, the JavaScript runtime engine converts the JavaScript data types to the appropriate database data type.

Warning

Since JavaScript does not support a packed decimal data type, the conversion may result in some loss of precision when reading and writing the packed decimal data type. Before updating the database, you should check the values and use the appropriate mathematical functions to make any corrections.

Each database supports different data types, so the rules for conversion vary according to the database vendor. Table 14.11 describes how the JavaScript runtime engine converts DB2 data types.

Table 14.11 Data Type Conversions for DB2

DB2 Data Type	JavaScript Data Type
`char(n)`, `varchar(n)`, `long varchar`, `clob(n)`	`String`
`integer`, `smallint`	`integer`
`decimal`, `double`	`floating point`
`date`, `time`, `timestamp`	`Date`
`blob`	`Blob`

Table 14.12 describes the data type conversions the JavaScript runtime engine makes for Informix.

Table 14.12 Data Type Conversions for Informix

Informix Data Type	JavaScript Data Type
`char`, `nchar`, `text`, `varchar`, `nvarchar`	`String`
`decimal(p,s)`, `double precision`, `float`, `integer`, `money(p,s)`, `serial`, `smallfloat`, `smallint`	`Number`
`date`, `datetime*`	`Date`
`byte`	`Blob`
`interval`	Not supported

The datetime data type of Informix allows the user to specify the precision of the date. The JavaScript runtime engine correctly handles the conversion of datetime data types with a precision of YEAR to SECOND. It does not correctly convert a precision such as MONTH to DAY. This effects the display of the information, but not the data format.

With ODBC there is a double translation. ODBC translates the vendor's data type to an ODBC data type. The JavaScript runtime engine converts the ODBC data type to a JavaScript data type. For information on how ODBC converts data types, see the vendor's documentation. Table 14.13 describes how the JavaScript runtime engine converts the ODBC data types.

Table 14.13 Data Type Conversion for ODBC

ODBC Data Type	JavaScript Data Type
SQL_LONGVARCHAR, SQL_VARCHAR, SQL_CHAR	String
SQL_SMALLINT, SQL_INTEGER, SQL_DOUBLE, SQL_FLOAT, SQL_REAL, SQL_BIGINT, SQL_NUMBERIC, SQL_DECIMAL	Number
SQL_DATE, SQL_TIME, SQL_TIMESTAMP	Date
SQL_BINARY, SQL_VARBINARY, SQL_LONGBINARY	Blob

Table 14.14 describes how the JavaScript runtime engine converts data types for Oracle.

Table 14.14 Data Type Conversions for Oracle

Oracle Data Type	JavaScript Data Type
long, varchar(n), varchar2(n), rowid	String
number(p,s), number(p,0), float(p)	Number
date	Date
raw(n), longraw	Blob

Table 14.15 describes the conversions the JavaScript runtime engine makes for Sybase data types.

Table 14.15 Data Type Conversions for Sybase

Sybase Data Type	JavaScript Data Type
char(n), varchar(n), nchar(n), nvarchar(n), text	String
bit, tinyint, smallint, int, float(p), double precision, real, decimal(p,s), numeric(p,s), money, small-money	Number*
datetime, smalldatetime	Date
binary(n), varbinary(n), image	Blob

On the client-side, Sybase limits numbers to 33 digits. If you attempt to insert a longer number, Sybase generates an error.

Except as noted for Informix, JavaScript converts all dates into the date object. To insert a new date, you need to create a new instance of the date object and then assign the new object to the database property as shown in the following example:

```
tmpDate = new Date()
cusorObj.orderDate=tmpDate
```

Warning

Livewire cannot handle dates after February 5, 2037.

Handling Database Errors

When writing scripts that interact with a database, you need to design your scripts to handle potential errors. When a SQL statement fails, the database returns an error message indicating a failure. When a LiveWire Database Service returns a value greater than zero, you need to perform the following steps:

1. Check the JavaScript status code.
2. If necessary, check the major error code from the database
3. If a vendor library error, check the minor error code

Warning

You need to handle the error immediately. If you execute another LiveWire method before handling the error, the JavaScript run-time engine resets the status code and the codes from the SQL server.

JavaScript Status Codes

All of the methods that return a status code use sets of status codes. A status code of zero indicates that the operation completed successfully.

A value between 1 and 27 indicates the nature of the error as described in Table 14.16

Table 14.16 Meaning of Status Codes

Status Code	Description	Status Code	Description
0	No error	14	Null reference parameter
1	Out of memory	15	Connection object not found
2	Object never initialized	16	Required information is missing
3	Type conversion error	17	Object cannot support multiple readers
4	Database not registered	18	Object cannot support deletions
5	Error reported by server	19	Object cannot support insertions
6	Message from server	20	Object cannot support updates
7	Error from vendor's library	21	Object cannot support updates
8	Lost connection	22	Object cannot support indices
9	End of fetch	23	Object cannot be dropped
10	Invalid use of object	24	Incorrect connection supplied
11	Column does not exist	25	Object cannot support privileges
12	Invalid position within object (bounds error)	26	Object cannot support cursors
13	Unsupported feature	27	Cannot open

Most of the errors reported by the status code are from the JavaScript runtime engine. However, if the status code has a value of 5 through 7, you need to check the major and minor error codes and messages.

SQL Error Messages

When the status code has a value of 5 or 6, you can get more information about the error or message with the `majorErrorCode()` method and the `majorErrorMess()` method.

The majorErrorCode() Method

The `majorErrorCode()` method returns a string indicating the error code from the database or ODBC. The syntax for the `majorError-Code()` method is as follows:

```
majorCode = objName.majorErrorCode()
```

The value of the major error code depends on the database vendor as follows:

- Informix returns the Informix error code
- ODBC reports the SQL message number from the SQL server
- Oracle returns the code generated by Oracle Call-level Interface (OCI)
- Sybase returns the DB Library error number or the SQL server message number

To translate the error code, refer to the vendor's documentation.

The majorErrorMess() Method

The `majorErrorMess()` method returns the error message received from the database server or ODBC. The syntax for the `majorErrorMess()` method is as follows:

```
majorMsg = objName.majorErrorMess()
```

The string returned by `majorErrorMess()` depends on the database vendor as follows:

- Informix returns "Vendor Library Error:" and an Informix error string
- Oracle returns "Server Error:" and an Oracle error string
- Sybase returns "Vendor Library Error:," "Server Error:," or no prefix, when the severity code is 0, plus a message string

The minorErrorCode() Method

The `minorErrorCode()` method returns a secondary error code from the database vendor's library. The syntax for the `minorError-Code()` method is as follows:

```
minorCode = objName.minorErrorCode()
```

The value of the minor error code returned by the `minorError-Code()` method depends on the database vendor as follows:

- Informix returns the ISAM error code or 0, if there is no ISAM error
- Oracle returns the operating system error code as reported by OCI
- Sybase returns the severity level

The minorErrorMess() Method

The minorErrorMess() method returns the secondary error message from the database vendor's library. The syntax for the minorErrorMess() method is as follows:

```
minorMsg = objName.minorErrorMess()
```

The value of the minor error message returned by the minorErrorMess() method depends on the database vendor as follows:

- Informix returns "ISAM Error:" and a string describing the error
- Oracle returns the server name
- Sybase returns the operating system error text

The following example shows how you might want to handle errors:

```
// this could be a part of a JavaScript procedure
function dispErr(statusCode, majorErr, majorMess, minorErr,
                minorMess) {
   write("<P>The following error occurred:</P>")
   write("<P>Status code: "+statusCode+"<BR>")
   if (statusCode==5 || statusCode==6 || statusCode==7) {
```

```
      if (majorErr!=0) {
         write("Major error code: "+majorErr+"<BR>")
         write("Major error message: "+majorMsg+"<BR>")
      }
      if (minorErr!=0) {
         write("Minor error code: "+minorErr+"<BR>")
         write("Minor error message: "+minorMsg+"<BR>")
      }
   }
   write("</P>")
}
// Other code
database.beginTransaction
custRec=database.cursor("SELECT * from customer where
   customerID = "+request.custID, true)
if (custRec.next()) {
   custRec.custName=request.custName
   custRec.custPhone=request.custPhone
   retCode=custRec.updateRow("customer")
   custRec.close()
   if (retCode==0) {
      database.commitTransaction()
   }
   else {
      dispErr(retCode, database.majorErrorCode(),
              database.majorErrorMess(),
              database.minorErrorCode(),
              database.minorErrorMess())
      database.rollbackTransaction()
   }
}
else {
   custRec.close()
   database.rollbackTransaction()
}
```

Summary

The LiveWire Database Service extends server-side JavaScript to act as a client to a SQL database server. Netscape 3.x servers are multithreaded servers, which allow multiple connections to a database. The `DbPool` and `Connection` objects support multiple connections to different users. However, the JavaScript runtime engine automatically builds the `database` object that supports a single database connection to one database user.

Once you have a connection to a database, you can use several methods to retrieve information. The `cursor()` method creates an instance of the `Cursor` object, which is a virtual table that reflects the SQL SELECT statement. If the cursor is updateable, you can add, change, or update rows in the cursor. You can also run stored procedures with the `storedProc()` method. The `storedProc()` method creates an instance of the `Stproc` object. If the stored procedure executes any SQL SELECT statements, the stored procedure creates result sets, which are read-only virtual tables. You use the `resultSet()` method to retrieve the result set and create an instance of the `Resultset` object. A column in the virtual table that contains binary data creates an instance of the `blob` object.

Databases have a much richer set of data types than does JavaScript. The JavaScript runtime engine automatically performs all data type conversions. In most cases, the JavaScript data type accurately reflects the original data. However, JavaScript has no equivalent for double precision data types. In these cases, you may have to perform some additional massaging of the data to maintain the precision.

The LiveWire Database Service handles errors through a status code and through methods that report errors from the SQL server. The error messages from the SQL server are different for each database vendor.

This chapter concludes the discussion of server-side JavaScript. The next chapter deals with the tools that can help you develop JavaScript applications.

Building JavaScript
Components

Topics in This Chapter

- What is a component?
- What is a JavaScript Bean (JSB) file?
- Creating JavaScript Bean files
- Packaging JavaScript Bean files

Chapter 15

The common way to build a JavaScript application is to use the cut-and-paste method, or to create JavaScript source files for common routines. The cut-and-paste method becomes a nightmare when making a change to a common routine that may appear in hundreds of Web pages. Incorporating common routines into JavaScript source files localizes the changes, but does little to aid the process of application development.

The next step in application development is to create reusable components that can be plugged together to create new applications. The idea of building applications using components is not new. Object-oriented programming languages, such as C++ and Java, treat the building of components as an integral feature of the language. CORBA, IIOP, and Sun's JavaBeans are technologies that extend the use of components in the building of applications.

The JavaScript Bean (JSB) file moves JavaScript into the world of building applications through the use of components. This chapter shows how to build a JavaScript Bean component.

To build JavaScript Bean components, you will need a text editor to add the necessary tags. To use JavaScript Bean components, you need a tool that builds applications from components, and works with JavaScript Bean components, such as Netscape's Visual JavaScript. To develop, test, and deploy applications in the Visual JavaScript Integrated Development Environment (IDE), you need Netscape's Component Developer's Kit (CDK). To package JavaScript Bean components, you need Sun's Java Develop Kit (JDK) 1.1 JAR packager. For debugging applications, it helps to have the Visual JavaScript debugger. With these tools, you are ready to build JavaScript components. Learning how to use these tools is a separate topic that is beyond the scope of this book.

Definition of a Component

A component is an application building block that possesses certain characteristics. A component is a modular, reusable segment of code, with a clearly defined interface. Examples of potential JavaScript components include a visual interface (such as a button, window, or form element), and nonvisual functions (such as, database connections, credit card checking routine, or data structures).

A component is modular because it is a self-contained element that performs a discrete task or related set of tasks. Since the component performs a discrete task, it is reusable throughout an application or in different applications. How a component performs these tasks is not relevant to the use of the component. To use a component, you only need to know its interface.

The traditional view of a component sees the interface as a set of hooks into the component. The hooks into the component are its runtime interface. The runtime interface enables the application to interact with the component. To add flexibility to the usability of a component, it also needs a design-time interface. The design-time interface allows the developer to customize selected aspects of the component's appearance and behavior.

In object-orient programming, the component is an object constructor. The application uses the object constructor to create instances of the object, which the application uses. The arguments passed to the constructor reflect the design-time interface, while the properties, methods, and event handlers of an instance of the object reflect the runtime interface.

Review of JavaScript Objects

Chapter 5, "JavaScript Object Model," presented the basics of JavaScript objects. This section expands on that initial discussion to give a more in-depth view of the differences between JavaScript and other object-oriented languages. This section establishes the basis for understanding how JavaScript fits into a component structure that relies on the features of object-oriented languages.

This section takes the position that JavaScript is an object-oriented language based on prototypes. In contrast, other object-oriented languages, such as Java and C++, are based on classes.

A *class* defines all of the properties that characterize a set of objects. A class is an abstract entity and not a member of the set of objects that it describes. An *instance* of a class is the instantiation of a class. For instance, Smith would be an instance of the employee class. An instance only has the properties of its parent class.

A prototype-based language only has objects and makes no distinction between a class and an instance of the class. A prototype-based language uses a *prototypical* object as a template for the initial properties of a new object. Unlike an instance of a class, the new object's properties are not fixed. Any object can acquire new properties or have properties removed. The changes to an object can occur when it is created or at run-time. In addition, any object can become a prototype for another object.

In a class-based language, the *class definition* is a separate file. The definition includes *constructor methods* that are used to create instances of the class. When you create an instance with the new operator, the constructor can establish the initial properties and perform other processing necessary to create an instance of the class.

As a prototype-based language, JavaScript does not maintain a separate class definition. Instead of having a separate constructor method, JavaScript uses a constructor function to create objects with an initial set of properties and values. In addition, any JavaScript function can serve as a constructor by simply using the new operator with the function.

A class-based language creates a hierarchy of classes by specifying a new class as a subclass of another class in the class definition file. The subclass inherits all of the properties of the parent class and can add new properties as part of the definition of the subclass.

Since JavaScript has no class definition files, it simulates a hierarchy by associating an object with a constructor function. A constructor function initiates the hierarchy as shown in the following example:

```
function customer () {
   this.custID = ""
   this.custName = ""
}
```

The next step is to create other functions that use the customer() constructor function and then add a prototype property to the function. The following example creates an order() constructor function and then adds a prototype property to the function:

```
function order() {
   this.orderNo = ""
   this.orderDate = ""
}

order.prototype = new customer
```

The next step is to use the order() constructor function to create a new object as shown in the following example:

```
orderObj = new order
```

The orderObj has the properties of the customer() constructor and the order() constructor function. Thus, JavaScript can simulate the hierarchical feature of class-based languages. For those who adopt a very strict view of what constitutes an object-orient language, JavaScript is an object-based language. For those who adopt a more liberal view, JavaScript is an object-oriented language. In either case, JavaScript contains the features necessary to build JavaScript Bean components that can be connected to Java and CORBA-compliant components. If you want to pursue this question, read the Netscape white paper entitled "Object Hierarchy and Inheritance in JavaScript." You can find this white paper at the following URL:

```
http://developer.netscape.com/library/documentation/index.html
```

The JavaScript Bean File

A JavaScript Bean (JSB) file encapsulates a JavaScript object and its supporting properties, methods, and events into a text file with the ".jsb" file extension. The JSB file then becomes a component to any tool that recognizes the JSB format.

The JSB file contains metainformation that allows a tool, such as Visual JavaScript, to make connections between components, and to manipulate and inspect components during the design process. To provide the ability to integrate with other components, the JavaScript Bean file is modeled after the JavaBeans beaninfo class, with extensions to support the Netscape ONE development environment.

The metainformation in a JSB file consists of text tags that encapsulate a single component definition. Like HTML, the tags are enclosed in angle brackets and can be nested. The `<JSB> </JSB>` tags bracket the component definition. Additional tags then define the following information:

- The `<JSB_DESCRIPTOR>` tag defines the component
- The `<JSB_ICON>` tag associates an icon with the component in Visual JavaScript
- The `<JSB_PROPERTY>` tag defines the public properties of a component
- The `<JSB_EVENT>` tag defines how the component handles events
- The `<JSB_INTERFACE>` tag defines the interface for external objects to a component's events
- The `<JSB_METHOD> </METHOD>` tags define the methods of the component
- The `<JSB_PARAMETER>` tag defines any parameters of a method
- The `<JSB_CONSTRUCTOR> </JSB_CONSTRUCTOR>` tags contain the actual code for the methods and events of the component

Each of the tags has attributes that provide specific details about the component. Although each component has variations according to the requirements of the component, the overall structure of a JSB file looks like the following:

```
<JSB>
    <JSB_DESCRIPTOR ...>
    <JSB_ICON ...>
    <JSB_PROPERTY ...>
    . . .
    <JSB_METHOD ...>
    . . .
        <JSB_PARAMETER ...>
        . . .
    </JSB_METHOD>
    . . .
    <JSB_EVENT ...>
    . . .
    <JSB_INTERFACE ...>
    . . .
    <JSB_CONSTRUCTOR ...>
    . . .
    </JSB_CONSTRUCTOR>
</JSB>
```

Since it is a text file, you need a text editor to write a JSB file. However, the Component Developer's Kit for the Windows platform includes JSBeanBuilder (now, NetObjects JavaScript Bean Builder).

With the JSB file, you can accomplish the following tasks:

- Define components that only contain JavaScript.
- Define HTML files, with the ".hi" file extension, that Visual JavaScript uses to retrieve information for properties and events of an object that are generated at runtime from the HTML tag.
- Define metainformation for a Java class, while hiding the actual implementation. This is the only way to instantiate a Java class from JavaScript in a server-side component.

Creating a JavaScript component for Visual JavaScript involves the following three steps:

1. Create a JavaScript Bean file.
2. If the component has multiple files, package the component into a JAR file.
3. Load and test the component in Visual JavaScript.

Creating a JavaScript Bean File

The following sections describe the tags used in writing a JSB file in the order that they normally appear in a file. However, in actual practice, you will probably write the JavaScript that is included in the `<JSB_CONSTRUCTOR>` `</JSB_CONSTRUCTOR>` tags first.

The <JSB> </JSB> Tags

The `<JSB>` `</JSB>` tags encapsulate the component definition. A JSB file contains only a single set of these tags since the JSB file contains a single component.

The <JSB_DESCRIPTOR> Tag

The `<JSB_DESCRIPTOR>` tag provides general information about the component, such as the component's name, display name, and runtime environment. Table 15.1 provides a brief description of the `<JSB_DESCRIPTOR>` tag's attributes.

Table 15.1 Attributes of the <JSB_DESCRIPTOR> Tag

Attribute	Description
CUSTOMIZER	An optional field that specifies a Java class to customize the component.
DISPLAYNAME	A required field that specifies a name for the component for display purposes.
ENV	An optional field that specifies the runtime environment. The default value is "either."
EVENTMODEL	An optional field that specifies the event model used by the component.
HELP_URL	An optional string that specifies a URL for a page containing help about the component.
ISHIDDEN	An optional field that specifies a tool in which the component does not appear in the WYSIWIG view of the page.
NAME	A required field that specifies a unique name for the component.

Table 15.1 Attributes of the <JSB_DESCRIPTOR> Tag (Continued)

Attribute	Description
NEEDSFORM	An optional field that indicates the component is related to an HTML form.
SHORTDESCRIPTION	An optional field that specifies a short description of the component for display in Visual JavaScript tool tips.
VISUAL	An optional field that specifies a Java class to provide the design time visual appearance of the component.

Note

In addition to the attributes defined in Table 15.1, you can add your own custom attributes. Any custom attributes must conform to standard SGML syntax formatting specifications. Custom attributes are mapped into corresponding attributes supported by the Java FeatureDescriptor base class.

At a minimum, the <JSB_DESCRIPTOR> tag requires the NAME and DISPLAYNAME attributes. Following is an example of a <JSB_DESCRIPTOR> tag.

```
<JSB_DESCRIPTOR NAME="myPackage.statusCodeToStatusMsg"
    DISPLAYNAME="Status Code To Status Msg"
    ENV="server"
    SHORTDESCRIPTION="Return Status Message">
```

The CUSTOMIZER Attribute

The CUSTOMIZER attribute is an optional attribute that specifies a Java class used to customize the component. The syntax for the CUSTOMIZER attribute is as follows:

```
CUSTOMIZER="packageName.packageClass"
```

The *packageName* is the name of the Java package that contains *packageClass*, which is the name of the Java class. For Visual JavaScript, the Java class used for customizing a component must derive from or extend the NSCustomizer class.

The DISPLAYNAME Attribute

The `DISPLAYNAME` attribute is a required attribute that contains the name Visual JavaScript displays for the component. The syntax for the `DISPLAYNAME` attribute is as follows:

```
DISPLAYNAME="componentClassName"
```

The *componentClassName* usually reflects the class name or constructor name of the object that implements the component.

The ENV Attribute

The `ENV` attribute is an optional attribute that specifies the runtime environment for the component. The syntax for the `ENV` attribute is as follows:

```
ENV="runtimeEnvironment"
```

Table 15.2 describes the values for the runtime environment.

Table 15.2 Values for the <JSB_DESCRIPTOR> ENV Attribute

Value	Description
`"client"`	The component is strictly a client-side component. When Visual Java-Script processes the JSB file, it automatically wraps the code with the `<SCRIPT> </SCRIPT>` tags.
`"server"`	The component is strictly a server-side component. When Visual Java-Script processes the JSB file, it automatically wraps the code with the `<SERVER> </SERVER>` tags.
`"both"`	Visual JavaScript generates both a client-side and server-side instance of the component. If you use this attribute, you also need to specify the ENV attribute for each property and method of the component.
`"either"`	The application developer decides whether the component is a client-side component or a server-side component. This is the default value for the ENV attribute.

The EVENTMODEL Attribute

The EVENTMODEL attribute is an optional attribute that specifies the event model for the component. The syntax for the EVENTMODEL attribute is as follows:

```
EVENTMODEL="model"
```

Table 15.3 describes the values for the EVENTMODEL attribute. Visual JavaScript uses the EVENTMODEL attribute to determine how it connects components. If you do not specify the attribute for the <JSB_DESCRIPTOR> tag, you need to specify an EVENTMODEL attribute for each event and property that uses an event.

Table 15.3 Values for the EVENTMODEL Attribute

Value	Description
"JS"	Visual JavaScript creates a method and assigns it to the JavaScript object.
"AWT11"	At runtime, add and remove listener methods connect components.
"HTML"	Permits connection to HTML objects (such as form elements). Although this is not actually an event model, it allows Visual JavaScript to construct functions for onchange and onclick events.

The HELP_URL Attribute

The HELP_URL attribute is an optional attribute that specifies the URL for a help page about the component. Application developers can view the help page in Netscape Communicator or Netscape Navigator by selecting More Info from the Visual JavaScript menu. The syntax for the HELP_URL attribute has the following two forms:

```
HELP_URL="uniformresourcelocator"
HELP_URL="$INSTALLDIRuniformresourcelocator"
```

In the first form, the URL is any valid URL. For a URL located on a server, the protocol is "http://." For local help files, the protocol is "file:///." If you preface the string with $INSTALLDIR, the value for *unformresourcelocator* is a pathname relative to the Visual JavaScript installation directory.

Tip

> The $INSTALLDIR option provides a platform independent of keeping the help files with a component archive and a given Visual JavaScript palette. This ensures that the help files for a project remain a part of the project, even if they are moved to another machine.

The ISHIDDEN Attribute

The `ISHIDDEN` attribute is an optional attribute that controls whether Visual JavaScript makes the component visible in the WYSIWIG view of an application page. The default is to display the component. The `ISHIDDEN` attribute has no values.

The NAME Attribute

The `NAME` attribute is a required attribute that specifies a unique name for the component. The syntax for the `NAME` attribute is as follows:

```
NAME="[packageName.]componentName"
```

If you package the component in a JAR file, you need to specify the name of the JAR file as the *packageName*. The *componentName* needs to be a unique name for the component.

The NEEDSFORM Attribute

The `NEEDSFORM` attribute is an optional attribute that indicates the component applies only to a form. If necessary, Visual JavaScript will generate the `<FORM> </FORM>` tags for the component. The `NEEDSFORM` attribute has no values.

The SHORTDESCRIPTION Attribute

The `SHORTDESCRIPTION` attribute is an optional attribute that provides a brief description of the component. The syntax for the `SHORTDESCRIPTION` attribute is as follows:

```
SHORTDESCRIPTION="tipString"
```

Visual JavaScript displays the *tipString* in its Tool Tips.

The VISUAL Attribute

The optional `VISUAL` attribute specifies a Java class that provides the design time visual appearance for the component. The syntax for the `VISUAL` attribute is as follows:

`VISUAL="packageName.packageClass"`

The *packageName* specifies the package that contains the Java *packageClass*. The VISUAL attribute controls the Layout View for Visual JavaScript. Visual JavaScript supports the following Java classes:

- HTMLFlowable
- HTMLContextMenu
- ActionListener
- RemovablePropertyChangeListener

The <JSB_ICON> Tag

The `<JSB_ICON>` tag tells Visual JavaScript to display any icon for the component. The `<JSB_ICON>` tag differs from the JavaBeans specification by allowing only one icon per component. The `ICONNAME` attribute is the only attribute of the `<JSB_ICON>` tag. The syntax for the `ICON-NAME` attribute is as follows:

`ICONNAME="filename"`

The *filename* refers to a file containing a 16x16 pixel color icon. Visual JavaScript appends "32" to the filename to retrieve an optional 32x32 pixel icon. For example, the file "myicon.gif" contains a 16x16 pixel icon, while the file "myicon32.gif" contains a 32x32 pixel icon.

The <JSB_PROPERTY> Tag

The `<JSB_PROPERTY>` tag declares that a property of the component object is a public property. For a component object to have properties, the constructor function needs to assign the properties to a component object. If the component has no public properties, then you don't need a `<JSB_PROPERTY>` tag. Table 15.4 provides a brief description of the attributes of the `<JSB_PROPERTY>` tag.

Table 15.4 Attributes of the <JSB_PROPERTY> Tag

Attribute	Description
DEFAULTVALUE	An optional attribute that specifies the default value for a parameter.
DEFAULT_VALUE	An alternative to DEFAULTVALUE.
DESIGNTIMEREADONLY	An optional attribute that indicates that the application designer can view, but not set, the property.
DISPLAYNAME	A required attribute that specifies the name of the property for display purposes.
ENV	An optional attribute that specifies the runtime environment in which the application retrieves or sets the property's value.
EVENTMODEL	An optional attribute that specifies the event model used by the property.
ISBOUND	An optional attribute that indicates that the property requires an on-change event handler.
ISDEFAULT	An optional attribute that indicates this is the default property.
ISEXPERT	An optional attribute that controls whether Visual JavaScript's Inspector can display this property.
NAME	A required attribute that specifies a unique identifier for the property.
PROPERTYEDITOR	An optional attribute that specifies a Java class for editing the property in Visual JavaScript.
PROPTYPE	A required attribute that specifies how the property is stored in an HTML document and how to treat a bound property.
READMETHOD	An optional attribute that specifies the get method used to retrieve the value of the property.
RUNTIMEACCESS	An optional attribute that specifies the runtime access for the property.
SHORTDESCRIPTION	An optional attribute that specifies the name for Visual JavaScript's Tool Tips.
TYPE	A required attribute that specifies the data type for the property.
WRITEMETHOD	An optional attribute that specifies the set method for the property.
VALUESET	An optional attribute that specifies a range of values for the property.

Note

> In addition to the attributes defined in Table 15.4, you can add your own custom attributes. Any custom attributes must conform to standard SGML syntax formatting specifications. Custom attributes are mapped into corresponding attributes supported by the Java FeatureDescriptor base class.

When you define default values to a component, Visual JavaScript passes the values to the constructor function as an object with the name "params." The following snippet shows the code generated by Visual JavaScript for passing default values to a constructor function:

```
var params = new JSObject()
params.prop_a = "value developer entered for a"
params.prop_b = "value developer entered for b"
params.id = "myObj1"
myObj1 = new com_xxx_myObj(params)
```

Since the purpose of the component is to build an object using the constructor function of the component, you can address the properties of the resulting object in the same manner that you address the properties of any JavaScript object. For example, to set the properties of myObj1, you could set the properties as follows.

```
myObj1.prop_a = "some value"
tempVar = myObj1.prop_a
```

Instead of working directly with the properties of an object, you can use get and set methods to update a property. Use a get method when the values of the properties are computed or when they depend on retrieving information from an outside source. You specify a get method with the READMETHOD attribute. If you need to edit the values before setting a property or need to update an outside source, use a set method for updating the property. The WRITEMETHOD attribute specifies the set method that you use to set a value for a property.

The DEFAULTVALUE Attribute

The `DEFAULTVALUE` attribute is an optional attribute that provides a default value for the property. The syntax for the `DEFAULTVALUE` attribute is as follows:

```
DEFAULTVALUE="value"
```

The property is assigned the specified *value*. You only use this function when the constructor function does not initialize the value of the property. The `DEFAULT_VALUE` attribute is equivalent to `DEFAULTVALUE`. The preferred choice is to use `DEFAULTVALUE`, since `DEFAULT_VALUE` exists for compatibility with earlier versions of Java-Beans.

The DESIGNTIMEREADONLY Attribute

The optional `DESIGNTIMEREADONLY` attribute indicates that the application designer can see the property, but not set the property to a new value. Visual JavaScript's Inspector shows this property in gray, which indicates that it cannot be set. There are no values for the `DESIGNTIMEREADONLY` attribute.

Use the `DESIGNTIMEREADONLY` attribute when the initial values are meaningless. The number of columns in a database cursor is a good example of a property that has no initial meaning since it depends on the format of the SQL SELECT statement.

The DISPLAYNAME Attribute

The `DISPLAYNAME` attribute is a required attribute that specifies the name Visual JavaScript uses in the object inspector. The syntax for the `DISPLAYNAME` attribute is as follows:

```
DISPLAYNAME="propertyName"
```

The ENV Attribute

The `ENV` attribute is a required attribute when the value of the ENV attribute in the `<JSB_DESCRIPTOR>` tag is "both." Visual JavaScript ignores the ENV attribute of the <JSB_PROPERTY> tag for all other values. The syntax for the ENV attribute is as follows:

```
ENV="runtimeEnvironment"
```

Table 15.5 lists the values for the ENV attribute and provides a brief description of each value.

Table 15.5 Values for the <JSB_PROPERTY> ENV Attribute

Value	Description
"client"	The component is strictly a client-side component. When Visual Java-Script processes the JSB file, it automatically wraps the code with the <SCRIPT> </SCRIPT> tags.
"server"	The component is strictly a server-side component. When Visual Java-Script processes the JSB file, it automatically wraps the code with the <SERVER> </SERVER> tags.
"both"	Visual JavaScript generates both a client-side and server-side instance of the component. If you use this attribute, you also need to specify the ENV attribute for each property and method of the component. This is the default value for the ENV attribute of the <JSB_PROPERTY> tag.

The EVENTMODEL Attribute

The EVENTMODEL attribute is an optional attribute that specifies the event model for the component. The EVENTMODEL attribute of the <JSB_PROPERTY> tag overrides the global EVENTMODEL attribute of the <JSB_DESCRIPTOR> tag. The syntax for the EVENTMODEL attribute is as follows:

```
EVENTMODEL="model"
```

Table 15.3 describes the values for the EVENTMODEL attribute. Visual JavaScript uses the EVENTMODEL attribute to determine how it connects components. If you do not specify the attribute for the <JSB_DESCRIPTOR> tag, you need to specify an EVENTMODEL attribute for each event and property that uses an event.

THE ISBOUND Attribute

The optional `ISBOUND` attribute indicates that a change in the value of the property triggers an onchange event. The type of event triggered depends on the value of the `PROPTYPE` attribute. This `ISBOUND` attribute has no values.

The ISDEFAULT Attribute

The optional `ISDEFAULT` attribute indicates that this property is the default property for the component. If none of the properties set the `ISDEFAULT` attribute, the first property defined by the `<JSB_PROPERTY>` tag becomes the default property. If more than one property has the `ISDEFAULT` attribute, the first one is the default property, and Visual JavaScript ignores all other `ISDEFAULT` attributes.

The ISEXPERT Attribute

The optional `ISEXPERT` attribute indicates that this is an *expert* property and the property does not appear in Visual JavaScript's Inspector. Expert properties are those that contain predefined or fixed values that the application designer should not change. At runtime, internal methods of the component may access the property, but the application developer does not need to add any code to directly access the property. Each property has an `isExpert()` method that returns true if the property is an expert property.

The NAME Attribute

The `NAME` attribute is a required attribute that specifies a unique name for the property, within the component. The syntax for the `NAME` attribute is as follows:

```
NAME="propertyName"
```

When the property has no get or set methods, direct references to the property use the *propertyName*.

The PROPERTYEDITOR Attribute

The optional `PROPERTYEDITOR` attribute specifies a Java class that Visual JavaScript's Inspector uses to edit the property. The syntax for the `PROPERTYEDITOR` attribute is as follows:

```
PROPERTYEDITOR="packageName.className"
```

The *packageName* is the name of the Java package that contains *packageClass*, which is the name of the Java class.

The PROPTYPE Attribute

The `PROPTYPE` attribute is a required attribute that determines how Visual JavaScript stores a property in an HTML document. The `PROPTYPE` attribute also determines how Visual JavaScript treats a bound property. The syntax for the `PROPTYPE` attribute is as follows:

```
PROPTYPE="value"
```

Table 15.6 lists the values for the `PROPTYPE` attribute.

Table 15.6 Values for the PROPTYPE Attribute

Value	Description
`"JS"`	Stores the property as a property of `JSObject` and passes the object to the constructor function.
`"TagAttribute"`	Stores a property in the HTML document as an attribute of the `<JSB_PROPERTY>` tag. The ".hi" files use this option for HTML form elements and other browser objects.
`"AWT11"`	Indicates that a property is accessed strictly through get and set methods.

The READMETHOD Attribute

The optional `READMETHOD` attribute specifies the name of the get method used to retrieve the value of the property at runtime. The syntax for the `READMETHOD` attribute is as follows:

```
READMETHOD="methodName"
```

The *methodName* corresponds to the name of a <JSB_METHOD> tag. If there is no get method for a property, the application developer can directly access the property for a JavaScript component. However, for a LiveWire component, Visual JavaScript uses the standard JavaBeans naming conventions to find the property.

Note

The data type of the get method's return value must correspond to the data type of the property as defined by the TYPE attribute. In addition, a get method must begin with the word "get," such as getMsg().

The RUNTIMEACCESS Attribute

The optional RUNTIMEACCESS attribute specifies the permitted access to the property at runtime. The syntax for the RUNTIMEACCESS attribute is as follows:

RUNTIMEACCESS="accessType"

Table 15.7 describes the possible values for the RUNTIMEACCESS attribute. The RUNTIMEACCESS attribute corresponds to a member of the PropertyProfile. Visual JavaScript's Connect Builder uses the RUNTIMEACCESS attribute to determine the allowable property connections.

Table 15.7 Values for the RUNTIMEACCESS Attribute

Value	Description
"FULL"	Property is read and write accessible at runtime. This is the default value.
"READONLY"	Property is read-only at runtime.
"NONE"	Property is not accessible at runtime and is not available for connection by Visual JavaScript.

The SHORTDESCRIPTION Attribute

The SHORTDESCRIPTION attribute is an optional attribute that provides a brief description of the property. The syntax for the SHORTDE-SCRIPTION attribute is as follows:

```
SHORTDESCRIPTION="tipString"
```

Visual JavaScript displays the *tipString* in its Tool Tips.

The TYPE Attribute

The TYPE attribute is a required attribute that specifies the data type for the property. The syntax of the TYPE attribute depends on whether the data type is a Java primitive data type, a Java class, or a JavaScript data type. Table 15.8 shows the syntax and possible values according to the origin of the data type.

Table 15.8 Syntax for the TYPE Attribute

Origin	Syntax	Values
Java primitive data class	TYPE="dataType"	The *dataType* is a value such as int or bool.
Java class	TYPE="package.class"	The *class* in the Java *package* defines the data type.
JavaScript data type	TYPE="JSDataType"	The JSDataType is string, number, boolean, or void.

The WRITEMETHOD Attribute

The optional WRITEMETHOD attribute specifies the name of the set method used to update the value of the property at runtime. The syntax for the WRITEMETHOD attribute is as follows:

```
WRITEMETHOD="methodName"
```

The *methodName* corresponds to the name of a <JSB_METHOD> tag. If there is no set method for a property, the application developer can directly access the property for a JavaScript component. However, for a

LiveWire component, Visual JavaScript uses the standard JavaBeans naming conventions to find the property.

Note

 The set method must have a single property that corresponds to the properties data type. In addition, the set method must begin with the word "set," such as `setMsg()`.

The VALUESET Attribute

The optional `VALUESET` attribute specifies the data values allowed for a property. The syntax for the VALUESET property is as follows:

```
VALUESET="valueString"
```

For string properties, the *valueString* is a comma-delimited set of string values as shown in the following example:

```
VALUESET="red, green, blue"
```

For numeric properties, the *valueString* is a comma-delimited set of numeric values, or a range of values. The syntax for specifying a range of values is *min:max*. As the following example illustrates, a range of values and specific values can appear in the *valueString*:

```
VALUESET="24:40, 65, 70"
```

The <JSB_METHOD> </JSB_METHOD> Tags

The `<JSB_METHOD> </JSB_METHOD>` tags define a public method. You need to define each public method with separate `<JSB_METHOD> </JSB_METHOD>` tags. The method tags refer to a method defined in the `<JSB_CONSTRUCTOR>` section of the component definition. If the method has parameters, you need to embed each parameter definition in the method definition with the `<JSB_PARAMETER>` tag. Following is an example of a method description:

```
<JSB_METHOD NAME="setMsg" TYPE="boolean">
  <JSB_PARAMETER NAME="recipient" TYPE="string">
```

```
<JSB_PARAMETER NAME="subject" TYPE="string">
</JSB_METHOD>
```

Table 15.9 lists the attributes of the `<JSB_METHOD>` tag and provides a brief description of each attribute.

Table 15.9 Attributes of the <JSB_METHOD> Tag

Attribute	Description
DISPLAYNAME	A required attribute that specifies the name of the method for display purposes.
ENV	An optional attribute that specifies the runtime environment for the method.
ISEXPERT	An optional attribute that controls whether Visual JavaScript's Inspector can display this method.
NAME	Specifies a unique name for the method.
SHORTDESCRIPTION	An optional attribute that specifies the name for Visual JavaScript's Tool Tips.
TYPE	Specifies the data type for the value returned by the method.

Note

In addition to the attributes defined in Table 15.9, you can add your own custom attributes. Any custom attributes must conform to standard SGML syntax formatting specifications. Custom attributes are mapped into corresponding attributes supported by the Java FeatureDescriptor base class.

The DISPLAYNAME Attribute

The `DISPLAYNAME` attribute is a required attribute that specifies the name Visual JavaScript uses in the object inspector. The syntax for the `DISPLAYNAME` attribute is as follows:

```
DISPLAYNAME="methodName"
```

The ENV Attribute

The ENV attribute is a required attribute when the value of the ENV attribute in <JSB_DESCRIPTOR> tag is "both." Visual JavaScript ignores the ENV attribute of the <JSB_METHOD> tag for all other values. The syntax for the ENV attribute is as follows:

```
ENV="runtimeEnvironment"
```

Table 15.5 lists the values for the ENV attribute and provides a brief description of each value.

The ISEXPERT Attribute

The optional ISEXPERT attribute indicates that this is an *expert* method and the method does not appear in Visual JavaScript's Inspector. Expert methods are internal support methods called by other methods. Application developers should never need to call an expert method. If they do, then the method should not be an expert method.

The NAME Attribute

The NAME attribute is a required attribute that specifies a unique name for the method, within the component. The syntax for the NAME attribute is as follows:

```
NAME="methodName"
```

The SHORTDESCRIPTION Attribute

The SHORTDESCRIPTION attribute is an optional attribute that provides a brief description of the method. The syntax for the SHORTDE-SCRIPTION attribute is as follows:

```
SHORTDESCRIPTION="tipString"
```

Visual JavaScript displays the *tipString* in its Tool Tips.

The TYPE Attribute

The TYPE attribute is a required attribute that specifies the data type for the return value of the method. The syntax of the TYPE attribute depends on whether the data type is a Java primitive data type, a Java class, or a JavaScript data type. Table 15.8 shows the syntax and possible values according to the origin of the data type.

The <JSB_PARAMETER> Tag

The <JSB_PARAMETER> tag defines a parameter for a method. Parameter tags are always embedded within the <JSB_METHOD> </JSB_METHOD> tags. Each parameter requires a separate <JSB_PARAMETER> tag. Table 15.10 lists the attributes of the <JSB_PARAMETER> tag and provides a brief description of the attribute.

Table 15.10 Attributes of the <JSB_PARAMETER> Tag

Attribute	Description
DISPLAYNAME	A required attribute that specifies the name of the parameter for display purposes.
NAME	Specifies a unique name for the parameter.
SHORTDESCRIPTION	An optional attribute that specifies the name for Visual JavaScript's Tool Tips.
TYPE	Specifies the data type for the parameter.

Note

In addition to the attributes defined in Table 15.10, you can add your own custom attributes. Any custom attributes must conform to standard SGML syntax formatting specifications. Custom attributes are mapped into corresponding attributes supported by the Java FeatureDescriptor base class.

The DISPLAYNAME Attribute

The DISPLAYNAME attribute is a required attribute that specifies the name Visual JavaScript uses in the object inspector. The syntax for the DISPLAYNAME attribute is as follows:

```
DISPLAYNAME="parameterName"
```

The NAME Attribute

The NAME attribute is a required attribute that specifies a unique name for the parameter, within the component. The syntax for the NAME attribute is as follows:

```
NAME="parameterName"
```

The SHORTDESCRIPTION Attribute

The SHORTDESCRIPTION attribute is an optional attribute that provides a brief description of the parameter. The syntax for the SHORTDE-SCRIPTION attribute is as follows:

```
SHORTDESCRIPTION="tipString"
```

Visual JavaScript displays the *tipString* in its Tool Tips.

The TYPE Attribute

The TYPE attribute is a required attribute that specifies the data type for the return value of the method. The syntax of the TYPE attribute depends on whether the data type is a Java class, or a JavaScript data type. Table 15.11 shows the syntax and possible values according to the origin of the data type.

Table 15.11 Syntax for the <JSB_PARAMETER> TYPE Attribute

Origin	Syntax	Values
Java class	TYPE="package.class"	The *class* in the Java *package* defines the data type.
JavaScript data type	TYPE="JSDataType"	The JSDataType is string, number, boolean, or void.

The <JSB_EVENT> Tag

Event handlers in a component allow the component to respond to external events, such as those generated by user actions. A component can also act as the source of events. The properties and methods of a component allow other components to interact with a component, but not the other way around. An event generated by a component acts as a trigger that can initiate activities outside of the component. Events generated by a component are similar to the onchange and onfocus events generated by HTML objects. If a Java class handles the events, then you need to define the interface to the Java class with the <JSB_INTERFACE> tag.

The <JSB_EVENT> tag is modeled along the lines of the EventSet-Descriptor object. The JavaBeans model for firing and receiving events centers on the concept of event producers and event listeners. With JavaBeans, any Bean that wants to be a receiver of an event, registers itself as an event listener with the Bean that produces the event. When the source Bean fires an event, it calls a predefined method on each of the registered listeners. For JavaScript Beans, Visual JavaScript insures a match between event producers and event listeners. The <JSB_EVENT> and <JSB_INTERFACE> tags provide Visual JavaScript the information needed to match event producers with event listeners.

Table 15.12 lists the attributes of the <JSB_EVENT> tag and provides a brief description of each attribute.

Table 15.12 Attributes of the <JSB_EVENT> Tag

Attribute	Description
ADDLISTENERMETHOD	Specifies the name of an event to add a listener method for the event.
DISPLAYNAME	A required attribute that specifies the name of the event for display purposes.
EVENTMODEL	Specifies the event model used by the event.
ISDEFAULT	An optional attribute that specifies that this is the default event for the component.
ISEXPERT	An optional attribute that controls whether Visual JavaScript's Inspector can display this event.
LISTENERTYPE	Specifies the Java class that implements the listener interface.

Table 15.12 Attributes of the <JSB_EVENT> Tag *(Continued)*

NAME	A required attribute that specifies a unique name for the method.
REMOVELISTENERMETHOD	Specifies the name of a method used to remove a listener method for an event.
SHORTDESCRIPTION	An optional attribute that specifies the name for Visual JavaScript's Tool Tips.

Note

In addition to the attributes defined in Table 15.12, you can add your own custom attributes. Any custom attributes must conform to standard SGML syntax formatting specifications. Custom attributes are mapped into corresponding attributes supported by the Java FeatureDescriptor base class.

The ADDLISTENERMETHOD Attribute

The ADDLISTENERMETHOD attribute specifies the name of the method used to add a listener method for an event generated by the component. The ADDLISTENERMETHOD is required for the AWT11 event model when the listener method belongs to another object. The syntax for the ADDLISTENERMETHOD is as follows:

```
ADDLISTENERMETHOD="addMethod"
```

The *addmethod* is the name of a method that adds a listener method for the event. The *addmethod* requires a matching method description using the <JSB_METHOD> </JSB_METHOD> tags.

The DISPLAYNAME Attribute

The DISPLAYNAME attribute is a required attribute that specifies the name Visual JavaScript uses in the object inspector. The syntax for the DISPLAYNAME attribute is as follows:

```
DISPLAYNAME="parameterName"
```

The EVENTMODEL Attribute

The EVENTMODEL attribute is an optional attribute that specifies the event model for the event. The EVENTMODEL attribute of the <JSB_EVENT> tag overrides the global EVENTMODEL attribute of the <JSB_DESCRIPTOR> tag. The syntax for the EVENTMODEL attribute is as follows:

```
EVENTMODEL="model"
```

Table 15.3 describes the values for the EVENTMODEL attribute. Visual JavaScript uses the EVENTMODEL attribute to determine how it connects components. If you do not specify the attribute for the <JSB_DESCRIPTOR> tag, you need to specify an EVENTMODEL attribute for each event and property that uses an event.

The ISDEFAULT Attribute

The optional ISDEFAULT attribute indicates that this event is the default event for the component. If none of the events set the ISDEFAULT attribute, the first event defined by the <JSB_EVENT> tag becomes the default event. If more than one event has the ISDEFAULT attribute, the first one is the default event, and Visual JavaScript ignores all other IS-DEFAULT attributes.

The ISEXPERT Attribute

The optional ISEXPERT attribute indicates that this is an *expert* event and the event does not appear in Visual JavaScript's Inspector. Expert events are internal events called events or methods belonging to the component. Application developers should never need to trigger an expert event. If they do, then the event should not be an expert event.

The LISTENERTYPE Attribute

The LISTENERTYPE attribute specifies the name of a Java class that implements the listener interface. The LISTENERTYPE is required with the AWT11 event model. The syntax for the LISTENERTYPE is as follows:

```
LISTENERTYPE="eventListener"
```

The value for *eventListener* corresponds to the name of a
`<JSB_INTERFACE>` tag.

The NAME Attribute

The NAME attribute is a required attribute that specifies a unique name
for the event. The syntax for the NAME attribute is as follows:

```
NAME="eventName"
```

The REMOVELISTENERMETHOD Attribute

The REMOVELISTENERMETHOD attribute specifies the name of a
method that removes a listener method for the event. The RE-
MOVELISTENERMETHOD is required for the AWT11 event model when
the listener method belongs to another object. The syntax for the RE-
MOVELISTENERMETHOD is as follows:

```
REMOVELISTENERMETHOD="removeMethod"
```

The *removeMethod* is the name of a method that removes a listener
method for the event. The *removeMethod* requires a matching method
description using the `<JSB_METHOD>` `</JSB_METHOD>` tags.

The SHORTDESCRIPTION Attribute

The SHORTDESCRIPTION attribute is an optional attribute that provides a brief description of the event. The syntax for the SHORTDE-
SCRIPTION attribute is as follows:

```
SHORTDESCRIPTION="tipString"
```

Visual JavaScript displays the *tipString* in its Tool Tips.

The <JSB_INTERFACE> Tag

The `<JSB_INTERFACE>` tag defines the Java package and class of a
Java event handler. The `<JSB_INTERFACE>` tag only has the NAME attribute. The syntax for the NAME attribute is as follows:

```
NAME="packageName.class"
```

The *packageName* is a fully qualified name of a Java package that contains the *class* that is the event handler.

The <JSB_CONSTRUCTOR> </JSB_CONSTRUCTOR> Tags

The <JSB_CONSTRUCTOR> </JSB_CONSTRUCTOR> tags encapsulate the JavaScript that constructs a component. The constructor tags contain either embedded JavaScript or use the SRC attribute that names a JavaScript source file. The only attribute of the <JSB_CONSTRUCTOR> tag is the SRC attribute, which has the following syntax:

SRC="*filename*"

Note

A server-side component requires the use of the SRC attribute.

The constructor function includes the following:

- A constructor function in the form of *packageName_componentName*. The *packageName* appears only when the component is part of a JAR file. The *component-Name* reflects the value of the NAME attribute in the <JSB_DESCRIPTOR> tag, with the exception that all dots in the NAME attribute are underscores in the constructor function name. For example, if the constructor function name is myPkg_examples_testObject, the NAME attribute of the <JSB_DESCRIPTOR> tag is myPkg.examples.testObj.
- A single argument that is an object containing the parameters for the constructor function.
- An optional return value.

When you place a component on a Visual JavaScript page, Visual JavaScript automatically encapsulates the function with the <SCRIPT> </SCRIPT> tags or the <SERVER> </SERVER> tags depending on the value of the ENV attribute. When an instance of the component is placed on the page, the constructor function is called to create the object.

Examples of JavaScript Components

Both Visual JavaScript and the Component Developer's Kit come with plenty of examples for JavaScript Bean Files. Table 15.13 lists them.

Table 15.13 Visual JavaScript's JavaScript Bean Examples

Name of JSB	Description
CheckBox.jsb	A client-side component that generates a JavaScript check box element.
Cursor.jsb	The LiveWire Cursor component is a server-side component that creates a cursor from the specified SQL query.
CustomTable.jsb	The Custom Server Table JSB creates a customizable server-side HTML table that contains the information from a database cursor.
DateDisplay.jsb	The Date Display is a client-side component that displays the current date or the last-modified date of the HTML document.
DBSelect.jsb	The Database Select List is a server-side script that uses a form selection list to query and format data from a database.
DBPool.jsb	The LiveWire DBPool component is a server-side component that establishes a database connection using the DBPool object.
DummyCursor.jsb	The JavaScript Dummy Cursor component is a client-side component that mimics a database cursor; for demonstration and testing.
FormAccept.jsb	The Database Form handler is a server-side component that forms submissions. The component inserts, deletes, and updates a row in a database table.
JSBufferedCursor.jsb	The JavaScript Client Cursor script is both a server-side and client-side component that executes a SQL query and buffers the results for the client-side script.
Label.jsb	The Server Label component is a server-side component for displaying a single element from a database cursor.
MailToLink.jsb	The Mail-to Link component is a client-side component that generates a link for sending messages.
RadioGroup.jsb	The JavaScript Radio Group is a client-side component that generates a radio buttons group form element.
ScrollingBanner.jsb	The Scrolling Banner component is a client-side component that scrolls a message in the browser status bar.
SelectBox.jsb	The JavaScript Select List component generates both client-side and server-side code for a select list form element.
SendMail.jsb	The Server Send Mail component is a server-side component that sends a mail message.

Table 15.13 Visual JavaScript's JavaScript Bean Examples *(Continued)*

Name of JSB	Description
`SimpleTable.jsb`	The Simple Server Table component is a server-side component that creates an HTML table from the results of a SQL query.
`ValidatedText.jsb`	The Validated Text component is a client-side component that validates a text form element.

Table 15.14 lists the JavaScript Bean files provided with the Component Developer's Kit (CDK). The JSB files in the CDK come with excellent tutorial Web pages. Many of these examples combine the use of JavaScript and Java related sets of components into a single JAR file.

Table 15.14 JavaScript Bean Files in the Component Developer's Kit

Name of Example	Description
`HellowWorldJSB`	A simple client-side component that shows how to write a JSB and package it in a JAR file.
`CustomDisplay`	This client-side example shows how to combine JavaScript, Java, and supporting images into a component.
`SimpleClientServer`	This example consists of a simple client-side component that controls a layer, a simple server-side component that echoes form contents. The purpose of the example is to show how to combine related components into a single JAR file.
`CustomJSB`	This client-side example includes a Customizer Java class for customizing the design-time behavior of a component.
`DatePicker`	This client-side example illustrates the use of firing and receiving events.
`DialogWidget`	A client-side example that creates a moveable dialog box.
`JSBDOC Tool`	This is an advanced example that uses JSB and Java Beans to build a documentation tool.
`Visual JavaScript Palette Item Source`	This is the source code to all palette items that ship with Visual JavaScript.
`SourceLoader`	This client-side component shows how to encapsulate Java functionality within JavaScript.
`FloatingWindow`	A client-side component that creates floating windows.

Packaging a Component

If the component consists of a single JSB file, you do not package the component. However, if the component consists of multiple files (such as JSB files, images, and JavaScript source files), you need to package the files before importing them into Visual JavaScript. You may also want to combine multiple related components into a single package file and then import the package into Visual JavaScript.

To package a component into a JAR file, you need the Java Development Kit (JDK) version 1.1. The JDK 1.0.2. transitional Beans specifications requires that the JAR file contain at least one component.

The steps for packaging a component into a JAR file are as follows:

- Create a directory structure that reflects the name of the package. For example, mystuff/samples (or mystuff\samples for the Windows platform) is the initial directory structure for all packages that begin with the name mystuff_samples.

- Create a subdirectory under the packages directory for the package you wish to build. For example, the new relative pathname is mystuff/samples/pkg1.

- If necessary, create another subdirectory for class files. This is required if the class file is part of a package.

- Create a manifest file in the package directory. The manifest file is an ASCII file that contains a list of all components that are part of the package. The manifest file name needs to have the ".mf" file extension, and it needs to be in uppercase letters. Listing 15.1 shows the format of a manifest file.

- Make sure the JDK bin directory is in your path name.

Listing 15.1 Example of a manifest file

```
Manifest-Version: 1.0

Name: mystuff/samples/pkg1/test.jsb
Java-Bean: True
```

To build the JAR file, use the following jar command syntax:

```
jar cfm jar-name manifest-name bean-name1[ bean-name2 ...]
```

For example, to build a JAR for the test.jsb component, the jar command is as follows:

```
jar cfm test.jar test.mf mystuff/samples/test.jsb
```

To examine the contents of a JAR file, use the following syntax for the jar command:

```
jar tf jar-name
```

Summary

JavaScript Beans are reuseable components that can combine with other components to create a Web page with component development tools such as Visual JavaScript. The JavaScript Bean uses a constructor function to create runtime objects that have the properties and methods defined by the constructor function. By itself, the JavaScript portion of a JavaScript Bean is just a flexible runtime module. You could place the code in a JavaScript source file, and use traditional tools to implement the module into your Web page.

The JavaScript Bean file uses HTML style tags to add the definitions required for a component development tool that implements JavaBeans. The JSB tags define the design-time interface for a component. The JSB tags define the public properties, public methods, and event handling for the component. The component development tool uses these definitions to construct connections to other components.

Instead of cutting and pasting, the application developer now uses a component development tool to build platform independent applications. The output of the component development tool is a standard HTML document that runs on any browser that supports JavaScript.

Tools are an important part of Web page development. The next chapter reviews some of the tools available for developing JavaScript applications.

JavaScript Tools

Topics in This Chapter

- Tools from Netscape
- Tools from third parties
- Tools for signing scripts

Chapter

16

To write a Web page that uses JavaScript, all you really need is a simple text editor. However, even developers who swear that any tool beyond a text editor is a waste, probably use a macro editor, which is a more advanced tool. Advanced text editors provide features that simplify the task of editing ASCII text files and developing Web pages.

Many of the tools in this chapter are customized text editors that help you perform advanced and specialized tasks. For example, instead of typing in tags, you just click a button to insert a tag. Some tools provide wizards that collect necessary information and then insert the results into your document. Other tools perform tasks such as debugging, packaging, and signing scripts. The purpose of these tools is to reduce the development effort involved in the building of web applications. They all provide something more than just letting you enter JavaScript code into an HTML document.

The tools described in this chapter are divided between those provided by Netscape, those provided by third parties, and special tools required to sign scripts. If I have left out your favorite tool, it is because either I was unaware of it, or I was unable to get answers from a vendor about the tool.

Tools Available from Netscape

Netscape is not the best place to look for tools to write JavaScript code. In my opinion, Netscape Navigator Gold 3.x and Netscape Communicator's Page Composer are fine for developing simple Web pages, but they are not great tools for developing JavaScript code. However, Netscape does offer JavaScript tools for the application developer who wants to develop client/server applications that integrate Java, JavaScript, and CORBA-compliant objects.

Visual JavaScript

Visual JavaScript is a component development tool for the development of crossware web applications. Crossware web applications are applications that run across different network and operating system platforms. Crossware web applications can easily extend to external partners and customers. Rather than installing application software on the client machine, the Web browser becomes the common client platform for all crossware applications. The crossware environment extends the limited client/server communications of HTTP through the use of distributed object and the Internet Inter-ORB Protocol (IIOP). For additional information on the role of crossware web applications in the Netscape ONE environment, check the following URL:

```
http://developer.netscape.com/library/wpapers/crossware/
index.html
```

Components are the building blocks used to construct crossware applications. JavaScript components, Java components, and reusable blocks of HTML, come together to form an application. The component development tool that brings these components together into a crossware web application is Visual JavaScript. The suggested design rules for the Netscape ONE environment are as follows:

* Use HTML to create the user interface (UI)

- Use JavaScript to connect UI elements together
- Use Java for computational-intensive functions, for accessing remote services using protocols such as LDAP and IIOP, or for graphical UI elements
- Use the JavaBeans component model for building applications

Visual JavaScript uses Sun's JavaBeans component model with extensions for JavaScript components. For CORBA-compliant objects, Visual JavaScript generates a JavaScript Bean component based on the Interface Definition Language (IDL) files that make use of IIOP to communicate over an Object Request Broker (ORB).

As mentioned in Chapter 15, "Building JavaScript Components," components have a runtime interface and a design-time interface. The design-time interface provides the Visual JavaScript tools (such as the Page Editor, Inspector, and Connection Builder) with the information needed to design the runtime behavior of a component.

The major features of Visual JavaScript are as follows:

- Visual development of crossware applications
- A WYSIWIG HTML editor
- Drag-and-drop assembly using components
- An extensible component palette of HTML, JavaBean, JavaScript, and CORBA components
- Event-oriented programming with automatic code generation
- Database integration
- Sample application and components
- Support for plug-ins and third-party components

Figure 16.1 shows a sample of the Visual JavaScript screen, with the component palette.

Visual JavaScript is not for everyone. It is a component development tool oriented towards the Netscape ONE development platform, and the server-side components are for the Netscape Enterprise server. However, this is an essential tool if you are working in a Netscape environment and you are developing crossware web applications.

Personally, I am biased towards the component development environment. It takes you beyond the cut-and-paste world of Web page development into the world of reuseable components. It takes work to

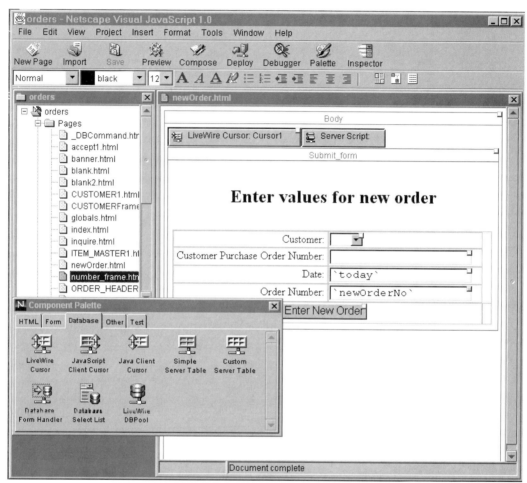

Figure 16.1 **Example of Visual JavaScript screen.**

develop good reuseable components, but the end result is well worth the effort.

Component Developer's Kit

If you use Visual JavaScript, then you will need the Component Developer's Kit (CDK). The CDK contains the following:

- The "Component Developer's Guide" provides information on how to develop reuseable Java, JavaScript, or CORBA-compliant components.

- Sample components for Java, JavaScript, and CORBA, along with detailed descriptions of each sample component.
- Resource listings to help component developers learn more about component design
- A component development pack ready to install in Visual Java-Script
- For the Windows platforms, the CDK includes NetObjects JavaScript BeanBuilder. NetObjects recently acquired Acadia Softwares JavaScript BeanBuilder, so the CDK still refers to it as the Acadia JavaScript BeanBuilder.

The starting point for exploring the CDK, and for learning about component development, is the Component Developer's Kit HTML based documentation of the CDK. Figure 16.2 shows a portion of the initial screen for the CDK documentation.

One of the sample components is actually a complete application for documenting the components that you build. The JavaScript Bean Documentation Tool creates JavaDoc style documentation for JavaScript Beans. Another of the samples provides the complete source code for the components that ship with Visual JavaScript. The CDK contains a lot of information, so plan on spending some time exploring its contents.

The JavaScript Debugger

The word "bug" is a word that I do not like to use. A "bug" implies that some gremlin attacked the code to create a "new feature." In my lexicon, when software fails to perform according to specification, it is a "defect." A "defect" is a failure in the software building process, for which there is assigned responsibility. Fixing a defect requires more than just fixing the software problem, it requires fixing the process that allowed the problem to occur. Unfortunately, the software industry continues to misapply the word "bug."

In spite of the moniker, a debugger is a useful tool in certain circumstances. I use a "debugger," when my thinking about the behavior of a statement differs from the machine's interpretation. My source code looks correct, but when I run the application it does not work the way I expected. This is when I use a "debugger" to help me understand where I made a mistake.

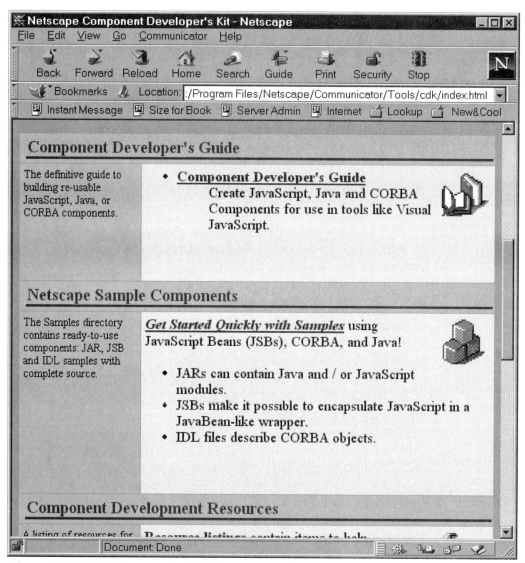

Figure 16.2   Initial page for CDK documentation.

For JavaScript applications, the defect finder that I recommend is Netscape's JavaScript Debugger. The JavaScript Debugger is a Java application and requires Netscape Communicator 4.0. The JavaScript Debugger is a client-side debugger that includes the following features:

- A watch mechanism

- Conditional breakpoints
- A breakpoint management window
- Error reporting
- Signed script support
- Stepping through code
- An object inspector
- Call stack to show current execution location

Figure 16.3 shows an example of the JavaScript Debugger window. Since the JavaScript Debugger needs to access otherwise forbidden information, you need to grant it permission to access the HTML document that you wish to check.

To install the JavaScript Debugger in Netscape Communicator 4.x, go to the following URL:

```
http://developer.netscape.com/products/jsdebug/index.html
```

When you click on "download JavaScript Debugger," you will get a license page. If you accept the license, click the "Accept" button and the JavaScript Debugger will download as a Smart Update. There are several permission requests that you need to accept to grant permission for Smart Update to install the JavaScript Debugger. Remember to bookmark the JavaScript Debugger Web page—you will use it to start the JavaScript Debugger.

Tools Available from Third Parties

The third-party products presented in this section are primarily tools that I have used to develop JavaScript applications. There are several HTML editors that allow you to enter JavaScript code in a text editor fashion. Those HTML editors do not qualify as JavaScript tools. If I have missed a good JavaScript tool, let me know and I will include it on the Web page for this book.

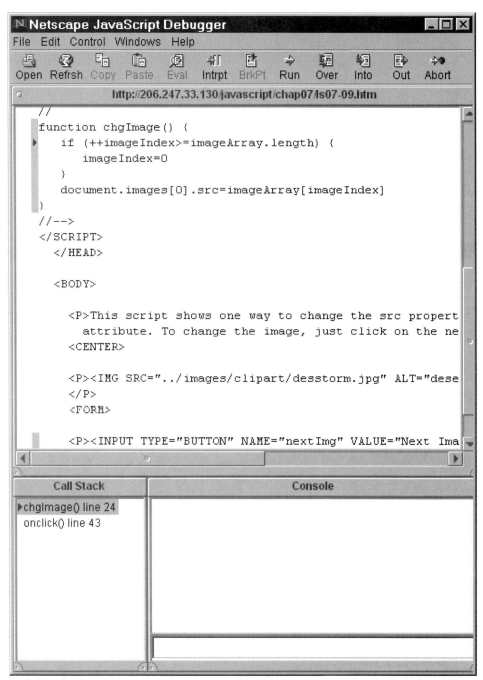

Figure 16.3 Example of JavaScript Debugger window.

NetObjects ScriptBuilder

NetObjects ScriptBuilder was Acadia Infuse until NetObjects bought the product from Acadia Software. ScriptBuilder combines a powerful script editor, drag-and-drop scripting, and a large knowledge base of scripting information. ScriptBuilder works with JavaScript, JScript, VB-Script, and HTML. The ScriptBuilder Inspector tool checks your scripts for browser compatibility.

ScriptBuilder is the first tool optimized for Web script editing. Script-Builder supports both client-side script editing and server-side script editing. ScriptBuilder is only available for the Windows 95/NT platforms. Figure 16.4 shows the ScriptBuilder Window after running the Script-Builder Inspector. To get the latest information on ScriptBuilder, surf to the following URL:

```
http://www.netobjects.com/
```

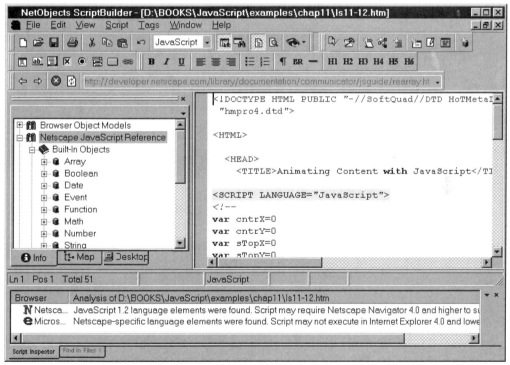

Figure 16.4 *Example of NetObjects ScriptBuilder.*

I recommend ScriptBuilder as an essential addition to the tool collection of anyone who writes a lot of scripts. ScriptBuilder does not have a fancy WYSIWIG interface for HTML, but HTML editing is not its primary purpose. I used the beta version of Acadia Infuse 2.0, the old name for ScriptBuilder, to create several of the scripts in this book.

NetObjects JavaScript Bean Builder

NetObjects JavaScript Bean Builder (formerly Acadia JSBeanBuilder) is a tool for building JavaScript Bean files. JavaScript Bean Builder comes with Netscape's Component Developer's Kit (under its former name). JavaScript BeanBuilder combines a tag editor for the JSB tags, and a script editor for the JavaScript code. JavaScript Bean Builder has many of the features of ScriptBuilder, but is optimized for building JavaScript Bean files. Figure 16.5 shows the JavaScript Bean Builder window.

There are two ways to build JavaScript Bean files; the hard way and the easy way. The hard way is using the Windows 95/NT version of the Component Developer's Kit. Instead, take the easy way to writing JavaScript Bean files, and use JavaScript Bean Builder. If you can use ScriptBuilder, then the learning curve for JavaScript Bean Builder is next to nothing.

HoTMetaL Pro 4.0

I am including a review of HoTMetaL Pro 4.0 because it comes with a JavaScript editing tool. Since HoTMetaL Pro 4.0 was released before ScriptBuilder 2.0, it uses Acadia Infuse version 1.02 as the tool for editing JavaScript files. With the exception of the view listings created with ScriptBuilder, I used HoTMetaL Pro 4.0 to create every listing in this book.

HoTMetaL Pro is not one tool, rather, it is a collection of tools that form a total package for Web page development. The major features of HoTMetaL Pro are as follows:

- Site Maker is a wizard that walks you through the creation of a Web site step by step. Site Maker automatically creates a customized Web site according to your specifications.
- HoTMetaL Pro Editor has three authoring environments: WYSIWIG, tag-on mode, and direct HTML source editing.
- HoTMetaL Pro Editor converts documents and spreadsheets

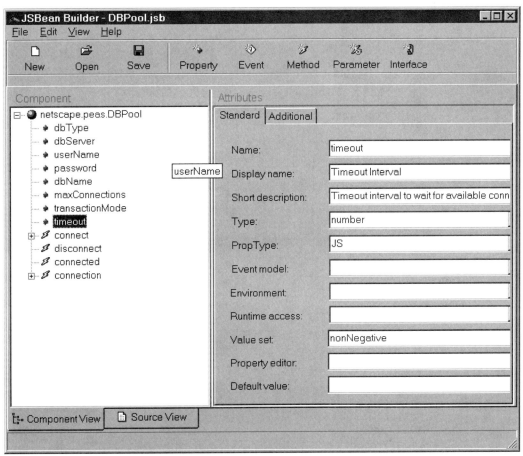

Figure 16.5 *Example of JavaScript Bean Builder.*

       into HTML format. HoTMetaL Pro supports Word, WordPerfect, AMI PRO, RTF, ASCII text, Excel, and other formats.

- HoTMetaL Pro Editor WYSIWIG editing of font size and color.
- HoTMetaL Pro Editor lets you drag and drop images and links into Web pages.
- HoTMetaL Pro Editor offers you the power of inline image map editing.
- HoTMetal Pro Editor validation feature checks your HTML syntax against different versions of HTML.
- HoTMetaL FX lets you drag and drop preconfigured Web en-

hancements (such as DHTML, image maps, and animated GIFs) into your Web pages.

- Ulead's PhotoImpact SE offers you built-in graphics editing.
- Ulead's GIF Animator lets you create animated GIF files.
- Information Manager is a site management tool.

In addition, HoTMetaL Pro comes with a collection of Power Tools. The Power Tools are products from other vendors that round out the Web page development tool set. The Power Tools provided are as follows:

- Aimtech's Jamba helps you to quickly and easily create Java applets.
- Acadia Infuse (now, NetObjects) ScriptBuilder version 1.02 lets you add JavaScript to your Web page. When you click the ScriptBuilder menu option it takes the page you are currently editing into ScriptBuilder. After you finish editing the Java-Script, it takes the revisions back into the HoTMetaL Pro editor. This is a nice feature, because it skips the exercise of constantly saving and opening the same file in different editors.
- StarBase's Versions provides logging and version control of your Web pages. Version control is a great extension to HoT-MetaL Pro. Even if you use a different HTML editor, I suggest that you take a look at the Versions package as a tool for source file management. Their URL is:

`http://www.starbasecorp.com.`

- ZBSoft's ZBZerver is an Internet/intranet server package for Windows.
- VReam's VRCreator creates 3D animations using the Virtual Reality Markup Language (VRML).
- DTL's Dataspot is an Internet accessible database service.

Figure 16.6 demonstrates the link between HoTMetaL Pro and ScriptBuilder. The ability to switch between editing an HTML document and editing JavaScript is the main reason I chose HoTMetaL Pro for developing the examples in this book. If you are looking for an excellent Web site development tool, I recommend that you try HoTMetaL Pro. The URL for their Web site is as follows:

`http://www.softquad.com`

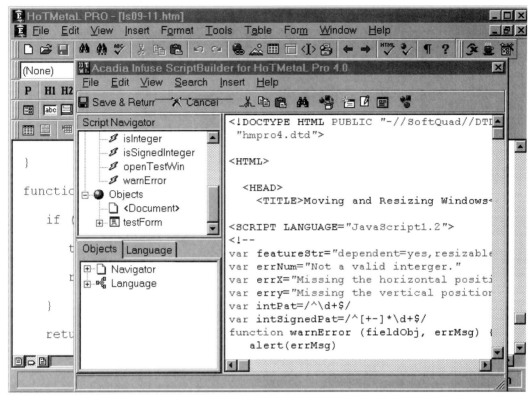

Figure 16.6   Example of HotMetal Pro integration to ScriptBuilder.

Products from Other Vendors

There are a few JavaScript tools that deserve mentioning. Even though I was unable to evaluate them, you might find that they fit your specific requirements.

Borland's IntraBuilder is a visual development tool that uses both client-side and server-side JavaScript to access databases. IntraBuilder uses the Borland Database Engine instead of the LiveWire DataBase Service. If you are looking for a tool to build Web applications that require database access, you should try Borland's IntraBuilder. For more information about Intrabuilder, navigate your way to the Borland web site at:

`http://www.borland.com/intrabuilder/`

OnDisplay's CenterStage is an extranet middleware product that integrates alternative data sources such as Web-enabled applications, web data, legacy applications, e-mail, and reports, with other application middleware products. CenterStage uses both JavaScript and LiveWire. The product really applies to corporate Web application developers. More information about the product is available from:

```
http://www.ondisplay.com/OnDisplayHome.htm
```

Tools for Signing Scripts

Before you can sign a script, you need an object-signing certificate. Object-signing certificates are available from two sources:

- An independent Certificate Authority (CA) that authenticates your identity and charges a fee for their service. For signed scripts that are distributed on the Internet, you need to use an independent CA. The URLs certificates authorities that currently provide object-signing certificates are as follows:

```
http://digitalid.verisign.com/nosintro.htm
http://www.thawte.com/
```

- A corporate CA running Netscape's Certificate Server. The corporate CA applies to signed scripts distributed to an intranet or extranet.

Once you have an object-signing certificate, you need the necessary tools to sign scripts. The tools required to sign scripts are as follows:

- Zigbert is a stand-alone command-line tool that uses the JAR format to sign files. You then package the JAR file using a ZIP utility. You can get the current version of Zigbert at the following URL:

```
http://developer.netscape.com/products/zigbert/index.html
```

- Perl Signer is a Perl script that runs on top of Zigbert to create JAR files that contain digital signatures and related information. Perl Signer is part of the Command Line Tools package which also contains Zigbert.

The version of Zigbert available at the time of this writing does not support the signing of inline scripts. Until Zigbert supports both Java-Script source files and inline JavaScript, there are two signing procedures. If you are only signing JavaScript source files, you only use Zigbert. If you are signing inline JavaScript, you need to use the Perl Signer, which massages the files before invoking Zigbert. Since Zigbert is an evolving tool, you need to read the latest documentation which you can find at the following URL:

```
http://developer.netscape.com/library/documentation/signedobj/
zigbert/index.htm
```

Summary

Although there are a lot of tools available to the Web page developer, there are only a few tools that provide more than editing functions for JavaScript. This chapter reviewed the tools available from Netscape and third-party software vendors.

Every JavaScript developer should install the JavaScript Debugger, since it only costs the time it takes for downloading and installation. NetObjects ScriptBuilder is another tool that anyone who does a lot of scripting should consider adding to their toolbox.

To the best of my knowledge, HoTMetaL Pro 4.0 is the only HTML editor that integrates a JavaScript editing tool with the HTML editor. The current version of HoTMetaL Pro uses what was Acadia Infuse ScriptBuilder version 1.02, which only supports JavaScript 1.1. With the acquisition of Acadia Software's products by NetObjects, the next version of HoTMetaL Pro should include the latest version of NetObjects ScriptBuilder.

For those who want to develop components for the Netscape ONE environment, the tools required are Visual JavaScript and the Component Developer's Kit. The Component Developer's Kit for the Windows platforms includes NetObjects JavaScript Bean Builder.

For those looking for high-end products that support development in an enterprise environment with integration to databases, there are a number of available products that support JavaScript. Borland's Intra-Builder provides integration to a wide variety of databases and has a visual development environment.

Appendix A:
Color Codes

Color	Red	Green	Blue
aliceblue	F0	F8	FF
antiquewhite	FA	EB	D7
aqua	00	FF	FF
aquamarine	7F	FF	D4
azure	F0	FF	FF
beige	F5	F5	DC
bisque	FF	E4	C4
black	00	00	00
blanchedalmond	FF	EB	CD
blue	00	00	FF
blueviolet	8A	2B	E2
brown	A5	2A	2A
burlywood	DE	B8	87

Color	Red	Green	Blue
cadetblue	5F	9E	A0
chartreuse	7F	FF	00
chocolate	D2	69	1E
coral	FF	7F	50
cornflowerblue	64	95	ED
cornsilk	FF	F8	DC
crimson	DC	14	3C
cyan	00	FF	FF
darkblue	00	00	8B
darkcyan	00	8B	8B
darkgoldenrod	B8	86	0B
darkgray	A9	A9	A9
darkgreen	00	64	00
darkkhaki	BD	B7	6B
darkmagenta	8B	00	8B
darkolivegreen	55	6B	2F
darkorange	FF	8C	00
darkorchid	99	32	CC
darkred	8B	00	00
darksalmon	E9	96	7A
darkseagreen	8F	BC	8F
darkslateblue	48	3D	8B
darkslategray	2F	4F	4F
darkturquoise	00	CE	D1
darkviolet	94	00	D3
deeppink	FF	14	93
deepskyblue	00	BF	FF
dimgray	69	69	69
dodgerblue	1E	90	FF
firebrick	B2	22	22
floralwhite	FF	FA	F0
forestgreen	22	8B	22

Color	Red	Green	Blue
fuchsia	FF	00	FF
gainsboro	DC	DC	DC
ghostwhite	F8	F8	FF
gold	FF	D7	00
goldenrod	DA	A5	20
gray	80	80	80
green	00	80	00
greenyellow	AD	FF	2F
honeydew	F0	FF	F0
hotpink	FF	69	B4
indianred	CD	5C	5C
indigo	4B	00	82
ivory	FF	FF	F0
khaki	F0	E6	8C
lavender	E6	E6	FA
lavenderblush	FF	F0	F5
lawngreen	7C	FC	00
lemonchiffon	FF	FA	CD
lightblue	AD	D8	E6
lightcoral	F0	80	80
lightcyan	E0	FF	FF
lightgoldenrodyellow	FA	FA	D2
lightgreen	90	EE	90
lightgrey	D3	D3	D3
lightpink	FF	B6	C1
lightsalmon	FF	A0	7A
lightseagreen	20	B2	AA
lightskyblue	87	CE	FA
lightslategray	77	88	99
lightsteelblue	B0	C4	DE
lightyellow	FF	FF	E0
lime	00	FF	00

Color	Red	Green	Blue
limegreen	32	CD	32
linen	FA	F0	E6
magenta	FF	00	FF
maroon	80	00	00
mediumaquamarine	66	CD	AA
mediumblue	00	00	CD
mediumorchid	BA	55	D3
mediumpurple	93	70	DB
mediumseagreen	3C	B3	71
mediumslateblue	7B	68	EE
mediumspringgreen	00	FA	9A
mediumturquoise	48	D1	CC
mediumvioletred	C7	15	85
midnightblue	19	19	70
mintcream	F5	FF	FA
mistyrose	FF	E4	E1
moccasin	FF	E4	B5
navajowhite	FF	DE	AD
navy	00	00	80
oldlace	FD	F5	E6
olive	80	80	00
olivedrab	6B	8E	23
orange	FF	A5	00
orangered	FF	45	00
orchid	DA	70	D6
palegoldenrod	EE	E8	AA
palegreen	98	FB	98
paleturquoise	AF	EE	EE
palevioletred	DB	70	93
papayawhip	FF	EF	D5
peachpuff	FF	DA	B9
peru	CD	85	3F

Color	Red	Green	Blue
pink	FF	C0	CB
plum	DD	A0	DD
powderblue	B0	E0	E6
purple	80	00	80
red	FF	00	00
rosybrown	BC	8F	8F
royalblue	41	69	E1
saddlebrown	8B	45	13
salmon	FA	80	72
sandybrown	F4	A4	60
seagreen	2E	8B	57
seashell	FF	F5	EE
sienna	A0	52	2D
silver	C0	C0	C0
skyblue	87	CE	EB
slateblue	6A	5A	CD
slategray	70	80	90
snow	FF	FA	FA
springgreen	00	FF	7F
steelblue	46	82	B4
tan	D2	B4	8C
teal	00	80	80
thistle	D8	BF	D8
tomato	FF	63	47
turquoise	40	E0	D0
violet	EE	82	EE
wheat	F5	DE	B3
white	FF	FF	FF
whitesmoke	F5	F5	F5

Appendix B:
Resource Library

JavaScript References

- `http://developer.netscape.com/one/`
  `javascript/index.html`

The JavaScript Developer Central page is the starting point for the latest information on JavaScript from Netscape. Check this page on a regular basis for the latest news on JavaScript.

- `http://developer.netscape.com/news/`
  `viewsource/index.html`

The View Source e-zine has regular articles on JavaScript, and is one of the best sources for information on using JavaScript. You should subscribe to the mailing list for notification of the release of new issues.

- `http://www.netscapeworld.com/`

Netscape Enterprise Developer has articles, sample code, and monthly articles on JavaScript. You should subscribe to the e-mail notification so that you don't miss an issue.

- `http://www.cnet.com/Content/Builder/`
- `http://www.cnet.com/Content/Builder/`
  `Programming/?st.bl.gptb.prog`

CNET's BUILDER.COM site is an important site for Web page development. BUILDER.COM has a special section for Web programming and scripting.

- `http://www.webreference.com/js/`

This is another good site for keeping track of what is happening in JavaScript. The JxPharamacy page contains a lot of useful information on JavaScript development.

- `http://www.infohiway.com/javascript/`
  `indexf.htm`

Cut-N-Paste is an e-zine that has monthly articles on JavaScript. This sight also has a large collection of sample scripts.

- `http://www.webreference.com/javascript/`
- `http://www.webcoder.com/index_real.html`

Although JavaScript Tip of the Week is no longer being updated, the site does have a collection of useful scripts and JavaScript information. The author of the site now writes for WebCoder.com, which is a Web site devoted to JavaScript and DHTML.

- `http://www.planetwidemarket.com/equinox/`
  `codersarchive/archives/tips.html`

A site devoted to Netscape that posts a new tip every week, many of which are for JavaScript.

- `http://www.emf.net/~mal/cookiesinfo.html`

Malcolm's Guide to Persistent Cookie Resources provides an introduction to cookies and contains links to other cookie sites.

- `http://www.microsoft.com/JScript/`

This Web page is the starting point for Microsoft's documentation on JScript. You may have to do a bit of searching to find all of the pieces.

- Windsor, Janice and Brian Freedman, *Jumping JavaScript*, Prentice Hall, 1997

This book contains a lot of examples for accomplishing specific tasks. Although the book is based on JavaScript 1.1, it is still a good reference book.

- Kent, Peter, and Kent Multer, *Netscape JavaScript 1.2 Programmer's Reference, Windows, MacIntosh and Unix Edition,* Ventana Press, 1997

This book is strictly a reference book with very few examples. Although the book differs slightly from the current and final version of JavaScript 1.2, it is handy quick reference guide.

JavaScript Tutorials

- `http://rummelplatz.uni-mannheim.de/~skoch/js/`

Voodoo's Introduction to JavaScript is one of the oldest JavaScript tutorial sites, and it does have tutorials for JavaScript 1.2. If you have a hard time connecting to the site in Germany, you can switch to one of the mirror sites from the home page.

- `http://www.webteacher.com/javatour/`

JavaScript Tutorial for the Non-Programmer takes you step by step through the fundamentals of JavaScript. It is a good site for those who have a background in HTML, but lack any background in programming.

- `http://www.cnet.com/Content/Builder/Programming/Javascript/`

CNET's JavaScript for Beginners is another site for the beginner in JavaScript.

- `http://www.useractive.com/tutorial/js_tutorials/`

UserActive's JavaScript Laboratory takes a rather unique approach to learning JavaScript. In addition to the tutorial, you build scripts that you can then save and execute.

- `http://rampages.onramp.net/~jnardo/javascript/zen.html`

The Way of JavaScript Tutorial is a brief JavaScript tutorial inspired by the verse of Zen Patriarch—Kakuan.

- `http://www.freqgrafx.com/411/`

JavaScript 411 has a tutorial, a library of JavaScript routines, and a JavaScript FAQ. The library contains a sizeable collection of useful JavaScript code.

JavaScript Repositories

- `http://planetx.bloomu.edu/~mpscho/jsarchive/`
- `http://www.tradepub.com/javascript/`
- `http://www.web-development.com/jscript/`
- `http://www.javascripts.com/`
- `http://www.livesoftware.com/jrc/index.html`
- `http://www.btinternet.com/~martin.webb/search.html`
- `http://www.serve.com/hotsyte/reserve.html`
- `http://www.serve.com/hotsyte/wildman/`
- `http://www.essex1.com/people/timothy/js-index.htm`
- `http://leden.tref.nl/ageytenb/jswr/`
- `http://www.javascripts.com/`
- `http://javascriptsource.com/main.html`

These sites all contain collections of JavaScript code. Some have only a few examples and some have large collections. With a little searching, you will find an example that meets your needs.

JavaScript News Groups

- `http://www.livesoftware.com/jrc/index.html#news`

Live Software has a JavaScript Development group and a JavaScript Examples group.

- snews://secnews.netscape.com/
  netscape.devs-javascript

The Netscape JavaScript group is only open to members of DevEdge.

- news:comp.lang.javascript

The Usenet group for JavaScipt.

CGI References

- http://www.perl.com/

This is a general site for the Perl scripting language, but it also has a good collection of CGI scripts.

- http://www.cgi-resources.com/

This site has a wealth of information on CGI including almost 1,000 CGI programs. The site also has a list of books on CGI programming.

Java References

- http://java.sun.com/

This is the site for Java. The first thing you must do is download the latest release of Java.

- http://developer.netscape.com/one/java/
  index.html

Netscape's Java Developer Central is the starting point for Netscape's Java related information.

- http://www.javaworld.com/

JavaWorld is a good e-zine for finding the latest information on Java. Occasionally, JavaWorld has articles on JavaScript.

- Horstmann, Cay S., and Gary Cornell, *Core Java 1.1, Volume 1—Fundamentals*, Prentice Hall, 1997.

Core Java 1.1, Volume 1 is written for the experienced programmer who wants to put Java to work on real problems. This book is an excellent Java reference for understanding how Java works.

- Naughton, Patrick, *The Java Handbook*, Osborne McGraw Hill

Patrick Naughton is one of the people who developed Java. His book is a good introduction to the Java language, and as a bonus, the end of the book tells you the story of the birth of Java.

Plug-in References

- `http://developer.netscape.com/one/plugins/index.html`

Netscape's Plug-ins Developer Central is the home page for plug-in information.

- Young, Douglas A., *Netscape Developer's Guide to Plug-ins*, Prentice Hall, 1997

If you want to write a plug-in, this book is a comprehensive guide to the subject of writing plug-ins.

Appendix C: JavaScript and the Year 2000

JavaScript per se does not have a year 2000 problem. However, when you work with dates, you need to consider how different browsers handle years. As JavaScript evolved, the behavior of the `getYear()` method of the Date object changed.

Netscape Navigator 2.x and Microsoft Internet Explorer 3.x start number years by subtracting 1900 from the four-digit year. For the twentieth century all years are two digit values (such as 86 and 98). The year 2000 and beyond simply continue the formula by starting with the number 100. With these browsers, you only need to add the 1900 to the value returned by the `getYear()` method to obtain the four digit year. However, there are a few caveats as follows:

- Netscape Navigator 2.x does not correctly handle years before 1970
- Microsoft Internet Explorer 3.x does not correctly handle years before 1900

The getYear() method for Netscape Navigator 3.x, Netscape Communicator 4.x, and Microsoft Internet Explorer 4.x returns the year according to the following rules:

- Years prior to 1900 are returned as four digit years
- Years for the twentieth century are returned as two digit years
- Years from 2000 and beyond are returned as four digit years

As browsers start to comply to the ECMAScript standard, the getYear() method may undergo yet another change. The ECMAScript standard specifies that the getYear() method return years prior to 1900 as negative values. The ECMAScript standard also added the getFullYear() method. Microsoft Internet Explore 4.x and Netscape Communicator 4.04 implement the getFullYear() method.

The script shown in Listing C.1 displays the results of the getYear() method for the years 1899, 1969, 1999, and 2000. The results of running this test using Netscape Communicator 4.04 are shown in Figure C.1.

Listing C.1 Browser Date Test

```
<HTML>
  <HEAD>
    <TITLE>Browser Date Test</TITLE>
  </HEAD>
  <BODY>
    <H1 ALIGN="CENTER">Browser Date Test</H1>
<SCRIPT LANGUAGE="JavaScript">
<!--
tstDate=new Date()
document.write("<P> The current year is "
          +tstDate.getYear()+"</P>")
tstDate.setYear(1899)
document.write("<P> When set to 1899, the year is "
          +tstDate.getYear()+"</P>")
tstDate.setYear(1969)
document.write("<P> When set to 1969, the year is "
          +tstDate.getYear()+"</P>")
tstDate.setYear(1999)
```

```
document.write("<P> When set to 1999, the year is "
          +tstDate.getYear()+"</P>")
tstDate.setYear(2000)
document.write("<P> When set to 2000, the year is "
          +tstDate.getYear()+"</P>")
//-->
</SCRIPT>
  </BODY>
</HTML>
```

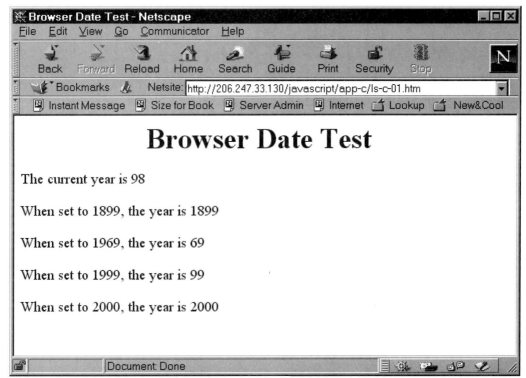

Figure C.1   Results of Browser Date Test.

With the variations between browsers, you need to convert dates according to the version of each browser. The "Ultimate JavaScript Client Sniffer" from Netscape is a comprehensive routine that checks for all current variations of client-side browsers. The following URL provides more details on the browser detection routine:

```
http://developer.netscape.com/library/examples/javascript/
```

`browser_type.html`

The script in Listing C.2 tests the ability of a browser to correctly convert a year into a four digit year. The script uses the "Ultimate JavaScript Client Sniffer" to determine the browser version.

Listing C.2 Date Conversion Test

```
<HTML>
  <HEAD>
    <META NAME="GENERATOR"
    CONTENT="NetObjects ScriptBuilder 2.0">
    <TITLE>Date Conversion Test</TITLE>
<SCRIPT LANGUAGE="JavaScript">
<!--
// Ultimate client-side JavaScript client sniff.
// (C) Netscape Communications 1998.  Permission granted
// to reuse and distribute.

// Everything you always wanted to know about your
// JavaScript client but were afraid to ask ... "Is" is
// the constructor function for "is" object,
// which has properties indicating:
// (1) browser vendor:
//     is.nav, is.ie, is.opera
// (2) browser version number:
//     is.major (integer indicating major version
//               number: 2, 3, 4 ...)
//     is.minor (float   indicating full  version
//               number: 2.02, 3.01, 4.04 ...)
// (3) browser vendor AND major version number
//     is.nav2, is.nav3, is.nav4, is.ie3, is.ie4
// (4) JavaScript version number:
//     is.js (float indicating full JavaScript version
//            number: 1, 1.1, 1.2 ...)
// (5) OS platform and version:
//     is.win, is.win16, is.win32, is.win31, is.win95,
//     is.winnt, is.win98
//     is.os2
//     is.mac, is.mac68k, is.macppc
```

```
//      is.unix
//          is.sun, is.sun4, is.sun5, is.suni86
//          is.irix, is.irix5, is.irix6
//          is.hpux, is.hpux9, is.hpux10
//          is.aix, is.aix1, is.aix2, is.aix3, is.aix4
//          is.linux, is.sco, is.unixware, is.mpras,
//          is.reliant, is.dec, is.sinix, is.freebsd, is.bsd
//      is.vms
//
// See
//http://home.kiss.de/~i_thum/JS_tutorial/bstat/navobj.html
// for a detailed list of userAgent strings.


function Is ()
{   // convert all characters to lowercase to simplify
    // testing
    var agt = navigator.userAgent.toLowerCase()

    // *** BROWSER VERSION ***
    this.major = parseInt(navigator.appVersion)
    this.minor = parseFloat(navigator.appVersion)

    this.nav = ((agt.indexOf('mozilla')!=-1)
                && ((agt.indexOf('spoofer')==-1)
                && (agt.indexOf('compatible') == -1)))
    this.nav2 = (this.nav && (this.major == 2))
    this.nav3 = (this.nav && (this.major == 3))
    this.nav4 = (this.nav && (this.major == 4))
    this.navonly = (this.nav
                && (agt.indexOf(";nav") != -1))

    this.ie   = (agt.indexOf("msie") != -1)
    this.ie3  = (this.ie && (this.major == 2))
    this.ie4  = (this.ie && (this.major == 4))

    this.opera = (agt.indexOf("opera") != -1)

    // *** JAVASCRIPT VERSION CHECK ***
    // Useful to workaround Nav3 bug in which Nav3
    // loads <SCRIPT LANGUAGE="JavaScript1.2">.
```

```
if (this.nav2 || this.ie3) this.js = 1.0
else if (this.nav3 || this.opera) this.js = 1.1
else if (this.nav4 || this.ie4) this.js = 1.2
// NOTE: In the future, update this code when newer
// versions of JS are released. For now, we try to
// provide some upward compatibility so that future
// versions of Nav and IE will show they are at
// *least* JS 1.2 capable. Always check for JS version
// compatibility with > or >=.
else if ((this.nav && (this.minor > 4.05))
          || (this.ie && (this.major > 4)))
      this.js = 1.2
else this.js = 0.0 // HACK: always check for JS version
                   // with > or >=


// *** PLATFORM ***
this.win   = ((agt.indexOf("win")!=-1)
              || (agt.indexOf("16bit")!=-1) )
// NOTE: On Opera 3.0, the userAgent string includes
//       "Windows 95/NT4" on all Win32, so you can't
//       distinguish between Win95 and WinNT.
this.win95 = ((agt.indexOf("win95")!=-1)
              || (agt.indexOf("windows 95")!=-1))


// is this a 16 bit compiled version?
this.win16 = ((agt.indexOf("win16")!=-1)
           || (agt.indexOf("16bit")!=-1)
           || (agt.indexOf("windows 3.1")!=-1)
           || (agt.indexOf("windows 16-bit")!=-1) )

this.win31 = (agt.indexOf("windows 3.1")!=-1)
           || (agt.indexOf("win16")!=-1)
           || (agt.indexOf("windows 16-bit")!=-1)


// NOTE: Reliable detection of Win98 may not be
//       possible. It appears that:
//       - On Nav 4.x and before you'll get plain
//         "Windows" in userAgent.
//       - On Mercury client, the 32-bit version will
//         return "Win98", but the 16-bit version
//         running on Win98 will still return "Win95".
```

```
this.win98 = ((agt.indexOf("win98")!=-1)
              || (agt.indexOf("windows 98")!=-1))
this.winnt = ((agt.indexOf("winnt")!=-1)
              ||(agt.indexOf("windows nt")!=-1))
this.win32 = this.win95 || this.winnt || this.win98
              || ((this.major >= 4)
                 && (navigator.platform == "Win32"))
              || (agt.indexOf("win32")!=-1)
              || (agt.indexOf("32bit")!=-1)

this.os2 = (agt.indexOf("os/2")!=-1)
           || (navigator.appVersion.indexOf("OS/2")!=-1)
           || (agt.indexOf("ibm-webexplorer")!=-1)

this.mac    = (agt.indexOf("mac")!=-1)
this.mac68k = this.mac && ((agt.indexOf("68k")!=-1) ||
                          (agt.indexOf("68000")!=-1))
this.macppc = this.mac && ((agt.indexOf("ppc")!=-1) ||
                          (agt.indexOf("powerpc")!=-1))

this.sun    = (agt.indexOf("sunos")!=-1)
this.sun4   = (agt.indexOf("sunos 4")!=-1)
this.sun5   = (agt.indexOf("sunos 5")!=-1)
this.suni86= this.sun && (agt.indexOf("i86")!=-1)
this.irix   = (agt.indexOf("irix") !=-1)     // SGI
this.irix5  = (agt.indexOf("irix 5") !=-1)
this.irix6  = ((agt.indexOf("irix 6") !=-1)
              || (agt.indexOf("irix6") !=-1))
this.hpux   = (agt.indexOf("hp-ux")!=-1)
this.hpux9 = this.hpux && (agt.indexOf("09.")!=-1)
this.hpux10= this.hpux && (agt.indexOf("10.")!=-1)
this.aix    = (agt.indexOf("aix")  !=-1)     // IBM
this.aix1   = (agt.indexOf("aix 1")  !=-1)
this.aix2   = (agt.indexOf("aix 2")  !=-1)
this.aix3   = (agt.indexOf("aix 3")  !=-1)
this.aix4   = (agt.indexOf("aix 4")  !=-1)
this.linux = (agt.indexOf("inux")!=-1)
this.sco    = (agt.indexOf("sco")!=-1)
              || (agt.indexOf("unix_sv")!=-1)
this.unixware = (agt.indexOf("unix_system_v")!=-1)
this.mpras    = (agt.indexOf("ncr")!=-1)
```

```
    this.reliant  = (agt.indexOf("reliantunix")!=-1)
    this.dec    = (agt.indexOf("dec")!=-1)
            || (agt.indexOf("osf1")!=-1)
            || (agt.indexOf("dec_alpha")!=-1)
            || (agt.indexOf("alphaserver")!=-1)
            || (agt.indexOf("ultrix")!=-1)
            || (agt.indexOf("alphastation")!=-1)
    this.sinix = (agt.indexOf("sinix")!=-1)
    this.freebsd = (agt.indexOf("freebsd")!=-1)
    this.bsd = (agt.indexOf("bsd")!=-1)
    this.unix  = (agt.indexOf("x11")!=-1) || this.sun
                || this.irix || this.hpux || this.sco
                ||this.unixware || this.mpras
                || this.reliant || this.dec || this.sinix
                || this.aix || this.linux || this.freebsd

    this.vms   = (agt.indexOf("vax")!=-1)
                || (agt.indexOf("openvms")!=-1)
}

var is = new Is()

// function to convert year to full year
function convYear(dateObj) {
            // ie3 fails to handle dates before 1900
            // nav2 needs to be checked for how it handles dates
            // before 1900
            if (is.nav2 || is.ie3) {
            return (dateObj.getYear()+1900)
    }
            if (is.nav3 || (is.nav && is.minor<4.04) || is.opera)
{
            var yearRet=dateObj.getYear()
            if (yearRet<100) yearRet+=1900
            return yearRet
            }
            return dateObj.getFullYear()
}
//-->
</SCRIPT>
  </HEAD>
```

```
<BODY>
   <H1 ALIGN="CENTER">Date Conversion Test</H1>
<SCRIPT LANGUAGE="JavaScript">
<!--
tstDate=new Date()
tstDate.setYear(1899)
document.write("<P> When set to 1899, the year is "
               +convYear(tstDate)+"</P>")
tstDate.setYear(1969)
document.write("<P> When set to 1969, the year is "
               +convYear(tstDate)+"</P>")
tstDate.setYear(1999)
document.write("<P> When set to 1999, the year is "
               +convYear(tstDate)+"</P>")
tstDate.setYear(2000)
document.write("<P> When set to 2000, the year is "
               +convYear(tstDate)+"</P>")
//-->
</SCRIPT>
  </BODY>
</HTML>
```

The `convYear()` function in Listing C.2 converts dates for Netscape Navigator 2.x and Microsoft Internet Explorer 3.x to a four digit year by adding 1900 to the value returned by the `getYear()` method. The problem with Netscape Navigator 2.x is how to detect and handle dates before 1970. Microsoft Internet Explore 3.x presents the same problem with dates before 1900.

For Netscape Navigator 3.x through Netscape Communicator 4.03, the `convYear()` function treats all years less than 100 as belonging to the twentieth century and adds 1900 to the year. Any value equal to or greater than 100 is simply returned as is. This conversion nicely handles years from 100 to 9999. The `convYear()` function assumes that the Opera browser handles dates in the same manner as Netscape Navigator 3.x.

The `convYear()` function considers all other browsers as complying to the ECMAScript standard and uses the `getFullYear()` method of the `Date` object. Unless the `getFullYear()` method changes its behavior in future versions of JavaScript, it should reliably work for all current and future browser releases. Figure C.2 shows the results of using the `getFullYear()` method in Netscape Communicator 4.04.

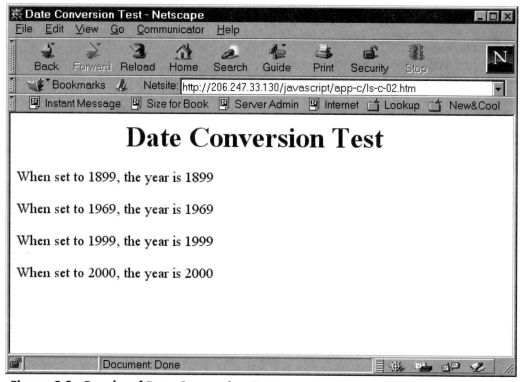

Figure C.2   Results of Date Conversion Test.

The year 2000 is not far away. If you use the `Date` object to determine the difference between two future dates, you need to modify your scripts to correctly handle the behavior of the `getYear()` method.

Index

About the CD-ROM

Overview

The CD-ROM contains the complete source code for every example shown in the book. In addition, the HandiScripts directory has the first two JavaScript solutions in the growing collection of HandiScripts. The tools directory contains an evaluation copy of NetObjects Scriptbuilder 2.0, and the CBT has a computer-based training course for the JavaScript object model from CBT Systems (please see the readme for more specific instructions).

System Description

All of the examples work with Netscape Navigator 4.04 or greater. Most of the examples work with older version of Netscape Navigator and Microsoft Internet Explorer 3.x and 4.x. NetObjects Scriptbuilder is a editing tool for JavaScript. Most of the scripts in the book were written with the aid of earlier versions of ScriptBuilder. The CBT computer-based training course for the JavaScript object model represents provides access to training material that normally costs $225.

How to use the CD-ROM

As you proceed through the book, you can run the examples from the CD-ROM. To gain more experience with writing scripts, you can modify or develop new scripts using NetObjects ScriptBuilder. As you proceed through the chapters describing the JavaScript object model, you can review what you have learned by studying the corresponding units in the CBT computer-based training course.

Operating Systems

To obtain full benefit from the examples on the CD-ROM, you need the latest version of Netscape Navigator on any platform. The examples for Chapter 13 require either Netscape FastTrack server 3.x or Netscape Enterprise server 3.x. NetObjects ScriptBuilder and CBT's training course run only under Microsoft Windows 95 or Microsoft Windows NT.

For More Information

For additional HandiScripts, visit http://www.nilenet.com/~billa/HandiScripts. To purchase NetObjects ScriptBuilder, go to http://www.netobjects.com. For more information on courses offered by CBT Systems, go to http://www.cbtsys.com. If you are interested in instructor-led JavaScript training, check out http://www.trainix.com.

Technical Support

Prentice Hall does not offer technical support for the software on the CD-ROM. However, if there is a problem with the CD, you may obtain a replacement copy be emailing us with your problem at:

```
discexchange@phptr.com
```

You can obtain support information about NetObjects Scriptbuilder at

```
http://www.netobjects.com.
```